POSTCARDS

ALASKA

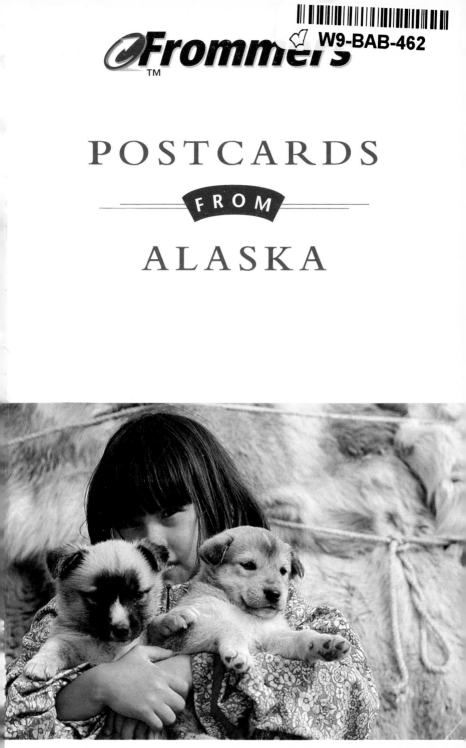

A Native girl with Alaskan husky puppies in Kotzebue, 26 miles north of the Arctic Circle near the Bering Strait. See chapter 10. © Clark James Mishler/Alaska Stock Images.

The Starr Hill neighborhood in downtown Juneau. Built up a mountain on the side of the Gastineau Channel and surrounded by the Juneau Icefield, the city is the only state capital in the U.S. that cannot be reached by road. See chapter 5. © Mark Kelley/Alaska Stock Images.

Chilkat dancer Charles Jimmie, Sr., in front of the Tlingit tribal house at Fort William Seward in Haines. The Chilkat Dancers, formed in 1957, perform regularly in town and have toured all over the world. See chapter 5. © Kim Heacox Photography/Ken Graham Agency.

Denali State Park borders the southeast corner of Denali National Park, and provides wonderful views of the south side of Mt. McKinley. See chapter 8. © Mike Jones/Ken Graham Agency.

A kayaker exploring near icebergs in Tracy Arm. The South Sawyer Glacier, located at the end of the Arm, calves off many tons of ice daily, giving the channel an otherworldly look. See chapter 5. © Jeff Foott/Alaska Stock Images.

A sled dog race in Fairbanks. The city and the surrounding area host the Yukon Quest International Sled Dog Race in February and the North American Sled Dog Championships in March. See chapter 9. © Gary Schultz/Alaska Stock Images.

Glaciers flow down from Mt. McKinley, the tallest peak in North America. The dark streaks in the glacial ice are called moraine, and are accumulations of rock pushed to the side as the glacier flows slowly downhill. Those in the center of the flow are called median moraine, and are produced when two glaciers flow together. See chapter 8. © Ken Graham/Ken Graham Agency.

A baby Arctic ground squirrel shopping for groceries. See the appendix for a guide to Alaska's wildlife. © Paul McCormick/The Image Bank.

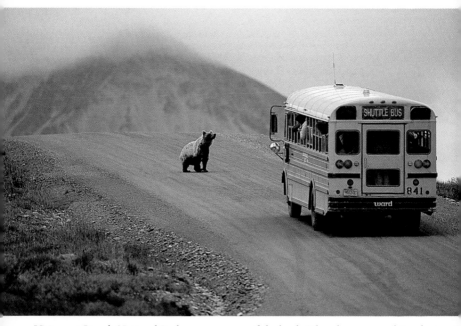

Visitors at Denali National Park encounter one of the locals. Though some complain about the buses, which are the only way to traverse the park in a vehicle, it's a system that keeps visitors from overwhelming the ecosystem, so the animals are still there to watch and their behavior remains essentially normal. It may be the only $20 safari in the world. See chapter 8. © Kim Heacox Photography/Ken Graham Agency.

A totem pole in Juneau. One of the most distinctive representations of Native culture in Southeast Alaska, totems are carved to depict the genealogy and history of their people. You'll see them throughout the region, particularly at Ketchikan's several totem parks and heritage centers and at the Sitka National Historic Park, which has a totem trail and a workshop where Native artists craft new poles. *See chapter 5.* *© Randy Brandon/Alaska Stock Images.*

In the summer, moose are most often seen standing in forest ponds eating the weeds from the bottom or pruning streamside willows, their all-time favorite food; at Denali, moose most often show up along the first few miles of the park road, in the willowy forest. See chapter 8. © Ken Graham/Ken Graham Agency.

Though Anchorage is Alaska's largest city, where 40% of the state's population resides, it sits so close to wild areas that anyone with a few hundred dollars for a float plane can be on a lake or river with the bears and salmon in a matter of minutes. See chapter 6. © Ken Graham/Ken Graham Agency.

Harry Gaines showing off his 80-pound trophy King salmon, caught in the Kenai River, home of the world's largest salmon. Kings come in two runs on the Kenai: The early run, from mid-May to the end of June, usually produces smaller fish in the 20- to 40-pound range; the second run comes during the month of July and includes massive fish that range up to 90 pounds. See chapters 2 and 7. © Ken Graham/Ken Graham Agency.

Dall sheep rams at Polychrome Mountain in Denali National Park. The Dall sheep's habitat is the high, rocky places, where their incredible agility makes them safe from predators. In Denali you'll typically see them from a great distance, using binoculars. Often the sheep move in herds of a dozen or more animals. See chapter 8. © Craig Blacklock/Larry Ulrich Stock.

A brown bear catching his dinner. In coastal areas where salmon are plentiful, such as Southeast Alaska or Katmai National Park, brown bears (also known as grizzlies) can grow to well over 1,000 pounds, and even approach the one-ton mark. The largest of all are found on salmon-rich Kodiak Island. See chapter 10. © Galen Rowell/Mountain Light.

A humpback whale breaching in Frederick Sound. No one knows for sure why they leap from the water like this—it may just be because they enjoy it. Humpbacks are easy to recognize by their huge, mottled tails; by the hump on their backs; and by their arm-like flippers, which can grow to be 14 feet long. See the appendix. © David Hoffmann/ Ken Graham Agency.

A bald eagle swoops down and makes off with its prey. Eagles are so common in Alaska that in most coastal towns a pigeon would cause a bigger stir among bird fanciers. In Southeast, Haines is a prime eagle-spotting area, where thousands congregate in the fall, and Sitka and Ketchikan both have raptor centers where you can see eagles up close. See chapter 5. © Dan Parrett/Alaska Stock Images.

Cruises are a popular way to see Alaska's coast, and the small cruise ships in particular—such as those operated by Alaska's Glacier Bay, Cruise West, American Safari Cruises, Clipper, and Special Expeditions—can really give you an up-close feeling for the rhythm of life in the region. Left: A Zodiac landing craft ferries passengers from the Yorktown Clipper *(© Wolfgang Kaehler Photography). Below: Passengers on the* Spirit of '98 *witness glacial calving at the South Sawyer Glacier in Tracy Arm (© Dave G. Houser Photography). See chapter 4.*

Fields of Nootka lupine along the shores of Turnagain Arm, at the foot of the Chugach Mountains. One of the world's great drives follows the Seward Highway roughly 50 miles from Anchorage south to Portage Glacier, passing through a magnificent, ever-changing, mostly untouched landscape full of wildlife. *See chapter 6.*

Lone canoeist on Lower Summit Lake on the Kenai Peninsula, just south of Anchorage. See chapter 7.

Other Great Guides for Your Trip:

Frommer's Alaska Cruises & Ports of Call

Frommer's Canada

Frommer's British Columbia & the Canadian Rockies

Frommer's Vancouver & Victoria

Frommer's Washington State

Frommer's Seattle & Portland

Here's what the critics say about Frommer's:

"Amazingly easy to use. Very portable, very complete."

—*Booklist*

♦

"The only mainstream guide to list specific prices. The Walter Cronkite of guidebooks—with all that implies."

—*Travel & Leisure*

♦

"Complete, concise, and filled with useful information."

—*New York Daily News*

♦

"The best series for travelers who want one easy-to-use guidebook."

—*U.S. Air Magazine*

Alaska

2001

by Charles P. Wohlforth

IDG Books Worldwide, Inc.
An International Data Group Company
Foster City, CA • Chicago, IL • Indianapolis, IN • New York, NY

About the Author

Charles P. Wohlforth is a lifelong Alaskan who has been a writer and journalist since 1986. After graduating from Princeton University, he worked as a newspaper reporter in the small town of Homer, Alaska, and then for the *Anchorage Daily News,* where he covered the *Exxon Valdez* oil spill. In 1992, Wohlforth went on his own as a freelance writer for various regional and national magazines and as the author of books such as this one. His *Frommer's Family Vacations in the National Parks* covers parks all over the United States based on insights from the Wohlforth family's own camping experiences. Wohlforth lives in Anchorage with his wife, Barbara, sons Robin and Joseph, and daughter, Julia.

Cruise chapter: Introductory comments by **Matt Hannafin** and Charles Wohlforth; cruise-planning information and big-ship reviews excerpted from *Frommer's Alaska Cruises & Ports of Call* by **Fran Wenograd Golden** and **Jerry Brown;** small-ship reviews by Matt Hannafin.

IDG Books Worldwide, Inc.

An International Data Group Company
909 Third Ave.
New York, NY 10022

Find us online at **www.frommers.com**

ISBN 0-02-863775-5
ISSN 1042-8283

Editor: Lisa Renaud and John Rosenthal/Dog-Eared Pages
Production Editor: Tammy Ahrens
Design by Michele Laseau
Cartographer: John Decamillis
Photo Editor: Richard Fox
Production by IDG Books Indianapolis Production Department

Special Sales

For general information on IDG Books Worldwide's books in the U.S., please call our Consumer Customer Service department at 1-800-762-2974. For reseller information, including discounts, bulk sales, customized editions, and premium sales, please call our Reseller Customer Service department at 1-800-434-3422.

Manufactured in the United States of America

5 4 3 2 1

Contents

4 Cruising Alaska's Coast 64

5 Southeast Alaska 80

6 Anchorage & Environs 186

7 The Kenai Peninsula & Prince William Sound 230

List of Maps

ACKNOWLEDGMENTS

I couldn't put together a book such as this without a lot of help in covering Alaska's great distances and tracking its fast-changing visitor businesses. Friends all over Alaska show me around when I drop in for one of my visits as a "professional tourist," but a few people in particular do much more. My wife, Barbara, almost a coauthor, visits sights and hotels and keeps our family in order and happy as we travel together. My children, Robin, Julia, and Joseph, always are good sports and provide unique perspectives for "our travel book," making the discoveries of travel a joy, as only children can. My assistants in Anchorage and journalistic colleagues all over Alaska enabled me to make this book as up-to-date as any you'll find: Angela Baily, Kathryn Gerlek, Lynn Englishbee, Terry Williams, Carolyn Minor, Tom Morphet, Kris Capps, Carol Sturgulewski, Will Swagel, Tom Begich, Kathleen Tassaro, Robin Mackey Hill, Joe Bridgman, and Dimitra Lavrakas. Others, who helped build previous editions, included Brian O'Donohue, Alex DeMarben, Wendy Feuer, Eric and Caroline Wohlforth, Eric Troyer, Mark Handley, Catherine Reardon, Dean Mitchell, and Laura Mathews. Many other friends offered help and advice, and I'm grateful to all of them.

—Charles P. Wohlforth

An Invitation to the Reader

In researching this book, we discovered many wonderful places—hotels, restaurants, shops, and more. We're sure you'll find others. Please tell us about them, so we can share the information with your fellow travelers in upcoming editions. If you were disappointed with a recommendation, we'd love to know that, too. Please write to:

Frommer's Alaska 2001
IDG Books Worldwide, Inc.
909 Third Ave.
New York, NY 10022

An Additional Note

Please be advised that travel information is subject to change at any time—and this is especially true of prices. We therefore suggest that you write or call ahead for confirmation when making your travel plans. The authors, editors, and Publisher cannot be held responsible for the experiences of readers while traveling. Your safety is important to us, however, so we encourage you to stay alert and be aware of your surroundings. Keep a close eye on cameras, purses, and wallets, all favorite targets of thieves and pickpockets.

What the Symbols Mean

✪ Frommer's Favorites

Our favorite places and experiences—outstanding for quality, value, or both.

The following abbreviations are used for credit cards:

AE	American Express	EC	Eurocard
CB	Carte Blanche	JCB	Japan Credit Bank
DC	Diners Club	MC	MasterCard
DISC	Discover	V	Visa
ER	enRoute		

Find Frommer's Online

www.frommers.com offers up-to-the-minute listings on almost 200 cities around the globe—including the latest bargains and candid, personal articles updated daily by Arthur Frommer himself. No other Web site offers such comprehensive and timely coverage of the world of travel.

The Best of Alaska

1

As a child, when my family traveled outside Alaska for vacations, I often met other children who asked, "Wow, you live in Alaska? What's it like?" I never did well with that question. To me, the place I was visiting was far simpler and easier to describe than the one I was from. The Lower 48 seemed a fairly homogeneous land of freeways and fast food, a well-mapped network of established places. Alaska, on the other hand, wasn't—and isn't—even completely explored. Natural forces of vast scale and subtlety still were shaping the land in their own way, inscribing a different story on each of an infinite number of unexpected places. Each region, whether populated or not, was unique far beyond my ability to explain. Alaska was so large and new, so unconquered and exquisitely real, as to defy summation.

In contrast to many places you might choose to visit, it's Alaska's unformed newness that makes it so interesting and fun. Despite the best efforts of tour planners, the most memorable parts of a visit are unpredictable and often unexpected: a humpback whale leaping clear of the water, the face of a glacier releasing huge ice chunks, a bear feasting on salmon in a river, a huge salmon chomping onto your line. You can look at totem poles and see Alaska Native cultural demonstrations, and you can also get to know living indigenous people who still know and live by many of the traditional ways. And sometimes grand, quiet moments come, and those are the ones that endure most deeply.

As the writer of this guidebook, I aim to help you get to places where you may encounter what's new, real, and unexpected. Opening yourself to those experiences is your job, but it's an effort that's likely to pay off. Although I have lived here all my life, I often envy the stories visitors tell me about the Alaska places they have gone to and what happened there. No one owns Alaska, and most of us are newcomers here. In all this immensity, a visitor fresh off the boat is just as likely as a lifelong resident to see or do something amazing.

1 The Best Views

- **A First Sight of Alaska:** Flying north from Seattle, you're in clouds, so you concentrate on a book. When you look up, the light from the window has changed. Down below, the clouds are gone, and under the wing, where you're used to seeing roads, cities, and farms on most flights, instead you see only high, snowy mountain peaks, without the slightest mark of human presence, stretching as far as the horizon. Welcome to Alaska.

Alaska

MILEAGE CHART Approximate driving distances in miles between cities.	Anchorage	Circle	Dawson City	Eagle	Fairbanks	Haines	Homer	Prudhoe Bay	Seattle	Seward	Skagway	Tok	Valdez
Anchorage		520	494	501	358	775	226	847	2234	126	832	328	304
Circle	520		530	541	162	815	746	1972	2271	646	872	368	526
Dawson City	494	530		131	379	548	713	868	1843	619	430	189	428
Eagle	501	541	131		379	620	727	868	1974	627	579	173	427
Fairbanks	358	162	379	379		653	584	489	2121	484	710	206	364
Haines	775	815	548	620	653		1001	1142	1774	901	359	447	701
Homer	226	746	713	727	584	1001		1073	2455	173	1058	554	530
Prudhoe Bay	847	1972	868	868	489	1142	1073		2610	973	1199	695	853
Seattle	2243	2271	1843	1974	2121	1774	2455	2610		1361	1577	1931	2169
Seward	126	646	619	627	484	901	173	973	1361		958	454	430
Skagway	832	872	430	579	710	359	1058	1199	1577	958		504	758
Tok	328	368	189	173	206	447	554	695	1931	454	504		254
Valdez	304	526	428	427	364	701	530	853	2169	430	758	254	

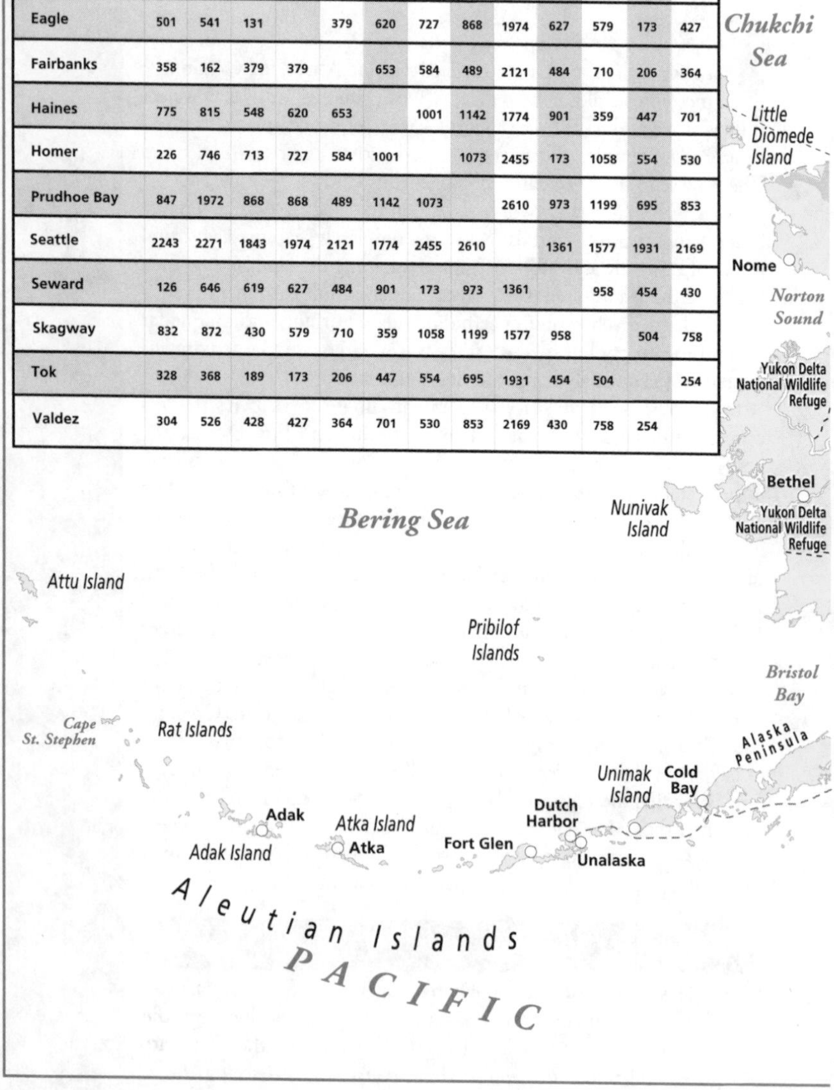

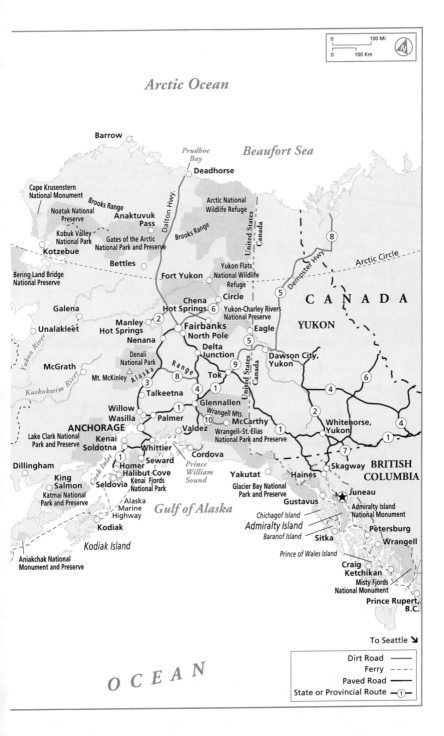

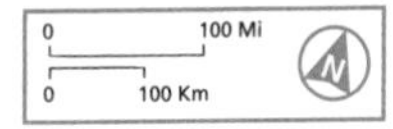

Arctic Ocean

Barrow
Prudhoe Bay
Beaufort Sea
Deadhorse
Cape Krusenstern National Monument
Brooks Range
Noatak National Preserve
Anaktuvuk Pass
Dalton Hwy.
Arctic National Wildlife Refuge
Brooks Range
United States
Canada
Kobuk Valley National Park
Gates of the Arctic National Park and Preserve
Kotzebue
Dempster Hwy.
Arctic Circle
Bettles
Bering Land Bridge National Preserve
Fort Yukon
Yukon Flats National Wildlife Refuge
Circle
CANADA
Galena
Chena Hot Springs
Yukon-Charley Rivers National Preserve
Manley Hot Springs
Unalakleet
Fairbanks
Eagle
YUKON
Yukon River
North Pole
Nenana
Delta Junction
Dawson City, Yukon
Denali National Park
McGrath
Alaska Range
Tok
United States
Canada
Mt. McKinley
Kuskokwim River
Talkeetna
Glennallen
Willow
Wrangell Mts.
Wasilla
Palmer
McCarthy
ANCHORAGE
Valdez
Whitehorse, Yukon
Lake Clark National Park and Preserve
Kenai
Wrangell-St. Elias National Park and Preserve
Soldotna
Whittier
Cordova
Seward
Prince William Sound
Dillingham
Homer
Cook Inlet
Halibut Cove
Skagway
BRITISH COLUMBIA
Yakutat
Haines
King Salmon
Seldovia
Kenai Fjords National Park
Glacier Bay National Park and Preserve
Juneau
Katmai National Park and Preserve
Alaska Marine Highway
Gulf of Alaska
Gustavus
Admiralty Island National Monument
Chichagof Island
Admiralty Island
Kodiak
Baranof Island
Sitka
Petersburg
Kodiak Island
Wrangell
Aniakchak National Monument and Preserve
Prince of Wales Island
Craig
Ketchikan
Misty Fjords National Monument
Prince Rupert, B.C.

To Seattle ↘

OCEAN

Legend	
Dirt Road	
Ferry	
Paved Road	
State or Provincial Route	

- **Punchbowl Cove** (Misty Fjords National Monument): A sheer granite cliff rises smooth and implacable 3,150 feet straight up from the water. A pair of bald eagles wheels and soars across its face, providing the only sense of scale. They look the size of gnats. See chapter 5.
- **From the Chugach Mountains Over Anchorage, at Sunset:** The city sparkles below, on the edge of an orange-reflecting Cook Inlet, far below the mountainside where you stand. Beyond the pink and purple silhouettes of mountains on the other side of the Inlet, the sun is spraying warm, dying light into puffs of clouds. And yet it's midnight. See chapter 6.
- **Mount McKinley from the Air** (Denali National Park): Your bush pilot guides his plane up from the flatlands of Talkeetna into a realm of eternal white, where a profusion of insanely rugged peaks rises in higher relief than any other spot on earth. After circling a 3-mile-high wall and slipping through a mile-deep canyon, you land on a glacier, get out of the plane, and for the first time realize the overwhelming scale of it all. See chapter 8.
- **The Northern Lights** (Alaska's Interior): Blue, purple, green, and red lines spin from the center of the sky, draping long tendrils of slow-moving light. Bright, flashing, sky-covering waves wash across the dome of stars like ripples driven by a gust of wind on a pond. Looking around, your companions' faces are rosy in a silver, snowy night, all gazing straight up with their mouths open. See chapter 9.

2 The Best Alaska Cruises

Cruises provide comfortable, leisurely access to the Inside Passage and the Gulf of Alaska. Here are some of the best bets. See chapter 4 for details.

- **Best Up-Close Alaska Experience:** Alaska's Glacier Bay Tours and Cruises' *Wilderness Adventurer* and *Wilderness Explorer* sail itineraries that shun overcrowded port towns in favor of wilderness areas and small fishing villages. Both carry sea kayaks for off-ship exploration, and both feature naturalist-led hikes as central features of the experience. The line is owned by an Alaska Native corporation and the ships are small (carrying 74 and 36 passengers, respectively) and very casual. They're not fancy, but that's the point—it's where they take you that counts.
- **Best Itinerary:** World Explorer Cruises' *Universe Explorer* is unmatched, offering a 14-day round-trip itinerary from Vancouver that includes all the major ports of call and a few others, too. They also offer a 9-night round-trip out of Vancouver, featuring the best of the Inside Passage. The ship is large, though not huge, and stresses education rather than the typical big-ship cruise diversions.
- **Most Comfortable Small Ships:** Cruise West's *Spirit of Endeavor* and *Spirit of '98* (a 19th-century coastal steamer re-creation) and Clipper's *Yorktown Clipper* offer a higher level of comfort than the other small ships in Alaska while still giving you an intimate, casual, up-close small-ship experience.
- **Most Luxurious Big Ships:** *Crystal Harmony* is the top-of-the-line ship in the Alaska market, with superb cuisine, elegant service, lovely surroundings, great cabins, and sparkling entertainment. If you want a more casual kind of luxury, Radisson Seven Seas' *Seven Seas Navigator* (which is slightly smaller than the *Harmony*) offers just that. Among the mainstream cruise ships, Celebrity's *Mercury* and *Galaxy* are the big winners, offering cutting-edge modern ships with great service, dining, and design.
- **Best Cruisetours:** Holland America Line and Princess are the leaders in linking cruises with land tours into the interior, either before or after your cruise. They

own their own hotels, deluxe motor coaches, and railcars, and after many years in the business, they both really know what they're doing. Princess concentrates more on the Anchorage/Denali/Fairbanks routes, while Holland America has many itineraries that get you to the Yukon territory's Dawson City and Whitehorse.

3 The Best Glaciers

More of Alaska—more than 100 times more—is covered by glacier ice than is settled by human beings.

- **Grand Pacific Glacier** (Glacier Bay National Park): Two vast glaciers of deep blue meet at the top of an utterly barren fjord. They rubbed and creased the gray rock for thousands of years before just recently releasing it to the air again. Boats that pull close to the glaciers seem surrounded by the intimidating walls of ice on three sides. See chapters 4 and 5.
- **Childs Glacier** (Cordova): Out the Copper River Highway from Cordova, this is a participatory glacier-viewing experience. The glacier is cut by the Copper River, a quarter mile broad; standing on the opposite shore (unless you're up in the viewing tower), you have to be ready to run like hell when the creaking, popping ice gives way and a huge berg falls into the river, potentially swamping the picnic area. Even when the glacier isn't calving, you can feel the ice groaning in your gut. See chapter 7.
- **Exit Glacier** (Seward): You can drive near the glacier and walk the rest of the way on a gravel path. Then it towers above like a huge blue sculpture, the spires of broken ice close enough to breathe a freezer-door chill down on watchers. See chapter 7.
- **College Fjords** (Prince William Sound): In this area of western Prince William Sound, you can see a couple of dozen glaciers in a day. Some of these are the amazing tidewater glaciers that dump huge, office-building-sized spires of ice into the ocean, each setting off a terrific splash and outward-radiating sea wave. See chapters 4 and 7.

4 The Most Beautiful Drives & Train Rides

There aren't many highways in Alaska, but all are worth exploring. You'll find a description of each in chapter 9 under "Alaska's Highways à la Carte." Here are some highlights:

- **White Pass and Yukon Route Railway** (Skagway to Summit): The narrow-gauge excursion train, sometimes pulled by vintage steam engines, climbs the steep grade that was chiseled into the granite mountains by stampeders to the Klondike gold rush. The train is a sort of mechanical mountain goat, balancing on trestles and steep rock walls far above deep gorges. See chapter 5.
- **Seward Highway** (Turnagain Arm): Just south of Anchorage, the highway has been chipped into the side of the Chugach Mountains over the surging gray water of Turnagain Arm. Above, Dall sheep and mountain goats pick their way along the cliffs, within easy sight. Below, white beluga whales chase salmon through the turbid water. See chapter 7.
- **Alaska Railroad** (Anchorage to Seward): The line follows the same stretch of Turnagain Arm as the Seward Highway, then splits off as it rises into the mountains of the Kenai Peninsula, rumbling close along the face of a glacier and clinging to the edge of a vertically walled gorge with a roaring river at the bottom. See chapter 7.

- **Denali Highway:** Leading east-west through the Alaska Range, the Denali Highway crosses terrain that could be another Denali National Park, full of wildlife and with views so huge and grand, they seem impossible. See chapter 8.
- **Richardson Highway:** Just out of Valdez heading north, the Richardson Highway rises quickly from sea level to more than 2,600 feet, switching back and forth on the side of a mountain. With each turn, the drop down the impassable slope becomes more amazing. North of Glennallen, the highway rises again, bursting through the tree line between a series of mountains and tracing the edge of long alpine lakes, before descending, parallel with the silver skein of the Alaska Pipeline, to Delta Junction. See chapter 9.
- **Top of the World and Taylor Highways:** Leading over the top of rounded, tundra-clothed mountains from Dawson City, Yukon Territory, to the Alaska Highway near Tok, this gravel route floats on a waving sea of terrain, with mountains receding to the infinite horizon in every direction. See chapter 9.
- **The Roads Around Nome:** You can't drive to Nome, but 250 miles of gravel roads radiate from the Arctic community into tundra that's populated only by musk oxen, bear, reindeer, birds, and other wildlife. See chapter 10.

5 The Best Fishing

The quality of salmon fishing in Alaska isn't so much a function of place as of time. See chapter 2 for how to find out where the fish will be when you arrive.

- **Bristol Bay:** This is the world's richest salmon fishery; lodges on the remote rivers of the region are an angler's paradise. See chapter 2.
- **Prince of Wales Island:** Fly-in trips or roadside streams yield some of the most prolific salmon fishing and peaceful fly-fishing anywhere. See chapter 5.
- **Copper River Valley, Cordova:** The Copper itself is silty with glacial runoff, but feeder streams and rivers are rich with trout, Dolly Varden, and salmon. See chapter 7.
- **The Kenai River:** The biggest king salmon—up to 98 pounds—come from the swift Kenai River. Big fish are so common in the second run of kings that there's a special, higher standard for what makes a trophy. Silvers and reds add to a mad, summer-long fishing frenzy. See chapter 7.
- **Homer:** Alaska's largest charter-fishing fleet goes for halibut ranging into the hundreds of pounds. Beyond the road system, Unalaska has the biggest halibut. See chapters 7 and 10.
- **Kodiak Island:** The bears are so big because they live on an island that's crammed with spawning salmon in the summer. Kodiak has the best roadside salmon fishing in Alaska, and the remote fishing, at lodges or fly-in stream banks, is legendary. See chapter 10.

6 The Best Tips for Cooking Salmon

Now that you've caught a Pacific salmon, you need to know how to cook it—or order it in a restaurant—to avoid spoiling the rich flavor.

- **Freeze As Little As Possible:** It's a sad fact that salmon loses some of its richness and gets more "fishy" as soon as it's frozen. Eat as much as you can fresh, because it'll never be better. (Ask if the salmon is fresh when you order it in a restaurant.) Most fishing towns also have sport-fish processors who will flash-freeze or smoke the rest; they'll often trade your fish for stuff that's already processed. Don't overlook smoking, the traditional Native way of preserving fish for the winter.

- **Choose the Best Fish:** The finest restaurants advertise where their salmon comes from on the menu. In early summer, Copper River kings and reds are the richest in flavor; later in the summer, Yukon River salmon are best. King, red, and silver are the only species you should find in a restaurant. The oil in the salmon gives it the rich, meaty flavor; the fish from the Copper and Yukon are high in oil content.
- **Keep It Simple:** When ordering salmon or halibut in a restaurant, avoid anything with cheese or heavy sauces. When salmon is fresh, it's best with light seasoning, perhaps just a little lemon, dill weed, and pepper and salt, and basted with soy sauce; or without anything on it at all, grilled over alder coals.
- **Don't Overcook It:** Salmon should be cooked just until the moment the meat changes color and becomes flaky through to the bone, or slightly before. A minute more, and some of the texture and flavor are lost. That's why those huge barbecue salmon bakes often are not as good as they should be—it's too hard to cook hundreds of pieces of fish just right and serve them all hot.
- **Fillets, Not Steaks:** Salmon is cut two ways in Alaska: lengthwise fillets or crosswise steaks. The fillet is cut with the grain of the flesh, keeping the oil and moisture in the fish. Do not remove the skin before cooking—it holds in the oils, and will fall off easily when the fish is done.

7 The Best Bear Viewing

There are many places to see bears in Alaska, but if your goal is to make *sure* you see a bear—and potentially lots of bears—these are the best places:

- **Anan Wildlife Observatory:** When the fish are running, you can see many black bear feeding in a salmon stream from close at hand. Access is easiest from Wrangell. See chapter 5.
- **Pack Creek** (Admiralty Island): The brown bears of the island, which is more thickly populated with them than anywhere else on earth, have learned to ignore the daily visitors who stand on the platforms at Pack Creek. Access is by air from Juneau. See chapter 5.
- **Katmai National Park:** During the July and September salmon runs, dozens of giant brown bears congregate around Brooks Camp, where, from wooden platforms a few yards away, you can watch the full range of their behaviors. Flight services from Homer and Kodiak also bring guests at any time of the summer to see bears dig clams on the park's eastern seashore. See chapters 7 and 10.
- **Denali National Park:** The park offers the best and least expensive wildlife-viewing safari in the state. Passengers on the buses that drive the park road as far as the Eielson Visitor Center usually see at least some grizzlies. See chapter 8.

8 The Best Marine Mammal Viewing

You've got a good chance of seeing marine mammals almost anywhere you go boating in Alaska, but in some places it's almost guaranteed.

- **Frederick Sound** (Petersburg): A humpback jumped right into the boat with whale-watchers here in 1995. Petersburg boats also see otters and baby seals sitting on icebergs floating in front of LeConte Glacier. See chapter 5.
- **Point Adolphus** (Gustavus): Humpback whales show up off the point in Icy Strait, just a few miles from little Gustavus, a town of luxurious country inns, and in Bartlett Cove within Glacier Bay National Park. See chapter 5.

- **Sitka Sound:** Lots of otters and humpback whales show up in the waters near Sitka. In fall, when the town holds its Whale Fest, you can spot them from a city park built for the purpose. See chapter 5.
- **Kenai Fjords National Park** (near Seward): You don't have to go all the way into the park—you're pretty well assured of sea otters and sea lions in Resurrection Bay, near Seward, and humpbacks and killer whales often show up, too. See chapter 7.
- **Prince William Sound:** Otters, seals, and sea lions are easy—you'll see them on most trips out of Valdez, Whittier, or Cordova—but you also have a good chance of seeing both humpback and killer whales in the Sound. See chapter 7.

9 The Best Encounters with Native Culture

- **Chilkat Dancers** (Haines): The Tlingit dances of Haines are authentically loose—children learn their new parts by being thrown into the dance and picking it up. The totem-carving studio is wonderfully casual, standing open for visitors to wander in and meet the artists. See chapter 5.
- **Saxman Totem Park** (just south of Ketchikan): A Tlingit Native corporation owns a major totem pole collection and clan house here, providing tours and cultural demonstrations for visitors. The informal part of the experience, meeting carvers in the workshop, is the real highlight. See chapter 5.
- **Alaska Native Heritage Center** (Anchorage): All of Alaska's Native groups joined together to build this grand new living museum and gathering place, where dance and music performances, storytelling, art and craft demonstrations, and simple meetings of people happen every day. See chapter 6.
- **Alutiiq Museum** (Kodiak): The Koniag people are recovering their culture from the ground and from artifacts repatriated from the world's museums. Visitors can even join in archaeological fieldwork. See chapter 10.
- **Museum of the Aleutians** (Unalaska): Built by Aleuts to preserve and exhibit their own heritage, the new museum stands right beside a major dig still in progress. See chapter 10.
- **Inupiat Heritage Center** (Barrow): Another brand-new living museum, this is a place to meet and enjoy performances by the Native people who built the place, and to see extraordinary artifacts they have made and recovered from frozen digs. See chapter 10.
- **NANA Museum of the Arctic** (Kotzebue): Eskimos of this still-traditional city/village proudly show off their Inupiat way of life with a combination of high-tech and age-old entertainment. See chapter 10.

10 The Best Community Museums & Historic Sites

- **Sitka National Historical Park:** The site of the 1804 battle between the Tlingits and Russians, in a totem pole park and seaside stand of old-growth forest, allows you to really appreciate what the Native people were fighting for. Inside the visitor center, Native craftspeople carry on their traditional work and talk with visitors. See chapter 5.
- **The Alaska State Museum** (Juneau): This richly endowed museum doesn't just show off its wealth of objects—it also uses them to teach about the state. A visit will put Alaska's Native cultures and pioneer history entirely in context. See chapter 5.

- **Anchorage Museum of History and Art:** Alaska's largest museum has the room and expertise to tell the story of Native and white history in Alaska, and to showcase contemporary Alaskan art and culture. See chapter 6.
- **The Pratt Museum** (Homer): The Pratt explains the life of the ocean in an intimate and clear way you'll find nowhere else in Alaska. See chapter 7.
- **University of Alaska Museum** (Fairbanks): The wealth of the university's study of Alaska, in all its forms, is put on display in galleries and daily shows, from equipment used to study the aurora borealis to a petrified bison. See chapter 9.

11 The Best Gold Rush Sites

The Klondike Gold Rush of 1898 transformed Alaska from a blank map at the periphery of America's consciousness to a fast-growing frontier and magnet for thousands of dreamers with visions of wealth. A century later, Alaska's best historic sites preserve that extraordinary time.

- **Skagway:** The little town at the top of Lynn Canal was where most of the gold rush stampeders got off the boat to head over the mountains to the Klondike. Spared from fire, flood, or even much significant economic development other than tourism, Skagway contains a large collection of gold rush era buildings protected by the National Park Service. See chapter 5.
- **Fairbanks:** The gold rush in Fairbanks, just after the turn of the century, is not entirely done yet—there's a big new mine north of town. The city is large enough to provide lots of interesting and fun activities that exploit gold rush history. See chapter 9.
- **Dawson City:** A group of prospectors made the Klondike gold strike in 1896 and returned to tell of it in 1897, and in 1898 tens of thousands of greedy gold seekers arrived after an arduous stampede. Dawson City is ground zero, and the town is dedicated to preserving and sharing the history of the gold rush phenomenon. See chapter 9.
- **Eagle:** Unlike the other tourist-thronged gold rush towns, Eagle is a forgotten backwater where the gold rush was the last significant thing to happen. The town is real and unspoiled, with lots to see but few other people to see it with. See chapter 9.

12 The Best Winter Destinations

- **Sitka:** Much of historic Sitka is just as good in winter as at any other time of year, but with fewer crowds and lower prices. The humpback whale watching is exceptional in the late fall and early winter, as the whales stop off here on their migration. See chapter 5.
- **Anchorage:** The Fur Rendezvous and Iditarod sled dog races keep a winter-carnival atmosphere going through much of February and March, but those who enjoy participatory winter sports will enjoy Anchorage most, with some of the best Nordic and telemark skiing anywhere, close access to three downhill skiing areas, dog mushing, and lake skating. See chapter 6.
- **Alyeska Resort** (Girdwood): Alaska's premier downhill skiing area has lots of snow over a long season, fantastic views, new lifts, and a luxurious hotel. See "The Best Hotels," below, and chapter 6.
- **Chena Hot Springs Resort:** A 90-minute ride from Fairbanks and you're out in the country, where the northern lights are clear on a starry winter afternoon and night. The resort has lots of activities to get you out into the snowy countryside, or you can just relax in the hot mineral springs. See chapter 9.

13 The Best Unspoiled Small Towns

- **Gustavus:** It's a lovely little town near Glacier Bay National Park, except it isn't really a town. There's no local government or town center—just a collection of luxurious country inns and lodges in a setting of great scenic beauty, close to some of the best fishing, whale watching, and sea kayaking in Alaska. See chapter 5.
- **Petersburg:** The town is so accessible (it's right on the Inside Passage ferry route), that it's incredible it has kept its quaint, small-town identity. Out of town, there's a wonderfully diverse choice of outdoor activities. See chapter 5.
- **Cordova:** This fishing town off the beaten track is a forgotten treasure, caught at some mythical point in the past when Norman Rockwell's paintings were relevant. That atmosphere combines with great bird watching, fishing, scenic grandeur, and other outdoor activities to make Cordova one of Alaska's most charming and attractive destinations. See chapter 7.
- **Halibut Cove:** Halibut Cove has no roads, only the calm green water in an ocean channel between docks and floats and houses on boardwalks. There are three art galleries, but the main activities are slowing down, paddling around, and walking in the woods. See chapter 7.
- **Kodiak:** This is the hub for an area, virtually untouched by visitors, with the biggest bears, most plentiful salmon, richest wilderness, best sea kayaking waters, and much other natural beauty. In town there are narrow, winding streets, Russian and Native historic sites, and wonderfully hospitable people. See chapter 10.

14 The Strangest Community Events

- **Cordova Ice Worm Festival:** The truth is, ice worms do exist. Really. This winter carnival celebrates them in February. The highlight is the traditional annual march of the ice worm (a costume with dozens of feet sticking out) down the main street. See chapter 7.
- **Snow Man Festival** (Valdez): A community that counts its winter snowfall by the yard makes the most of it in March, with a winter carnival that includes ice bowling, snowman building, and a drive-in movie projected on a snowbank. See chapter 7.
- **Midnight Sun Baseball Game** (Fairbanks): The semipro baseball game, played without lights, doesn't begin until 10:30pm on the longest day of the year. See chapter 9.
- **Bering Sea Ice Golf Classic** (Nome): The greens are Astroturf, as the sea ice won't support a decent lawn in mid-March. Hook a drive and you could end up spending hours wandering among the pressure ridges, but you must play the ball as it lies. See chapter 10.
- **Nome Polar Bear Swim/Bathtub Race:** Nome has so *many* strange community events. Memorial Day is marked by the polar bear swim, sea ice permitting. Labor Day is celebrated by a bathtub race down Front Street, with water and a bather in each tub. See chapter 10.
- **Pillar Mountain Golf Classic** (Kodiak): The course is one hole, par is 70, and elevation gain is 1,400 feet. Having a spotter in the deep snow of late March is helpful, but use of two-way radios, dogs, and chain saws is prohibited. Also, there's no cutting down power poles, and cursing tournament officials carries a $25 fine. See chapter 10.

- **Community Softball** (Barrow): Play in the Arctic requires some special considerations. Spectators watch from their cars, and if a ball disappears in a puddle so that no part of it is showing, runners can advance no more than two bases. See chapter 10.

15 The Best Hotels

- **Westmark Cape Fox Lodge** (Ketchikan; ☎ **907/225-8001**): Standing in its own little forest atop a rocky promontory that dominates downtown Ketchikan, this cleanly luxurious hotel has the feel of a mountain lodge or resort. A funicular tram carries visitors to the Creek Street boardwalks, or you can take the wooded cliff-side path. The rooms and common areas, accented with masterpieces of Tlingit art, have exceptional views of the city and Tongass Narrows through the trees. See chapter 5.
- **Hotel Captain Cook** (Anchorage; ☎ **800/843-1950**): This is the grand old hotel of downtown Anchorage, with a heavy nautical theme, teak paneling, and every possible amenity. It also remains the state's standard of service and luxury. See chapter 6.
- **Westin Alyeska Prince Hotel** (Girdwood; ☎ **800/880-3880**): The first sight of this ski resort hotel—designed in a château style and standing in an undeveloped mountain valley—is enough to make you catch your breath. Wait till you get inside and see the starscape and polar bear diorama in the lobby atrium, or the large swimming pool, with its high-beamed ceiling and windows looking out on the mountain. The cozy rooms are full of cherry wood. A tram carries skiers and diners to the top of the mountain. See chapter 6.
- **Land's End** (Homer; ☎ **907/235-0400**): The hotel itself has some nice touches, but it wouldn't be in a class with the others on this list if not for its location. The low, wood buildings lie like a string of driftwood beached on the tip of Homer Spit, out in the middle of Kachemak Bay. Nothing stands between the rooms or restaurant and the ocean, across the beach. Sometimes whales and otters swim along the shore, just outside the windows. See chapter 7.
- **River's Edge Resort Cottages** (Fairbanks; ☎ **800/770-3343** or 907/474-0286): A village of trim little cottages with nicely appointed rooms watches the Chena River flow by from patios with sliding-glass doors. The owners thought of building the place when they saw how guests in their RV park enjoyed socializing. You feel like you've moved into a friendly neighborhood. Guests can canoe right from their front yards. See chapter 9.
- **Fairbanks Exploration Inn** (☎ **907/451-1920**): Alaska's best historic inn doesn't look so exciting from the outside—it's just a group of bungalows under the birch trees—but the bedrooms and common sitting rooms, full of light on bare wood floors, have a cool elegance and authenticity that make them that much more luxurious. See chapter 9.
- **The Grand Aleutian Hotel** (Unalaska/Dutch Harbor; ☎ **800/891-1194**): Not long ago, it wasn't much of a distinction to be the best hotel in the Alaska Bush. Then the UniSea fish company built this large, lodge-style luxury hotel, which is competitive with the best in the state and gets extra points for the sheer audacity of building it on this remote, volcanic island. The hotel's existence creates a unique opportunity for those who want to stay in a fine hotel and see the Bush, with the best unexploited fishing and wildlife and bird watching. See chapter 10.

16 The Best Bed & Breakfasts

- **Alaska Ocean View Bed and Breakfast** (Sitka; ☎ **907/747-8310**): Here a family has set out to turn its home into perfect accommodations. Among other details, the elaborate decor in each room matches a unique packet of souvenir wildflower seeds given to each guest. See chapter 5.
- **Pearson's Pond Luxury B&B Inn and Adventure Spa** (Juneau; ☎ **888/658-6328**): Diane Pearson takes the prize for the most obsessive attention to detail at any B&B in Alaska. Not only are the bathrooms stocked with condoms and computers, but the private pond, with a spraying fountain, is stocked with fish. See chapter 5.
- **Glacier Trail Bed & Breakfast** (Juneau; ☎ **907/789-5646**): The hosts built their house to be the perfect B&B, with Jacuzzi tubs, stunning glacier views from the bedrooms, and many amenities. Others could have done that, but only this fascinating and very Alaska couple could make their guests feel so welcome. See chapter 5.
- **Aurora Winds Inn B&B Resort** (Anchorage; ☎ **907/346-2533**): This enormous house on the hillside above Anchorage has rooms so completely and theatrically decorated you'll feel as if you're sleeping in a movie set. See chapter 6.
- **The Oscar Gill House Bed and Breakfast** (Anchorage; ☎ **907/258-1717**): It's no longer hard to find beautifully restored historic B&Bs, but I've found no others like this one, where, despite being overwhelmed with business, the hosts keep their rates low just because they're decent people who know how it feels to be overcharged when you're traveling. See chapter 6.
- **The Northern Nights Inn** (Cordova; ☎ **907/424-5356**): Located in a historic hillside house with just a few rooms, the inn is operated by an old Cordova family with lots of energy and hospitality. The upstairs rooms have every amenity and are furnished with antiques, but rent for very low rates. See chapter 7.
- **Forget-Me-Not Lodge and the Aurora Express Bed and Breakfast** (Fairbanks; ☎ **907/474-0949**): The owners bought an old-fashioned railroad train, hauled it up the side of a mountain above Fairbanks, and remodeled the cars in luxurious theme decor as a bed-and-breakfast. See chapter 9.

2

Planning Your Trip: The Basics

Planning a trip to Alaska can be a bit more complicated than traveling in the rest of the United States. Besides the vast distances and range of climatic conditions, the best places book up far ahead for the high summer season. This chapter provides the general information to get oriented, then covers when and how to travel to Alaska, including guides, outfitters, and package tour operators. I've also included advice on fishing and shopping for Alaska Native art.

Internet resources are covered in **"Planning Your Trip: An Online Directory,"** on p. 48.

1 The Regions in Brief

SOUTHEAST ALASKA The Southeast Panhandle is the relatively narrow strip of mountains and islands that lies between Canada and the Gulf of Alaska. To Alaskans, it's Southeast, but to the rest of the country, it's more like the northernmost extension of the lush Pacific Northwest. It's a land of huge rain-forest trees, glacier-garbed mountains, and countless islands ranging in size from the nation's third largest to tiny, one-tree islets strewn like confetti along the channels and fjords. The water is the highway of Southeast Alaska, as the land is generally too steep and rugged to build roads, but there are lots of towns and villages reachable by the ferry system or cruise ships. Southeast contains **Juneau,** Alaska's capital and third-largest city, and **Ketchikan,** next in size to Juneau. Southeast's towns are as quaint and historic as any in Alaska, especially **Sitka,** which preserves the story of Russian America and its conflict with the indigenous Native people. Alaska Native culture—Tlingit and Haida—is rich and close to hand. No other region is richer in opportunities for boating or seeing marine wildlife. Likewise, no other region is as crowded with tourists; some half a million of them are passengers of cruise ships that dock in the tiny towns all summer. The weather is wet and temperate.

SOUTHCENTRAL ALASKA As a region, Southcentral is something of a catch-all. The area is roughly defined by the arc of the Gulf of Alaska from the Canadian border on the east to Cook Inlet and the end of the road network to the west. It's a microcosm of the state, containing **Prince William Sound,** which is similar to the wooded island habitat of Southeast; the **Kenai Peninsula,** a roaded fishing, boating, and outdoor mecca; **Anchorage,** the state's modern, major city; and

Alaska by the Numbers

This chart shows some comparative indicators for 17 of Alaska's most popular destinations. The third column is the best season to visit, when there's enough going on and weather is suitable (that includes weather that's good for winter sports). The "Transportation" column shows ways of getting to each destination (see more on this in "Getting There," later in this chapter).

Place	Population	Season	Transportation	Precip. (inches)	Snow (inches)
Anchorage	259,391	May–Sept/ Feb–Mar	Road, air, rail	15.4	69
Barrow	4,438	June–Aug	Air	4.7	28
Denali National Park	169	June–Sept	Road, rail	15.0	54.8
Fairbanks	83,773	May–Sept/ Feb–Mar	Road, air, rail	10.4	68
Glacier Bay National Park	377	May–Sept	Air, boat	53.9	70.2
Homer	4,154	May–Sept	Road, air, ferry	24.9	58
Juneau	30,189	May–Sept	Air, ferry	52.9	100
Kenai	7,005	May–Oct	Road, air	18.9	59.3
Ketchikan	13,961	May–Sept	Air, ferry	155.2	37
Kodiak Island	12,158	May–Sept	Air, ferry	74.3	80
Kotzebue	2,932	June–Aug	Air	9.0	47.6
Nome	3,615	June–Aug/ Mar	Air	15.6	56
Petersburg	3,415	May–Sept	Air, ferry	105.8	102
Seward	3,010	May–Sept	Road, rail, ferry, air	67.7	79.9
Sitka	8,681	May–Sept/ Nov	Air, ferry	86.8	40.7
Skagway	825	May–Sept	Road, ferry, air	23.0	35.7
Valdez	4,164	May–Sept/ Mar	Road, air, ferry	61.5	32.0

the **Matanuska and Susitna Valleys,** an agricultural and suburban region of broad flatlands between steep mountains. Southcentral dominates Alaska, with most of the state's population and a more highly developed transportation system than elsewhere, including a network of highways and the Alaska Railroad. Southcentral's weather is influenced by the ocean, keeping it from being very hot or very cold. The coastal areas are wet, while just behind the coastal mountains the weather is drier.

THE INTERIOR The vast central part of the state is crossed by highways and by rivers that act as highways. Big river valleys lie between great mountain ranges, the largest of which are the Alaska Range, which contains **Mount McKinley,** North America's tallest peak, and the Brooks Range, the northern end of the cordillera that includes the Rockies. McKinley is the centerpiece of **Denali National Park,** Alaska's premier road-accessible wildlife-viewing destination. The region's dominant city is **Fairbanks,** Alaska's second largest, which lies on the lazy Chena River roughly in the middle of the state. The natural environment is drier and less abundant than Southeast or Southcentral. The Athabascans, the Interior's first people, still subsist from this sparse land in tiny villages and river fish camps. Summers can be hot and winters very cold in the Interior, because of the distance from the ocean.

THE BUSH Bush Alaska is linked by lifestyle rather than by geography. One good definition would be that the Bush is that part of the state that's closer to the wilderness than to civilization. It's also the only part of the state where Native people outnumber whites and other relative newcomers. In many Bush villages, readily accessible to the outside world only by small plane, people still live according to age-old subsistence hunting-and-gathering traditions. The Bush region includes the majority of Alaska outside the road network, ranging from the north end of the Canadian border all the way around the coast, out the Aleutians, and the Alaska Peninsula and Kodiak Island, south of Anchorage. But some towns in each of the other regions also could be called "Bush villages." The Bush contains many regions, including the Arctic, Northwest, and Southwest Alaska.

2 Visitor Information

The **Alaska Tourism Industry Association,** P.O. Box 143361, Anchorage, Alaska 99514-3361 (☎ **907/929-2200;** e-mail info@alaskatia.org), handles inquiries for the whole state and sends out a free "vacation planner." The agency was in flux as of this writing, however; it does have a Web site at **www.alaskatia.org** at the moment, but it needs work, and will surely be further developed in the coming months.

For outdoor recreation, the **Alaska Public Lands Information Centers** are centralized sources of information on all government lands, which include more than 85% of the state. The centers, in Anchorage, Fairbanks, Ketchikan, and Tok, are operated cooperatively by many land agencies, including the National Park Service and U.S. Forest Service. The Anchorage center is at 605 W. Fourth Ave., Suite 105, Anchorage, AK 99501 (☎ **907/271-2737,** TTY 907/271-2738; www.nps.gov/aplic). See the Fairbanks and Tok listings in chapter 9 for the centers there. Information on the facility in Ketchikan, called the Southeast Alaska Discovery Center, is in chapter 5.

We have covered Internet travel-planning resources in **"Planning Your Trip: An Online Directory,"** on p. 48. Information for specific destinations, on the Internet or otherwise, is in each of the relevant section throughout the book.

3 Money

Alaska is an expensive destination any way you slice it. In popular spots, a good standard motel room is rarely available for less than $100 in the high season, and is more often over $120. Airfare from Seattle to Anchorage fluctuates

Native Art: Finding the Real Thing

In a gift shop in Southeast Alaska, a woman who said she was an artist's assistant was sanding a Tlingit-style carving. When I asked who made the carving, the artist said, "It's my work." At the time, that seemed like an odd way of putting it. Only later did I learn from one of the artist's former assistants that his "work" involved ordering the carvings from Southeast Asia and shipping them to Alaska, where he hired locals to pretend to be working on them in the shop. A journalist friend of mine met a boy in the alley behind a gift store in Ketchikan removing "Made in Taiwan" stickers from merchandise with a razor blade. Several years ago, the Federal Trade Commission fined an art dealer for peddling fake Native art. He was able to go on selling carvings signed by a person with a made-up, Native-sounding name along with the name of an Alaska village. The artist was Cambodian and had spent only a few months in the village.

You may not care if the gifts and souvenirs you buy in Alaska really come from Alaska. But if you do, especially if you plan to spend a lot of money on authentic Alaska Native art, you must pay attention.

The most serious kind of counterfeit is fake Alaska Native fine art. Pieces sell for $500 or more, and the scam both defrauds the buyer and takes food off the tables of Alaska's village artists, who can't compete in price with Indonesian carvers. In 1995, *Anchorage Daily News* reporter Bruce Melzer documented that copying original Native art is a widespread practice. He found villages in Bali where hundreds of workers were turning out Eskimo masks and moose, otter, and sheep carvings from fossilized walrus ivory, whalebone, and other Alaskan materials, using designs taken from books sent from Alaska. (I am indebted to Melzer for much of the information in this essay.)

wildly with competition among the airlines, but a $300 round-trip, with 14-day advance purchase, is a fair deal. (Flying is cheaper than driving or taking the ferry and bus.) You can easily pay twice that to fly to an Alaska Bush community. Even the train is expensive, with a one-way fare from Anchorage to Fairbanks (a 350-mile trip) costing $160 on the least luxurious of three choices of cars.

A couple ordering a good salmon dinner, appetizers, and wine will likely pay $100 in a fine restaurant, including tip. One reason cruise ships have become such a popular way to visit Alaska is that, for the same quality level, they're less expensive on a daily basis than independent travel, and offer the chance to see remote coastal areas that can be quite costly to get to for land-based visitors. (See chapter 4 for details on cruising.)

To travel at a standard American comfort level, a couple should allow $120 per person, per day, for room and board. The cost of an activity such as flightseeing, wildlife cruises, or guided fishing typically is $75 to $250 per person. Also add ground transportation—you may need to rent a car, the best way to see much of the state. An economy car rents for around $55 a day from the major national firms, although you can do better with an unknown brand. Weekly rentals generally cost the same as renting for 5 individual days. You also may need train and ferry tickets.

Ask some questions before you buy. Any reputable art dealer will provide you with a biography of the artist who created an expensive work. Ask specifically if that artist actually carved the piece: Some Native artists have sold their names and designs to wholesalers who produce knockoffs. Price is another tip-off. An elaborate mask is more likely to cost $3,000 than $300. Another indicator is the choice of materials; most soapstone carvings are not made in Alaska.

The **Alaska Arts Council** (☎ **907/269-6610**) validates Native art and crafts with a **silver hand** label, which assures you it was made by the hands of an Alaska Native. But the program isn't universally used, so the absence of the label doesn't mean the work definitely isn't authentic. Other labels aren't worth much—an item could say **Alaska Made** even if only insignificant assembly work happened here. Of course, in Bush Alaska, and in some urban shops, you can buy authentic work directly from craftspeople. Buying in Native-owned co-ops also is safe.

For gifts that don't claim to be made by Natives but do at least purport to originate in the state, a symbol of two bears that says **Made in Alaska** indicates that **Make It Alaskan Inc.** (☎ **907/258-2878**) has determined it was at least substantially made here. Non-Natives produce Alaskan crafts of ceramics, wood, or fabric, but not plastic—if it's plastic, it probably was not made in Alaska. Again, price is an indicator: As with anywhere else in the United States, the cheapest products come from Asia.

Mostly, finding something real is up to you. When Melzer interviewed dealers selling fake Alaska Native arts and crafts, they said they tell customers where the work comes from if asked. But most people don't ask.

Of course, you also can trim down your costs by cutting your demands. You'll learn more about the real Alaska staying in bed-and-breakfast accommodations than in a standard hotel room. Expect to pay $85 to $95 for a decent room with a shared bathroom, $90 to $110 for a private bathroom. The free breakfast cuts down on your food costs, too. And there are plenty of family restaurants where you can eat a modest dinner for two for $30, with a tip and a glass of beer. Traveling in that style will bring the cost of room and board down to about $80 per person, per day, for a couple.

Another way to save money is to travel in the shoulder season, before and after the peak summer season. Hotel and guided activity prices drop significantly, typically 25% or more. May and September are solidly in the shoulder season, and sometimes you get bargains as late as June 15 or as early as August 15. Traveling in the winter is a whole different experience, but certainly saves a lot of money—where hotels are open, you'll find their rates typically running half of their high-season levels. For other considerations on off-season and shoulder-season travel, see "When to Go," later in this chapter.

You can save the most money by giving up a private room every night and cooking some of your own meals. Camping is a fun way to really see Alaska and costs only $8 to $12 a night in state and federal government campgrounds. Hostels are available in most towns, typically for around $12 a night.

Thousands of young people come to Alaska each summer and spend almost nothing, replenishing their funds when necessary with stints working at a fish cannery or restaurant—low-wage, long-hour jobs are usually available in the summer (see "For Students" under "Tips for Travelers with Special Needs," later in this chapter).

Even the small Bush communities now have ATMs; the main exceptions these days are remote outdoor destinations. In the "Fast Facts" section for each town in this book, I'll tell you if there's an ATM and where to find it. There's even a Web site where you can locate the nearest Plus Network ATM wherever you are in the world: **www.visa.com/pd/atm/**. Alaska ATMs generally are on the Cirrus, Plus, or MAC networks, and other major ATM networks.

In larger towns, you'll find that every business you'd expect to take credit, charge, or debit cards at home will accept them. Even bed-and-breakfasts and inexpensive restaurants usually take cards now. Few businesses of any kind will take an out-of-state personal check. Traveler's checks are good just about anywhere, but there's no reason to go through the hassle and expense anymore.

4 When to Go

CLIMATE & SEASONS

The weather in Alaska can be extreme and unpredictable. We're the first to get whatever Arctic Siberia or the void of the North Pacific have to throw at North America. The extremes of recorded temperatures are a high of 100°F and low of –80°F. At any time of year your vacation could be enlivened by weeks of unbroken sunny weather or weighed down by weeks of unbroken rain. All you can do is play the averages, hope for the best, and, if you do get bad weather, get out and have fun anyway—that's what Alaskans do. My own subjective summary of the visitor season in various Alaska places is found below in the chart "Alaska's Climate, by Months & Regions."

JUNE, JULY & AUGUST Summer in Alaska is a miraculous time, when the sun refuses to set, the salmon run up river, and people are energized by limitless daylight. The sun dips below the horizon in Anchorage for only about 4 hours on June 21, the longest day of the year, and the sky is light all night. The state fills with people coming to visit and to work in the seasonal fishing, timber, and construction industries. Weather gets warmer, although how warm depends on where you go (see the chart below). June is the driest of the 3 summer months, July the warmest, and August generally the rainiest month of the brief summer, but warmer than June. In most respects, June is the best summer month to make a visit, but it does have some drawbacks to consider: In the Arctic, snow doesn't all melt until mid-June; in Southcentral Alaska, trails at high elevation or in the shade may be too muddy or snowy; and not all activities or facilities at Denali National Park open until late June. It's also the worst time for mosquitoes.

Summer also is the season of high prices. Most operators in the visitor industry have only these 90 days to make their year's income, and they charge whatever the market will bear. July is the absolute peak of the tourist season, when you must book well ahead and when crowds are most prevalent. (Of course, crowding is relative. With a population density of roughly one person per square mile, Alaska is never *really* crowded.) Before June 15 and after

Alaska's Climate, by Months & Regions

	Jan	Feb	Mar	Apr	May	June	July	Aug	Sept	Oct	Nov	Dec
Anchorage: Southcentral Alaska												
Average high**	21	26	33	43	54	62	65	63	55	41	27	23
Average low**	8	12	18	29	39	47	52	50	42	29	15	10
Hours of light*	6:30	9:15	12:00	15:00	17:45	19:30	18:15	15:30	12:00	9:15	7:00	5:30
Sunny days†	12	10	13	12	11	10	9	9	9	10	10	10
Rainy or snowy days	8	8	8	6	7	8	11	13	14	12	10	11
Precipitation‡	0.8	0.8	0.7	0.7	0.7	1.1	1.7	2.4	2.7	2	1.1	1.1
Barrow: Arctic Alaska												
Average high**	–7	–12	–9	5	24	38	45	42	34	18/	3	–5
Average low**	–19	–24	–21	–9	14	30	34	33	27	9	–7	17
Hours of light*	0:00	7:30	12:00	17:00	24:00	24:00	24:00	18:00	12:00	8:00	0:00	0:00
Sunny days†	7	18	21	18	8	9	11	5	4	6	8	4
Rainy or snowy days	4	4	4	4	4	5	9	11	11	11	6	5
Precipitation‡	0.2	0.2	0.2	0.2	0.2	0.3	1	1	0.6	0.5	0.3	0.2
Cold Bay: Aleutian Archipelago												
Average high**	33	32	35	38	44	50	55	56	52	44	39	35
Average low**	24	23	25	29	35	41	46	47	43	35	30	27
Hours of light*	8:00	10:00	12:00	14:30	16:30	17:30	16:30	14:30	12:00	10:00	8:00	7:00
Sunny days†	8	6	8	4	3	3	3	2	4	6	6	7
Rainy or snowy days	19	17	18	16	17	16	17	20	21	23	22	21
Precipitation‡	2.8	2.3	2.2	2	2.3	2.1	2.5	3.2	4.4	4.3	4.2	3.7
Fairbanks: Interior Alaska												
Average high**	–2	7	24	41	59	70	72	66	55	32	11	2
Average low**	–18	–14	–2	20	38	50	53	47	36	18	–6	–15
Hours of light*	5:15	9:00	12:00	15:45	19:00	22:00	20:00	16:00	12:00	9:00	5:30	3:45
Sunny days†	15	14	17	14	16	13	12	10	10	9	12	12
Rainy or snowy days	8	7	6	5	7	11	12	12	10	11	11	9
Precipitation‡	0.5	0.4	0.4	0.3	0.6	1.4	1.9	2	0.9	0.9	0.8	0.8
Juneau: Southeast Alaska												
Average high**	29	34	39	47	55	61	64	63	56	47	37	32
Average low**	19	23	27	32	39	45	48	47	43	37	27	23
Hours of light*	7:30	9:30	12:00	14:45	17:00	18:15	17:30	15:00	12:00	10:00	7:30	6:30
Sunny days†	8	7	7	8	8	8	8	9	6	4	6	5
Rainy or snowy days	18	17	18	17	17	15	17	17	20	24	20	21
Precipitation‡	4.5	3.7	3.3	2.8	3.4	3.1	4.2	5.3	6.7	7.8	4.9	4.4
Valdez: Prince William Sound												
Average high**	26	30	36	44	52	59	62	61	54	43	32	28
Average low**	15	18	22	30	38	44	48	46	40	33	22	18
Hours of light*	7:00	9:15	12:00	15:00	17:45	19:30	18:00	15:30	12:00	9:15	7:00	5:30
Sunny days†	9	9	11	11	9	8	8	10	8	8	10	7
Rainy or snowy days	17	14	16	14	17	15	17	17	20	20	16	18
Precipitation‡	5.6	5.1	4.7	3.2	3.8	3.1	3.8	6	8.4	8	5.5	6.8

*Hours of light is an approximation of the possible daylight on the 20th day of each month.

**All temperatures are given in degrees Fahrenheit.

†Sunny days includes the average observed clear and partly cloudy days per month.

‡Precipitation is the average water equivalent of rain or snow.

August 15, the season begins to decline, providing occasional bargains and more elbow room. But the length and intensity of the visitor season vary widely in different areas, and in some places it stays quite busy from Memorial Day to Labor Day.

MAY & SEPTEMBER More and more visitors are coming to Alaska during these shoulder months to take advantage of the lower prices, absence of crowds, and special beauty.

May is the drier of the 2 months and can be as warm as summer, if you're lucky, but as you go farther north and earlier in the month, your chances increase of finding cold, mud, and even snow. In Alaska, we don't have spring—the melt of snow and resultant seas of mud are called **break up.** Flowers show up with the start of summer. Many outdoor activities aren't possible during break up, which can extend well into May. Before May 15, most tourist-oriented activities and facilities are still closed, and a few don't open until Memorial Day or June 1. Where visitor facilities are open, they often have significantly lower prices. Also, the first visitors of the year always receive an especially warm welcome. The very earliest salmon runs start in May, but for a fishing-oriented trip it's better to come later.

Sometime from late August to mid-September, weather patterns change, bringing clouds, frequent rainstorms, and cooling weather, and signaling the trees and tundra to turn bright, vivid colors. For a week or two (what week it is depends on your latitude), the bright-yellow birches of the boreal forest and rich red of the heathery tundra make September the most lovely time of year. But the rain and the nip in the air, similar to late October or November in New England, mean you'll likely have to bundle up; and September is among the wettest months of the year. Most tourist-oriented businesses stay open, with lower prices, till September 15, except in the Arctic. After September 15, it's potluck. Some areas close up tight, but the silver salmon fishing hits prime time on the Kenai Peninsula, and the season stays active until the end of the month. A lucky visitor can come in September and hit a month of crisp, sunny, perfect weather, and have the state relatively to him- or herself. Or, it can be cold and rainy all month. Cruise ships continue to ply the Inside Passage well into October, while the sky dumps torrential rains: Ketchikan averages 22 inches and 24 rainy days in the month.

WINTER One of the most spectacular trips I ever took was a train ride from Fairbanks to Anchorage in January. Outside the windows, Mount McKinley stood clear and so vivid in a vast, smooth landscape of pale blue and rich orange that I felt as if I could reach out and touch it. A young woman from South Africa was on the train. When I asked her why she came to Alaska in January, she only had to point out the window.

She was right, but visitors and the people who serve them generally haven't figured that out yet. Some towns (such as Skagway and Dawson City) close down almost completely. In others—most places on the ocean, for example—nearly all activities and attractions are closed for the season, but services remain open for business travelers. Where facilities are open, hotel prices are often less than half of what you'd pay in the high season. Quite luxurious rooms sometimes go for the cost of a budget motel. Visitors who seek out places of interest can have an exceptional and memorable time, enjoying some of the best alpine, Nordic, and backcountry skiing, outdoor ice-skating, dog mushing, snowmobiling, and aurora and wildlife watching available anywhere, at any time. The best time to come is late winter, from February through mid-March, when the sun is up longer and winter carnivals and competitive dog mushing hit their peak.

WHAT TO WEAR

SUMMER You're not going to the North Pole, and you don't need a down parka or winter boots weighing down your luggage. But you do need to be ready for a variety of weather, from sunny, 80° days to windy, rainy 50° outings on the water. The way Alaskans prepare for such a range is with layers. The content of the layers depends on what you'll be doing, but everyone should bring at least this: warm-weather clothes, long-sleeved shirts and pants, a wool sweater, a warm jacket, and a raincoat. Gloves and wool hats are a good idea, too, especially for boating trips. Combining these items, you'll be ready for any summer conditions. If you will do any hiking, bring sturdy shoes or cross trainers.

WINTER Normal alpine and Nordic skiing garb is adequate for skiing in Southcentral Alaska. Cross-country skiing in the Interior may require you to dress more warmly than you're accustomed to. Snowmobiling or dog mushing in winter requires the warmest possible clothing. On guided trips, they'll tell you what to bring or provide it for you. A full outfit for backcountry travel—including the stoutest Sorel or Air Force bunny boots, insulated snow pants, thermal underwear, a heavy down parka with a hood, thick mittens (not gloves), and a wool hat or face-covering mask—costs more than $500. You can buy what you need in Anchorage or Fairbanks when you arrive.

If you're not planning anything so rugged, you can get by in a city with a normal greatcoat, hat, gloves, and wool socks; if you're like most Alaskans, you'll just make a quick dash from car to heated building when really cold weather hits.

Alaska Calendar of Events

Here are some of the biggest community events of the year in Alaska's cities and towns. You'll also find fishing derbies going on all summer almost anywhere you go in Alaska. The dates, in many cases, are estimates, simply because of the early publication date of this book. Don't plan a vacation around them without calling the organizers or visitor information centers listed in each of the towns for up-to-date details.

February

- **The Yukon Quest International Sled Dog Race** (☎ **907/452-7954;** www.yukonquest.org/), held in mid-February, starts or finishes in Fairbanks (Fairbanks has the start in even-numbered years; Whitehorse, Yukon Territory, in odd-numbered years). Mushers say this rugged 1,000-mile race is even tougher than the Iditarod. Midmonth.
- **The Anchorage Fur Rendezvous Winter Carnival** (☎ **907/277-8615**) is a huge, citywide winter celebration, with many community events, fireworks, craft fairs, snowshoe softball, dogsled rides, and other fun. The main event is the **World Champion Sled Dog Race** (☎ **907/562-2235**), a 3-day sprint event of about 25 miles per heat. Second and third weekends of the month.

March

- **The Nenana Ice Classic** (☎ **907/832-5446;** www.ptialaska.net/~tripod), in Nenana, starts with a weekend celebration of dance performances, dog mushing, and other activities; the classic is a sweepstakes on who can guess closest to the exact date and time the ice will go out on the Tanana River. You can buy tickets all over Alaska. First weekend in March.

✪ **The Iditarod Trail Sled Dog Race** (☎ **907/376-5155;** www.iditarod.com/) starts the first Saturday in March with much fanfare from **Anchorage,** then the teams are loaded in trucks for the **Iditarod Restart,** in **Wasilla,** which is the real beginning of the race. Here the historic gold rush trail becomes continuous for the dogs' 1,000-mile run to Nome. The event enlivens Wasilla at the end of a long winter. The finish in Nome is the biggest event of the year in the Arctic, drawing world media attention and turning Nome into a huge party for a few days (they even play golf out on the sea ice). The race solicits volunteers to help, which is a much better way to experience it than just watching.

✪ **The World Ice Art Championships** (☎ **907/451-8250;** www.icealaska.com/), held in early to mid-March, brings carvers from all over the world to sculpt immense clear chunks cut from a Fairbanks pond. Among ice carvers, Fairbanks's ice is famous for its clarity and the great size of the chucks. Some spectacular ice sculptures stand as tall as a two-story building. Mid-March.

April

- **The Alaska Folk Festival,** Juneau. A community-wide celebration drawing musicians, whether on the bill or not, from all over the state. Call ☎ **907/364-2658** for information. Mid-April.
- **The Garnet Festival,** the third week of April, marks the arrival of the sea lions, hooligans, shorebirds, and bald eagles on the Stikine River Delta, a spring tornado of wildlife in the region's largest coastal marshes. Community activities take place in town while jet boat tours traverse the delta. Call ☎ **800/367-9745** or 907/874-3901 for information.

May

- **Copper River Delta Shorebird Festival** (☎ **907/424-7260;** www.ptialaska.net/~midtown) revolves around the coming of dizzying swarms of shorebirds—estimates range from 5 to 22 million—that use the delta and beaches near the town as a migratory stopover in early May. The whole community gets involved to host bird watchers and put on a full schedule of educational and outdoor activities.
- **The Kachemak Bay Shorebird Festival,** Homer (☎ **907/235-7740;** homeralaska.org/shorebird.htm), held in early May, includes guided bird-watching hikes and boat excursions, natural history workshops, art shows and performances, a wooden boat festival, and other events. It's organized by Alaska Maritime National Wildlife Refuge and the Homer Chamber of Commerce to mark the return of the annual migration in early May.
- **Little Norway Festival,** Petersburg (☎ **907/772-4636;** www.petersburg.org), celebrating the May 17, 1814, declaration of independence of Norway from Sweden. The town goes wild, and 4 days of community events are planned the third full weekend of the month.
- **Kodiak Crab Festival** (☎ **907/486-5557;** www.kodiak.org/crabfest.html), lasting 5 days over Memorial Day weekend, is the town's biggest event of the year and includes a carnival, parade, ultramarathon, and rubber duck race, and also the solemn blessing of the fleet and memorial service for lost fishermen.

June

✪ **The Sitka Summer Music Festival** (☎ **907/747-6774;** www.sitkamusicfestival.org/), a chamber-music series that began in 1972, draws musicians from all over the world for 3 weeks in June. Performances take place Tuesdays and Fridays, and other events all week.

- **Midnight Sun Baseball Game,** Fairbanks. A summer-solstice event—the local semipro baseball team, the Fairbanks Goldpanners, plays a game without artificial lights beginning at 10:30pm. Call ☎ **907/451-0095** for information. Around June 21.
- **Midnight Sun Festival,** Nome. Celebrates the summer solstice, when Nome gets more than 22 hours of direct sunlight, with a parade, softball tournament, bank holdup, raft race, and similar events. Call ☎ **907/443-5535** for information. June 21.
- ✪ **The Last Frontier Theater Conference** (☎ **907/834-1612;** www.uaa.alaska.edu/pwscc/) brings famous playwrights and directors to the community for seminars and performances in June. Arthur Miller, Edward Albee, and other famous writers have met the public here in fairly intimate settings.

July

- **The Yukon Gold Panning Championships and Canada Day Celebrations,** Dawson City. The Canadian equivalent of the Fourth of July. July 1.
- ✪ **Independence Day.** Most of the small towns in Alaska make a big deal of the Fourth of July. Seward always has a huge celebration, exploding with visitors, primarily from Anchorage. Besides the parade and many small town festivities, the main attraction is the **Mount Marathon Race,** from the middle of town straight up rocky Mount Marathon to its 3,022-foot peak and down again. **Seldovia, Ketchikan, Skagway,** and **Juneau** also have exceptional Fourth of July events. See the individual town write-ups for more information.
- **The Fairbanks Summer Arts Festival** (☎ **907/474-8869;** www.fsaf.org/). Over 2 weeks in late July and early August, the festival brings artists of international reputation for workshops and performances in music, dance, theater, opera, and the visual arts.

August

- **The Southeast Alaska State Fair** and **Bald Eagle Music Festival** (☎ **907/766-2476**), Haines. Held for 5 days in early August; it's a regional small-town get-together, with livestock, cooking, a logging show, a parade, music, and other entertainment.
- **The Alaska State Fair** (☎ **907/745-4827;** www.akstatefair.org/), Palmer. The biggest event of the year for the Matanuska Valley, and one of the biggest for Anchorage. It's a typical state fair, except for the huge vegetables. The good soil and long days in the Valley grow cabbages the size of a beanbag chair. A mere beach ball–sized cabbage wouldn't even make it into competition. The 11 days before Labor Day.

October

- **Alaska Day Festival,** Sitka. Alaska Day, commemorating the Alaska purchase on October 18, 1867, is a big deal in this former Russian and U.S. territorial capital city.

November

- **Sitka WhaleFest** (☎ **907/747-5940;** www.sitka.org/whale.htm). Over a weekend in early November, during the fall and early winter period when humpback whales congregate in Sitka Sound. There are workshops, whale-watching tours, a concert, and other community events. The event coordinates with the Alaska Bald Eagle Festival.

- **The Alaska Bald Eagle Festival** (☎ **907/766-2202;** www.baldeaglefest.org), Haines. Seminars and special events mark an annual congregation of 3,000 eagles near Haines. It's timed to allow visitors to also attend the WhaleFest in Sitka.
- **Great Alaska Shootout Men's Basketball Tournament,** Anchorage. The University of Alaska Seawolves host a roster of the nation's top-ranked NCAA Division I teams at the Sullivan Arena. For tickets call ☎ **800/GR8-SEAT,** or point your browser to www.goseawolves.com. Thanksgiving weekend.
- **Christmas Tree Lighting,** Anchorage. Takes place in town square, with Santa arriving behind a team of real reindeer. It's usually followed by a performance of The Nutcracker in the Alaska Center for the Performing Arts. Call ☎ **907/276-5015** for information. The Saturday after Thanksgiving.

5 Escorted Tour or Do-It-Yourself?

Hundreds of thousands of visitors come to Alaska each year on escorted package tours, leaving virtually all their travel arrangements in the hands of a single company that takes responsibility for ushering them through the state for a single, lump-sum fee. But more and more visitors are cutting the apron strings and exploring Alaska on their own, and finding a more relaxed, spontaneous experience. There are advantages and disadvantages to each approach, and which way you choose to visit depends on how you value those pros and cons. Unfortunately, some people make the choice based on expectations that aren't valid, so it's important to know what you're getting into.

An escorted package tour provides security. You'll know in advance how much everything will cost, you don't have to worry about making hotel and ground transportation reservations, you're guaranteed to see the highlights of each town you visit, and you'll have someone telling you what you're looking at. Often, a package price saves money over traveling at the same level of comfort independently. If there are weather delays or other travel problems, it's the tour company's problem, not yours. Everything happens on schedule, and you never have to touch your baggage other than to unpack when it magically shows up in your room. If you sometimes feel like you're a member of a herd on an escorted tour, you'll also meet new people, a big advantage if you're traveling on your own. Most passengers on these trips are retired, over age 65.

If you're short on time, escorted package tours make the most of it, often traveling at an exhausting pace. Passengers get up early and cover a lot of ground, with sights and activities scheduled solidly through the day. Stops last only long enough to get a taste of what the sight is about, not to dig in and learn about a place you're especially interested in. On an escorted trip, you'll meet few if any Alaska residents, since most tour companies hire college students from *"Outside"* (a term coined by Alaskans to refer to anyplace that's not in Alaska) to fill summer jobs. You'll stay in only the largest hotels and eat in the largest, tourist-oriented restaurants—no small, quaint places loaded with local character. For visiting wilderness, such as Denali National Park, the quick and superficial approach can, in my opinion, spoil the whole point of going to a destination that's about an experience, not just seeing a particular object or place.

Studies by Alaska tourism experts have found that many people choose escorted packages to avoid risks that don't really exist. Alaska may still be untamed, but that doesn't mean it's a dangerous or uncomfortable place to travel. Visitors who sign up for a tour to avoid having to spend the night in an igloo or use an outhouse may wish they'd been a bit more adventurous when they arrive and find that Alaska has the same facilities found in any other state. Except for tiny Bush villages that you're unlikely to visit anyway, you can find the standard American hotel room almost anywhere you go. The tourism infrastructure is well developed even in small towns—you're never far from help unless you want to be.

It's also possible for an independent traveler to obtain some of the predictability a package tour provides. You can reserve accommodations and activities and control your expenses by using a good travel agent experienced in Alaska travel. Some even offer fixed-price itineraries that allow you to travel on your own (see "Independent Travel Planning" at the end of this section). But independent travelers never have the complete security of those on group tours. Once you're on the road, you'll be on your own to take care of the details, and weather delays and other cancellations can confound the best-laid plans. If you can't relax and enjoy a trip knowing unforeseen difficulties could happen, then an escorted package tour is the way to go.

LARGE TOUR COMPANIES

Three major tour and cruise-ship companies dominate the Alaska package-tour market with "vertically integrated" operations that allow them to take care of everything you do while in Alaska with tight quality control. Each also offers tours as short as a couple of hours to independent travelers who want to combine their own exploring with a more structured experience. All can be booked through any travel agent.

Holland America Westours/Gray Line of Alaska. 300 Elliot Ave. West, Seattle, WA 98119. ☎ **800/544-2206.** www.graylinealaska.com or www.hollandamerica.com.

The Holland America cruise line became the giant of Alaska tourism by buying local tour companies such as Gray Line and Westours to carry visitors in buses, trains, and boats, and the Westmark hotel chain to put them up for the night. Today the Alaska/Yukon operation employs 2,000 workers operating 184 buses, 13 rail cars, and 2 day boats. Most clients arrive in the state on one of the company's ships (see chapter 4), but even within Alaska, chances are that any tour you sign up for other than Princess or Alaska Sightseeing (see below) will put you on a Gray Line coach and exclusively in Westmark hotels. I've included descriptions of Westmark hotels in most of the towns where they're found. The quality is not consistent—the Westmark Cape Fox in Ketchikan is among the best hotels in the state while the hotel in Skagway is below usually accepted standards. Most are adequate properties with standard American rooms. On a group tour, you don't spend much time in the room, as schedules generally are tightly planned and daily departures early. You'll find a description of the company's rail cars on the Anchorage-Denali-Fairbanks run in chapter 8. Gray Line coaches are first rate, especially several superluxurious, extralong vehicles that bend in the middle and have a lounge in the back. And the company goes more places than any other, with a catalog that covers just about anything in the state that could possibly be done with a group. Some of its boat and tour excursions—on the Yukon River between Dawson City and Eagle, for example—are entirely unique. Prices depend on a variety of factors, but in general a tour of a week is about $1,500 per person.

Princess Cruises and Tours. 2815 Second Ave., Suite 400, Seattle, WA 98121-1299. ☎ **800/426-0442.** www.princess.com.

The Princess cruise line has built its land-tour operation from the ground up instead of buying it (as Holland America did), and the result is a smaller but consistently top-quality collection of properties. The four Princess hotels—two near Denali National Park, and one each in Fairbanks and Cooper Landing, on the Kenai Peninsula—all are exceptionally good. Princess operates its own coaches and has superb rail cars on the Alaska Railroad route to Denali. Descriptions of each hostelry can be found in the appropriate chapter. Most people on the tours come to Alaska on a cruise ship, but tours are for sale separately, too. The company's network of tours is less extensive than Holland America's but visit the places most people want to go.

Alaska Sightseeing/Cruise West. Fourth and Battery Bldg., Suite 700, Seattle, WA 98121. ☎ **800/888-9378.** www.cruisewest.com.

This relatively small company, started by Alaska-based tourism pioneers, offers a more intimate experience compared to the Princess and Holland America giants. Its ships, which carry around 100 passengers each compared to Holland America's and Princess's 1,500-plus, can navigate into more interesting places, and the company has taken the trouble to contract with some of the most knowledgeable small-town companies for tours rather than trying to do everything with their own hired college students. The land tours are marketed primarily as add-ons to small-vessel cruises, but are available separately, and cover most of the state. The company doesn't own its own hotels and uses the Alaska Railroad's cars on the train ride to Denali National Park, joining the train in Talkeetna.

INDEPENDENT TRAVEL PLANNING

Using this guidebook, you can book everything yourself, but for a long trip it can get quite complicated to keep track of all your dates and deposits. If you use a trusted travel agency from home, use the reviews in this book to become a smart consumer. Read through the book, make your choices, and bring the agent as detailed a plan as possible, derived from your own research, and just have him/her do the bookings for you. Most agents who don't specialize in Alaska are aware of only the biggest attractions and best-marketed companies. Another option is to use a travel agency or trip-planner based in Alaska. They'll know much more about the place and can help you more in picking out what you want to do. I've listed a few below.

Unfortunately, there are cautions to be offered in using the agencies. They work on commission, which means they're being paid by the establishments you're buying from. Of course, a good agent will disregard the size of the commission and really look out for you, but I've encountered too many visitors on poorly planned itineraries not to advise caution. Many travel agents book visitors on trips to far-flung corners of the state in quick succession, so they wind up staying only briefly in expensive places and then zooming off somewhere else, all with little concern for the visitors' true interests. Your best defense is to do enough research so you can actively participate in the planning.

Here I've gathered the names of some agencies that book Alaska trips. Expect to pay booking fees and to have the agent collect commissions from the businesses you use. My knowledge of these agencies is limited to contacting them as a journalist. I have removed any about whom I received justified complaints.

Online booking agencies are listed in "Planning Your Trip: An Online Directory," on p. 48.

Alaska Bound. 321 East Lake St., Petoskey, MI 49770. ☎ **888/ALASKA-7** or 231/439-3000. www.alaskabound.com.

This Michigan-based agency started as a cruise planner, working primarily with Holland America, but now plans many independent trips, too, charging $100 per person. Although they don't take credit cards, they will use yours to book your stays, so you get the security and frequent-flier mileage.

All Ways Travel. 302 G St., Anchorage, AK 99501. ☎ **800/676-2946** or 907/276-3644. E-mail: allways@alaska.net.

This is a solid old travel agency in downtown Anchorage, with many years of experience in arranging Alaska trips. Fees depend on the effort expended and type of bookings you need. Owner Anna Mae Rocker is a respected community volunteer with many years of experience.

Fantasia Travel. 290 N. Yenlo, L-2, Wasilla, AK 99654. ☎ **800/478-2622** or 907/376-2622. www.alaskaflights.com

This agency, under the same ownership as Camp Alaska Tours, gladly puts clients in B&Bs and cabins, not just the high-priced places most agents prefer to use. Sign up for notification of airfare sales by e-mail on their Web site.

Sport Fishing Alaska. 9310 Shorecrest Dr., Anchorage, AK 99515. ☎ **907/344-8674.** www.alaskatripplanners.com.

Choose this company for a fishing vacation. The owners, former guides and float-, charter-, and air-taxi operators, Larry and Sheary Suiter, know where the fish will be week-to-week. They charge a $95 up-front fee. (See "Fishing," below.)

Viking Travel. P.O. Box 787, Petersburg, AK 99833 ☎ **800/327-2571** or 907/772-3818. alaska-ala-carte.com.

An entrepreneur in the small Southeast Alaska town of Petersburg built this travel agency, initially specializing in independent trips emphasizing the outdoors but now planning trips for the whole state. Instead of a fee or percentage, he charges a package price. The firm also books Alaska and B.C. ferries without surcharge; get on their list and they will book your cabins and vehicle reservations on the first day the system makes them available.

6 Sample Itineraries

Many visitors to Alaska feel compelled to cover the whole state, traveling to each region, and planning everything around seeing certain famous wilderness parks. By doing so, they spend a lot more time and money than is necessary. Each of Alaska's regions, by itself, has most of what you're coming to Alaska for—wildlife, mountains, glaciers, historic sites, cute little towns—and you can have a better trip touring one or two regions in greater depth than spending precious time going from region to region.

The other mistake some people make is traveling only to the largest and most famous destinations. Such a goal-oriented style of travel misses the fun, offbeat places you can discover. Alaska's greatest sights certainly are worth your time, but visitors often tell me those were not their most memorable moments. Instead, save time for chance encounters with wildlife or interesting local people, or simply to enjoy a peaceful moment all alone in the woods.

Finally, remember why you're going to Alaska. Surely it's not to visit museums or tourist attractions, but instead to see one of the most beautiful, unspoiled places on earth. To do that, you need to get outside; there's only so much you can see and learn through the glass of a car or bus window. Take a chance on a sea kayaking excursion, a day hike, or a mountain-bike ride. There will never be a better chance to try it.

To help readers understand how Alaska destinations can fit together, I've set up a series of itineraries in 1-week loops or tours. For 2- or 3-week itineraries, link these together, spend more time in each place, or add trips to the many places I haven't included in these loops, which include some of my favorites. This isn't intended as a menu, just as inspiration to create your own trip. If you're driving *to* Alaska, add a week to each end of your trip.

NORTHERN SOUTHEAST ALASKA

Day 1: Fly to Juneau.

Day 2: Take a look at the State Museum and other sights in town and Mendenhall Glacier, or take a day hike or sea-kayaking excursion.

Day 3: Take the Auk Nu passenger ferry to Gustavus, with a whale-watching excursion on the way. Spend the night at one of the charming inns there.

Day 4: See Glacier Bay National Park on a boat tour. Spend another night in Gustavus.

Day 5: Fly on a small plane to Haines, spending the day there seeing the eagles and attending the Native dancing and checking out the totem-carving studio.

Day 6: Take the passenger ferry to Skagway to see the historic sites and take the train excursion, or take a hike or mountain-bike ride.

Day 7: Take the Alaska ferry back to Juneau and fly home.

SOUTHERN SOUTHEAST ALASKA

Day 1: Arrive in Ketchikan by ferry from Prince Rupert.

Day 2: Tour the cultural sites in Ketchikan or take a hike in the rain forest.

Day 3: Take a boat tour and flightseeing day trip from Ketchikan to Misty Fjords National Monument, or take a charter-fishing or sea-kayaking excursion.

Day 4: Take the ferry to Sitka.

Day 5: See the historic sites and museums in Sitka.

Day 6: Get outdoors in Sitka, hiking, fishing, sea kayaking, or on a whale-watching and sea otter cruise.

Day 7: Take the ferry or fly to Juneau, then fly out.

KENAI FJORDS & DENALI NATIONAL PARKS

Day 1: Fly to Anchorage.

Day 2: Spend a day taking in the city, with a visit to the museum, zoo, or Native cultural center. Or spend your day outdoors, riding a bike on the coastal trail or hiking in Chugach State Park.

Day 3: Take the train to Seward and take a boat ride into Kenai Fjords National Park. Spend the night in Seward.

Day 4: Enjoy Seward and Exit Glacier, perhaps taking a hike or a sea kayak paddle, returning to Anchorage on the evening train.

Day 5: Rent a car and drive to Denali National Park, taking an afternoon hike or raft ride in the entrance area.

Day 6: Take a shuttle bus into the park for wildlife viewing and day hiking.

Day 7: Drive back to Anchorage and fly out.

PRINCE WILLIAM SOUND LOOP

Day 1: Fly to Anchorage.

Day 2: Rent a car and drive all day to Wrangell–St. Elias National Park (take the van over the gravel road unless you are covered for your rental car). Stay at a lodge in McCarthy or Kennicott.

Day 3: See Kennicott and take a hike near the glacier.

Day 4: Drive to Valdez and see the sights in town, fish for salmon, or take a hike.

Day 5: Take a boat ride to Columbia Glacier and go sea kayaking or sailing there.

Day 6: Take the car ferry from Valdez to Whittier and drive to Girdwood for a hike or tram ride.

Day 7: Drive to Anchorage and fly home.

FAIRBANKS INTERIOR LOOP

Day 1: Fly to Fairbanks and rent a car.

Day 2: Spend a day in Fairbanks exploring the city and its attractions.

Day 3: Drive to Denali National Park, taking an afternoon hike or raft ride in the entrance area.

Day 4: Take a shuttle bus into the park for wildlife viewing and day hiking.

Day 5: Drive via the Denali Highway and Richardson Highway back to Fairbanks, then drive out Chena Hot Springs Road to the resort, or to camp in the Chena Hot Springs State Recreation Area.

Day 6: Swim at the Hot Springs and hike in the recreation area.

Day 7: Return to Fairbanks and fly out.

WINTERTIME CHOICES

Arrive in **Anchorage** in February, during the Fur Rendezvous sled dog races, or in March, to see the start of the Iditarod. If you're a Nordic skier, enjoy **Kincaid Park.** After checking on avalanche conditions, rent a car and make a day trip into **Chugach State Park** or to **Turnagain Pass,** south of Anchorage, or ski into one of many public cabins in **Chugach National Forest.**

Alpine skiers should spend at least a few days in **Girdwood** at the Alyeska Resort. Besides exceptional skiing, this is a good place for a dog-sled or snow-machine ride, and there are others at each stop on the itinerary.

After Girdwood, catch the train from Anchorage to **Fairbanks,** spending the night in Fairbanks and catching the sled-dog races or ice-carving festivals in February or March. The following day, take the van out to the **Chena Hot Springs Resort,** for outdoor explorations, swimming, and aurora watching, returning and flying out of Fairbanks when your trip is over.

7 Planning an Outdoor Vacation

Alaska is unique for its scenery, wildlife, and immense, untouched wilderness, and that's why most people visit. Experiencing wilderness is about being alone in natural places. It's ironic, then, that so many visitors spend their time in crowded ships, buses, trains, and airplanes, all of which are the antithesis of wilderness. You do need technology to get to the wilderness of Alaska, but unless you at least partly let loose of that umbilical cord, you'll never really arrive at your destination.

Every town in Alaska is a threshold to the wild. There's always a way to go hiking, biking, or sea kayaking, or to get on the bank of a stream or the deck of a boat to hook into a furiously fighting wild salmon. In the evening, you

Outdoor Choices

Here are the outdoor activities we've covered in our pages. Checks mark places where the activity is good and developed for visitors. Stars are our favorites. Note, this chart is not exhaustive, and is certainly subjective.

	Backpacking	Bear Viewing	Bird Watching	Canoeing	Day Hiking	Diving	Fishing (Halibut)	Fishing (Salmon)	Mountain Biking	River Floating	Skiing (Alpine)	Skiing (Nordic)	Sea Kayaking	Whale Watching
Southeast														
Ketchikan					✔		✔	✔					✔	
Prince of Wales				★	✔	★	✔	★	✔					
Wrangell		★			✔		✔	✔	✔	★			✔	
Petersburg	✔				★		✔	✔	✔			✔	✔	★
Sitka			✔		★	★	✔	✔	✔				✔	✔
Juneau	✔	★	✔	✔	★	✔	✔	✔	✔		✔	✔	✔	✔
Glacier Bay/ Gustavus			✔		✔		★	✔	✔				★	★
Haines			★		✔		✔	✔	✔	★			✔	
Skagway	✔				✔				✔					
Anchorage (includes day trips from Anchorage)	★	✔	✔	✔	★			✔	★	✔	★	★	✔	
Kenai Peninsula/ PWS														
Chugach NF	★			✔	★			✔	★	✔				
Whittier			✔				✔	✔					✔	✔
Seward/Kenai Fjords NP	✔		★		✔		✔	★	✔				★	★
Cooper Landing	★				✔			★	✔	✔				

	Backpacking	Bear Viewing	Bird Watching	Canoeing	Day Hiking	Diving	Fishing (Halibut)	Fishing (Salmon)	Mountain Biking	River Floating	Skiing (Alpine)	Skiing (Nordic)	Sea Kayaking	Whale Watching
Kenai/Soldotna/ Kenai NWR				★				★		✔				
Homer/Halibut Cove/Seldovia	✔	✔	✔		★		★	✔	★			✔	✔	
Valdez			✔		✔		✔	★	✔	✔	✔	✔	✔	
Cordova	✔		★	★	✔		✔	✔	★	★	✔		✔	✔
Denali NP	★	★	✔		★				✔	✔				
Interior														
Fairbanks			✔	✔	✔				✔	✔	✔	✔		
Chena Hot Springs Rd	★			✔	★				✔	★		✔		
Steese Hwy	✔			✔	✔				✔	✔				
Dalton Hwy	✔		✔		✔									
Dawson City/Eagle				✔						✔				
Wrangell– St. Elias NP	★				✔				✔	★				
Bush														
Kodiak		✔			✔		✔	★	✔				✔	
Katmai NP	✔	★			✔			★						
Dutch Harbor/ Unalaska			★		✔		★	✔						
Pribilof Is			★		✔									
Nome			★		✔				★ (must bring bike)					
Kotzebue			✔							✔				
Barrow			✔						✔					

can be back in a comfortable hotel room. Or take it a step further: Plan to go out overnight, perhaps with a friendly local guide at first, and then on your own. I've included lots of details on how to do this throughout the book. Scary? If it weren't a little scary, it would be Disneyland, and it's not. It's real, and that's why it's worth doing.

Wilderness lodges are listed in the following sections: Gustavus, Prince of Wales Island and Admiralty Island in chapter 5; across Kachemak Bay from Homer in chapter 7; and in Denali National Park and near Talkeetna in chapter 8. Remote Forest Service cabins in Tongass and Chugach national forests are covered in chapters 5 and 7, respectively.

For more information about using the Internet to book your adventure trip, see **"Planning Your Trip: An Online Directory"** on p. 48.

ACTIVITIES

BACKPACKING Alaska's best backpacking country for trail hikes is in **Chugach State Park** near Anchorage (chapter 6), on Chena Hot Springs Road and on the Steese Highway near Fairbanks (chapter 9), and in the **Chugach National Forest** on the Kenai Peninsula (chapter 7). For hiking beyond trails, go to **Denali and Wrangell–St. Elias national parks** (chapters 8 and 9). Alaska trail hikes require the same skills as backpacking anywhere else, plus preparation for cold and damp. Hiking beyond the trails is a glorious experience, but you need to know how to cross rivers and find your way—it's best if you have some outdoor experience first. Or go with a guide; they're listed below. See section 10, later in this chapter, for tips on avoiding bears in the wilderness.

BIKING Most every town in Alaska has a bike-rental agency. There are excellent biking trails all over the state and few restrictions on where you can ride. A bike is a great way into Denali National Park (chapter 8); Anchorage has great paved trails and mountain biking routes (chapter 6); and in Haines and Skagway (chapter 5), **Sockeye Cycles** leads mountain biking tours. See **Alaska Bicycle Adventures,** below, for longer tours.

CANOEING Paddling a canoe on a remote Alaska lake or river is the best way for outdoors people to get into the wilderness without a guide or a great deal of expense. For beginners, it's easy to rent a canoe in Fairbanks (chapter 9) for a day trip. If you're ready to go overnight, the choices of routes are extraordinary, including the rivers of the Interior (chapter 9), canoe routes with rental cabins in Southeast Alaska's Tongass National Forest (chapter 5), the bird-watching country of the Copper River Delta near Cordova, or the supreme lake canoe routes of the Kenai National Wildlife Refuge (both in chapter 7), where there also is a wonderful opportunity for guided lake canoeing.

CAR CAMPING Campgrounds are almost everywhere in Alaska, many in extraordinarily beautiful natural places. Public campgrounds far outnumber

Tips on Tipping

As a general rule, tip fishing guides and outfitters $10 to $20 per person per day. For outings of less than a day, adjust the tip accordingly. At wilderness lodges, which normally have all-inclusive rates, it's often best to add the tip to your final payment when you leave and let the proprietor distribute it to the staff rather than try to do it at each meal. A blanket tip of $15 per day is acceptable.

commercial ones. They're usually located where they are because there's something special about the place: a great view or beach, an exceptional fishing stream or trailhead. Rarely will you find running water or flush toilets; most are seasonal, with hand pumps for water. (When it's time to wash up, stay at a commercial campground, which I've noted in each town section in the destination chapters throughout this book.) I've mentioned some great campgrounds throughout the book, but there are many more than I had space to cover. A map that lists all the public campgrounds is available from the Alaska Public Lands Information Centers (see "Visitor Information," above) for 25¢.

FISHING Fishing in Alaska may spoil you for fishing anywhere else. The world's largest salmon and halibut were caught here in recent years, and Pacific salmon are so plentiful that catching and processing them still provides the state's largest source of employment. Fly fishermen also come for our thriving wild stocks of steelhead, cutthroat, and rainbow trout and Dolly Varden char.

There's no room here to tell you how to fish in Alaska—the best way is to pick it up from anglers, most conveniently by going with a guide on your first outing. You can also study up by getting a detailed guidebook, such as the encyclopedic *Alaska Fishing,* by Rene Limeres and Gunnar Pederson, published by Foghorn Press (www.foghorn.com). The best all-around source of information is the **Alaska Department of Fish and Game Sport Fish Division** (☎ **800/874-8202** or 907/465-4180; www.state.ak.us/local/akpages/FISH.GAME/sportf/sthome.htm). The agency not only produces printed guides and a handy Web site (including fishing licenses for sale online), but also will field questions from the public and records exhaustive sportfishing hot lines for various areas around the state. Local visitor centers and sporting goods stores also can get you on the right track, if you just want to give fishing a try one day of your trip. Even better, spend a day fly-in fishing; the flight service will set you up with gear and drop you in a hot fishing spot (you can do it from virtually any town listed in chapter 5, 6, or 7).

If fishing is the primary goal of your trip, think about booking time at a fishing lodge. The remote rivers of the Bristol Bay region have Alaska's most prolific salmon fishing, and the only way out there is to take a floatplane to a remote site. You'll be on streams jammed with salmon and with few other anglers to compete with. But you'll waste your money if you book a date that's not near the peak of the local salmon run (that does happen). Consequently, I've listed few river-fishing lodges in the book. (The exceptions: on the Kenai River in Cooper Landing and Kenai-Soldotna, in chapter 7; and ocean fishing lodges in Ketchikan and on Prince of Wales Island, in chapter 5, and on Kachemak Bay outside Homer, in chapter 7.) Instead, I recommend booking through **Sport Fishing Alaska,** 9310 Shorecrest Dr., Anchorage, AK 99515 (☎ **907/344-8674;** www.alaskatripplanners.com). The business is run by a couple, Larry and Sheary Suiter, with years of experience on the Kenai River and in Southwest Alaska. After receiving a $95 advance fee, they plan a fishing vacation tailored to your budget that puts you right where fishing is hot at the time when you can travel.

FLIGHTSEEING No one should come to Alaska without seeing the scenery at least once from a small plane. The most spectacular rides of all are the Mount McKinley flights from Talkeetna (chapter 8) and the Glacier Bay National Park flights from Haines or other surrounding communities (chapter 5). But just about anywhere you go is worth seeing from the air; only then can you grasp how huge and complex the land is and how little changed by mankind. Fixed-wing flights give you the most time aloft for your money,

A Salmon Primer

In Alaska, it's not so much where you wet your line, but when. The primary catch, Pacific salmon, lives in saltwater but spawns in freshwater, with each fish returning to the stream of its birth during a certain, narrow window of time called a "run." When the salmon are running, fishing is hot; when they're not running, it's dead. And the runs change day-to-day, typically lasting only a few weeks. (Halibut, on the other hand, are bottom-dwelling ocean fish; you can fish them from a boat every day when the tide is right.) You can fish salmon all over the state in fresh- and saltwater, but the closer you are to the ocean, the better the fish are; salmon flesh softens in fresh water and their skin turns dull and red. Salmon right from saltwater that haven't started their spawning cycle are called silver bright—when you see one, you'll understand why. No Pacific salmon feeds in fresh water, but kings and silvers, meat eaters at sea, strike out of habit when they reach the river.

There are five species of Pacific salmon, each preferring its own habitat, and, even when the habitat overlaps, each timing its run differently. Each species has two names.

King (or **chinook**) are the most coveted, best-fighting fish, commonly growing to over 30 pounds in 5 to 7 years at sea (the sport record, from the Kenai River, was 97 pounds, and the largest ever, taken by commercial fishermen near Petersburg, was 126 pounds). It takes a lot of effort to find and land a big king, but it's the ultimate in Alaska fishing. You also need a special king stamp from the Alaska Department of Fish and Game, in addition to your fishing license. King runs come mostly from late May to early July.

The **silver** (or **coho**) is smaller than the king, typically topping out around 12 pounds, but fights and jumps ferociously, so it is nearly as big

with seats going for around $100 for an hour-long flight. If you can't afford that, consider taking scheduled prop service between small communities, which can cost less than $50 and allow you to see almost as much.

RAFTING Letting an Alaskan river pull you through untouched wild country in a raft provides a unique perspective without the sweat and toil of backpacking. Alaska has many great rivers, virtually all undeveloped and, with perhaps a single exception, never crowded. White-water guides operate on some of the best. River day trips go from around Anchorage (chapter 6), Denali National Park (chapter 8), Cooper Landing (chapter 7), the Kennicott/McCarthy area (chapter 9) and, on calmer water, Talkeetna (chapter 8), Haines and Juneau (both in chapter 5). Outfitters also lead trips deep in Alaska, using the rivers to visit extraordinary places that can be reached no other way. Those trips most commonly traverse Wrangell–St. Elias National Park, the Arctic National Wildlife Refuge, and lands in the western Arctic near Kotzebue, or the backcountry of Glacier Bay National Park, where the Tatshenshini and Alsek rivers have been called the world's wildest, with huge rapids passing among rock and glaciers. Many companies offer floats; some are listed below and still others are in the destination chapters throughout this book.

SEA KAYAKING Kayakers understandably love the waters of Prince William Sound, of Homer's Kachemak Bay, of Kenai Fjords National Park (all a prize. Silvers run mostly in the fall, beginning in August and lasting into October in some streams.

Red (or **sockeye**) salmon, so named for their tasty red flesh, are the trickiest to catch. They usually weigh 4 to 8 pounds and can run in any of the summer months, depending on the region and stream. Reds feed primarily on plankton at sea, and when they strike a fly, it's out of an instinct that no one really understands; you need perfect river conditions to catch reds legally.

Pinks (or **humpies**) grow to only a few pounds and aren't as tasty as the other three species; their flesh lacks the fat that makes salmon so meaty in flavor. Pinks are so plentiful that Alaska anglers usually view them as a nuisance to get off the line, but visitors often enjoy catching them: There's nothing wrong with a hard-fighting 4-pound fish, especially if you use light tackle.

Chum (or **dog**) salmon return mostly to streams in western and Arctic Alaska and are rarely targeted by anglers. Like pinks, they lack flavorful fat and are mostly used for subsistence by Alaska Natives, who smoke or dry the fish for winter use or freeze them to feed dog teams. Chums commonly weigh 7 to 18 pounds.

The gear you use depends on the species you are after and the regulations for the area you're fishing. You have to catch the fish in the mouth; snagging is allowed only in special circumstances. On saltwater, boats troll for kings and silvers with herring bait and gear to hold it down. Lures, salmon eggs, or flies will work on silvers and kings in the rivers, but regulations vary. Flies work best with reds. Most Alaska fishermen use spinning gear on the larger salmon species, as landing such a large fish is iffy with a fly rod.

covered in chapter 7), and Kodiak (chapter 10), and around all the little islands, deep fjords and glaciers of Southeast Alaska (chapter 5). Just about every coastal town has a kayak outfitter taking visitors on day trips or expeditions. I think it would be a shame for any fit person to come to Alaska and not take a sea-kayaking day trip. It is your best chance to get close enough to really know the place, and see whales, sea otters, sea birds, and marine life in an intimate way. Local guides are listed in almost every coastal town in the book. Outfitters offering longer trips to a variety of places are listed below.

OUTFITTERS & OUTDOOR PACKAGE TRIPS

Besides the outfitters and tour guides listed below, I've noted other operators in the destination chapters covering the towns where they primarily operate. Browse through those destination chapters before deciding on a trip, because the local guides often know their own areas best, and the small towns are often the most interesting.

Alaska Bicycle Adventures. 907 E. Dowling Rd. no. 29, Anchorage, AK 99518. ☎ **800/770-7242** or 907/243-2329. www.alaskabike.com.

The well-run operation provides all the arrangements for bicycle expeditions over Alaska's rural highways, including a support van that follows the group and ferries bicyclists over the dangerous or boring patches of road, or picks them up just because they're tired. Sea-kayaking and fishing excursions break up some trips. Choose from many itineraries; one appealing program lasts a week, looping from Anchorage, over the Denali Highway, down the Richardson Highway, a little bit into Wrangell–St. Elias National Park, then to Valdez and across Prince William Sound (by boat) and back to Anchorage. It costs $2,395.

Alaska Discovery. 5130 Glacier Hwy., Juneau, AK 99801. ☎ **800/586-1911** or 907/780-6226. www.akdiscovery.com.

A homegrown ecotourism pioneer that's developed a national reputation, Alaska Discovery still offers some of the best sea-kayaking trips in Southeast Alaska, including Glacier Bay and Admiralty Island outings that cater to both beginners and the truly rugged. Their inn-to-inn trips are essentially outdoor-oriented package tours, taking groups to the best spots for day activities like kayaking, rafting, or watching wildlife. Extended river trips float through the Arctic and on the Tatshenshini and Alsek Rivers. They also offer outdoor packages for complete vacations. A 3-day kayak expedition near Juneau is $495 or $595, while 10 days in the Arctic is around $3,000.

Alaska Wildland Adventures. P.O. Box 389, Girdwood, AK 99586. ☎ **800/334-8730** or 907/783-2928. www.alaskawildland.com.

This Alaska-based company specializes in trips for regular folks who may not have done a lot of arduous outdoor activities before. Concentrating in the area from Denali National Park to the Kenai Peninsula, where they operate four wilderness lodges, most of the company's trips link together a series of outdoor day activities, such as rafting, hiking, or wildlife watching, with beds and indoor plumbing in the evening. A 10-day safari is $3,895; trips for families with kids or with tent camping included are available, too.

Alaskan Wilderness Sailing & Kayaking Safaris. P.O. Box 1313, Valdez, AK 99686. ☎ **907/835-5175.** www.alaskanwilderness.com.

Based on an island near Prince William Sound's Columbia Glacier, Jim and Nancy Lethcoe share the waters they love with warmth and a great depth of knowledge. Crusaders for protecting the Sound long before the *Exxon Valdez* oil spill, they have written a shelf of books about its history, nature, and best spots. Their offerings include day sailing and short paddles in inflatables and longer expeditions on a yacht or in a rigid kayak.

Camp Alaska Tours. P.O. Box 872247, Wasilla, AK 99687. ☎ **800/376-9438** or 907/376-9438. E-mail: campak@alaska.net.

Readers often tell me about the wonderful time they had with these folks, traveling in a van with only 12 adults and camping each night along the way. Trips last 6 days to 2 weeks, with hiking, rafting, kayaking, and an opportunity to see the outdoors with a new group of outdoors-oriented friends. Their philosophy is to keep things loose and allow people to pursue their own interests. Prices are around $125 per day, and one itinerary is available for families with children as young as age 10.

Colors of Nature. P.O. Box 24106, Santa Barbara, CA 93121. ☎ **888/385-5595.** www.colorsofnature.com.

Rich Reid, an accomplished professional nature photographer, leads tours for photographers and those who just want to observe closely. Rather than workshops, these are trips oriented to seeing: Reid takes his groups, limited to nine, where they can expect good lighting and spectacular sights, such a migrations, foliage, or the aurora. They stay in comfortable lodgings and ride in a 15-passenger van. A 10-day tour is $2,895.

Equinox Wilderness Expeditions. 618 W. 14th Ave., Anchorage, AK 99501. ☎ **907/274-9087.** www.equinoxexpeditions.com.

Karen Jettmar, author of *The Alaska River Guide,* the standard guidebook on floating Alaska's rivers, leads challenging rafting, sea-kayaking, and hiking trips and base camp wildlife viewing each summer in some of the wildest and most exotic places around the state. Her groups are tiny, with five to eight members, and she specializes in trips for women; family and coed trips are available, too. A 10-day Arctic float trip costs around $3,000.

Nova. P.O. Box 1129, Chickaloon, AK 99674. ☎ **800/746-5753** or 907/745-5753. novalaska.com.

These guys started commercial rafting on Alaska's rivers in 1975, but as the industry developed, they kept the company small, keeping their base in a tiny village on the Matanuska River, northeast of Anchorage, and primarily employing Alaskan guides. Their catalog covers longer expeditions on some of the state's wildest rivers, but also includes itineraries of 2 or 3 days that more of us could afford. Two days on the Matanuska costs $275; three days on the Talkeetna, including the 14-mile long, Class IV rapids of the Talkeetna Canyon, costs $950.

St. Elias Alpine Guides. P.O. Box 111241, Anchorage, AK 99511. ☎ **888/933-5427** or 907/345-9048; summer 907/554-4445. www.steliasguides.com.

When you're ready for a real expedition, these are the real professionals to contact. Having given up on McKinley years ago as too crowded, they specialize in trekking, climbing, and floating the deep and rugged wilderness of Wrangell–St. Elias National Park. Theirs is the only trip catalog I know of that offers first ascents as part of the product line; so far, they've taken clients to the top of unclimbed mountains 45 times. More details are in chapter 9.

8 Getting There & Getting Around

BY PLANE

Anchorage is the main entry hub, served by several major carriers to the rest of the United States, primarily through Seattle, including **United Airlines** (☎ **800/241-6522;** www.ual.com), **Delta Air Lines** (☎ **800/221-1212;** www.delta-air.com), and, with the most flights, **Alaska Airlines** (☎ **800/252-7522;** TDD 800/682-2221; www.alaskaair.com). There's also much more limited service from **America West** (☎ **800/235-9292;** www.americawest.com), **American** (☎ **800/433-7300;** www.americanair.com), **Continental** (☎ **800/525-0280;** www.flycontinental.com), **Northwest** (☎ **800/225-2525;** www.nwa.com), and **TWA** (☎ **800/221-2000;** www.twa.com), and a handful of smaller Alaska-based carriers and charter operators.

The Seattle-Anchorage route is competitive and prices are volatile, sometimes as low as $200 if you're lucky, so shop around before booking. You can usually count on paying $300 with advance purchase. Summer sales sometimes hit in April. If you can make a last-minute decision, sign up for Web specials on the Alaska Airlines site and other airline sites, as there often are bargains to be had you can't get any other way. Most airlines also continue to Fairbanks, but **Alaska Airlines** is the only jet carrier to Southeast Alaska and most of Alaska's small towns. It also has arrangements with commuter lines that fan out from its network to smaller communities.

To fly to the smallest villages, or to fly between some small towns without returning to a hub, you take a **Bush plane.** The legendary Alaska Bush still connects Alaska's villages by small plane and flies air taxi passengers to fishing sites, lodges, remote cabins, or just about anywhere else you might want to go. An authentic Alaskan adventure is to be had by taking a Bush mail plane round-trip to a village and back. The ticket price is generally much less than a flightseeing trip, and you'll have at least a brief chance to look around a Native village. Cordova, Kodiak, Nome, Kotzebue, Barrow, and Fairbanks are places from which you can do this. See those destinations chapters for details.

BY SHIP

The most popular way to get to Alaska is on a **cruise ship.** Chapter 4, "Cruising Alaska's Coast," provides an in-depth look at your options.

For a more intimate and affordable trip, with a chance to stop as long as you like along the way, take the **Alaska Marine Highway System** (☎ **800/642-0066;** TDD 800/764-3779; www.dot.state.ak.us/external/amhs/home.html). It's my favorite way to travel. The big blue, white, and gold ferries ply the Inside Passage from Bellingham, Washington, and Prince Rupert, B.C., to the towns of Southeast Alaska, with road links to the rest of the state at Haines and Skagway. One ferry a month connects from that system across the Gulf of Alaska to the central part of the state. From there, smaller ferries connect towns in Prince William Sound and the Kenai Peninsula to Kodiak Island and the Aleutian Archipelago. For a complete discussion of the system and its intricacies, see "Getting Around by Ferry: The Alaska Marine Highway" in chapter 5.

BY RAIL

You can't get to Alaska by train, but you can get close. **Amtrak** (☎ **800/USA-RAIL;** www.amtrak.com) serves Bellingham, Washington, a couple of times a day; from there, you can catch the Alaska ferry north from a dock near the depot. From the east, it makes more sense to catch the ferry in Prince Rupert, B.C., getting there on Canada's **Via Rail** (☎ **888/VIA-RAIL;** www.viarail.ca/). U.S. residents can book this through Amtrak. Within Alaska, the **Alaska Railroad** (☎ **800/544-0552;** www.akrr.com) runs from Seward north through Anchorage and Denali National Park to Fairbanks (see those sections for details).

BY CAR OR RV

Driving to Alaska is a great adventure, but it requires thousands of miles on the road, and you have to have plenty of time. By car, Anchorage is 2,250 miles from Seattle and 3,400 miles from Los Angeles.

Some of the 1,400-mile **Alaska Highway** is dull, but there are spectacular sections of the route, too, and few experiences give you a better feel for the size and personality of Alaska. Putting your car on the ferry cuts the length of the trip considerably, but raises the cost; you could rent a car for 2 weeks for the same price as carrying an economy car on the ferry one way from Bellingham to Haines. I love riding the ferry up the Inside Passage, but I usually rent a car or bike to get around in the towns on the way. Details on the Alaska section of the Alaska Highway, and other highways, are contained in chapter 9. ***The Milepost*** (www.themilepost.com/), published by Morris Communications, contains mile-by-mile logs of all Alaska highways and approaches, and is sold widely (the commercial listings are advertisements, and are not objective, by the way).

The Cheapest Way to Alaska

Flying is the cheapest and by far the simplest way to get to Alaska. Take other means only for the adventure, not for the cost. Round-trip bus fare from Skagway to Anchorage costs as much as a full-fare plane ticket from Seattle to Anchorage and back. To get to Skagway from Bellingham on the ferry costs even more. Driving costs more yet, when you count rooms, food, and wear on your vehicle. Fuel alone for the 4,500-mile drive from Seattle to Anchorage would cost about $350 in a car that gets 20 miles to the gallon—more than a plane ticket. (Okay, maybe a foursome in a car, camping every night, and eating rice and beans can do it cheaper.)

Renting a car is the easiest way to see the Interior and Southcentral part of the state. All the major national car-rental companies are represented in Anchorage as well as many local operators, who may have lower prices for older cars, and possibly will allow you to drive on gravel roads (see chapter 6). In smaller cities and towns, there are usually a couple of agencies; our town descriptions provide details on which firms are in each town. Base rates for major rental companies are in the range of $50 a day for an economy car.

One-way rentals between Alaska towns are an attractive way to travel, but you generally pay steep drop-off charges, so a more popular plan is to fly into and out of Anchorage and use it as a base to pick up and return the car. There are two popular circular routes from Anchorage: to Denali and Fairbanks on the Parks Highway and back on the Richardson and Glenn Highways, or to Valdez by ferry from Whittier and back on another part of the Richardson Highway and the Glenn Highway.

Many retirees come to Alaska in their motor homes, park the RV by a salmon stream, and spend the summer. Sounds nice, but for most of the rest of us, with limited time, it makes more sense to rent an RV after flying to Alaska. It's not any cheaper to travel in a rented RV than to travel with a rental car, staying in hotels and eating in restaurants (starting around $1,400, plus gas and possibly mileage charges in high season); what you'll gain is freedom, without the need to reserve everything far in advance, schlepp in and out of hotels, or set up tents. A further advantage is that the RV insulates you better than a car or a tent from rainy or cold weather. I've listed two major rental agencies in Anchorage (see chapter 6). There are big savings to be had in the spring and fall and one-way rentals to Alaska are available, for a price.

9 Tips for Travelers with Special Needs

FOR TRAVELERS WITH DISABILITIES

The Americans with Disabilities Act and economic competition have sped the process of retrofitting hotels and even B&Bs to be accessible for people with disabilities. They're often the best rooms in the house. Hotels without such facilities now are the exception; however, check when making reservations.

There are several Alaska agencies for people with disabilities. **Challenge Alaska,** P.O. Box 110065, Anchorage, AK 99511 (☎ **907/344-7399;** www.challenge.ak.org/), is a nonprofit organization dedicated to providing accessible outdoor activities. They have a skiing center on Mount Alyeska (☎ **907/783-2925**), in Girdwood, and also offer summer camping, sea kayaking, fishing, and other trips; get on their mailing list for current listings. Prices are low: a 2-day sea kayaking outing was only $115, and volunteer helpers can go free.

Challenge Alaska also keeps track of tourism operators who are authentically accessible and welcomes inquiries.

Alaska Welcomes You! Inc., P.O. Box 91333, Anchorage, AK 99509-1333 (☎ or TTY **800/349-6301,** or 907/349-6301; www.accessiblealaska.com), books accessible cruises, tours in Southcentral Alaska, extended travel packages to Denali National Park and the Kenai Peninsula, and does trip planning for independent travelers with special needs. The operator is a respected community worker for the disabled.

FOR SENIORS

People over age 65 get reduced admission prices to most Alaska attractions, and some accommodations have special senior rates. National parks offer free admission and special camping rates for people over 62 with a Golden Age Passport, which you can obtain at any of the parks for $10 and which never expires. Most importantly, mention your age when booking your airfare; most domestic airlines offer senior discounts.

Most towns have a senior citizens center where you'll find activities and help with any special needs. The **Anchorage Seniors Center** (☎ **907/258-7823**) offers guidance for visitors, as well as use of the restaurant, showers, gift shop, and fitness room; a big band plays Friday nights for dancing. **Elderhostel,** 75 Federal St., Boston, MA 02110-1941 (☎ **877/426-8056;** TTY 877/426-2167; from overseas, ☎ 978/323-4141; www.elderhostel.org), operates many weeklong Alaska learning vacations for groups of people 55 and older.

FOR GAY & LESBIAN TRAVELERS

Anchorage, Juneau, and Fairbanks have active gay and lesbian communities. In Anchorage, **Identity Inc.** (☎ **907/258-4777;** www.alaska.net/~identity) offers referrals, publishes a newsletter called *Rainbow Borealis,* sponsors potluck dinners, and holds a gay pride picnic the last Sunday in June on the Delaney Park Strip. The **S.E. Alaska Gay/Lesbian Alliance** (☎ **907/586-4297;** www.ptialaska.net/~seagla) is a similar organization in Juneau. **QnetAK** is a Web site with statewide information, at www.mosquitonet.com/~qnetak. **Apollo Travel Agency,** 714 W. 76th Ave., Anchorage, AK 99518 (☎ **907/561-0661;** e-mail: apollo@alaska.net), is a member of the International Gay Travel Agencies Association and can guide you to businesses, such as B&Bs and tour operators, that cater specifically to gays and lesbians.

Nationally, **The International Gay & Lesbian Travel Association** (☎ **800/448-8550** or 954/776-2626; www.iglta.org) links travelers up with the appropriate gay-friendly service organization or tour specialist and has Web links to similar organizations. Members are kept informed of gay and gay-friendly hoteliers, tour operators, and airline and cruise-line representatives.

FOR STUDENTS

Most museums offer free or reduced admission for students and anyone under 18, although sometimes you have to ask. Make sure to bring a student ID card.

There are hostels in most major towns in Alaska; except for those in Anchorage and Fairbanks, they tend to be open in the summer only. You'll find them listed in the text for each town, and most are listed by **Hostelling International/American Youth Hostels,** 733 15th St. NW, Suite 840, Washington, DC 20005 (☎ **202/783-6161;** www.hiayh.org), on their Web site or in a directory, *Hostelling North America,* which you can order there or by phone (free to members, $3 for nonmembers). Membership gives you discounts at member hostels, and is free for youths 17 and under. For age 18 to 54, membership is $25, 55 and over $15.

Many students travel to Alaska for summer work. It's usually possible to get a job in a fish cannery in most coastal towns. Work on the slime line is hard and unpleasant and the pay is low, but if the season is good and you work long hours, camping to keep your expenses low (most canneries have tent cities of summer workers nearby), you can take home more money for your summer's work than you would normally earn. Hillary Rodham Clinton worked an Alaska slime line when she was in school, and you can, too. Stay onshore, however, as offshore fish-processing ships are a truly miserable and dangerous place to work and if the ship doesn't get any fish, you don't make any money. Also, don't come north expecting to make fabulous wages. The stories of college students making huge crew shares on fishing boats are legends—there are plenty of experienced deckhands to take those jobs before boats hire raw hands they have to train. Jobs are always available in the tourism industry, too, although you'll have to plan ahead more for that. The **Alaska Department of Labor Job Service** posts job openings and advice on its Web site, **www.labor.state.ak.us/esjobs/jobs**. A search function allows you to narrow it down by area and field—just point your Web browser to seafood processing.

FOR FAMILIES

When we researched our first edition of this book, my son, Robin, was 3, and my daughter, Julia, was 6 months. Now Robin is 8, Julia is 5, and new arrival Joseph is 1, and, along with my wife, Barbara, we still travel around Alaska together updating "our Alaska travel book" (we also write *Frommer's Family Vacations in the National Parks* together). Yes, it's a great job, and bringing the family along is the best part.

Alaska's magnificent scenery is something even young children can understand and appreciate. Also, an Alaska vacation is largely spent outdoors, which is where kids like to be. Robin never gets enough ferry riding, even after we've been doing it for weeks, and all three children enjoy camping immensely. Our experience camping with babies, even as young as 3 months, has been entirely positive. Having everyone sleep in the tent, at baby level, is an infant's idea of vacation paradise.

There are drawbacks to Alaska as a family destination. The primary one is the expense. The airlines' half-off companion fares are inconsistently applied, and we haven't yet gotten one on the Alaska route. Activities like flightseeing and tour boat cruises tend to have less-than-generous children's discounts and cost too much for most families. Often, bed-and-breakfast rooms are too small for a family. Hotel rooms and restaurant meals are expensive in Alaska. Car camping solves many of those problems, with stops in a hotel every few days to get everyone cleaned up. I wouldn't take kids over the Alaska Highway, however; instead, I'd fly to Anchorage and rent a car and any bulky camping gear there (see "Getting Outside; Equipment" in chapter 6).

You have to be careful in choosing your itinerary and activities with children. The highways in Alaska are long and children will require a gradual approach to covering ground. They also need time to play, to explore, and to rest. Children often don't enjoy activities like wildlife watching. It takes a long time to find the animals, and when you do, they're usually off in the distance—kids younger than 8 often don't have the visual skills or patience to pick out the animals from the landscape. Don't overtax children with walks and hiking trips; it'll just make everyone miserable. We keep track of the longest hike we've managed without excessive whining, then try to extend that record just a little bit each time out. Short sea-kayaking excursions, on the other hand, are great for children who are old enough, riding in the front of a double-seat boat with a parent in back; we began with Robin at age 7, and I have friends who have done it with a 3-year-old. In practice, age limits depend on the outfitter and your child's responsibility level.

If you're flawed mortals like us, after the end of a few weeks on the road, you'll be getting on each other's nerves. We found success by leaving time for low-key kid activities, like beachcombing and playing in the park, while one grown-up splits off for a museum visit, shopping, or a special, more expensive activity. Of course, if you want to preserve your marriage, you'll have to be scrupulously fair about who gets to go flightseeing and who has to stay behind and change diapers, as you won't have my all-purpose excuse (research).

If you're interested in a package tour with your family, most of the companies listed in this chapter will take children, but research carefully to make sure you will have enough down time. A better choice would be an outdoor-oriented trip designed for by an outfitter; several are listed above under "Outfitters & Outdoor Package Trips"). **Alaska Wildland Adventures** (☎ **800/334-8730**) has various trips for kids as young as 12, and even offers a "Family Safari" for families with children ages 6 through 11 that strings together day trips in various places with stays at wilderness lodges, including a float trip on the Kenai River and several days in Denali National Park. The 8-day trip costs $3,595 for adults and $3,395 for kids, exclusive of air travel. **Alaska Discovery** (☎ **800/586-1911**) takes children as young as 10 on some of its extended Southeast Alaska sea-kayaking trips, which start at $495 to $595 for 3 days and 2 nights.

10 Health, Safety & Traveler's Insurance

CRIME & EMERGENCY SERVICES

CRIME Sadly, crime rates are not low in Alaska's larger cities, although muggings are rare. Take the normal precautions you'd take at home. You're safe in daylight hours anywhere tourists commonly go, less so late at night leaving a bar or on a wooded bike trail. Women need to be especially careful on their own, as Alaska has a disproportionately high rate of rape. Most women I know avoid walking by themselves at night, especially in wooded or out-of-the-way areas. The late-night sunlight can be deceiving—just because it's light out doesn't mean it's safe. Sexual assaults occur in towns big and small. Women should never hitchhike alone. If you are a victim of a crime, you can reach police almost anywhere by calling 911, or, if it is not an emergency, using the numbers listed under "Fast Facts" in each community section.

MEDICAL EMERGENCIES You'll find modern, full-service hospitals in each of Alaska's larger cities, and even in some small towns that act as regional centers. There's some kind of clinic even in the smallest towns, although they often are staffed by physicians' assistants rather than medical doctors. I've listed the address and phone numbers for medical facilities in each destination under "Fast Facts." Call those numbers, too, for referrals for a dentist or other health professional. In an emergency, call 911.

If you suffer from a chronic illness, consult your doctor before your departure. For conditions like epilepsy, diabetes, or heart problems, wear a **Medic Alert Identification Tag** (☎ **800/ID-ALERT;** www.medicalert.org), which will immediately alert doctors to your condition and give them access to your records through Medic Alert's 24-hour hot line.

OUTDOORS HEALTH & SAFETY

BEARS & OTHER WILDLIFE Being eaten by a bear is probably the least likely way for your vacation to end. Deaths from dog bites are much more common, for example. But it's still wise to be prepared for bears, and know how to avoid being trampled by moose.

The first rule of defense is simple: Don't attract bears. All food and trash must be kept in airtight containers when you're camping (when car camping, the trunk of the vehicle will do), and be careful when you're cooking and cleaning up not to spread food odors. Never keep food or pungent items in your tent. Clean fish away from your camp site.

When walking through brush or thick trees, make lots of noise to avoid surprising a bear or moose—bells you can hang on your belt are for sale at sporting good shops, or you can sing or carry on loud conversation.

At all costs, avoid coming between a bear and its cubs or a bear and food. Moose are strongly defensive of their young, too, and can attack if they feel you're getting too close.

If you see a bear, stop, wave your arms, make noise, and, if you're with others, group together so you look larger to the bear. Don't tempt the bear to chase; depart by slowly backing away, at an angle. If the bear follows, stop. Once in a great while, the bear may bluff a charge; even less often, it may attack. If you're attacked, fall and play dead, rolling into a ball face down with your hands behind your neck. The bear should lose interest. In extremely rare instances, a bear may not lose interest, because it's planning to make a meal of you. If this happens, fight back for all you're worth. Many Alaskans carry a gun for protection in bear country, while some carry pepper spray or bear "mace" that's available in sporting-goods stores. In either case, you have to hold back the weapon as a last resort, when the bear is nearly upon you in the process of an attack. If you take a gun, it had better be a big one. Even a .45-caliber handgun won't stop a bear in time if you don't get off a precise shot. A .300-Magnum rifle or 12-gauge shotgun loaded with rifled slugs is the weapon of choice.

BOATING SAFETY Going out on the water or floating a cold, fast river is more hazardous in Alaska than in most other places, and you should go only with an experienced, licensed operator unless you really know what you're doing. The weather can be severe and unpredictable, and there's no margin for error if you fall into the water or capsize—you have only minutes to get out and get warm before hypothermia and death. A life jacket will keep you afloat, but it won't keep you alive in 40°F water. If you're sea kayaking or canoeing, stay close to shore and take along everything you need in dry bags to quickly warm a person who gets wet (see "Hypothermia," below).

HYPOTHERMIA Sometimes known as exposure, hypothermia is a potentially fatal lowering of core body temperature. It can sneak up on you, and it's most dangerous when you don't realize how cold you are, on a damp mountain hike or wet boating trip. The weather doesn't have to be very cold if you're damp and not adequately dressed in a material (whether wool or synthetic) that keeps its warmth when wet. Overheating and getting sweaty also can create a hypothermia danger, summer and winter, so the layer of clothing next to your skin is especially important. Among the symptoms of hypothermia are cold extremities, shivering, being uncommunicative, displaying poor judgment or coordination, and sleepiness. The cure is to warm the victim up—getting indoors, forcing him or her to drink hot liquids, and, if shelter is unavailable, applying body heat from another person, skin on skin, in a sleeping bag.

INSECT BITES The good news is that Alaska has no snakes or poisonous spiders. The bad news is that Alaska makes up for it with mosquitoes and other biting insects. They're not dangerous, but they can ruin a trip. Insect repellent is a necessity, as is having a place where you can get away from them. Hikers in the Interior, where mosquitoes are worst, sometimes use head nets. Mosquitoes can bite through light fabric, which is why people in the Bush wear heavy Carhart pants and jackets even on the hottest days. You might want to pack Benadryl or some other antihistamine cream to relieve itching if you do get bitten.

DANGEROUS PLANTS Two shrubs common in Alaska can cause skin irritation, but we've got nothing as bad as poison ivy or poison oak. **Pushki,** also called cow parsnip, is a large-leafed plant growing primarily in open areas, up to shoulder height by late summer, with white flowers. The celerylike stalks break easily, and the sap has the quality of intensifying the burning power of the sun on skin. Wash it off quickly to avoid a rash. **Devil's Club,** a more obviously dangerous plant, grows on steep slopes and has ferocious spines that can pierce through clothing. Also, don't eat anything you can't positively identify, as there are deadly poisonous mushrooms and plants.

RIVER CROSSINGS Hiking in Alaska's backcountry often requires crossing rivers without bridges. Use great caution: It's easy to get in trouble. Often, the water is glacial melt, barely above freezing and heavy with silt that makes it opaque, and it can quickly fill your pockets and drag you down. If in doubt, don't do it. If you do decide to cross, unbuckle your pack, keep your shoes on, face upstream, use a heavy walking stick if possible, and rig a safety line. Children should go in the eddy behind a larger person, or be carried.

SHELLFISH Don't eat mussels, clams, or scallops you pick or dig from the seashore unless you know they're safe. To find out, call the **Alaska Department of Environmental Conservation** (☎ **907/269-7501**), which tests the beaches. Most of Alaska's remote beaches are not tested and so are not safe. The risk is paralytic shellfish poisoning, a fatal malady caused by a naturally occurring toxin. It causes total paralysis, including your breathing. A victim may be kept alive with mouth-to-mouth respiration until medical help is obtained.

SWIMMING Ask about lake water before swimming in it. In recent years, some lakes have been infested with a bug that causes an itchy rash.

WATER Authorities advise against drinking unpurified river or lake water. Hand-held purification devices (not just filters), available from sporting-goods stores for around $75, are the most practical way of dealing with the problem (I swear by my Voyageur purifier, made by Pur). Iodine kits and boiling also work. The danger is *Giardia,* a bug that causes diarrhea and has been spread to thousands of water bodies all over the United States by dog feces. It may not show up until a couple of weeks after exposure and could last up to 6 weeks. If you get symptoms after getting home, tell your doctor you may have been exposed so you can get tested and cured.

DRIVING SAFETY

SUMMER Keep your headlights on all the time for safety on the highway. Drivers are required to pull over at the next pull-out whenever five or more cars are trailing on a two-lane highway, regardless of how fast they're going. This saves the lives of people who otherwise will try to pass. When passing a truck going the other way on a gravel highway, slow down or stop and pull as far as possible to the side of the road to avoid losing your windshield to a flying rock. Always think about the path of rocks you're kicking up toward others' vehicles. Make sure you've got a good, full-sized spare tire and jack if driving a gravel highway. For remote driving, take a first-aid kit, emergency food, a tow rope, and jumper cables.

WINTER Drivers on Alaska's highways in winter should be prepared for cold-weather emergencies far from help. Take all the items listed for rural summer driving, plus a flashlight, matches and materials to light a fire, chains, a shovel, and an ice scraper. A camp stove to make hot beverages also is a good idea. If you're driving a remote highway, such as the Alaska Highway, between November and April, take along gear adequate to keep you safe from the cold even if you have to wait 24 hours with a dead car at –40°F (that would include parkas, boots, hats, mittens, blankets, and sleeping bags). Never drive a road marked "Closed" or "Unmaintained in Winter." Even on maintained rural roads, other vehicles come by rarely. All Alaska roads are icy all winter. Studded tires are a necessity—nonstudded snow tires or so-called "all-weather" tires aren't adequate. Also, never leave your car's engine stopped for more than 4 hours in extreme cold (–10°F or colder). Alaskans generally have electrical head-bolt heaters installed to keep the engine warm overnight; you'll find electrical outlets everywhere in cold, Interior Alaska areas.

TRAVEL INSURANCE

There are three kinds of travel insurance: trip-cancellation, medical, and lost-luggage coverage. Trip-cancellation insurance is a must if you have paid the large cash deposits demanded by many Alaska outfitters, fishing guides, wilderness lodges, package tour operators, and cruise companies. A premium of 8% of the cost of the trip is well worth the protection against the uncertainty of Alaska weather (most deposits are lost in case of weather delays or cancellations) or unexpected crises that might prevent you from being able to depart as planned.

Medical insurance for travelers from outside the United States is a worthwhile investment, too, but probably doesn't make sense for most travelers from the U.S., who most likely are already covered under their regular health insurance. Likewise, your baggage is probably covered under your homeowner's policy or credit card benefits. Besides, if the airline loses your bags, they are usually responsible for up to $2,500 per piece on domestic flights, $640 on international flights; don't check baggage worth more than that. Some credit- and charge-card companies may also insure you against airplane crashes and other travel accidents if you buy tickets with their cards. It's a cheap benefit for them to offer because claims are so rare; for the same reason, buying such insurance yourself doesn't make economic sense.

Various companies sell travel insurance; you can conveniently buy online. Reputable firms include **Access America** (☎ **800/284-8300;** www.accessamerica.com) and **Travel Guard International** (☎ **877/216-4885;** www.travel-guard.com).

●

Fast Facts: Alaska

Area Code All of Alaska is in area code **907.** In the Yukon Territory, the area code is **867.** When placing a toll call within the state, you must dial 1, the area code, and the number. See "Telephone," below, for important tips.

Banks & ATMs There are banks and automated teller machines in all but the tiniest towns.

Business Hours In the larger cities, major grocery stores are open 24 hours a day and carry a wide range of products (even fishing gear) in addition to food. At a minimum, **stores** are open Monday through Friday from 10am to 6pm, on Saturday afternoon, and closed on Sunday, but many are open much longer hours, especially in summer. **Banks** may close an hour earlier and, if open on Saturday, usually are open only in the morning. Under state law, **bars** don't have to close until 5am, but many communities have an earlier closing, generally around 2am.

Cellular Phone Coverage Most towns in the populated portion of the state have cellular coverage. Your cell phone provider should be able to give you a brochure detailing roaming charges.

Emergencies Generally, you can call ☎ **911** for medical, police, or fire emergencies. On remote highways there sometimes are gaps in 911 coverage, but dialing 0 will generally get an operator, who can connect you to emergency services. Citizens Band channels 9 and 11 are monitored for emergencies on most highways, as are channels 14 and 19 in some areas.

Holidays Besides the normal national holidays, banks and state and government offices close on two state holidays: Seward's Day (the last Monday in March) and Alaska Day (October 18, or the nearest Friday or Monday if it falls on a weekend). See chapter 3 for a listing of national holidays.

Internet/E-mail Access The easiest way to connect is to go to the local Internet cafe or public library, listed under "Fast Facts" in each town write-up. See "Planning Your Trip: An Online Directory" for tips on how to get your e-mail on the road. If you want to dial up the Internet from your own laptop, you may have to call long distance to your home access number; since long-distance phone lines in Alaska's smaller towns can be poor, you may not succeed. Major networks have local numbers in Anchorage and Fairbanks, where the phone connections are crystal clear.

Liquor Laws The minimum drinking age in Alaska is 21. Most restaurants sell beer and wine, while a minority have full bars that serve hard liquor as well. Packaged alcohol, beer, and wine is sold only in licensed stores, not in grocery stores, but these are common and are open long hours every day. More than 100 rural communities have laws prohibiting the importation and possession of alcohol (this is known as being "dry") or only the sale but not possession of alcohol (known as being "damp"). With a few exceptions, these are tiny Bush communities off the road network; urban areas are all "wet." Of the communities featured in this book, Kotzebue and Barrow are damp, and the rest are wet. Before flying into a Native village with alcohol, ask about the law, as bootlegging is a serious crime (and serious bad manners), or check a list on the Alcoholic Beverage Control Board Web site, at www.revenue.state.ak.us/abc/localopt.htm.

Maps I've noted the best trail maps in each applicable section throughout this book. For the most popular areas, I recommend the excellent trail maps published by **National Geographic Maps Trails Illustrated** (☎ **800/962-1643** or 303/670-3457; www.trailsillustrated.com). They're sold in park visitor centers, too. The maps are printed on plastic, so they don't get spoiled by rain; however, they don't cover the whole state. Buy **official topographic maps** from the U.S. Geological Survey directly at USGS-ESIC, 4230 University Dr., Anchorage, AK 99508

(☎ **907/786-7011**), open Monday to Friday, 8:30am to 4:30pm, or online at edcwww.cr.usgs.gov/. ***The Alaska Atlas and Gazetteer,*** published by DeLorme Mapping (☎ **800/452-5931;** www.delorme.com), contains topographical maps of the entire state, most at 1:300,000 scale. It's widely available in Alaska.

Newspapers The state's dominant newspaper is the *Anchorage Daily News* (www.adn.com); it's available everywhere but is not easy to find in Southeast Alaska. Seattle newspapers and *USA Today* are often available, and in Anchorage you can get virtually any newspaper.

Taxes There is no state sales tax, but most local governments have a sales tax and a bed tax on accommodations. The tax rates are listed in each town section throughout the book under its "Fast Facts."

Telephone I am assured that all major calling cards will work in Alaska, but this certainly hasn't been the case in the past. To make sure, contact your long-distance company, or buy a by-the-minute card. (For further information, see "Fast Facts: For the Foreign Traveler" in chapter 3.)

Time Zone Although the state naturally spans five time zones, in the 1980s, Alaska's central time zone was stretched so almost the entire state would lie all in one zone, known as Alaska time. It's 1 hour earlier than the U.S. West Coast's Pacific time. Crossing over the border from Alaska to Canada adds an hour and puts you at the same time as the West Coast. As with almost everywhere else in the United States, daylight saving time is in effect from 1am on the first Sunday in April (turn your clocks ahead 1 hour) until 2am on the last Sunday in October (turn clocks back again).

Tipping Guides As a general rule, tip fishing guides and outfitters $10 to $20 per person per day. For outings of less than a day, adjust the tip accordingly. At wilderness lodges, which normally have all-inclusive rates, it's often best to add the tip to your final payment when you leave and let the proprietor distribute it to the staff rather than try to do it at each meal. A blanket tip of $15 per day is acceptable.

Planning Your Trip: An Online Directory

When I first wrote this book, five years ago, only statewide organizations and universities had Web sites, and most of them didn't tell you much. Today, as you'll see from flipping our pages, virtually every mom-and-pop B&B has a site and most tourism businesses sell their wares online (a few don't bother with any other medium). From your computer, you can read the community news in Seldovia (www.seldovia.com), look at the clouds in Kaltag (www.akweathercams.com), and check the status of the Aurora Borealis (www.gi.alaska.edu or www.spaceweather.com). Never before have you been able to know more or shop more effectively in advance of a vacation.

This chapter is intended to help with some of the tools. First, I offer general advice on how and when to use the Internet; next I list general Internet resources for booking any trip; then I've listed some of the many Alaska-oriented online guides, booking agencies and government information sites. No site has paid for inclusion here, and the reviews are my own opinions. Please remember, however, that the Internet changes faster than the weather, and you will doubtless find some dead links or outdated information here that were correct at the time of this writing.

I welcome e-mail from readers, especially complaints or praise about businesses listed in the book. Your experiences have a great impact on how and whether I include particular establishments. My e-mail address is wohlforth@gci.net. I try to answer requests for advice, too, if I can, but be forewarned that I'm often traveling or too busy with paying work to be able to help out visitors looking for free trip-planning help. My best trip-planning advice is already contained in this book.

1 The Ways of the Web

Here are some tips and warnings gleaned from my own experience and the advice of experts about using the Internet to plan a trip.

SHOULD YOU BOOK ONLINE?

I use the Internet, and I use travel agents, and I book by telephone directly with operators. Each method has its pros and cons.

INTERNET ADVANTAGES The Web is by far the fastest and most complete source of information about Alaska travel. No other medium allows you to see so much and get the particular fact you are looking for so quickly. It's a great way to comparison shop. You also

Credit-Card Security on the Net

Credit-card companies have adjusted their policies to take most of the risk out of using a card on the Internet. Using an encrypted Web browser, your card number is no more at risk on the Web than over the telephone. (Don't send card numbers unless you are on a secure server; you can tell by the key in the lower left corner of Netscape's browser, or the padlock on Internet Explorer.) Of course, if you are dealing with an unscrupulous operator, you can get fleeced online or in person.

can sometimes save money booking on the Internet, as airlines often offer sales and discounts for using their sites to buy tickets. Since they have cut their commissions to travel agents, you usually have to pay a fee to use an agent, sometimes with the result of paying more for your ticket over all. Car-rental reservations also work well online, and when it comes to unique accommodations, such as wilderness lodges or bed and breakfast stays, the Internet is a far better avenue than a typical travel agent, who likely has little knowledge or patience to deal with such obscure businesses. I've sometimes shopped the Internet and then called an agent to see if they can beat the deal.

INTERNET DISADVANTAGES You wouldn't think it, but using the Internet to plan a trip takes a lot longer than the traditional methods. When you use a travel agent, you rely on that person's knowledge to filter out all the bad choices and offer only the good. On the Internet, you have to sift through everything. For complex airline reservations, including trips with stopovers, companion fares, or more than one leg, it simply doesn't pay to use the Internet; if the system will work at all, it will take forever to figure it out and you won't know if you got a good deal.

Internet information also can be unreliable. One problem is the many out-of-date or abandoned sites that keep sending out wrong information year after year. I don't rely on Web sites at all to research this book; I check every fact with a real person.

A bigger problem is objectivity. You expect businesses to make themselves sound as good as possible in their ads, but most seemingly objective online guides really are just advertising vehicles, too, and they tend to portray their advertisers in too positive a light. Unlike the print world, where you've learned to tell an ad from and article, it's often impossible to tell on the Web.

Other sites, such as the big booking sites, show everything as equal. A quick search on Expedia turns up a copious array of hotels in Anchorage, including some dives where you wouldn't even get out of the cab if you were unfortunate enough to arrive with a reservation. Making the same search on other sites turns up much of the same bad information. That's why I'm pretty sure I'll be employed for a long time. The Internet is merely a medium; the information you get from it is only as good as what someone puts in at the other end. If you want to know where to stay, you still need an objective report, such as this book.

2 All-Purpose Booking Sites

There are three ways to deal with the airlines, car-rental agencies, and chain hotels online: Contact them directly, at their own Web sites; use a large online travel agent; or use an online discounter.

Check Out Frommer's Site

We highly recommend **Arthur Frommer's Budget Travel Online** (**www.frommers.com**) as an excellent travel-planning resource. Of course, we're a little biased, but you'll find indispensable travel tips, reviews, monthly vacation giveaways, and online booking. Among the most popular features of this site are the regular "Ask the Expert" bulletin boards, which feature Frommer's authors answering your questions via online postings.

Subscribe to Arthur Frommer's Daily Newsletter (**www.frommers.com/newsletters**) to receive the latest travel bargains and inside travel secrets in your e-mailbox every day. You'll read daily headlines and articles from the dean of travel himself, highlighting last-minute deals on airfares, accommodations, cruises, and package vacations.

Search our Destinations archive (**www.frommers.com/destinations**) of more than 200 domestic and international destinations for great places to stay and dine, and tips on sightseeing. Once you've researched your trip, the online reservation system (**www.frommers.com/booktravelnow**) takes you to Frommer's favorite sites for booking your vacation at affordable prices.

ONLINE AGENCIES The great thing about agencies such as Expedia and Travelocity is the window they offer on booking networks that allow you to search for the best price among many different providers. These sites give you a lot of new power. You don't have to buy, or usually even register, to use these tools. You can check flight schedules and fares, hotel availability, car-rental prices, and even the exact location of a flight that's already in the air. On the other hand, they don't always yield the best price, and they can be cumbersome to use if you are not doing the simplest of trips. Discount airlines may not appear; Southwest, the largest discounter, generally isn't available. Other airlines may block their best fares (read on for ways to beat this system). Also, it's hard to get a reasonable price on a multileg trip or a one-way car rental (Expedia at least prices one-way rentals). Airfare pricing systems are insanely complicated, and if you don't know the rules, it can be just too frustrating.

BOOKING DIRECT You can also book airline tickets, rental cars, cruises, and chain hotel rooms online directly with the provider. These companies often offer sales or bonus frequent-flier mileage on their own Web sites that you can't get anywhere else. I've sometimes used Expedia or one of the other online agents to narrow down a selection of carriers or rental agencies at a particular location; then I've gone directly to the least expensive provider's site to see if I can save even more by buying direct. Go with whoever offers the best deal.

LAST-MINUTE DISCOUNTS Most travelers to Alaska will need to plan ahead, but if you can manage an impulse trip, or need to come on business without warning, there's a chance you can snag a great deal on airfare or a cruise through the Internet. Airlines and other companies use their Web sites to fill unsold seats at a discount. It's like the remainder bin at the record store, and, like the remainder bin, it's not a place to find the day's best sellers. Since airline loads are heavy for peak summer travel to Alaska, waiting to get a bargain fare is not a good strategy at that time. Shoulder and off-season is a better bet. Most Web specials are announced on Tuesday or Wednesday and are valid for travel the following weekend. The best way to grab a last-minute bargain is to sign up for e-mail alerts at the airlines' sites or one of the sites listed below; when a fare you like comes up, make your decision and go. Using a similar strategy, you may be able to save on a cruise, too. Or use one of the sites that gathers all this information for you.

TRAVEL BOOKING & BARGAIN SITES

Dozens of sites provide access to national booking networks or their own discounted offerings. Here are some of the best.

✪ 1travel.com. **www.1travel.com**

This bargain site offers a bunch of ways to beat the system, including the ability to search for better fares on different days, searches of consolidators, "white label" fares that connect passengers with airlines that would prefer the world not know how cheap they'll go, and e-mail notification of good deals. A long menu offers deals on cruises and other kinds of travel.

✪ Expedia.com. **expedia.com**

This Microsoft product really works. You can use it for domestic and international flights, hotels and B&Bs, and car-rental booking. You don't need to register to search and get prices. Expedia makes it easy to handle flights, hotels, and car bookings on one itinerary, so it's a good place for one-stop shopping.

The entry page has been made much simpler and more inviting; the site's biggest strengths are the lack of clutter and that it doesn't try to pull you in certain directions. Expedia also has come out first with some features that really challenge the travel agents: you can look for one-way car rentals, if you rent between airports, and you can search for airline fares by route, getting back a calendar of when the lowest fare applies. Also, unlike Travelocity, you can easily find out which airlines are covered; go to the pull-down menu on the round-trip search page.

The hotel and B&B listings, with crisp, zoomable maps, are comprehensive, but offer little information upon which to make a choice and contain irrelevant information (the nearest airport to the Hilton Anchorage is listed as Merrill Field, which in fact serves private pilots). They also carry "content" on travel news, destinations, and the like; my spot check on Alaska found it thin and out of date.

Go4less.com. **www.go4less.com**

Check here before booking a cruise. When I last checked, 16 Alaska cruises were listed, half of them with discounts of 50% or more. You may have to grab a last-minute deal to save that money, but there are worse things in life than unexpectedly taking off on a cruise.

Priceline.com. **www.priceline.com**

This is the choice for gamblers. You tell the Web site when and where you want to go, how much you're willing to pay, and give them your credit card number. Within an hour or so, you either have nothing, or you have irrevocably bought an airline ticket or rented a car from a company that was willing to meet your price. You can't back out after you find out which company you've got or what time of day you are flying. For hotel rooms, it's a bit less scary: You're under no obligation until you get the quote and the name of the place, but you'll likely find only chains with standard rooms bidding for your business anyway (the names of the hotels participating is secret). That may make sense for business travelers, but I think the hotel you stay in is too big a part of your vacation to leave it up to chance. On the other hand, if your plans are certain and you have already shopped, why not bid for the lowest plane fare and rental-car price? First, get the best price you can online or with your travel agency, then bid below that price. Note, however, that you get no extras: No frequent-flyer miles are awarded, no one-way or stopover tickets, no special meals. Tickets are nonrefundable and can't be exchanged for another flight. Cars rentals are paid for in advance and can't be changed; for extensions, you're at the agency's mercy.

Smarter Living. www.smarterliving.com
This is essentially a bargain travel news service. After signing up, with your name and other personal information, you'll be sent e-mail updates on airline specials and many other travel deals, customized to your interests.

Travelocity. www.travelocity.com
Travelocity is easy to use, but not as flexible as Expedia: You can't rent a car one way, and it's harder to figure out the cheapest times to travel. However, you can get more information without committing to a reservation, and American Airline's Sabre system, originally developed for travel agents, works quickly. I find the site cluttered, however, and there is a tendency to try to lure you in directions that may not be right for you. Get around all that by using the same system through Yahoo (go to Yahoo.com and click on "Travel" near the top of the page). Like Expedia, the hotel system doesn't make much sense, mixing dives and luxurious places. When I checked for Anchorage airport hotels, I got back one in Denali National Park, more than 200 miles away. It is hoped its information will improve in the next year, as Frommer's has partnered with Travelocity to provide content for this site. Travelocity does have an edge for serious bargain hunters—you can have it e-mail you about fare changes on routes you choose. As the Alaska market is highly volatile, with extreme discounts sometimes appearing and disappearing quickly, you could use this feature to time your purchase.

✪ Trip.com. www.trip.com
This site is intended for business travelers, but I like it for several reasons. It's fast and not cluttered with ads. It's innovative, with ideas like the Flight Tracker, which lets you find out exactly where any flight is in the air right now (and its speed, altitude, and other information) and when it will arrive. And it's a little subversive. Two examples: They book blocks of rooms in hotels so customers can get into sold-out places for a $20 surcharge (kind of like scalping concert tickets); and they have an engine that can search the airlines' own Web sites, so you can find out about the cheapest discount fares that are blocked from the major online booking systems.

WebFlyer. www.webflyer.com
This site, with lots of news and resources aimed at frequent fliers, allows you to shop the airlines' weekend Web specials by city without clogging your e-mail box with unwanted information.

Airline Links

If you're looking for an airline Web site, you'll find virtually every one on earth linked at the FAA's site, at **www.faa.gov/passenger.htm**.

FINDING ACCOMMODATIONS ONLINE

The Internet isn't as well suited to selling hotel rooms as it is to selling airline tickets and rental cars. That's because hotel rooms aren't all created equal; the chains keep trying, but cute, interesting places continue to crop up that don't fit the cookie cutter. Web sites that list tens of thousands of establishments can't judge them all. Unlike the publishers of this book, they don't have someone going out to inspect every listing, and there's always the possibility of advertising coloring the opinions you get.

These systems work best for predictable chain hotels. On the other hand, systems that put you in the hands of the establishments' own Web sites can be highly useful as a first step in research—just don't use them as your only information source, since they're not objective.

All Hotels on the Web. **www.all-hotels.com**
Use this site to book hotels and B&Bs you already have researched, or to find accommodations on your way to Alaska. The Alaska listings are extensive, but not without errors and certainly not universal—some Alaska towns are not represented at all. Each listing is paid for by the establishment.

Go Camping America. **www.gocampingamerica.com/main.html**
These nationwide campground listings include at least one campground in most Alaska towns on the road system, a list of facts about each, and, most useful of all, links to their own sites, in many cases.

InnSite. **www.innsite.com**
Lots of B&Bs and inns are listed in Alaska, and many thousands all over the United States. Unlike some sterile and uncommunicative hotel directories, these pages link you right to the establishment's own, independent Web site, which will usually give you a much better feel for what it is like.

TravelWeb. **www.travelweb.com**
You will mostly find standard chain hotels on this easy-to-use directory. There is enough information to make a choice, but take it with a grain of salt: Descriptions are written in brochure-speak. The site's big advantage is fast, simple online booking.

3 Alaska Traveler's Tools

Local sources usually have the best information, and that is certainly true through the medium of the Internet. Throughout this book, I've integrated the best Web sites into the text along with the businesses and towns they relate to. Most towns have excellent sites that act as portals to activities and businesses in their areas. Here you'll find some of the more general Internet information that applies statewide.

ATM LOCATORS

Visa's Plus Network is at www.visa.com/pd/atm/. MasterCard and the Cirrus and Maestro networks are at www.mastercard.com/atm. Either way, entering your address brings back the three closest ATMs.

AURORA PREDICTIONS

University of Alaska's Geophysical Institute. **www.gi.alaska.edu**
The university is a leading center of aurora research. They post a prediction of exactly which parts of the state will see the aurora each night. For more on the subject, also check www.spaceweather.com.

PERFORMING ARTS & SPECTATOR SPORTS

Tickets.com recently bought Alaska's dominant ticket agency (CarrsTix, at www.carrstix.com). **Festival Finder (www.festivalfinder.com)** lists some of Alaska's music festivals, with links to each, as well as thousands nationwide.

WEATHER & TIDE

The most complete Alaska site belongs to the National Weather Service, at www.alaska.net/~nwsar/. For national weather, and prettier graphics, check Intellicast (www.intellicast.com). A really cool site, with weather cams in remote places around the state, is operated by the FAA at www.akweathercams.com.

To check the tide anywhere in Alaska or around the United States, and a lot of other interesting nautical and astronomical information, go to NOAA's **Center for Operational Oceanographic and Observational Services** (co-ops.nos.noaa.gov/co-ops.html).

OBJECTIVE INFORMATION SITES

Government and established media form an island of objectivity in the commercial world of the Internet. Use these sites to get straight information about the outdoors, transportation, culture, and services, though you'll get little or nothing about individual businesses.

Alaska Public Lands Information Centers. **www.nps.gov/aplic**
This interagency office is a clearinghouse of outdoor information.

✪ Anchorage Daily News. **www.adn.com**
The state's dominant newspaper offers an exhaustive online visitors' guide for the whole state, including a regional weekly fishing report that reveals which streams are hot, and a cultural event calendar covering the region.

Bureau of Land Management. **wwwndo.ak.blm.gov/**
This Department of the Interior agency manages much of Alaska and has a site loaded with useful information on rivers and rural highways, if you look diligently.

Fairbanks News Miner. **www.newsminer.com**
This Interior newspaper produces a good online visitors' guide for the whole region.

National Forest Service, Alaska Region. **www.fs.fed.us/r10/**
The Tongass, the nation's largest national forest, operates an excellent site, with information on trails, public cabins, and many other subjects. Chugach National Forest is slowly catching up.

✪ National Park Service. **www.nps.gov**
I use this one a lot. Each park has its own site, with much helpful information.

National Recreation Reservation Service. **www.reserveusa.com**
Use this Forest Service contractor to book cabins and campsites online (for important details, see "Exploring Southeast Alaska" in chapter 5 and "Chugach National Forest" in chapter 7).

Maps

Driving maps and directions are available from many sites, including **Expedia.com**. **MapQuest** (www.mapquest.com) provides much other information as well. For a less cluttered version of the same product, click on "Maps" at the top of the home page at **Yahoo.com**.

Using the Internet on the Road

Don't take your laptop on vacation. For one thing, it's pathetic. For another, it's unnecessary. Even tiny Alaska towns have some kind of Web access these days; most have a trendy Internet cafe of some kind, while in others you can log on at the public library. Internet access for each Alaska community is listed in the appropriate section of the book. The **Net Café Guide** (www.netcafeguide.com/mapindex.htm) helps you find them all over the world. Relying on this kind of access is far easier than lugging a computer around, worrying about it being stolen, and trying to connect through spotty phone lines on weird hotel phone systems. Typically, you can find the information you want for only a few dollars.

There are three ways to get your e-mail on the Web, where you can check it from any computer. One: Your Internet Service Provider may have a Web-based interface. Just find out how it works before you leave home. Two: You can open an account on a free, Web-based e-mail provider before you leave home, such as Microsoft's **Hotmail** (hotmail.com) or **Yahoo! Mail** (mail.yahoo.com), checking it anywhere. Your home ISP may be able to forward your home e-mail to the Web-based account automatically. Or, three: Use www.mail2web.com. This amazing free service allows you to type in your regular e-mail address and password and retrieve your e-mail from any Web browser, anywhere, so long as your home ISP hasn't blocked it with a firewall.

Southeast Alaska Tourism Council. **www.AlaskaInfo.org**
This is a booster organization for cooperating communities. The site is beautiful and allows you to link to individual towns, which have their own sites linking to individual businesses.

✪ State of Alaska. **www.state.ak.us**
The state's home page is the easiest starting point for navigating to some extremely useful sites, allowing you to avoid typing in long addresses. Here are some of the best:

Alaska Department of Fish and Game: Anglers, hunters, and wildlife enthusiasts should stop in for resources, including online fishing licenses, a fascinating Wildlife Notebook, fishing information (down to the individual stream level), and even scientific papers.

Division of State Parks (within Alaska Department of Natural Resources): Some of Alaska's most accessible wild lands are in its state parks, many of which are on par with national parks in their beauty and size. Public-use cabins also are online.

Alaska Marine Highway System (within the Department of Transportation): The state's indispensable ferry system operates a useful if primitive site. Several other agents also offer online ferry information and reservations; see "Ferry System Booking Tips," in chapter 5.

Road Reports (Department of Transportation and Public Facilities): It's often said that Alaska has only two seasons: winter and road construction. The road guys offer updates and warnings for each on the state's highways.

The **Alaska Tourism Industry Association** (**www.alaskatia.org**) is the official point of contact for visitor inquiries, but had not yet put up a useful Web site at this writing.

COMMERCIAL TRAVEL SITES

These commercial sites are useful, if you remember what your relationship to them is. Many try to gain your trust by looking like news or information organizations, when in fact they are online stores trying to sell products and tailoring their content to help their advertisers. Having worked as a journalist in the online world, I have learned from experience that the ethics of print journalism have not made the leap onto the Web. Unless you know otherwise, you should suspect all online information is tainted by commercial bias.

360 Alaska. **www.360alaska.com**
A gimmick, but a cool gimmick: The site tries to sell you on its advertisers with 360° images of beautiful places that you can scroll through.

Alaska Internet Travel Guide. **www.AlaskaOne.com/travel**
This site contains an astounding number of links to travel businesses, each of which has its own, informative page.

Alaska Wilderness and Tourism Association. **www.awrta.org/**
This is an environmental advocacy organization, rather than just a tourism sales channel; that means they often take tough stands and that you can count on the member outfitters, guides, and lodges to care about the environment. Some were founded to teach about beautiful places and to help save them. Most of the best in the state are on the site, which provides handy comparative information.

Alaskan.com. **www.alaskan.com**
Formerly, and more accurately, called the Great Alaskan Mall, this site contains links to thousands of advertisers that have been organized by subject area that makes them easy to find on uncluttered pages.

AlaskaOutdoors. **www.alaskaoutdoors.com**
Look here for links to many outfitters, fishing guides, lodges, and the like all over the state.

✪ Alcanseek. **www.alcanseek.com**
This is a sort of Yahoo! of the north, with links and reports on the Alaska Highway and related regions organized by topic channels. Anyone planning to drive the highway should take a look. (The name Alcan is a nickname for the Alaska Highway, which runs from British Columbia through the Yukon to Alaska.)

Great Alaskan Tour Saver. **www.TourSaver.com**
This link will take you to the homepage for a potentially money-saving Alaska travel coupon book, and access to Anchorage travel expert Scott McMurren.

✪ Great Outdoor Recreation Pages. **www.gorp.com**
GORP is the original and best of the outdoor Web sites. It is loaded with feature stories, online communities, useful links, and listings; you can find a lot of handy outdoor information without ever encountering the outfitters and lodges that are paying to be there. That journalistic approach appropriately builds reader trust, something other sites should emulate.

inAlaska.com. **www.inalaska.com**
This site, to which I have occasionally contributed, aims to do more than list links to advertisers; it carries feature articles, stories about timely happenings, and straight travel guide data.

For Foreign Visitors

3

Visitors from the rest of the United States sometimes say Alaska is like a foreign country full of Americans. If you are coming from overseas, it may be doubly unfamiliar. This chapter aims to help you through the details so you can better enjoy the differences.

Information on border crossings between the United States and Canada on the Alaska Highway is contained in chapter 9.

1 Preparing for Your Trip

ENTRY REQUIREMENTS

Check at any U.S. embassy or consulate for current information and requirements. You can also obtain a visa application and other information online at **U.S. State Department's** Web site, at **travel.state.gov**.

DO YOU NEED A VISA? Most tourists coming to the United States do not need a visa. Canadian citizens only need proof of residence (not even a passport), and citizens of 29 other countries need hardly more under the U.S. State Department's **Visa Waiver Pilot Program.** At press time, the list included: Andorra, Argentina, Austria, Australia, Belgium, Brunei, Denmark, Finland, France, Germany, Iceland, Ireland, Italy, Japan, Liechtenstein, Luxembourg, Monaco, The Netherlands, New Zealand, Norway, Portugal, San Marino, Singapore, Slovenia, Spain, Sweden, Switzerland, the United Kingdom, and Uruguay. Citizens can enter for up to 90 days of pleasure travel with only a valid passport and a round-trip air or cruise ticket in their possession upon arrival. If they first enter the United States, they may also visit Mexico, Canada, Bermuda, and/or the Caribbean islands and return to the United States without a visa. Further information is available from any U.S. embassy or consulate.

Citizens of all other countries must obtain visas.

OBTAINING A VISA To obtain a visa, a traveler must submit a completed application form (either in person or by mail) along with a $45 fee and two photos (1½ inches or 37 × 37 mm square), and must demonstrate binding ties to a residence in the home country. If you cannot go in person, contact the nearest U.S. embassy or consulate or check the State Department Web site (travel.state.gov) for directions on applying by mail. Your travel agent or airline office may also be able to provide you with visa applications and instructions.

MEDICAL REQUIREMENTS Unless you're arriving from an area known to be suffering from an epidemic (particularly cholera or yellow fever), inoculations or vaccinations are not required for entry into the United States. If you have a disease that requires treatment with narcotics or syringe-administered medications, carry a valid signed prescription or letter from your physician to allay any suspicions that you may be smuggling narcotics.

Upon entering the United States, foreign nationals are required to declare any dangerous contagious diseases they carry, which includes infection with HIV, the AIDS virus. Anyone who has such a disease is excluded from entry as a tourist. However, you may be able to apply for a waiver if you are attending a conference or have another compelling non-tourism reason for your visit. If you will be entering the country in Alaska, contact the **Immigration and Naturalization Service Anchorage Port Director** (☎ **907/271-3521;** www.ins.usdoj.gov) to inquire about a waiver or related issues. If you're entering the United States at another point, contact the **INS** at ☎ **800/375-5283** (TTY 800/767-1833). Doubtless many HIV-positive visitors come in without declaring their condition, their way of dealing with an archaic law that was originally intended to halt the spread of tuberculosis and the like.

DRIVER'S LICENSES Foreign driver's licenses are mostly recognized in the United States, although you may want to get an international driver's license if your home license is not written in English.

CUSTOMS

WHAT YOU CAN BRING IN

Personal effects, such as cameras and fishing rods, are exempt from duties. In addition, every visitor over 21 years of age may bring in the following without paying duties: (1) 1 liter of wine or hard liquor; and (2) 200 cigarettes, or 50 cigars (but not from Cuba), or 3 pounds of smoking tobacco; and (3) $100 worth of gifts (including up to 100 additional cigars, but no alcohol). To claim the gift exemption, you must spend at least 72 hours in the United States and cannot have claimed it within the preceding 6 months.

The duty on goods exceeding these exemptions is 10% of the value on the first $1,000; above that amount, it depends on the item. Importation of most raw food and plant material is prohibited or requires a special license. Foreign tourists may bring in or take out up to $10,000 in U.S. or foreign currency, traveler's checks or securities with no formalities; larger sums must be declared to U.S. Customs on entering or leaving and paperwork filed.

Declare any medicines you are carrying and be prepared to present a letter or prescription from your doctor demonstrating you need the drugs; you may bring in no more than you would normally use in the duration of your visit.

For many more details on what you can and cannot bring, go to the informative U.S. Customs Web sit at **www.customs.ustreas.gov/** and click on "Traveler Information," or call ☎ **202/927-1770.**

WHAT YOU CAN BRING HOME

WILDLIFE PRODUCTS Alaska Native art and crafts made from protected marine mammals are perfectly legal (even though possessing the raw animal pelts is not legal for non-Natives), but you do need to get permits to take these items out of the country. Permits also are required to export products made from brown or black bear, bobcat, wolf, lynx, or river otter. The best solution is to have the shop where you buy the item mail it to you insured, and have them take care of the paperwork. If you carry it with you, or buy from a shop that can't handle the paperwork, you'll need to get your own permits. To go into or through Canada, get a Personal Effects Exemption Certificate for the item by calling the **U.S. Fish and Wildlife Service** in Anchorage (☎ **907/271-6198**). They can handle it in a few days. Call them also for permits for products made of nonmarine mammals. To take **marine mammal products** to a country other than Canada, you need a permit from the **Fish and Wildlife Service** in Washington, D.C. (☎ **800/358-2104;** www.fws.gov). It can take a month to get these permits. There may be other regulations for bringing walrus ivory into your home country because of the international ban on elephant ivory. It's important to note that Alaska Natives have used these materials for thousands of years, and their harvest poses no threat to the species.

OTHER GOODS Rules governing what you can bring back duty-free vary from country to country, and generally are posted on the Web. **Canadians** should check the booklet *I Declare,* which your can download or order from Revenue Canada (☎ **613/993-0534;** www.ccra-adrc.gc.ca). **British** citizens should contact HM Customs & Excise (☎ **020 7202 4227;** www.hmce.gov.uk). **Australians** can contact the Australian Customs Service (☎ **1-300/363-263** within Australia, 61-2/6275-6666 from outside Australia; www.customs.gov.au/). **New Zealand** citizens should contact New Zealand Customs (☎ **09/359-6655;** www.customs.govt.nz/).

INSURANCE

Although it's not required of travelers, health insurance is highly recommended. Unlike many European countries, the United States does not usually offer free or low-cost medical care to its citizens or visitors. Doctors and hospitals are expensive, and in most cases will require advance payment or proof of coverage before they render their services. Travel-insurance policies can cover everything from the loss or theft of your baggage and trip cancellation to the guarantee of bail in case you're arrested. Good policies will also cover the costs of an accident, repatriation, or death. Packages such as **Europ Assistance** in Europe are sold by automobile clubs and travel agencies at attractive rates. **Worldwide Assistance Services, Inc.** (☎ **800/777-8710,** ext. 409, or 703/204-1897; www.worldwideassistance.com) is the agent for Europe Assistance in the United States.

Though lack of health insurance may prevent you from being admitted to a hospital in nonemergencies, don't worry about being left on a street corner to die: The American way is to fix you now and bill the living daylights out of you later.

I also strongly recommend trip-cancellation and interruption insurance if you place deposits on Alaska services or accommodations. Insurance providers are covered under "Health, Safety & Traveler's Insurance" in chapter 2.

MONEY

The most common **bills** are the $1 (colloquially, a "buck"), $5, $10, and $20 denominations; $50 and $100 bills usually are not welcome as payment for small purchases. Four denominations of **coins** are commonly used: 1¢ (1 cent, or a penny); 5¢ (5 cents, or a nickel); 10¢ (10 cents, or a dime); 25¢ (25 cents, or a quarter). Occasionally you will also encounter coins for 50¢ (50 cents, or a half dollar) and any of three designs of the $1 piece. New designs for U.S. currency have been introduced, but the old-style bills and coins are still legal tender. See chapter 2 for a discussion of **credit cards, ATMs, traveler's checks,** and other payment methods in Alaska.

Though traveler's checks are widely accepted, ***make sure that they're denominated in U.S. dollars,*** as foreign-currency checks are often difficult to exchange. Remember: You'll need identification, such as a driver's license or passport, to change a traveler's check.

The "foreign-exchange bureaus" so common in Europe are rare even at airports in the United States, and nonexistent outside major cities. The only such business in Alaska is **Thomas Cook Currency Services,** at 311 F St. in Anchorage (☎ **907/278-2822;** www.thomascook.com). It's best not to change foreign money (or traveler's checks denominated in a currency other than U.S. dollars) at a small-town bank. Obtain U.S. dollars before you leave home. You can pay for almost anything with a credit or charge card, with the exchange automatically made by your bank.

SAFETY

Robberies (like muggings) are quite rare in Alaska, even in Anchorage, but the incidence of rape is quite high. Precautions are covered in chapter 2. Of course, thefts can happen anywhere; the only time anyone has tried to steal from me in Alaska was in a tiny village. Keep control of your belongings and lock your car and hotel doors. Don't leave valuables in sight in the car. Guns are ubiquitous in Alaska; avoid getting into an argument in a rough bar.

2 Getting to the United States

Most flights to Alaska come from domestic airports, requiring trips from overseas to pass through Seattle or another major city, but service may be available direct to Anchorage from Japan, Germany, or South Korea. Canadians can drive to Alaska over the Alaska or Top of the World highways, covered in chapter 9, or on an Alaska Marine Highway System ferry from Prince Rupert, B.C., covered in chapter 5.

Some major American carriers—including Delta and Continental—offer travelers on their transatlantic or transpacific flights special low-price tickets on U.S. continental flights under the **Discover America** program (sometimes called **Visit USA,** depending on the airline). Offering one-way travel between U.S. destinations at significantly reduced prices, this coupon-based airfare program is the best and easiest way to tour the United States at low cost.

These discounted fare coupons are not available in the United States, and must be purchased abroad in conjunction with your international ticket. You should ask your travel agent or the airline reservations agent about this program well in advance of your departure date—preferably when you buy your international ticket—since the regulations may govern your trip planning, and conditions can change without notice.

Getting through immigration control and customs can take 2 or 3 hours, especially if you enter the country at a big-city airport on a busy summer day. Leave at least that much time to connect to a domestic flight. Passing between Alaska and Canada takes no time at all unless you have special complications. See chapter 9 for Canadian border requirements.

Fast Facts: For the Foreign Traveler

See "Fast Facts" in chapter 2 for information not listed here.

Automobile Organizations Auto clubs will supply maps, suggested routes, guidebooks, accident and bail-bond insurance, and emergency road service. The **American Automobile Association (AAA)** is the major auto club in the United States. If you belong to an auto club in your home country, inquire about AAA reciprocity before you leave. You may be able to join AAA even if you're not a member of a reciprocal club; to inquire, call ☎ **800/222-4357,** or visit **www.aaa.com**. AAA is actually an organization of regional auto clubs, so look under "AAA

Automobile Club" in the White Pages of the telephone directory. AAA has a nationwide emergency road service telephone number (☎ **800/AAA-HELP**).

Currency & Currency Exchange See section 1 of this chapter.

Electricity Like Canada, the United States uses 110 to 120 volts AC (60 cycles), compared to 220 to 240 volts AC (50 cycles) in most of Europe, Australia, and New Zealand. If your small appliances use 220 to 240 volts, you'll need a 110-volt transformer and a plug adapter with two flat parallel pins to operate them here. Downward converters that change 220 to 240 volts to 110 to 120 volts are difficult to find in the United States, so bring one with you.

Embassies & Consulates All embassies are located in Washington, D.C. If your country isn't listed, call for directory information in Washington, D.C. (☎ **202/555-1212**) for the number of your national embassy. **Australia:** Embassy, 1601 Massachusetts Ave. NW, Washington, DC 20036 (☎ **202/797-3000;** www.austemb.org). **Canada:** Embassy, 501 Pennsylvania Ave. NW, Washington, DC 20001 (☎ **202/682-1740;** www.canadianembassy.org). **Ireland:** Embassy, 2234 Massachusetts Ave. NW, Washington, DC 20008 (☎ **202/462-3939;** www.irelandemb.org). **Japan:** Embassy, 2520 Massachusetts Ave. NW, Washington, DC 20008 (☎ **202/238-6700;** www.embjapan.org). **New Zealand:** Embassy, 37 Observatory Circle, Washington, DC 20008 (☎ **202/328-4800;** www.emb.com/nzemb). **United Kingdom:** Embassy, 3100 Massachusetts Ave. NW, Washington, DC 20008 (☎ **202/588-6500;** www.britainusa.com). The following nations have consulates general in Anchorage: **Japan,** 550 W. Seventh Ave (☎ **907/279-8428**), and **South Korea,** 101 W. Benson Blvd. (☎ **907/561-5488**). Various other countries have consulates or honorary consuls who may be of some assistance, each listed in the local telephone directory, but generally the nearest full consulate offices are outside the state.

Emergencies Call ☎ **911** to report a fire, call the police, or get an ambulance almost anywhere in the United States. This is a toll-free call (no coins are required at public telephones).

Gasoline (Petrol) Petrol/gasoline stations are known as both gas stations and service stations. Gasoline costs about half as much here as it does in Europe (about $1.50 per gallon at press time), and taxes are already included in the printed price. One U.S. gallon equals 3.8 liters or .85 Imperial gallons.

Holidays Banks, government offices, post offices, and many stores, restaurants, and museums are closed on the following legal national holidays: January 1 (New Year's Day), the third Monday in January (Martin Luther King Day), the third Monday in February (Presidents' Day, Washington's Birthday), the last Monday in May (Memorial Day), July 4 (Independence Day), the first Monday in September (Labor Day), the second Monday in October (Columbus Day), November 11 (Veterans' Day/Armistice Day), the fourth Thursday in November (Thanksgiving Day), and December 25 (Christmas). Additionally, banks and state government offices in Alaska close on two state holidays: the last Monday in March (Seward's Day) and October 18 (Alaska Day, which is celebrated on the nearest Friday or Monday if the 18th falls on a weekend).

Legal Aid If you are stopped for a minor traffic infraction (such as speeding), never attempt to pay the fine directly to a police officer; this could be construed as attempted bribery, a much more serious crime. Pay fines by mail, or directly into the hands of the clerk of the court. Alaska law carries harsh penalties, including mandatory jail time, for drunk driving. Even some traffic tickets, such as speeding more than 15 miles per hour over the limit, can involve a mandatory court appearance, a major inconvenience that is worth avoiding by slowing down. If accused of a serious crime, say and do nothing before consulting a lawyer. Here the burden is on the state to prove a person's guilt beyond a reasonable doubt, and everyone has the right to remain silent, whether he or she is suspected of a crime or actually arrested. Once arrested, a person can make one telephone call to a party of his or her choice. Call your embassy or consulate.

Mail The location of the post office in each town in this book is listed in the appropriate Fast Facts sections. You can send mail from your hotel or the post office. Mail in the United States must have a five-digit postal code (or ZIP code), after the two-letter abbreviation of the state to which the mail is addressed. At press time, domestic postage rates were 20¢ for a postcard and 33¢ for a letter. For international mail, mailing a first-class letter of up to one-half ounce costs 60¢ (48¢ to Canada and 40¢ to Mexico), a first-class postcard 55¢ (45¢ to Canada and 40¢ Mexico).

Taxes In neither the United States nor the state of Alaska is there a value-added tax (VAT) or sales tax, but most communities, with the exception of Anchorage, levy their own sales taxes, and all communities impose taxes on hotel rooms and rental cars. See the individual town sections "Fast Facts" for local tax rates.

Telephone & Fax Before using a telephone in a hotel, check for surcharges on long-distance and local calls, which can be astronomical. If so, you're better off using a **public pay telephone,** which you'll find clearly marked in most public buildings and private establishments as well as in hotel lobbies and on the street. Many convenience stores sell **prepaid calling cards** in denominations up to $50; these can be the least expensive way to call home. **Local calls** made from public pay phones usually cost 25¢. Read the instructions on the phone; in smaller Alaska communities, you may have to wait for the person you are calling to answer before quickly putting the money in the phone. Pay phones do not accept pennies or anything larger than a quarter.

Most long-distance and international calls can be dialed directly from any phone. For **long-distance calls within Alaska and the United States and to Canada,** dial 1 followed by the three-digit area code and the seven-digit number. For **international calls to places other than Canada,** dial 011 followed by the country code, city code, and the telephone number of the person you are calling. U.S. area codes and international country codes are listed in the front of the White Pages telephone directory, or dial 0 to get a country code. If you're calling the **United States** from another country, the country code is 01.

For **reversed-charge, collect, operator-assisted, and person-to-person calls,** dial 0 (the number zero) followed by the area code and number you want; an operator will then come on the line, and you should specify that you are calling collect, or person-to-person, or both. If your operator-assisted call is international, ask for the overseas operator.

For **local and national directory assistance** ("information"), dial ☎ **411;** for a number in a particular area code, dial the area code followed by ☎ 555-1212. Typically, you'll be charged around 50¢ for this service.

There are two kinds of telephone directories in the United States. The so-called **White Pages** list private households and business subscribers in alphabetical order; the **Yellow Pages** list businesses and organizations categorized by the

Travel Tip

Calls to area codes **800, 888,** and **877** are toll-free. However, calls to numbers in area codes **700** and **900** (chat lines, bulletin boards, "dating" services, and so on) can be very expensive—usually a charge of 95¢ to $3 or more per minute, and they sometimes have minimum charges that can run as high as $15 or more.

services they provide. In Alaska, the two directories are contained in the same book in all communities except Anchorage. Look in the front of the White Pages for emergency contact numbers and instructions on how to make long-distance calls. Blue pages near the front of the White Pages directory list numbers for government agencies. Sometimes it's easier to find phone numbers online. Yahoo.com is one site offering this free service.

Most hotels have **fax machines** available for guest use, often with expensive per-page charges. I have listed business services such as fax, copy, mailing, and computer centers in the "Fast Facts" section on each community.

Time Most of the United States is divided into **six time zones.** From east to west, they are: eastern, central, mountain, Pacific, Alaska, and Hawaii/Aleutian. For example, noon in New York City is 11am in Chicago, 10am in Denver, 9am in Los Angeles, 8am in mainland Alaska, and 7am in Honolulu and the outer Aleutians.

Daylight saving time is in effect from 1am on the first Sunday in April through 1am the last Sunday in October, except in Arizona, Hawaii, part of Indiana, and Puerto Rico. Daylight saving time moves the clock 1 hour ahead of standard time.

Tipping Tips make up a major part of the compensation for many service workers. To leave no tip in a restaurant is socially unacceptable.

In restaurants, bars, and nightclubs, tip your server 15% to 20% of the check, depending on the quality of service. Tip **bartenders** 10% to 15%, tip **check-room attendants** $1 per garment, and tip **valet-parking attendants** $1 per vehicle. Tipping is not expected in cafeterias or fast-food restaurants where you order at a counter. In hotels, tip **bellhops** $1 per bag ($2 to $3 if you have a lot of luggage) and tip the **housekeeper** at least $1 per day. Tip **cab drivers** 15% of the fare, tip **skycaps** at airports $1 per bag ($2 to $3 if you have a lot of luggage), and tip **hairdressers** and **barbers** 15% to 20%. Do not tip gas-station attendants and ushers at movies and theaters.

See "Fast Facts" in chapter 2 for tipping of guides and outfitters.

Toilets You won't find public toilets (or "rest rooms") on the streets in most U.S. cities, but they can be found in hotel lobbies, bars, restaurants, museums, department stores, railway and bus stations, or service stations.

4 Cruising Alaska's Coast

Alaska is one of the top cruise destinations in the world, with almost three quarters of a million people sailing the state's coast annually, visiting the towns and wilderness areas of Southeast and the Gulf of Alaska by day and burrowing into their ships for effortless travel by night. This element of cruise travel—the fact that it's *easy*—is one of its main drawing cards for visitors to Southeast, where the lack of roads between towns makes the waters of the Inside Passage the region's de facto highway. You could do the same routes on the Alaska State Ferry, but you'd have to be willing to invest more time, both for the actual traveling and for the planning.

Now for the bad news: All those cruise ships aren't necessarily good for Alaska and its residents. Alaskans are known for their hospitality, but we all have our limits. Imagine living in a coastal settlement and having an entire town full of new people arriving all at once—as many or more as live there—mobbing your streets and hiking trails, spewing pollution into the air and water, and creating a tremendous racket of helicopters. Imagine it happened every day, without respite, all summer. Suppose all the old, community businesses on the waterfront area were driven out by seasonal gift shops? You might not mind if you were one of the few local visitor-industry entrepreneurs who snags fleeting cruise-ship spending, but most people would find their sense of hospitality wearing thin.

For years, the cruise ship industry exploited the hospitality of Southeast Alaska as if it were an inexhaustible resource, but a dam of resentment burst when two of the lines, Royal Caribbean and Holland America, were caught and convicted of felonies for dumping pollution such as dry cleaning fluid, photo chemicals, and used oil in the pristine waters of the Inside Passage, and then lying about it. Marine pilots—the local experts who guide the ships through tricky passages—disclosed that some of the lines routinely asked to be brought to small "doughnut holes" of water just outside the state's 3-mile limit of control to dump sewage. Those sites also happened to be Alaska's prime whale-watching grounds. Huge plumes of black smoke some ships belched into the air of Southeast towns also turned out to be illegal.

Juneau residents voted in a $10 head tax on cruise-ship visitors (it is included in your fare). Holland America struck back by reducing charitable contributions in town and Princess announced it would pull out of Juneau earlier in the evening, denying local shops key shopping hours. Bills in the 2000 legislature would have imposed new pollution regulations and a $50 per-passenger tax, but the industry managed to kill both in committee, and instead offered unverifiable voluntary controls on dumping.

You'll find the residents of Southeast Alaska remain warm to visitors, whether they come from cruise ships or travel independently, but the tide of public sentiment about the industry has turned. Many feel the environmental damage and cultural bulldozing brought by these floating cities is not worth the economic benefit. After years of fast growth, the industry, too, has begun talk of a "carrying capacity." Perhaps a bit late, they are recognizing that quaint little towns aren't such fun to visit if overrun by other visitors. Whether any change occurs, however, probably depends on what the lines hear from their customers. Your enjoyment of a trip is the cruise lines' stock in trade, and few would enjoy these beautiful places so much with the knowledge they were contributing to their demise.

In this chapter we'll go through the cruise options available in the state, focusing primarily on those that give a real in-depth experience. For even more information, pick up a copy of *Frommer's Alaska Cruises & Ports of Call.*

1 Weighing Your Cruise Options

Your two main questions in choosing a cruise in Alaska are, "Where do I want to go?" and "How big a ship?"

INSIDE PASSAGE OR THE GULF OF ALASKA?

Typically, the cruise lines offer two basic weeklong itineraries. Inside Passage cruises generally sail round-trip from Vancouver, British Columbia, visiting three or four port towns (typically Juneau, Skagway, Ketchikan, and either Sitka, Haines, or Victoria, B.C.) along the Inside Passage, spending a day in Glacier Bay or one of the other glacier areas, and spending 2 days "at sea," meaning they just cruise along, allowing you to relax and enjoy the scenery.

Gulf of Alaska cruises generally sail north- and southbound between Vancouver and Seward (the port for Anchorage) in alternating weeks, visiting many of the same towns and attractions as the Inside Passage cruises but—since they don't have to turn around and sail back to Vancouver—also tagging on a visit to Valdez, Hubbard Glacier, College Fjord, or one or more of the other Gulf towns or natural attractions.

Though most of the major operators stick pretty closely to these two basic routes, the small-ship cruise lines tend to offer more **small-port and wilderness-oriented itineraries,** some sailing round-trip from Juneau or Sitka, some sailing between Juneau and Ketchikan, and one even sailing between Juneau and Glacier Bay. Many of these ships visit the major ports of call, but may also include visits to small ports that aren't accessible to the bigger ships, towns like Petersburg, Wrangell, Gustavus, Elfin Cove, and possibly the Native village Metlakatla. Some ships sail itineraries where passengers can explore by kayak or on hiking treks.

Cruisetours combine a cruise with a land tour, either before or after the cruise. Typical packages link the cruise with a 3- to 5-day Anchorage/Denali/Fairbanks tour, a 7-day Yukon tour (which visits Anchorage, Denali, and Fairbanks on the way), or a 5- to 7-day tour of the Canadian Rockies. Holland America, Princess, and Cruise West (a distant third) are the three leaders in the cruisetour market. Even if you book with another cruise line, chances are your land tour will be through one of these operators.

BIG SHIP OR SMALL?

Imagine an elephant. Now imagine your pet pug dog, Sparky. That's about the size difference between your options in the Alaska market: behemoth modern megaships and small, more exploratory coastal vessels.

The **big ships** offer you heated pools, theatrical productions, organized activities, spas, jogging tracks, discos, generally spacious accommodations, fine dining, and more, but their size comes with three major drawbacks for passengers: (1) they can't sail into narrow passages or shallow-water ports, (2) their size and inflexible schedules limit their ability to stop or even slow down when wildlife is spotted, and (3) when their passengers disembark in a town, they tend to overwhelm that town, limiting your ability to see the real Alaska.

The **small ships** offer little in terms of amenities: they usually have small cabins, only one lounge/bar and dining room, and no exercise facilities, entertainment, or organized activities. Despite all of this, they're universally more expensive than the big ships, and offer fewer discounts. That's the minus side. On the plus side, (1) they can sail almost anywhere (including far into Misty Fjords, where no large ship can penetrate), (2) since they tend to have more flexibility in their schedules than the large ships, they can usually take time to linger if whales or other wildlife are sighted nearby, (3) their small size doesn't scare off wildlife as easily as the big ships, and the fact that you're at or near the waterline (rather than 10 stories up, as on the large ships) means you get a more close-up view, and (4) they're almost all completely casual—no dressing up required.

Visitors aboard large ships may physically be in Alaska, but unless they're reminded of it they might never know, such is the disjoin between the glitzy modern ships and the real world outside. Visitors aboard small ships, however, get an experience that's many times more intimate, allowing them to really get in touch with the place they've come to see. For all these reasons, my advice to anyone wanting to experience Alaska rather than just get a postcard impression of it is to spend the extra money for a small-ship cruise. As with any product, you get what you pay for, and by paying extra in the short term for a more intimate cruise you're almost guaranteed of having an Alaska experience that you'll remember your whole life.

2 The Best Cruise Lines in Alaska

Cruise lines are in the business of giving their guests a good time, so they've all got something going for them. Here's my pick of Alaska's best, though, in a few different categories.

- **Best Line for an Up-Close Alaska Experience:** There's almost no contest here. **Alaska's Glacier Bay Tours and Cruises** is the only line offering itineraries that take you into the heart of natural Alaska, avoiding the usual tourist towns entirely on their adventure-oriented cruises and concentrating instead on hiking, kayaking, and wildlife watching. The overall experience is 100% casual and the spartan ships act more like base camps than resorts.
- **Best Lines for an Educational Experience:** With its single old ocean liner, **World Explorer Cruises** focus on wildlife education and on helping passengers really learn about Alaska and Alaska Native culture. The ship is budget and casual all the way, but its staff of naturalists and guest lecturers is among the best in the business. Among small ships, **Clipper Cruise Line, Lindblad Expeditions,** and **Glacier Bay Tours and Cruises** all focus on education, with naturalists giving lectures on board and leading groups ashore.
- **Best Lines for a Stress-Free Cruise:** For years, **Holland America**'s stock-in-trade has been providing a comfortable, low-key vacation experience for older travelers, and though the line has been making some changes to attract a younger clientele as well, it's still the best bet for someone wanting to visit Alaska in reassuring comfort. On the small-ship side, **Cruise West** caters to many older

passengers, though those who want to add some excitement to their trip can opt for boating, kayaking, and biking excursions.

- **Best Lines for Pampering:** If you want to cruise in style, sailing through Alaska like a pasha in a sedan chair, you've got a few choices. **Crystal Cruises** and **Radisson Seven Seas Cruises** are the two real luxury lines in the market, offering a white-glove experience. Among mainstream ships, **Celebrity Cruises** is the best by far, with exceptional service, dining, and decor. In the small-ship category, **American Safari Cruises** offers an experience that's as close as you can get to sailing aboard a private yacht. Its two ships carry only 12 and 22 passengers each, with all expenses included, including excursions and alcoholic beverages.

3 Booking Your Cruise

Almost every cruise line publishes brochure prices that are the travel equivalent of a new car's sticker price: wildly inflated in the hope that someone, somewhere might take them at face value. In reality, especially as sailings gets close and it looks as if the line will get stuck with unsold space, cruise lines are almost universally willing to sell their cruises for much, much less. (The small-ship lines tend to be the exception to this rule. Since they have less space to sell and appeal to a more specific market niche, they can often get their initial asking price.)

More than ever, there are numerous ways to book a cruise and find the best discounts. In the United States, 90% to 95% of all cruise bookings are arranged through **travel agents,** but instead of using the services of a traditional travel agent, these days you can also head for your computer and check out what the **online cruise agencies and discounters** are offering; a handful even allow you to actually submit your credit card online and make a reservation without ever having to talk to a soul. And some cruise lines, like Carnival, NCL, Royal Caribbean, and Celebrity, even have their own booking sites (although at press time, they aren't particularly user-friendly).

BOOKING A SMALL-SHIP CRUISE

The small-ship companies in Alaska—Alaska's Glacier Bay Tours and Cruises, American Safari Cruises, Clipper, Cruise West, and Lindblad Expeditions—all offer real niche-oriented cruise experiences, attracting passengers who have a very good idea of the kind of experience they want (usually educational and/or adventurous, and always casual and small-scale). In many cases, a large percentage of passengers on any given cruise will have sailed with the line before. Because of all this, and because the passenger capacity of these small ships is so low (from 12 to 138), in general you're not going to find the kind of deep discounts you do with the large ships. Still, for the most part these lines rely on agents to handle their bookings, taking very few reservations directly. (Clipper is the exception to this rule, taking most of their Alaska bookings directly, rather than through agents.) All of the lines have a list of agents with whom they do considerable business and can hook you up with one or another of them if you call (or e-mail) and ask for an agent near you.

AGENCIES SPECIALIZING IN MAINSTREAM CRUISES

The following cruise-only and full-service agencies have solid reputations in selling mainstream cruises such as Princess, Carnival, Royal Caribbean, Celebrity, Holland America, and Norwegian Cruise Line, and operate from a combination of walk-in business and 800-number telephone-based business.

- **Admiral of the Fleet Cruise Center,** 12920 Bluemound Rd., Elm Grove, WI 53122 (☎ **800/462-3371** or 262/784-2628).

- **Admiral of the Fleet Cruise Center,** 3430 Pacific Ave. SE, Ste. A-5, Olympia, WA 98501 (☎ **800/877-7447** or 360/866-7447).
- **The Cruise Company,** 10760 Q St., Omaha, NE 68127 (☎ **800/289-5505** or 402/339-6800).
- **Cruises By Brennco,** 508 E. 112th St., Kansas City, MO 64131 (☎ **800/955-1909** or 816/942-1000).
- **Cruise Value Center,** 6 Edgeboro Rd., East Brunswick, NJ 08816 (☎ **800/231-7447**).
- **Hartford Holidays,** 129 Hillside Ave., Williston Park, NY 11596 (☎ **800/828-4813** or 516/746-6670).
- **Just Cruisin' Plus,** 5640 Nolensville Rd., Nashville, TN 37211 (☎ **800/888-0922** or 615/833-0922).
- **Kelly Cruises,** 1315 W. 22nd St., Ste. 105, Oak Brook, IL 60523 (☎ **800/837-7447** or 630/990-1111).
- **Mann Travel** and **Cruises American Express,** 4400 Park Rd., Charlotte, NC 28209 (☎ **800/849-2301** or 704-556-8311).
- **National Leisure Group,** 100 Sylvan Rd., Ste. 600, Wobrun, MA 01801 (☎ **800/435-7683** or 617/424-7990).
- **The Travel Company,** 220 Congress Park Dr., Delray Beach, FL, 33445 (☎ **800/242-9000;** www.mytravelco.com).

ONLINE CRUISE SELLERS & TRAVEL COMPANIES

This is a sampling of reputable Web-based cruise sellers; the first three are cruise-only and the last four are travel generalists that sell cruises along with airfare, tour packages, and car rentals.

- **Icruise.com**
- **Cruise.com**
- **Cruise411.com**
- **mytravelco.com**
- **Previewtravel.com**
- **Travelocity.com**
- **Expedia.com**

THE COST: WHAT'S INCLUDED & WHAT'S NOT

However you arrange to buy your cruise, what you basically have in hand at the end is a contract for transportation, lodging, dining, entertainment, housekeeping, and assorted other miscellaneous services that will be provided to you over the course of your vacation. It's important, though, to remember what extras are not included in your cruise fare. Aside from airfare, which is usually not included in your cruise fare (see more on air arrangements below), the most pricey addition to your cruise fare, particularly in Alaska, will likely be shore excursions. Ranging from about $29 for a bus tour to $250 or more for a helicopter or fixed-wing flightseeing excursion, these sightseeing tours are designed to help cruise passengers make the most of their time at the ports the ship visits, but they can add a hefty sum to your vacation costs.

You'll also want to add to your calculations **tips for the ship's crew.** Tips are given at the end of the cruise, and passengers should reserve at least $9 per person, per day ($63 per passenger for the week) for tips for the room steward, waiter, and busboy. (In practice, I find that most people tend to give a little more.) Additional tips to other personnel, such as the head waiter or maître d', are at your discretion. On the small ships, all tips often go into one pot, which the crew divides up after the cruise.

All but a very few ships charge extra for **alcoholic beverages** (including wine at dinner) and for soda. Nonbubbly soft drinks such as lemonade and iced tea are included in your cruise fare.

Port charges, taxes, and other fees are usually included in your cruise fare but not always, and these charges can add as much as $175 per person onto the price of a 7-day Alaska cruise. Make sure you know whether these are included in the cruise fare when you are comparing rates.

Of course, just as at a hotel, you also pay extra for items like ship-to-shore phone calls or faxes, e-mails, spa treatments, and so on.

MONEY-SAVING STRATEGIES

Cruise pricing is a fluid medium, and there are a number of strategies you can use to save money off the booking price.

LATE VS. EARLY BOOKING

More than ever before, there are no steadfast rules about pricing—policies differ from line to line, and from week to week, depending on supply and demand. If there's empty space on a ship as the sailing date nears, lines would rather sell a cabin for a lower fare than not sell it at all. While booking early will still get you as much as a 50% discount off the brochure rates and give you a better pick of cabins, booking late (just a few weeks or month or two before sailing) will often get you an even better rate. Of course, you have to consider when booking at the last minute that if you have to fly to the port of embarkation, you may have to pay an airfare so high that it cancels out your savings on the cruise. You'll find last-minute deals advertised online and in the travel section of your Sunday newspaper. You should also check with a travel agent or an agency or discounter that specializes in cruises.

SHOULDER-SEASON DISCOUNTS

You can think of the Alaska cruise season as three distinct periods: (1) peak season, late June, July, and early to mid-August; (2) value/standard season, early June and late August; and (3) budget season, May and September. You can save by booking a cruise during this last period, in the shoulder months of May or September, when cruise pricing is lower. The weather might be a little chillier, and September is known for rain, but a lot fewer people visit during those months, allowing you a bit more pristine experience of the place, especially if you're sailing on a small ship. Frommer's cruise editor took an early May sailing with Glacier Bay Tours and Cruises in 1998 and reported that he felt like he had the state all to himself.

DISCOUNTS FOR THIRD & FOURTH PASSENGERS & GROUPS

Most ships offer highly discounted rates for third and fourth passengers sharing a cabin with two "full-fare" passengers (even if those two have booked at a discounted rate). It may mean a tight squeeze, but it'll save you a bundle. Some lines offer special rates for kids, usually on a seasonal or select-sailings basis, that may include free or discounted airfare. Those under age 2 generally cruise free.

One of the best ways to get a cruise deal is to book as a **group** of at least 16 people in at least eight cabins. The savings include not only a discounted rate, but at least the cruise portion of the 16th ticket will be free. A "group" in this instance can be a real group (friends, relatives, and so on) or simply a block of passengers booked by a travel agency on the same cruise. You don't have to even pretend you know these people, but the savings are the same. Ask your travel agent about any group deals they may offer.

SENIOR-CITIZEN DISCOUNTS

Senior citizens may be able to get extra savings on their cruise. Some lines will take 5% off the top for those 55 and up, and the senior rate applies even if the second person in the cabin is younger. Membership in groups such as AARP is not required, but such membership may bring additional savings.

BOOKING AIR TRAVEL THROUGH THE CRUISE LINE

Except during special promotions, airfare to the port of embarkation is rarely included in the cruise rates, so you'll have to purchase airfare on your own or buy it as a package with your cruise through your travel agent or online cruise site. You can usually find information on these "air/sea" programs in the back of cruise line brochures, along with prices. The benefit of booking through the cruise line is that round-trip transfers between the airport and the ship are usually included. Also, the cruise line will know your airline schedule, and in the event of delayed flights and other unavoidable snafus, will be able to do more to make sure you and the other people on your flight get on the ship; if you've booked your air transportation separately, you're on your own. On the downside, air add-ons may not be the best deal and it might be cheaper to book your own airfare. Also, you probably won't be able to use any frequent-flier miles you may have accumulated.

CHOOSING YOUR CABIN

Cruise-ship cabins run from tiny boxes with accordion doors and bunk beds to palatial multiroom suites with hot tubs on the balcony. Which is right for you? Price will likely be a big factor here, but so should the vacation style you prefer. If, for instance, you plan to spend a lot of quiet time in your cabin, you should probably consider booking the biggest room you can afford. If, conversely, you plan to be out on deck all the time checking out the glaciers and wildlife, you might be just as happy with a smaller (and cheaper) cabin to crash in at the end of the day. Cabins are either inside (without a window or porthole) or outside (with), with the latter being more expensive. On the big ships, the more deluxe outside cabins may also come with private verandas.

SPECIAL MENU REQUESTS

The cruise line should be informed at the time you make your reservations about any special dietary requests you have. Some lines offer kosher menus, and all will have vegetarian, low-fat, low-salt, and sugar-free options available.

4 The Small-Ship Cruise Lines

Small ships allow you to see Alaska from sea level, without the kind of distractions you get aboard the big ships—no glitzy interiors, no big shows or loud music, no casinos, no spas, and no crowds, as the largest of these ships carries only 138 passengers. You're immersed in the 49th state from the minute you wake up to the minute you fall asleep, and for the most part left alone to form your own opinions. Personally, I feel that, despite these ships' higher cost, they provide by far the better cruise experience for those who really want to get the feel of Alaska.

Small-ship itineraries can be categorized as **port-to-port,** meaning they mimic the larger ships in simply sailing between port towns; **soft-adventure,** meaning they provide some outdoors experiences like hiking and kayaking, while not requiring participants to be trained athletes; and **active-adventure,** meaning the hiking and kayaking will be the real focus of the trip, and may be strenuous.

On all of these types of cruise, the small-ship experience tends toward an education rather than glitzy entertainment. You'll likely get **informal lectures** and sometimes video presentations on Alaska wildlife, history, and Native culture. Meals are served in open seatings, so you can sit where and with whom you like, and time spent huddled on the outside decks scanning for whales fosters great camaraderie among passengers.

Cabins on these ships don't generally offer TVs or telephones and tend to be very small and sometimes spartan (see the individual reviews for exceptions). Alaska Sightseeing's *Spirit of '98* and *Spirit of Oceanus* and Clipper Cruise Line's *Clipper Odyssey* have elevators, but in general the small ships are not good choices for travelers who require the use of wheelchairs or have other mobility problems.

ALASKA'S GLACIER BAY TOURS & CRUISES

226 2nd Ave. West, Seattle, WA 98119. ☎ **800/451-5952** or 206/623-2417. Fax 206/623-7809. www.glacierbaytours.com.

Alaska's Glacier Bay Tours and Cruises—the only Native-owned cruise line in Alaska—offers three types of cruises: soft-adventure (aboard the Wilderness Explorer), active-adventure (aboard the Wilderness Adventurer), and port-to-port (aboard the slightly more luxurious Executive Explorer). The Wilderness Discoverer is a hybrid, sailing itineraries that mix 3 days of adventure activities with 3 days spent visiting popular ports of call.

The adventure sailings are for a particular type of traveler, one interested in exploring Alaska's wilds rather than its towns. On the *Wilderness Explorer's* soft-adventure cruises, for example, the biggest town you're likely to encounter after departing Juneau is tiny little Elfin Cove, population around 30 to 35 (at least in the summer). Other than this, days are spent hiking in remote regions, exploring the glaciers, cruising the waterways looking for whales and other wildlife, and **kayaking**—the *Wilderness Adventurer, Wilderness Explorer,* and *Wilderness Discoverer* carry fleets of stable two-person sea kayaks, which are launched from dry platforms at the ships' sterns. A week-long sailing typically includes three kayak treks. **Naturalists** sail with every cruise to point out natural features and lead off-ship expeditions, all of which are included in the cruise price. On board, the atmosphere is casual and friendly, with the staff establishing a friendly, casual rapport with passengers, providing just enough attention while leaving you the space to enjoy your vacation however you want. Entertainment facilities on all ships are minimal: board games, books, and a TV/VCR in the lounge, on which passengers can view tapes on wildlife, Alaska history, Native culture, and a few feature films.

TYPICAL PASSENGERS On the *Wilderness Explorer, Adventurer,* and *Discoverer,* passengers tend to be on the youngish side, with as many couples in their 40s and 50s as in their 60s and 70s, and a scattering of 30-somethings (and a few 80- or 90-somethings) filling out the list. Whatever their age, passengers tend to be active and interested in nature and wildlife. On the *Executive Explorer,* passengers tend to be older (60 and up) and less active and adventurous, though they still enjoy the same informality as aboard the line's other vessels.

SHIPS The 49-passenger catamaran-style ***Executive Explorer*** is Glacier Bay's most luxurious ship, sailing port-to-port itineraries. The spartan, 74-passenger ***Wilderness Adventurer*** and almost identical 86-passenger ***Wilderness Discoverer*** are the line's soft-adventure ships, outfitted with sea kayaks and kayak dry-launch platforms in their sterns. The 36-passenger ***Wilderness Explorer*** is the line's most basic ship, with tiny cabins and bunk-style beds. It visits no ports, instead offering the most active cruise experience available in Alaska, with cruises structured so passengers are out kayaking and hiking most of each day and only use the vessel to eat, sleep, and get from place to place. **Sample rates per person:** Lowest-price inside cabins $2,415, lowest outside $2,735 for 7-night cruise; no suites.

AMERICAN SAFARI CRUISES

19101 36th Ave., West, suite 201, Lynnwood, WA 98036. ☎ **888/862-8881.** Fax 425/776-8889. www.americansafaricruises.com.

Directed to the demanding high-end traveler, American Safari Cruises promises an intimate, all-inclusive yacht cruise to some of the more out-of-the-way stretches of the Inside Passage. The company books only 12 to 22 people per cruise, guaranteeing unparalleled flexibility and privacy. Black-bear aficionados can chug off in a Zodiac boat for a better look; active adventurers can explore the shoreline in one of the yacht's four kayaks; and lazier travelers can relax aboard ship. Another big plus: All off-ship excursions—including flightseeing and trips to boardwalked cannery villages and Tlingit villages—are included in the cruise fare, as are drinks. The price is considerable, as is the pampering.

TYPICAL PASSENGERS Passengers, almost always couples, tend to be more than comfortably wealthy and range from 45 to 65 years of age. Most hope to get close to nature without sacrificing luxury.

SHIPS More private yachts than cruise ships, the 22-passenger ***Safari Quest*** and 12-passenger ***Safari Spirit*** look like Ferraris, all sleek, contoured lines and dark glass. Cabins are comfortable, and sitting rooms are intimate and luxurious, almost as if they had been transported whole from a spacious suburban home. A big-screen TV in the main lounge forms a natural center for impromptu lectures during the day and movie-watching at night. **Sample rates per person:** Lowest-price outside cabins $3,423 for 7-night cruise; no inside cabins or suites.

CLIPPER CRUISE LINE

7711 Bonhomme Ave., St. Louis, MO 63105. ☎ **800/325-0010** or 314/727-2929. Fax 314/727-6576. www.clippercruise.com.

Honored by *Condé Nast Traveler* as one of the top-10 cruise lines in the world, Clipper's operation is more sophisticated and service-oriented than most other lines with ships this size. Its ships sail port-to-port itineraries, and as aboard Alaska's other small-ship lines, the onboard atmosphere is casual, and what lies out there beyond the ship's rail is most passengers' real focus. Lectures and videos on Alaska make up the bulk of the entertainment program, and a nightly social hour encourages passengers to mix and mingle. Motorized landing craft, carried aboard the ship, ferry passengers to remote beaches, pristine forests, small villages, and wildlife refuges, where naturalists and/or historians and other experts may conduct walking tours.

TYPICAL PASSENGERS Passengers are generally over 55, educated, and financially sound, with relatively high expectations when it comes to food, comfort, and overall experience. While they want to experience Alaska's natural wonders—whales, glaciers, woodlands—they're not necessarily run-the-rapids types.

SHIPS Along with Alaska Sightseeing's *Spirit of Endeavor* and *Spirit of Oceanus* and Glacier Bay's *Executive Explorer*, the 128-passenger ***Clipper Odyssey*** and 138-passenger *Yorktown Clipper* are two of the best choices in Alaska for someone who wants small-ship intimacy and flexibility but doesn't want to skimp on comfort. Their public rooms are larger and more appealing that aboard competing ships, and all cabins are outside. Except for those at the lowest level, all have picture windows, and the top suite on the *Odyssey* offers a private veranda. **Sample rates per person:** Lowest-price outside cabins $2,310 for 7-night cruise; no inside cabins on either ship; suites only on *Odyssey* ($7,900 for 10-night cruise).

CRUISE WEST

2401 4th Ave., Suite 700, Seattle, WA 98121. ☎ **800/426-7702** or 206/441-8687. Fax 206/441-4757. www.smallship.com.

Cruise West is the largest operator of small ships in Alaska, offering port-to-port itineraries, friendly service, and a casual onboard atmosphere. As with Clipper Cruise Line, Cruise West's ships are for people who want to visit Alaska's port towns and see its wilderness areas up close and in a relaxed, small-scale environment without big-ship distractions; they're not for people who want to spend their days hiking and kayaking.

The line's friendly, enthusiastic staffs are a big, big plus, making guests feel right at home. A cheerful and knowledgeable cruise coordinator accompanies each trip to answer passengers' questions about Alaska's flora, fauna, geology, and history, and Forest Service rangers, local fishermen, and Native Alaskans sometimes come aboard to give informal talks about the culture and industry of the state.

TYPICAL PASSENGERS Cruise West passengers tend to be older (typically around 60 to 75), financially stable, well educated, and independent-minded.

SHIPS The 70-passenger ***Sheltered Seas*** is a cabinless excursion ship that cruises Alaska's waterways by day and deposits passengers at a hotel ashore at night, generally after the crowds from larger cruise ships have left and in time to enjoy some nightlife. If you can't decide between cruising Alaska and seeing it by land, this is an option worth exploring. The 96-passenger ***Spirit of '98,*** a replica of a 19th-century steamship, carries its Victorian flavor so well that fully two-thirds of the people I met onboard thought the ship had been a private yacht at the turn of the 20th century. (Note: The *'98* is the only small ship in Alaska that has an elevator and a cabin that's wheelchair friendly.) The 78-passenger ***Spirit of Alaska*** and ***Spirit of Columbia,*** 84-passenger ***Spirit of Discovery,*** and 52-passenger ***Spirit of Glacier Bay*** are all spartan ships designed to get passengers into small ports and allow them to see the state up close. The 102-passenger ***Spirit of Endeavor,*** on the other hand, offers among the highest levels of small-ship comfort of any small ship in Alaska, comparable to Clipper's *Yorktown Clipper* and Glacier Bay's *Executive Explorer.* At press time, Cruise West had just announced the acquisition of a new vessel, the 114-passenger ***Spirit of Oceanus*** (the former *Renaissance V* of Renaissance Cruises). It will be the largest and, from the sound of it, poshest vessel in the fleet, with 12 high-end cabins boasting private teak balconies. **Sample rates per person:** Lowest-price inside cabins $2,495, lowest outside $3,295, lowest suite $4,545 for 7-night cruise.

LINDBLAD EXPEDITIONS

720 Fifth Ave., New York, NY 10019. ☎ **800/397-3348** or 212/765-7740. Fax 212/265-3770. www.specialexpeditions.com.

Lindblad Expeditions specializes in environmentally sensitive, soft-adventure vacations that are explorative and informal in nature, designed to appeal to the intellectually curious traveler seeking a cruise that's educational as well as relaxing. Days aboard are spent learning about the Alaskan outdoors from high-caliber expedition leaders trained in botany, anthropology, biology, and geology, and observing the world around you either from the ship or on shore excursions, which are included in the cruise package. Educational films and slide presentations aboard ship precede nature hikes and quick jaunts aboard Zodiac boats.

TYPICAL PASSENGERS Passengers tend to be over 55, educated, relatively well off, and physically active (even so, the ships become very quiet not long after dinner; everyone crashes early to store up energy for the next day).

SHIPS The shallow-draft, 70-passenger ***Sea Lion*** and ***Sea Bird*** are identical twins. With just two public rooms and utilitarian cabins, they're very similar to other "expedition style" small ships, such as Glacier Bay's *Wilderness Adventurer* and ASCW's *Spirit of Alaska* (as a matter of fact, the *Spirit of Alaska* and the two Special Expedition ships all sailed at one time for the now-defunct Exploration Cruise Lines). Cabins are small and functional, and public space is limited to the open sundeck and bow areas, the dining room, and an observation lounge that serves as the nerve center for activities. **Sample rates per person:** Lowest-price outside cabins $3,689 for 7-night cruise; no inside cabins or suites.

5 Midsized Educational Cruising

WORLD EXPLORER CRUISES

555 Montgomery St., San Francisco, CA 94111-2544. ☎ **800/854-3835** or 415/393-1565. Fax 415/391-1145. www.wecruise.com.

This is a real one-of-a-kind Alaska cruise experience that combines a relatively large ship (the dowdy, 740-passenger Universe Explorer) with an education-oriented approach more typical of a small-ship line. The ship offers an incredible itinerary—a 14-night round-trip cruise out of Vancouver that visits all the popular ports of call along with Haines, Wrangell, Valdez, and Seward—an educational lecture series, an atmosphere of friendly informality, and some truly high-caliber shore excursions. There's also a library stocked with 16,000 volumes (many on Alaska nature, history, and culture), a 150-seat cinema for movie watching, and a 16-terminal computer learning center operated by a company called SeniorNet. Entertainment-wise, one night it might be a string quartet, the next a cello soloist, a classical pianist, or an operatic soprano, cabaret singer, or ballad singer. The ship's lecture circuit features talks on ecology and the cultures of Alaska, presented by experts in their subject.

TYPICAL PASSENGERS The *Universe Explorer* tends to attract an older clientele, though the average age of its passengers is declining, mostly due to bike/hike-and-cruise options that allow passengers to bike or hike their way through the ports of call. These more active shore excursions appeal to a family market. It's not unusual for the ship to sail with between, say, 15 and 30 teens and preteens on board. There is a youth program and a team of counselors.

SHIPS The 739-passenger ***Universe Explorer*** has nice but not spectacular public spaces and adequate if not palatial cabins. The bulk of the ship is taken up with double-occupancy rooms with twin beds (convertible to queen-size). Some also are capable of accommodating third passengers in foldaway sofa beds. Public areas are fairly spartan. The ship has a functional reception area, lounge/bar facilities, a comfortable but not glamorous show room, and a huge library, with many selections on nature and wildlife. **Sample rates per person:** Lowest-price inside cabins $1,988, lowest outside $2,885, lowest suite $3,990 for 14-night cruise.

6 The Big-Ship Cruise Lines

The ships featured in this section vary in size, age, and offerings, but share the common thread of having more activities and entertainment options than any one person can possibly take in over the course of a cruise. You'll find swimming pools, health clubs, spas, nightclubs, movie theaters, shops, casinos, multiple restaurants, bars, and special kids' playrooms, and in some cases sports decks, virtual golf, computer rooms, and cigar clubs, as well as quiet spaces where you can get away from it all. In most cases you'll find lots and lots of onboard activities including games, contests, classes, and lectures, plus a variety of entertainment options and show productions, some very sophisticated.

CARNIVAL CRUISE LINES

3655 NW 87th Ave., Miami, FL 33178-2428. ☎ **800/CARNIVAL.** Fax 305/471-4740. www.carnival.com.

Carnival is the big kahuna of the cruise industry, but translating the line's warm-weather "24-hour orgy of good times" philosophy to Alaska's "look at the bears and whales!" temperament isn't an easy trick. In one of its Alaska brochures, the line says that, like the prospectors, you might find yourself shouting "Eureka"—but in the ship's casino, not at a gold rush site. Kinda makes you wonder why you aren't just going to Vegas.

On the plus side, entertainment is among the industry's best, with each ship boasting a dozen dancers, a 12-piece orchestra, comedians, jugglers, and numerous live bands, as well as a big casino. Activity is nonstop. Cocktails begin to flow before lunch, and through the course of the day you can learn to country line-dance or ballroom dance, take cooking lessons, learn to play bridge, watch first-run movies, practice your golf swing by smashing balls into a net, join in a knobby-knee contest, or just eat, drink, shop, and then eat again. Alaska-specific naturalist lectures are delivered daily. In port, Carnival offers more than 60 **shore excursions,** divided into categories of easy, moderate, and adventure. For kids, the line offers Camp Carnival, an expertly run children's program with activities that include Native arts and crafts sessions, lectures conducted by wildlife experts, and special shore excursions for teens.

TYPICAL PASSENGERS Overall, Carnival has some of the youngest demographics in the industry: mostly under 50, including couples, lots of singles, and a good share of families. It's the same Middle America crowd that can be found in Las Vegas and Atlantic City and at Florida's megaresorts.

SHIPS The 2,112-passenger, 84,000-ton ***Carnival Spirit*** is not yet in service at this writing, but advance PR says it'll have a wedding chapel, conference center, and, in addition to the formal dining room and casual buffet restaurant, an alternative restaurant sitting high up by the ship's smokestack. The ship will also have more of what makes Carnival tick, including a two-level gym, balconies on over half the cabins, a large children's center, and two consecutive decks of bars, lounges, and nightspots, one with an outdoor wraparound promenade. **Sample rates per person:** Lowest-price inside cabins $1,582, lowest outside $1,929, lowest suite $2,926 for 7-night cruise.

CELEBRITY CRUISES

1050 Caribbean Way, Miami, Fl 33132. ☎ **800/437-3111** or 305/539-6000. Fax 800/437-5111. www.celebrity-cruises.com.

Celebrity Cruises offers a great combination: a classy, tasteful, and luxurious cruise experience at a moderate price—it's definitely the best in the midpriced category. The line's ships are real works of art; its cuisine—guided by Michel Roux, one of the top French chefs in Britain—is outstanding; its service first-class, friendly, and unobtrusive; and its spa facilities among the best in the business.

A typical day might offer bridge, darts, a culinary art demonstration, a trapshooting competition, a fitness fashion show, an art auction, a volleyball tournament, and a none-too-shabby stage show. Lectures on the various ports of call, the Alaskan environment, glaciers, and Alaskan culture are given by resident experts. For children, Celebrity ships employ a group of counselors who direct and supervise a camp-style children's program. Activities are geared toward different age groups. There's an impressive kids' play area and a separate lounge area for teens.

TYPICAL PASSENGERS The typical guest is less party-oriented, more sophisticated, and more independent-minded than aboard a lot of other megaships. You'll find everyone from kids to retirees.

SHIPS Sleek, modern, and stunningly designed, both the 1,870-passenger ***Mercury*** and the larger, 1,950-passenger ***Infinity*** have a lot of open deck space and lots of large windows that provide access to the wide skies and the grand Alaskan vistas. Overall, there are no really bad cabins on these ships—inside cabins are about par for the industry standard, outside cabins are larger than usual, and suites (which come with butler service) are particularly spacious. Startlingly modern art—by the likes of Robert Rauschenberg, Jasper Johns, David Hockney, Pablo Picasso, Andy Warhol, and Richard Serra—is scattered throughout both vessels. Both ships (but especially *Infinity*) feature incredible spas with hydrotherapy pools, steam rooms, and saunas, plus health and beauty services and exceptionally large fitness areas. **Sample rates per person:** Lowest-price inside cabins $1,750, lowest outside $2,480, lowest suite $5,782 for 7-night cruise.

CRYSTAL CRUISES

2049 Century Park East, Suite 1400, Los Angeles, CA 90067. ☎ **800/446-6620** or 310/785-9300. Fax 310/785-3891. www.crystalcruises.com.

Luxury all the way. Crystal offers all the amenities of much bigger ships, but in a more luxurious and intimate atmosphere, with only 940 passengers. Everything is first class, with fine attention paid to detail and to making guests feel comfortable. Service on the ship is nothing short of superb. The ship carries a battery of Alaska naturalists, environmentalists, and National Park Service rangers to educate and entertain passengers in the wilderness areas of the 49th state. The line's food-and-wine series presents well-known chefs and wine experts who put on food preparation demonstrations, lecture on the art of cookery, and prepare dinner one night during the cruise. A PGA-approved golf pro accompanies practically every Harmony cruise, conducting clinics along the way. The Harmony also has a flourishing computer room on board, with training for the uninitiated. There's dazzling show-lounge entertainment, first-run movies, and a casino operated by Caesar's World, parent company of Caesar's Palace.

TYPICAL PASSENGERS Passengers aboard Crystal tend to be successful businesspeople who can afford to pay for the best. Many are under 50, with the average age probably closer to 60 than 70. Whatever their age, they tend to be people who like to dress up rather than down. "Casual night" doesn't mean the same thing to Crystal guests as it means to other people.

SHIPS A handsome ship by any standard, the 940-passenger ***Crystal Harmony*** has one of the highest passenger-space ratios of any cruise ship. Its cabins are large, well appointed, and tastefully decorated with quality fittings and in agreeable color tones. Almost half of them have private verandas. Public rooms are classy throughout. Two alternative restaurants, Prego (Italian, mostly northern) and Kyoto (Asian/Japanese), introduce variety to the dining experience. **Sample rates per person:** Lowest-price inside cabins $4,032, lowest outside $4,395, lowest suite $9,900 for 12-night cruise.

HOLLAND AMERICA LINE

300 Elliott Ave. W., Seattle, WA 98119. ☎ **800/426-0327** or 206/281-3535. Fax 206/286-7110. www.hollandamerica.com.

Holland America can be summed up in one word: tradition. The company was formed way back in 1873 as the Netherlands-America Steamship Company, and its ships today strive to present an aura of history and dignity, like a European hotel where they never let rock stars register. Service is provided primarily by Filipino and Indonesian staff members who are uniformly fantastic—gracious and friendly without being cloying.

Though most of the line's Alaskan fleet is relatively young, the ships are designed with a decidedly "classic" feel—no flashing neon lights here. Similarly, Holland America's ships are heavy on more mature, less frenetic kind of activities. You'll find good bridge programs and music to dance (or just listen) to in the bars and lounges, plus health spas and the other amenities found on most large ships. The line has improved its nightly show-lounge entertainment, which was once, frankly, not so hot. Each week includes a crew talent show in which the Indonesian and Filipino staff members perform their countries' songs and dances. Club HAL is one of the industry's more creative children's programs, though the children's playrooms (often no more than a meeting room stocked with a few toys) are no match for what you find on the latest Princess or Celebrity megaships.

TYPICAL PASSENGERS Though it still caters mostly to the older crowd that's long been its bread and butter, the average age is dropping, partly thanks to an increased emphasis on its children's program.

SHIPS The 1,266-passenger ***Ryndam, Statendam,*** and ***Veendam*** are more or less identical. All cabins have a sitting area and lots of closet and drawer space, and even the least expensive inside cabins run almost 190 square feet, quite large by industry standards. Outside doubles have either picture windows or verandas. The striking dining rooms, two-tiered showrooms, and Crow's Nest forward bar/lounges are among these ships' best features. The newer, 1,440-passenger ***Volendam*** and ***Zaandam*** are larger and fancier, with triple-decked oval atriums, 197 suites and deluxe staterooms with private verandas, five showrooms and lounges, and an alternative restaurant designed as an artist's bistro, featuring drawings and etchings. The smallest cabin is a comfortable 190 square feet. The very long, stately, 1,494-passenger ***Westerdam*** is reminiscent of an old-time ocean liner, with portholes on some decks, a wide wraparound promenade, a truly lovely showroom, and spacious cabins and lounges. Cabins are large, though none have verandas. **Sample rates per person:** Lowest-price inside cabins $1,407, lowest outside $2,087, lowest suite $3,689 for 7-night cruise.

NORWEGIAN CRUISE LINE

7665 Corporate Center Dr., Miami, FL. 33126. ☎ **800/327-7030.** Fax 305/448-7936. www.ncl.com.

Norwegian Cruise Line (NCL) offers an informal and upbeat onboard atmosphere on both the medium-sized *Norwegian Wind* and the megaship *Norwegian Sky,* sailing from Seattle. The line excels at activities, and its recreational and fitness programs are among the best in the industry. Last year NCL inaugurated a casual-dining policy that allows passengers to dine when they want (within a certain time frame), with whomever they want, dressed however they want.

In Alaska, NCL offers an Alaskan lecturer, wine tastings, art auctions, trap shooting, cooking demonstrations, craft and dance classes, incentive fitness program, and bingo, among other activities. Passengers can choose from a good selection of soft-adventure shore excursions, including hiking, biking, and kayaking. Entertainment is generally strong, and includes Broadway-style musical productions. For kids, there's an activity room, video games, an ice-cream bar, and guaranteed baby-sitting aboard, plus sessions with park rangers and escorted shore excursions.

TYPICAL PASSENGERS In Alaska, the demographic tends more toward retirees than on the line's warmer-climate sailings, but you'll find families as well, including grandparents bringing along the grandkids.

SHIPS The 2,002-passenger ***Norwegian Sky*** is the newest and biggest ship in the NCL fleet, with an Internet cafe, a huge sundeck (complete with a driver in a golf cart delivering drinks), a basketball court and batting cage, and a wedding chapel (for in-port ceremonies only). In contrast to its large public spaces, standard cabins are small at 154 square feet and have little storage space. The smaller, less fancy, 1,700-passenger ***Norwegian Wind*** has three main dining rooms, an alternative restaurant, and the typical range of lounges, bars, and entertainment facilities. Closet and drawer space in cabins is quite limited, so pack lightly. **Sample rates per person:** Lowest-price inside cabins $1,400, lowest outside $1,899, lowest suite $4,452 for 7-night cruise.

PRINCESS CRUISES

10100 Santa Monica Blvd., Los Angeles, CA 90067. ☎ **800/LOVE-BOAT** (568-3262) or 310/553-1770. Fax 310/277-6175. www.princesscruises.com.

Consistency is Princess's strength. With new ships joining its fleet like so many cars off a Detroit assembly line, you'd think that maintaining acceptable service standards could be a problem. All things considered, though, Princess accomplishes this rather well. Throughout the fleet, the service in all areas—dining room, lounge, cabin maintenance, and so on—tends to be of consistently high quality.

Princess passengers can expect enough onboard activities to keep them going morning to night, if they've a mind to, and enough nooks and crannies to allow them to do absolutely nothing, if that's their thing. Kids are well taken care of, with especially large children's playrooms. On shore, the line's shore-excursion staffs get big points for efficiency.

TYPICAL PASSENGERS Typical Princess passengers are likely to be between, say, 50 and 65. Recent additional emphasis on its youth and children's facilities has begun to attract a bigger share of the **family market,** resulting in the passenger list becoming more active overall.

SHIPS The 1,950-passenger ***Dawn, Sea, Sun,*** and ***Ocean Princes*** are virtually indistinguishable from one another except for cosmetics. Despite their size, you'll probably never feel crowded; there always seems to be lots of space on deck, in the buffet dining areas, and in the lounges. There are beautiful libraries, patisseries for pastries and cappuccino, and pizzerias for good made-to-order Italian fast food. The ships have extensive children's playrooms with ball drop, castles, computer games, puppet theaters, and more. As for cabins, even the smallest is a spacious 175 square feet, and more than 400 have private verandas. The 1,590-passenger ***Regal Princess*** is warm and inviting inside, and on the outside looks like—what? A spaceship? A *Star Wars* storm trooper's helmet? Spacious, well-furnished cabins are one of the ship's better features (standard dimensions are about 190 square ft.), and there are some interesting public rooms, like the huge observation lounge/casino/bar. **Sample rates per person:** Lowest-price inside cabins $1,848, lowest outside $2,030, lowest suite $4,102 for 7-night cruise.

RADISSON SEVEN SEAS CRUISES

600 Corporate Dr., Suite 410, Fort Lauderdale, FL 33334. ☎ **800/285-1835.** www.rssc.com.

Radisson offers the best in food, service, and accommodations in an environment that's a little more casual and small-shiplike than Crystal's more determined luxury.

The line assumes for the most part passengers want to entertain themselves on board, so organized activities are limited, but they do include lectures by local experts, well-known authors, and the like, plus facilities for card and board games and the occasional dance lesson. There are three computers in the library to allow guests to send e-mail and use CD-ROMs. Entertainment includes production shows, cabaret acts, and local acts that come on board at ports. The library stocks books and also movies guests can play on their in-cabin VCRs. The line has a no-tipping policy, and offers creative shore excursions.

TYPICAL PASSENGERS Radisson tends to attract high-income, low-key passengers aged 50 and up. The typical passenger is well educated, well traveled, and inquisitive.

SHIPS Cabins on the 490-passenger ***Seven Seas Mariner*** are all ocean-view suites, most with private verandas. The standard suite is a large 301 square feet; some suites can interconnect if you want to book two for additional space. In the public areas, the show lounge is designed to resemble a 1930s nightclub. There are two additional lounges plus a casino and the Connoisseur Club, a cushy venue for predinner drink and after-dinner fine brandy and cigars. The ship's spa offers Judith Jackson European spa treatments using a variety of herbal and water-based therapies. **Sample rates per person:** Lowest-price suite $2,730 for 7-night cruise; no inside or standard outside cabins.

ROYAL CARIBBEAN INTERNATIONAL

1050 Caribbean Way, Miami, FL 33132. ☎ **800/327-6700** or 305/539-6000. www.rccl.com.

Royal Caribbean sells a mass-market style of cruising that's reasonably priced and offered aboard casual, well-run ships that offer plenty of the standard cruise line fare—craft classes, horse racing, bingo, shuffleboard, deck games, line-dancing lessons, wine-and-cheese tastings, cooking demonstrations, art auctions, and the like—plus elaborate health clubs and spas, covered swimming pools, large open sundeck areas, and innumerable bars, lounges, and other entertainment centers. The Viking Crown Lounge and other glassed-in areas make excellent observation rooms to see the Alaska sights. Royal Caribbean spends big bucks on entertainment, which includes high-tech show productions. Headliners are often featured. Port lectures are offered on topics such as Alaska wildlife, and the line offers some 65 shore excursions. The line's children's activities are some of the most extensive afloat.

TYPICAL PASSENGERS The crowd on Royal Caribbean ships, like the decor, rates pretty high on the whoopee scale, though not quite at the Carnival level. Passengers represent an age mix from 30 to 60, and a good number of families are attracted by the line's well-established and fine-tuned kids' programs.

SHIPS The 2,000-passenger ***Rhapsody*** and ***Vision of the Seas*** are almost identical, and offer plenty of nice touches that give them the feel of top-flight shore resorts. You'll find sumptuous, big-windowed health club/spas and loads of fine shopping, dining, and entertainment options. Cabins are not large but do have small sitting areas. All outside cabins on both ships' Bridge and Commodore decks have balconies and can sleep up to four quite comfortably. The 2,100-passenger ***Radiance of the Seas*** will also be sailing in Alaska in 2001, but had not been launched at press time, so details are not available. **Sample rates per person:** Lowest-price inside cabins $1,100, lowest outside $2,330, lowest suite $3,100 for 7-night cruise.

5 Southeast Alaska

Rich, proud people have lived in Southeast Alaska for thousands of years, fishing its salmon and hunting all through its primeval forests, where the tree trunks grow up to 10 feet thick. In canoes, they explored the hundreds of misty, mossy, enchanted islands where the animals, trees, and even the ice had living spirits. The salmon lived under the sea in human form, becoming fish in the summer to swim in seething masses up the rivers and streams as a gift of food to feed their kin, the people. In return, the people treated the salmon with respect and ceremony, allowing their spirits to return to human form under the sea to live another year. So blessed, the Tlingit and Haida built great, carved houses and poles, fought wars, owned slaves, traded with faraway tribes, and held rich contests of giving called potlatches, where they passed on the stories that still help explain their mysterious world. Even for a modern non-Native walking in the grand quiet of the old-growth rain forest, it's easy to find yourself listening for the spirits of the trees speaking their mysteries.

Discovery subsists on mystery, and Southeast Alaska is still being discovered. A honeycomb of limestone caves under Prince of Wales Island wasn't found until 1987. Explorers continue to map its endless miles of caverns, finding the bones of extinct animals, the leavings of some of North America's earliest prehistoric people, bear dens, strange eyeless shrimp that live nowhere else, and even underground streams that host spawning salmon. The caves network at every step into passages that lead straight up or down or off to either side, some only large enough to carry a cool wind. The unfathomable intricacy is exhilarating but also a bit disquieting, like a breath of the supernatural, for it is proof of the unknowable.

Southeast Alaska itself unfolds like the intricate, hidden world below the tree roots. This land of ice and forest may not look as large on the map as other parts of Alaska, but the better you know it, the bigger it becomes, until you have to surrender to its immensity. You don't need to go underground to experience the sensation—you can experience it by gazing from a boat at the fractal geometry of the endlessly folded, rocky shoreline. The discoveries you make depend only on how closely you look. On a cruise through the Inside Passage, you'll marvel at all the little beaches and rocky outcroppings you pass—hundreds of inviting spots each day you steam through. If you were to stop at random on any one of those uninhabited beaches in a skiff or kayak, you'd find you could spend a day surveying just a few acres of rocks, the overhanging forest, and the tiny pools of water left behind by the tide. And if you gazed down into any one of those pools, you'd find a complex world all its own, where tiny predators and prey live out their own drama of life in the space of a few square feet.

The area stands apart from Alaska, and not only because most of it can't be reached by road. No other part of the state shares the mysterious, spirit-ridden quality of the coastal rain forest. No other area has such mild weather, more akin to the Pacific Northwest than to the heart of Alaska. Certainly no other area in Alaska gets so much rain, nor do many other places on earth. The traditional Native people here differed from other Alaska Natives, too: They were far richer and left behind more physical artifacts. The Tlingit, Haida, and Tsimshian exploited the wealth nature gave them and amplified it by being successful traders with tribes to the south and over the mountains in today's British Columbia and Yukon Territory. In their early contact, the Tlingits even briefly defeated the Russian invaders in the Battle of Sitka, and after white dominance was established, managed to save many of their cultural artifacts and stories.

Along with its other riches and complexities, Southeast Alaska also has many charming small towns and villages that seem to have grown organically from mountainsides bordering the fjords and channels of the islands. With economies that predate Alaska's oil boom, they developed slowly, their fishermen building houses to hand down to their children. The smaller towns remain completely exempt from the American blight of corporate sameness. The real, old-fashioned main streets are prosperous with family businesses where the proprietors know their customers by first name.

1 Exploring Southeast Alaska

A unique and inviting aspect of traveling in Southeast Alaska is that no roads connect most of the communities. People are forced to get out of their speeding cars and get on boats, where they can meet their fellow travelers and see what's passing by—slowly. The islands of the region form a protected waterway called the **Inside Passage,** along which almost all of the region's towns are arrayed. Thanks to the **Alaska Marine Highway** ferry system, it's inexpensive to travel the entire passage, hopping from town to town and spending as much time in each place as you like. And if you're short on time, air service is frequent, with jets to the major towns and commuter planes to the villages.

GETTING AROUND BY FERRY: THE ALASKA MARINE HIGHWAY

The state-run **Alaska Marine Highway System,** 1591 Glacier Ave., Juneau, AK 99801-1427 (☎ **800/642-0066** or 800/764-3779 TDD; fax 907/277-4829; www.dot.state.ak.us/external/amhs/home.html), is a subsidized fleet of blue-hulled, ocean-going ferries whose mission is to connect the roadless coastal towns of Alaska for roughly the same kind of cost you'd pay if there were roads and you were driving. Call for a free schedule or download it from the Web site.

PROS & CONS The ferry system's strengths are its low cost, frequent summer sailings, exceptional safety, and the fact that it's about the most fun form of family travel I can imagine—kids love it. In the summer, Forest Service guides offer interpretive talks on board. Its weaknesses are crowding during the July peak season, sometimes many-hour delays, generally lackluster food, and a shortage of cabins, which means that most people camp on deck or in chairs during overnight passages.

Ferry System Booking Tips

The **Alaska Marine Highway's** statewide toll-free number (☎ **800/642-0066**) has been chronically understaffed, but there are ways around that problem. You can reserve online at **www.dot.state.ak.us/external/amhs/**. Or, if you need to talk to someone, call the staff at the office in Anchorage, where they have less to do, at ☎ **907/272-7116.** The office is staffed for walk-ins, too, in the Alaska Public Lands Information Center, at Fourth and F streets in Anchorage.

In addition, the contractors who operate ferry terminals in Kodiak (☎ **800/526-6731;** www.akferry.com) and Homer (☎ **800/382-9229;** www.akmhs.com) maintain toll-free numbers and Web sites where you can reach an agent quickly, get detailed advice, and reserve for anywhere in the system.

You can avoid crowds on the boats by scheduling around them. Ferries are crowded northbound in June and southbound in August and both ways in July. If you're planning to fly one way and take the ferry the other, go against the flow (southbound in June and northbound in August) and you'll have the ship more to yourself.

ROUTES The system mostly serves Southeast, though it does cover most of coastal Alaska, with one sailing a month connecting Southeast Alaska with the Southcentral region nearer Anchorage, and two smaller ferries there that link communities all the way out the Aleutian Chain (see chapters 7 and 10).

To the south, five large, main-line ferries call on Prince Rupert, British Columbia, and run about 37 hours north to Haines and Skagway. Each of these towns is connected to the rest of the world by roads, but none of the towns in between are. In the summer, the large ships stop daily (although sometimes in the middle of the night) in Ketchikan, Wrangell, Petersburg, Juneau, Haines, and Skagway. Some make a side-trip to Sitka on the way. Juneau is the hub, with many extra sailings north on the Lynn Canal to Haines and Skagway. One ship, the *Columbia,* goes all the way south to Bellingham, Washington; from there, it makes a 37-hour nonstop run to Ketchikan before continuing up through the other towns to Haines.

The two smaller, feeder ferries, the *LeConte* and *Aurora,* connect the larger towns to tiny towns and villages up and down the coast. They mostly take local residents back and forth to their villages, so they're rarely crowded. They are the definition of "off the beaten track," offering the cheapest and easiest way to the real wilderness of the Alaska Bush. The feeder ferries have restaurants but no cabins.

CONNECTIONS **From the south:** The appeal of taking the ferry to Alaska from Bellingham, Washington, is obvious, but it does not save money over flying and it takes 2 days just to get to Ketchikan. The popular alternative is to board in Prince Rupert, B.C., which you can reach by rail (see "Getting There & Getting Around" in chapter 2), by car (Park Avenue Corner Store, ☎ **888/437-1373,** offers secured parking for $5 a day Canadian, and provides a shuttle to the dock), or by riding the **B.C. Ferries** system, 1112 Fort St., Victoria, B.C., Canada V8V 4V2 (☎ **250/386-3431;** www.bcferries.bc.ca). That route allows you to tour British Columbia's Victoria Island, although you would need a car. Get to the island from the south by ferry at Nanaimo or Victoria from Vancouver or Port Angeles, Washington, respectively, then drive north to Port Hardy, where the B.C. ferry connects to Prince Rupert, docking right next to the Alaska ferry.

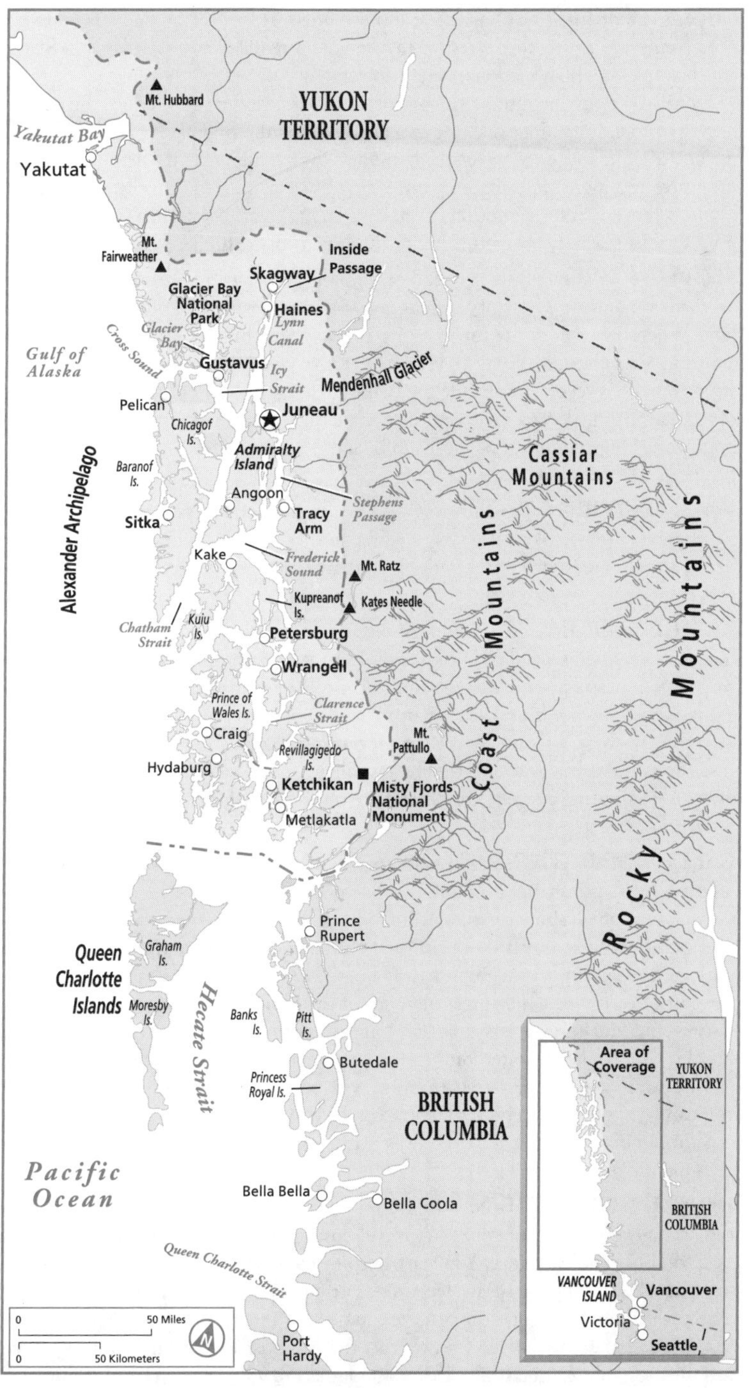

Mt. Hubbard
YUKON TERRITORY
Yakutat Bay
Yakutat
Mt. Fairweather
Inside Passage
Skagway
Glacier Bay National Park
Haines
Lynn Canal
Glacier Bay
Cross Sound
Gulf of Alaska
Gustavus
Icy Strait
Mendenhall Glacier
Pelican
Juneau
Chicagof Is.
Admiralty Island
Cassiar Mountains
Alexander Archipelago
Baranof Is.
Angoon
Stephens Passage
Tracy Arm
Sitka
Kake
Frederick Sound
Mt. Ratz
Kupreanof Is.
Kates Needle
Chatham Strait
Kuiu Is.
Petersburg
Wrangell
Coast Mountains
Rocky Mountains
Prince of Wales Is.
Clarence Strait
Craig
Mt. Pattullo
Revillagigedo Is.
Hydaburg
Ketchikan
Misty Fjords National Monument
Metlakatla
Prince Rupert
Queen Charlotte Islands
Graham Is.
Moresby Is.
Hecate Strait
Banks Is.
Pitt Is.
Butedale
Princess Royal Is.
BRITISH COLUMBIA
Pacific Ocean
Bella Bella
Bella Coola
Queen Charlotte Strait
Port Hardy
0
50 Miles
0
50 Kilometers
N
Area of Coverage
YUKON TERRITORY
BRITISH COLUMBIA
VANCOUVER ISLAND
Vancouver
Victoria
Seattle

From the north: The choices are more limited: rent a car or ride a bus. Two bus lines connect Skagway to the rest of the state, and rental cars are available in Skagway and Haines. See those sections, below, for details.

By air: By flying to your staring point, you can save time and reduce the chance of having to spend the night sleeping in a chair on board. Long hauls on the ferry can be uncomfortable and don't save much money over flying, but the ferry is much less expensive and more appealing for connecting towns within the Southeast region itself. Fly into Juneau, Sitka, or another sizable town and plan a ferry trip from there, stopping various places before returning to catch your plane home.

STOPPING OVER Buying ahead or booking round-trip tickets saves you nothing on the ferry, and stopovers of any length add little to the cost of your passage. Use the ferry system to explore the towns along the way, grabbing the next ferry through to continue your journey. If you travel without a vehicle, you generally don't need reservations (major exceptions include the Bellingham sailings and passages across the Gulf of Alaska). Bring along a bike, or even a sea kayak, to have total freedom in exploring Southeast. Don't count on port calls to be long enough to see the towns; if the boat is running late, they may not let you off at all.

WALK-ON FARES The adult walk-on fare from Prince Rupert to Skagway is $130. Bellingham to Ketchikan is $164, Bellingham to Skagway $252. Juneau to Sitka is $26. Fares for children 11 and under is roughly half price, while children 2 and under ride free.

BRINGING VEHICLES You must reserve a place to take a vehicle on the ferry in the summer, often several months ahead. Fares vary according to the size of the car as well as your destination; a passage from Prince Rupert to Haines for a typical 15-foot car is $283, or $578 from Bellingham. You also have to buy a ticket for each person, including the driver. Compare the cost of **renting a car** at your destination, as it could cost the same or less and save the inconvenience and wear-and-tear of bringing your own. You can bring a kayak, canoe, or bike on the ferry for around a third of the cost of an adult ticket.

CABIN RESERVATIONS Sometimes you can snag a cabin from the standby list (approach the purser upon boarding), but generally you must reserve ahead for the summer season. Cabins on the Bellingham run book up many months ahead. An overnight, two-berth **outside cabin** (one with a window) is around $50 on most sailings, or $121 from Prince Rupert to Haines, $271 from Bellingham to Haines, plus the cost of your ticket. The great majority of the cabins are small and spartan, coming in two- and four-bunk configurations, but for a premium you can reserve a more comfortable unit (called a "stateroom" in the ferry literature) with a sitting room attached. Most cabins have tiny private bathrooms with showers. Try to get an outside cabin so you can watch the world go by. Cabins can be stuffy, and the windowless units can be claustrophobic as well. The staterooms don't cost that much more and provide your own private observation lounge.

DO YOU NEED A CABIN? If you do a lot of layovers in Southeast's towns, you can arrange to do most of your ferry travel during the day. But you'll probably have to sleep on board at least once. You can't sleep in your vehicle. One of the adventures of ferry travel is finding a chair to sleep in or setting up a tent on deck with everyone else. The covered, outdoor solarium, on the top deck, is the best sleeping spot on board, in part because the noise of the ship covers other sounds. The recliner lounges are comfortable, too, but can be stuffy. If the ship looks crowded, grab your spot fast to get a choice location. **Showers** are available, although there may be lines. Lock the valuables and luggage you don't need in the **coin-operated lockers.** If you're tenting, the best place is behind the solarium, where it's not too windy. On the *Columbia,* that space is small, so grab it early. Bring duct tape to secure your tent to the deck in case you can't find a sheltered spot, as the wind over the deck of a ship in motion blows like an endless gale. If all that sounds too rugged, or if you have small children and no tent, reserve a cabin. It offers a safe and private home base and a good night's rest, and there's a certain romance to having your own compartment on a public conveyance.

FERRY FOOD If you can, bring your own food on the ferry. Ferry food isn't positively bad, but it's quite inconsistent from one ship to the next. It's often greasy, and you can get awfully tired of it after several meals in a row. Also, during peak season, the food lines are sometimes unreasonably long. We usually bring a cooler or picnic basket. Even if you're traveling light, you can pick up some bagels and deli sandwiches on a stopover or long port call.

THE BEST RUNS Going to Sitka through **Peril Straits,** the ferry fits through extraordinarily narrow passages where no other vessel of its size ventures; the smooth, reflective water is lovely, and you may see deer along the shore. The **Wrangell Narrows,** between Petersburg and Wrangell, also are an incredible ride, day or night, as the ship accomplishes a slalom between shores that seem so close you could touch them, in water so shallow the schedules must be timed for high tide. **Frederick Sound,** between the Narrows and Wrangell, offers prime waters for whale sightings. Approaching Skagway through the towering mountains of the **Lynn Canal** fjord also is especially impressive.

GETTING AROUND BY AIR & ROAD

BY AIR Air travel is the primary link between Southeast's towns and the rest of the world. Major towns without road access have jet service, provided by **Alaska Airlines** (☎ **800/252-7522;** www.alaskaair.com), currently the region's only major airline. Juneau is Southeast Alaska's travel hub. Ketchikan and Sitka each have a few flights a day, while Wrangell, Petersburg, and Yakutat each have one flight going each direction daily. Gustavus is served from Juneau once daily during the summer. Some of these "milk runs" never get very far off the ground on hops between small towns: On the 31-mile Wrangell-to-Petersburg flight, the cabin attendants never have time to unbuckle. Haines and Skagway, which have highway connections, don't receive visits from jets, but all the towns and even the tiniest villages have scheduled prop service.

If you can possibly afford it, you'll want to take a **"flightseeing" trip** at some point during your trip. The poor man's way of doing this is to fly a small prop plane on a scheduled run between two of your destinations instead of taking the ferry. If you ask, the pilot may even go out of his or her way to show you the sights; even if not, you'll gain an appreciation for the richness and extreme topography of the region. Each operator also offers flightseeing tours, which cost as little as $50 for a brief spin. Flight services are listed in each town section.

Like the ferries, the planes can be quite late. Each of the airports in Southeast has its own challenges caused by the steep, mountainous terrain and the water. In bad weather, even jet flights are delayed or they "overhead"—they can't land at all at the intended destination and leave their passengers somewhere else. Your only protection against these contingencies are travel insurance, a schedule that allows plenty of slack in case you're significantly delayed, and low blood pressure.

BY ROAD Three Southeast Alaska communities are accessible by road: Haines, Skagway, and the village of Hyder, which lies on the British Columbia border east of Ketchikan and is accessible from the gravel Cassiar Highway through Canada. If you're

Why There Are No Highways

A tectonic plate that underlies the Pacific Ocean brought the islands of the Southeast Alaska Panhandle from across the globe and squished them up against the plate that carries the land mass of Canada. Along the line of this glancing collision, large glacial mountains thrust up, and the islands themselves were stretched and torn into the fractured geography that makes the area so interesting. In short, it's just too expensive to build roads through those icy mountains and across the steep, jumbled terrain of the islands. In 2000, Gov. Tony Knowles shelved a plan to build a road to Juneau, the capital city, because of the cost, electing to add more ferries instead.

driving the Alaska Highway, passing through Haines and Skagway adds 250 miles of very scenic driving to the trip. Take the ferry the 15 miles between the two towns (they're separated by 362 road miles). This ferry route is not as heavily booked as the routes heading between either town and Juneau, but it's a good idea to reserve ahead anyway. You also can rent a car from Haines or Skagway for travel to the rest of the state at the end of a ferry journey (Haines will save you only 60 miles over Skagway); buses serve Skagway; details are listed in the sections on each of those towns. If you're driving the highway in winter, you should be prepared for weather as cold as 40°F below zero. Alaska winter driving information is under "Health, Safety & Insurance" in chapter 2.

Bikes make a lot of sense for getting around Southeast's small towns, which tend to be compact. You can rent one almost anywhere you go or bring your own on the ferry. The networks of abandoned or little-used logging roads on some islands offer limitless routes for mountain biking. Elsewhere, Forest Service hiking trails are often open for riding.

GETTING OUTSIDE IN THE TONGASS NATIONAL FOREST

Nearly all of Southeast Alaska, stretching 500 miles from Ketchikan to Yakutat, is in Tongass National Forest. The towns sit in small pockets of private land surrounded by 17 million acres of land controlled by the U.S. Forest Service—an area nearly as large as the state of Maine, and considerably larger than any other national forest or any national park in the United States. The great majority of this land has never been logged, and the rate of logging has dropped dramatically in recent years, preserving one of the world's great temperate rain forests in its virgin state. It's an intact ecosystem full of wildlife, and mostly free of human development. Indeed, you quickly forget it *is* the Tongass National Forest. Since it always surrounds you when you're in this region, it's simply the land.

FOREST SERVICE CABINS

One of the best ways to get into Southeast's wilderness is by staying at one of the scores of remote Forest Service Public Recreation Cabins. These are simple cabins, generally without electricity or running water, where you can lay your sleeping bag on a bunk and sit by a warm wood stove, out of the rain. You need to bring everything with you, as if camping, but it's a good deal more comfortable than a tent. And you will probably find yourself in a stunningly beautiful spot, perhaps with your own lake and a boat for fishing. Cabins are along canoe trails, on beaches best reached by sea kayak, on high mountain lakes accessible only by floatplane, and along hiking trails.

GETTING CABIN INFORMATION I've listed a few of the cabins in the text with the towns they're nearest, but for complete information check the Tongass Web site (**www.fs.fed.us/r10/tongass**) or get copies of the **Public Recreation Cabin catalogs** published by the Forest Service. A free booklet is distributed for each of the three major areas in the national forest: the Ketchikan Area, which includes Prince of Wales Island and Misty Fjords; the Stikine Area, around Petersburg and Wrangell; and the Chatham Area, around Juneau, Sitka, and Admiralty Island. Each cabin is briefly described. You can get the booklets from the visitor centers and ranger offices listed with each town, or write ahead to the **Forest Service Information Center,** Centennial Hall, 101 Egan Dr., Juneau, AK 99801 (☎ **907/586-8751** or 907/586-7894 TTY; fax 907/586-7928).

You'll need a good map to figure out where the cabins are, and an idea of how to get there and how much travel will cost—generally, this will be many times the cabin rental of $25 to $45 a night. Few cabins can be reached without a boat or aircraft. Often, a flight service can help you choose according to your interests and how far you can afford to fly. You may be able to rent the gear you need, but you'll have to reserve that ahead, too. The solution to these puzzles is different for each town; I've listed where to find help in the town sections later in this chapter.

RESERVING A CABIN The cabins are reserved through a new national system. (The locals aren't too happy about that, because now outsiders can grab their favorite spots just as easily as they can.) Don't rely on the reservation operators or Web site for advice or cabin information—they're in upstate New York—but pose your questions instead to the ranger station nearest where you plan to go. The rangers are friendly and have probably stayed in the cabin you're interested in. Use the reservation system when you've made your decision and are ready to book; you can check cabin availability dates and reserve on the Internet (**www.reserveusa.com**). Contact this **National Recreation Reservations Service (NRRS),** operated by **Reserve America,** at ☎ **877/444-6777,** 877/833-6777 TDD, or 518/885-3639 with toll from overseas. The phone lines are open summer daily 8am to midnight EST, winter daily 10am to 7pm. They take American Express, Discover, MasterCard, and Visa, or you can reserve on the phone and then pay by certified check. Cabins are available for reservation on a first-come, first-served basis, starting 180 days ahead.

2 Ketchikan: On the Waterfront

Had they known about it, the film noir directors of the 1950s would have chosen the Ketchikan (*ketch*-e-kan) waterfront for Humphrey Bogart to sleuth. One can picture the black-and-white montage: A pelting rain drains from the brim of his hat, suspicious figures dart through saloon doors and into the lobbies of concrete-faced hotels, a forest of workboat masts fades into the midsummer twilight along a shore where the sea and land seem to merge in miles of floating docks. Along Creek Street, salmon on their way to spawn swim under houses chaotically perched on pilings beside a narrow boardwalk; inside, men are spawning, too, in the arms of legal prostitutes. Meanwhile, the faces of totem poles gaze down on the scene disapprovingly, mute holders of their own ancient secrets.

Today, the director hoping to re-create that scene would have his work cut out for him removing the T-shirt shops and bright street-front signs that seek to draw throngs of cruise passengers in to buy plastic gewgaws. Not so long ago, Ketchikan was a rugged and exotic intersection of cultures built on the profits of logging Southeast's rain forest, but in just a few years it has transformed into a tourist center, softening its rough edges while selling their charm to visitors. And the changes can only accelerate. More and bigger ships are coming, and Southeast Alaska's last major timber mill—the Louisiana Pacific–owned pulp plant in Ward Cove, north of town—closed in 1997 due, in part, to environmental concerns. A major portion of the mill was blown up in 1999; they sold tickets to see who would get to press the button on the explosives, but the occasion was less than festive, as former employees saw the scene of their work lives disappear into dust. A smaller, more labor-intensive wood-products operation, sawing lumber and making veneer, is trying to take the place of Louisiana Pacific, but in the meantime, the economy is moving on.

On summer days, the white cruise ships tower above the town like huge new buildings on the dock facing Front Street, the downtown's main drag. Each morning their gangways disgorge thousands of visitors, clogging the streets and, for a few hours, transforming the town into a teeming carnival. With only a few hours to spend, the passengers explore the closest of the twisting streets, see the museum at the Southeast Alaska Discovery Center, or take a tour to one of the totem pole parks. Then evening comes, the streets empty, and the cruise ships slide off quietly on the way to their next port.

That is when a sense of the old, misty, mysterious Ketchikan starts to return. Visitors with a little more time to spend, and the willingness to explore beyond the core tourist areas, can drink fully of the history and atmosphere of the place, staying in a quaint old hotel, hiking a boardwalk path through the primeval rain forest, and making unique discoveries.

There certainly is plenty to see. Ketchikan is a center of Tlingit and Haida culture, and there are two replica **clan houses** and **totem pole parks,** as well as the only museum dedicated solely to preserving the old, original poles from the days when the Tlingit and Haida peoples' cultural traditions were more intact. Two other museums preserve and explain the broader culture and natural history of the area. There are several art galleries that feature serious local work.

Ketchikan also makes a great jumping-off point for some spectacular outdoor experiences, including a trip to **Misty Fjords National Monument** (see section 3, later in this chapter). As the state's fourth-largest city, Ketchikan is the transportation hub for the southern portion of Southeast Alaska. (The nickname "Gateway City" refers to its geographical location and transportation function.) Seaplanes based on docks along the waterfront are the taxis of the region, and a big interagency visitor center can get you started. Ketchikan also is one of the wettest spots on earth, with rain measured in the hundreds of inches; quality rain gear is requisite for any activity, in the wilds or in the streets of town.

ESSENTIALS

GETTING THERE

BY AIR **Alaska Airlines** (☎ **800/252-7522** or 907/225-2145; www.alaskaair.com) provides Ketchikan with nonstop jet service from Seattle and with flights to the north stopping in Petersburg, Wrangell, Sitka, Juneau, and Anchorage. Commuter lines run wheeled and floatplanes from Ketchikan to the neighboring communities, as well as offering fishing packages and flightseeing.

The airport is on a different island from the town and can be reached only by a ferry that runs each way every half hour (more frequently at peak times). Typically, it leaves the airport on the hour and half hour, and leaves the Ketchikan side on quarter hours. Believe the airline when it tells you when to catch the ferry for your plane. The fare is $2.50 for adults, $1.50 ages 6 to 11, and free under 6. Returning the same day is free. The fare for cars is $5 each way, no matter how soon you come back. You'll need a vehicle (or a cab) to get to town from the airport ferry (see "Getting to Town," below).

BY FERRY The dock is 2½ miles north of downtown. **Alaska Marine Highway** ferries (see more info in section 1 of this chapter) run 6 hours north to Wrangell and

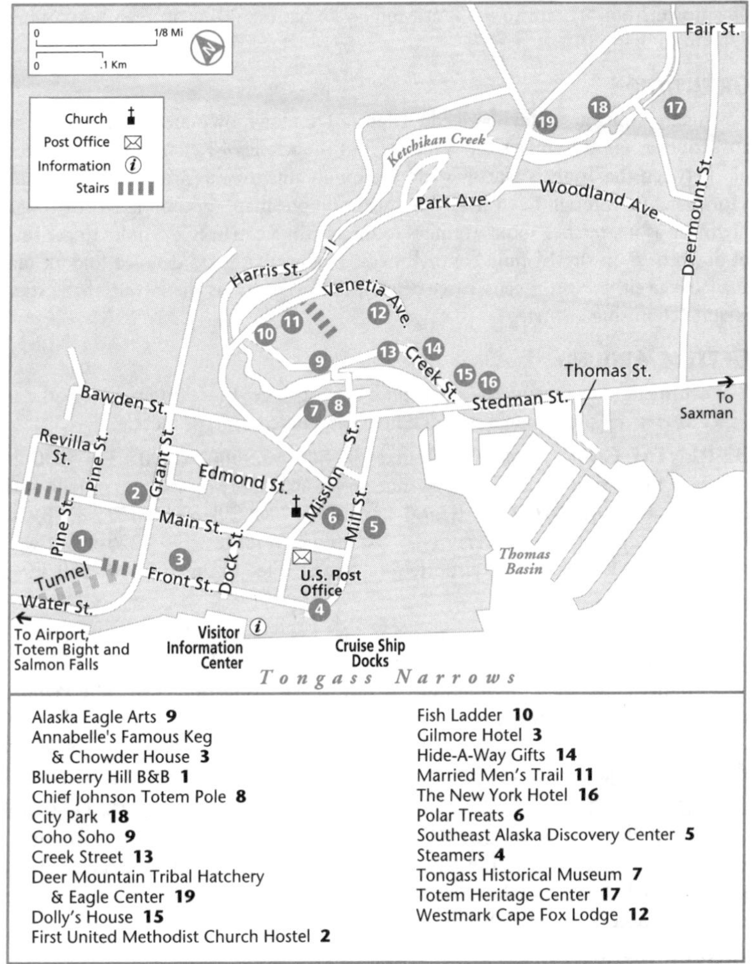

6 hours south to Prince Rupert, B.C. The walk-on fare from Prince Rupert is $38, from Wrangell it's $24, children under 12 go half price. For updated arrival and departure times, call the local terminal at ☎ **907/225-6181.**

GETTING TO TOWN A shuttle, taxi, or city bus can get you into town from the ferry terminal or the airport ferry. The **Airporter Shuttle** (☎ **907/225-5429**) meets each flight and picks up at the major hotels according to a schedule you can get at the front desk. They'll pick up anywhere else by arrangement. The $15 fare downtown is comparable to what you'd pay for a taxi, and includes the airport ferry fare.

The local taxis, mostly minivans, charge reasonable prices compared to some Alaska communities. Try **Yellow Taxi** (☎ **907/225-5555**) or **Sourdough Cab** (☎ **907/225-5544**). Take the cab just to the airport ferry dock and walk on the ferry; unless you've got dozens of steamer trunks, you don't need the taxi to go across on the ferry with you (or pay the expensive fee for doing so).

A **bus** operated by the Ketchikan Gateway Borough (☎ **907/225-6800**) runs roughly every half hour from the airport ferry parking lot and state ferry terminal downtown from 5:15am to 9:45pm Monday to Saturday and once an hour Sunday 8:45am to 3:45pm.

Orientation

Ketchikan is on huge **Revillagigedo Island.** The downtown area with most of the attractions is quite compact and walkable, but the whole of Ketchikan is long, strung out between the Tongass Narrows and the mountains. A waterfront road goes under various names through town (it's Water Street on our map), becoming North Tongass Highway as it stretches about 16 miles to the north. Saxman is 2½ miles to the south of downtown on the 14-mile South Tongass Highway. A good detailed foldout map, available at either visitor center (see below), is a necessity, as the layout of the streets is quite confusing at first.

Getting Around

You can spend a day seeing the sights on foot, but to get to the totem pole parks and other interesting places you'll need a rented car, guided tour, or bicycle.

BY RENTAL CAR **Alaska Car Rental** (☎ **800/662-0007** or 907/225-5000) has offices at the airport and at Third Avenue and Tongass, or will pick up or deliver the car for free. **Southeast Auto Rental** (☎ **800/770-8778** or 907/225-8778) is a budget agency and also delivers. **Avis** (☎ **800/230-4898** or 907/225-4515; www.avis.com) has a desk at the airport, too. Rental rates begin at about $50 for an economy car.

BY BIKE A bike is a good way to get around Ketchikan. A 2½-mile bike trail runs along the water to Saxman, stopping a few blocks short of the totem pole park there, and another goes north 6.4 miles to the Ward Lake Recreation Area. **The Pedalers,** on Spruce Mill Way, near the Southeast Alaska Discovery visitors center (☎ **907/225-0440**), rents bikes for $6 an hour or $25 a day. If you rent two bikes for the day, they'll deliver them to you.

BY BOAT & SEA KAYAK Harbor cruises are available from **Alaska Cruises** (☎ **800/228-1905** or 907/225-6044) at $50 for a ride lasting 60 to 90 minutes. A sea kayak gets you closer to the watery part of the city and the marine life of the surrounding area. **Southeast Exposure** (☎ **907/225-8829**) offers a 3½-hour tour, no experience necessary, for $50. They also rent bikes.

Visitor Information

The **Southeast Alaska Discovery Center,** 50 Main St., Ketchikan, AK 99901 (☎ **907/228-6220** or 907/288-6237 TDD; fax 907/228-6234; www.nps.gov/aplic), is much more than a visitor center. Housed in a large, attractive building of log and concrete a block from the cruise-ship dock, the center contains an exceptional museum of the region's natural and cultural history and contemporary society. Curators have managed to tell the truth without offending either side in the community's hot debate over logging and the environment. There's also an auditorium showing a high-tech slide show. Admission to those facilities costs $4 in summer, free in winter. Without paying, you can get guidance about planning your time and activities in the outdoors. An information kiosk and bookstore are located near the entrance, and downstairs you'll find a trip-planning room that contains information about outdoor pursuits all around the state, a luxurious library of material in various media, and an information desk where you can ask questions and get help on the details. The center is open May to September daily 8am to 5pm, October to April Tuesday to Saturday from 8:30am to 4:30pm.

You can reach the Forest Service through the **Ketchikan Ranger District,** at 3031 North Tongass Ave., Ketchikan, AK 99901 (☎ **907/225-2148;** www.fs.fed.us/r10/tongass).

The **Ketchikan Visitors Bureau,** 131 Front St. (at Mission Street), Ketchikan, AK 99901 (☎ **800/770-2200** or 907/225-6166; fax 907/225-4250; www.visit-ketchikan.com), stands right on the cruise-ship dock, offering town information and booths where tourism businesses sell their wares, including tickets for tours. The center is open daily in the summer from 8am to 5pm and when cruise ships are in town; weekdays only in winter.

The **Ketchikan Chamber of Commerce** (☎ **907/225-3184;** www.ketchikanchamber.com) has links to virtually every business in town on its useful Web site.

SPECIAL EVENTS

There's a detailed **events calendar** on the Web at **www.ketchikanchamber.com/calyear.html**.

Celebration of the Sea, a 10-day event beginning around the first of May, includes a variety of art, music, and community events; you can get a schedule from the Ketchikan Visitors Bureau. The Chamber-sponsored **King Salmon Derby,** a 50-year-old tradition, takes place at the end of May and the beginning of June.

The Fourth of July celebration is huge, with a long parade watched on Front Street by mobs of locals and cruise-ship passengers. After the parade, there's a **Timber Carnival** with an all-afternoon loggers' competition at the baseball field near City Park on Park Avenue; admission is free.

The Blueberry Arts Festival, held the second Saturday of August, has booths, music, and food, and is put on by the Ketchikan Area Arts and Humanities Council, 338 Main St. (☎ **907/225-2211;** www.ketchikanarts.org/). Check with the council for winter performing arts events, too.

FAST FACTS: KETCHIKAN

Several **banks** have ATMs, including the one at 306 Main St., as do grocery stores and the Salmon Landing Market.

Ketchikan General Hospital is at 3100 Tongass Ave. (☎ **907/225-5171**).

Cyber-by-the-Sea (☎ **907/247-6904;** www.cyberbythesea.com), at 5 Salmon Landing, offers Internet access via Mac, PC, or WebTV in a light, trendy room. There's a $6 minimum charge, or $10 per hour.

If you need the **police,** call ☎ **907/225-6631** for nonemergencies.

The main **post office** is at 3609 Tongass Ave. A more convenient downtown substation is at the Great Alaska Clothing Company, 422 Mission St.

Sales tax is 5.5%. Room taxes for accommodations total 11.5%.

EXPLORING KETCHIKAN

Schoolteacher Lois Munch, of **Classic Tours** (☎ **907/225-3091;** www.classictours.com), makes her tours fun: She wears a poodle skirt to drive visitors around in her '55 Chevy. A 2-hour tour to the Saxman totem poles is $50; a 3-hour tour adds a natural history stop and costs $65. Rates are per person and include the admission to Saxman. The maximum group size is five. Check at the town visitor center for many more choices; tour companies sell wares from booths there.

TLINGIT, HAIDA & TSIMSHIAN CULTURAL HERITAGE

The Ketchikan area has two totem pole parks and a totem pole museum, as well as a wealth of contemporary Native art displayed all over town. Notable pieces stand at

Whale Park at Mission and Bawden streets and at the Westmark Cape Fox Lodge. Most of what you see in Southeast Alaska is Tlingit—the Haida and Tsimshian generally live to the south and east in British Columbia—but Ketchikan is near the boundary between the three peoples, so their similar cultures mix here.

Totem Heritage Center. 601 Deermount St. ☎ **907/225-5900.** Admission $4 in summer, free in winter. Summer daily 8am–5pm; winter Mon–Fri 1–5pm.

Located near City Park, the center contains the largest collection of original 19th-century totem poles in existence. The poles are displayed indoors, mostly unpainted, many with the grass and moss still attached where they were when the poles were rescued from the elements in villages where they had been mounted up to 160 years ago. Totem poles were never meant to be maintained or repainted—they generally disintegrate after about 70 years, and were constantly replaced—but these were preserved to help keep the culture alive. A high ceiling and muted lighting lend to the spiritual grandeur of the art. Well-trained guides are on hand to explain what you're looking at, and there are good interpretive signs. The gift shop carries authentic Native crafts in the summer.

✪ **Totem Bight State Historical Park.** 10 miles out of town on N. Tongass Hwy. Ketchikan Ranger Station, 9883 N. Tongass Hwy. ☎ **907/247-8574.** www.dnr.state.ak.us/parks/units/totembgh.htm.

The park presents poles and a clan house carved beginning in 1938 by elders working with traditional tools to copy fragments of historic poles that had mostly rotted away. The project, funded by the New Deal's Civilian Conservation Corps, helped save a Tlingit culture that had been essentially outlawed until that time. The setting, the site of a traditional fish camp, is a peaceful spot on the edge of Tongass Narrows, at the end of a short walk through the woods, so the experience is both aesthetic and educational. The park also stands out for its excellent interpretive signs and a printed guide and Web site that explain what you're looking at.

Saxman Native Village Totem Pole Park. In Saxman, 2½ miles south of Ketchikan on the S. Tongass Hwy. ☎ **907/225-4421** for tour times and tickets. Admission $30 adults, $15 children 12 and under.

Saxman's park has artifacts similar to those at Totem Bight park, but with an added resource: Accomplished carvers are still at work here in the building to the right of the park, and the Native corporation that owns the park puts on tours. The drawback of the site for independent travelers is that Cape Fox Corp. caters mainly to cruise-ship passengers, and no interpretive material is available other than its 2-hour tour. The tour includes a visit to the clan house for a short performance of a Tlingit legend and a demonstration of traditional dance and song by the Cape Fox Dancers, and a visit to the carving center to see work in progress. If you want those elements, be sure to buy your ticket from Cape Fox, as others sell tours to the park that don't go inside. The tour schedule is different each day, depending on the ships.

A Stroll Through Town

Get the clearly presented *Official Historic Ketchikan Walking Tour Map* free from the visitor center; its three routes cover everything of interest downtown. Here are the highlights.

Creek Street was Ketchikan's red-light district until fairly recently. Now its quaint, meandering boardwalks are a tourist attraction thronged with visitors. Prostitution was semilegal in Alaska until 1952, recently enough to survive in local memories but distant enough from life today to have made Creek Street historic and to transform the women who worked there from outcasts to icons. Dolly Arthur, who started in business for herself on the creek in 1919 and died in 1975, lived through both eras, and her home became a commercial museum not long after her death. **Dolly's House** is amusing, mildly racy, and a little sad. Admission is $4; it's open 9am to 4pm during the summer and when cruise ships are in town.

Creek Street has some interesting shops, described below, but it's fun mostly just for a walk on the creek-side boardwalk, into the forest above, and over the "Married Men's Trail"—a discreet way for married men to reach the red-light district—through the woods from the street to where the Westmark Cape Fox Lodge now stands. **The Cape Fox Hill–Creek Street Funicular** (known as "the tram"), a sort of diagonal elevator, also runs 211 feet from the boardwalk up to the Westmark Cape Fox Lodge on top of the hill. Take it up and then enjoy the walk down through the woods. The summertime fare is $1, but if no one is around, just press the "up" button and go.

If you need a place to recharge, stop at the attractively situated **Ketchikan Public Library,** 629 Dock St. Its big windows look out on the foaming rapids, and the children's section downstairs has a play area with lots of toys. In the same building is the **Tongass Historical Museum** (☎ **907/225-5600**), a one-room museum that presents the history and Native heritage of Ketchikan, along with an annually revolving exhibit. Although it's too small to hold your attention for long, its contents are informatively displayed. It's open daily 8am to 5pm in the summer; Wednesday to Saturday afternoons in the winter. Admission is $2. The library is open Monday to Wednesday from 10am to 8pm, Thursday through Saturday from 10am to 6pm, and on Sunday from 1 to 5pm.

Following the creek upstream, take a look at the **fish ladder** at the Park Avenue bridge, then continue to the **Deer Mountain Tribal Hatchery,** 1158 Salmon Rd. (☎ **907/225-6760**), a small king and silver salmon hatchery where you can see fry swimming in large tubs and even feed them. The hatchery is combined with the educational **Eagle Center,** which exhibits captive bald eagles and other raptors. Besides the indoor cages, there's a large outdoor eagle enclosure that takes in some trees and a section of the salmon stream. Visitors can go inside, a perfect setting for photos; when we visited, an eagle perched just 10 feet away. The birds are flightless or otherwise injured, some of them from Sitka's Alaska Raptor Rehabilitation Center, which is a sort of bird hospital. The center and hatchery are open in summer daily 8:30am to 4:30pm, in winter only by arrangement. Admission is $6.95.

Beyond the hatchery is **City Park,** where Ketchikan Creek splits into a maze of ornamental pools and streams once used as a hatchery; my young son and I found it a magical place. The Totem Heritage Center, listed above, opens on the park. Continuing past the center to Deermount Street, you round the hill back to the waterfront. Turn right on Stedman, past the Thomas Basin boat harbor, to the starting point.

The brand-new **Great Alaskan Lumberjack Show,** behind the Alaska Discovery Center (☎ **888/320-9049;** www.lumberjackshow.com/alaska.html) is put on by a nationally touring team based in Wisconsin that does lumberjack stunts and competitions. Tickets are $29 adults, half price ages 5 to 12. Times vary, so call ahead or check the Web site.

SHOPPING

Ketchikan has become a shopping and art destination thanks to the explosion of visitors. If you want something authentically Alaskan, however, you have to be careful. For some important tips, see "Native Art—Finding the Real Thing," in chapter 2.

Soho Coho, at 5 Creek St., is worth a visit even if you aren't a shopper. Owner Ray Troll is Alaska's leading fish-obsessed artist. His gallery shows his work and that of other Ketchikan artists from the same school of surreal rain forest humor. In Troll's art, subtle ironies and silly puns coexist in a solidly decorated interior world. T-shirts are his most popular canvas; "Spawn Till You Die" is a classic. Troll displays his art on a gorgeous Web site at www.trollart.com. The gallery is open summer daily from 9am to 6pm; winter, Wednesday to Saturday 11am to 5:30pm, Sunday 11am to 4pm.

Adjacent to Soho Coho, **Alaska Eagle Arts** is a serious gallery featuring the bold yet traditional work of Native artist Marvin Oliver. Upstairs, stop in at **Parnassus Books,** a cubbyhole with a broad and sophisticated selection of Alaskana, great for browsing.

Down the boardwalk at 18 Creek St., expert craftsmen create indigenous art and interact with visitors at **Hide-A-Way Gifts,** which carries carvings and Native crafts.

At 123 Stedman St., near the bridge over the creek, **Blue Heron Gallery and Gifts** (☎ **907/225-1982**) carries Alaska arts and crafts that appeal to locals as well as visitors: jewelry, stained glass, clothing, jam, prints, and so on.

The Wood Shop, at 632 Park, on the way to the hatchery and City Park, sells wonderful wooden toys, jewelry, and other underpriced crafts made and sold by participants in a program for the mentally ill.

The **Salmon Landing Market,** on the waterfront, contains several shops of potential interest, including **Fairweather Prints,** an outdoor gear store, an Internet cafe, and **The Edge,** a popular espresso shop.

On the city streets near the cruise-ship dock, check out **Scanlon Gallery,** at 318 Mission St., which carries Alaska contemporary art, Alaska Native art, and affordable prints and other items in various media. **Exploration Galley,** 633 Mission St., uniquely specializes in antique maps, and also carries pottery and Native art. The varied inventory is a nice break from the sameness you'll see in most of the shops. The Ketchikan Arts and Humanities Council operates the **Main Street Gallery,** at 338 Main St. (www.ketchikanarts.org/mainstreetgallery.html), with shows by Alaska artists changing monthly.

On Mission Street, try the local chocolate and beer. **Ketchikan Brewing Company,** 607 Mission, brews right in the storefront, and offers free samples to adults. They don't have a bottling operation, however, so you can only buy it by the half gallon jug or order on tap at local bars. **KetchiCandies,** at 315 Mission St., caters to visitors and the many locals addicted to their homemade chocolates and other candies.

GETTING OUTSIDE

There's lots to do outdoors around Ketchikan, but most of it will require a boat or plane; drive-by attractions are limited. See the sections on Misty Fjords National Monument and Prince of Wales Island (both later in this chapter) for more day-trip options. In any event, your first stop should be the trip-planning room at the Southeast Alaska Discovery Center (see "Visitor Information," near the beginning of the Ketchikan section), where a forest ranger can provide detailed information on trails, fishing, and dozens of available U.S. Forest Service cabins.

SPECIAL PLACES

REMOTE CABINS The U.S. Forest Service maintains more than 50 **cabins** around Ketchikan; all are remote and primitive, but at $25 to $45 a night, you can't beat the price or the settings. This is a chance to be utterly alone in the wilderness; many of the lake cabins come with a boat for fishing and exploring. For details and descriptions of all the cabins, contact the **Southeast Alaska Discovery Center**

(☎ **907/228-6214;** www.fs.fed.us/r10/tongass). The reservation system to use when you're actually ready to book a cabin is described in "Getting Outside in the Tongass National Forest" in section 1 of this chapter.

You'll need all your camping gear except a tent, including sleeping bags, a camp stove, and your own cooking outfit, a lantern, and so on. **Alaska Wilderness Outfitting and Camping Rentals,** 3857 Fairview St. (☎ **907/225-7335;** www.latitude56.com/camping/index.html), rents some of the gear you need, as well as small outboards for the skiffs, and will even take care of your grocery shopping. They don't rent sleeping bags and some other necessities. (The same folks have a water taxi, kayak delivery, and charter service called **Experience One Charters,** listed below in the Misty Fjords section of this chapter.)

The cabins are remote. You can hike or take a boat to some of them, but most are accessible only by floatplane. Expect to pay around $300 an hour for a three-passenger Cessna 185, $450 or more for a five-passenger DeHavilland Beaver, for a plane to drop you off and go back and get you when you're ready to come out. The weight of your gear will determine how many people can ride in the plane. **Island Wings Air Service,** 1285 Tongass Ave. (☎ **888/854-2444** or 907/225-2444; www.islandwings.com), a well-regarded two-plane operation, offers flat round-trip fares ($225 to $400 per person) to each of the cabins, with a list on their informative Web site. They also welcome calls to help visitors figure out where to go and how to set up the trip.

SCENIC TRAILS The **Ward Lake Nature Trail** circles 1.3 miles around a smooth lake among old-growth Sitka spruce large enough to put you in your place. Ward Creek has steelhead and cutthroat trout, Dolly Varden char, and silver salmon; check current regulations before fishing. To reach the trail, campgrounds, and picnic area, travel about 7 miles out North Tongass Highway and turn right on Revilla Road just before the sawmill.

For a slightly more challenging hike, **Perseverance Lake Trail** climbs up boardwalks with steps from the CCC campground, 1.4 miles up the road, to another lake 2.3 miles away.

Deer Mountain Trail can be a challenging overnight trek, starting only half a mile from Ketchikan, but most people instead use it for a scenic day hike. There are dramatic views 1 mile up the trail and at the summit, which comes after a 2½-mile, 3,000-foot climb. The trail continues through the mountains from there, to the Deer Mountain Forest Service cabin, across another summit, through some summer snow and ice, and ends at another trailhead 10 miles away. The main trailhead is ½ mile up Ketchikan Lakes Road. Pick up a trail guide sheet from the Forest Service at the Southeast Alaska Discovery Center.

Outdoor Activities

FISHING The **Alaska Department of Fish and Game,** 1255 W. Eighth St. (P.O. Box 25526), Juneau, AK 99802-5526 (☎ **907/465-4180;** www.state.ak.us/local/akpages/FISH.GAME/adfghome.htm), produces a 24-page fishing guide to Ketchikan, with details on where to find fish in both fresh- and saltwater, listing 17 spots accessible from the roads. You can also pick up a copy at the Southeast Alaska Discovery Center. For licenses and other help, the local **Fish and Game office** is at 2030 Sea Level Dr., Suite 205, Ketchikan, AK 99901 (☎ **907/225-2859**).

Guided fishing charters can get out on the water for salmon and halibut, and bareboat rental also is available. The Ketchikan Visitors Bureau or Chamber of Commerce can put you in contact with an operator. A day-long guided charter costs around $200 per person, half day about $130. If you want to devote your time in Ketchikan to fishing, check out the fishing lodges listed below.

SEA KAYAKING The islands, coves, and channels around Ketchikan create protected waters rich with life and welcoming for exploration by kayak. Any reasonably fit adult can enjoy a kayaking outing. **Southeast Exposure,** 515 Water St. (☎ **907/225-8829;** www.southeastexposure.com/), rents kayaks and guides trips. Their harbor tour lasts 2½ hours and costs $50. A 6-day trip is $950 per person. They'll put together a special trip for groups of three or more, including longer day trips.

ACCOMMODATIONS

In addition to the hotels and B&Bs listed below, the **Ketchikan Reservation Service,** 412 D-1 Loop Rd., Ketchikan, AK 99901 (☎ **800/987-5337** or phone/fax 907/247-5337; www.ketchikan-lodging.com), books many bed-and-breakfasts and outfitted apartments.

EXPENSIVE

Best Western Landing. 3434 Tongass Ave., Ketchikan, AK 99901. ☎ **800/428-8304** or 907/225-5166. Fax 907/225-6900. www.landinghotel.com. 75 units, 1 2-bedroom apt. TV TEL. High season $120–$130 double; $155 suite. Low season $90–$110 double; $110 suite. Year-round $200 apt. AE, CB, DC, DISC, MC, V.

This is a well-run, regularly remodeled establishment with a wide variety of rooms, from simple hotel rooms to a two-bedroom apartment. The best are in the new wing, but all have microwave ovens, refrigerators, coffeemakers, and hair dryers. The location, right across from the ferry dock, is distant from the downtown sights, so you'll need to rent a car or use the courtesy van, which runs back and forth regularly.

The hotel has a traditional **family restaurant** with something for everyone on the menu. Dinner entrees range from $11 to $26. Hours are 6am to 9pm off-season, until 10pm in summer. Drinks are available from **Jeremiah's** bar, upstairs, which serves a somewhat more sophisticated menu of Italian dishes and bar food. Smoking and no-smoking areas each have their own fireplace, and there's a deck overlooking the water across the highway.

Salmon Falls Resort. 16707 N. Tongass Hwy. (P.O. Box 5700), Ketchikan, AK 99901. ☎ **800/247-9059** (reservations) or 907/225-2752. Fax 907/225-2710. www.salmonfallsresort.net. 52 units. TEL. $139 double. Extra person $10. MC, V. Closed Sept 15–May 15.

This huge fishing lodge has its own waterfall where silver salmon spawn in August, as well as a dock on Clover Passage with boats for all the guests. Inclusive fishing packages start at $900 per person, double occupancy, for a 3-day stay with 2 days on the water, self-guided. With a guide, the price is $1,300 per person. The lodge is on the Tongass Highway 16.7 miles north of town, so you save the cost of flying to a comparable lodge off the island. The rooms are comfortable and well decorated; the new building is best.

But it's the restaurant and bar that are really amazing: a massive log octagon held up in the center by a section of the Alaska pipeline, with great views from all tables and a well-prepared menu of steak and seafood ranging from $18 to $29. It's worth a drive out the road for dinner, even if you aren't staying here.

✪ **Westmark Cape Fox Lodge.** 800 Venetia Way, Ketchikan, AK 99901. ☎ **800/544-0970** (central reservations) or 907/225-8001. Fax 907/225-8286. www.westmarkhotels.com. 72 units. TV TEL. High season $159–$169 double. Low season $129–$139 double. Year-round $200 suite. AE, DC, DISC, MC, V.

This is the most beautiful hotel in Southeast Alaska. It's owned by the Cape Fox Native corporation and run by the Westmark chain. The hotel's understated but inspired design and masterpieces of Tlingit art lend a sense of the peace and spirit of the rain forest. All but a dozen rooms share Ketchikan's most spectacular view, looking out among huge trees over the edge of a cliff that dominates the city and waterfront (rooms on the opposite side are $10 less). To get down the cliff merely requires stepping aboard the Creek Street funicular, which drops you in the middle of the town's most charming and popular tourist area. Even if you can't afford to stay, the elegance and view are worth a visit. Rooms have coffeemakers, clock radios, and double phone jacks, and suites are furnished with quilts and other homey features.

The **Heen Kahidi** restaurant shares the wonderful view, and the food is generally good, placing it among the best in the less-than-stellar field of Ketchikan's restaurants. Lunch entrees are around $10, and dinner $18 to $32.

MODERATE

Blueberry Hill B&B. 500 Upper Front St. (P.O. Box 9508), Ketchikan, AK 99901. ☎ **877/449-2583** or 907/247-2583. Fax 907/247-2584. www.ptialaska.net/~blubrry. 4 units. TEL. High season $85–$100 double; $125 suite. Extra person $25. Rates include full breakfast. AE, DISC, MC, V. Closed in winter.

This gracious 1917 house, once a residence for nuns, stands atop the rocky cliff that bounds the north side of the downtown waterfront, above the tunnel. It's a short drive, or 115 steps down a public stairway, to the center of the action; but up here all is peaceful in common rooms with high ceilings and stately dimensions and trim. Each of the guest rooms also is large and light, with handmade quilts and crisp, elegant furnishings. No smoking.

Edgewater Bed and Breakfast. 2070 S. Tongass Hwy. (P.O. Box 9302), Ketchikan, AK 99901. ☎ **907/247-3343.** Fax 907/247-3343. www.edgewaterbb.com. 4 units. TV TEL. $100–$125 double; $150 suite. Rates include continental breakfast. MC, V.

On the coastal bike trail about 1½ miles south of town, the rooms at this new B&B are reached from private entrances on wraparound decks right on Tongass Narrows. Guests can fish from their front doors, freezing the catch for later or cooking it up right there on the barbecue. You can watch eagles at their nest out your window, part of the close-up waterfront view. The large common room includes a full stocked kitchen for guests' use, and there are free laundry facilities. It's possible to use a bike for transportation while based here, but having a car would be a major plus.

The Narrows Inn. 4871 N. Tongass Hwy. (P.O. Box 8296), Ketchikan, AK 99901. ☎ **888/686-2600** or 907/247-2600. Fax 907/247-2602. www.narrowsinn.com. 44 units. TV TEL. High season $95–$129 double. Low season $79 double. Extra person $10. AE, CB, DC, DISC, MC, V.

It's on the water near a boat dock 1½ miles north of the ferry terminal, so you'll want to rent a car if staying here, but these fresh, waterfront accommodations could make staying here worthwhile. The rooms and bathrooms in the two-story motel-style buildings are small, but they're clean and light, and have natural woodwork; some have private balconies. The inn will book fishing trips that leave from its own small marina below the riprap shore.

The **Narrows Inn Restaurant** serves a steak and seafood menu, with dinner entrees generally near $20, and all the usual American choices for lunch. Meals are hearty and consistently good. The dining room is spacious and bright with its ocean frontage, but doesn't have the character or style fitting the fine-dining menu and prices.

INEXPENSIVE

Captain's Quarters Bed & Breakfast. 325 Lund St., Ketchikan, AK 99901. ☎ **907/225-4912.** Fax 907/225-4912. www.ptialaska.net/~captbnb. 3 units. TV TEL. High season $85 double. Low season $69 double. Extra person $20. Rates include continental breakfast. MC, V. No children allowed.

These large, quiet rooms, with sweeping views of the city and ocean, and a self-contained, self-service breakfast room, rival the best hotel rooms in Ketchikan, but cost half as much. A nautical theme carries through with oak woodwork. One room has a full kitchen. The house is perched in a mountainside neighborhood just north of the tunnel where half the streets are stairs. It's a reasonable walk from downtown. There's no smoking in the house.

Gilmore Hotel. 326 Front St., Ketchikan, AK 99901. ☎ **800/275-9423** or 907/225-9423. Fax 907/225-7442. www.gilmorehotel.com. 40 units. TV TEL. High season $72–$85 double; $129 suite. Low season $58–$68 double; $105 suite. Extra person $5. AE, CB, DC, DISC, MC, V.

This 1927 concrete structure on the waterfront tries for a historic feel to match the high ceilings, dignified facade, and views over the cruise-ship dock. The front rooms are the most desirable, while some others are tiny nearly to the point of claustrophobia. About two-thirds have shower stalls in the bathrooms, while the balance have shower-tub combinations. The service and style—including the courtesy van, room service, and free coffee in the lobby—suggest a more expensive place.

Annabelle's Famous Keg and Chowder House, the hotel restaurant, serves a good steak and seafood menu, with entrees ranging from $18 to $49 (most dishes are around $25). The dining room is well appointed in a lavish turn-of-the-century style, with nicely spaced tables on a floral carpet. The mahogany and brass continues into the bar, where you will find many lunch and dinner choices of pasta, seafood, sandwiches, and salads for around $10.

✪ **New York Hotel.** 207 Stedman St., Ketchikan, AK 99901. ☎ **907/225-0246.** 8 units. TV TEL. High season $69–$79 double. Low season $39–$59 double. Rates include continental breakfast. AE, MC, V.

This funny little 1924 building, in a perfect central location just off Creek Street, contains charming, antique-furnished rooms that look out on a small boat harbor. The rooms have more attractive amenities than other hotels in town that cost much more, and were sparkling clean when I visited. The tasteful 1991 restoration of the New York saved the building, now on the National Register of Historic Places, while keeping its quirks and charms—including the tiny lobby and narrow stairs.

The attached **New York Café** serves inexpensive food in a bright little room containing a perfect restoration of an old-fashioned lunch counter. Huge windows and a high ceiling pour light onto the black-and-white tiled floor. It can be smoky, and currently is open only in the summer. Lunch prices range from $5 to $8; dinner entrees are about $15 to $20.

A Hostel

First United Methodist Church. 400 Main St. (P.O. Box 8515), Ketchikan, AK 99901. ☎ **907/225-3319.** www.hiayh.org/ushostel/islreg/ketchi.htm. 23 beds. $10 per person. Closed Sept–May.

Open only June through August, this church-run hostel, affiliated with Hostelling International, is 1 block up hill from the tunnel in the downtown area. Free pastries and hot drinks are provided, and guests have use of the church kitchen. Bring a sleeping bag. The office is open from 7 to 9am and 6 to 11pm.

CAMPING

Three Forest Service campgrounds with a total of 47 sites are located at **Ward Lake** (see "Special Places," above). A salmon stream runs through the middle of the lakeside Signal Creek Campground, which, along with the Last Chance Campground, can be reserved through the national system described in "Getting Outside in the Tongass National Forest," in section 1 of this chapter.

Eighteen miles out North Tongass Highway, the **Settler's Cove State Park** includes a sandy beach (a good place to watch whales, beachcomb, or even swim) and the 1-mile Lunch Falls Loop Trail, a handicapped-accessible path to a spectacular waterfall. There are 14 campsites, half of which will take rigs of up to 30 feet, without hookups. Camping costs $10 a night. For information, contact the **Alaska Division of Parks** (☎ **907/247-8574**), 9883 N. Tongass Hwy.

If you need hookups for an RV, try **Clover Pass Resort,** about 13 miles north of the ferry terminal on North Point Higgins Road (☎ **800/410-2234** outside Alaska only, or 907/247-2234). They charge $26 a night.

DINING

Ketchikan lacks memorable restaurants. The hotels house the best restaurants, which I've described under "Accommodations," above, specifically in the Westmark Cape Fox Lodge, Gilmore Hotel, Salmon Falls Resort, The Narrows Inn, Best Western Landing, and New York Hotel listings.

The local favorite espresso place is **The Edge,** at 5 Salmon Landing Market, in an airy water-view corner space (☎ **907/225-1465**), where people gather on comfy furniture around a coffee table for hot drinks, bagels, and pastries. They also have traditional tables and chairs.

Ocean View Restaurante. 3159 Tongass Ave. ☎ **907/225-7566.** Lunch $6–$9; dinner $8–$17. MC, V. Daily 11am–11pm. MEXICAN/ITALIAN.

Off the usual tourist path, ¼ mile south of the ferry terminal, this bustling family restaurant packs in the locals by doing many things well: steak and seafood, sizzling fajitas and other Mexican dishes, submarine sandwiches, pizza, pasta, and even Greek appetizers. The smoke-free dining rooms are small, making reservations a wise move during rush hours, but there's nothing fancy about the place. The reasonable prices make meals here the best deal in town, with few entrees over $14. Bowls of chips and salsa hit the Formica table as soon you sit down. The pizza, delivered free, is the best in town. They do not have a liquor license.

Polar Treats. 410 Mission St. ☎ **907/247-6527.** Lunch $5–$6.50. MC, V. High season daily 7am–9pm. Low season Mon–Sat 7am–5pm. DELI/WRAPS.

The chairs are plastic and the tableware disposable, but if you're looking for a quick, inexpensive, and delicious lunch break while sightseeing, you'll do no better. The wraps are huge, messy, and flavorful, with wonderfully exotic combinations of ingredients. The panini and other sandwiches are good, too. At least stop in for the hand-packed ice cream. There are only four tables and a lunch counter, so much of the business is takeout or delivered.

Steamers. 76 Front St. ☎ **907/225-1600.** Average complete lunch $10; average complete dinner $17–$50. AE, DC, DISC, MC, V. Daily 11am–11pm. STEAK/SEAFOOD.

On the third floor right on the dock (take the corner elevator to the top), this huge bar and grill tries for a Seattle feel, with 20 beers on tap and a complete menu of seafood and beef, available as full dinners or à la carte. Dinner prices demand this be a place for a special meal—a fish-and-chips dinner is $17, and you can easily spend more than $50 per person; lunches are around $10. Each meal I've had here has been nicely seasoned and done to perfection—fish grilled not a moment too long. The bright dining room of light oak has towering ceilings and huge windows, with tables well separated; service was professional. They have live music during the day in the high season.

NIGHTLIFE

Historically, Ketchikan has been a hard-drinking town. Trap doors remain in the floors of some Creek Street buildings where bootleggers would pass booze up from boats underneath. The bars on Front Street are generally authentic waterfront places: dark gritty rooms where you can meet commercial fishermen and other locals. **Annabelle's** is a more genteel, refurbished version of an old-fashioned Front Street bar. **Steamers,** described under "Dining," above, has a comfortable bar with live music and a great view. Bowling, live music, and ball games on TV, as well as meals and drinks, are available at the **Roller Bay Cafe,** at 2050 Sealevel Dr.

3 Misty Fjords National Monument

Among the vast, uninhabited islands, bottomless bays and fjords, massive trees, and inconceivably towering cliffs of the southern Alaska Panhandle are 2.3 million acres of inviolate wilderness, which Pres. Jimmy Carter set aside as a national monument with a stroke of his pen in 1978. It's still waiting to be discovered. There are sheer cliffs as high as Yosemite Valley's that rise straight from remote Punchbowl Cove, where only those fortunate enough to explore by boat, kayak, or floatplane are likely to see them. There's no question that this land, larger than Yellowstone National Park, qualifies scenically as among America's greatest wild places—and without roads or trails it feels more like a great national park a century ago than the busy places we know now. Here, a seemingly endless untouched wilderness forces you to admit that your own imagination is sadly puny by comparison with its huge trees and extraordinary geology.

As with all uncrowded places, access to Misty Fjords is rationed, in this case by cost. There's no cheap way to see the bulk of the monument; the only practical way to get there is by boat or floatplane. The only places to stay are 14 rustic U.S. Forest Service cabins. The most popular way to see the monument is on a tour boat from Ketchikan. The monument is also a good place for sea kayaking—that's how the backcountry Forest Service rangers get around.

There are several noteworthy places to see. **New Eddystone Rock,** standing in the middle of Behm Canal, is a 237-foot-tall exclamation point of weathered rock, the remaining lava plug from an eroded volcano. **Rudyerd Bay** is like a place where the earth shattered open: The cliffs in its Punchbowl Cove rise vertically 3,150 feet from the surface of water that's 900 feet deep—topography in a league with the Grand Canyon. Waterfalls pound down out of the bay's granite. The **glaciers** of the northern part of the monument also are impressive, although they require a plane to visit.

Don't go to Misty Fjords to see animals. You may see harbor seals, but here the attraction is the land itself and its outrageous geology. Also, the name is accurate: It's misty. Or it could be pouring rain. This is among the rainiest spots on earth.

ESSENTIALS

GETTING THERE

BY BOAT The most affordable way to see the fjords is to go on one of the tour boat excursions offered by Ketchikan operators. The largest and most experienced of these is **Alaska Cruises,** owned by Juneau's Goldbelt Native corporation, 220 Front St., Ketchikan (☎ **800/228-1905** or 907/225-6044; www.goldbelttours.com). They run a high-speed, 92-passenger catamaran on daily daylong trips out to Rudyerd Bay and back. Most passengers take the boat 4 hours one way, then fly 20 minutes back to Ketchikan on a floatplane, seeing the same amazing scenery from the air. The tour travels up the Behm Canal, past New Eddystone Rock, then drifts through Punchbowl Cove before finally coming to a floating dock at the head of Rudyerd Bay, where passengers board the floatplanes. (This controversial dock currently has no permit to be here, so the situation could change.) The fare is $198 for adults, $160 for children 2 to 11. If you take the boat both ways, you'll hear the narration twice, but you'll pay only $145 ($115 for kids). They serve a continental breakfast on the outbound trip, snacks and chowder on the way back. If you're susceptible to seasickness, try to have an alternative date set aside to go in case of bad weather; the water is generally smooth in the fjords but rough on the way there. (Take your Dramamine *before* you set out; once you're underway, it's generally too late.) They drop off kayakers, too (see "By Kayak," below).

If you have a larger group, consider a private charter, of which many are available in Ketchikan. **Experience One Charters,** 3857 Fairview, Ketchikan (☎ **907/225-7335;** www.latitude56.com), takes groups of up to 16 to Misty Fjords on a vessel and itinerary you control. It's quite expensive, however, because you must pay for a minimum of 8 to 10 passengers, at $200 to $275 each. They also haul kayaks for groups and specialize in outfitting visits to Forest Service cabins.

BY KAYAK There are few more spectacular places for overnight kayak expeditions. If you have only a few days, concentrate on Rudyerd Bay. Don't miss Punchbowl Cove or the trail to Punchbowl Lake, where there is a shelter and good camping, or a trail and shelter at Nooya Lake. Both lakes have public rowing skiffs. The Forest Service produces useful **Recreation Opportunity Guides** for Misty Fjords and other areas around Ketchikan.

Southeast Exposure, 507 Stedman St., Ketchikan (☎ **907/225-8829;** www.southeastexposure.com), offers guided trips to the monument, starting at 4 days for $700 per person. They also rent kayaks for $30 to $50 a day; a 90-minute training class is mandatory.

I don't recommend an unguided trip deep into the fjords for first-time kayakers, but I can't imagine a more appealing destination for experienced paddlers. **Alaska Cruises** (see "By Boat," above) drops off or picks up kayakers at Rudyerd Bay for $200 per person. Larger groups can charter a boat, gaining the advantage of a choice of drop-off points. **Experience One Charters** (see "By Boat," above) offers that service and rents camping equipment.

BY PLANE You can cover a lot more ground a lot faster this way, and flying over the cliffs, trees, and glaciers is an experience all its own. Several air-taxi operators in Ketchikan take flightseeing day trips or drop clients at remote places. You can also use them to get to a remote cabin (see below) or other outings in the area. **Island Wings Air Service,** 1285 Tongass Ave., Ketchikan (☎ **888/854-2444** or 907/225-2444; www.islandwings.com), is one such operator. They charge $149 per person for a 2-hour flight that includes 45 minutes on the ground at the Fjords. They also can help you plan a custom trip.

ON FOOT The tiny town of **Hyder** is 18 miles by trail from Misty Fjords, but it's at the end of the long Portland Canal, so most of the monument is not readily accessible from there. There's an opportunity to **watch black and brown bears feeding from a Forest Service platform on Fish Creek**—the most unregulated, accessible bear viewing in the state—and the area has good birding. Hyder can be reached by the Cassiar Highway from British Columbia.

Visitor Information

The **Southeast Alaska Discovery Center,** 50 Main St., Ketchikan, AK 99901 (☎ **907/228-6220;** www.nps.gov/aplic), can give you a trip-planning packet about Misty Fjords. Get the names of charter operators from the **Ketchikan Visitors**

Bureau, 131 Front St. (at Mission Street), Ketchikan, AK 99901 (☎ **800/770-2200** or 907/225-6166; fax 907/225-4250; www.visit-ketchikan.com).

The monument is part of the Tongass National Forest, and that agency is the best source of information before you travel. **Misty Fiords National Monument offices** are at the U.S. Forest Service Ketchikan Ranger District, 3031 Tongass Ave., Ketchikan, AK 99901 (☎ **907/225-2148;** www.fs.fed.us/r10/tongass).

ACCOMMODATIONS

The only lodgings are 14 **U.S. Forest Service cabins** and several three-sided shelters. Many are little used and extremely remote, and all those on lakes come with their own rowboats.

The cabins cost $25 to $45 per night, but that's only a small part of the cost of using them. You also have to pay for a floatplane (about $300 to $450 an hour) to take you there and back. I've listed the names of air-taxi and gear-rental operators in "Getting Outside," in section 2 of this chapter.

Winstanley Island Cabin is a good destination for kayakers, and there's a chance of seeing bears. **Big Goat Lake Cabin** overlooks an alpine lake near a 1,700-foot waterfall; it's accessible only by plane, and because it's so beautiful, a lot of plane traffic comes by. **Ella Lake** is relatively near Ketchikan—so it's a shorter, cheaper trip to get there—but it's still very secluded. You can fly to it, or take a boat to a 2.3-mile hiking trail to the lake, then row across the lake to the cabin. Right off Rudyerd Bay, beautiful **Nooya Lake** has a three-sided shelter.

These are just highlights; for a complete listing of cabins, contact the Forest Service or check its Web site. For reservation information, see "Getting Outside in the Tongass National Forest," in section 1 of this chapter.

4 Prince of Wales Island

If you have plenty of time, the Alaska Bush is just a short ferry or small-plane ride from Ketchikan, ready to be explored by car. Prince of Wales Island, known locally as "POW," is 135 miles long and 45 miles wide, making it the third-largest island in the United States (after Alaska's Kodiak Island and Hawaii's Big Island), yet it is populated by only a few tiny towns and Native villages. What makes the island unique in Alaska is that it's traversed by a network of more than 1,000 miles of gravel roads, built and maintained by the U.S. Forest Service to facilitate logging. That means you can drive to beautiful places rich with fish, exploring without the expense of an airplane or boat, but rarely seeing another person. It can be a strange feeling to drive for hours without seeing a building or another car. The flip side of such accessibility is that large clear cuts now mar many once-beautiful parts of the island.

Fishing, in both salt- and freshwater, is by far the biggest reason to visit the island. The Forest Service lists 32 good fishing streams and maintains some 20 public cabins, built mainly for their access to remote fishing lakes and streams. Many fishing lodges operate on the island, mostly taking guests out on boats to fish salmon in the ocean; most visitors to the island have booked inclusive packages at one of the lodges well in advance.

But some people discover more of the island. Divers find clear waters and a rich profusion of marine life; two canoe routes cross wilderness areas of the island; and few other places offer families such opportunities for solitude and discovery along the road and trails. Plus, POW contains hundreds of barely explored caves, two of which casual visitors can safely enter, albeit with some effort.

ESSENTIALS

GETTING THERE & GETTING AROUND You can fly to Prince of Wales on a plane or floatplane with any of the air-taxi operators in Ketchikan. **L.A.B. Flying Service** (☎ **800/426-0543** or 907/247-5220; www.labflying.com) offers plane service; **Promech Air** (☎ **800/860-3845** or 907/225-3845) uses floatplanes.

If you fly, and you're not at a lodge or on a package, you'll need to rent a car. **Wilderness Rent-a-Car,** at Log Cabin Sporting Goods in Craig (☎ **800/949-2205** or 907/826-2205), charges $69 to $79 a day plus 30¢ a mile after 100 miles, which can add up fast if you explore the whole island. If you plan to drive a lot on the island, you'll do better by renting a car in Ketchikan and taking it over on the ferry. The **Alaska Marine Highway** serves Hollis roughly once a day (see section 1 of this chapter, "Exploring Southeast Alaska"; the number on Prince of Wales is ☎ **907/826-3432**). The fare for a small car from Ketchikan to Hollis is $41, and each passenger is $20 more. It's safest to reserve a ferry spot a week or two in advance in high season, but it's entirely possible to just show up and luck into a space, too. If you arrive in Hollis without a car, **Sea Otter Taxi** (☎ **907/755-2362**), in Klawock, can pick you up.

VISITOR INFORMATION Before going to Prince of Wales, stop at the **Southeast Alaska Discovery Center** at 50 Main St. in Ketchikan (☎ **907/228-6220;** www.nps.gov/aplic), and pick up the Forest Service recreation guides and the $4 road guide, which is a large map showing the roads and topography and listing the cabins and facilities available around the island. Fishermen will also want to get a copy of the Alaska Department of Fish and Game's ***Sport Fishing Guide*** for the island, as well as other guidance from the **Ketchikan Division of Sport Fish** office, at 2030 Sealevel Dr., Suite 207, Ketchikan, AK 99901 (☎ **907/225-2859**). You also can order the map and get tourist information from the **Prince of Wales Chamber of Commerce,** P.O. Box 497, Craig, AK 99921 (☎ **907/826-3870;** fax 907/826-5467; princeofwalescoc.org).

ORIENTATION The largest town is **Craig,** on the west side of the island. Here you'll find three good hotels, restaurants, a bank with an ATM, various stores, and a floatplane dock. Seven miles east is **Klawock,** a large Native village with the island's major paved landing strip, a shopping center, more restaurants and accommodations, and a rotting totem pole park built under the New Deal in the 1930s. The other towns and villages on the island are quite small and have limited services. **Hollis,** where the ferry lands on the east side of the island, has few visitor services.

GETTING OUTSIDE

FISHING The fishing opportunities on Prince of Wales are legendary. Fly-fishermen I know have returned from POW looking like they've been yanked back from a visit to paradise. They talk of rain forest surrounding streams and lakes that are seemingly virgin to the fishhook and yield steelhead, cutthroat, and other trout by the dozen in a day's fishing.

Many lodges on the island offer river or ocean trips, and guides are booked up many months in advance. Some are described below. You can also go on your own, using the Forest Service cabins or camping. Some cabins come with boats that allow access away from the road, or you can rent a canoe (see below). Even without a boat, there are enough roads and enough good fishing that anyone with a car and a copy of the ***Sport Fishing Guide*** (see above) can find a no-fail fishing spot.

CAVING The limestone of Prince of Wales Island contains a honeycomb of miles of caves. Though they're wet, cold, and challenging, advanced cavers consider these to be among the world's most exciting caves, for their complexity and for the wonder of exploring areas that have never been seen by humans. The caves weren't discovered until 1987, and there's still plenty left to be mapped by explorers led by the Forest Service.

Two caves have been developed for the public. Forest Service guides lead visitors on highly recommended 2-hour treks into **El Capitan** cave three times a day Thursday to Saturday during the summer (reservations required). Although the tour goes only about 600 feet into the 12,000-foot cave, it feels like you've been to the center of the earth in these incredibly complex, twisting chambers. The hike is only for the fit and starts with a climb up 350 steps to the mountainside cave opening. Visitors can wade into the grottolike **Cavern Lake Cave** on their own—you never lose daylight in this broad crack in the earth. Tall rubber boots or other preparations for the flowing cavern stream will help. The caves are a 3-hour drive from Craig, and you'll need the Forest Service's **road guide** (see above) to find them. Contact the **Thorne Bay Ranger District,** 1312 USFS Dr. (P.O. Box 19001), Thorne Bay, AK 99919 (☎ **907/828-3304;** www.fs.fed.us/r10/tongass).

DIVING Craig Sempert's **Craig Dive Center,** 107 Main St., Craig (☎ **907/826-3481** or 800/380-DIVE in Alaska only; craigdiv@ptialaska.net), offers rentals and fully guided diving packages to the island. The water here is clearer and the invertebrate and marine mammal life even richer than in the Inside Passage part of Southeast Alaska. Plankton blooms can cloud things up in the summer, but winter is always clear. Sempert dives in wet and dry suits, and tailors packages to visitors' interests, diving in unexplored areas, and even in caves. He also rents out a pair of attractive kitchenette apartment units by the night, for $85 double—a great place for families to stay, whether divers or not.

CANOEING A couple of lovely backwoods canoe routes cross parts of the island, on Sarkar Lake and through the Honker Divide, each with Forest Service cabins along the way. Here's an inexpensive way into deep wilderness, with the relative comfort of a roof over your head at night. You can bring your own canoe or rent one from **Log Cabin Sporting Goods** in Craig (☎ **800/949-2205** or 907/826-2205). They charge $20 a day for a canoe or kayak; they also rent camping packages and carry anything else you might need to buy.

ACCOMMODATIONS & DINING

IN CRAIG

Also see the description of the rooms at **Craig's Dive Shop,** mentioned above.

Haida Way Lodge. P.O. Box 90, Craig, AK 99921. ☎ **800/347-4625** or 907/826-3268. Fax 907/826-4020. www.haidawaylodge.com. 25 units. TV TEL. High season $112 double. Low season $85 double. Extra person $5. AE, CB, DC, DISC, MC, V.

This is a surprisingly good hotel, renting crisp standard rooms even to people not on fishing packages. The packages, including 3 days of charter fishing, start at $1,760 per person. They book up quite early for the summer season.

The same owners operate **Sunnahae Lodge,** also in Craig (☎ **907/826-4000**), with comfortable, smoke-free rooms available with packages.

IN KLAWOCK

Try **Fireweed Lodge,** Klawock (☎ **907/755-2930;** www.fireweedlodge.com/), which has its own dock and a wilderness feel, but is near the airport and shopping center. **Papa's Pizza** (☎ **907/755-2244**), in the shopping center in Klawock, has some of the island's best food and free delivery.

ON THE NORTHERN END OF POW

McFarland's Floatel. P.O. Box 19149, Thorne Bay, AK 99919. ☎ **888/828-3335** or 907/828-3335. 4 cabins. $220 per night. MC, V.

This unique place has four two-bedroom cabins on the beach, overlooking the dock where the lodge and boats float on placid water. Cabins have full kitchens and guests cook their own meals. You can fly right to the lodge and rent a Chevy Suburban there for $65 a day ($80 for nonguests) to tour the island, paying no mileage charges. The proprietors offer guided charter fishing on a 32-foot boat for $150 to $200 per person. After you've gotten your bearings on a charter, rent a skiff for $65 a day ($80 if you're not a guest) to fish or explore on your own. As with all POW lodges, reserve well ahead.

Waterfall Resort. P.O. Box 6440, Ketchikan, AK 99901. ☎ **800/544-5125** outside Alaska only, or 907/225-9461. Fax 907/225-8530. www.waterfallresort.com. 4-day, 3-night trips, including meals, guided boat fishing, and floatplane from Ketchikan, from $2,960 per person. AE, DISC, MC, V.

One of the state's best-known luxury lodges, Waterfall is reached only by floatplane. Located on the western side of the island, it occupies a converted cannery that was built here beginning in 1912 to exploit the incredible abundance of salmon in the area.

CAMPING

If you enjoy roughing it, nothing could be more appealing than a stay on POW in a primitive **Forest Service cabin** on a remote lake all your own. Several of the cabins on Prince of Wales are reached by skiffs that the Forest Service leaves tied up at the bank by the road—you load your gear and row to your lodgings. This accessibility makes them far more affordable than cabins elsewhere in the forest that can be reached only with a floatplane or charter boat. See section 2 of this chapter, on Ketchikan, for information on renting camping gear, and "Outside in the Tongass National Forest," in section 1, for info on how to rent a cabin.

If you don't need a solid roof, you can camp almost anywhere on the island. The **Eagles Nest Campground,** a mile toward Thorne Bay on the Thorne Bay Road from the Control Lake Junction, has 11 well-separated sites among huge trees by the edge of Balls Lake. A ½-mile boardwalk along the edge of the lake ends at Control Creek among a grove of Sitka spruce of staggering girth and height. Sites can be reserved through the same system as cabins.

5 Wrangell

Wrangell, valued for its position near the mouth of the Stikine River, began as a Tlingit stronghold and trading post and became the site of a Russian fort built in 1834. The British leased the area from the Russians in 1840, and their flag flew until the U.S. purchase of Alaska in 1867. Over the balance of the 19th century, Wrangell experienced three gold rushes and the construction of a cannery and sawmill.

Then time pretty much stopped.

While the world outside changed, Wrangell stayed the same from the mid–20th century on. It even moved backward. Elsewhere, Wal-Mart and shopping malls were invented and small town main streets deflated, then people noticed what they had lost and tried to bring back their communities. Not here, beyond the road system. With little incentive for anyone to visit, Wrangell stayed as it was after a 1952 fire burned the downtown: a burly, blue-collar American logging town, simple and conservative.

Wrangell cut trees, processed them, and shipped them. The bars stayed busy and no one thought of opening a health food restaurant. As long as there were trees to saw into lumber, the future was safe in the past.

Or so it seemed until environmental and economic concerns closed the mill. Some feared the town would die, too. Sawing lumber had sustained the local economy for more than 100 years, and a third of the paychecks in town came from that one plant. But, as it turned out, change hasn't destroyed Wrangell. The town is quieter, and some trailer houses have disappeared, but the year-round population is down only modestly, at about 2,500. In its new incarnation, Wrangell is working to improve on its positive qualities, and the residents show an endearing eagerness to please. A big new museum is planned, and two ecotourism operators are offering kayaking, hiking, and the like. Tour boats take guests up the wild Stikine River, out on the water for Southeast's great salmon fishing, and over to the mainland to see hordes of bears at the Anan Wildlife Observatory. The U.S. Forest Service maintains gravel roads that lead to some spectacular places. The town even built a golf course called Muskeg Meadows—leave it to Wrangell to name a golf course for a hummocky swamp.

Wrangell can't change its stripes—it's still a muscular town with narrow horizons—but that's part of the attraction. The town still has a nonthreatening, small-scale feel that allows a family to wander comfortably and make friends. My family and I were invited home to dinner by another family we had just met. There is no crime, so there is no fear of strangers. We picnicked in one of the totem pole parks, hiked in the rain forest, and looked at ancient art strewn across Petroglyph Beach. We were sorry to have to leave. On the ferry back to Juneau, a class of Wrangell sixth graders sat next to us. They talked with excited innocence of all the new things they hoped to experience in the state capital, the most electrifying of which seemed to be the prospect of eating for the first time at McDonalds. Wrangell, I thought, still has a long way to go to catch up with the rest of the world, and that is a condition much to be envied.

ESSENTIALS

GETTING THERE **Alaska Airlines** (☎ **800/252-7522;** www.alaskaair.com) serves Wrangell once daily with a jet flying 28 minutes north from Ketchikan and another 19 minutes south from Petersburg, a flight that skims low over the treetops the entire way.

Wrangell is on the main line of the **Alaska Marine Highway System** (☎ **800/642-0066;** www.dot.state.ak.us/external/amhs/home.html), with landings six times a week in the summer. The voyage through the narrow, winding **Wrangell Narrows** north to Petersburg is one of the most beautiful and fascinating in Southeast Alaska. It's quite a navigational feat to watch as the 400-foot ships squeeze through a passage so slender and shallow the vessel's own displacement changes the water level on shore as it passes. The route, not taken by cruise ships (which approach through larger waterways), is also a source of delays, as the water in the narrows is deep enough for passage only at high tide. The walk-on fare is $24 from Ketchikan, $18 from Petersburg. The terminal is downtown (☎ **907/874-3711**), a block from the Stickeen Inn.

VISITOR INFORMATION The small office of the **Wrangell Chamber of Commerce Visitor Center** is located in the Stikine Inn (P.O. Box 49), Wrangell, AK 99929 (☎ **800/367-9745** or 907/874-3901; www.wrangell.com/Chamber), facing the city dock, where cruise ships tie up. The center is open Monday to Friday 10am to 4pm in summer, and other hours when a cruise ship is in town.

The U.S. Forest Service also has an information desk at the **Wrangell Ranger District Office,** 525 Bennett St. (P.O. Box 51), Wrangell, AK 99929 (☎ **907/874-2323;** www.fs.fed.us/r10/tongass), located on the hill behind town. Here you can draw on local

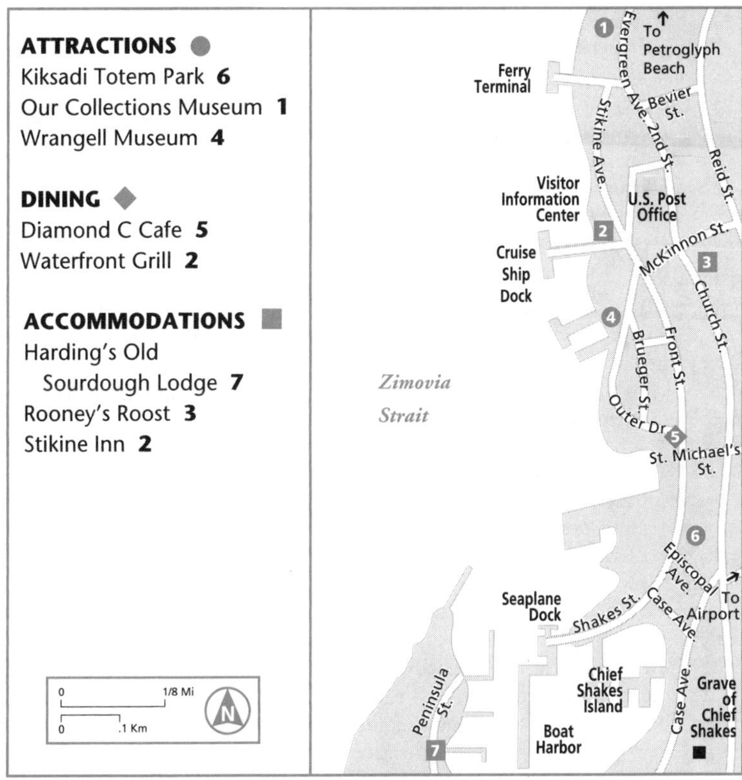

knowledge of the logging roads and fishing holes, obtain guides to each Forest Service cabin and path, and, for $4, buy a detailed Wrangell Island Road Guide topographic map that shows and describes the island's outdoor attractions. The office is open Monday to Friday only, 8am to 5pm in summer and 7:30am to 4:30pm in winter.

ORIENTATION The main part of town is laid out north to south along the waterfront at the northern point of Wrangell Island. **Front Street** is the main business street, leading from the small-boat harbor and **Chief Shakes Island** at the south to the city dock and the ferry dock at the north. Most of the rest of the town is along **Church Street,** which runs parallel a block higher up the hill. **Evergreen Avenue** and **Bennett Street** form a loop to the north which goes to the airport. The only road to the rest of the island, the **Zimovia Highway,** heads out of town to the south, paved for about 12 miles, then connects to over 100 miles of gravel logging roads built and maintained by the Forest Service, most of which are usable for two-wheel-drive vehicles in the summer.

GETTING AROUND You can do the town on foot, but you will need wheels for the airport or Zimovia Highway.

The guys at **Practical Rent A Car** are friendly; they're at the airport (☎ **907/874-3975**), or you can have them deliver the car to you.

For a **taxi,** try **Porky's Cab Company** (☎ **907/874-3603**).

Rent **bikes** from **Solo Cat Sports** (☎ **907/874-2920**), described in more detail below.

FAST FACTS: WRANGELL A **bank** at 115 Front St. has an ATM.

Wrangell General Hospital, at 310 Bennett St. (☎ **907/874-3356**), has a walk-in clinic.

SeaPac.net, a cybercafe where you can check your e-mail, is on Main Street (☎ **907/874-4010**).

For nonemergency calls to the **police,** dial ☎ **907/874-3304.**

There's a **post office** at 105 Federal Way, near the ferry dock.

The local **sales tax** is 7%. Rooms carry a $4 bed tax on top of that.

SPECIAL EVENTS **The Garnet Festival,** the third week of April, marks the arrival of the sea lions, hooligan, shorebirds, and bald eagles on the Stikine River Delta, a spring tornado of wildlife in the region's largest coastal marshes. Community activities take place in town while jet boat tours traverse the delta. **The Wrangell King Salmon Derby,** the last 2 weeks of May and first part of June, started in 1953. Contact the Wrangell Chamber of Commerce (listed above under "Visitor Information"), or check their Web site for details.

EXPLORING WRANGELL & ENVIRONS

Before white settlers arrived, the Tlingits already had warred for centuries over this strategic trading location near the mouth of the Stikine River. The first Chief Shakes was a successful conqueror who enslaved his enemies, then handed down power through the female line, in the Tlingit tradition, for 7 generations. Charlie Jones was recognized as the last of the line, Chief Shakes VII, at a potlatch in 1940, but the position had long since lost most of its status. The decline began after the Alaska purchase, in 1867. Word came of the Emancipation Proclamation, which theoretically freed a third of the residents of the coast's Tlingit villages. Chief Shakes VI sent his slaves in canoes to dry halibut; they kept paddling home to Puget Sound, never looking back. (An excellent pamphlet, "Authentic History of Shakes Island and Clan," by E. L. Keithhahn, sells for $4 at the Wrangell Museum, described below.)

Chief Shakes Island, a tiny islet in the middle of the small-boat harbor, is the site of a Tlingit clan house and collection of totem poles constructed by Native workers, using traditional tools, in the Civilian Conservation Corps during the 1930s. Unlike some CCC clan house replicas in the region, which mix Tlingit styles, this house is an exact, scaled-down copy of the 1834 house in which Chief Shakes VI lay in state in 1916. The inside of the clan house is fascinating, both in the sense it gives of the people's ways, and for some extraordinary artifacts. Unfortunately, it takes some effort to get inside if you're not traveling on a cruise ship. The tribal association opens the house regularly only when ships are in town, when you can enter for $2 (or perhaps $2.50) and hear an explanatory talk. If there's no cruise ship, call Nora Rinehart at ☎ **907/874-2023,** or, if you can't reach Nora, Margret Sturdevant at ☎ **907/874-3747.** For a $20 minimum fee, they'll come down and open the house and give you the talk. Even if you can't manage that, visit the island to see the rotting totem poles and the charming setting (and, with extra time, visit the overgrown grave of

Center of Attention

A new $4.5 million home for Wrangell Museum is expected to be completed by the 2001 visitor season, but the project has already been delayed once. The new waterfront location will be Wrangell's centerpiece, serving not only as an exhibit space, but as a cultural and civic center for the entire town.

Chief Shakes V, on Case Avenue just across the harbor). There's a resident otter that you can often see near the island's footbridge, sometimes feeding its young.

The carved house posts in the clan house are replicas of the mid 18th-century originals that now stand in the **Wrangell Museum,** 318 Church St. (☎ **907/874-3770**). These are probably the oldest and certainly the best-preserved Tlingit house posts in existence, still bearing the original fish egg and mineral paints, and a gash where, during a potlatch, a chief hacked off an image that a visitor admired and gave it to him—a gesture that, as intended, demonstrated the extent of his wealth. The museum has many other important Alaska Native pieces, and a lot of other just plain old stuff that tells the story of Wrangell, one of Alaska's most historic towns. As director Theresa Thibalt told me, "We were the economic center of Alaska at one time—for a short time—believe it or not." This is a special museum, connecting visitors and locals in many ways other than just showing off artifacts. Admission is $3 for adults, free ages 16 and under. Summer hours are Monday to Friday 10am to 5pm, Saturday 1 to 5pm, and when the ships are in. In winter, they're open Tuesday to Friday 10am to 4pm.

One of the museum's projects has been the preservation of an impressive set of petroglyphs that lie on the beach a mile north of town. The 50 carvings of **Wrangell Petroglyph Beach State Historic Park** probably represent the work of forgotten indigenous people predating the Tlingit, and were made over a long period of time. The images, chipped into rocks, are of animals and geometric forms. Their purpose is lost to time. Walk north on Evergreen Avenue and follow the signs down to the beach (don't go within an hour of high tide). Replicas of the petroglyphs were recently carved so that visitors who want to take rubbings will not destroy the originals; also try not to step on them. The great pleasure here is simply to search for the carvings—they're just lying out there, and it takes some looking—and to wonder at their meaning and age.

Wrangell has one more museum, a good place to stop on the way back from the Petroglyph Beach, meet a delightful old lady, and see her favorite things. Elva Bigelow maintains her **Our Collections Museum** in a big old boat shed on Evergreen Avenue (☎ **907/874-3646**). It's an all-inclusive gathering of her family's 60 years in Wrangell: old tools, nautical equipment, and sewing machines, a collection of 60 dolls, a large diorama of the town assembled for the 1967 centennial celebration, and anything else you can imagine. Mrs. Bigelow's museum is open when cruise ships are in town, or you can reach her by phone and she'll gladly show it to you—she loves visitors. Donations are appreciated, and Mrs. Bigelow sells her own crochet work and other crafts.

On Front Street near the center of town, the **Kiksadi Totem Park** was built by the Sealaska regional Native corporation in the mid-1980s on the former site of a clan house. The grass is a comfortable place to sit, and the totem poles truly beautiful.

GETTING OUTSIDE: ON WRANGELL ISLAND

Wrangell Island's network of gravel roads, maintained by the Forest Service, leads to places of awesome beauty rarely visited by non-Alaskans. There are a few day-hike trails, some lovely campsites, and paths to remote cabins and fishing lakes you can have to yourself. There are a couple of calm and scenic places to start a kayak paddle.

There's only one way out of town: south on the Zimovia Highway along narrow Zimovia Strait. The Forest Service map (see "Visitor Information," above) is helpful for anything you might want to do along this route.

The first stop is **City Park,** just south of town. Besides having a picnic area on the shore among big trees, it's a fine **tide pooling** spot. Go a couple of hours before a good, low tide.

Five miles out Zimovia Highway you reach the **Shoemaker Bay Recreation Area,** with a small boat harbor, campground, and picnic sites (see "Camping," below).

Continuing south, **Eight Mile Beach** is a good stop for a ramble, and don't miss **Nemo Point,** a high, ocean-side overlook from which you can see more than 13 miles along Zimovia Strait all the way back to town. The campsites here are gorgeous.

All the way across the island, about 45 minutes from town, **Earl West Cove** gives access to the protected wilderness waters on the Eastern Passage. There's a good campground there, too.

HIKING Across the road from the Shoemaker Bay Recreation Area, the **Rainbow Falls Trail** climbs steeply for just under a mile (and 500 feet in elevation gain) on a boardwalk with steps, up a ridge between two creeks, forested with big, mossy Sitka spruce and western hemlock. The falls seem to tumble down between the branches. From that point, you can continue another 2.7 miles and another 1,100 feet higher into open alpine terrain on the **Institute Creek Trail** to the Shoemaker Overlook, where there are great views, a picnic area, and a shelter. Marie Oboczky, who owns **Rainwalker Expeditions** (☎ **907/874-2549;** www.rainwalkerexpeditions.com), leads nature walks on the lower part of the trail, and longer hikes all over the island. The advantage of going with Oboczky is that she is a skilled naturalist and teacher and knows all the best places to go.

The Rainbow Falls Trail is the island's busiest, especially when cruise ships are in town. If you want to assure you won't see anyone, take one of the less developed walks you can reach along the logging roads—the Forest Service can point the way. One good choice is the **Salamander Ridge Trail,** which leads a mile to subalpine terrain, where you can take off for off-trail hiking. The trail begins 27 miles from Wrangell on Salamander Road, also known as Forest Road 50050. The **Long Lake Trail** leads over a half-mile boardwalk to a public shelter and rowboat on the lake, on Forest Road 6271 (you'll need a map).

BIKING A paved bike trail leads all the way from town, between the Zimovia Highway and the water, to the **Shoemaker Bay Recreation Area,** 5 miles south. There are many more miles of appealing mountain bike routes, on Forest Service roads and single-track trails, all over the island. **Solo Cat Sports** (☎ **877/874-2923** or 907/874-2920; www.thetongass.com/solocat.htm), owned by the warm and enthusiastic Steve Prysunka, leads backcountry tours and rents quality mountain bikes and other gear out of his home at 441 Church St. Prices range from $32 a day for a standard bike to $69 for a full suspension model. They also have child trailers.

SEA KAYAKING **Solo Cat Sports** (see "Biking," above) and **Alaska Vistas** (☎ **907/874-3006;** www.alaskavistas.com) both offer guided sea kayaking and rentals from Wrangell. Solo Cat aims to make independent sea kayakers of beginners; Alaska Vistas offers a wide variety of ecotourism services and has been around longer. Either will do day trips starting from the boat harbor, or guided trips of many days.

An interesting longer day trip starts from Earl West Cove, on the east side of the island. Solo Cat uses it as a launch point. Among the destinations is Berg Bay, where there's a Forest Service cabin for rent, excellent bird watching, and an old mining trail for hiking.

One of Alaska Vistas' most popular trips starts with a jet-boat trip on the Stikine River to Shakes Lake, and then paddles back to Wrangell with stops at the natural hot springs and other sites along the way.

You can rent all the equipment you need in Wrangell, including boats and camping gear, or bring it on the ferry. Water taxis cost $90 to $120 an hour.

FISHING Wrangell Island allows anglers access to rarely visited streams and lakes, some with public cabins, that you can reach by car or a drive and short hike. The Forest Service provides a list, and the Alaska Department of Fish and Game publishes a 20-page ***Petersburg Wrangell Sport Fishing Guide*** (for a copy, call ☎ **907/465-4180,** or go to the Web at www.state.ak.us/local/akpages/FISH.GAME/adfghome.htm), or go with a guide. **Marlin Benedict** (☎ **907/874-2590;** www.flyfishingwrangell.com/) guides fly-fishing outings on shore. On most days, he doesn't see another angler while targeting salmon, cutthroat trout, or Dolly Varden char. He also partners with an ocean fishing charter boat. May and June are the prime months for king salmon fishing, silvers start in July, and halibut are available all summer.

The well-run **Alaska Waters,** listed below, offers a long day of saltwater fishing for $200 per person. I've also heard good things about **Tenacious Charters** (☎ **907/874-3723**), run by an experienced commercial fisherman who does charters between his regular work, on a stable, 42-foot vessel. You can probably arrange to take part of the day for sightseeing and wildlife watching, too. Many other charter boats are available at the harbor—pick up information about them at the visitor center.

GETTING OUTSIDE: OFF THE ISLAND

Wrangell is in an extraordinary place, surrounded by vast, rich wild lands for fishing, rafting, sea kayaking, or simply enjoying. I've described two of the main off-island destinations below—the Stikine River and the Anan Wildlife Observatory—but there are many more, too many to mention. The guides I've listed can give ideas, or contact the Forest Service to get a list of the cabins they rent to the public, many of which provide exclusive access to exceptional fishing.

To get anywhere, you need a boat or floatplane. You can go independently, hiring a water taxi for $90 to $120 an hour; it costs about $450, one-way, to get to a remote Forest Service cabin. That service is offered by various operators, including the impressive, Native-owned **Alaska Waters,** 241 Berger St. (☎ **800/347-4462** or 907/874-2378; www.alaskawaters.com). They also rent all the outdoor stuff you'll need, including camping equipment and canoes, and offer guided fishing, Stikine River jet boat tours and expeditions, and trips to the Anan Wildlife Observatory. Commentary includes natural history and Tlingit cultural traditions and legends.

If you're going by air, **Sunrise Aviation** (☎ **800/874-2311** or 907/874-2319; www.pnw.com/sunrise/) is a Wrangell-based operator.

THE STIKINE RIVER

The Stikine's gray, glacial water rushes all the way from the dry Interior of British Columbia to a broad, shallow delta in the rain forest a few miles from Wrangell. It's among the fastest navigable rivers anywhere, and in early gold rush years was a route over the mountains. Tours that sometimes go as far as Telegraph Creek, B.C., use high-powered jet boats that can accelerate like a hot rod. (Two major operators for such tours are described just above.)

The shallow delta is an exceptionally rich wildlife-viewing area, with sea lions, eagles, and many other species of birds. When the salmon are running, you can see them thrashing in their spawning pools. Farther upriver, tours see Sitka black tailed deer, moose, brown and black bears, mountain goats, river otters, and beavers.

The Garnet Ledge, near the river's mount, still yields gems 130 years after its discovery. It's probably not worth the somewhat arduous visit for most travelers, but the story is interesting. The ledge was exploited from 1907 to 1936 by the first all-woman corporation in the nation, a group of investors from Minneapolis. Today, only children have the right to remove the stones since the deposit's last owner deeded the mine to the Boy Scouts and the children of Wrangell in 1962. Information on the history and recreational mining of the ledge is available at the Wrangell Museum and the visitor center, and you can buy garnets from the ledge from children who set up card tables at the ferry and cruise-ship docks when the ships are in, and often elsewhere, too.

Traveling upriver, tours usually stop at the **Shakes Glacier** and **Shakes Lake,** where there are 3,000-foot cliffs and some 50 waterfalls. Bring a swimsuit for a dip in the Forest Service–owned **Chief Shakes Hot Springs,** where there's an indoor and an outdoor tub for public bathing. The temperature is adjustable up to 120°F. Some tours go all the way to Telegraph, B.C., 160 miles upriver, where Alaska Waters (see above) brings travelers to a remote homestead lodge. A 3-day, 2-night package is $575. The going rate for a 6-hour jet-boat tour from Wrangell is around $145.

Rafting the Stikine offers fast water, expansive scenery, and the potential for a remote, many-day journey. The two firms listed above under "Sea Kayaking," Alaska Vista and Solo Cat Sports, offer these guided trips, lasting about 10 days to 2 weeks, for an inclusive price of around $2,500 per person. Solo Cat also takes kayakers down the river. Alaska Vista and Alaska Waters also rent rafts and other gear for floating the Stikine. A raft is about $100 a day.

ANAN WILDLIFE OBSERVATORY

When the pink salmon are running in July and August (peak is mid-July to August 20), more than 40 **black and brown bears** gather at a waterfall on Anan Creek, on the mainland southeast of Wrangell Island, often walking close to a platform where visitors stand watching. Outside this season, you won't see any bears, however. Forest Service guides are on duty during the bear months; visitors must also follow safe bear behavior (they'll brief you when you arrive; also, see "Outdoors Health & Safety" in chapter 2). Most visitors will enjoy a guided day trip from Wrangell more than going on their own. **Alaska Waters** goes by boat, charging about $145 per person for the hour-long run from Wrangell and a few hours with the bears. Sunrise Air flies the 29 miles. It's also possible to go without a guide, and no permit is needed; there's even a Forest Service cabin for rent, although it's in high demand during the bear season. The walk to the observatory is half a mile from the shore where you land, on a good trail.

ACCOMMODATIONS

Buness Bed and Breakfast. 327 First St. (P.O. Box 66), Wrangell, AK 99929. ☎ **907/874-2036.** E-mail: buness@seapac.net. 1 unit. TV TEL. Summer $70 double. Winter $60 double. Rates include continental breakfast. No credit cards.

This B&B has just one fresh, attractively decorated room with a VCR, coffeemaker, microwave, refrigerator, and claw-footed tub with shower, and a nearby sauna. The family, pillars of the community, also rents a floating cabin 20 miles from town for $95 a night.

Harding's Old Sourdough Lodge. 1104 Peninsula (P.O. Box 1062), Wrangell, AK 99929. ☎ **800/874-3613** or 907/874-3613. Fax 907/874-3455. www.akgetaway.com. 16 units. TEL. $85 double; $135 triple or quad; $150–$195 suite. Rates include continental breakfast. AE, DC, DISC, MC, V.

The energetic Bruce Harding, a large dog, and a cat run the hotel in the style of a fishing lodge. Harding rents the rooms alone or as part of fishing or jet-boat tour packages and offers other local guide services for kayaking, rafting, flightseeing, and so on. The attractive building with a wraparound porch is about a mile from the center of town in a waterfront area, but Harding will drive you where you want to go. Some rooms are small, and most have only shower stalls, not tubs. Decoration is on an outdoors theme. The suites are huge. All rooms have access to a central sauna and steam bath, and a self-service laundry. Fresh seafood dinners are served nightly, family style—you eat what they cook. Dinner prices are $16 to $24 per person, and nonguests can partake with reservations.

Rooney's Roost Bed and Breakfast. 206 McKinnon (P.O. Box 552), Wrangell, AK 99929. ☎ **907/874-2026.** E-mail: rroost@seapac.net. 5 units, 3 with private bathroom. TV TEL. $75 double. Rates include full breakfast. MC, V.

Located downtown, this attractive old house with dormer windows was recently remodeled and updated by members of the family that has operated it for years.

Stikine Inn. 107 Front St. (P.O. Box 990), Wrangell, AK 99929. ☎ **888/874-3388** or 907/874-3388. Fax 907/874-3923. www.stikine.com. 34 units. TV TEL. High season $80–$90 double; $110 suite. Low season $70–$80 double; $90 suite. Extra person over age 12 $5. AE, DISC, MC, V.

The town's main hotel is close to the ferry dock and stands right on the water's edge. It's a bustling place, a center of community activity. The visitor center is in the same building. Rooms are spacious, comfortable, and clean, but somewhat worn and generally outdated. The more modern units have only one bed. The suites are well worth the price. I could hear the water lapping the shore outside the window as I fell asleep, and had a view of the sunset over the ocean.

The restaurant is described under "Dining," below. The art gallery and gift shop on the ground floor, **River's Edge Fine Arts & Gifts,** is the largest in town, with fine art, pottery, and inexpensive gifts. Sometimes artists give demonstrations there.

Hosteling & Camping

Wrangell Hostel is at the First Presbyterian Church, 220 Church St., Wrangell, AK 99929 (☎ **907/874-3534**). They're open mid-June to Labor Day, and the rate is $10 a night.

There are several attractive campgrounds in Wrangell. I've never seen a campground in a spot like the mountaintop **Nemo Point Forest Service Campground** (see "Getting Outside: On Wrangell Island," earlier in this section), but it's more than a dozen miles out of town. Five miles south of town, the **Shoemaker Bay Recreation Area** has sites by the road overlooking the boat harbor, right across from the Rainbow Falls Trail. There are water and electric hookups for RVs. Contact the **Wrangell Recreation and Parks Department** at ☎ **907/874-2444** for information. They also manage **City Park,** right at the edge of town on Zimovia Highway, where camping is permitted. For a full hookup RV site, try **Alaska Waters'** small park, at 241 Berger St. (☎ **907/874-2378**). They charge $15 a night, and $3 for access to the shower room. Showers also are available for $3 at the town swimming pool, at the school.

Dining

You don't go to Wrangell for the dining, but you can get an adequate meal there. The best restaurant in town is the **Waterfront Grill** at the Stikine Inn (see "Accommodations," above). It's a typical family restaurant serving three meals a day. When you sit down for dinner, they bring two menus, one for fine dining and another for the less expensive fare favored by the locals. Nothing is terribly expensive or terribly exciting among the steak, seafood, sandwiches, or pizza. The dining room is trim and bright, with superb ocean views.

Harding's Old Sourdough Lodge (see "Accommodations," above) serves meals to guests, and to others by reservation. It's a family-style dinner without a menu.

The **Diamond C Cafe,** at 215 Front St. (☎ **907/874-3677**), is a comfortable small-town coffee shop open 6am to 3pm daily in summer, closing at 1pm Sundays in the winter. It's lighter, cleaner, and better decorated than these places usually are, and the service is fast and friendly. Besides the hearty breakfasts, they serve burgers and sandwiches in the $4 to $8 range.

6 Petersburg: Unvarnished Threshold to the Outdoors

Petersburg is the perfect small town, the sort of prosperous, picturesque, quirky place that used to be mythologized in Disney films. Except that Petersburg would never let Disney in the door. People here are too smart for that, and too protective of a place they know would be spoiled by too much attention. For the same reason, Petersburg is just as glad the big cruise ships can't enter their narrow harbor. They've got something too good going here to spoil it with throngs of tourists and seasonal gift shops. Instead, locals spend the money that keeps Nordic Drive, the main street, thriving with family owned grocery and hardware stores, restaurants, a fish market, a cybercafe, and other businesses. Wooden streets over Hammer Slough still serve utilitarian purposes, making them far more appealing than if they were prettied up as tourist areas. When you walk along Sing Lee Alley and check out the stylish little bookstore, you rarely see others like yourselves—instead, you see Norwegian fishermen in pickup trucks and blond-haired kids on bikes.

Keeping Petersburg insular and authentic also means the outdoor opportunities to which it provides an entryway are sublime but little used. There are wonderful trails, mountain-biking routes, and secret places. On the water, the humpback whale watching is as reliable as anywhere in Alaska, and still undiscovered. There's a glacier to visit, terrific fishing, and limitless sea-kayaking waters. The in-town attractions are few—a day is plenty for simple sightseeing—and little attempt has been made to accommodate lazy gawkers. But Alaska's best is waiting for those willing to spend the effort to look.

Petersburg is named for its founder, Peter Buschmann, who killed himself after living here for only 4 years. But that shouldn't be a reflection on the town, which is in an ideal location and has flourished since that inauspicious beginning. In 1898, or thereabouts (historians differ), Buschmann founded a cannery on Mitkof Island facing the slender, peaceful Wrangell Narrows in what was to become Petersburg. The stunning abundance of salmon and halibut and a nearby source of ice—the LeConte Glacier—made the site a natural. Buschmann had emigrated from Norway in 1891 and, as a proud old Son of Norway told me, he always hired Norwegians. Any Norwegian who came to him, he hired. In a few years, the cannery failed. Perhaps an excessive payroll? My suggestion was met with an icy glance and a change of subject. Teasing aside, Buschmann's mistake was merging his cannery with a firm trying to challenge a monopolistic canning operation, and they went down together.

Buschmann's suicide followed his financial reverses, but the promise of Petersburg remained. The Norwegians stayed, and slowly built a charming town of white clapboard houses with steeply pitched roofs, hugging the water. Their living came from the sea, as it still does. Appropriately, the downtown area doesn't stop at water's edge. Roads, boardwalks, and buildings continue over the smooth waters of Wrangell Narrows, out to the cannery buildings that survive on long wooden piers, and into the boat harbors, which branch out in a network that far surpasses the city streets.

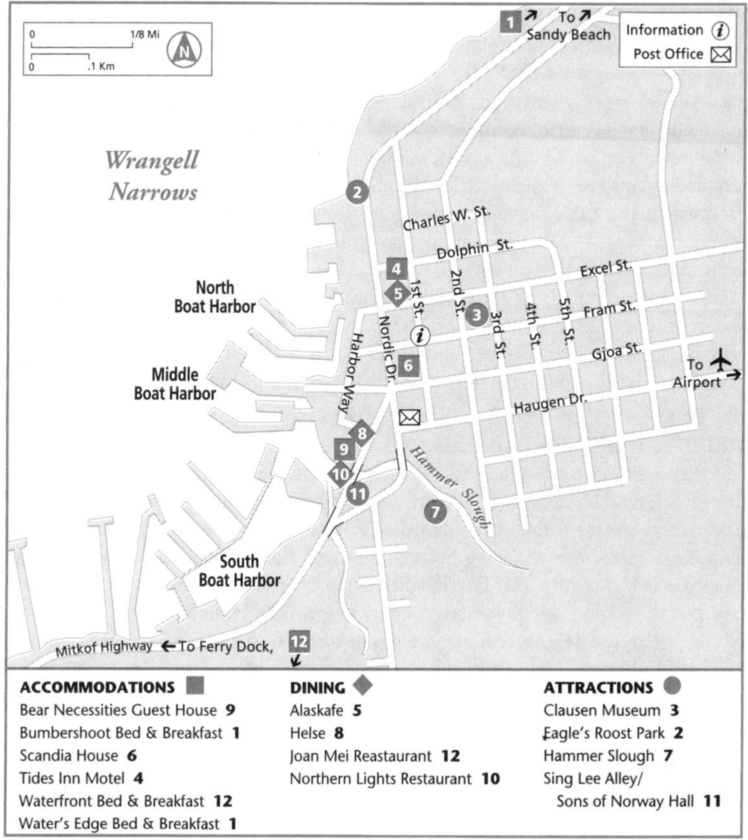

Today the town's economy, based on fishing and government work—the Stikine Ranger District of the Tongass National Forest is headquartered here—makes for a wealthy, sophisticated, and stable population.

ESSENTIALS

GETTING THERE Petersburg has the most welcoming **ferry terminal** in the system (☎ **907/772-3855**), with a grassy lawn and a pier from which to watch the boats and marine animals. It's about a mile to the town center. To the north, the **Alaska Marine Highway** (☎ **800/642-0066;** www.dot.state.ak.us/external/amhs/home.html) can take you from Juneau directly (an 8-hour run), or by way of Sitka (10 hours to Sitka from Juneau, then 9 more from Sitka to Petersburg). The fare is $18 from Wrangell (3 hours), $26 from Sitka, and $44 from Juneau.

Petersburg is served by **Alaska Airlines'** jets (☎ **800/252-7522;** www.alaskaair.com) once north and once south each day, with the nearest stops on the puddle jumper being Juneau and Wrangell. **L.A.B. Flying Service** (☎ **800/426-0543** or 907/772-4300; www.labflying.com) connects Petersburg to Juneau with prop service, stopping in Kake on the way. From the airport, call **Maine Cab** (☎ **907/772-6969**) for a taxi into town.

VISITOR INFORMATION The Petersburg Chamber of Commerce and the U.S. Forest Service jointly operate the informative **Visitor Information Center,** corner of First and Fram streets (P.O. Box 649), Petersburg, AK 99833 (☎ **907/772-4636;** www.petersburg.org). A ranger offers detailed guidance on the outdoor opportunities that really make Petersburg fun as well as trail guides and natural history publications. A chamber helps with hiring a boat, finding lodgings, and other arrangements to make it happen. This also is the place for details on Forest Service cabins in the ranger district, which you can reserve through the national system described in "Getting Outside in the Tongass National Forest," in section 1 of this chapter. The center is open in summer daily from 9am to 5pm, winter Monday to Friday 10am to 2pm.

In a new building, the full-service **Viking Travel agency,** corner of Nordic Drive and Sing Lee Alley (☎ **800/327-2571** or 907/772-3818; alaska-ala-carte.com or www.alaskaferry.com), also specializes in booking local guides for tours, kayaks, whale watching, flights, fishing charters, and other activities. Owner David Berg is knowledgeable and helpful. They also sell custom Alaska tour packages.

ORIENTATION Petersburg is on Mitkof Island, divided from the much larger Kupreanof Island by the long, slender channel of the Wrangell Narrows. There are three small-boat harbors, and so many docks, boardwalks, and wooden streets that the town seems to sit on the ocean. **Nordic Drive** is the main street, running from the ferry dock through town, then becoming **Sandy Beach Road** as it rounds Hungry Point to the north. At Sandy Beach, you can circle back, past the cannery worker's tent city and the airport, which stands above the town, to **Haugen Drive,** which meets Nordic again near **Hammer Slough,** right in town. To the south, Nordic becomes the **Mitkof Highway,** which runs to the undeveloped balance of the island.

GETTING AROUND You can walk downtown Petersburg, but you'll need wheels or a boat to get to most outdoor activities.

The **Tides Inn Motel** and **Scandia House** (see "Accommodations," below) both rent cars, but not many are available in town, so book well in advance for summer.

Biking is a great way to see Petersburg. You can rent a bike for $4 to $5 an hour or $20 a day from **Northern Bikes,** located in the Scandia House Hotel (☎ **907/772-3978;** e-mail: THE-YODA@webtv.net). They're open 11am to 5pm Monday to Saturday in the summer.

The Scandia House also rents small boats, a wonderful way to explore Wrangell Narrows and get to trails across on the other side, or go fishing inexpensively. An 18-footer with a 40-horse outboard rents for $150 a day, gas included, $25 less for guests of the hotel. They don't provide fishing gear.

FAST FACTS There are **ATMs** at two banks, both at the corner of Nordic Drive and Fram Street.

The **Petersburg Medical Center** is the local hospital, at Second and Fram streets (☎ **907/772-4291**).

There are three **Internet** places in town. The best is **AlasKafe,** upstairs at 306 N. Nordic (☎ **907/772-5282**), which offers access for $7 an hour; you can also get lunch and a haircut here (see "Dining," below).

The **police and fire station** is on Nordic Drive near Haugen. Call ☎ **907/772-3838** for nonemergencies.

The **post office** has been at 12 N. Nordic Dr., at the corner of Haugen Drive, but a new one is under construction at 1201 Haugen, next to the grocery store.

Sales tax is 6%. The **room tax** on accommodations totals 10%.

SPECIAL EVENTS **The Little Norway Festival,** which celebrates the May 17, 1814, declaration of independence of Norway from Sweden, is an occasion for

Petersburg to go wild. The 4-day schedule of events is the third full weekend of the month, with a street fair, parade, beauty pageant, seafood feast, and so on. **The King Salmon Derby** offers $30,000 in prizes over Memorial Day weekend.

The Canned Salmon Classic lasts June 1 through August 15, with a first prize of up to $4,000 going to the person who guesses how many cans of salmon will be packed in Petersburg during the season. **Oktoberfest,** lasting all month, includes lots of events. **Julebukking,** a Norwegian tradition, happens on Christmas Eve, when merchants offer food and drink to their customers and the streets fill with people.

For information on any of the above events, contact the **Petersburg Chamber of Commerce** (☎ **907/772-3646**).

EXPLORING PETERSBURG

A walk around Petersburg should include the boardwalk streets of **Hammer Slough,** the tidal mouth of a creek that feeds into the waterfront. **Sing Lee Alley** leads from North Nordic Drive at the charming center of town, passing by several interesting little shops, including **Sing Lee Alley Books,** at no. 11 (☎ **907/772-4440**), where there's a good collection on natural history and local culture. Petersburg has so many thriving little shops because of its isolation and healthy economy—so far, it's been too small to attract the predation of Wal-Mart and other chains.

Sing Lee Alley turns from solid ground to wooden dock before you reach the **Sons of Norway Hall,** a town center where a large model Viking ship used in the Little Norway Festival is often parked. Next door, also on pilings, is a large plaza with flags and plaques memorializing Petersburg residents. Across the street, on the outboard side, **Tonka Seafoods** (☎ **907/772-3662;** www.tonkaseafoods.com) is a specialty fish processor with a shop and mail-order operation. They offer tours ($5) during the summer, 1 to 3pm Monday to Saturday. Call ahead if you're really interested, as times can change.

Continue on to Nordic Drive, then turn left, crossing back over the slough to **Birch Street,** which follows the slough's bank on pilings upstream past old, weathered houses that hang over the placid channel. Many have one door for the road and another for the water. It's a charming, authentic place. Step out of the way of cars on the one-lane dock/street.

Back down at the waterfront, stroll the harbor floats to see the frenetic activity of the huge commercial fishing fleet in the summer, then continue north on Nordic Drive to **Eagle's Roost Park,** where there is a grassy area to sit and a stairway that leads down to the water. At low tide, an interesting if rugged beach walk starts here. You're almost guaranteed to see eagles, which congregate for the fish waste from the nearby cannery. Look in the tops of the trees. (In fact, you can see eagles almost anytime and anywhere along the water in Petersburg.)

The **Clausen Memorial Museum,** at Second and Fram streets (☎ **907/772-3598;** www.alaska.net/~cmm/html/index.htm), interprets Petersburg and its history for the people who live here. It has a living, community feel. When I last visited, a portfolio of old photographs was on display with post-it notes for visitors to write down the names of anyone they could identify and other memories. The office of a leading fish packer is displayed just as he left it in the 1970s, a time capsule of the ordinary that says much about the town. No doubt the local fishermen are fascinated by the obsolete fishing gear, rugged old nautical equipment, and a model fish trap, outlawed in 1959 when Alaska became a state. It's like being invited into the town's collective memory. The museum is open in summer Monday through Saturday from 10am to 4:30pm; winter Wednesday and Saturday 12:30 to 4pm. Admission is $2 for adults, free for children 11 and under.

GETTING OUTSIDE

I have listed only a few highlights from Petersburg's wealth of outdoor opportunities. For other choices, many of them just as good as those I've written about here, or for the detailed trail and backcountry information you'll need, contact the U.S. Forest Service at either of two locations in Petersburg—the visitor center, listed above, or the **Petersburg Ranger District** offices at 12 North Nordic Drives (P.O. Box 1328), Petersburg, AK 99833 (☎ **907/772-3871;** www.fs.fed.us/r10/tongass).

Some of the best places to go around Petersburg require a boat. **Viking Travel** (see "Visitor Information," above) books most of the dozen or so small charter boats that are operating from the harbor at any one time, allowing them to consolidate small groups into 6-person boatloads for whale watching, sightseeing, or fishing.

Some operators have made a specialty of natural history and environmentally responsible tours. Barry Bracken, a retired marine fish biologist, offers these kinds of trips on his 28-foot vessel. Contact **Kaleidoscope Cruises** (☎ **800/TO-THE-SEA** or 907/772-3736; www.alaska.net/~bbsea). Ron Compton's **Alaska Scenic Waterways** (☎ **800/ASW-1176** or 907/772-3777; akscenic.com) also specializes in natural-history cruises using his aluminum jet boat, the *Motivator,* which has a landing craft bow that makes it easy to stop for picnics or beach walks.

SPECIAL PLACES

SANDY BEACH It's an easy bike ride or a longish walk 1.6 miles up Nordic Drive, around Hungry Point, at the northern tip of the island, then along Sandy Beach Road, to the beach and picnic area. Return by way of the airport, coming back into town on Haugen Drive. The beach itself is coarse sand and fine gravel, and you wouldn't swim in the frigid water, but it's a lovely spot, facing Frederick Sound on the east side of Mitkof Island.

If you go at high tide, you can beachcomb and bird watch—a great blue heron was hanging out last time I visited—but a better plan is to time your visit at a low tide (free tide books are widely available, or ask at the visitor center). At tides of one foot or lower, you can see the outlines of ancient fish traps built on the beach beginning 2,000 years ago. They look like V-shaped rows of rocks, and at times you can see stakes. The indigenous people who built them knew how to create channels that would corral salmon at high tide, leaving them stranded to be gathered up when the water receded. These ancient people presumably also created the petroglyphs on rocks near the traps, which may depict the traps or could have something to do with the sun. Finding the traps and petroglyphs isn't easy—it's best if you can get someone to lead you, perhaps by joining the occasional Forest Service walks that you can ask about at the visitor center. But, if you have the time and inclination to explore, walk out to the left from the picnic area, to the edge of the lagoon near the house with the greenhouse. A major petroglyph is on a black bedrock face, visible when you are looking back toward the picnic area, and the traps are just offshore from there.

RAVEN TRAIL & RAVEN'S ROOST CABIN About 4 miles up the steep but spectacular Raven Trail, which begins behind the airport off Haugen Drive near the water tower (roughly a mile from town), the Raven's Roost Forest Service cabin sits atop a mountain with a sweeping view of the town and surrounding waters and islands. It's the sort of place that inspires artists and poets. Allow 3 to 4 hours for the climb along a boardwalk, then up a steep muddy slope, then along a ridge, with an elevation gain of over 1,000 feet. It's possible to continue hiking over the steep, subalpine terrain of the Twin Ridge Ski Trail another 4.9 miles to the Twin Creek Road, and then get a ride 11 miles back to town. Check with the visitor center for trail

conditions. You'll need sleeping bags, cooking gear, lights, and food. Reserve the cabin through the national system described in section 1 of this chapter, "Getting Outside in the Tongass National Forest," and check there for information sources on the other 19 cabins in the area, most of which are reached by plane or boat.

MITKOF ISLAND The Mitkof Highway, leading south from Petersburg, opens most of Mitkof Island, with its king salmon fishing; views of swans, fish, and glaciers; salmon hatchery; hiking trails; lakes; and many miles of remote roads for mountain biking. The town's swimming hole and ice-skating pond are out the road, too. Anyone can enjoy a day's sightseeing drive over the island, and if you enjoy hiking and the outdoors, you'll find days of fun. Pick up the $4 *Forest Service Mitkof Island Road Guide* map at the visitor center or ranger office; it shows what you'll find along the way.

The Three Lakes Loop Road intersects with the highway twice, once 10 miles from Petersburg, and again 20 miles from town. From the north intersection, the one closest to town, it's 15 more miles to the level, 4.5-mile boardwalk **Three Lakes Trail,** which circles four small lakes, each of which contains trout, and three of which have Forest Service rowboats for public use. Besides the fish, it's a place of abundant wildflowers and berries, where you may see deer, beavers, bear, and many birds, including seasonal sandhill cranes.

Thirteen miles off Mitkof Highway, you come to **The Dip,** a declivity in the road where high school seniors have long painted their names and classes on the road. A mile farther, a quarter-mile boardwalk leads across the damp, hummocky ground of the rain forest muskeg to **Blind River Rapids,** a peaceful spot with a three-sided shelter where you can watch and fish for king salmon in June and silvers in September, and sometimes watch eagles and bears feeding on the fish. A mile-long loop leads farther into the forest and muskeg.

At 17 miles, somewhat hidden in the trees on the right, a bird-watching blind looks out on **Blind Slough,** where trumpeter swans winter. Swans normally will be gone by mid-March.

At 18 miles, at the end of the pavement, you'll reach the **Blind Slough Recreation Area,** where locals go to swim in the amber water in the summer. Water warms in the narrow slough, more than 5 miles from Wrangell Narrows. These are appealing canoeing or sea-kayaking waters, too. In the winter much of the town congregates here for ice-skating and bonfires.

A branch road at the recreation area leads over the slough to the **Crystal Lake Hatchery** (☎ **907/772-4772**), which raises king and silver salmon. I've toured a lot of hatcheries, but never enjoyed one as much as this place, simply because it's so informal—they get so few visitors that you just wander through on your own and ask questions of the friendly technicians. A guy who was using a machine to count millions of fish let us watch and help. Unfortunately, the hatchery may close, so call ahead.

At 22 miles from Petersburg, you reach the **Ohmer Creek campground,** with a 1-mile trail, a floating bridge over a beaver pond, and access to king salmon in June and July and trout and some salmon in late summer. The road continues from here along the south shore of Mitkof Island, with great ocean views, to its end at mile 32.

For a Take-Out Lunch

Stop in at **Coastal Cold Storage,** at Excel Street and Nordic Drive (☎ **907/772-4177**), where they sell seafood from freezers and live from tanks. Order burgers, sandwiches, fish specials, and ice-cream cones at the counter.

PETERSBURG CREEK The lovely, grassy Petersburg Creek area can be an afternoon's family frolic among the meadows of wildflowers that meet the water, or the start to a challenging 21-mile, multiday hike into the **Petersburg Creek–Duncan Salt Chuck Wilderness.** You'll need a skiff or sea kayak, or get a charter to drop you off, as the creek is on Kupreanof Island, across Wrangell Narrows from town; the state maintains a dock there. **Guided sea-kayak day trips** go up the creek (see "Sea Kayaking," below), which contains four species of salmon and two of trout. The trail is maintained by the Forest Service and has miles of boardwalks and two cabins, one at Petersburg Lake and one at East Salt Chuck, each with a boat for public use (reservations are required). Petersburg Lake has trout, and odds are good you'll see ducks, geese, loons, trumpeter swans, bald eagles, and black bears. The Kupreanof dock also provides access to the 3-mile, 3,000-foot trail that climbs Petersburg Mountain, a challenging hike that has spectacular views from the top.

LECONTE GLACIER/STIKINE RIVER DELTA Ice calving from the glacier has choked the waters in front, making approach difficult, but in June you can see seal pups on the floating ice and possibly mountain goats. A bit farther on is the Stikine River Delta, a wildlife habitat of grasslands, braided channels, and marshes with excellent bird watching in late April and early May, when the hooligan run, more than 1,500 bald eagles congregate, and some two million other birds rest on their West Coast migration. The charter operators listed above can take you, or Viking Travel can book one of the others who offer these trips. Boat tours based in Wrangell specialize in going to the Delta, too, and they're closer to the river. The going rate for a 4- to 5-hour tour to LeConte Glacier from Petersburg is about $90 per person. Going on to the delta would be more like $175 per person and take all day.

ACTIVITIES

FISHING There are many fishing streams and lakes you can reach on the roads—several are mentioned above, under "Mitkof Island." For more choices, check at the visitor center, or send away before you come for a *Petersburg/Wrangell Sport Fishing Guide* from the **Alaska Department of Fish and Game,** 1255 W. Eighth St. (P.O. Box 25526), Juneau, AK 99802-5526 (☎ **907/465-4180;** www.state.ak.us/local/akpages/FISH.GAME/adfghome.htm).

For expert advice and regulation information, you also can contact the Petersburg office (☎ **907/772-3801**). The boat harbor has a couple of dozen licensed charter fishing boats, mostly six-passenger vessels. As elsewhere, halibut and salmon are usually the target. You can get a list of operators at the visitor center, or book through **Viking Travel** (see "Visitor Information," above). Salmon charters usually last half a day and cost around $100 per person, while halibut charters go all day and average $165.

MOUNTAIN BIKING The largely abandoned logging roads on the island and on surrounding islands that can be reached by boat provide long bike rides without seeing cars or other people. **Northern Bikes,** in the Scandia House Hotel (☎ **907/772-3978**) rents gear and can give ideas on where to go.

SEA KAYAKING The waters of Wrangell Narrows are protected and interesting, with plenty to see. On longer trips of 3 days to a week, you can get out among the glaciers, Stikine River Delta, and even the whales—there's as much variety here, among these rain-forest islands, as anywhere in the region. It's possible to set up a trip linking some of the Forest Service cabins, too, or to use one as a base camp for a few days of exploration. **Tongass Kayak Adventures** (☎ **907/772-4600;** www.tongasskayak.com) offers guided and unguided versions of each of these adventures (they rent equipment, too). Their 4-hour paddle crosses Wrangell Narrows from the harbor and penetrates Petersburg Creek, where they stop for a snack and often see bear and deer. No experience is required; they charge $55 for adults and $30 for children 11 and under. A 3-night base camp tour costs $675 per person, an 8-night version begins at $1,320.

✪ **WHALE WATCHING** Most summers, **Frederick Sound** is one of the best places in the state to see humpbacks when they're feeding. Whale-watching charters go every day from May 15 to September 15, but the height is July and August. You'll likely see stunning bubble-net feeding, when the whales confine a school of fish in a circle of bubbles, then lunge upward to scoop them up, bursting through the surface in a great swoosh. Whales have even been known to spyhop, poking their heads as high above the surface as possible in order to look down into the boats that are watching them. In summer 1995, a humpback jumped right into one of these boats, presumably accidentally. (No one was injured, but a few people fell into the water.) Several charter operators offer trips in small, six-passenger boats. Some, including Kaleidoscope Cruises (under "Getting Outside," above), have hydrophones on board, so you may be able to hear the whales' vocalizations while waiting for them to surface, if their feeding behavior and the water conditions are right. Book through Viking Travel or directly with one of the operators I've mentioned above. Trips usually leave around 8am and stay out 6 to 10 hours, with several hours with the whales. Prices are $120 to $175 per person.

ACCOMMODATIONS

If these places are full, the visitor center can direct you to other choices.

Bear Necessities Guesthouse. 18 Sing Lee Alley (P.O. Box 923), Petersburg, AK 99833. ☎ **907/772-2279.** www.alaska.net/~bearbnb. 1 unit. TV TEL. $90 double. Extra person $10. Rates include continental breakfast. MC, V.

This is a nice one-bedroom apartment unit. Although it lacks a view, the decor is cute and the facilities are perfect for a family, with a full kitchen, lots of beds, and all expected amenities, plus extras like a fax machine and ironing board and iron. It's on pilings right on Sing Lee Alley.

Bumbershoot Bed and Breakfast. 909 Sandy Beach Rd. (P.O. Box 372), Petersburg, AK 99833. ☎ **907/772-4683.** Fax 907/772-4627. E-mail: ohknigs@pobox.alaska.net. 4 units, 2 with shared bathroom. $80–$90 double. Extra person $10. Rates include continental breakfast. DISC, MC, V.

The industrious Gloria Ohmer, who also owns the Tides Inn Motel (see below), has opened her extraordinary waterfront home on Frederick Sound to guests as well. The rooms are large, decorated with quilts she made. Gloria and her husband, Don Koenigs, also will share their beadwork, woodwork, sewing, stained glass, lapidary, music room, fish-cleaning room, and deck barbecue with you. It's hard to come away without gaining a little of their enthusiasm for life. Rooms with water views—and the water is only barely beyond your reach—rent for $10 more. For $150 a night, you can rent the entire downstairs apartment, with two rooms, a kitchen, and a large living room with a fireplace. They also lend bicycles, offer free use of the laundry machines, and arrange transportation from the ferry dock or airport.

Scandia House. 110 Nordic Dr. (P.O. Box 689), Petersburg, AK 99833. ☎ **800/722-5006** or 907/772-4281. Fax 907/772-4301. E-mail: scandia@alaska.net. 33 units. TV TEL. $90–$110 double, $130 double with kitchenette; $165 suite. Extra person over age 12 $10. Rates include continental breakfast. AE, CB, DC, DISC, MC, V.

Rebuilt in the town's distinctive Norwegian style after a fire in 1995, this building's solid simplicity puts it in a class by itself. White rooms with blonde-wood trim are blessed with natural light. You have a choice: front rooms with king-size beds, rooms with kitchenettes, twin-bedded rooms, or a magnificent fourth-floor suite with towering ceilings. Most rooms have only one bed and a few have shower stalls, not tubs. When I inspected, the housekeeping was immaculate. A courtesy van is available. The hotel rents skiffs (see "Getting Around," above) and has four cars for rent ($50 a day). Book rooms well in advance for the busy summer season.

Tides Inn Motel. 307 N. First St. (P.O. Box 1048), Petersburg, AK 99833. ☎ **800/665-8433** or 907/772-4288. Fax 907/772-4286. E-mail: tidesinn@alaska.net. 48 units. TV TEL. $85 double. Extra person $10. Rates include continental breakfast. AE, DC, DISC, MC, V.

Few hotels in Alaska have such good rooms at such affordable prices. The kitchenette rooms, which rent for the same rate, are an incredible bargain. The biggest difference among the rooms is the views. Those in the older part face an air shaft, while no-smoking units in the front of the new section get a sweeping view. I watched bald eagles doing aerobatics less than 50 feet from my front window. The management is efficient and committed to quality, slowly remodeling rooms while keeping those that remain out-of-date in clean, attractive condition. The hotel acts as the local Avis car-rental franchise, and keeps coffee on around the clock. The hotel is a block above Nordic Drive; a courtesy van or free taxi shuttles guests to the ferry or airport.

Waterfront Bed and Breakfast. Nordic Dr. near the ferry dock (P.O. Box 1364), Petersburg, AK 99833. ☎ **907/772-9300.** Fax 907/772-9308. www.alaska.net/~h20frbnb. 3 units. $95–$105 double. Rates include full breakfast. MC, V.

The building, designed as a bed-and-breakfast as well as a family home, sits on pilings over the Wrangell Narrows near the ferry dock. It combines supreme ocean views and the essential, watery sense of Petersburg. The kids' yard is on the wooden pier, and the canoe down below is free for guests to borrow. Rooms are decorated with Mission-style oak furniture and comforters; they have shower stalls, not tubs. Two rooms each have a single queen-size bed while the third, with two doubles, costs $10 more; the rate is the same no matter how many are in the room. Guests can use a microwave, fridge, coffeemaker, washer/dryer, and barbecue, as well as a sitting room with a VCR. The ferry is within walking distance, and they'll drive you to the airport.

Water's Edge Bed and Breakfast. 705 Sandy Beach Rd. (P.O. Box 1201), Petersburg, AK 99833. ☎ **800/TO-THE-SEA** (800/868-4373) or phone/fax 907/772-3736. www.alaska.net/~bbsea. 2 units. High season $90 double. Low season $70 double. Extra person $10. 2-night minimum stay. Rates include continental breakfast. No credit cards. No smoking. No children under 12.

Barry and Kathy Bracken's house sits right on the beach on Frederick Sound, about a mile from town, with a creek running next to one room. Kathy will pick you up from the airport or ferry terminal. You can sit in the large common room and bird-watch from there, or borrow the canoe for a paddle along the shore. Guests may also use bikes and laundry facilities. Probably the best thing to do here is to book a package combining a stay at the B&B and an excursion on Barry's 28-foot boat. A retired state marine fish biologist, he leads natural history and whale-watching excursions. His knowledge of the area is deep and his enthusiasm infectious. Book well ahead, as it's a rare and popular opportunity.

CAMPING

Petersburg's most famous campground is the **Tent City** at 1800 Haugen Dr. (☎ **907/772-4224;** ci.petersburg.ak.us/~park&rec/). The summer's young cannery workers set up tents and plastic sheeting on 50 wooden platforms for $5 a night. It's a bit rowdy for most tourists, but young people looking to make friends should enjoy it. A central pavilion has coin-op showers, sinks, phones, cooking areas, and firewood.

The closest natural camping is found 22 miles out the Mitkof Highway at **Ohmer Creek** (see "Special Places: Mitkof Island," above). **Twin Creek RV Park** is 6.5 miles out the highway (☎ **907/772-3244**), charging $18.85 for full hookups.

DINING

Petersburg mostly has typical small-town family restaurants, and not much else that rises above that level. Besides those listed below, the **Northern Lights Restaurant** (☎ **907/772-2900**) recently opened on the dock on Sing Lee Alley, a spot with great water views where restaurants have been going out of business regularly for years. Let's hope they make it, for the kind of dining they offer is much needed in Petersburg: three meals a day, with a lunch and dinner menu that ranges in price from $6.75 to $20, including burgers, salads, pasta, seafood, and prime rib.

AlasKafe. Upstairs at 306B N. Nordic, at the corner of Excel St. ☎ **907/772-JAVA.** All items $6–$9.25. No credit cards. Summer, Mon–Fri 7:30am–5pm, Sat 7:30am–midnight, Sun 9am–1pm. Winter, Tues–Sat 7:30am–5pm. COFFEEHOUSE.

It looks like a coffee shop, but they also serve delicious panini sandwiches, pasta, soup, vegetarian food, salad, and a kid's menu—in fact, it's the best lunch we've had in Petersburg. You can log onto the Internet, talk or read on the couch, or even get your hair cut—Glenn and Valerie Ing-Miller started the place as a hair salon, and their customers wouldn't let them shut down the salon in the back rooms when they decided to shift to selling food and coffee. On summer nights, they sometimes add live music, poetry readings, and the like.

Helse. 17 Sing Lee Alley. ☎ **907/772-3444.** All meals $2.25–$7.25. No credit cards. Mon–Fri 8am–4pm, Sat 10am–2:30pm. SANDWICHES/HEALTH FOOD.

This health-food store/restaurant serves hearty plates of food—mostly sandwiches plus daily specials—and I enjoyed my shrimp and cream cheese on grainy bread. The dining room is small and a little grubby, each table hanging at one end from a rope. The early '70s thing wears a bit thin.

Joan Mei Restaurant. 1103 S. Nordic, across from the ferry dock. ☎ **907/772-4222.** Average complete lunch $6.25–$14.50, average complete dinner $6.25–$20. MC, V. Mon–Tues and Thurs–Fri 11am–8:30pm, Sat–Sun 7am–8pm. CHINESE.

The whole family works together in this large, bright dining room, serving flaky egg rolls and entrees with vegetables that remain crisp and flavorful rather than being smothered or overcooked. Locals come here for a nice dinner out, and we saw many happy faces.

7 Sitka: Rich Prize of Russian Conquest

If I could visit only one Alaska town, it would probably be Sitka.

The history that Sitka preserves is interesting not only because of the Russian buildings that record Alaska's early white settlement, but more deeply for the story of the cultural conflict of Alaska Natives with the invaders, and their resistance and ultimate accommodation to the new ways. Here, 18th-century Russian conquerors who had successfully enslaved the Aleuts to the west met their match in battle against the rich, powerful, and sophisticated Tlingits. A visit to Sitka reveals the story of that war, and also the cultural blending that occurred in the uneasy peace that followed under the influence of the Russian Orthodox church—an influence that remained even after the Russians packed up (upon the U.S. purchase of Alaska in 1867), and continues today.

Sitka's history is Alaska's richest, and there's more of real interest in this town than anywhere else you might visit. The fact is, most Alaska towns haven't been on the map long enough to have accumulated much history. Those that have been around for a while often have been wiped out a time or two, leaving little to remind you of the distant past. There's usually a small museum and a few gold rush sites that can be seen in half a day. Not so in Sitka. Historic photographs bear a surprising resemblance to today's city. The National Park Service protects buildings and grounds of major historic significance—places where the pioneers spoke Russian, with ways so much more European than those of the rest of the American West. Even a superficial exploration of the attractions takes a day, and that without time for the out-of-the way points of interest or the outdoors.

In 1799, the Russians chose these protected waters on Sitka Sound, on the ocean side of Baranof Island, for a new fort as part of a strategy of pushing their sea otter hunting operations and territorial claims east and south along the west coast of North America. The Tlingit understandably considered this to be an invasion, and in 1802 they attacked the Russian's redoubt and killed almost everyone inside. The Russians counterattacked in 1804 with the cannons of the ship *Neva* and a swarm of Aleut warriors, eventually forcing the Tlingit chief, Katlian, to withdraw. But the Russians never rested easy in their new capital, named New Archangel, and the hostility of the proud and dangerous long remained.

Some Russian laborers intermarried and essentially adopted Tlingit culture, but the bureaucrats and naval officers sent to run the colony for the czar tended to view Alaska as purgatory and left as soon as they could. Under their ineffective and uninterested control, the Russians made surprising little impression on the great mass of Alaska. They failed to explore the Interior and held only tenuous control of the vast coastline.

The departing Russians rushed home, leaving only three significant towns—Unalaska, Kodiak, and Sitka—of which only Sitka retains more than a single Russian building. During their century of rule the Russians had nearly wiped out the sea otter and the culture of the Aleuts, but both would eventually bounce back. The Russian Orthodox church stood as their only lasting cultural gift. Thanks to the efforts of one extraordinary cleric, Father Ivan Veniaminov, Alaska Natives were able to worship in their own languages, winning many villages' continuing loyalty over less tolerant Protestant churches that came under American rule.

Besides its historic significance, Sitka also is fun to visit. Somehow it has retained a friendly, authentic feel, despite the crush of thousands of visitors. Perhaps because cruise-ship travelers must ride shuttle boats to shore, or because Sitka is a slightly inconvenient, out-of-the-way stop on the Alaska Marine Highway's main-line ferry routes, the city's streets haven't been choked by solid rows of seasonal gift shops, as has occurred in Ketchikan, Skagway, and a large part of Juneau. It remains picturesque, facing Sitka Sound, which is dotted with islands and populated by feeding eagles. Tourism is important here, but Sitka's community remains its center. The process of being "spoiled" hasn't even begun.

Even beyond the town and its history, Sitka is a gateway to a large, remote portion of Southeast Alaska, in the western coastal islands. This area contains some of Tongass National Forest's least-used outdoor opportunities. The ocean halibut and salmon fishing are excellent and not overexploited, the bird and wildlife watching exceptional.

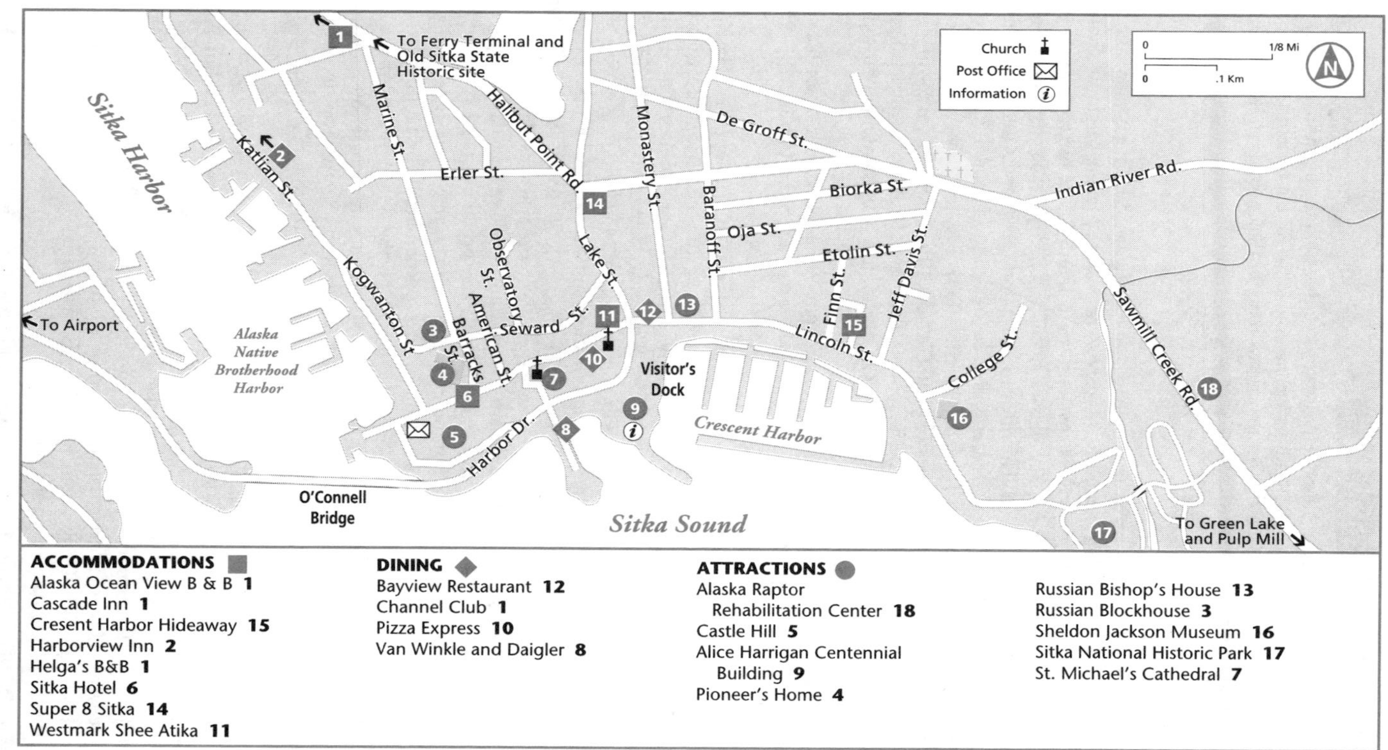
To Ferry Terminal and Old Sitka State Historic site
Church
Post Office
Information
0
1/8 Mi
0
.1 Km
N
Sitka Harbor
Katlian St.
Marine St.
Halibut Point Rd.
Erler St.
Monastery St.
De Groff St.
Baranoff St.
Biorka St.
Oja St.
Etolin St.
Indian River Rd.
Jeff Davis St.
Finn St.
Lake St.
Observatory St.
Seward St.
American St.
Barracks St.
Kogwanton St
To Airport
Alaska Native Brotherhood Harbor
Lincoln St.
College St.
Sawmill Creek Rd.
Visitor's Dock
Crescent Harbor
Harbor Dr.
O'Connell Bridge
Sitka Sound
To Green Lake and Pulp Mill
ACCOMMODATIONS
Alaska Ocean View B & B 1
Cascade Inn 1
Cresent Harbor Hideaway 15
Harborview Inn 2
Helga's B&B 1
Sitka Hotel 6
Super 8 Sitka 14
Westmark Shee Atika 11
DINING
Bayview Restaurant 12
Channel Club 1
Pizza Express 10
Van Winkle and Daigler 8
ATTRACTIONS
Alaska Raptor Rehabilitation Center 18
Castle Hill 5
Alice Harrigan Centennial Building 9
Pioneer's Home 4
Russian Bishop's House 13
Russian Blockhouse 3
Sheldon Jackson Museum 16
Sitka National Historic Park 17
St. Michael's Cathedral 7

Thank You. No, Thank *You*.

In 1867, Russia's Czar Alexander feared he couldn't hold the unprofitable colony of Alaska and saw a political advantage in doing his American allies the favor of selling it to them. Ironically, the Americans thought they were doing Russia a favor by buying it.

ESSENTIALS

GETTING THERE Sitka sits on the west side of Baranof Island, a detour from the Inside Passage. The big, main-line ferries on the **Alaska Marine Highway System** (☎ **800/642-0066;** www.dot.state.ak.us/external/amhs/home.html) don't always stop here, but the small *LeConte* adds more connecting trips each week, often stopping at villages in the region. The ride through narrow Peril Straits into Sitka is definitely worth the trip. The shore seems close enough to touch, and if you look closely you can sometimes see deer. The fare from either Juneau (9 hours away) or Petersburg (10 hours) is $26. The ferry dock (☎ **907/747-3300**) is 7 miles out of town.

Alaska Airlines (☎ **800/252-7522,** or 907/966-2422 locally; www.alaskaair.com) links Sitka daily to Juneau and Ketchikan, flights that then continue nonstop to Seattle and Anchorage.

Sitka Tours charges $3 to get to town from the airport, with buses meeting all arrivals. From the ferry dock their one-way fare is $5. **Sitka Cab** is at ☎ **907/747-5001;** the ride from the ferry dock is around $15.

VISITOR INFORMATION Although only a desk, the city-operated **Harrigan Centennial Hall Visitor Center,** 330 Harbor Dr., next to the Crescent Boat Harbor (☎ **907/747-3225**), provides refreshingly straightforward printed information. They're open in summer Monday through Wednesday 8am to 10pm, Thursday and Friday and most weekend days 8am to 5pm; in winter, Monday through Friday 8am to 5pm. If you are writing ahead for information, instead contact the **Sitka Convention and Visitors Bureau,** at P.O. Box 1226, Sitka, AK 99835 (☎ **907/747-5940;** fax 907/747-3739). They maintain a very useful Web site at **www.sitka.org**.

The **Sitka National Historical Park Visitor Center,** 106 Metlakatla St., Sitka, AK 99835 (☎ **907/747-6281;** www.nps.gov/sitk), run by the National Park Service, maintains the most important historic sites in Sitka, and is an essential stop where you can gather information and learn about what happened here. The Historic Sites of Sitka map produced by the Park Service and Sitka Historical Society is an indispensable guide to the buildings and parks around town. You can easily see Sitka's history on foot with one of these maps. The center is open daily 8am to 5pm in summer, Monday to Friday 8am to 5pm in winter. Also see "Exploring Sitka," below, for more on the park.

ORIENTATION Sitka, on the west side of Baranof Island, has only a few miles of road. The **ferry terminal** is located at its north end, 7 miles out, on **Halibut Point Road;** the site of the abandoned pulp mill is at the south end, 5 miles out **Sawmill Creek Boulevard.** The town faces Sitka Sound. Across Sitka Channel is **Japonski Island** and the **airport** (don't worry, it only looks as if your plane is going to land in the water). **Lincoln Street** contains most of the tourist attractions. A free map provided by the Sitka Convention and Visitors Bureau at the visitor center will help you navigate the initially confusing downtown streets.

GETTING AROUND The airport has locations of **Avis** (☎ **800/331-1212** or 907/966-2404; www.avis.com) and **Allstar/Practical** (☎ **800/722-6927** or 907/966-2552; www.ptialaska.net/~rfahey).

The Visitor Transit Bus operated by **Sitka Tribal Tours,** 456 Katlian St. (☎ **888/270-8687** or 907/747-7290; www.sitkatribe.org), makes a continuous circuit of the sites May to September, Monday to Friday, 12:30 to 4:30pm, with added hours when cruise ships are in. The fare is $5 all day, and kids ride free.

Right by the harbor, **S.E. Diving and Sports,** 105 Monastery St. (☎ **800/824-3483** in Alaska only, or 907/747-8279), rents bikes for $5 an hour or $20 a day. Top-quality bikes are for sale from Clay's Dive Shop, listed below under "Diving."

FAST FACTS There are **ATMs** at grocery stores and at banks at 300 and 318 Lincoln St.

The **Sitka Community Hospital** (☎ **907/747-3241**) is at 209 Moller Dr.

Highliner Cafe, in the Seward Square Mall (☎ **907/747-4924**), offers **Internet access** for $5 for the first half hour, and serves food.

Call ☎ **907/747-3245** for **police** nonemergencies.

The downtown **post office** is at 338 Lincoln St., and is open Saturday.

Sales tax is 5%. The tax on **rooms** totals 11%.

SPECIAL EVENTS The **Starring Ceremony,** in early January (with the exact date depending on the church calendar), marks Russian Orthodox Christmas with a procession through the streets and song and prayer at the doors of the faithful. Call St. Michael's Cathedral for information (☎ **907/747-8120**).

The **Sitka Salmon Derby** occurs at the end of May and beginning of June, when the kings are running; contact the Sitka Sportsman's Association (☎ **907/747-8886**). The **Sitka Summer Music Festival,** a chamber-music series that began in 1972, is one of Alaska's biggest cultural events, drawing musicians from all over the world for three weeks in June. Performances take place Tuesdays and Fridays, and other events all week. Contact the festival office for information (☎ **907/747-6774;** www.sitkamusicfestival.org).

Alaska Day, October 18, commemorating the Alaska purchase, is a big deal in this former Russian capital city; the **Alaska Day Festival** lasts 4 days leading up to the big event. The Convention and Visitors Bureau has information. The **Sitka Grind,** a music and arts celebration at varying sites around town, takes place the third Saturday of each month from October to March. The **Sitka WhaleFest** (☎ **907/747-5940;** www.sitka.org/whale.htm) takes place over a weekend in early November, during the fall and early winter period when humpback whales congregate in Sitka Sound. There are workshops, whale-watching tours, a concert, and other community events. Consider combining it with the Haines Bald Eagle Festival, coordinated to follow (see section 11 of this chapter, on Haines).

EXPLORING SITKA

Sitka Tribal Tours (see above) and **Sitka Tours** (☎ **907/747-8443**), which offers a more Russian perspective, offer a variety of town tours by bus and on foot, mostly serving cruise-ship passengers who are shorter on time than are independent travelers. Prices range from about $12 for a brief downtown tour to $33 for a longer town tour that includes most of the attractions, with admission to either the Native or Russian dancing, depending on which firm you go with. Or join **Sitka Walking Tours** (☎ **907/747-5354**) to find some of the lesser-known places—Jane Eidler does a great job, charging $9 for a 90-minute walk.

SITKA'S TLINGIT & RUSSIAN HERITAGE

✪ **Sitka National Historical Park.** 106 Metlakatla St. ☎ **907/747-6281.** Free admission. Visitor center open summer daily 8am–5pm; winter, Mon–Fri 8am–5pm. Park open summer daily 6am–10pm, winter daily 7am–8pm.

In 1799, the Russian America Company, led by Alexander Baranof, landed from their base in Kodiak, established Redoubt St. Michael (today the **Old Sitka State Historic Site,** 7½ miles north of town—just a grassy picnic area with interpretive signs), and claimed the Pacific Northwest of America for Russia. The Tlingit, who were sophisticated traders and already had acquired flintlocks, attacked with knives, spears, and guns, and destroyed the redoubt in mid-June 1802, killing almost all of the Russians. The Natives immediately began building fortifications on the site now within the national historical park, anticipating a Russian counterattack, which came in 1804. Baranof returned with an attacking force of a Russian gunship and a swarm of Aleut kayaks, which towed the becalmed vessel into position to begin the bombardment. The Tlingits withstood the siege for 6 days, then vacated their fort at night, after taking heavy losses from the shelling and from a bomb-laden canoe. The Russians founded and heavily fortified the town of New Archangel, and in 1808 it became their administrative capital. But the Tlingit name is the one that stuck: Shee Atika, since contracted to Sitka.

The historic significance of the battle site was recognized early, and Pres. Benjamin Harrison, a friend of Alaska missionary Sheldon Jackson, set it aside in 1890. In 1905, a collection of totem poles from around Southeast was brought here (the originals are in storage; replicas are on display). The historic park emphasizes the Native perspective. In the visitor center, a display explains the history, and Alaska Native artisans from the Southeast Alaska Indian Cultural Center work in a series of windowed workshops in wood, silver, and cloth, making traditional carvings, jewelry, drums, and regalia. An auditorium shows films and other programs.

I found the totem park and battle site most impressive. The totems stand tall and forbidding along a pathway through massive spruce and hemlock, where misty rain often wanders down from an unseen sky somewhere above the trees. The battle site is along the trail—only a grassy area now—but among the trees and totems, with the sound of the lapping sea and raven's call, you can feel deep down what the Tlingits were fighting for.

And, in fact, the park and center are full of evidence of the Tlingit's living heritage. In 1996, a gathering of clans erected a major new pole in front of the center to explain their story from before the Russians' arrival, back to mankind's beginnings in North America. It took quite a bit of debate to settle the story the pole would tell. For example, the crests of the eagle and raven tribal moieties are traditionally never shown on the same pole, but they had to be to tell the whole history of the Tlingits. The obvious success of the project speaks from the beauty of the pole, a strong symbol of cultural renewal.

The Russian Bishop's House. Lincoln and Monastery sts. No phone; call Sitka National Historical Park Visitor Center (☎ **907/747-6281**). Admission $3 per person or $6 per family. Summer daily 9am–1pm and 2–5pm; by appointment in winter.

Father Ivan Veniaminov (aka Bishop Innocent), born in 1797, translated the Bible into Tlingit and trained deacons to carry Russian Orthodoxy back to their Native villages. Unlike most of the later missionaries of other faiths (who were led by Sitka's other historic religious figure, Sheldon Jackson), Veniaminov allowed parishioners to use their own language, a key element to saving Native cultures. When the United States bought Alaska in 1867, few Russians remained, but thanks to Veniaminov's work, the Russian Orthodox faith remains strong in Native Alaska; today there are 89 parishes, primarily in tiny Native villages. In 1977, Veniaminov was canonized as St. Innocent in the Orthodox faith.

In 1842, the Russian America Company retained Finnish shipbuilders to construct this extraordinary house, Sitka's oldest surviving Russian building, as a residence, school, and chapel for Bishop Innocent. It survived many years of neglect in part because its huge beams were fit together like a ship's. The National Park Service bought and began restoring the building in 1972, and today it makes for a fascinating visit. Downstairs is a self-guided museum; upstairs, the bishop's quarters are furnished with original and period pieces. The tour concludes with a visit to a tiny chapel with many of the original icons Innocent brought from Russia.

✪ **Sheldon Jackson Museum.** 104 College Dr. ☎ **907/747-8981.** www.eed.state.ak.us/lam/museum/sjhome.html. Admission $4 adults, free for ages 18 and under. Mid-May to mid-Sept, daily 8am–5pm; mid-Sept to mid-May, Tues–Sat 10am–4pm.

One of the best collections of Alaska Native artifacts on display anywhere is kept here in Alaska's first concrete building (circa 1895), now a state museum run by the Alaska Department of Education on the campus of Sheldon Jackson College. Jackson, a Presbyterian missionary and major figure in Alaska history, started the collection in 1888. Although his assimilationist views today appear tragically destructive to Native cultures, Jackson also advanced Native education and economic opportunity and campaigned against exploitation and abuse. He imported domesticated reindeer to Alaska to create rural industry. This museum's small octagonal building is like a jewel box, but the overwhelming wealth is displayed in such ingenious ways that it avoids feeling cluttered. Some of the drawers in the white cabinetry open to reveal more displays. Some of the artifacts, despite their antiquity, are as fresh as if they had just been made. More are produced by Native artists who demonstrate their skill summer days. Find authentic Native art in the gift shop.

St. Michael's Cathedral. Lincoln and Cathedral sts. ☎ **907/747-8120.** $2 donation requested. Summer Mon–Fri 9am–4pm, Sat–Sun noon–3:30pm and for services. Call for winter hours.

The first Orthodox cathedral in the New World stands grandly in the middle of Sitka's principal street, where it was completed in 1848 by Father Veniaminov (see above). The cathedral contains icons dating from the 17th century, including the miraculous *Sitka Madonna.* The choirmaster or another knowledgeable guide is on hand to answer questions or give talks when large groups congregate. The original building burned down in a fire that took much of Sitka's downtown in 1966, but the icons were saved, and Orthodox Christians all over the United States raised the money to rebuild it exactly as it had been, completing the task in 1976.

OTHER ATTRACTIONS IN TOWN

Performances by the **New Archangel Dancers** (☎ **907/747-5516**) are one of the most popular attractions in the state, and most cruise-ship passengers go to their crowd-pleasing shows in the Harrigan Centennial Hall. Although the performers aren't Russian—the Russians left when they sold Alaska to the United States in 1867—the all-woman troupe performs male and female roles in traditional Russian and Ukrainian dances commemorating Sitka's Russian heritage. Shows are geared to ship arrivals—the times are posted at the hall, or phone for information. Admission is $6.

Also at the Centennial Hall, the free **Isabel Miller Museum** (☎ **907/747-6455;** sitka.org/historicalmuseum) shows exhibits on town history by the Sitka Historical Society, including a diorama of early Sitka. The one-room museum is open 8am to 5pm daily in the summer, 10am to 4pm Tuesday to Saturday in the winter.

The Sitka Tribe (☎ **888/270-8687** or 907/747-7290; www.sitkatribe.org) sponsors performances of **traditional Tlingit dance** daily at the Tribal Community House near the Pioneers' Home. The dancers explain the dances and interact with the audience; my son was entranced. The 30-minute show is $6 for adults, $4 for children. Call the numbers above for performance times.

Since 1980, injured eagles, hawks, owls, and other birds of prey have been brought to the **Alaska Raptor Center,** 1101 Sawmill Creek Blvd. (☎ **907/747-8662;** www.blommers.org/ARRC/A.R.R.C.html), for veterinary treatment, convalescence, and release or, if too badly injured, to reside permanently with more than 20 others at the center. The main attraction for visitors is seeing these impressive birds close up in large enclosures with natural habitats, and to watch staff treating birds and teaching them to fly again. Admission is $10 for adults and $5 for children under 12, money which helps the nonprofit center in its work. They're open 8am to 4pm daily April 15 to October 1. Call for hours in winter.

WALKING DOWNTOWN Get a copy of the "Sitka Through Four Seasons" brochure from the visitor center, which includes a map of the historic sites. Here are some of the high points:

The brick **Pioneers' Home,** a state-run residence for retired people who helped settle Alaska, stands on a grassy park at Lincoln and Katlian, where the Russians had their barracks and parade ground. Stop to talk to one of the old-timers rocking on the porch—each probably has more Alaska in his or her little finger than all the tour guides you'll meet all summer. Just north on Marine Street is a replica of a **Russian Blockhouse;** across Lincoln Street to the south and up the stairs is **Castle Hill,** a site of historic significance for the ancient Tlingits, for the Russians, and for Native Alaskans. The first American flag raised in Alaska was hoisted here in 1867. There are historic markers and cannons. Walking east past the cathedral and Crescent Harbor, several quaint historic buildings are on the left. My favorite is **St. Peter's by-the-Sea Episcopal Church,** a lovely stone-and-timber chapel with a pipe organ, consecrated in 1899. At the east end of the harbor is a **public playground;** continue down the street to **Sheldon Jackson College** and the national historical park.

SHOPPING

There are some good shops and galleries in Sitka, mostly on Lincoln and Harbor streets. Several are across the street from St. Michael's Cathedral, on the uphill side, including **Sitka's Artist Cove Gallery** at 241 Lincoln St. (closed January to March), and **Impressions,** right next door at 239 Lincoln St., selling contemporary Alaska prints and originals. Just down the street is **Fairweather Prints,** at 209 Lincoln St., a T-shirt shop with a difference: original wearable art made in Sitka. A couple of doors down is a quaint bookstore, **Old Harbor Books,** at 201 Lincoln St., a good browsing store with an excellent selection of Alaska books. **The Backdoor** espresso shop, at 104 Barracks St., in the back of the bookstore, has a relaxing art scene atmosphere for reading the newspaper or playing chess. We enjoyed an inexpensive breakfast there. The **Sitka Rose Gallery** occupies a lovely Victorian house at 419 Lincoln St., featuring sculpture, painting, and jewelry. The **Sheldon Jackson Museum Gift Shop,** 104 College Dr., has authentic Native arts and crafts from all over the state. The output of Sitka's own **Theobroma Chocolate Company** is sold all over town.

GETTING OUTSIDE: ON THE WATER

The little islands and rocks that dot Sitka Sound are an invitation to the sea otter in all of us; you must get out on the water. Humpback whales tend to show up in large groups in the fall but are also sometimes seen in the summer. There are so many bald eagles that you're pretty well guaranteed of seeing them from shore. But the lowly sea otter is the most common and, in my experience, most amusing and endearing of marine mammals, and you'll certainly see them from a boat tour. Otters seem so friendly and happy it's hard not to anthropomorphize and envy them.

Sightseeing & Wildlife Tours

Tour boats visit **St. Lazaria Island,** a bird rookery where you can expect to see puffins, murres, rhinoceros auklets, and storm petrels by the hundred thousand, as well as other pelagic birds. The volcanic rock drops off straight down into deep water, so even big boats can come close. Trips also commonly encounter otters and sometimes whales. The public tubs at **Goddard Hot Springs,** 17 miles south of town, are another possible stop for charters.

Many boats are available for **wildlife tours** or **saltwater fishing.** Sitka Convention and Visitors Bureau (see "Visitor Information," above) keeps a detailed charter boat list, including rates, that goes on for pages.

The **Sitka Wildlife Quest** operated by Allen Marine Tours (☎ **888/747-8101** or 907/747-8100; www.allenmarinetours.com) does a terrific job, with well-trained naturalists to explain the wildlife. You have a good chance of encountering humpback whales and sea otters. The 2-hour cruise costs $49 adults, $30 children, and leaves from the Crescent Harbor Visitors Dock Wednesday at 6pm and Saturday and Sunday at 9am late May to August. The Sunday excursion includes a visit to St. Lazaria Island. Buy tickets on board. These are different excursions from the ones offered to cruise-ship passengers.

For a more personal bird- and wildlife-watching tour to St. Lazaria Island, Walt Cunningham's **Educational Marine Tours,** 709 Lincoln St. (☎ **907/747-4900;** www.puffinsandwhales.com), takes up to four guests on his 26-foot boat. Walt is a gregarious character with more than 30 years experience on Alaska waters, studying marine mammals and homesteading an island off Kodiak. He charges $200 per person for a full-day trip, $100 for a half-day. He and his wife also run the Crescent Harbor Hideaway B&B (see below).

Sea Kayaking

Sitka's protected waters and intricate shorelines are perfect for sea kayaking. Four companies offer sea kayaking in Sitka; links to all are found at **www.sitka.org/tours.htm**, or call the visitor center. **Baidarka Boats,** 201 Lincoln St. (☎ **907/747-8996;** www.kayaksite.com), has been around the longest. They have a shop that rents the boats and offers instruction and guided paddles for every experience level, including raw beginners. The cost of the guided trips depends on the number in your group: A half-day trip is $95 for one person alone, $180 for six together.

Diving

These waters tend to be clear and biologically rich, making them appealing to divers. Winter is best, when plankton isn't blooming, but good periods come in summer, too. **Clay's Dive Shop,** 246 Katlian St. (☎ **907/747-7871**), is one of two dive shops in town.

GETTING OUTSIDE: ON SHORE

Fishing

Anglers should pick up the ***Sitka Area Sport Fishing Guide,*** which has lots of tips on streams, lakes, and methods in the area. You can write ahead for it from the **Alaska Department of Fish and Game,** 1255 W. Eighth St. (P.O. Box 25526), Juneau, AK 99802-5526 (☎ **907/465-4180;** www.state.ak.us/local/akpages/FISH.GAME/adfghome.htm). The local Fish and Game office is at 304 Lake St., Room 103, Sitka, AK 99835 (☎ **907/747-5355**).

Forest Service Cabins

The **Sitka Ranger District,** 201 Katlian St., Suite 109, Sitka, AK 99835 (☎ **907/747-4420;** www.fs.fed.us/r10/tongass), maintains two dozen wilderness cabins on Baranof, Chichagof, and Kruzof islands, in coves and on remote fishing lakes, where rowing skiffs generally are provided. The cabins and their facilities are described in a booklet titled *Public Recreation Cabins: Chatham Area Tongass National Forest,* which you can get from the Sitka Ranger District (much of the same information is on the Web site).

The cabins are simply shelter: you provide the camping gear. Renting a cabin is $35 to $45 a night, but your major cost is getting to the cabin—for each, it takes either a floatplane, boat, or helicopter. Perhaps the most affordable way is via **Sitka Sound Water Taxi** (☎ **907/747-5970;** home.gci.net/~snewell/). Small air taxis operating from Sitka include **Air Sitka,** 485 Katlian St. (☎ **907/747-7920**), and **Harris Air Services,** 400 Airport Rd. (☎ **907/966-3050**). Check "Getting Outside in the Tongass National Forest," in section 1, for information on researching and reserving a cabin.

Hiking

There are a dozen U.S. Forest Service hiking trails accessible from the roads around Sitka and another 20 you can get to by plane or boat. The best source for guidance, including printed trail maps, is the National Forest's **Sitka Ranger District,** 201 Katlian St., Suite 109, Sitka, AK 99835 (☎ **907/747-4220;** www.fs.fed.us/r10/tongass).

Two trailheads are walking distance from downtown. The 5½-mile **Indian River Trail** is a relaxing rain-forest walk rising gradually up the river valley to a small waterfall. Take Indian River Road off Sawmill Creek Road east of the Alaska State Troopers Academy. For a steeper mountain-climbing trail to alpine terrain and great views, the **Gavan Hill–Harbor Mountain Trail** is just past the house at 508 Baranof St., near downtown. It gains 2,500 feet over 3 miles to the peak of Gavan Hill, then continues another 3 miles along a ridge to meet Harbor Mountain Road.

At the north end of Halibut Point Road, 7½ miles from downtown, a broad boardwalk circles a grassy estuary, rich with birds and fish. The **Estuary Life Trail** and **Forest Muskeg Trail,** totaling about a mile, are exquisitely developed and accessible to anyone. It's a place of peaceful beauty. The new **Mosquito Cove Trail,** nearby, wends 1¼ miles through the old-growth forest to end at the cove's shore. The Forest Service distributes a superb guide map to this whole area at the end of the road.

Tide Pooling & Shore Walks

Halibut Point State Recreation Area, 4.4 miles north of town on Halibut Point Road, is a great place for a picnic, ramble, and tide pooling. To find the best low tides, check a tide book, available all over town. It's best to go on the lowest tide possible, arriving on the shore an hour or 2 before the low. To identify the little creatures you'll see, buy a plastic-covered Field Guide at the National Park Service visitor center at the historical park.

Whale Watching

Humpback whales stop to feed in Sitka Sound on their way south in the winter migration. During October, November, December, and March, you can watch from shore—the local government has even built a special park for the purpose. At **Whale Park,** 3½ miles south of town on Sawmill Creek Blvd., spotting scopes are mounted on platforms along a boardwalk and at the end of staircases that descend the dramatic, wooded cliffs. Excellent interpretive signs, located near surfacing concrete whales in the parking lot, explain the whales. The Sitka WhaleFest, in November (see "Special

Events," above), is the best time for whale enthusiasts; you can watch whales in the company of cetacean scientists from all over the west coat.

ACCOMMODATIONS

In addition to the places below, I can recommend the **Cascade Inn,** 2035 Halibut Point Rd. (☎ **800/532-0908** outside Alaska, or 907/747-6804), which has many amenities and waterfront balconies, but is 2.1 miles out from the downtown area. Downtown, you'll find good standard rooms with many extras in a quiet building at the **Super 8 Sitka,** 404 Sawmill Creek Blvd. (☎ **800/800-8000** for reservations, or phone/fax 907/747-8804). For something a bit more exotic, the **Rockwell Lighthouse** (☎ **907/747-3056**) is a mock lighthouse on an island built to rent to guests. It goes for $150 double in summer, $125 in winter.

The **Sitka Convention and Visitors Bureau** (☎ **907/747-5940;** www.sitka.org) has links to many B&Bs on its Web site, and can send you a printed list as well.

✪ **Alaska Ocean View Bed and Breakfast.** 1101 Edgecumbe Dr., Sitka, AK 99835. ☎ **907/747-8310.** Fax 907/747-3440. www.sitka-alaska-lodging.com. 3 units. TV TEL. High season $109–$159 double; extra person $15–$20. Low season $79–$119 double; extra person $10. Rates include breakfast. AE, MC, V. No smoking.

Ebullient Carol Denkinger and her husband, Bill, have a passion for making their bed-and-breakfast one you'll remember. They've thought of everything—the covered outdoor spa where you can watch the eagles, toys and games for the kids, thick robes and slippers, an open snack counter and big full breakfast, even wildflower seeds to take home. All rooms have coffee pots, refrigerators, microwaves, VCRs, CD players, clocks, hair dryers, irons, and modem jacks. They're located on a residential street with a view of the water about a mile from the historic district.

Crescent Harbor Hideaway. 709 Lincoln St., Sitka, AK 99835. ☎ and fax **907/747-4900.** www.ptialaska.net/~bareis/B&B.htm. 2 units. TV. High season $95–$125 double. Low season $75–$95 double. Extra person $25. Rates include continental breakfast. No credit cards. No smoking, even outside.

This stately 1897 house, one of Sitka's oldest, stands across a quiet street from Crescent Harbor and the lovely park at the harbor's edge, with a glassed-in porch to watch the world go by. One room is a large, one-bedroom apartment with a full kitchen and a private patio and phone line. The other nestles adorably under the eaves. Both have VCRs, clocks, radios, and hair dryers. Everything is clean and fresh. The operators are an artist and local radio host and a skipper of ecotours (his company is Educational Marine Tours). They enjoy telling stories of their life homesteading in Alaska's Bush. The common areas are shared with an Australian shepherd.

Harborview Inn. 713 Katlian St., Sitka, AK 99835. ☎ **800/354-6017** or 907/747-8611. Fax 907/747-5810. 35 units. TV TEL. High season $90 double; $100–$200 suite. Low season $60 double; $90–$200 suite. AE, MC, V.

These reasonably priced standard motel rooms are located in a business district a mile from the historic area. There's a coin-op laundry and a fish-cleaning and -freezing facility in the hotel, and free coffee in the lobby. Seven kitchenette suites are available, and some of these have a good water view. A courtesy van will take you to the ferry dock, airport, or downtown.

Helga's Bed and Breakfast. 2827 Halibut Point Rd. (P.O. Box 1885), Sitka, AK 99835. ☎ **907/747-5497.** 4 units. TV TEL. $75 double. Extra person $20. Rates include continental breakfast. AE, MC, V.

Helga Garrison offers three large, light rooms and a two-bedroom apartment overlooking Sitka Sound in a house several miles out Halibut Point Road. You'll need a car to stay here, but you have the advantage of close proximity to the Channel Club, an excellent restaurant. The rooms are a great bargain—modern and very clean, with all the comforts of home, including coffeemakers, microwave ovens, refrigerators, and radios. Three rooms have large shower stalls, while the suite has a shower-tub combination. There's also a coin-op laundry. Helga speaks German, too.

Sitka Hotel. 118 Lincoln St., Sitka, AK 99835. ☎ **907/747-3288.** Fax 907/747-8499. www.sitkahotel.com. 60 units, 45 with private bathroom. TV TEL. $60 double with shared bathroom, $75 double with private bathroom. Extra person $7. AE, MC, V.

If you choose carefully among these rooms, which vary in size and quality, you could come up with a real bargain on a comfortable room right across from the Russian parade grounds. Some, however, are not up to par; none are reserved exclusively for nonsmokers; and I wouldn't recommend the 14 rooms with shared bathrooms, which have only two showers between them. Common areas in the 1939 building are nicely done in heavy Victorian decor. Besides the central location, many rooms have good views. A coin-op laundry is available and a bar and restaurant are on site.

Westmark Shee Atika. 330 Seward St., Sitka, AK 99835-7523. ☎ **800/544-0970** for reservations, or 907/747-6241. Fax 907/747-5486. www.westmarkhotels.com. 99 units. TV TEL. High season $129–$139 double; $175–$225 suite. Low season $119–$129 double; $152–$175 suite. Extra person $15. AE, DC, DISC, MC, V.

This brown, four-story wood structure overlooking Crescent Harbor in the heart of the historic district is the community's main upscale hotel, where events and meetings take place. The restaurant, lounge, and most rooms have good waterfront views; rooms facing the harbor are $10 more. Rooms are clean and equipped with such extras as coffeemakers and hair dryers; the furniture tends to be worn and out-of-date. In the summer you can book tours and activities in the lobby.

The **restaurant** is reliably good, its menu reasonably priced for all three meals a day, including everything you'd expect from an upscale hotel restaurant, plus a large variety of seafood entrees in the evening.

HOSTELLING & CAMPING

Hostelling International—Sitka is located at 303 Kimsham St. (☎ **907/747-8661**), more than a mile from downtown. The 20 beds are $9 per night, but they don't provide linens. It's open June to August; office hours are 6pm to 10pm.

The Forest Service's **Starrigavan Campground,** at the north end of Halibut Point Road, 7½ miles from town and ½ mile from the ferry dock, is one of the loveliest in Alaska. One loop of sites branches from the Estuary Life Trail, widely separated under huge trees. The other loop is at the water's edge, with some sites situated next to the ocean to make you feel like you're way out in the wilderness. The 28 sites, with pit toilets, are first-come, first-served, with an $8 fee, open May 1 to Labor Day.

RV parks are located near the ferry dock and on Japonski Island, close to downtown.

DINING

Bayview Restaurant. 407 Lincoln St. ☎ **907/747-5440.** Main courses $5.50–$27. AE, DISC, MC, V. Spring–fall, Mon–Sat 5am–9pm, Sun 5am–8pm. Winter, Mon–Thurs 7am–8pm, Fri–Sat 7am–9pm, Sun 8am–8pm. BURGERS/PASTA/SEAFOOD.

The view of the boat harbor, the reasonable prices, and the good food make this second-story restaurant popular year-round, although it's sometimes noisy and a bit cramped. The Russian dishes are for the tourists, but everything I've tried from the extensive menu has been well prepared and served. The clam chowder sings, and people come back for the halibut and burgers. They serve beer and wine.

You Got Your Tacos on My Pizza

To find the **Nahiku Coffee Shop, Smoked Fish Stand,** and **Ti Gallery,** watch for **Pizza Express,** 236 Lincoln St., Suite 106 (☎ **907/966-2428**), serves an excellent pizza and hearty Mexican food, and they'll bring it right to your room.

✪ **Channel Club.** 2906 Halibut Point Rd. ☎ **907/747-9916.** Reservations recommended. Main courses $12–$40. AE, DC, MC, V. Sun–Thurs 5–10pm, Fri–Sat 5–11pm. STEAK/SEAFOOD.

The dining room looked like a typical small-town bar and restaurant. A young guy in a baseball cap was grilling steaks against one wall, the menu was posted over the salad bar, and the service was casual to a fault. Imagine my surprise, then, to receive the best steak I've had in years and the most fascinating and delicious salads served anywhere in Alaska. This diamond in the rough is located several miles out Halibut Point Road, but a courtesy van will come get you and take you home at the end of the evening. They've got a full liquor license.

Van Winkle and Daigler. 228 Harbor Dr. ☎ **907/747-3396.** Reservations required in high season, recommended low season. Lunch items $5–$9; dinner main courses $16–$20. AE, MC, V. High season, Mon–Sat 11:30am–2:45pm; daily 5–9:45pm. Low season, Mon–Sat 11:30am–2pm and 5–8:45pm, Sun 5–9pm. STEAK/SEAFOOD/PASTA.

VanWinkle and Daigler are cousins—one tends the bar, the other the kitchen—and their place is a nice balance of the casual and fine. The dining room has shelves of old cookbooks and tablecloths on the tables. The cuisine concentrates on Sitka-caught seafood, prepared with a well-informed simplicity: With fresh fish this good, it's important to know how to let the natural flavor shine through. A few creative dishes let the chef show off. Portions are huge and service quick, and the wine list and entrees are well priced. There's a full liquor license.

8 Juneau: Forest Capital

Juneau (*June*-oh) hustles and bustles like no other city in Alaska. The steep downtown streets echo with the mad shopping sprees of cruise-ship passengers in the summer tourist season and the whispered intrigues of the politicians during the winter legislative session. Miners, loggers, and ecotourism operators come to lobby for their share of Southeast's forest. Lunch hour arrives, and well-to-do state and federal bureaucrats burst from the office buildings to try the latest trendy restaurant or brown bag on one of the waterfront wharves, the sparkling water before them and gift store malls behind. The center of town becomes an ad hoc pedestrian mall as the crush of people forces cars to creep.

My Juneau is close at hand, but very different. As a child, at a magical age, I lived here with my family in a house on the side of the mountains above downtown. My Juneau is up the 99 steps that lead from the cemetery to the bottom of Pine Street—the way I walked home from school—and then to the top of residential Evergreen Avenue, where the pavement gives way to a forest trail among fiddlehead ferns and massive rain-forest spruces. That trail leads to the flume (a wooden aqueduct that used to bring water down from the mountains), upon which we would walk into the land of bears and salmon, the rumbling water at our feet. It's still a short walk from the rackety downtown streets to a misty forest quiet, where one can listen for the voices of trees.

Juneau is Alaska's third-largest city (Anchorage and Fairbanks are larger), with a population of 30,000, but it feels like a small town that's just been stuffed with people. Splattered on the sides of Mount Juneau and Mount Roberts along Gastineau Channel, where there really isn't room for much of a town, its setting is picturesque but impractical. Further development up the mountains is hemmed in by avalanche danger; beyond is the 1,500-square-mile **Juneau Icefield,** an impenetrable barrier. Gold-mine tailings dumped into the Gastineau created the flat land near the water where much of the downtown area now stands. The Native village that originally stood on the waterfront is today a little pocket of mobile homes several blocks from the shore. There's no road to the outside world, and the terrain forbids building one. Jets are the main way in and out, threading down through the mountains to the airport.

Gold was responsible for the location; it was found here in 1880 by Joe Juneau and Richard Harris, assisted by the Tlingit chief Kowee, who told them where to look. All three men are buried in the Evergreen Cemetery. Their find started Alaska's first modern development—the territory's first significant roads and bridges and its first electrical plant were built here, well before the Klondike Gold Rush. Hard-rock mining, which continued into the 1940s, removed more value in gold in a few years than the United States paid for all of Alaska, as attested by a photograph in the State Museum showing comparative piles of gold. There's plenty of gold left, but getting it out is too expensive under modern environmental controls. A company tried and failed recently to get the mines started again. There are several interesting gold mining sites to see around town. The Treadwell Mine on Douglas Island gives the ghostly sense of a thriving city abandoned and overgrown by the rain forest.

In 1900, Congress moved the territorial capital here from Sitka, which had fallen behind in the rush of gold rush development. Alaskans have been fighting over whether or not to keep it here for many decades since, but Juneau's economy is heavily dependent on government jobs, and it has successfully fought off a series of challenges to its capital status, most recently in 1994. The closest the issue came was in the 1970s, when the voters approved moving the capital, but then balked at the cost of building a whole new city to house it—a necessity since neither Anchorage nor Fairbanks (which have their own rivalry) would support the move if it meant the other city got to have the capital nearby.

There's plenty to see in Juneau, and it's a good town to visit because the relatively sophisticated population of government workers supports excellent restaurants and amenities not found elsewhere in Southeast. Alaska's most accessible glacier, the Mendenhall, is in Juneau, and businesses ranging from the fish hatchery to the brewery have set up tours for visitors. There are two good museums, too. Juneau is also a starting point for outdoor travel all over the northern Panhandle. Because the city is a travel hub, you'll likely pass through on your way to Glacier Bay or virtually anywhere else you want to go in the region. But you don't have to go that far to get into the outdoors from Juneau: You can start from the capitol building for a hike to the top of Mount Juneau or Mount Roberts, or up the Perseverance Trail that leads in between. Sea-kayaking and whale-watching excursions are nearby, as well as some of Alaska's most scenic tide pooling and beach walking.

Downtown, the crush of visitors can be overwhelming when many cruise ships are in port at once, and the streets around the docks have been entirely taken over by shops and other touristy businesses. Many of these are owned by people from outside who come to the state for the summer to sell gifts made outside to visitors. But only a few blocks away are quiet mountainside neighborhoods of houses with mossy roofs, and only a few blocks farther are the woods and the mountains, populated by bear, eagles, and salmon.

ESSENTIALS

GETTING THERE

BY AIR Jet service is available only from **Alaska Airlines** (☎ **800/252-7522;** www.alaskaair.com), with several daily nonstop flights from Seattle and Anchorage and from the smaller Southeast Alaska towns. Many of the region's commuter and air-taxi operators also maintain desks at the airport and have flights out of Juneau, including **L.A.B. Flying Service** (☎ **907/789-9160;** www.labflying.com) and **Wings of Alaska** (☎ **907/789-0790;** www.wingsofalaska.com).

BY FERRY All the ferries of Southeast's main-line **Alaska Marine Highway System** (☎ **800/642-0066;** www.dot.state.ak.us/external/amhs/home.html) stop at the terminal in Auke Bay (☎ **907/465-3940**), 14 miles from downtown. The *Malaspina* runs daily up the Lynn Canal to Haines and Skagway and back in the summer, leaving Juneau at 7am, arriving at Haines at 11:30am, arriving at Skagway at 1:45pm, then leaving Skagway at 4:15pm going back to Haines and returning to Juneau at 11pm. The passenger fare is $24 to Haines, $32 to Skagway. Cabins with outside windows have been made into inexpensive private day rooms, a relaxing, private way to travel.

GETTING INTO TOWN FROM THE AIRPORT & FERRY TERMINAL **Capital Cab** (☎ **907/586-2772** or 907/364-3349) offers **taxi service** (as well as tours by the hour). A cab in from the airport will cost you nearly $20. An express **Capital Transit city bus** (☎ **907/789-6901**) comes to the airport at 11 minutes past the hour on weekdays from 8:11am to 5:11pm and costs $1.25; however, your luggage has to fit under your seat or at your feet.

A cab from the ferry dock costs even more than from the airport, but **Mendenhall Glacier Transport (MGT;** ☎ **907/789-5460;** www.mightygreattrips.com) meets the boats May to September with a blue school bus and charges only $5 to town. They'll also take you from the ferry to the airport, but won't take passengers from the airport to downtown. Call between 6 and 8pm the night before your ferry leaves to arrange a pickup.

ORIENTATION

Juneau has three main parts: downtown, the Mendenhall Valley, and Douglas. Downtown Juneau is a numbered grid of streets overlying the uneven topography like a patterned quilt over a pile of pillows. As you look at Juneau from the water, Mount

Flying to Juneau

Don't schedule anything tightly around a flight to Juneau: The mist-shrouded airport, wedged between ocean and mountain, is tough to get into and can be a hair-raising place to land. It even has its own verb: *to overhead.* That means that when you fly to Juneau, you could end up somewhere else instead. The airline will put you on the next flight back to Juneau when the weather clears, but they won't pay for hotel rooms or give you a refund. Your only protection is travel insurance and a loose itinerary. This situation is such an ingrained part of Juneau's way of life that a channel on the cable TV system broadcasts the view from the airport 24 hours a day, showing the weather over the Gastineau Channel (it's called the Channel Channel, 23 on the dial). Residents know the view so well they can tell from the silent image if they'll get out that day.

Juneau is on the left and Mount Roberts on the right; Mount Roberts is a few hundred feet taller, at 3,819 feet. **Franklin Street** extends south of town 5½ miles to good hiking trails and the hamlet of Thane. When the city outgrew its original site downtown, housing spread to the suburban **Mendenhall Valley,** about a dozen miles out the Egan Expressway or the parallel, two-lane Glacier Highway to the north. The glacial valley also contains the Juneau International Airport, University of Alaska Southeast, and the **Auke Bay** area, where the ferry terminal is located. The road continues 40 miles, to a place generally called **"The End of the Road."** Across a bridge over the Gastineau Channel from downtown Juneau is Douglas Island. Turn left for the town of **Douglas,** mostly a bedroom community for Juneau, and turn right for the North Douglas Highway, which leads to the ski area and some beautiful rocky beaches.

GETTING AROUND

BY RENTAL CAR A car is a hindrance in compact downtown Juneau, but if you're going to the Mendenhall Glacier or to any of the attractions out the road or on Douglas Island, renting a car for a day or two is a good idea. Major car-rental companies are based at the airport.

BY BIKE Bikes make good sense in Juneau, where separated paths parallel many of the main roads and downtown traffic is slow. The 24-mile round-trip to Mendenhall Glacier keeps you on a bike path almost all the way. There are several bike shops. **Mountain Gears,** at 126 Front St. (☎ **907/586-4327**), rents 21-speed mountain bikes for $6 an hour or $25 a day, full suspension for $35. This full-service bike shop can give you ideas for mountain biking rides and provide maps and directions. If you're staying in the valley, try **Adventure Sports,** in the Nugget Mall at 8757 Glacier Hwy. and at the Auke Bay Harbor (☎ **907/789-5696**).

VISITOR INFORMATION

The **Davis Log Cabin Visitor Center,** 134 Third St., Juneau, AK 99801 (☎ **888/581-2201** or 907/586-2201; fax 907/586-6304; www.traveljuneau.com), located at Seward Street, near the capitol building in the center of downtown, is a replica of Juneau's first school, a log cabin with a little log belfry. Operated by the Juneau Convention and Visitors Bureau, the center distributes the usual commercial visitor information, a readable Juneau map, and a brochure called *Free Things to See and Do in Juneau.* Their *Juneau Travel Planner,* on line or on paper, contains exhaustive listings of hotels and B&Bs, charter boats, tours, and other services of business, including information like rates that booster organizations usually don't publish. The center is open Monday to Friday 8:30am to 5pm, Saturday and Sunday 9am to 5pm in summer; Monday to Friday 9am to 5pm in winter.

Volunteers also staff a **visitor information desk** at the airport, near the door in the baggage-claim area, during the summer. On the Web, **www.Juneaualaska.com** is a deep and well-organized site with lots of community information as well as travel lists and links.

The 17-million-acre Tongass National Forest maintains its headquarters' visitor center in an alcove in the convention center lobby, the **U.S. Forest Service Visitor Information Center,** in the Centennial Hall, 101 Egan Dr., Juneau, AK 99801; ☎ **907/586-8751;** fax 907/586-7928; www.fs.fed.us/r10/tongass). The rangers behind the desk are a critical link to the outdoors of the region, answering questions about trips and hikes; selling a fine collection of trail guides, field guides, and maps; distributing permits for Pack Creek bear viewing; and providing the lowdown on public recreation cabins around Juneau. They're open Monday to Friday 8am to 5pm.

FAST FACTS: JUNEAU

There are numerous **banks** in Juneau, and ATMs are available in most grocery stores.

Bartlett Regional Hospital, 3260 Hospital Dr. (☎ **907/586-2611**), is 3 miles out the Glacier Highway.

The organic **Cafe Myriad,** 230 Seward St. (☎ **907/586-3433;** www.myriadcafe.com), charges $3.50 for the first 15 minutes of **Internet access,** and $8 an hour thereafter.

The **police department** is at 210 Admiral Way. For nonemergency business, call ☎ **907/586-2780.**

The main **post office** downtown is in the federal building, 709 W. Ninth St., and in Mendenhall Valley at 9491 Vintage Blvd., by the airport.

Sales tax is 5%. You pay 12% tax on **rooms.**

SPECIAL EVENTS

An exhaustive event calendar is posted on the visitors' bureau Web site: www.traveljuneau.com/discover.

The Alaska Folk Festival (☎ **907/463-3316**) is an annual community-wide celebration drawing musicians from all over the state, April 16 to 22, 2001. **The Juneau Jazz and Classics Festival** (☎ **907/463-3378;** www.juneau.com/music), May 18 to 27, 2001, includes concerts at various venues. **Gold Rush Days** (☎ **907/586-2497**) at Riverside Park includes logging and mining events and competitions anyone can join, June 29 and 30, 2001.

The Golden North Salmon Derby (☎ **907/789-2399;** www.salmonderby.org) held annually since 1947, targets kings and silvers August 17 to 19, 2001. Unlike some other such derbies around the state, this isn't just a tourist thing—it empties the town, and is even covered live on the radio.

DOWNTOWN ATTRACTIONS & ACTIVITIES

✪ **Alaska State Museum.** 395 Whittier St. ☎ **907/465-2901.** www.educ.state.ak.us/lam/museum/asmhome.html. Admission $5 adults, free for ages 18 and under. Winter discount $4. High season, Mon–Fri 9am–6pm, Sat–Sun 10am–6pm; winter, Tues–Sat 10am–4pm.

The museum contains a huge collection of Alaska art and Alaska Native and historical artifacts, but it doesn't seem like a storehouse at all because the objects' presentation is based on their meaning, not their value. Come here to put the rest of your visit in context. A clan house in the Alaska Native Gallery contains authentic art you'd really find in its functional place. The Lincoln Pole is here, carved by an artist who used a picture of the president as his model to represent his clan's first encounter with whites. Native cultures from around the state contributed superb artifacts, presented to explain the lifestyle of those who made them. The ramp to the second floor wraps around the natural history display, with an eagle in a tree, and at the top a state history gallery uses significant pieces to tell Alaska's story. The children's area is among the best we've seen, with a ship they can play in—I just about needed a crowbar to get my son out. The gift store carries authentic Native arts and crafts, plus books, maps, and so on.

The Juneau-Douglas City Museum. At the corner of Fourth and Main sts. ☎ **907/586-3572.** www.juneau.lib.ak.us/parksrec/museum/. Admission $3 adults ($2 in winter), free for ages 18 and under. High season, Mon–Fri 9am–5pm, Sat–Sun 10am–5pm. Low season, Fri–Sat noon–4pm and by appointment.

This fun little museum displays artifacts and photographs from the city's pioneer and mining history in a meaningful way. Multilayered glass maps of the mines under Juneau are especially interesting. There are gorgeous stained-glass windows. The tiny book shop is stocked with handy information for your visit, including the historic hike guide booklet, historic walking-tour map, and maps of the Evergreen Cemetery and the old Treadwell Mine. The plaza in front is where the 49-star U.S. flag was first raised in 1959—they didn't make many of those, as Hawaii was admitted as the 50th within a year, but you'll still find one flying here.

The Last Chance Mining Museum. 1001 Basin Rd. (From downtown, take Gold St. to the top, then turn left, continuing up the valley to the end of Basin Rd.) ☎ **907/586-5338.** Admission $3. Daily 9:30am–12:30pm and 3:30–6:30pm. Closed Oct to mid-May.

The museum is in old mining buildings on forested Gold Creek, amid intact old mine shafts that penetrated many miles through the mountains—annually, the local historic society leads expeditions through them. The museum preserves the equipment and story of hard-rock gold mining in Juneau, once among the world's biggest centers of the industry. They have layered glass maps of mines, a mock tunnel, and one of the world's largest air compressors.

Mount Roberts Tramway. 490 South Franklin St., at the waterfront near the cruise-ship dock. ☎ **888/461-8726** or 907/463-3412. All-day pass $19.75 adults, $10.50 children 12 and under, tax included. Daily 9am–9pm. Closed Oct–Apr.

The tram takes only 6 minutes to whisk passengers from tourist-clogged Franklin Street to the clear air and overwhelming views at the tree line (1,760 ft.), a destination that used to require a day of huffing and puffing to witness. The tram itself can be crowded; it's once you're up there that the beauty hits you. The Alaska Native owners seem to understand that, and they have done a good job of building a network of paths to take advantage of the views, passing through a fascinating alpine ecosystem, and have even carved artwork into the living trunks of some of the trees. If you're energetic, you can start a 6-mile round-trip to Mount Roberts's summit (at 3,819 ft.), or you can hike the 2.5 miles back to downtown. There's an auditorium at the top tram station showing a film on Tlingit culture and a multimedia performance on wildlife. A bar and grill serves three meals a day. Don't bother with the tram on a day of fog or low overcast, as it's not worth the trip without the view.

A Juneau Walking Tour

Start: At the cruise-ship dock, or skip the first three paragraphs and start at the Capitol Building.
Finish: Gold Street
Time: 1 to 1½ hours for standard tour; 2½ hours for the extended tour, with minimal stops.

1. **The Marine Park waterfront area** is thronged with cruise-ship passengers and tour operators selling their services on most summer days. Juneau's downtown attractions are within walking distance. There's a visitor information kiosk to ask seasonal questions and pick up a map.

   Among the most popular sites in town is right at the dock, the statue of a small dog facing the ships as they come in. This is **Patsy Ann,** a bull terrier that in the 1930s always seemed to know when a steamer was arriving and faithfully stationed herself on the dock to meet the disembarking passengers.
2. The **Juneau Public Library,** atop the parking garage at the waterfront on South Franklin Street (☎ **907/586-5249**), has a large kids section, views of the water and Douglas Island, and impressive stained glass. A steel sculpture outside depicts an eagle and raven, representing the two halves of the Tlingit people. In

Downtown Juneau Walking Tour

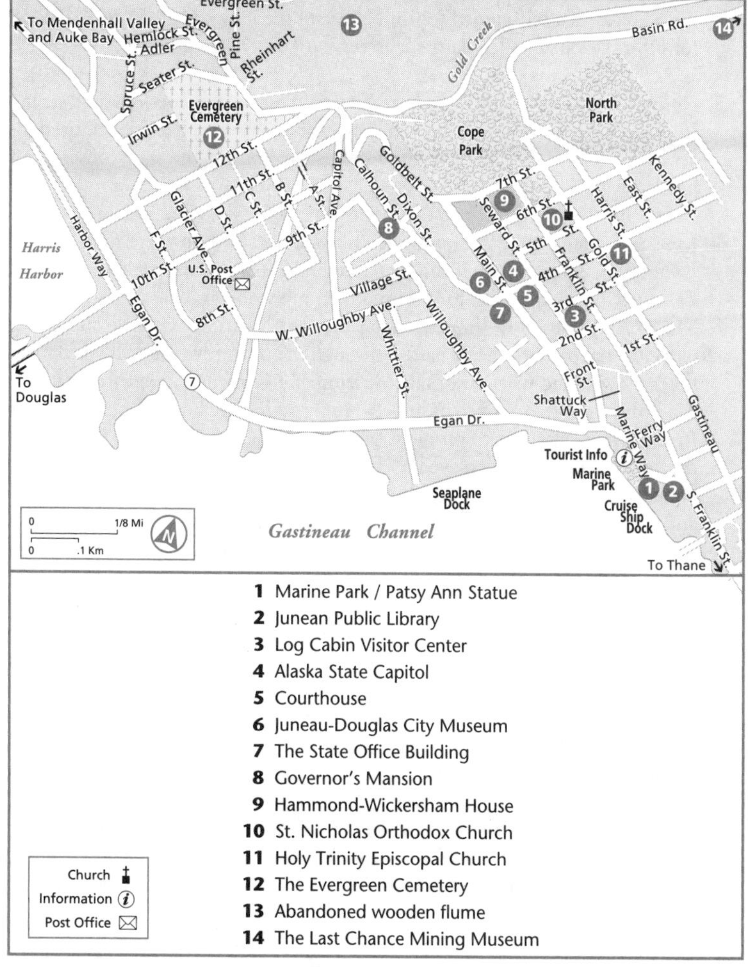

their matrilineal tradition, marriage was permitted only to a member of the opposite moiety, an eagle to a raven. Hours are Monday to Thursday 11am to 9pm and Friday to Sunday noon to 5pm.

Walk several blocks uphill on Franklin Street, to see some of the town's most interesting shops (see "Shopping," below) and turn 1 block left on Third Street to the:

3. **Davis Log Cabin Visitor Center,** at Third and Seward streets. It's a replica of a log school house, and is described above under "Visitor Information."

Another block uphill brings you to the:

4. **Alaska State Capitol,** standing on Fourth Street between Main and Seward. The federal government built the nondescript brick building in 1931; it may be the least impressive state capitol in the most beautiful setting in the nation. Inside, some of the old fashioned woodwork and decorative details are interesting, and the building is mostly without security to block your wanderings. During the summer, free tours start every half hour, 9am to 4:30pm, except Saturdays; other

times, pick up a self-guided tour brochure in the lobby. Call ☎ **907/465-3800** for information. The legislature is in session January to early May.

Across Fourth is the:

5. **Courthouse,** with a statue of a bear in front. This bear defines Alaska taste in art: It replaced a hated abstract steel sculpture called *Nimbus* that was removed by an act of the legislature, finally coming to rest in front of the state museum a few blocks away.

   On the opposite, northwest corner is the:

6. **Juneau Douglas City Museum,** described above. Stop in there now to buy the Evergreen Cemetery map if you plan to include that in your walk, or the *Historic Downtown Juneau Guide,* to learn more on the whole walk.
7. **The State Office Building** stands on the fourth corner. It's built into the edge of a cliff that forms a major barrier through the downtown area; if you're headed for the lower land where the State Museum and Centennial Hall are located, you can avoid eight flights of steps in between by taking the building's elevator down. In any event, visit the towering atrium, with its great views and a 1928 movie theater pipe organ that's played on Fridays at noon. The **state library historical collections** (☎ **907/465-2923**), off the lobby, contains historic photographs and artifacts, some of which are often on exhibit. They're open Monday to Friday 1 to 5pm. On sunny days, the patio off the atrium is a warm place for a picnic, with a fabulous view.

   Returning out the door you entered, turn left and follow Calhoun Street around the curve. An outdoor staircase here leads down to the flat area of town down below (but you know about taking the elevator). Those lowlands originally were mostly underwater and this embankment stood just above the shoreline, which continued along Front and South Franklin streets, before mine tailings created the fill that's now much of Juneau. The pedestrian overpass across Calhoun is used by the governor and his dog, Shadow, a black lab, to get to the Capitol from the white, neoclassical:

8. **Governor's Mansion** that's on the left. It was built by the federal government in 1912. If you see a tall, slender man with dark hair running a dog in the yard, that's Gov. Tony Knowles. A Democrat from Anchorage, he was elected to a second four-year term in 1998.

   Continuing down Calhoun, you'll come to Gold Creek, where you can turn right to peaceful **Cope Park,** which has a playground and tennis courts.

   To continue this walk to Evergreen Cemetery and up to the top of the town and through the woods on the flume—a long, strenuous walk—continue straight ahead. That's covered below under "The Extended Walk." Otherwise, backtrack from Gold Creek to Goldbelt Street, which branches from Calhoun on a seemingly impossible upward slope and circles back to the interesting and historic neighborhood behind the capitol.

   From Goldbelt, follow Seventh Avenue toward the mountains. On the right, you'll pass the well-marked:

9. **Hammond-Wickersham House.** A typical large frame house, it was built my a mine superintendent in 1899 and was bought in 1928 by Judge James Wickersham, revered by Alaskans for bringing law to Interior Alaska in Eagle, Nome, and Fairbanks, for exploring the Denali area and helping make it a national park, for convincing the federal government to build the Alaska railroad, and for winning Alaska's right to make its own laws when he represented

the territory in Congress. At this writing, a group was hoping to open the house for tours.

If you were to continue to the end of Seventh and climb the public stairs, you would come to Basin Road, which, after a considerable walk to the left up Gold Creek and over a wooden bridge, would lead to the **Last Chance Mining Museum** (see "The Extended Walk," below). For a shorter walk, turn right on Gold Street and follow it to the corner of Fifth, site of the tiny:

10. St. Nicholas Orthodox Church, a significant architectural landmark. The octagonal chapel was built in 1893–94 by Slavic miners and Tlingits. Many Tlingits chose the Russian Orthodox faith in the 19th century when government-sponsored missionaries sought to convert Alaska Natives to Christianity, for it was the only faith that allowed them to worship in their own language. Father Ivan Veniaminov (see page 124) had translated the Bible into Tlingit 50 years earlier when the Russians were still in Sitka. Today, Alaska Natives make up the bulk of the Russian Orthodox church in Alaska, and St. Nicholas still has an active Tlingit parish. Lengthy services are sung in English, Tlingit, and Slavic for Saturday vespers at 6pm and on Sunday morning at 10am; the congregation stands throughout the service. Otherwise, a guide is on hand 9am to 6pm, May 15 to September, to answer questions, and excellent written guides are available, too. A $2 donation is requested.

11. Holy Trinity Episcopal Church, a block down Gold at Fourth, also is worth a stop for its peaceful turn-of-the-century sanctuary of dark wood under a steeply pitched roof; it's unlocked all day. The church was built in 1896 by Alaska's first Episcopal bishop, when he established their first mission in Juneau. A little-known piece of church history: As an undersized acolyte at age 8, I almost smashed the stained glass in the back of the church when I lost control of the heavy crucifix and had to run down the aisle to keep up with it.

THE EXTENDED WALK

This long walk will take most of an afternoon, and includes some steep stairways and streets. Follow the walking tour until you reach Gold Creek (see number 8, above), then cross the creek and stay on the same road, bearing right as it becomes Martin Street.

12. The Evergreen Cemetery slopes toward the ocean, opening a wonderful vista over the clear green lawn. One reason it's so broad and open is that the markers are flush with the ground. The old Alaska Native graves are in the wooded portion on the far side. Joe Juneau and Richard Harris, the city's founders, are buried near the cross at this top end of the cemetery.

Across the road from the cross, Rheinhart Street reaches a little way into the mountainside. Follow the steep public stairs on the left up to the bottom of Pine Street. This is the walk I described in the introduction. The views get better and better as you rise to the top of Pine Street then go right on Evergreen Street, following to where it gives out among shadowy spruce and western hemlock. Continue on the peaceful forest trail among the ferns and evergreens up the valley from here, coming to the:

13. Abandoned wooden flume. Once the town's aqueduct, it now is maintained as a boardwalk for walks into the forest. Since it carried water, it's nearly level, but watch your step in wet weather, as it crosses some the high trestles over gullies.

At the end of the flume, cross over the valley to Basin Road. Stop here to see:

14. **The Last Chance Mining Museum,** described above under "Downtown Attractions & Activities."

To the left is the Perseverance Trail, described below, which continues up between the mountains, and the trailhead for a challenging hike up Mount Juneau. To get back to town, follow Basin Road back down the valley. It will leave you downtown, at the top of Gold Street, where you can complete the walking tour described above starting at paragraph 10.

SHOPPING

Juneau, like Ketchikan and Skagway, has developed a shopping district catering primarily to the cruise ships. When the last of more than 500 port calls are over late in the summer, many of the shops close their doors. If you're looking for authentic Alaska Native art and crafts, be warned that counterfeiting has become widespread. For buying tips, read "Native Art—Finding the Real Thing" in chapter 2.

For serious galleries, check out **Portfolio Arts,** 210 Ferry Way, Suite 101 (☎ **907/586-8111**), a gallery of Native and contemporary Alaskan art. **The Raven's Journey,** 175 S. Franklin (☎ **907/463-4686**), a brightly lit, museumlike gallery, shows Tlingit and other Northwest Indian carvings and masks, and whalebone, ivory, and fossil ivory carvings and jewelry from the Yup'ik and Inupiat of western and northern Alaska.

Rie Muñoz paints in Juneau, and her prints and tapestries are shown downtown at the **Decker Gallery,** 233 S. Franklin (☎ **907/463-5536**), and in the Mendenhall Valley at the **Rie Muñoz Gallery,** at 2101 Jordan Ave. (☎ **907/789-7411;** www.riemunoz.com). Her simple, graphic watercolors represent coastal Alaska communities and Native people with a cheerful but observant sensibility.

For gifts, try **Annie Kaill's** fine arts and crafts gallery, 244 Front St. It's a little out of the cruise-ship shopping area and gets most of its business from locals. It has a rich, full, homey feeling, with local work at various price levels. The long-established **Ad Lib,** at 231 S. Franklin St., also is reliable and oriented to items made in Alaska, with a charming variety of things that look and feel real. **Galligaskins,** 219 S. Franklin St. (www.galligaskins.net), features clothing with Alaska-theme designs. **Hearthside Books** is a cubbyhole of a bookstore at the corner of Franklin and Front streets, but has a good selection for its size. (Their larger branch is in the Mendenhall Valley's Nugget Mall, at 8745 Glacier Hwy.) The pleasingly dusty **Observatory,** at 235 Second St. (☎ **907/586-9676**), sells rare books, maps, and prints about Alaska.

Bill Spear sells his own brightly colored metal pins from his studio upstairs at 174 S. Franklin (☎ **907/586-2009**). Alaskans collect the vividly executed fish, birds, and other natural subjects, and treasure Spear's witty, provocative, and special-issue pins, too. He's a local original.

Taku Smokeries, at 550 S. Franklin, across the parking lot from the tram station (☎ **800/582-5122** or 907/463-3474; www.takusmokeries.com), is worth a stop even if you're not in the market for the pricey delicacies in the case: It's interesting to watch workers fillet, smoke, and pack salmon through large windows, and to read the explanatory signs about what they're doing. They'll ship the smoked fish anywhere.

ATTRACTIONS BEYOND WALKING DISTANCE

Mendenhall Glacier Transport (☎ **907/789-5460**) does a 2½-hour town and Mendenhall Glacier tour for $17.50. **Alaska Travel Adventures** (☎ **800/478-0052** in Alaska, 800/791-2673 outside Alaska, or 907/789-0052; www.alaskaadventures.com), offers a 90-minute mining-history tour in summer, complete with gold panning; the cost is $37 for adults and $25 for children 12 and under.

Juneau Beyond Downtown

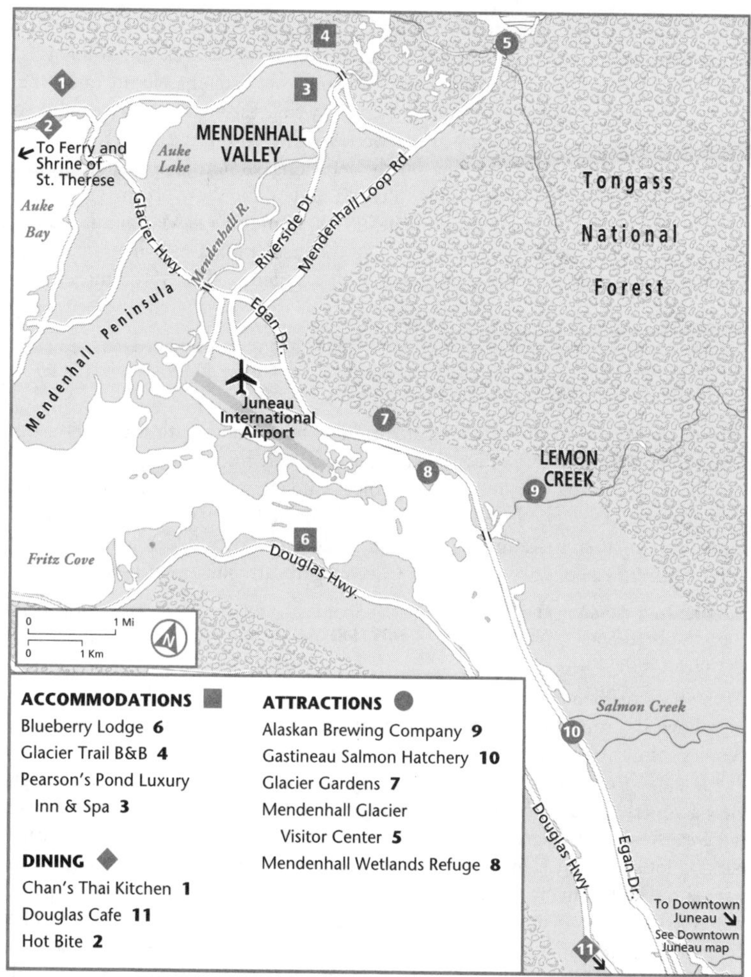

Alaskan Brewery and Bottling Company. 5429 Shaune Dr. ☎ **907/780-5866.** www.alaskanbeer.com. May–Sept, Mon–Sat 11am–4:30pm. Oct–Apr, Thurs–Sat 11am–4:30pm. Turn right from Egan Dr. on Vanderbilt Hill Rd., which becomes Glacier Hwy., then right on Anka St. and right again on Shaune Dr.

Beer lovers and aspiring capitalists will enjoy the tour of Alaska's most popular craft brewery. Now too big to still be called "micro," the brewery started in 1986 when 40 friends bet $5,000 each on Geoff and Marcy Larson's idea of bringing a local gold rush–era brew back to life. It worked, and now Alaskan Amber is everywhere in Alaska and in much of the Northwest, and the brewery has won a long list of national and international awards for its brews. The short but informative free tour includes tasting of the Amber, Pale Ale, and ESB beers, and starts every half hour.

Gastineau Salmon Hatchery. 2697 Channel Dr. (3 miles from downtown, turn left at the first group of buildings on Egan Dr.). ☎ **877/463-2486** or 907/463-5114. www.alaska.net/~dipac. Admission $3 adults, $1 children ages 12 and under. Summer, Mon–Fri 10am–6pm, Sat–Sun 10am–5pm. Sept 15–May 15, call ahead.

The hatchery, commonly known as DIPAC (Douglas Island Pink and Chums), was ingeniously designed to allow visitors to watch from outdoor decks the whole process of harvesting eggs and fertilizing them with milt for hatching. From mid-June to October, salmon swim up a 450-foot fish ladder, visible through a window, into a sorting mechanism, then are "unzipped" by workers who remove the eggs. You can often see seals and other wildlife feeding on the returning salmon just offshore from the hatchery at these times. Inside, large saltwater aquariums show off the area's marine life as it looks in the natural environment. It's less impressive in May and June, before the fish are running, when the tour includes the incubation area, where the fish eggs develop in racks of trays. Hatchery tours don't take long; allow 45 minutes for your entire visit.

Glacier Gardens. 7600 Glacier Hwy. (1 mile from the airport, beyond the Fred Meyer store). ☎ **907/790-3377.** www.ptialaska.net/~ggardens. Admission $14.95 adults, $8.95 ages 6–12. Summer daily 9am–6pm. Closed off-season.

This recently developed botanical garden, built by a family with a greenhouse and landscaping business, shows off both the native rain forest and subalpine flora of Southeast Alaska and also the brilliant colors gardeners can draw from this climate with such plants as rhododendrons and azaleas. Trails weave through the wooded formal garden, then head up the mountainside to a level of 500 feet, with broad views and a different ecological community. Covered golf carts shuttle visitors through.

Mendenhall Glacier. At the head of Glacier Spur Rd. (right from Egan Dr. on Mendenhall Loop to Glacier Spur). Visitor Center (☎ **907/586-6640**) open daily in summer 8am–6pm; call for winter hours.

At the head of Mendenhall Valley, the Mendenhall Glacier glows bluish white, looming above the suburbs like an ice-age monster that missed the general extinction. Besides being a truly impressive sight, Mendenhall is the most easily accessible glacier in Alaska and one of the state's most visited attractions. The parking lot has a great view across the lake to the glacier's face, with several short paths and a covered viewing area. A wheelchair-accessible trail leads down to the lake. The land right near the parking lot shows the signs of the glacier's recent passage, with little top soil, stunted vegetation, and in many places bare rock that shows the scratch marks of the glacier's movement. Atop a bedrock hill, reached by stairs or an elevator chipped out of the bedrock, the recently remodeled Forest Service visitor center contains a glacier museum, with excellent explanatory models, computerized displays, and ranger talks. Admission is $3 for adults, free for children. In late summer, you can watch red and silver salmon spawning in **Steep Creek,** just short of the visitor center on the road.

There are several trails at the glacier, ranging from a half-mile nature trail loop to two fairly steep, 3½-mile hikes approaching each side of the glacier. At the visitor center and a booth near the parking lot, the Forest Service distributes a brochure, "Mendenhall Glacier: Carver of a Landscape," which includes a trail map. The **East Glacier Loop Trail** is a beautiful day hike leading through the forest to a waterfall near the glacier's face and parts of an abandoned rail tram and an abandoned dam on Nugget Creek; the trail has steep parts but is doable for school-age children. The **West Glacier Trail** is more challenging, leaving from 300 yards beyond the skater's cabin and campground off Montana Creek Road and following the edge of the lake and glacier, providing access to the ice itself for experienced climbers with the right equipment.

In the winter, Mendenhall's lake and the surrounding paths in front of the glacier are groomed for cross-country skiing. A loop circles on the lake ice—flat skiing, but with a great view of the glacier. Don't go beyond the orange safety markers near the glacier's face. Other trails weave through the pothole lakes across from the glacier. Start at the Skater's Cabin—follow the loop road past the Glacier Spur Road, turn right on Montana Creek Road, and right again on Skater's Cabin Road. That's also the way to the lakeside and riverside Mendenhall Lake Campground.

ATTRACTIONS & ACTIVITIES OUT THE ROAD

On sunny summer weekends, Juneau families get in the car and drive out the road (northwest along the Glacier Highway, as it's officially known). The views of island-stippled water from the paved two-lane highway are worth the trip, but there also are several good places to stop. To use this road guide, set your trip odometer to zero at the ferry dock (which is 14 miles from downtown Juneau).

The **Auke Village Recreation Area** is a mile beyond the ferry dock and is a good place for picnics and beach walks. Less than a mile farther is a Forest Service campground.

The **Shrine of St. Therese** (☎ **907/780-6112;** www.juneau-diocese.addr.com), 9 miles beyond the ferry dock, stands on a tiny island reached by a foot trail causeway. The wonderfully simple chapel of rounded beach stones, circled by markers of the 15 stations of the cross, stands peaceful and mysterious amid trees, rock, water, and the cries of the raven, seeming to be of another world. The setting is truly spiritual. The vaguely Gothic structure was built in the 1930s of stone picked up from these shores and dedicated by Alaska's first Catholic bishop to St. Therese of Lisieux, who died in 1899 at the age of 24. Liturgy services are held June to August at 1:30pm. The Juneau Catholic Diocese maintains a log retreat hall on the shore facing the island; be quiet when descending the gravel driveway from the highway. They also have cabins for rent. The shrine's island is a good vantage from which to look around in the **Lynn Canal** for marine mammals or, at low tide, to go tide pooling among the rocks.

Eagle Beach, 14 miles beyond the ferry dock, makes a good picnic area in nice weather, when you can walk among the tall beach grass or out on the sandy tidal flats and look for eagles, or go north along the beach to look for fossils in the rock outcroppings.

The road turns to gravel, then comes to **Point Bridget State Park,** 24 miles beyond the ferry dock (see "Getting Outside: On Shore," below). Two miles farther, the road comes to an end, 40 miles from Juneau at pretty **Echo Cove.**

GETTING OUTSIDE: ON SHORE

ALPINE (DOWNHILL) SKIING The city-owned **Eaglecrest Ski Area** (☎ **907/790-2000;** www.juneau.lib.ak.us/eaglecrest/) is a large, steep local ski area, challenging enough to train Olympic silver medalist Hillary Lindh, Juneau's favorite daughter. A chair goes right to the top of Douglas Island, opening 360° views that defy description, and 640 acres of skiing terrain. More than 30 trails have a total vertical drop of 1,400 feet. It's only 12 miles from downtown on North Douglas Highway. An all-day lift ticket is $25 for adults.

BIRD WATCHING Bald eagles are more common than pigeons in Juneau. A few years ago, one of them made off with a tourist's Chihuahua, starting a statewide debate about whether it was funny or horrible. Eagles are most common on the shoreline, especially where fish are plentiful, such as at the hatchery. For more variety, the drive out the four-lane Egan Drive to the Mendenhall Valley crosses tidal flat bird habitat; there's a viewing platform as you near the airport.

HIKING I've mentioned two good hikes at Mendenhall Glacier, above. The **Juneau Trails** guide, available from the Forest Service visitor center for $4, describes 27 more routes in the Juneau area. ***In the Miner's Footsteps,*** a guide to the history behind 14 Juneau trails, is available for $3 from the Juneau-Douglas City Museum. The Juneau

Gearing Up for Juneau's Outdoors

You can rent all the gear you'll need for outings or Forest Service Cabin visits. **Mountain Gears,** listed above under "Getting Around," has mountain bikes and offers guidance on where to ride. **Adventure Sports,** in the Valley's Nugget Mall, at 8757 Glacier Hwy. and at the Auke Bay Harbor (☎ **907/789-5696**), rents sea kayaks, mountain bikes, and camping gear. **Juneau Outdoor Center,** in the Douglas boat harbor at 101 Dock St. (☎ **907/586-8220;** home.gci.net/~juneauoutdoorcenter) rents sea kayaks, camping gear, and skiffs with outboard motors you can use for fishing or exploring. Any of these can recommend one of the several water taxis doing remote drop-offs.

---

city **Department of Parks and Recreation** (☎ **907/586-5226;** www.juneau.lib.ak.us/parksrec/) leads hikes in summer and cross-country skiing in winter on Wednesdays for adults and on Saturdays for all ages. **Gastineau Guiding Company** (☎ **907/586-2666;** www.ptialaska.net/~hikeak) also leads day hikes.

The **Perseverance Trail** climbs up the valley behind Juneau and into the mining history of the area it accesses. It can be crowded in summer. To reach the trailhead, go to the top of Gold Street and follow gravel Basin Road; the trailhead is about a mile from the capitol building. The trail is 3 miles of easy walking on the mountainside above Gold Creek to the Perseverance Mine, at the Silverbow Basin, which operated intermittently from 1885 to 1921. Use caution on icy patches, as it can be dangerous. Be sure to pick up the well-documented $1 historic guide to the trail at the Juneau-Douglas City Museum.

Two trails start from points along the Perseverance. The challenging **Mount Juneau Trail** rises more than 3,500 feet in about 2 miles from a point 1 mile from the Perseverance trailhead. Go only in dry weather to avoid disastrous falls. The **Granite Creek Trail,** starting 2 miles in, climbs 1,200 feet over 1.5 miles to an alpine basin. Either trail will allow escape from crowds on the Perseverance Trail.

Another hike right from downtown climbs **Mount Roberts**—just follow the stairway from the top of Sixth Street, a neighborhood called Star Hill. The summit is 4½ miles and 3,819 vertical feet away, but you don't have to go all the way to the top for incredible views and alpine terrain. At the 1,760-foot level, you come to the restaurant at the top of the Mount Roberts tram, mentioned above. Of course, its easier to take the tram up and hike down, or start from the tram stop to hike to the summit.

The **Treadwell Mine Historic Trail,** on Douglas Island, is a fascinating hour's stroll through the ruins of a massive hard-rock mine complex that once employed and housed 2,000 men. Since its abandonment in 1922, big trees have grown up through the foundations, intertwining their roots with rails and machinery and adding to the site's exceptional power over the imagination. A well-written and indispensable guide by the Taku Conservation Society is available from the Juneau-Douglas City Museum. This is a great hike for kids. To find the trailhead, drive over the bridge to Douglas, turn left, then continue, staying as close to the water as possible, until you reach Savikko Park, also known as Sandy Beach Park, leaving your car at the far end. The trail starts near the tall stamp mill.

Another great family outing is to the **Outer Point Trail,** 1.3 miles on a forest boardwalk to a beach with good tide pooling, lots of eagles, and possible whale sightings. Nowhere else I know are there so many kinds of lovely places in such a short walk: the mossy rain forest, the stunted muskeg swamp, a glassy little creek, and the pebbled beach and bedrock ocean pools. From there, on the western point of Douglas Island—the opposite side from Juneau—you can see Auke Bay and the airport back to the east, Admiralty Island to the west, and the tiny islands of Stephens Passage before you. The only drawback is crowding, especially when tour groups tromp through; avoid them by going early or late. To get there, drive over the bridge to Douglas, then right on North Douglas Highway 11½ miles to the trailhead.

Out the road at mile 38 on the Glacier Highway, **Point Bridget State Park** (Office: 400 Willoughby Ave., 4th floor, ☎ **907/465-4563;** www.dnr.state.ak.us/parks/units/ptbridg1.htm) is less used but has easy, scenic trails. From the beach toward the end of the trail you may see sea lions and possibly humpback whales. The flat 3½-mile path leads through forest, meadow, marsh, and marine ecosystems. It's good for cross-country skiing, too. There are two public use cabins on the trail, for rent for $35 a night, 2.5 and 3.4 miles from the trailhead. Reserve at the State Parks office, or pick up the free trail-guide brochure from the Forest Service visitor center in Centennial Hall or the Web site.

NORDIC (CROSS-COUNTRY) SKIING Juneau's warm, damp winters don't always provide enough snow for good cross-country skiing at the lower elevations, but many of the hiking trails into the mountains become winter backcountry routes, and snow does stick up there. Before going out, always check with the Forest Service for advice on your route and on avalanche conditions. Several of the Forest Service cabins also serve as winter warm-up houses during the day, and make good skiing destinations. If conditions permit, a network of trails is set around the Mendenhall Glacier (see above), and Eaglecrest, the alpine area, has 12 kilometers of trail.

RAFTING The Mendenhall River isn't a wild or scary ride, so the guides on the Native-owned **Auk Ta Shaa Discovery,** 76 Egan Dr. (☎ **800/820-2628;** www.goldbelttours.com), offer commentary on Native legends and natural history. Although the float starts at the Mendenhall Glacier, this is far from a wilderness area—the river flows through the Mendenhall Valley suburbs. Still, you are likely to see eagles, and the river will look natural, not built up. The 4-hour rides cost $89 for adults, $44.50 children 8 to 16. Transportation from downtown is included in the price.

U.S. FOREST SERVICE CABINS Five U.S. Forest Service cabins are accessible from Juneau's road system by trails ranging from 3.3 to 5.5 miles. The **Peterson Lake** cabin has a skiff for Dolly Varden and cutthroat trout from the lake; silver and pink salmon and steelhead trout run in the nearby stream. The **John Muir** cabin sits on a 1,500-foot ridge top above Auke Bay, up the Auk Nu Trail. The large **Dan Moller** cabin is located on Douglas Island right across from town. The **Eagle Glacier** cabin overlooks the glacier upriver from Eagle Beach, reached by the Amalga Trail. The **Windfall Lake** cabin is lakeside, near fishing streams, with a big porch. Each rents for $35 a night, and generally there's a 2-night maximum stay. All these cabins are popular and must be reserved well in advance.

Several more cabins are reached only by air or water, including the **Berner's Bay** cabin, on a sandy beach an 8-mile sea-kayak paddle from Echo Cove. Two cabins, reached by float plane, are on **Turner Lake** in alpine terrain off Taku Inlet, each with a skiff and spectacular scenery. A bunch of cabins sit on trails and remote lakes and beaches on Admiralty Island, less than a half-hour floatplane ride from Juneau (see "Getting Outside: On Admiralty Island," below). The sea-kayaking and canoeing opportunities there are exceptional, and the island is mobbed with brown bears.

You'll need camping gear (see "Gearing Up for Juneau's Outdoors," above) to stay at the primitive cabins. The only things you can be sure of are a bunk for your sleeping bag and a roof over your head.

Get information on cabins from the **U.S. Forest Service Visitor Information Center,** in the Centennial Hall, 101 Egan Dr., Juneau (☎ **907/586-8751;** www.fs.fed.us/r10/tongass), then reserve through the national system described in "Getting Outside in the Tongass National Forest" in section 1 of this chapter.

GETTING OUTSIDE: ON THE WATER

SEA KAYAKING The protected waters around Juneau welcome sea kayaking, and the city is a popular hub for trips on the water farther afield. Besides the sublime scenery, you'll almost certainly see eagles, sea birds, and seals, and possibly humpback whales.

I recently counted five operators offering sea-kayaking excursions (and undoubtedly there are more), but the area's most established ecotourism operator is ✪ **Alaska Discovery,** 5310 Glacier Hwy. (☎ **800/586-1911** or 907/780-6226; www.akdiscovery.com), with trips all over Southeast and beyond. Part of the company's ethic and reason for being is to build support for protecting Southeast's wild places. A multiday kayak trip is your chance to really know the Alaska wilderness. Alaska Discovery will even custom-design a trip for your group. If you haven't spent much time in the outdoors but would like to see real Alaska wilderness, I couldn't recommend a better introductory trip than the Coastal Escape, a 3-day, 2-night camping trip to Berner's Bay, on Lynn Canal north of the end of the road. Besides paddling, groups spend plenty of time exploring the beaches and rain-forest shorelines. Fit beginners will do fine, with teens as young as 14 normally invited; some trips may include kids as young as 10. The cost is $495 to $595 per person. No whiners, however: There's a good chance of rain, you'll sleep in a two-person tent, and paddling is work. Alaska Discovery's other trips range up to 12 days and go some truly incredible places, including Glacier Bay National Park (see section 9 of this chapter); they're best for those with some sea-kayaking experience.

If you don't have that kind of time, Alaska Discovery and the Native-owned **Auk Ta Shaa Discovery** (☎ **800/820-2628** or 907/586-8687; www.goldbelttours.com) jointly offer a wildlife-watching sea-kayak day trip starting from an unspoiled spot way out the road for $95 per person, $47.50 ages 12 to 16. The 7-hour trip includes 5 hours of kayaking and a beach picnic.

Other operators offer even shorter tours, often in waters closer to town or with larger groups. If you're very short of time, **Alaska Travel Adventures** (☎ **800/478-0052** in Alaska, 800/791-2673 outside Alaska, or 907/789-0052; www.alaskaadventures.com) does a 3½-hour trip, with 2½ hours on the water, for $75 adults, $50 children. Their tours, composed mostly of cruise-ship passengers, start from Auke Bay.

Several businesses that rent kayaks are listed under "Gearing Up for Juneau's Outdoors" (p. 148). Typically, you'll pay about $40 a day for a single, $50 for a double. Delivery is easy to arrange on the road system.

FISHING & WHALE WATCHING The closest I ever came to a humpback whale—I almost touched it—was on the way back from king salmon fishing out of Juneau on a friend's boat. More than two dozen charter companies offer fishing from Juneau and Auke Bay; you can go to **watch whales** or fish, or both. Juneau is well protected behind layers of islands, so the water generally is calm.

There are a lot of companies offering trips. The Juneau Convention and Visitors Bureau maintains a list of businesses with details on their services and prices; their Web site has links to many. **Juneau Sportfishing and Sightseeing,** 2 Marine Way, Suite 230 (☎ **907/586-1887;** www.juneausportfishing.com), is one of the largest operators, and their rates are typical: $185 per person for a full day of fishing, $110

A Day Trip to Tracy Arm

I receive more consistently positive comments from readers about the ✪ **boat tours to Tracy Arm,** south of Juneau, than about anything else. One reason, I suspect, is that the fjords of the Tracy Arm–Fords Terror Wilderness (part of Tongass National Forest) are relatively unknown outside the area, but the scenery and wildlife viewing easily rival Glacier Bay National Park, which was rated as the best national park to visit by the readers of *Consumer Reports.* For those not riding a cruise ship, Tracy Arm has a significant advantage over Glacier Bay: It's much easier and less expensive to get to. Day trips to Tracy Arm from Juneau cost about $110 and take 8 hours; a trip to Glacier Bay costs at least three times as much and is exhausting as a day trip—it's wiser to overnight there, though that adds still more to the cost.

The Tracy Arm fjord is a long, narrow, twisting passageway into the coastal mountains, with peaks up to a mile high that jut straight out of the water, waterfalls tumbling thousands of feet down their sides. At its head, Sawyer Glacier and South Sawyer Glacier calve ice into the water with a rumble and a splash. Whales and other wildlife usually show up along the way. And, as at Glacier Bay, John Muir paid a visit. No second-best here!

The largest operator is the Native-owned **Auk Nu Tours** (part of Goldbelt, which owns most of the big tourism businesses in town), 76 Egan Dr., Juneau (☎ **800/820-2628** or 907/586-8687; www.goldbelttours.com). They offer a daylong trip daily at 9am in the summer. A naturalist provides commentary on the high-speed catamaran. Light meals and the use of binoculars are included in the price.

Other large boats compete, and you can shop around. The family operated **Adventure Bound Alaska,** at 215 Ferry Way, Juneau (☎ **800/228-3875** or 907/463-2509; www.adventureboundalaska.com), prides itself on slower tours that allow more time to soak up the sights. The total time on the water is 90 minutes more than Auk Nu and is priced $10 less. The 56-foot single-hull boat has deck space all the way around.

Another way to go is to charter a six-passenger boat. Although it may cost twice as much or more per person, you'll decide when to linger with the animals or ice. Check with the visitor center for a referral, or **Juneau Sportfishing and Sightseeing** (☎ **907/586-1887**), listed in this section under "Fishing & Whale Watching."

for 4 hours, or $85 for a 2½-hour whale-watching trip. They'll pick you up at your hotel and process or smoke your fish.

Juneau isn't known particularly for its stream fishing, but there are a few places on the roads where you can put in a line. The ***Northern Southeast Alaska and Yakutat Sport Fishing Guide,*** published by the Alaska Department of Fish and Game Division of Sport Fish, 1255 W. 8th Ave. (P.O. Box 3-2000), Juneau, AK 99801 (☎ **907/465-4180;** www.state.ak.us/local/akpages/FISH.GAME/adfghome.htm), contains all the information you'll need.

For a remote fly-in experience with fly or spinning gear, contact **Alaska Fly'N'Fish Charters,** 9604 Kelly Court (☎ **907/790-2120;** www.alaskabyair.com). A guided 4-hour trip is $350 per person, with a two-person minimum.

CRUISING A sailing or motor yacht can put you in the Inside Passage wilderness in perfect comfort, but with the freedom usually reserved only for hardy outdoors people. Imagine motoring up to a glacier or landing on a remote beach on an uninhabited island for a picnic, or catching your own salmon dinner and watching humpback whales from your own deck. Of course, it's also quite expensive to go this way.

Various Juneau operators offer multiday cruising charters on motor yachts, including **Adventures Afloat** (☎ **800/323-5628** or 907/789-0111; www.ptialaska.net/~valkyrie/) and **Alaska Yacht Charters** (☎ **800/725-3913** or 907/789-1978; www.alaskayachtcharters.com). **ABC Alaska Yacht Charters** (☎ **800/780-1239** or 907/789-1239; www.abcalaska.com) represents a fleet of 27- to 140-foot vessels. You may enjoy daydreaming with their Web site even if you can't afford it. The all-inclusive prices for a cruise with a crew start around $2,000 a day. They also charter bareboat motor yachts, without skippers, starting around $2,200 a week for the smallest vessels.

Southeast's lone bareboat sailing charter operator operates from Juneau, **58° 22'–North Sailing Charters** (☎ and fax **907/789-7301;** alaskasailing.com), and they're busy enough that you should reserve the previous fall. They have two 36-foot Catalinas, for which they charge $356 a day. Inside Passage wind can be weak and fluky, blowing through the narrow channels between the mountains, but sailing is a peaceful way to explore the wilderness.

DIVING The **Channel Dive Center,** 8365 Old Dairy Rd. (☎ **907/790-4665**), offers instruction, rentals, and guiding for dry-suit diving. From fall through spring, you can dive among sea lions. Diving is not as good in the summer, when plankton blooms tend to cloud the water.

GETTING OUTSIDE: ON THE ICE

The more than 36 major glaciers around Juneau flow from a single ocean of ice behind the mountains, the 1,500-square-mile **Juneau Icefield.** You can land on it in a helicopter just to touch the ice, or for a nature hike or dogsled ride. It's expensive, but there are few other places to see, let alone explore, the kind of ice sheet that carved North America in the last ice age. From the air, glaciers look unreal, like creations by a graphic artist, their sinuous lines of blue and white ice striped with darker gray gravel debris. Only standing on the ice, which on closer inspection resembles the crusty compressed snow of springtime snow berms, do you get a clear sense of this entirely unfamiliar kind of terrain.

It's worth noting that these tours have had some major mishaps in recent years. While these accidents represent a tiny fraction of all the safe flights, they're a reminder that flying a helicopter to a glacier is not like flying an airliner.

Era Helicopters (☎ **800/843-1947** or 907/586-2030; www.eraaviation.com/helicoptertours) is among Alaska's oldest and most respected operators. Their 1-hour glacier landing flight costs $179. They also offer a program of **dog-sled rides** on the ice. This is a neat idea: A lot of visitors to Alaska want to ride a dogsled, but it's a winter sport that really can't be re-created with sleds on wheels, as most dogsled tours try to do in the summer. Here, you do it on snow, as it's meant to be done. That excursion costs $305 per person. Wait for decent weather for a flightseeing trip; overcast weather with flat lighting makes it difficult to see the ice clearly.

Another company with its own helicopters specializes in hiking and teaching about glaciers: **NorthStar Trekking** (☎ **907/790-4530;** www.glaciertrekking.com). Their small groups (a maximum of 11, with two guides) go on hiking excursions of up to a few miles, with the speed determined by the group. The 4-hour trip, which includes half an hour of flight time, costs $289 per person.

GETTING OUTSIDE: ON ADMIRALTY ISLAND

The 900,000-acre land mass beyond Douglas Island from Juneau, at the entrances to the Gastineau Channel, is Admiralty Island, one of the largest virgin blocks of old-growth forest in the country. The vast majority of the island is the protected **Kootznoowoo Wilderness.** Kootznoowoo, Tlingit for "fortress of bears," is said to have the highest concentration of bears on earth. Despite the town of Angoon on the western side of the island, there are more bears than people on Admiralty. The island's ✪ **Pack Creek Bear Viewing Area** is the most famous and surefire place to see bears in Southeast. The area has been managed for bear viewing since the 1930s, when hunting was outlawed. There's a platform for watching the bears up close as they feed on salmon spawning in the creek in July and August. Peak viewing occurs in the middle of that period. The bears generally pay no attention to the people.

Only 25 miles from Juneau, Pack Creek is so popular that the Forest Service uses a permit system to keep it from being overrun during the day (from 9pm to 9am, no humans are allowed). There are no facilities in this wilderness area, but a platform allows safe bear viewing. Book early.

The easiest way to go is with a tour operator who has permits. The Forest Service visitor center at the Centennial Hall can give you a list of guides. **Alaska Discovery,** 5310 Glacier Hwy. (☎ **800/586-1911** or 907/780-6226; www.akdiscovery.com), has many permits for sea kayak trips. Their 1-day excursion flies out, then paddles to the creek; no experience is necessary, but you must be physically capable of hiking and paddling. It costs $450 per person. A 2-night campout and sea kayak near the creek offers more time to see the bears and appreciate the scenery. It costs $895 per person. **Alaska Fly 'N' Fish Charters,** 9604 Kelly Court (☎ **907/790-2120;** www.alaskabyair.com), also has permits for its 5½-hour fly-in visits, which cost $400 per person. Twelve permits per day go to the commercial operators and 12 to other people; 8 of those 12 can be booked in advance with the Forest Service, and the other 4 are held out to be distributed 3 days before they're good, or the previous Friday for Tuesday and Wednesday, at 9am at the Forest Service visitor center at the Centennial Hall. In the peak season, permits cost $50 for adults, $25 for those aged 16 or under or 62 and over. After you have the permit, you'll still need a way to get there, and it won't be cheap. **Alaska Fly 'N' Fish Charters,** for example, charges $200 per person round-trip to drop off customers with their own permits; the price drops to $140 for groups of three to five. You could also charter a boat, which would allow you to combine the bear watching with other sightseeing (see "Fishing & Whale Watching," above.

Protected **Seymour Canal,** on the east side of the island, is popular for canoeing and kayaking, and has two other sites besides Pack Creek where bears often show up: Swan Cove and Windfall Harbor. Outfitters are listed above. There are 15 Forest Service cabins on Admiralty, and the well-regarded **Thayer Lake Lodge,** Auke Bay (☎ **907/789-5646;** www.AlaskaOne.com/thayerlake/), is located on a wilderness inholding near Angoon. For information on the island, cabins, and an excellent $4 map, contact the **U.S. Forest Service Visitor Information Center,** in the Centennial Hall, 101 Egan Dr., Juneau (☎ **907/586-8751;** www.fs.fed.us/r10/tongass), or **Admiralty Island National Monument,** 8461 Old Dairy Rd., Juneau (☎ **907/586-8790;** www.fs.fed.us/r10/chatham/anm).

ACCOMMODATIONS

Hotel rooms are tight in the summer, so book ahead.

Bed-and-breakfasts are really the way to go in Juneau—the best B&Bs I know are here. You'll get a better room and have more fun for less money. The *Juneau Travel Planner,* published by the Juneau Convention and Visitors Bureau (☎ **888/581-2201**) contains a chart showing many of the hotels and B&Bs, with their features and price ranges. **Bed & Breakfast Association of Alaska, INNside Passage Chapter** communicates almost exclusively through its Web site (**www.accommodations-alaska.com/**), where you will find many B&Bs listed, most with links to their own pages.

EXPENSIVE

Baranof Hotel. 127 N. Franklin St., Juneau, AK 99801. ☎ **800/544-0970** or 907/586-2660. Fax 907/586-8315. www.westmarkhotels.com. 193 units. TV TEL. High season $159 double. Ask about discount packages. AE, CB, DC, DISC, MC, V.

In winter, the venerable old Baranof acts like a branch of the state capitol building for conferring legislators and lobbyists; in the summer, it's like a branch of the package-tour companies. The 1939 concrete building has the feel of a grand hotel, although some rooms are on the small side. The upper-floor rooms have great views on the water side. Remodeling there has successfully added fresh, modern comforts while retaining the old fashioned opulence of the building. Rooms below the 5th floor haven't gotten the same treatment, however, and are less desirable. Phones have voice mail and modem jacks; irons and ironing boards are in each room. Kitchenettes and large suites are available.

The art deco **Gold Room** restaurant is Juneau's most traditional fine-dining establishment. The dining room remarkably combines intimacy and grandeur, a real showplace of shining brass, frosted glass, and rich wood. The food varies in quality year to year, and on my last two visits, it was uninspired, not living up to the room or the high prices. The hotel cafe is popular and serves good basic meals.

Goldbelt Hotel Juneau. 51 W. Egan Dr., Juneau, AK 99801. ☎ **888/478-6909** or 907/586-6900. Fax 907/463-3567. www.goldbelttours.com. 105 units. TV TEL. High season $169–$179 double. Low season $139–$149 double. Extra person $15. AE, DC, DISC, JCB, MC, V.

The Goldbelt Native corporation bought this somewhat heartless upscale hotel near the water and brought its public spaces to life with masterpieces of Tlingit art, including a new totem pole out front, a huge yellow cedar bas-relief by Nathan Jackson in the lobby-restaurant area, and a museum-quality Chilkat blanket in a display case. The large bedrooms, with either two full-sized or one king bed, were upgraded with bold colors and new furniture in a wood finish like dark cherry. They're noticeably quiet and immaculate. Some have exercise equipment, and all come with standard extras such as data ports, voice mail, and ironing boards and irons. The rooms on the front have good views of the Gastineau Channel. A courtesy van runs to the airport and ferry dock.

The **restaurant,** Chinooks, is flooded with light from big windows. It serves three meals daily. For lunch, a burger is $8 and lamb shank $15. Dinner entrees are $13 to $36 on a short but varied menu. We found the cuisine, while adequate, fell short of its mark: the rosemary garlic chicken lacked flavor.

✪ **Pearson's Pond Luxury B&B Inn and Adventure Spa.** 4541 Sawa Circle, Juneau, AK 99801. ☎ **888/658-6328** or 907/789-3772. Fax 907/789-6722. www.pearsonspond.com. 4 units. TV TEL. High season $169–$259 double. Low season $70–$159 double. Extra person $30. AE, CB, DISC, DC, MC, V.

Imagine you're a slightly obsessed bed-and-breakfast host and you decide to give your guests every amenity you can possibly think of. Now go to Diane Pearson's house and count how many you missed. A refrigerator and coffee machine? Child's play: Pearson provides a kitchenette stocked with food, wine, and her own home-baked bread. Maybe you thought of a private duck pond with a dock, a rowboat, and a fountain? But did you stock the pond with fish? And did you remember VCRs, CD players,

Downtown Juneau

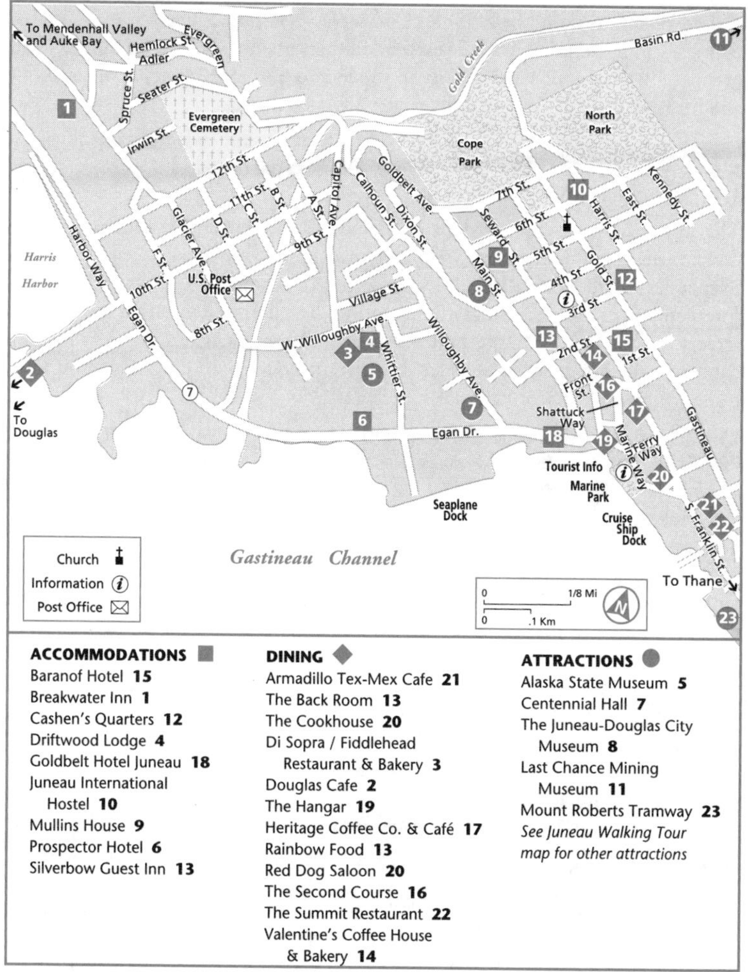

bicycles, fishing rods, massage, yoga, two separate hot tubs in the garden, and a business center, modem ports and a laptop in your room, e-mail accounts, and free laundry? There's more, but you'll have to spend the night here to see it all. Book far ahead. Pearson's is located in the Mendenhall Valley, 15 minutes from downtown. Pearson also offers travel booking and rents condos downtown by the week.

Moderate

Breakwater Inn. 1711 Glacier Ave., Juneau, AK 99801. ☎ **800/544-2250** or 907/586-6303. Fax 907/463-4820. www.breakwaterinn.com. 40 units, 8 apts. TV TEL. High season $109–$119 double. Low season $79 double. Extra person $10. AE, CB, DC, DISC, MC, V.

This two-story building near the small-boat harbor, a long walking distance to the central downtown area, has newly remodeled standard motel rooms. The waterside rooms, which cost $10 more, have balconies but also significant highway noise. On the mountain side, all 20 rooms have kitchenettes with microwave ovens.

The **restaurant** on the second floor serves traditional steak and seafood in a nautical dining room. After 30 years, it still gets good reviews. The dinner menu is extensive, with main courses mostly in the $18 to $28 range. They're open for lunch and breakfast, too.

Cashen's Quarters. 315 Gold St., Juneau, AK 99801. ☎ **907/586-9863.** Fax 907/586-9861. www.cashenquarters.com. 5 units. TV TEL. $100 double; $175 suite. Extra person $10. Rates include self-service breakfast. DISC, MC, V.

The 1914 guest house, next door to friendly Dan and Cindy Cashen's home right downtown, contains five large, self-contained units with full kitchens, satellite TV, telephones on their own lines with answering machines, extra phone lines for the Internet, hair dryers, irons, and ironing boards. The homey decoration shows a certain artistry on Cindy's part; she pulled together diverse elements for a funky sort of country style. For breakfast, she stocks the refrigerator with everything you need to make your own heavy or light meal.

✪ **Glacier Trail Bed & Breakfast.** 1081 Arctic Circle, Juneau, AK 99801. ☎ **907/789-5646.** Fax 907/789-5697. www.juneaulodging.com. 3 units. TV TEL. High season $120–$145 double. Low season $85–$100 double. Extra person $20. Rates include full breakfast. AE, MC, V.

You wake up to an expansive view of the Mendenhall Glacier filling a picture window in a big, quiet, tastefully decorated room. Luke and Connie Nelson built the house with this moment in mind. Before beginning construction, they researched B&Bs all over the country, which no doubt inspired them to include microwaves, coffeemakers, and fridge in each soundproof room. Then they added extras like Jacuzzi bathtubs, free bicycles, and private phone lines. The Nelsons are fascinating, literate people with varied interests and a lifetime of experience with Alaska's outdoors. Luke's family owns a lodge on Admiralty Island, and with them he does Pack Creek tours (see "Getting Outside: On Admiralty Island," above). You'll need to rent a car if you stay here. The Nelsons also rent kayaks for outings on nearby Mendenhall Lake. A family apartment downstairs is a perfect choice for large groups.

Prospector Hotel. 375 Whittier St., Juneau, AK 99801-1781. ☎ **800/331-2711** or 907/586-3737. Fax 907/586-1204. www.prospectorhotel.com. 58 units. TV TEL. High season $110 double; $135–$145 double with kitchenette. Low season $80 double; $95–$120 double with kitchenette. AE, DC, DISC, MC, V.

This is a comfortable hotel right on the waterfront, with large, standard rooms in attractive pastel colors. More than two dozen rooms have kitchenettes, and some of the more expensive ones equate to a nice furnished apartment. Those facing the channel have good views, but suffer from highway noise. The carpet, wall coverings, and light oak furniture were all recently renewed. The lower level, called the first floor, is a half-basement; it's somewhat dark and lacks an elevator. A parking garage takes care of the chronic shortage of downtown parking, and the hotel is planning to add an exercise room.

T. K. Maguire's, the restaurant, features an extensive dinner menu ranging in price from $11 to $22, with lots of fresh fish and a special prime rib. Lunch is sandwiches, salads, and fish in the $7 to $16 range.

Silverbow Guest Inn. 120 Second St., Juneau, AK 99801. ☎ **800/586-4146** or 907/586-4146. Fax 907/586-4242. www.silverbowinn.com. 6 units. TV TEL. High season $125 double. Low season $88 double. Extra person $15. $10 surcharge for 1-night stays. Rates include continental breakfast. AE, MC, V.

The young proprietors have found an original and oddly pleasing style in their little downtown hotel. The lobby mixes the wood floors and stained glass of a real old

Travel Tip

Generally, **smoking** is not permitted at bed-and-breakfasts and inns; smokers should ask when they book if smoking is allowed even outside.

Victorian building with funky plastic kitsch they've collected from junk shops and the Home Shopping Network. In the rooms, the overlay of new on old is a charming Pottery Barn style. One triple and one quad room are available. Breakfast from the family bakery (famed for its authentic bagels) is included in the price, as is an afternoon social house, where they serve wine and cheese in the lobby. Phones are direct and the televisions are small. (See the restaurant description below; an art house cinema also is on site.)

Inexpensive

Blueberry Lodge. 9436 N. Douglas Hwy., Juneau, AK 99801. ☎ and fax **907/463-5886.** www.blueberrylodge.com. 5 units, all with shared bathroom. High season $85–$95 double. Low season, $75 double. Extra person over age 4 $15. Rates include full breakfast. AE, DISC, MC, V.

Staying here is like visiting a first-class wilderness lodge, except you're only 6 miles from downtown Juneau. Jay and Judy Urquhart built the spectacular log building themselves in the woods of Douglas Island, looking out on an eagle's nest and the Gastineau Channel's Mendenhall Wetlands Refuge. They keep a spotting scope in the living room and will lend you binoculars and rubber boots for an exploration by the water. Rooms are large, contemporary, and very clean, with rich colors that contrast with the huge logs of the walls. It's possible to be alone and to enter without passing through the family's quarters, but the general atmosphere is social, with two teenagers, two dogs, and a cat in residence. Judy serves a big, luxurious breakfast and offers her laundry machines free for guests to use. You'll need to rent a car for the 10-minute drive to town.

The Driftwood Lodge. 435 Willoughby Ave., Juneau, AK 99801. ☎ **800/544-2239** or 907/586-2280. Fax 907/586-1034. www.driftwoodalaska.com. 63 units. TV TEL. High season $78 double; $95 suite. Low season $62 double; $89 suite. Extra person $7. AE, CB, DC, DISC, MC, V.

This downtown motel, next door to the State Museum, is popular with families, and houses legislators and aides in the winter in its apartmentlike kitchenette suites. Although the building can't hide its cinderblock construction and old-fashioned motel exterior, or its lack of elevators, the rooms have been remarkably comfortable whenever we have visited. They all have coffee machines and some other extras you would expect only in a more expensive hotel. The management is doing a good job keeping prices low while constantly improving the place. For the price of an ordinary room elsewhere, you can get a huge suite with a full kitchen here. A round-the-clock courtesy car saves guests money getting to the airport, and offers inexpensive town tours. There's a coin-op laundry and coffee in the lobby and bike rental on site.

A Hostel

Juneau International Hostel. 614 Harris St., Juneau, AK 99801. ☎ **907/586-9559.** www.home.gci.net/~juneauhostel. 47 beds. $10 per person nonmembers, $7 members.

This exceptional hostel is conveniently located in a historic yellow house among the downtown sights. The office is open from 7 to 9am and 5 to midnight in the summer, 8 to 9am and 5 to 10:30pm in the winter. Kitchen and laundry facilities are available. Prepaid reservations are essential in July and August.

CAMPING

Juneau has two Forest Service campgrounds open mid-May through mid-September. Each is exceptional in its own way. For information, call the Juneau Ranger District at ☎ **907/586-8800;** www.fs.fed.us/r10/tongass. **The Mendenhall Glacier Campground,** overlooking the lake and glacier and next to the Mendenhall River, has 68 sites, 18 of which offer full hookups for RVs. New bathrooms with showers and flush toilets were built in 1999. To get there, turn right on Montana Creek Road from Back Loop Road, also known as Mendenhall Loop Road. Tent sites are $8, RV sites $18; no reservations are accepted. **The Auke Village Campground,** 1.7 miles north of the ferry dock, lies along an ocean beach, with pit toilets and running water. Sites are $8 per night.

Auke Bay RV Park, less than 2 miles from the ferry terminal (☎ **907/789-9467**), has sites with full hookups for $22 a night, and showers and laundry facilities on-site. Reservations are recommended. **Spruce Meadow RV Park,** at 10200 Mendenhall Loop Rd. (☎ **907/789-1990;** www.juneaurv.com), was brand-new in 2000.

DINING

EXPENSIVE

DiSopra/The Fiddlehead Restaurant and Bakery. 429 W. Willoughby Ave. ☎ **907/586-3150.** Reservations recommended for DiSopra. Main courses $8.25–$24; lunch $8–$13. 15% gratuity added for parties of 6 or more. AE, DISC, MC, V. Summer, DiSopra daily 5–10pm; Fiddlehead, daily 7am–10pm. Winter, DiSopra Tues–Sat 5–9pm; Fiddlehead, daily 7am–9pm. SEAFOOD/ITALIAN.

What was a rather stale Birkenstock-and-whole grain kind of place downtown has been reinvigorated by a team of classically trained chefs into a remarkable fine dining experience. That's upstairs, at the aptly named DiSopra ("up above" or "upstairs" in Italian). Meanwhile, downstairs, the Fiddlehead lives on, with a long list of vegetarian dishes remaining, and more exciting, updated choices added for lunch or dinner that draw on the sophisticated Italian tastes introduced by the new owners. Its dining room still has butcher block tables, knotty pine paneling, and ferny stained glass. It's a refreshing lunch spot or inexpensive but rewarding place for dinner, with entrees that top out at $13. Upstairs, the big windows, mural, and solicitous service help create an elegant setting for beautifully crafted food.

The Summit Restaurant. 455 S. Franklin St. ☎ **907/586-2050.** Reservations recommended. Main courses $15–$28. AE, CB, DC, DISC, MC, V. Daily 5–11pm. STEAK/SEAFOOD.

An intimate dining room with only 10 tables looks over the cruise-ship dock from big windows, making the wonderfully formal service seem only the more opulent. This air of easy, world-weary elegance can't be faked, and the Summit is the only restaurant in Alaska that really has it. If you're lucky enough to get a reservation during the summer season, you'll find the seafood and vegetables from the constantly changing, sometimes creative menu perfectly prepared. A great place for a romantic meal. Upstairs is the Inn at the Waterfront, listed above.

MODERATE

The Back Room. 120 Second St. ☎ **907/586-4146.** www.silverbowinn.com. Main courses $6.50–$22. DISC, MC, V. Tues–Fri 11:30am–2pm and 5:30–10pm; Sat 8am–2pm, 5:30pm–10pm; Sun 8am–2pm. (In winter, they close at 9pm Tues-Sat, and don't open until 9am on Sun). SANDWICHES/ECLECTIC.

An architect and an urban planner met in graduate school in Seattle, married, and took over the historic Silverbow Inn, with its bakery and restaurant. With them they

Quick Bites in Juneau

You can pick up a picnic at the deli at the **Rainbow Food** health-food grocery at the corner of Seward and Second streets (☎ **907/586-6476**). **Hot Bite,** a stand at the Auke Bay boat harbor, is a local secret, serving charcoal-broiled burgers and mind-blowing milkshakes.

The Second Course, 213 Front St. (☎ **907/463-5533**), one of Juneau's best restaurants, is open only for lunch (Monday to Friday noon to 2pm), except for private banquets in the evening. The lunch buffet is $10.45, including tax. The warm and cheerful Heidi Grimes prepares and presides over tasty and interesting "New Asian Cuisine."

Downtown Juneau's young, professional population supports several good coffee houses. **Valentine's Coffee House and Bakery,** 111 Seward St. (☎ **907/463-5144**), serves soups, salads, pizza, and calzone, as well as microbrews, in an authentic old-fashioned storefront. **Heritage Coffee Co. and Café,** 174 S. Franklin St. (☎ **907/586-1087**), also serves light meals and is a good people-watching place. Near the cruise-ship dock, **The Cookhouse,** 200 Admiral Way (☎ **907/463-3777**), specializes in massive hamburgers and other big helpings, catering mainly to tourists in a pleasant dining room.

brought a cosmopolitan sensibility new to Juneau. At this writing, the place was doubling as an art house cinema 3 nights a week, funded in part by a Juneau Arts Council grant. The dining room, with its rough redbrick walls, high ceilings, and faux Victorian details, is decorated with campy plastic toys and junk that the rock group Devo would have loved—ray guns and the like. The food comes from an equally eccentric menu, which includes a Philly cheese steak sandwich with Cheese Whiz, an Indonesian peanut pasta, and a teriyaki salmon grill. Prices are reasonable. Microbrews are on tap and many exotic beers sold by the bottle.

Douglas Cafe. 916 Third St., Douglas (turn left after crossing the bridge from Juneau, then continue until you see the cafe on the left). ☎ **907/364-3307.** Lunch items $6.50–$9; dinner main courses $8.25–$17. MC, V. Summer, Tues–Fri 11am–8:30pm, Sat 9am–8:30pm, Sun 9am–1:30pm. Closed Tues in winter. ECLECTIC.

It's a great pleasure to find a place like this hiding in the guise of an ordinary small-town burger joint. The key, I'm convinced, is the two owners working in the kitchen, indistinguishable from the other young guys in baseball caps back there. They turn out creative seafood, meat, and vegetarian dinners, drawing on world cuisines and using some combinations rarely thought of before. The small dining room is lively, bright, and casual, but a bit cramped, and the wooden benches get hard by the end of a meal. Weekend breakfasts are an event, filling the place with townspeople. Service is quick and casual. Alaskan Amber and other craft brews are on tap.

The Hangar. 2 Marine Way. ☎ **907/586-5018.** Reservations recommended. Main courses $12–$21. AE, DISC, MC, V. Sun–Thurs 11am–1am; Fri–Sat 11am–3am. Kitchen closes at 10pm. STEAK/SEAFOOD.

Situated in a converted airplane hangar on a wooden pier with large windows, this bar and grill has great views and a jolly atmosphere. It can be smoky, but the atmosphere and camaraderie draw in the local and tourist crowds for a fun time. It's a great place to drink beer (24 brews on tap), listen to live music, or play at one of the three pool tables.

INEXPENSIVE

Armadillo Tex-Mex Cafe. 431 S. Franklin St. ☎ **907/586-1880.** Main courses $6–$16. MC, V. Summer daily 11am–10pm. Winter Mon–Sat 11am–9pm. TEX-MEX.

You order lunch at a counter and choose drinks from a cooler, but this casual, infectiously cheerful place is where some of Alaska's best Southwestern food comes from. Locals, who swear by it, know the restaurant merely as "Tex-Mex." Chicken is a specialty, and the homemade salsa is famous, served free with a basket of chips for each diner. The tiny dining room is located near the docks. They serve wine and beer, brewing their own brand periodically. With an output of only 32 barrels a year, they've kept supply well below demand.

Chan's Thai Kitchen. 11820 Glacier Hwy. (in Auke Bay, across the boat harbor). ☎ **907/789-9777.** Main courses $8–$12. MC, V. Tues–Thus 11am–2pm and 5–8pm, Fri 11am–2pm and 5–8:30pm, Sat 4:30–8:30pm. THAI.

The small, overlit dining room in the half-basement level of a steak house sees few tourists, but locals brag to each other about how long they were willing to stand in the small entrance area to get a table. For a year after it opened, everyone I met would ask me, "Have you been to the Thai place yet?" When I did finally go, I became a believer, too—the authentic Thai food is that good, the service quick and professional, and the atmosphere, if lacking in polish, conducive to a good time. Reservations are not accepted and they do not have a liquor license (it's BYO).

NIGHTLIFE

Two **salmon bakes** take place nightly during the summer, each offering entertainment with the fish. Alaska Travel Adventures has offered its **Gold Creek Salmon Bake** for almost 30 years. It's touristy, yes, but fun, with marshmallow roasting, music, and other entertainment—great for families. (I'd avoid it in the rain, though.) The cost is $24 for adults, $16 for children. Call ☎ **907/789-0052** to arrange pickup by van.

The Gold Nugget Revue plays summer nights at 7pm at the Thane Ore House, 4 miles out Thane Road, south of Juneau (☎ **907/586-1462**). The show includes cancan dancing and a gold rush melodrama—corny, but people leave smiling. The meal of salmon, halibut, or beef ribs costs $27, or skip the meal and pay $8.50 for the show alone. There is indoor or outdoor seating.

For more substantial performances, try to catch a show by Juneau's **Perseverance Theatre,** Alaska's largest professional theater. Their stage is usually dark midsummer, but the winter season often starts in September and sometimes lasts until early June. To find out what's playing, contact the theater's office at 914 Third St., Douglas (☎ **907/364-2421**), or check the Web site at www.juneau.com/pt.

A political scandal or two have put a damper on some of the infamous legislative partying that once occurred in Juneau, far away from home districts, but there still are good places to go out drinking and dancing. The **Red Dog Saloon,** at 278 S. Franklin St., is the town's most famous bar, with a sawdust-strewn floor and slightly contrived but nonetheless infectious frontier atmosphere. It's a fun place, with walls covered with lots of Alaska memorabilia. The nightly live music is free of cover charge. Across the street, **The Alaskan Bar,** 167 S. Franklin, is in an authentic gold rush hotel, with a two-story Victorian bar room that's the scene of boisterous parties and music all year. **The Hangar,** listed above under "Dining," is the place for beer drinkers, with two dozen brews on tap. They have a big-screen TV and live music Friday and Saturday nights, as well as pool and darts.

9 Glacier Bay National Park

Glacier Bay is a work in progress; the boat ride to its head is a chance to see creation unfolding. The bay John Muir discovered in a canoe in 1879 didn't exist a century earlier. Eighteenth-century explorers had found instead a wall of ice a mile thick where the entrance to the branching, 65-mile-long fjord now opens to the sea. Receding faster than any other glacier on earth, the ice melted into the ocean and opened a spectacular and still-unfinished land. The land itself is rising 1½ inches a year as it rebounds from the weight of now-melted glaciers. As your vessel retraces Muir's path—and then probes northward in deep water where ice stood in his day—the story of this new world unravels in reverse. The trees on the shore get smaller, then disappear, then all vegetation disappears, and finally, at the head of the bay, the ice stands at the water's edge surrounded by barren rock, rounded and scored by the passage of the ice but not yet marked by the waterfalls cascading down out of the clouds above.

Glacier Bay, first set aside by Pres. Calvin Coolidge in 1925, is managed by the National Park Service, which has the difficult job of protecting the wilderness, the whales, and the other wildlife while showing them to the public. This is a challenge, since this rugged land the size of Connecticut can be seen only by boat or plane, and the presence of too many boats threatens the park. The whales appear to be sensitive to the noise of vessels and, since the 1970s, when only a single whale returned all year, the park service has used a permit system to limit the number of ships that can enter the bay. Any tour boat sees several other ships on a day's journey up the bay, but how much it bothers the whales really can't be proved. After a bitter controversy, the park service increased the number of cruise ships entering the bay recently, and whale sightings have continued to be quite frequent.

On my most recent trip, I saw humpback whales breaching (leaping all the way out of the water) every day. I saw orcas, too. One day, while fishing for halibut from a small boat in foggy Icy Strait, just outside the park, I heard a sound like thunder not far off. Like thunder, the sound repeated, growing closer, but its source remained hidden behind the white circle of fog that surrounded us. Then the smooth water suddenly bulged and a huge, barnacled creature shot upward and crashed down with a sharp clap and a splash that rocked the boat. And then it happened again. The whale went on performing for most of an hour. A day later, I encountered the same spectacle while sea kayaking in the park's Bartlett Cove.

Consumer Reports readers in 1996 voted this the best of all the national parks to visit. Leaping whales and falling glaciers are hard to beat. But the park also has major drawbacks to consider. Sightings aren't guaranteed, so there's a risk that you'll spend a lot of money and not see any whales. And even though this is a huge wilderness, the opportunities to see it are limited and therefore crowded. The lone concessionaire-operated tour boat into the bay costs $175 per person and is usually full of people. The large cruise ships that bring most visitors to the park view the scenery without getting up close to the shore or wildlife and miss the shore-based attractions. Smaller ships see more, with smaller groups and more chances to get outdoors. Independent travelers can spend a few days in some of Alaska's most attractive wilderness accommodations, in Gustavus, with great fishing, hiking, sea kayaking and tour boat rides into the park. But the only way to see the heart of the park in true solitude is on a boat you charter for yourself (out of range of most budgets) or on a rugged overnight sea-kayaking adventure.

As an alternative, consider the other places to see Alaska's glaciers and whales that are easier and less expensive to visit. If you're in Juneau, consider a day trip to Tracy

Arm instead. In Southcentral Alaska, plan a day-trip from Whittier to see the glaciers of western Prince William Sound or from Seward to see Kenai Fjords National Park. There are other places in Southeast rich with marine wildlife, as well. Still, Glacier Bay beats them all—and just about anyplace on earth—for the combination of lots of whales and lots of big glaciers.

ESSENTIALS

GETTING THERE

Gustavus, covered in the next section of this chapter, is the gateway to Glacier Bay. Unless you're on a cruise ship, you'll fly or take a passenger ferry to Gustavus. Those arrangements are covered in that section. Vans to the park headquarters at Bartlett Cove meet planes and boats and cost $10 to make the 10-mile trip to the park, plus $2 for baggage. If you are staying in Gustavus, most of the inns and lodges there offer free transfers to the park.

BY TOUR BOAT The ***Spirit of Adventure*** tour boat is the main way for independent travelers to see the park. It is operated by park concessionaire **Alaska's Glacier Bay Tours,** based at 226 Second Ave. W., Seattle, WA 98119 (☎ **800/451-5952** or 206/623-2417; fax 206/623-7809; www.glacierbaytours.com) or, locally, in the summer only, at P.O. Box 199, Gustavus, AK 99826 (☎ **907/697-2226;** fax 907/697-2408). The boat is fast and quiet, carrying up to 250 passengers in upper and lower lounges. Its shortcomings are inadequate outdoor deck space and a tendency for the windows to fog up inside. Some find the table-oriented seating arrangements a bit confining, and the 9-hour voyage is too long for most children. There's a snack bar and a simple lunch is provided. Bring good rain gear and layers of warm clothing. Binoculars, a necessity, are provided. A park service ranger does the commentary, so you can count on accuracy and a didactic approach missing from most commercial tours. The fare is $175 for adults, half price for children.

The company offers a same-day trip from Juneau, Haines, or Skagway, but it makes for too long a day, and the schedule leaves no shore time in Glacier Bay or Gustavus. The package fare from Juneau is $346.50, more from Haines or Skagway. A better choice is to take their 2-day package, riding from Juneau to Gustavus on the *Auk Nu* passenger ferry, including a whale-watching trip in Icy Strait (see the Gustavus section, below), then spend the night at Bartlett Cove and do the *Spirit of Adventure* tour the second day, and fly back to Juneau, Haines, or Skagway. That package costs $481 from Juneau. See the Gustavus section for more choices.

BY SMALL CRUISE SHIP If your budget allows, there may be no better way to see Glacier Bay than on a small cruise ship on an excursion of a couple of days or more. **Alaska's Glacier Bay Tours and Cruises** has developed a whole small-ship cruise fleet around this idea, and visitors come back overjoyed. The four vessels—including the ***Wilderness Explorer*** and the larger ***Wilderness Adventurer,*** which carry racks of sea kayaks—carry only 36 to 86 passengers each, and offer a range of itineraries. See chapter 4 for a complete review.

Another highly recommended small-ship cruise line that includes Glacier Bay in its itinerary is **Cruise West.** Its offerings and prices can also be found in chapter 4.

Smaller operators based in Gustavus also do these trips. If you have a large group, you can have a boat and guide to yourself. Mike Nigro, a former backcountry ranger and 25-year resident, takes groups of four to six for $1,400 to $1,650 per day on a 42-foot yacht. **Gustavus Marine Charters** is reached at ☎ **907/697-2233** or www.gustavusmarinecharters.com.

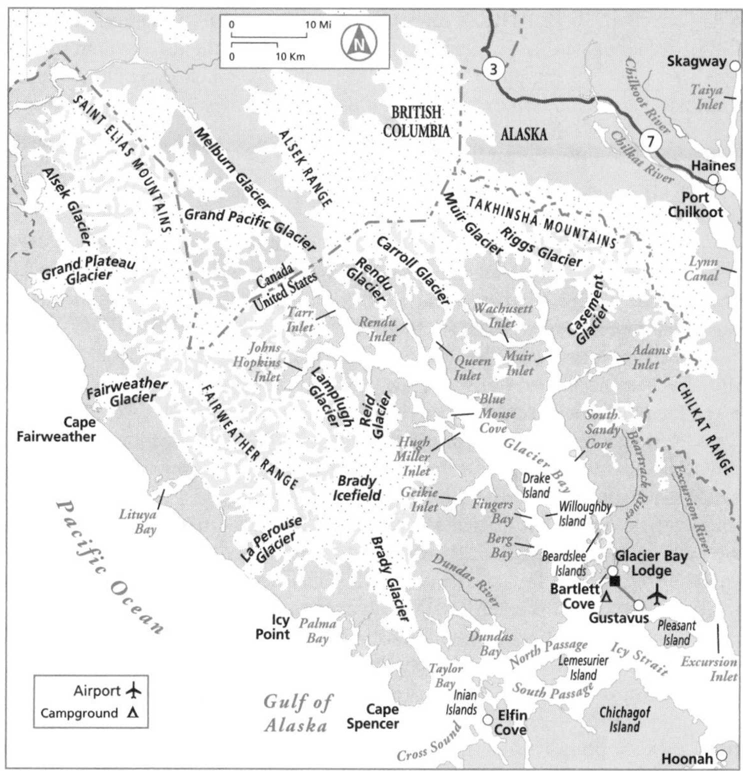

Visitor Information

Contact the **Glacier Bay National Park and Preserve** at P.O. Box 140, Gustavus, AK 99826 (☎ **907/697-2230;** www.nps.gov/glba/). The park service interprets the park mainly by placing well-prepared rangers on board all cruise and tour vessels entering the bay. The park also maintains a modest visitor center with displays on the park on the second floor of the lodge at wooded Bartlett Cove. Nearby are the park's offices, a free campground, a backcountry office, a few short hiking trails, a dock, sea-kayak rental, and other park facilities. Rangers lead daily nature walks and present an evening slide show.

ACTIVITIES AT THE PARK

AT BARTLETT COVE There are three short hiking trails through the rain forest of Sitka spruce and western hemlock at Bartlett Cove. Each weaves through the cool, damp quiet that these huge trees and the moss create on the forest floor. Wet spots often are crossed by boardwalks with railings. A free trail guide is available at the visitor center.

The **Forest Loop** is an easy trail about 1 mile long, beginning at the lodge and passing through the woods and past some park buildings to the cove's pebble beach. The **Bartlett River Trail** is a 4-mile round-trip leading to the Bartlett River Estuary, a good bird-watching spot, especially during migrations. The **Bartlett Lake Trail** branches off the Bartlett River Trail after about 0.25 mile, a 3-mile one-way forest hike to the lake.

KAYAKING IN THE PARK You won't forget seeing a breaching humpback whale from a sea kayak, sitting just inches off the water, and feeling the waves from its stupendous splash passing under your hull. Here, it's a common experience. When we breathlessly told our innkeepers about this life-expanding revelation, they smiled politely. They hear the same descriptions every day.

Inexperienced paddlers should choose a guided trip. ✪ **Alaska Discovery,** 5310 Glacier Hwy., Juneau (☎ **800/586-1911** or 907/780-6226; www.akdiscovery.com), is Alaska's best large sea-kayak guide organization. They offer paddles ranging from 6 hours to 8 days in Glacier Bay. A 6-hour guided paddle from Bartlett Cove is the best choice for beginners. Although the trip goes nowhere near the glaciers, the paddlers stand a good chance of seeing whales, sometimes quite close up. The guides are well trained and know how to teach and make the trip an adventure. Any fit person could enjoy the trip. It costs $125, including a tasty lunch and a ride from your lodgings or the airport. The longer tours also are well guided and outfitted, but I wouldn't recommend a week of sea kayaking to anyone who hasn't tried it before. You should have spent enough time in a kayak and camping to know you'll enjoy such a remote, physically demanding trip even if it rains the whole time. If you're up to it, however, this is the most intimate and authentic way to experience this wilderness, with almost unlimited time to see the glaciers and wildlife. The 5-day trip to the bay's more visited west arm is $1,695; 8 days in the spectacular but forgotten east arm is $1,995. The company also has a simple bed-and-breakfast in Gustavus, for 1- or 2-night stays at the beginning or end of a sea-kayaking excursion.

It's also possible to paddle around Bartlett Cove or near Gustavus without a guide. Raw beginners can try it, but a safer course is to take a guided outing first. **Glacier Bay Sea Kayaks,** based in Gustavus (☎ **907/697-2257;** www.he.net/~kayakak), is the park service concessionaire, operating May 1 to September 30. They offer day rentals, which begin with an instructional briefing, for $50 a day. Drop-offs up the bay are $167.50 round-trip. You will need a backcountry permit from the park service to make such a self-guided trip, and you'll have to attend their briefing. Permits are readily available at the park headquarters, but research what to bring before you leave for the park.

FLIGHTSEEING The other way to get into the park is by flightseeing. **Frontier Air,** based in Gustavus (☎ **907/697-2386**), offers flights from the Bartlett Cove visitor center. Other companies offer tours from various towns, Haines being the closest (see section 11, below). You'll see the incredible rivers of ice that flow down into the bay, and may even see wildlife. What you give up is a lingering, up-close look and the awesome sense of having all that ice and rock above you.

ACCOMMODATIONS, CAMPING & DINING

Glacier Bay Lodge. Bartlett Cove (P.O. Box 199), Gustavus, AK 99826. ☎ **800/451-5952** or 907/697-2226. Fax 206/623-7809 or 907/697-2408. www.glacierbaytours.com. 56 units. TEL. $165 double. Extra person $9. Hostel bunks $28 per person. AE, DC, DISC, MC, V. Closed mid-Sept to mid-May.

Operated by the park concessionaire, Alaska's Glacier Bay Tours and Cruises, this is the only place to stay in the park (although Gustavus, 10 miles down the road, has some of the most attractive accommodations in Alaska). The lodge rooms are comfortable but, for the price, nothing special. Although well maintained, they're in need of updating. The buildings' setting, accessed from the main lodge by boardwalks and steps, is amid the soothing quiet of large rain forest trees.

The **restaurant** has huge windows looking onto Bartlett Cove, where you can sometimes see whales. There are inexpensive main courses on the dinner menu, but mainly it's a fine-dining establishment with white tablecloths and dishes in the $20 range. Breakfast is available as early as 5:30am and dinner as late as 10pm. Drinks are served in the restaurant or on a deck over the cove; on rainy days, visitors congregate around the fire in the comfortable lobby. Laundry facilities and bike rentals are available.

The area's least expensive beds are the bunks in men's and women's dorms with six beds each. The lodge also provides public showers for the free park service **campground.** About ¼ mile from the dock, the campground lacks running water but has a warming hut, firewood, and bear-resistant food caches. You have to cook in a fire ring in the intertidal zone and observe other bear avoidance rules the rangers will explain. Get a camping permit at the ranger station when you arrive; the campground is almost never full.

10 Gustavus: Country Inns & Quiet

The unincorporated town of Gustavus (gus-*tave*-us) remains an undiscovered treasure—or at least it succeeds in making itself feel that way. It's wonderfully remote, accessible only by air or a small passenger ferry, but has a selection of comfortable and even luxurious inns and lodges, plus several days' worth of outdoor activities, including excellent salmon and halibut fishing, nearly surefire whale watching, close access to the sea kayaking and other activities at Glacier Bay National Park, and places for casual hiking and bicycle outings. Neither large cruise ships nor the Alaska State Ferry land here, leaving the roads free of their throngs of shoppers. Miraculously, the 400 townspeople have been smart enough to value what they've got and build on it. Even the gas station is a work of art. Walking, biking, or driving down the quiet roads, everyone you pass—every single person—waves to you.

The buildings, mostly clapboard houses and log cabins, are scattered widely across an oceanfront alluvial plain. Several of the founding homesteads were farms, and the broad clearings of sandy soil wave with hay and wildflowers. The setting is unique in Alaska, and when I had a choice to go anywhere in the state recently for a four-day trip with extended family, this is the place I chose. Each of us took something lasting from the trip. My older son, age 8, learned what it was like to be able to bike anywhere at will, making discoveries in the woods and friends on the quiet lanes without his parents reining him in. My parents, in their 60s, glowed when they returned from kayaking among the breaching humpback whales in the park's Bartlett Cove. I reminisce about a day at the beach when I built dams and sand castles with the children, looking up to see a family of orcas romping just off shore. My cousin won't forget the huge platters of Dungeness crab that came for dinner one night at the inn.

The problem with Gustavus is the expense (and the dampness, but you get used to that). The best outdoor activities involve charters or rentals, which add as much as $200 a day to the cost of your trip. Most accommodations have all-inclusive plans, which include great meals but come with price tags typically around $150 per person per night. Less expensive B&Bs exist, but there is little choice of restaurants for dinner.

ESSENTIALS

GETTING THERE The **Auk Nu** passenger ferry, a high-speed catamaran (☎ **800/820-2628** or 907/789-5701; www.auknutours.com), leaves Juneau's Auke

Be Prepared

Gustavus isn't formally a town; it has no bank and the few other businesses. Bring cash and anything you may need.

Bay harbor from 11789 Glacier Highway, near the ferry terminal, at 11am daily mid-May through mid-September. The adult fare is $45 one way, $85 round-trip; children 3 to 12 $30 and $60. The *Auk Nu* lands at the Gustavus dock at 1:15pm, goes on an afternoon whale-watching cruise in Icy Strait (sightings guaranteed or your money back), then leaves for Juneau at 5:45pm, arriving at 8pm. Adding the whale watch, which I recommend unless you are planning to see the whales of Icy Strait some other way, brings the adult round-trip fare to $139 (more on that below). On the ferry run, they also carry kayaks, bikes, and other cargo, for an added fee, and serve light meals—a choice of chili or chowder when we went. It can't hurt to bring snacks.

During the summer, **Alaska Airlines** (☎ **800/252-7522;** www.alaskaair.com) flies a jet once a day from Juneau to Gustavus and back in the late afternoon. The fare is around $100, round-trip. Various commuter carriers serve Gustavus from Juneau and other nearby towns, including **L.A.B. Flying Service** (☎ **800/426-0543** or 907/766-2222; www.labflying.com), which charges $74 each way.

VISITOR INFORMATION There are no public buildings in Gustavus because there is no government. Only the informal community association holds sway. Generally, you contact a lodge, and once you're comfortable with them, allow them to advise you and book your activities. Be certain you reserve a place to stay before showing up in Gustavus.

GETTING AROUND There are just a few roads. The main one starts at the airport and runs about 10 miles to **Bartlett Cove,** the Glacier Bay National Park base of operations. **Dock Road** branches off to the left, at the gas station, and leads to the ocean dock. Most businesses will give you a good free map, which shows everything in town, for exploring by bicycle. Many inns and B&Bs have courtesy vans and free bicycles. **TLC Taxi** (☎ **907/697-2239**) will carry you and your kayak; the fare from the Gustavus Dock to Bartlett Cove is $8, plus $10 per kayak (reserve ahead if you need the taxi).

EXPLORING GUSTAVUS

Everything to do in Gustavus involves the outdoors.

✪ **WHALE WATCHING & FISHING** Whales keep their own schedule, but you're almost certain to see them on a whale-watching excursion from Gustavus, where the swirling current of Icy Strait creates such a rich feeding ground that humpbacks come back every summer without fail. Whale-watching trips aboard the ***Auk Nu,*** a large, comfortable catamaran, leave the town dock for Point Adolphus every day at 2pm. The commentary is first rate, and a good, light meal is included in the price. The fare for the 3-hour cruise is $78, and you get your money back if you don't see whales—which virtually never happens.

Other, smaller operators will provide a more intimate experience on smaller boats, usually getting you closer to the whales. They'll also combine the trip with superb halibut and salmon fishing if salmon are running. The advantage of halibut fishing here is fish in spectacular, protected waters; seasickness generally is not a concern. Your inn host in Gustavus can make the arrangements. A boat typically charters for $200 or more per person for a full day, plus the cost of having your fish professionally packed and shipped home to you.

SEA KAYAKING **Alaska Discovery,** 5310 Glacier Hwy., Juneau (☎ **800/586-1911** or 907/780-6226; www.akdiscovery.com), offers an easy 2½-day, 2-night kayaking expedition among the whales for $795 per person. They take a boat to a base camp, then kayak among the whales from there. The outing is suitable for fit beginners and older children. Gustavus-based **Spirit Walker Expeditions** (☎ **800/KAYAKER**

or 907/697-2266; www.seakayakalaska.com), has a good reputation locally. They lead guided 1- to 7-day trips to the whale-watching grounds and beyond. **Sea Otter Kayak** (☎ **907/697-3007;** www.he.net/~seaotter) rents kayaks on Dock Road.

HIKING & BICYCLING There are few cars in Gustavus—they have to be hauled here on a barge—but most inns provide bikes. The roads are fun to explore, and the sandy beaches, accessed from the town dock, are great for a walk and a picnic, to watch eagles and other birds and wildlife. You can go many miles, if you are of a mind for a run or long walk, but we saw little reason to go far before stopping to play and picnic on a broad sand beach undisturbed by any human footprint but our own.

There's also a primitive 9-hole **golf course** mowed from the meadows near the beach; inquire with your host for information, or just go to the first tee, paying your fee and borrowing clubs on the honor system at a shed there.

ACCOMMODATIONS & DINING

Gustavus contains many of Alaska's best remote accommodations. There are many more good places to stay than I have room to describe here, some of them so good they'd be the best on the list in most other Alaska towns. The competition in Gustavus is extraordinary. I can wholeheartedly recommend these, which I list here in increasing order of price and luxury: **Blue Heron Bed and Breakfast at Glacier Bay,** off Dock Road (☎ and fax **907/697-2293;** www.blueheronbnb.net); **Growley Bear Inn,** Dock Road (☎ **907/697-2730;** www.growleybear.com); and the **Glacier Bay Country Inn,** Tong Road (☎ **800/628-0912** or 907/697-2288; www.glacierbayalaska.com).

Most accommodations are "Gustavus style," which means charging a single daily price for comfortable, unique rooms, breakfast and dinner served family style, brown bag lunches, bicycles and some other outdoor equipment, transportation around the area, and someone to make all the arrangements for fishing, sea kayaking, hiking, and Glacier Bay tours. It's expensive, but it's a great way to visit. Another set of accommodations charges less, but leaves you on your own for lunch and dinner and other details.

Unfortunately for those who choose the less costly, à la carte approach, Gustavus is short on restaurants. Each of the full-service inns serves meals to nonguests by prior arrangement, and the Glacier Bay Lodge serves three meals a day—but it's 10 miles away at the park's Bartlett Cove headquarters. Several free-standing restaurants have gone out of business periodically around town; your innkeeper can direct you to one that's currently operating. One that's been going strong for several years is **A Bear's Nest Cafe,** on Rink Creek Road (☎ **907/697-2440**), where the barefoot and braided Lynne Morrow serves organic dishes, homemade bread, seafood specials, soup, and sandwiches in a dining room that's also the ground floor of her house, 1 to 8pm daily in the summer. She accepts Discover, MasterCard, and Visa. Also, a country store on dock road sells basics for picnics.

Some of the inns do not have licenses to serve alcohol; if that's a consideration, be sure to ask before you book your stay.

Glacier Bay's Bear Track Inn. 255 Rink Rd., Gustavus, AK 99826. ☎ **888/697-2284** or 907/697-3017. Fax 907/697-2284. www.beartrackinn.com. 14 units. $393 per person, double occupancy; discounts for additional nights. Rates include round-trip air from Juneau and all meals. AE, DISC, MC, V. Closed Nov–Jan.

Six miles from Gustavus, this extraordinary log building faces its own field of wildflowers, which, if you walk half a mile across it, leads to the sea. You look out on this scene from a lobby with a huge fireplace, a ceiling 28 feet high, and a wall of windows. The immense logs of the walls and the isolation give the place the feeling of a wilderness lodge, but the rooms are as good as any upscale hotel, and have the advantage of large dormer windows with sweeping views. Objectively, it's the best place in Gustavus, and one of the best remote lodges in Alaska; however, I found it too perfect to hold much charm. Unlike other lodges and inns in Gustavus, meals are cooked to order from a varied menu; the inn serves beer and wine. Those not staying here can buy dinner for $30. The lodge offers many services, including baby-sitting and car rental.

✪ **Gustavus Inn at Glacier Bay.** Gustavus Rd. (P.O. Box 60), Gustavus, AK 99826. ☎ **800/649-5220** or 907/697-2254. Fax 907/697-2255. 11 units. $150 per person per night. Children under 12 half price. Rates include all meals. AE, MC, V. Closed Sept 16–May 15.

This is the original and still the best of the Gustavus full-service inns. By objective standards of modern luxury, imitators have surpassed the old homestead farmhouse, but no one could duplicate the extraordinary hospitality of the Lesh family, honed over 35 years of running the inn. They know how to make guests feel immediately a part of the place. The site is unsurpassed, too, standing at the center of the community, amid blowing grass and with a huge vegetable garden that provides much of the dining room's wonderful food. Dave, the chef, has published a cookbook. The seasonings he uses on seafood are a real revelation, served on big, inexhaustible platters in the dining room, where there's also a beer and wine bar. Before going, talk over what you want to do with Dave or his father, Jack, and let them book everything. They drive guests around, offer free bikes and fishing rods (bring your own tackle), and laundry service.

Meadow's Glacier Bay Guest House. Off Dock Rd. (P.O. 93), Gustavus, AK 99826. ☎ **877/766-2348** or 907/697-2348 (phone or fax). www.glacier-bay-alaska.com. 5 units, 4 with private bathroom. TEL. $119 double with shared bathroom, $139–$199 double with private bathroom. Extra person $69. Rates include full breakfast. MC, V.

At high tide the sea comes to the base of the lawn by the grassy meadow and estuary where this house stands, a rich foreground for stunning views in every direction. If any house could live up to such a setting, this is it. Designed by owner Chris Smith's father, its cool, airy spaces interpret those outside with big geometric shapes, shining wood floors, and great white walls hung with some of the best of Alaska's contemporary art. Each guest room is its own small work of the decorator's art: fashionable, immaculate, and perhaps a little too good for mere mortals. Smith's wife, Meadow Brook, presides, serving elaborate breakfasts and providing advice and equipment for the area's outdoors.

A Puffin's Bed and Breakfast. Rink Creek Rd. (P.O. Box 3), Gustavus, AK 99826. ☎ **800/478-2258** in Alaska, or 907/697-2260. Fax 907/697-2258. www.puffintravel.com. 3 cabins, 1 house. $95 cabin for 2; $125 house for 2. Extra adult $25 in cabin, $20 in house; extra child age 2–12 $10 in room. Cabin rates include full breakfast. No credit cards.

The simple cabins are set among the thick spruce woods, connected by paths to each other and a central lodge where breakfast is served and the busy hosts run their charter and booking businesses. It's an economical choice for a visitor who doesn't need to be treated like a sultan. The cabins, with vinyl floors, have their own bathrooms with shower stalls, microwave ovens, coffeemakers, and refrigerators. The two-bedroom house, with a complete kitchen and laundry facilities, is a good choice for families; it does not include breakfast, but you can stock up at a country store nearby. They offer car rental, a courtesy car, laundry machines, free bicycles, and many packages for visiting Gustavus and Glacier Bay.

11 Haines: Eagles & the Unexpected

For years we always just passed through Haines on the way from the ferry up the highway. I didn't know what I was missing until I stopped and took a couple of days to really investigate. Now Haines is one of my favorite Alaska towns.

Haines is casual, happy, and slightly odd. It waits for you to find it, but once found, it unveils wonderful charms. If you're looking for the mythical town of Cicely from television's *Northern Exposure,* you'll get closer in Haines than anyplace else I know (in fact, the producers scouted here before choosing to shoot in Roslyn, Washington). As I walked down a sidewalk, I saw a sign in a storefront that said to look in the big tree across the street. I looked, and there was an eagle peering back at me. At the Alaska Indian Arts Native cultural center, seeking an office or a ticket window or someone in charge, I wandered into a totem pole studio where a carver was completing a major commission. He gladly stopped to talk. It turned out there wasn't anyone in charge.

The **Chilkat Dancers** have performed here for almost 40 years, and are respected for authentically carrying on Tlingit cultural heritage. But their membership is undefined, and their performances, while impressive, are also funny and slightly strange. Whites dance beside Natives, and rehearsals are never held; the new generation learns by being thrown into the performances, sometimes before the age of 5. Issues that are a big deal in some other towns just aren't in Haines.

Haines's dominant feature, **Fort William H. Seward,** gives the town a pastoral atmosphere. The fort is a collection of grand, white clapboard buildings arranged around a 9-acre parade ground, in the middle of which stands a Tlingit clan house—out of place, yes, but wonderfully symbolic of Haines. The town is a friendly, accessible center of Tlingit culture as well as a retired outpost of seemingly pointless military activity.

And Haines has ✪ **bald eagles**—always plenty of bald eagles, and in the fall, a ridiculous number of bald eagles. More, in fact, than anywhere else on earth. The chance to see the birds draws people into the outdoors here. There are well-established guides for any activity you might want to pursue, all cooperating and located together. There are some excellent hiking trails right from town, as well as protected sea kayaking waters. Also, it's well worth noting that due to its location in relation to the flow of weather, Haines is not as rainy as elsewhere in Southeast.

ESSENTIALS

GETTING THERE The **Alaska Marine Highway System,** 1591 Glacier Ave., Juneau, AK 99801-1427 (☎ **800/642-0066,** or 907/766-2111 locally; www.dot.state.ak.us/external/amhs/home.html), is how most people get to Haines, and the cruise on the Lynn Canal fjord from Juneau or Skagway is among the most beautiful in the Inside Passage. The fare is $24 from Juneau and $17 from Skagway. The dock is 5 miles north of town. Unfortunately, since this is the northern highway connection where nearly all vehicles get off or on, there often are delays.

If you're just going to or from Skagway without a car, a good alternative is one of the privately operated passenger ferries. The Haines-Skagway Fast Ferry, operated by **Chilkat Cruises and Tours** (☎ **888/766-2103** or 907/766-2100; www.chilkatcruises.com), runs a 150-passenger catamaran, the *Fairweather Express,* at least three round-trips a day on the 40-minute trip. It leaves from the Port Chilkoot dock, below Fort William Seward, where they have a booking service and serve meals. Adult round-trips are $36, one way $24; children 12 and under pay half price.

The Haines-Skagway Water Taxi and Scenic Cruise (☎ **888/766-3395** or 907/766-3395; www.lynncanal.com) makes the run to Skagway and back a sightseeing cruise, following the shoreline and stopping for wildlife sightings. The 80-passenger vessel leaves from the small boat harbor, charging adults $35 round-trip, $22 one-way; children under 12 go half price. Unlike the state ferry, the private shuttles operate only in the summer.

If you're driving, the **Haines Highway** leads 155 miles to Haines Junction, Yukon Territory, an intersection with the Alaska Highway (you must pass through Canadian customs—see the "Alaska Highway" section in chapter 9 for rules). The road runs along the Chilkat River and the bald eagle preserve, then climbs into spectacular alpine terrain. Anchorage is 775 driving miles from Haines, Fairbanks is 653. One-way car rentals to Anchorage, Fairbanks, and Skagway are available from **Avis,** at the Hotel Hälsingland (☎ **907/766-2733**), with a $300 drop-off charge plus the rental cost; you can sometimes get a special deal at the end of the season, when the rental companies are shuffling cars around and shipping many back to the Lower 48. You can also rent an RV one way to Anchorage. **ABC Motorhome Rentals,** 3875 W. International Airport Rd., in Anchorage (☎ **800/421-7456** or 907/279-2000; www.abcmotorhome.com), charges $500 plus a 1-week rental, starting around $1,400 in the high season.

Three air services offer schedule prop service, air taxi, and flightseeing tours to surrounding communities. One is **L.A.B. Flying Service,** based at Main Street and 4th Avenue (☎ **800/426-0543** or 907/766-2222; www.labflying.com), with frequent flights, charging $80 one way for the 30-minute trip from Juneau.

VISITOR INFORMATION The small but well-staffed and -stocked **Haines Convention and Visitors Bureau Visitor Information Center,** Second Street near Willard (P.O. Box 530), Haines, AK 99827 (☎ **800/458-3579** or 907/766-2234; www.haines.ak.us), is operated by the city government, which also sends out a vacation-planning packet. It's open Monday to Friday 8am to 8pm, Saturday and Sunday 9am to 4pm in summer; in winter, hours are Monday to Friday 8am to 5pm.

ORIENTATION Haines sits on the narrow Chilkat Peninsula near the north end of the Southeast Alaska Panhandle. Highways run north and east on either side of the peninsula; the one on the east side goes to the ferry dock, 5 miles out, and ends after 11 miles at **Chilkoot Lake.** The other is the **Haines Highway,** which leads to the Canadian border, the Alaska Highway, and the rest of the world.

The town itself has two parts: the sparsely built downtown grid and, down Front Street or Second Avenue, a short walk to the west, the Fort William Seward area. Vans and buses that meet the ferry offer free or inexpensive transfers, seeking to take you on a town tour. Hotel Hälsingland books tours, too, but your feet or a bicycle will get you around handily.

GETTING AROUND Bikes are available from **Sockeye Cycle,** just uphill from the Port Chilkoot Dock on Portage Street in the Fort William Seward area (☎ **907/766-2869;** www.cyclealaska.com), for $6 an hour or $30 a day.

Haines Taxi and Tours can be reached at ☎ **907/766-3138.**

Avis car rental has an outlet at the Hotel Hälsingland. **Affordable Cars** is at the Captain's Choice Motel (see "Accommodations," below).

FAST FACTS There are two **ATMs,** at the First National Bank of Anchorage, Main Street and Second Avenue; and at Howsers Supermarket, a few doors down Main.

The **Haines Medical Clinic** (☎ **907/766-2521**) is on First Avenue, near the visitor center.

Mountain Market, at Third Avenue and the Haines Highway (☎ **907/766-3340**), charges $8 an hour for **Internet access.** But at the **Haines Borough Library,** Third Avenue and Willard Street (☎ **907/766-2545**), you can log on for free.

The city **police** can be reached in nonemergency situations at ☎ **907/766-2545.** Outside city limits, call the **Alaska State Troopers** at ☎ **907/766-2552.**

There's a **post office** at 55 Haines Hwy.

The local **sales tax** is 5.5%.

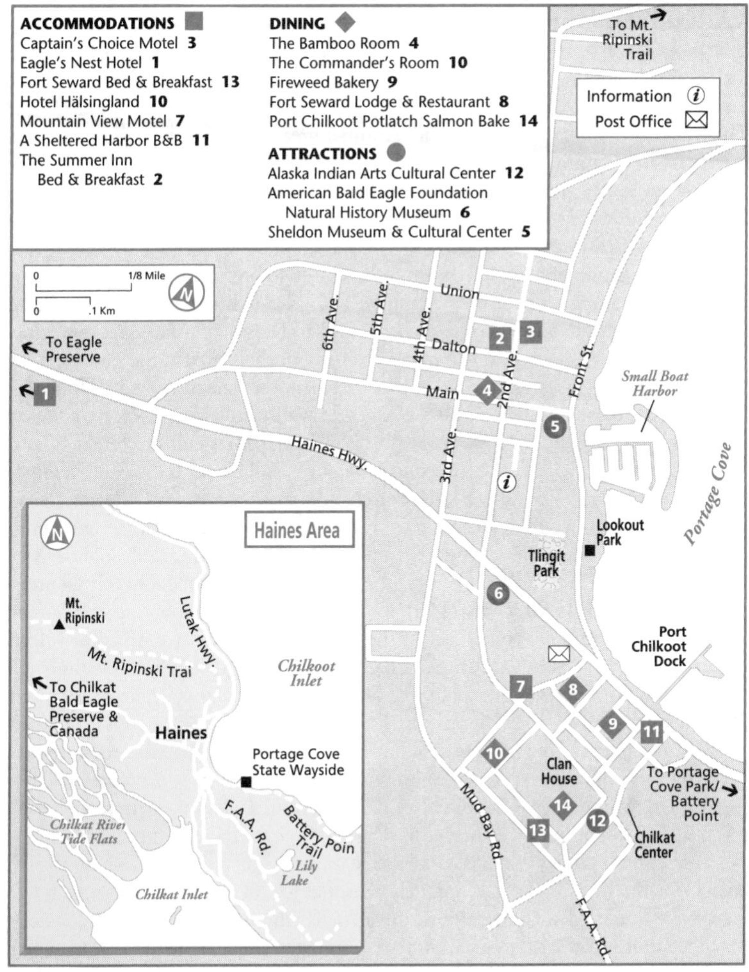

SPECIAL EVENTS The **Great Alaska Craftbeer and Homebrew Festival** (☎ **800/542-6363**) takes place over 3 days in mid-May. The **Kluane to Chilkat International Bike Relay** (☎ **907/766-2202**) is held around the summer solstice, June 21, heading down the Haines Highway, with more than 1,000 entrants; it's quite a downhill.

The **Southeast Alaska State Fair** and **Bald Eagle Music Festival** (☎ **907/766-2476**) is the biggest event of the summer, held for 5 days in early August; it's a regional small-town get-together, with livestock, cooking, a logging show, a parade, music, and other entertainment. Buildings constructed for the filming of the movie *White Fang* were donated to the fair, and now form the nucleus of a retail area there. (One stop of interest there, at any time, is the local microbrewery, Haines Brewing Co., which offers samples and informal tours.)

The **Alaska Bald Eagle Festival** (☎ **907/766-2202;** www.baldeaglefest.org) offers seminars and special events to mark the annual eagle congregation. It's held in mid-November, timed to allow visitors to also attend the WhaleFest in Sitka.

EXPLORING HAINES

The main feature of Haines is **Fort William H. Seward,** a collection of large, white, wood-frame buildings around sloping parade grounds overlooking the magnificent Lynn Canal fjord. (Get the informative walking-tour map of the National Historic Site from the Haines Convention and Visitors Bureau.) The fort led a peaceful life, for a military installation. By the time the U.S. Army built it, in 1903, the Klondike gold rush was over, and there's no evidence it ever deterred any attack on this little peninsula at the north end of the Inside Passage. It was deactivated at the end of World War II, when it was used for training.

In 1947, a group of five veterans from the Lower 48 bought the fort as surplus, with the idea of forming a planned community. That idea didn't really work out, but one of the new white families helped spark a Chilkat Tlingit cultural renaissance in the 1950s. The Heinmillers, who still own a majority of the shares in the fort, were looking for something to do with all that property when someone suggested a Tlingit tribal house on the parade grounds. The project, led by a pair of elders, took on a life of its own, and the ✪ **Chilkat Dancers** and **Alaska Indian Arts** cultural center followed. Lee Heinmiller, a member of the second generation, still manages the dance troupe his father started in 1957 as a Boy Scout project and participates in the performances with his pale, spreading paunch gleaming in abbreviated traditional Native dress. He has been adopted as a member of the tribe and given a name that accords high respect.

The dancers, who have been all over the world, perform at the **Chilkat Center for the Arts** (☎ and fax **907/766-2160**), an auditorium just off the southeast corner of the parade grounds, and sometimes at the clan house. Check at the Visitor Information Center or the Alaska Indian Arts Cultural Center for show times. Admission is $10 for adults, $5 for students, and free for children 5 and under. The cultural center is open from 9am to 5pm Monday to Friday and evenings when cruise ships are in town. It occupies the old fort hospital on the south side of the parade grounds and has a small gallery and a carvers' workshop where you can see work in progress.

In the downtown area, the **Sheldon Museum and Cultural Center,** 11 Main St. (☎ **907/766-2366;** www.sheldonmuseum.org), contains an upstairs gallery of well-presented Tlingit art and cultural artifacts; downstairs is a collection on the white history of the town. There's a uniquely personal feel to the Tlingit objects, some of which are displayed with pictures of the artisans who made them and the history of their relationship with the Sheldons, for whom the museum is named. It's open in summer, daily from 1 to 5pm, plus mornings and evenings that are posted weekly; call for winter hours. Admission is $3 for adults, free for children under 12.

The entirely unique **American Bald Eagle Foundation Natural History Museum,** at 115 Haines Hwy. (☎ **907/766-3094;** www.baldeagles.org), is essentially a huge, hair-raising diorama of more than 100 eagles and other animal mounts. Dave Olerud sits in a wheelchair behind the desk and will talk your ear off about the museum if you want him to—he worked on it for 18 years and was paralyzed in a fall during construction. Admission is $2.50 adults, $1 ages 8 to 12. It's open summer Monday to Thursday 9am to 10pm, Friday 9am to 5pm, Saturday and Sunday 1 to 5pm. Winter hours are Monday and Wednesday 1 to 4pm.

GETTING OUTSIDE

✪ **EAGLE VIEWING** Haines is probably the best place on earth to see bald eagles. The **Chilkat Bald Eagle Preserve** protects 48,000 acres of river bottom along the Chilkat River. From October to January, up to 3,000 eagles gather in the cottonwood trees (also known as western poplar) on a small section of the river, a phenomenon known as the Fall Congregation. (A healthy 200 to 400 are resident the rest of the year.) The eagles come for easy winter food: A very late salmon run spawns here into December in a 5-mile stretch of open water known as the Council Grounds.

During the Congregation, dozens of eagles stand in each of the gnarled, leafless cottonwoods on the riverbanks, occasionally diving for a fish. The best places to see them are pull-out, paths and viewing areas along the Haines Highway from mile 18 to 21. Don't walk on the flats, as that disturbs the eagles. The preserve is managed by Alaska State Parks, 400 Willoughby, 3rd Floor, Juneau, AK 99801 (www.dnr.state.ak.us/parks/units/eagleprv.htm), but the Haines Convention and Visitors Bureau may be a better source of information for planning a visit.

Local guides offer trips to see the eagles by raft, bicycle, or bus—mostly in the summer, when the eagles are fewer but visitors more numerous. **Chilkat Guides,** based on Beach Road on the waterfront below the fort (☎ **907/766-2491;** www.raftalaska.com), does a rafting trip twice a day during the summer down the Chilkat to watch the eagles. The water is gentle—if it's too low, there's a chance you'll be asked to get out and push—and you'll see lots of eagles, mostly at a distance. The company is run by young people who create a sense of fellowship with their clients. The 4-hour trip, with a snack, costs $80 for adults, $40 for children.

Sockeye Cycle (see "Biking," below) has guided bike tours to see eagles and Fort Seward on a 90-minute trip that costs $42, and **Alaska Nature Tours** (☎ **907/766-2876;** kcd.com/aknature) takes 3-hour bus and hiking tours to the preserve for $50 per person in summer.

BIKING **Sockeye Cycle,** at 24 Portage St., near the dock (☎ **907/766-2869;** www.cyclealaska.com), leads a variety of guided trips—a couple of hours, half or full day, or even a 9-day trek. A 3-hour ride along Chilkoot Lake costs $90. Or you can go on your own for $30 a day. The area is quite conducive to biking.

FISHING There are several charter operators in Haines, for halibut or salmon, or guided freshwater fishing for king and silver salmon, halibut, Dolly Varden, or cutthroat trout. The Haines Convention and Visitors Bureau can help you find a guide through the links on their Web site or the list of operators they keep at the office. **Chilkat Cruises and Tours** (☎ **888/766-2103** or 907/766-2100; www.chilkatcruises.com) is one reputable operator. Expect to pay about $100 per person for half a day fishing salmon in saltwater, about $180 for halibut or all-day salmon. For self-guided fishing advice, contact the local office of that Alaska Department of Fish and Game at ☎ **907/766-2625** (www.state.ak.us/local/akpages/fish.game/sportf/sf_home.htm).

✪ **FLIGHTSEEING** This is one of Alaska's best flightseeing trips. The Inside Passage is beautiful, and one mountain away is Glacier Bay National Park; the ice field and the glaciers spilling through to the sea are a sight you can't forget. It's possible to land on an immense glacial ice field and see the sun slicing between the craggy peaks. **Alaska Mountain Flying and Travel,** 132 2nd Ave. (☎ **800/954-8747** or 907/766-2665; www.flyglacierbay.com), offers these flights; the owner and pilot is known for his glacier and beach landings. Prices range from $115 to $259 per person, and reservations are recommended. **L.A.B. Flying Service** (☎ **800/426-0543;** www.labflying.com) is a larger operator, offering flights from Haines starting at $105 per person.

HIKING There are several good trails near Haines, ranging from an easy beach walk to a 10-mile, 4,000-foot climb of **Mount Ripinsky,** north of town (it starts at the top of Young Street). Get the *Haines Is for Hikers* trail guide from the visitor center. The easiest for families is the **Battery Point Trail,** which goes 2.4 miles along the beach from the end of the shore road that leads southeast from the Port Chilkoot cruise-ship dock. **Mount Riley** is south of town, with three trail routes to a 1,760-foot summit that features great views and feels much higher than it is; get the trail guide or ask directions to one of the trailheads. **Seduction Point Trail** is 7 miles long, starting at Chilkat State Park at the end of Mud Bay Road south of town and leading to the end of the Chilkat Peninsula. It's a beach walk, so check the tides; they'll give you a tide table at the visitors bureau.

SEA KAYAKING **Deishu Expeditions,** a half mile south of Fort Seward on Beach road (☎ **800/552-9257** or 907/766-2427; www.seakayaks.com), offers instruction, short guided trips, longer expeditions, and rentals ($35 a day for a single, plus $20 for getting dropped off somewhere). A half-day guided paddle is $85, including a snack; a full day, including lunch, is $125.

ACCOMMODATIONS

Many towns have a lot of chainlike hotels and only one or two unique places with character. In Haines, the situation is reversed.

Besides the hotels I've listed, you'll find good economy rooms at these other places: **A Sheltered Harbor B&B,** 57 Beach Rd. (☎ and fax **907/766-2741;** www.geocities.com/asheltered); **Mountain View Motel,** at Mud Bay Road and Second Avenue (☎ **907/766-2900**); **Fort Seward Lodge, Restaurant & Saloon,** in the old fort exchange (☎ **800/478-7772** or 907/766-2009; www.ftsewardlodge.com); and **Eagle's Nest Motel,** Mile 1, Haines Hwy. (☎ **800/354-6009**).

Captain's Choice Motel. 108 N. Second St. at Dalton St. (P.O. Box 392), Haines, AK 99827. ☎ **800/478-2345** or 907/766-3111. Fax 907/766-3332. www.capchoice.com. 39 units. TV TEL. High season $104 double; $145 suite. Low season $76 double; $120 suite. Extra person $5. AE, CB, DC, DISC, MC, V.

These trim, red-roofed buildings house the one standard chainlike motel in town, with all the anticipated amenities. Yet it still has a certain amount of charm, making it—objectively, anyway—probably the best hotel in town. The room decor is on the dark side, with paneling, and somewhat out-of-date, but quite clean, and many of the rooms have good views on a large sundeck. Each has a coffeemaker and refrigerator, Showtime movies, a clock radio, and a telephone with a modem port. They offer a courtesy van, rent cars and pickup trucks, and book activities.

✪ **Fort Seward Bed and Breakfast.** 1 Fort Seward Dr. (P.O. Box 5), Haines, AK 99827. ☎ **800/615-NORM** or phone/fax 907/766-2856. www.haines.ak.us/norm. 6 units, 2 with private bathroom. TV. High season $84–$115 double. Low season $74 double. Extra person $20. Rates include full breakfast. DISC, MC, V. Closed Oct 15–Apr 7.

The fort surgeon's quarters overlook the parade grounds and the Lynn Canal with a big wraparound porch and an unspoiled historic feel. Norm Smith has lived in this house most of his life and in 1981 started the B&B with his wife, Suzanne, a gifted hostess who instantly makes you feel like an old friend. The rooms have high ceilings, fireplaces, wonderful cabinetry—all kinds of authentic charm. It's a social place, with a barbecue on the porch, and guests are welcome to use the kitchen, where Norm produces a fine full breakfast. They'll pick you up where needed, and free bikes are available for guests. No smoking.

Hotel Hälsingland. Fort William Seward parade grounds (P.O. Box 1589), Haines, AK 99827. ☎ **800/542-6363** or 907/766-2000. Fax 907/766-2445. www.haines.ak.us/halsingland. 50 units, 45 with private bathroom. TV TEL. $59 double without bathroom, $93 double with private bathroom; $119 suite. AE, DC, DISC, MC, V. Closed mid-Nov to mid-Mar.

This National Historic Landmark has been operating continuously as a hotel in the same family since 1947, a year after it stopped functioning as the commanding officer's quarters at Fort William Seward. Owner Arne Olsson has worked hard to renew the rooms, however, and his work has paid off in upgrading the huge, white clapboard structure, although some of the furniture still looks not antique but just plain old. Every room is different, so it's wise to choose when you check in. Some are priced for backpackers, with fewer amenities. When I stayed in a big, oddly shaped room with a nonworking fireplace and windows on the parade grounds, I felt like I could almost hear the commander walking across the floor in his spurs. A courtesy van and Avis car rental are available, and the hotel serves as a center for tours, buses, and other arrangements.

The **Commander's Room** restaurant has a wide selection of fresh seafood with views of the ocean and parade grounds, and prompt service. It's open for breakfast and dinner. The small bar has craft brews on tap. It's a friendly, low-key place in the evening.

The Summer Inn Bed and Breakfast. 117 Second Ave. (P.O. Box 1198), Haines, AK 99827. ☎ and fax **907/766-2970.** www.summerinn.wytbear.com. 5 units, none with private bathroom. High season $80 double; $100 suite. Low season $70 double; $90 suite. Extra person $10. Rates include full breakfast. MC, V.

This lovely old clapboard house downtown has a big porch and living room, decorated in whites and pale, lacy fabrics, like Grandma's house. The five rooms are cozy but small, and share three bathrooms among them (bathrooms were immaculate when we last visited). The house was built by a reputed former member of Soapy Smith's gang in 1912 (see Skagway section for more on Soapy). No smoking or drinking is allowed.

DINING

Haines doesn't have a great restaurant, but you can eat well at the Hotel Hälsingland (see "Accommodations," above) during the summer, and there are lots of places for a burger or a slice of pizza. Among the best lunch places is the **Mountain Market & Cafe,** a health-food store at Third Avenue and the Haines Highway (☎ **907/766-3340**). A youthful hangout, it serves hearty and reasonably priced sandwiches, wraps, and soups. It's great for picnics, or stop by for coffee or breakfast.

The Bamboo Room. Second Ave. near Main St. ☎ **907/766-2800.** www.kcd.com/bamboo. Lunch $6–$12.50; dinner $6–$23. AE, DISC, DC, MC, V. Summer daily 6am–midnight. Winter daily 6am–8pm. DINER/SEAFOOD.

This small restaurant, in the same family for nearly 50 years, was recently rescued from being a smoky adjunct to the bar. It has been divided off by attractive etched glass and made into a first-class diner serving burgers, salads, pasta, and lots of seafood. Many light and healthful items are on the menu along with the solid fried foods. The new incarnation fits a building that started as a French restaurant during the gold rush era and then became a brothel and speakeasy before the Tengs family got it in 1953. The history is on the back of the menu.

Fireweed Bakery. Fort Seward Bldg. 37, Blacksmith Rd. ☎ **907/766-3838.** Lunch $6–$11; dinner $7–$11. MC, V. Summer, Mon–Sat 7am–9pm. Winter, Wed–Sat 8am–8pm. ORGANIC MEDITERRANEAN.

In this dining room just 2 blocks from the Port Chilkoot dock, in the Quartermaster's Building at old Fort Seward, thoughtful restoration has come closer than anywhere else in the fort to recreating the elegance enjoyed by turn-of-the-century officers. Captains chairs and eight tables made by a Haines craftsman sit amid ample hardwood, wainscoting, and local art—a clean, stylish look. The menu, posted on a blackboard, changes daily, but it is consistently wholesome and expertly seasoned, with items such as gyro sandwiches or mushroom ravioli. The bagels are top notch, as are all the sophisticated baked goods. At press time, a beer and wine license was still in the works.

Fort Seward Lodge, Restaurant and Saloon. Mile 0 Haines Hwy., in Fort William Seward. ☎ **907/766-2009.** www.ftsewardlodge.com. Lunch $8–$10; dinner $8–$25. DISC, MC, V. Summer daily 5–10pm. Winter daily 5:30–9pm. STEAK/SEAFOOD.

A favorite of the locals, the restaurant resides in a tall room in the old Post Exchange of the historic fort, where patrons have long speared dollar bills to the ceiling. It's now papered with money. This is a fun place, with a friendly and gregarious staff and partying tradition (although the bar is in a separate room). The food—simple, fresh fish, meat, and vegetables—may be the best in town. The prime rib especially is famous. The full bar has Alaska microbrews on tap.

Port Chilkoot Potlatch Salmon Bake. Fort William Seward parade grounds. ☎ **907/766-2000.** Reservations recommended. $21.75 per person. AE, DC, DISC, MC, V. Daily 5–8:30pm. Closed Oct–Apr. SALMON BAKE.

Salmon bakes are touristy by nature, but this long-established event is a *good* salmon bake. The sockeye is grilled on alder and not overcooked or ruined with overseasoning. Dining is at picnic tables, either in tents or in the clan house on the parade grounds. After you go through the line, waiters replenish your plate. One glass of beer or wine is included in the price as well as dessert and other trimmings.

12 Skagway: After the Gold Rush

It's only been 100 years since white civilization came to Alaska. There were a few scattered towns in Southeast before that—Juneau, Sitka, and Wrangell, for example—but until the Klondike Gold Rush, the great mass of Alaska was populated only by Natives who had never seen a white face, for only a few explorers and prospectors had ever ventured farther. Then, in a single year, 1898, the population exploded. (See "The Gold Rush in Context," in chapter 9.) It still stands as the greatest event in Alaska's short but eventful history, for the flow of people in a few short years set the patterns of development ever since. For Skagway, it created a long-term living based on showing off to visitors the wildest boom town of the era, a true Wild West outpost that in its biggest years was completely without law other than the survival of the meanest. And a good living it's been, for in today's Skagway, more money and more than 20 times as many visitors come through in a year as made the trip to the Klondike during the gold rush.

In 1896 there was a single log cabin in Skagway, in 1897 the word of the Klondike strike made it to the outside world, and in 1898 Skagway was a huge gold rush boomtown. In 1899 the gold rush was ending, and in 1903, 300 tourists arrived in a single day to see where the gold rush happened. By 1908, local businessmen had started developing their tourist attractions, moving picturesque gold rush buildings to Broadway, the main street, to create a more unified image when visitors arrived on the steamers. By 1920, tourism had become an important part of the economy. By 1933, historic preservation efforts had started. Today, you can see history in Skagway, and you can see the history of history.

With around 800 residents and nearly half a million visitors annually, the "real" town has all but disappeared, and most of the people you'll meet are either fellow visitors or summer workers brought north to serve them. Most of the tourists are from

Skagway

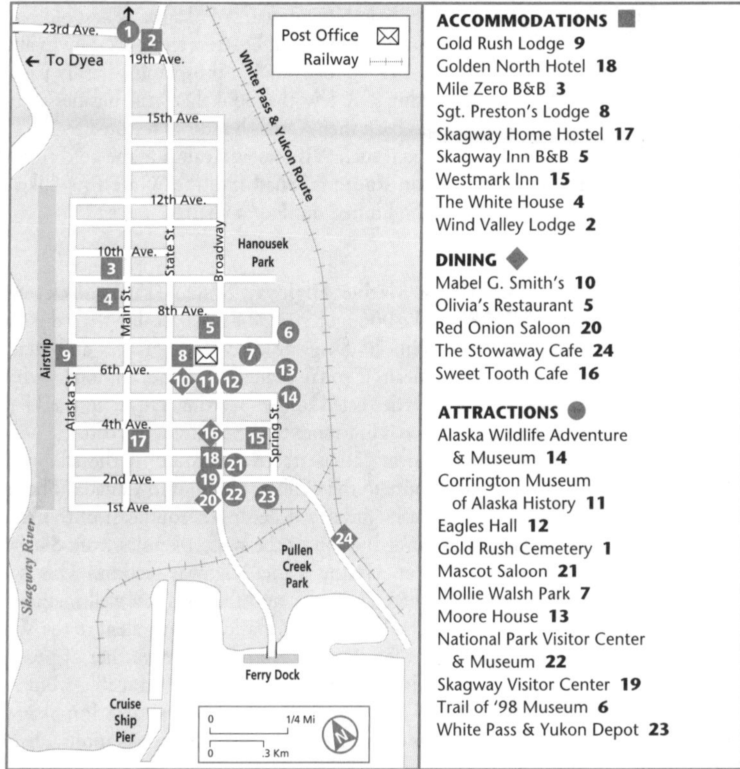

cruise ships—it's not unusual for several ships to hit town in a single morning, unleashing waves of people up the wharf and into the one historic street. There are plenty of highway and ferry travelers, too, and outdoor enthusiasts come to do the Chilkoot Trail, just as the stampeders did.

Is it worth all those visits? Skagway, spared from fire and recognized so long ago for its history, is probably the best-preserved gold rush town in the United States. What happened here in a 2-year period was certainly extraordinary, even if the phenomenon the town celebrates is one of mass insanity based on greed, inhumanity, thuggery, prostitution, waste, and, for most, abject failure. In the rush years of 1897 and 1898, Skagway or its ghost-town twin city of Dyea were the logical places to get off the boat to head off on the trek to the gold fields near the new city of Dawson. (That fascinating town is covered in chapter 9.) Skagway instantly grew from a single homestead to a population of between 15,000 and 25,000—no one knows exactly how many, in part because the people were flowing through so fast but also because there was no civil authority to count the people. Dawson City ended up with 30,000.

While Canada was well policed by the Mounties, Skagway was truly lawless—a hell on earth, as one Mountie described it. Soapy Smith, a con artist turned organized crime boss, ruled the city; the governor offered to put him officially in charge as a territorial marshal and rode with him in the 1898 Independence Day parade. Four days later, Smith was shot dead in a gunfight with Frank Reid, who led a vigilante committee upset over one of Smith's thefts. Reid died of his wounds in the shoot-out, too, but Smith's gang was broken. Of course, the gold rush was about to end anyway.

In 1976 the National Park Service began buying many of Skagway's best old buildings for the **Klondike Gold Rush National Historic District** and now it owns about 15, having completed restoration in 1999. Broadway is a prosperous, freshly painted 6-block strip of gold rush era buildings. A few that look like real businesses turn out to be displays showing how it was back then. Other buildings restored by the Park Service are under lease to gift shops and such. Visitors also can ride the gold rush-era narrow-gauge **White Pass and Yukon Route railroad** into the White Pass, hike the **Chilkoot Trail,** or join in some other, limited outdoor activities.

ESSENTIALS

GETTING THERE The **Alaska Marine Highway System** 1591 Glacier Ave., Juneau, AK 99801-1427 (☎ **800/642-0066,** or 907/983-2941 locally; www.dot.state.ak.us/external/amhs/home.html), connects Skagway daily with Haines and Juneau. The fare is $17 to Haines, $32 to Juneau. If you're headed to Haines without a vehicle, consider the two private passenger ferries listed under "Getting There" in the Haines section. Haines is 15 miles away by boat but more than 350 miles by road.

Since 1978, ✪ **Klondike Highway 2** has traced the route of the stampeders through the White Pass, a parallel route to the Chilkoot Trail, into Canada. The road runs 99 miles, then meets the Alaska Highway a dozen miles southeast of the Yukon capital of Whitehorse. The border is at the top of the pass, 14 miles from Skagway. (Information on customs is in chapter 9 in the Alaska Highway section.) This is one of the most spectacular drives anywhere in Alaska, and the road is a well-maintained two-lane highway with wide shoulders. The views are basically equivalent to the White Pass and Yukon Route railway, but a lot cheaper. Do it in clear weather, if possible, as in cloudy weather all you'll see is whiteout. Car rentals are available from **Avis** (☎ **800/331-1212** or 907/983-2247), with an office at the Westmark Inn Skagway, at Third and Spring streets. The **Gold Rush Lodge** (see "Accommodations," below) also has cars for rent.

Two bus lines have summer service from Whitehorse or Beaver Creek, where there are connections with Anchorage or Fairbanks. Gray Line's **Alaskon Express** (☎ **800/544-2206** or 907/983-2241; www.graylinealaska.com/alaskon.cfm) stops at the Westmark Inn Skagway, at Third and Spring streets. The fare is $215 from Anchorage. **Alaska Direct Busline** (☎ **800/780-6652**) operates the same route, charging $180.

Several air taxi operators serve Skagway. **L.A.B. Flying Service** (☎ **800/426-0543** or 907/983-2471; www.labflying.com) has scheduled flights from Juneau for $169 round-trip.

VISITOR INFORMATION In the restored railroad depot, the **National Park Service Visitor Center,** Second Avenue and Broadway (P.O. Box 517), Skagway, AK 99840 (☎ **907/983-2921;** www.nps.gov/klgo), is the focal point for activities in Skagway. Rangers answer questions, give lectures, and show films, and four times a day lead an excellent guided walking tour. The building houses a small museum that lays the groundwork for the rest of what you'll see. Most of the Park Service's programs are free. It's open daily 8am to 8pm from June to August, daily 8am to 6pm in May and September, and Monday to Friday 8am to 5pm from October to April. The park headquarters in the same building is open normal business hours, and the staff there will gladly answer questions or show a film.

The **Skagway Convention and Visitors Bureau Center,** 245 Broadway (P.O. Box 1025), Skagway, AK 99840 (☎ **888/762-1898** or 907/983-2854; fax 907/983-3854; www.skagway.org), occupies the historic Arctic Brotherhood Hall, the building with the driftwood facade. The Web site contains links to hotels, restaurants, and activities, or they'll send you the information on paper. Stop in especially for the informative **Skagway Walking Tour Map** of historic sites, the town's single handiest and most informative historic resource. It's open daily 8am to 6pm in the summer, Monday to Friday 8am to 5pm in the winter.

On the Web, check out **Skagway.com**, with well-organized links to many local resources and a message board where you can discuss a visit or Chilkoot Trail trip.

GETTING AROUND Skagway is laid out on a simple grid, with streets branching off from Broadway. All the main sights can be reached on foot.

If you want to go to Dyea (2 miles along Klondike Hwy. 2, then 8 miles on a gravel road) or the gold rush graveyard, a bike is a fun way to do it. **Sockeye Cycle,** on Fifth Avenue off Broadway (☎ **907/983-2851;** cyclealaska.com), rents good mountain bikes for $6 an hour and leads guided day trips (see "Getting Outside," below).

FAST FACTS **ATMs** are at a bank on Broadway at 6th Avenue, and in the Yukon and White Pass Route depot.

The **Skagway Medical Clinic,** staffed by a physician's assistant, can be reached at ☎ **907/983-2255** during business hours, or 907/983-2418 after-hours.

For **Internet/e-mail** access, try the library, at Eighth and State streets.

For nonemergency **police** business, call ☎ **907/983-2232.**

There's a **post office** on Broadway between Sixth and Seventh avenues.

The local **sales tax** is 4%. The **bed tax** totals 8%.

SPECIAL EVENTS **A Mini Folk Festival** in April is sponsored by the Skagway Fine Arts Council (☎ **907/983-2276**). **Skagway's July 4th Parade and Celebration,** organized by the city, has been a big deal since Soapy Smith led the parade in 1898. It includes an international softball tournament, involving teams from Canada. **The Klondike Road Relay,** a 110-mile overnight foot race over the pass, brings hundreds of runners in teams of 10 from all over the state. It's held in early September. Call the visitor center for information.

EXPLORING SKAGWAY

Many companies offer car, van, or bus tours of Skagway, but none goes to greater lengths for a unique experience than Steve Hites, whose **Skagway Streetcar Company,** 270 Second Ave. (☎ **907/983-2908**), uses antique touring vehicles with costumed guides who consider their work "theater without walls." The very personal and amusing 2-hour streetcar tour, based on a tour originally given to President Harding in 1923, is $35 for adults. Hites also offers a 90-minute van ride up the highway to the White Pass Summit for $29 and a 5-hour tour into the Yukon Territory for $69; children are charged half fare. Hites operates out of his big gift shop with an espresso counter and a theater, where he completes his tour. Book the tour at least 2 weeks in advance, as they're always sold out.

TOURING THE HISTORIC PARK

The main thing to do in Skagway is to see the old buildings and historic gold rush places. Do it with the *Skagway Walking Tour Map* or join a fascinating National Park Service guided walking tour (see "Visitor Information" above). Commercial tours are covered above, under "Getting Around."

Start with a visit to the **museum** at the National Park Service Visitor Center and next door. It helps put everything else in context. Of greatest interest is a collection of food and gear similar to the ton of supplies each prospector was required to carry over the pass in order to gain entry into Canada, a requirement that prevented famine among the stampeders, but made the job of getting to Dawson City an epic struggle.

While they prepared to go over the pass, gold rush greenhorns spent their time in Skagway drinking and getting fleeced in the many gambling dens and brothels. Nothing was against the law in the town's heyday because there was no civil authority. It's hard to picture at times, because everything looks so orderly now, but the Park Service has tried. For example, the **Mascot Saloon,** at Broadway and Third Avenue, has statues bellying up to the bar. It's open daily from 8am to 5pm and admission is free.

The Park Service offers free tours of the 1897 **Moore House,** near Fifth Avenue and Spring Street, 1pm to 5pm during the summer. Ten years before the gold rush happened, Capt. William Moore brilliantly predicted it and homesteaded the land that would become Skagway, knowing that this would be a key staging area. He built a cabin in 1887, which stands nearby. But when the rush hit, the stampeders simply ignored his property claims and built the city on his land without offering compensation. Years later, he won in court.

A block east, on Sixth Avenue, is **Mollie Walsh Park,** with a good children's play area, public rest rooms, and phones. A sign tells the sad story of Skagway's first respectable woman, who chose to marry the wrong man among two suitors and was killed by him in a drunken rage. The other suitor—who'd previously killed another rival for her affections—commissioned the bust of Walsh that stands at the park.

The **Gold Rush Cemetery** is 1½ miles from town, up State Street. Used until 1908, it's small and overgrown with spruce trees, but some of the charm and mystery of the place are lost because of the number of visitors and the shiny new paint and maintenance of the wooden markers. The graves of Soapy Smith and Frank Reid are the big attractions, but don't miss the short walk up to Reid Falls. A map is available at the visitor center. The closely spaced dates on many of the markers attest to the epidemics that swept through stampeders living in squalid conditions. Remember, there was no sanitation for the tens of thousands who passed this way in 1898.

About 9 miles north of Skagway is the ghost town of **Dyea,** where stampeders started climbing the Chilkoot Trail. It's a lovely coastal drive or bike ride: from Skagway, go 2 miles up Klondike Highway 2 and then turn left, continuing 8 miles on gravel road. Dyea is a lot more ghost than town. All that remains are a few boards, broken dock pilings, and miscellaneous iron trash. On a sunny day, however, the protected historical site is a perfect place for a picnic, among beach grasses, fields of wild iris, and the occasional reminder that a city once stood here. The National Park Service leads a guided history and nature walk once a week; check at the visitor center. (See "Getting Outside," below, for other ideas on going to Dyea.)

The little-visited **Slide Cemetery,** in the woods near Dyea, is the last resting place of many of the 60 to 70 men who died in an avalanche on the Chilkoot Trail on Palm Sunday, April 3, 1898. No one knows how many are here, or exactly who died, or how accurate the wooden markers are. In 1960, when the state reopened the Chilkoot Trail, the cemetery had been completely overgrown, and the markers were replaced. But somehow the mystery and forgetting make it an even more ghostly place, and the sense of anonymous, hopeless hardship and death it conveys is as authentic a gold rush souvenir as anything in Skagway.

MUSEUMS & ATTRACTIONS

The White Pass and Yukon Route. Second Ave. depot (P.O. Box 435, Dept. B), Skagway, AK 99840. ☎ **800/343-7373** or 907/983-2217. www.whitepassrailroad.com.

A narrow-gauge railroad line that originally ran to Whitehorse, the White Pass was completed after only 2 years in 1900. It's an engineering marvel and a fun way to see spectacular, historic scenery. The excursion ride begins at a depot with the spine-tingling sound of a working steam engine's whistle. The steamer pulls the train a couple of miles, then diesels take the cars—some of them originals more than 100 years old—up steep tracks that were chipped out of the side of the mountains. They "recommend" you don't get out of your seat, but it's a long ride on a slow train, and most people get up and socialize; however, you cannot move from car to car while the train is moving. The trick is to go in clear weather. When the pass is socked in all you see is white clouds. Tickets are expensive, however, and you have to reserve ahead. Take the gamble: cancellation carries only a 10% penalty and you can change dates for no charge. Also, try to go on a weekend, when fewer cruise ships are in town taking up all the seats; weekend trains can be booked as little as a week ahead, while midweek excursions book up months ahead. The summit excursion—which travels 20 miles with an elevation gain of 2,865 feet, then turns back—takes about 3 hours and costs $78, half price ages 3 to 12.

The biggest treat for train lovers is an 8-hour all-steam-powered round-trip to Lake Bennett, where the stampeders launched their boats for the trip to Dawson City. Leaving each Saturday morning June to August, the fare is $156. Lunch at Lake Bennett is included. A Lake Bennett trip by diesel engine happens 3 days a week for $128, and includes lunch and a walking tour at the lake. You can get all the way to Whitehorse on a train that meets a bus, for a $95 fare, one way. These days, the line operates only as a tourist attraction, closing down mid-September to mid-May.

Trail of '98 Historical Museum and Archives. Seventh and Spring sts. ☎ **907/983-2420.** Admission $2 adults, $1 students and children. Summer daily 9am–5pm. Winter by appointment only.

The museum contains a fine collection of gold rush artifacts, including Soapy Smith's Colt Deringer and the bloody tie he wore on the day of his fatal gunfight. The building is Skagway's most impressive, and one of the state's most dignified architectural landmarks, a crisp granite block standing among tall shade trees on the edge of town. It began life as a gold rush era college and later was a federal courthouse, city hall and jail. Extensive renovations were completed in 2000.

Alaskan Wildlife Adventure and Collection Showcase. Fourth and Spring sts. ☎ **907/983-3600.** Admission $19 adults, $17.50 seniors, $7.50 children under 12. Summer daily 9am–6pm. Closed winter.

This unique business contains an amazing collection of miscellaneous memorabilia from the long Alaska lives of Bob and Anna Groff and an immense display of their 76 animal mounts in a room built for the purpose. Bob and Anna show you around, and they are museum-quality examples of the solid, friendly, old-time Alaska type. Sadly, a recent price increase makes admission more expensive than I can recommend paying.

Corrington Museum of Alaska History. Fifth Ave. and Broadway, in Corrington's gift shop. Free admission. Mid-May to mid-Sept 9am–7pm. Closed winter.

The eclectic exhibit that leads into the gift shop is well worth a stop. Besides owning some interesting items, they've done a good job of putting it all together in an understandable way.

GETTING OUTSIDE

BACKPACKING The National Park Service and Parks Canada jointly manage the famous **Chilkoot Pass Trail,** publishing a trail guide and offering information at their offices in Skagway and Whitehorse. Some 20,000 stampeders used the trail to get from Dyea—9 miles from Skagway—to Lake Bennett, 33 miles away, where they could build and launch boats bound for Dawson City. Today about 3,000 people a year make the challenging hike, taking 3 to 5 days. The Chilkoot is not so much a wilderness trail as an outdoor museum, but don't underestimate it, as so many did during the gold rush.

To control the numbers, **Parks Canada,** 205-300 Main St., Whitehorse, Yukon Y1A 2B5 Canada (☎ **800/661-0486;** fax 867/393-6701; www.harbour.com/parkscan/ct), allows only 50 hikers with permits per day to cross the summit. To buy the permits, call with a Visa or MasterCard and the date you plan to start. If you mail the money, your reservation isn't guaranteed till it arrives. Permits are $40 for adults, $20 ages 6 to 15, plus an $11 per person reservation fee. Eight of the 50 daily permits are held for walk-ins, distributed along with any no-shows at the Park Service's visitor center in Skagway. Once over the pass, you're on Lake Bennett, on the rail line 8 miles short of the road. You can walk to the road, or get back to Skagway on the White Pass and Yukon Route railway (see "Museums & Activities," above), which runs at 1pm daily, June through August. The one-way fare to Frasier, B.C., is $25 for adults or children; the scenic 3-hour ride to Skagway is $65 adults, $32.50 children. Be certain to make your reservations well in advance. Although you can stock up on groceries in Skagway, you'll need to rent any equipment in Juneau or Whitehorse.

There are two **U.S. Forest Service cabins** near Skagway, and official access to both is by the White Pass and Yukon Route railway. Both are on trails described in the *Skagway Trail Map,* mentioned below. One cabin is an old, red White Pass caboose parked next to the tracks 6 miles up the line at the trailhead for the 4.5-mile **Denver Glacier Trail.** Another cabin is 1½ miles off the track, 14 miles up on the spectacular **Lawton Glacier Trail.** For either, you need a $35 cabin permit (see "Getting Outside in the Tongass National Forest," in section 1 of this chapter, for reservations information) and a train ticket from the railroad. For details, contact the National Park Service visitor center (see above), or the **Juneau Ranger District,** 8465 Old Dairy Rd., Juneau, AK 99801 (☎ **907/586-8800;** www.fs.fed.us/r10/tongass).

BIKING **Sockeye Cycle,** on Fifth Avenue off Broadway (☎ **907/983-2851;** cyclealaska.com), leads bike tours, including one that takes clients to the top of the White Pass in a van and coasts down on bikes; the 2-hour trip is $69. They also lead a tour of the quiet ghost town site of Dyea for $69, going over in a van. I rode to Dyea from Skagway on my own over the hilly, 10-mile coastal road, one of the most pleasant, scenic rides I can remember.

HIKING A ***Skagway Trail Map*** is available from the visitor center, listing 11 hikes around Skagway. An easy evening walk starts at the suspension footbridge at the north end of First Avenue, crossing the Skagway River to **Yakutania Point Park,** where pine trees grow from cracks in the rounded granite of the shoreline. Across the park is a shortcut taking a couple of miles off the trip to Dyea and to the **Skyline Trail and A.B. Mountain,** a strenuous climb to a 3,500-foot summit with great views. On the southern side of town, across the railroad tracks, a network of trails heads up from Spring Street between Third and Fourth avenues to a series of mountain lakes, the closest of which is **Lower Dewey Lake,** less than a mile up the trail.

HORSEBACK RIDING **Chilkoot Horseback Adventures** leads half-day horseback tours of Dyea and West Creek Glacier for $109, booked through Southeast Tours at Fifth Avenue and Broadway (☎ **907/983-3990**).

FLIGHTSEEING Skagway, like Haines, is a good place to choose for a flightseeing trip, as Glacier Bay National Park is just to the west. **L.A.B. Flying Service** (☎ **800/426-0543** or 907/983-2471; www.labflying.com) is one of several companies offering fixed-wing service. Expect to pay $120 to $280 per person. **Temsco Helicopters** (☎ **907/983-2900;** www.temscoair.com) takes 55-minute tours over the Chilkoot Trail, including a 25-minute landing on a glacier (not in Glacier Bay); those flights cost $160.

SHOPPING

With almost 100 years of experience, Skagway knows how to do gift shops, and now has more than 50. Of course, most are closed in winter, as the town has only about 800 year-round residents. And, as always, you must be cautious about counterfeits when buying Native artwork (see "Native Art—Finding the Real Thing," in chapter 2).

Corrington's, at Fifth and Broadway, is a large gift store with an entire free museum attached (see "Museums & Attractions," above). **Lynch and Kennedy,** at Fourth Avenue and Broadway, is in a building owned and restored by the National Park Service and leased to the current gift store; it carries fine art, jewelry, and high-quality gifts. **Inside Passage Arts,** on Broadway between Fourth and Fifth avenues, is a gallery of Alaska Native fine art.

ACCOMMODATIONS

All the accommodations in Skagway are within close walking distance of the historic district, except as noted. I cannot recommend the **Westmark Inn Skagway.** Although it's by far the largest and most expensive hotel in town, I found the rooms lacking.

In addition to the accommodations listed, you'll find good standard rooms, reasonably priced and about a mile from the sights, at **Wind Valley Lodge,** 22nd Avenue and State Street (☎ **907/983-2236;** www.alaskan.com/windvalleylodge). You'll also find inexpensive rooms at **Sgt. Preston's Lodge,** Sixth Avenue and State Street (☎ **907/983-2521**).

At The White House. Corner of Eighth and Main sts. (P.O. Box 41), Skagway, AK 99840-0041. ☎ **907/983-9000.** Fax 907/983-9010. www.skagway.com/whitehouse. 10 units. TV TEL. High season $104–$120 double. Low season $75–$85 double. Extra person $10. Rates include full breakfast. AE, DISC, MC, V.

The Tronrud family essentially rebuilt a burned 1902 gable-roofed inn, which has dormer and bow windows and two porticos with small Doric columns. They made the rooms comfortable and modern while retaining the style of the original owner, Lee Guthrie, a successful gambler and saloon owner of the gold rush years. The inn has hardwood floors and fine woodwork. Bedrooms vary in size, but all have the owner's homemade quilts on the beds, phones with direct lines, and ceiling fans. A courtesy van picks up guests.

Gold Rush Lodge. Sixth Ave. and Alaska St. (P.O. Box 514), Skagway, AK 99840. ☎ **877/983-3509** or 907/983-2831. Fax 907/983-2742. www.AlaskaOne.com/goldrush. 12 units, all with shower only. TV TEL. High season $80–$105 double. Low season $60–$75 double. Extra person $10. AE, DC, DISC, MC, V.

This is a clean, comfortable motel by the airstrip, 3 blocks from the historic district, with a grassy picnic area out back. The rooms are on the small side but modern and attractively decorated in light colors, and have microwaves, refrigerators, VCRs, fans, coffeemakers, and hair dryers. Bathrooms have shower stalls, no tubs. The hosts provide fruit, coffee, and a cookie jar in the lobby, and write the guests' names and hometowns on an erasable board so they can get to know each other. They offer a courtesy car and rent cars for $50 a day. No smoking.

Golden North Hotel. Third Ave. and Broadway (P.O. Box 343), Skagway, AK 99840. ☎ **888/222-1898** or 907/983-2294. Fax 907/983-2755. www.goldennorthhotel.com. 31 units, 27 with private bathroom. TEL. $75 double with shared bathroom; $105–$120 double with private bathroom. Extra person $10. Rates include continental breakfast. AE, DC, DISC, MC, V.

This big, yellow landmark on Broadway was built in 1898 and is Alaska's oldest operating hotel. It's a fun place to stay. New owners spent $1.6 million to restore the creaking wooden building while keeping its campy character intact, including the placards in each room about a different gold rush family and the big claw-footed tubs. Eight rooms have showers only, two have shower-tub combinations, and the remainder have only tubs. Four rooms share bathrooms. A courtesy car is available.

Historic Skagway Inn Bed and Breakfast. Seventh Ave. and Broadway (P.O. Box 500), Skagway, AK 99840. ☎ **888/752-4929** or 907/983-2289. Fax 907/983-2713. www.skagwayinn.com. 12 units, none with private bathroom. High season $99–$119 double. Low season $69–$75 double. AE, DISC, MC, V.

Built in 1897, this cute little Victorian inn has frilly rooms ranging from small single bedrooms to a large front room, above the street, with a porch. There are six bathrooms for the 12 guest rooms, and they're kept immaculate. The lobby is a welcoming parlor full of books where guests visit over tea. A courtesy van and a kennel are available.

A full breakfast is served in the windowed dining room, which at night becomes **Olivia's,** an intimate fine-dining establishment. Since it has only seven tables, guests can't help feeling special. The sometimes creative menu emphasizes fresh local seafood and garden produce. Reservations are usually necessary.

Mile Zero Bed & Breakfast. Ninth Ave. and Main St. (P.O. Box 165), Skagway, AK 99840. ☎ **907/983-3045.** Fax 907/983-3046. www.bbonline.com/ak/milezero. 7 units. TEL. High season $105 double; extra person $25. Low season $70 double; extra person $20. MC, V.

In 1995, Howard and Judy Mallory specially built this place to be a B&B, and they thought of everything. The large, immaculate rooms all have private bathrooms, telephone lines, and two entrances, from an internal hall and through French doors that lead to a porch. It's an exceptional place, located a few blocks from the historic area. A continental breakfast is served in a large common room, and they'll pick you up at the ferry and lend you a bicycle free of charge. No smoking.

HOSTELS & CAMPSITES

There's a free **National Park Service campground** at Dyea, with well-separated sites near the water. There are several RV parks. You'll find full hookups for $22 at **Garden City RV Park,** between 15th and 17th streets on State Street (☎ **907/983-2378**). The city also maintains the Pullen Creek/Skagway RV Park (☎ **800/936-3731** or 907/983-2768) near the small-boat harbor, with coin-operated showers open to the public. RV sites with power and water are $22, dry sites $16, or $12 if you have a tent and no vehicle.

Skagway Home Hostel. Third Ave. near Main St. (P.O. Box 231), Skagway, AK 99840. ☎ **907/983-2131.** www.ptialaska.net/~schave. 1 private room, 3 dorms. $15 per bunk, $40 double private room.

Frank Wasmer and Nancy Schave have really opened up their historic home to hostelers, sharing their meals, refrigerator, bathrooms, laundry machines, bicycles, and hospitality side by side with guests. The atmosphere is like off-campus shared housing at college, except the house is nicer and better kept. Bunks are in separate male and female dorm rooms. To reserve, you have to send the money ahead—they don't return long-distance calls. In winter, reservations are required, as Frank and Nancy might otherwise not be there. Summer registration hours are 5:30 to 10:30pm. No pets, alcohol, or smoking.

DINING

Restaurants go out of business and open up faster in Skagway's fully seasonal economy than anywhere else I know, so you may need to ask around for a current recommendation. Besides those listed here, also see **Olivia's,** in the Historic Skagway Inn, above. Stop off for espresso and baked goods at **Mabel G. Smith's** (☎ **907/983-2609**), a bakery, card, and coffee shop on Fifth Avenue off Broadway.

The Stowaway Cafe. End of Congress Way near the small boat harbor. ☎ **907/983-3463.** Reservations recommended. Dinner $12.50–$28.50. V. Summer daily 4–10pm. Closed winter. SEAFOOD/CAJUN.

In a small, gray clapboard house overlooking the boat harbor, a 5-minute walk from the historic sites, Jim and Kim Long's little restaurant is a labor of love—they met here when she hired him to fix it up, then married and bought the place. Jim expertly cooks the grilled and blackened salmon and halibut that anchor the menu; there's also beef, pasta, and all the usual waterfront restaurant items. Service is fast. The tiny dining room is decorated with a miscellaneous collection of knickknacks that will keep your attention almost as well as the harbor view. Avoid the alcove on the street side, however, where you're out of the flow and lose the view. Inexpensive lunches are available 11am to 4pm only from a take-out window. They have a beer and wine license.

Sweet Tooth Cafe. 315 Broadway. ☎ **907/983-2405.** Lunch $5.75–$7.25. MC, V. Daily 6am–3pm. DINER.

One of Skagway's few year-round restaurants, the Sweet Tooth makes it through the winter with good, simple food, quick service, reasonable prices, and hearty portions. The dining room is light and keeps with the town's quaint theme. Alcoholic beverages are not available.

NIGHTLIFE

Incredibly, the ***Days of '98 Show*** has been playing since 1927 in the Fraternal Order of Eagles Hall No. 25, at Sixth Avenue and Broadway (☎ **907/983-2545**). Jim Richards carries on the tradition each summer with actors imported from all over the United States, doing three shows a day. The evening shows begin mock gambling at a casino run by the actors. The performance includes singing, cancan dancing, a Robert Service reading, and the story of the shooting of Soapy Smith. Matinees are $12, and evening shows are $14; senior citizens pay $2 less, and children are charged half price.

The **Red Onion Saloon,** at Second Avenue and Broadway, is an authentic-feeling old bar that often has terrific live jazz and other styles of music, but the players sometimes jump up suddenly and leave—they're cruise-ship musicians who enjoy coming here to stretch out and jam, and they can't afford to miss the boat. It was a brothel originally—what wasn't in this town?—and a mock madam is on hand offering tours. **Moe's Frontier Bar,** at Fifth Avenue and Broadway, is more of a gritty local hangout.

6 Anchorage & Environs

As teenagers living in Anchorage, my cousin and I got a job from a family friend painting his lake cabin. He flew us out on his floatplane and left us there, with paint, food, and a little beer. There was a creek that ran past the lake so full of salmon that we caught one on every cast until we got bored and started thinking of ways to make it more difficult. We cooked the salmon over a fire, then floated in a boat on the lake under the endless sunshine of a summer night, talking and diving naked into the clear, green water. We met some guys building another cabin one day, but otherwise we saw no other human beings. When the week was over, the cabin was painted—it didn't take long—and the floatplane came back to get us. As we lifted off and cleared the trees, Anchorage opened in front of us, barely 10 minutes away.

The state's largest city, Anchorage—where 40% of Alaska's population resides—is accused crushingly of being just like a city "Outside," not really part of Alaska at all. It's true that the closer you get to Anchorage, the more the human development reminds you of the outskirts of Anytown, USA, with fast-food franchises, occasional traffic jams, and the ugly big-box retail development inflicted everywhere by relentless corporate logic. You often hear the joke, "Anchorage isn't Alaska, but you can see it from there," and writers piously warn visitors to land in Anchorage but move on as soon as possible, as if it's catching.

When I hear that advice, I think of the many great experiences I've had here—like painting that cabin, years ago. Anyone in Anchorage with a few hundred dollars for a floatplane can be on a lake or river with the bears and salmon in a matter of minutes, in wilderness deeper than any you could find in the Lower 48. **Chugach State Park** is largely within the city limits, but it's the size of Rocky Mountain National Park, and has similar alpine terrain, with the critical difference that most of it is virtually never visited. Yet you can be climbing those mountains in half an hour's journey from your downtown hotel. **Chugach National Forest,** the nation's second largest, is less than an hour down the road. In downtown's **Ship Creek,** people catch 40-pound salmon from under a freeway bridge. Even within the city, you can bike dozens of miles along the coast or through wooded greenbelts, or ski in one of the nation's best Nordic skiing parks. Anchorage is indeed a big American city, with big-city problems of crime and pollution, but it's also entirely unique for being surrounded by pristine and spectacular wild lands. Anywhere else, Anchorage would be known not for shortcomings, but as one of America's greatest major cities for outdoor enthusiasts.

ANCHORAGE YESTERDAY & TODAY

Anchorage isn't old enough to have a sharp identity as a city—its first generation is just now passing away. Anchorage started as a tent camp for workers mobilized to build the Alaska Railroad in 1915. A few houses and businesses went up to serve the federal employees who were building and later running the railroad, as Steve McCutcheon's father did. McCutcheon, who died in 1998, remembered a remote, sleepy railroad town, enlivened by a couple of large World War II military bases, but never more than strictly functional. As one visitor who came in the early 1940s wrote, the entire town looked like it was built on the wrong side of the tracks.

A couple of years ago, McCutcheon looked out the picture window from his living room on a placid lake surrounded by huge, half-million-dollar houses, each with a floatplane pulled up on the green front lawn, and he recalled the year people started to take Anchorage seriously. It was the year, he said, when they started thinking it would be a permanent city, not just an encampment where you went for a few years to make money before moving on—the year they started building Anchorage to last. That year was 1957. Oil was discovered on the Kenai Peninsula's Swanson River, south of here. It was around that time that McCutcheon built his own house, far out in the country with no neighbors anywhere in the area, all alone on a lake. At that time, you could homestead in the Anchorage bowl. Those who had the opportunity but chose not to—my wife's family, for example—gave it a pass only because it seemed improbable that the flat, wet acreage way out of town would ever be worth anything.

Oil fueled Anchorage's growth like nitrogen fertilizer poured on a shooting weed. Those homesteads that went begging in the 1950s and early 1960s now have shopping malls and high-rise office buildings on them. Fortunes came fast, development was haphazard, and a lot was built that we'd all soon regret. I had the bizarre experience of coming home from college to the town I'd grown up in and getting completely lost in a large area of the city that had been nothing but moose browse the last time I'd seen it. Visitors found a city full of life, but empty of charm.

In the last 15 years, that has started to change. Anchorage is slowly outgrowing its gawky adolescence. It's still young, prosperous, and vibrant—and exhausting when the summer sun refuses to set—but now it also has some excellent restaurants, a good museum, a new Native cultural center and a nice little zoo, and things to do in the evening besides the tourist melodramas you'll find in every Alaska town. People still complain that Anchorage isn't really Alaska—in Fairbanks, they call it "Los Anchorage" (and in Anchorage, Fairbanks is known as "Squarebanks")—yet the great wilderness around the city remains intertwined with its streets. Along with a quarter million people, Anchorage is full of moose—so many, they're becoming pests and wintertime hazards, inspiring debate about hunting them within the city limits. Bears and bald eagles also show up in town, though less frequently, on the system of greenbelts and bike trails that brings the woods into almost every neighborhood.

Anchorage stands on broad, flat sediment between the Chugach Mountains and the silt-laden waters of upper Cook Inlet. At water's edge, mud flats not yet made into land stretch far offshore when the tide is at its low point, up to 38 vertical feet below high water. There's a **downtown area** of about 8-by-20 blocks, near Ship Creek where it all started. Like many cities built since the arrival of the automobile, the layout is not particularly conducive to any other form of transportation. But the city's boundaries go far beyond the reach of cars, taking in the Chugach, Turnagain Arm all the

Anchorage

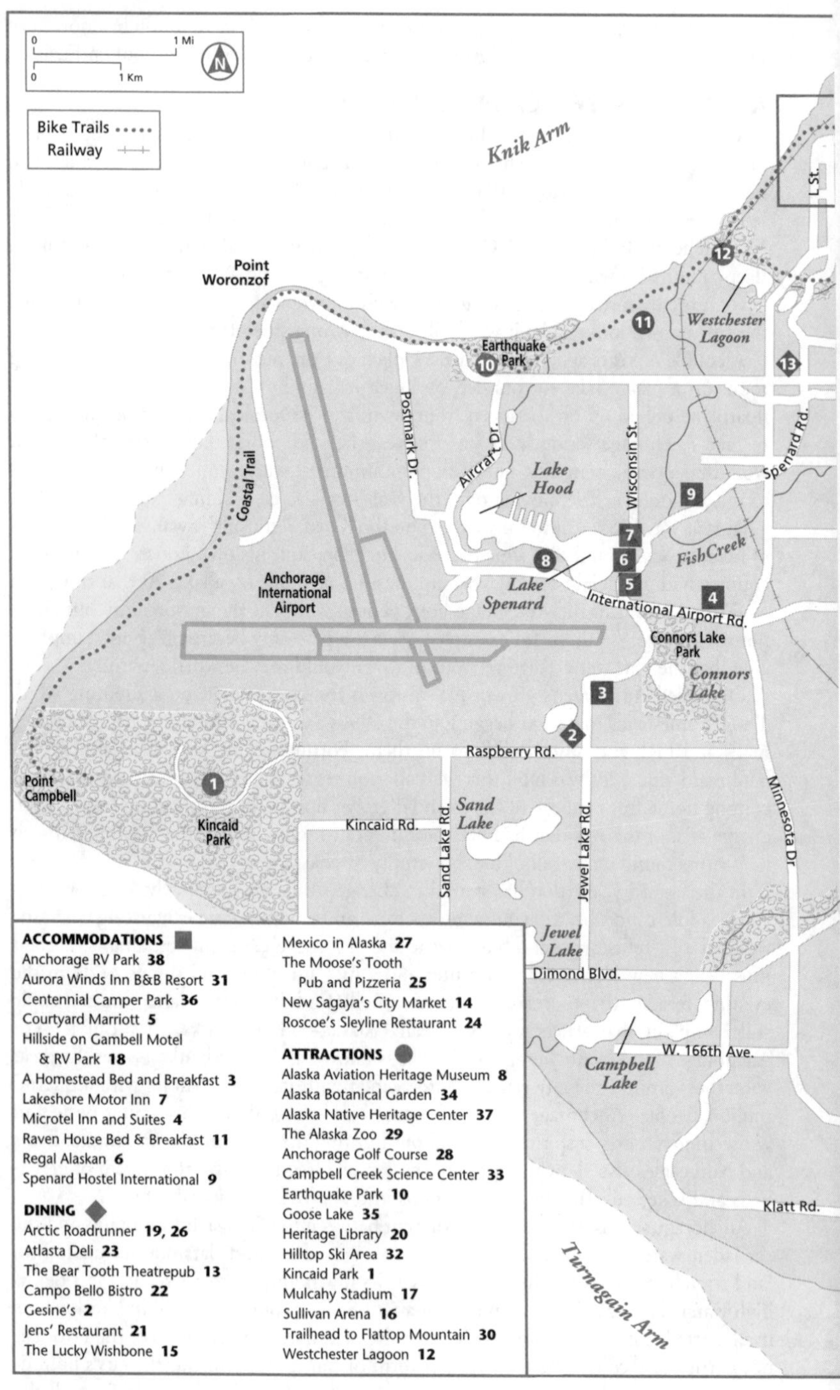

0
1 Mi
0
1 Km
N
Bike Trails
Railway
Knik Arm
L St.
Point Woronzof
Earthquake Park
10
11
12
Westchester Lagoon
13
Postmark Dr.
Aircraft Dr.
Lake Hood
Wisconsin St.
Spenard Rd.
9
7
6
5
8
Fish Creek
Coastal Trail
Anchorage International Airport
Lake Spenard
International Airport Rd.
4
Connors Lake Park
Connors Lake
3
2
Raspberry Rd.
Point Campbell
1
Kincaid Park
Kincaid Rd.
Sand Lake Rd.
Sand Lake
Jewel Lake Rd.
Minnesota Dr
Jewel Lake
Dimond Blvd.
W. 166th Ave.
Campbell Lake
Klatt Rd.
Turnagain Arm
ACCOMMODATIONS
Anchorage RV Park 38
Aurora Winds Inn B&B Resort 31
Centennial Camper Park 36
Courtyard Marriott 5
Hillside on Gambell Motel & RV Park 18
A Homestead Bed and Breakfast 3
Lakeshore Motor Inn 7
Microtel Inn and Suites 4
Raven House Bed & Breakfast 11
Regal Alaskan 6
Spenard Hostel International 9
DINING
Arctic Roadrunner 19, 26
Atlasta Deli 23
The Bear Tooth Theatrepub 13
Campo Bello Bistro 22
Gesine's 2
Jens' Restaurant 21
The Lucky Wishbone 15
Mexico in Alaska 27
The Moose's Tooth Pub and Pizzeria 25
New Sagaya's City Market 14
Roscoe's Sleyline Restaurant 24
ATTRACTIONS
Alaska Aviation Heritage Museum 8
Alaska Botanical Garden 34
Alaska Native Heritage Center 37
The Alaska Zoo 29
Anchorage Golf Course 28
Campbell Creek Science Center 33
Earthquake Park 10
Goose Lake 35
Heritage Library 20
Hilltop Ski Area 32
Kincaid Park 1
Mulcahy Stadium 17
Sullivan Arena 16
Trailhead to Flattop Mountain 30
Westchester Lagoon 12

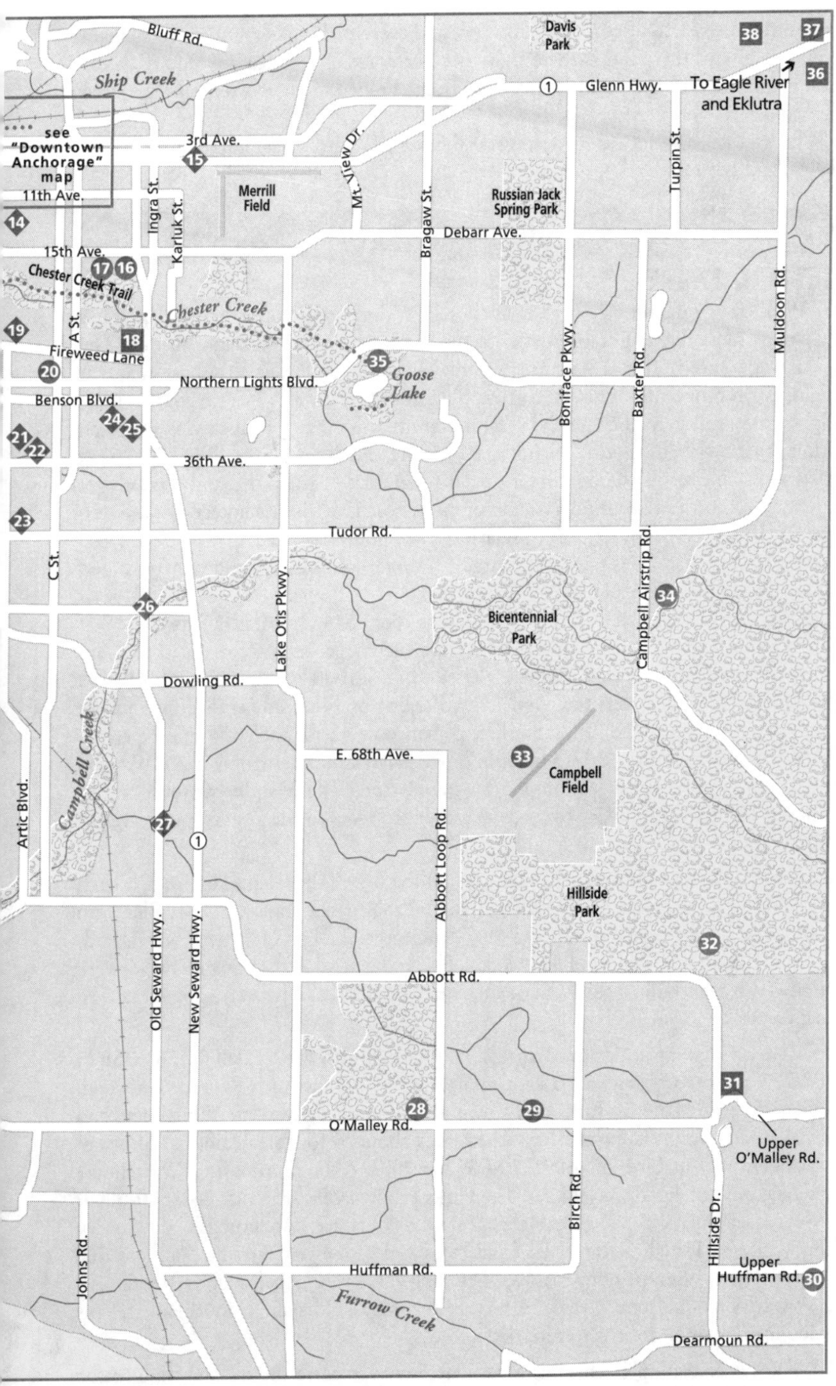
Bluff Rd.
Ship Creek
see "Downtown Anchorage" map
11th Ave.
3rd Ave.
Merrill Field
Mt. View Dr.
Davis Park
Glenn Hwy.
To Eagle River and Eklutra
Turpin St.
Russian Jack Spring Park
Bragaw St.
Debarr Ave.
Ingra St.
Karluk St.
15th Ave.
Chester Creek Trail
Chester Creek
A St.
Fireweed Lane
Northern Lights Blvd.
Goose Lake
Boniface Pkwy.
Baxter Rd.
Muldoon Rd.
Benson Blvd.
36th Ave.
Tudor Rd.
C St.
Lake Otis Pkwy.
Bicentennial Park
Campbell Airstrip Rd.
Dowling Rd.
Campbell Creek
E. 68th Ave.
Campbell Field
Artic Blvd.
Abbott Loop Rd.
Hillside Park
Old Seward Hwy.
New Seward Hwy.
Abbott Rd.
O'Malley Rd.
Upper O'Malley Rd.
Birch Rd.
Hillside Dr.
Johns Rd.
Huffman Rd.
Upper Huffman Rd.
Furrow Creek
Dearmoun Rd.

way to the Alyeska Ski Resort in Girdwood, and even reaching over to Prince William Sound. Most of that land is there only to be explored. I can't say for sure if all the mountain peaks in the municipality have been climbed, and far from all have been named.

This chapter also includes coverage of the suburbs in the Matanuska and Susitna valleys and beyond.

1 Essentials

GETTING THERE

BY PLANE You'll probably get to Anchorage at the start of your trip by air, as it has by far the most flights linking Alaska to the rest of the world on many airlines. The **Anchorage International Airport** is a major hub. Seattle has the most frequent flights, with numerous domestic carriers flying nonstop all day. Within Alaska, most flights route through Anchorage, even for communities that are much closer to each other than either is to Anchorage. **Alaska Airlines** (☎ **800/252-7522;** www.alaskaair.com) is the dominant carrier for Alaska destinations, and the only jet operator to most Alaska cities. Various commuter carriers link Anchorage to rural destinations not served by jet. **Era Aviation** (☎ **800/866-8394** or 907/266-8394; www.era-aviation.com) is one of the largest for Southcentral Alaska destinations and can be booked through Alaska Airlines.

A **taxi ride** downtown from the airport runs about $14. Try **Alaska Cab** (☎ **907/563-5353**). Taxis generally are expensive in Anchorage because of the spread-out urban design. The **Borealis Shuttle** (☎ **888/436-3600** or 907/276-3600; www.borealisshuttle.com) covers the whole city, charging by zones; to get downtown from the airport they charge $10 for the first person plus $2 for each additional person. **Alaska Tourquest** (☎ **907/344-6667;** www.alaskatourquest.com) runs between the airport and railroad station for $6 per person. The **People Mover** city bus system (☎ **907/343-6543;** www.peoplemover.org) goes to the airport, but service is infrequent.

BY CAR There's only one road to the rest of the world: the Glenn Highway. It leads to the Mat-Su Valley area, Glennallen, Tok, and the Alaska Highway, 330 miles from Anchorage. Thirty miles out of town the Glenn meets the Parks Highway, which leads to Denali National Park and Fairbanks. The other road out of town, the Seward Highway, leads south to the Kenai Peninsula. See "Alaska's Highways à la Carte," in chapter 9.

BY BUS Gray Line's **Alaskon Express,** 745 West Fourth Ave. (☎ **800/478-6388** or 907/277-5581; www.graylinealaska.com/alaskon.cfm), links Anchorage to Girdwood, Valdez, Denali National Park, and down the Alaska Highway to Whitehorse and Skagway, and points along the way. The fare is about $215 from Haines or Skagway. **Alaska Direct Bus Line** (☎ **800/770-6652** or 907/277-6652) runs from Whitehouse and Skagway for slightly lower fares. The **Parks Highway Express** (☎ **888/600-6001;** www.AlaskaShuttle.com) offers daily service between Anchorage's downtown Youth Hostel, Denali National Park, and Fairbanks (one-way fares are $40 and $60 respectively), with stops along the way, including Talkeetna. Other small vans and buses offer service to and from Seward, Homer, Fairbanks, and Denali National Park; see the sections on each of those places for details.

BY RV A recreational vehicle is a popular way to explore the region. High-season rates are around $1,400 a week, plus the large amount of fuel you use and possibly mileage charges. Major agencies include **ABC Motorhome Rentals,** 3875 W.

International Airport Rd. (☎ **800/421-7456** or 907/279-2000; www.alaskan.com/abcmotorhomes), and **Cruise America,** 8850 Runamuck Place (☎ **800/327-7799** or 907/349-0499; www.cruiseamerica.com). They offer one-way rentals to Anchorage from their other gateway centers around the country for an added fee of $750.

BY RAIL The **Alaska Railroad** (☎ **800/544-0552** or 907/265-2494, or 907/265-2620 TDD; www.akrr.com) connects Anchorage with Seward to the south and with Fairbanks and Denali National Park to the north. The run to and from Seward, which operates only in the summer, is truly spectacular; the fare is $50 one way, $86 round-trip, children ages 2 to 11 half off. Heading north, the line runs year-round 12 hours to Fairbanks (the summer fare is $160 one way), and in the summer to Denali ($120), or take full-dome cars with Princess Tours or Holland America–Westours. For details, see chapter 8 on Denali National Park.

ORIENTATION

Many visitors never make it beyond the **downtown** area, the old-fashioned grid of streets at the northwest corner of town where the large hotels and the gift shops are located. Street numbers and letters work on a simple pattern and navigation is easy. Beyond downtown, most of Anchorage is oriented to commercial strips, and you'll need a map to find your way. The map on p. 195 will suffice for major thoroughfares, but to find anything on smaller streets, pick up a detailed map at the visitor centers or in any grocery store. Some parts of greater Anchorage are in distinct communities outside the bowl formed by the Chugach Mountains, including **Eagle River** and **Eklutna,** out the Glenn Highway to the northeast, and **Girdwood** and **Portage,** on the Seward Highway, to the south. The suburban **Matanuska and Susitna valleys** lie north of the city on the Glenn and Parks highways.

GETTING AROUND

BY RENTAL CAR Most major car-rental companies operate in Anchorage, mostly from desks at the airport in a tunnel off the domestic baggage claim area. A compact car costs about $50 a day, with unlimited mileage. Cars can sell out in summer, so reserve ahead. I have found one obscure agency, **Levi Car Rental** (☎ **907/563-2279**), willing to rent older vehicles for use on Alaska's gravel highways; the others will not. They charge $65 a day for a Subaru Legacy.

BY BUS Bus fare all over town on the **People Mover** city bus system (☎ **907/343-6543;** www.peoplemover.org) is $1 for adults, 50¢ for ages 5 to 18, and there is a free zone in the downtown core. The transit center bus depot is at Sixth Avenue and G Street. Buses generally come every half hour but are less frequent on weekends.

BY BIKE A bike is a great way to explore, using the network of bike trails, but not a practical means of transportation for anyone but strong riders. The **Tony Knowles Coastal Trail** comes right downtown (see "Getting Outside," below). Bikes are usually for rent in Elderberry Park downtown, at the start of the Coastal Trail. Exact arrangements seem to change annually, but at the moment the provider is **CycleSights** (☎ **907/344-1771** or 907/227-6109). They charge $15 half day, $20 full day, and offer pickup and delivery. **The Bicycle Shop,** in midtown at 1035 W. Northern Lights Blvd. (☎ **907/272-5219**), rents and services a wide selection of bikes, charging $20 the first day, $15 for additional days, or $85 a week.

VISITOR INFORMATION

The **Anchorage Convention and Visitor Bureau,** 524 W. Fourth Ave., Anchorage, AK 99501-2212 (☎ **907/276-4118;** fax 907/278-5559; www.anchorage.net), offers information for the whole state at its centers and extensive Web site. The main location is the **Log Cabin Visitor Information Center,** downtown at Fourth Avenue and F Street (☎ **907/274-3531**). It's open June to August daily 7:30am to 7pm, May and Sept daily 8am to 6pm, October to April daily 9am to 4pm. If it's crowded, go to the storefront office right behind it. You'll also find visitor information desks at the airport—one in the baggage-claim area in the domestic terminal and two in the international terminal: in the lobby and in the transit area.

The ✪ **Alaska Public Lands Information Center,** located at 605 W. Fourth Ave. (across the intersection from the log cabin at Fourth and F), Suite 105, Anchorage, AK 99501 (☎ **907/271-2737,** or 907/271-2738 TTY; www.nps.gov/aplic), has guidance for anyone planning to spend time outdoors anywhere in Alaska, as well as exhibits of interest even for those who aren't. The center occupies a grand room with high ceilings in the 1930s post office and federal courthouse. All the land agencies are represented, you can buy ferry tickets from the Alaska Marine Highway System, there's an excellent selection of trail and field guides, and there are rangers who advise based on personal experience. They're open daily in summer 9am to 7pm; winter Monday to Friday 10am to 5:30pm.

SPECIAL EVENTS

For an exhaustive event listing, with something almost every day of the year, check www.anchorage.net. See the "Out from Anchorage" sections below for events in communities farther afield.

The **Anchorage Folk Festival** (☎ **907/566-2334**) brings together musicians from around the state the last 2 weekends of January. The ✪ **Fur Rendezvous Winter Carnival,** over 2 weekends in mid-February (☎ **907/277-8615**), is a huge, citywide winter celebration, with many community events, fireworks, craft fairs, snowshoe softball, dogsled rides, and other fun. The main event is the **World Champion Sled Dog Race** (☎ **907/562-2235**), a 3-day sprint event of about 25 miles per heat. The ✪ **Iditarod Trail Sled Dog Race** (☎ **907/376-5155;** www.iditarod.com) starts from Anchorage the first Saturday in March at 10am, then the teams are loaded into trucks a few miles out of town and restarted the next day in Wasilla for the 1,000-mile run to Nome (see the section on the Matanuska and Susitna valleys, later in this chapter, and the Nome section in chapter 10). **The Native Youth Olympics,** in April at the University of Alaska Sports Center, is a tough competition in traditional Native sports (☎ **907/265-5900**).

The **Saturday Market** is a big street fair and farmer's market held during the summer at Third Avenue and E Street (☎ **907/277-5634**). **Music in the Park** presents free band performances in the park at Fourth Avenue and E streets Wednesdays and Fridays at noon all summer (☎ **907/279-5650**). The **Mayor's Midnight Sun Marathon** (☎ **907/343-4474**) brings more than 2,000 runners for a race near the time of the summer solstice. The **Ship Creek Salmon Derby,** for 10 days in mid-June and again in August, offers a chance to win money and benefit charity by catching big salmon in downtown Anchorage (☎ **907/276-6472**).

The annual convention of the **Alaska Federation of Natives** (☎ **907/274-3611**), held in October, brings villagers from all over the state, and with them dance celebrations and an exceptional opportunity to buy Native crafts at a fair. The ✪ **Great Alaska Shootout Men's Basketball Tournament** brings top-ranked college teams to the Sullivan Arena over Thanksgiving weekend. **The Christmas Tree Lighting** (☎ **907/276-5015**) takes place in town square the Saturday after Thanksgiving, with Santa usually arriving behind a team of real reindeer. A performance of *The Nutcracker* often follows in the Alaska Center for the Performing Arts.

FAST FACTS: ANCHORAGE

A **bank** is rarely far away, and grocery stores also have **ATMs.** Downtown, **Key Bank** is at the corner of Fifth Avenue and F Street.

Kinko's Copies, at 2210 E. Northern Lights Blvd. (☎ **907/276-4228;** fax 907/276-8357), offers the usual business services. The **Z. J. Loussac Library,** at 3600 Denali St. (☎ **907/343-2975;** www.ci.anchorage.ak.us), offers **free Web access.**

There are two **hospitals** in Anchorage serving the general public: **Alaska Regional Hospital,** at 2801 DeBarr Rd. (☎ **907/276-1131**), and **Providence Alaska Medical Center,** at 3200 Providence Dr. (☎ **907/562-2211**).

The **Anchorage Police Department** has main offices at 4501 S. Bragaw Rd., south of Tudor Road; for a nonemergency call ☎ **907/786-8500.** For nonemergency police business outside the city, call the **Alaska State Troopers,** 5700 E. Tudor Rd. (☎ **907/269-5511**).

There are many **post offices** in town; in the downtown area, it's downstairs in the brown building at Fourth Avenue and D Street.

There's no **sales tax** in Anchorage. The bed tax is 8%.

2 Accommodations

Hotel rooms are overpriced in Anchorage, so you might prefer a B&B or a small, independent hotel. I've searched for such places, choosing those with character and reasonable prices. There are hundreds more, many of them just as good.

The main booking agency in town is **Alaska Private Lodgings,** P.O. Box 200047, Anchorage, AK 99520-0047 (☎ **907/258-1717;** fax 907/258-6613; www.alaskabandb.com). They cover the whole state and can help with itinerary planning. Their directory of B&Bs is on the Web site, with pictures. You also can drop in the downtown office at 704 W. Second Ave.

A large group of B&Bs maintains an impressive cooperative Web directory linking to its members: **Anchorage Alaska Bed and Breakfast Association** can be found at **www.Anchorage-BnB.com**. Their **B&B Hotline** (☎ **907/272-5909**) puts callers directly in touch with B&Bs.

DOWNTOWN

VERY EXPENSIVE

✪ **Hotel Captain Cook.** Fourth Ave. and K St. (P.O. Box 102280), Anchorage, AK 99510-2280. ☎ **800/843-1950** or 907/276-6000. Fax 907/343-2298. www.captaincook.com. 547 units. TV TEL. High season $230–$250 double; $240–$1,500 suite. Low season $125–$145 double; $135–$1,500 suite. Extra person $10. AE, DC, DISC, JCB, MC, V.

This is Alaska's great, grand hotel, where royalty and rock stars stay. Former governor Wally Hickel built the first of the three towers after the 1964 earthquake, and now the hotel fills a city block. Inside, the brown decor has a fully realized (maybe a little excessive) nautical theme, with art memorializing Cook's voyages and enough teak to build a square-rigger. The standard rooms are large, with great views from all sides—you don't pay more to be higher. The most recently remodeled rooms are in Tower 1 and have up-to-date bathrooms. The lobby contains 16 shops, and there's a concierge, tour desks, barbershop and beauty salon, and business center. The full-service health club in the basement has a decent-sized pool and a racquetball court.

Sophisticated continental food and elaborately formal service justifies the high prices at ✪ **The Crows Nest,** the city's most traditional fine dining restaurant, on the hotel's top floor. Pheasant, quail, bison, and venison were on recent menus, as well as the usual seafood, beef, and lamb. All tables have stupendous views, and high-backed booths lend a sense of intimacy. The deliberate service requires you to set aside a full evening for a special meal—the meal unfolds gradually, with almost theatrical formality. Main courses range from $26 to $50; a five-course fixed menu is $50 per person ($70 per person with wine). **Fletcher's,** off the lobby, is an English pub serving good Italian-style pizza and sandwiches. **The Pantry** is more than a typical hotel cafe, with excellent service and interesting entrees mixed in with the more predictable choices.

Expensive

The large **Hilton Anchorage,** 500 W. Third Ave. (☎ **800/445-8667** or 907/272-7411; www.hilton.com), is right at the center of downtown activities. The **Sheraton Anchorage,** 401 E. Sixth Ave. (☎ **800/325-3535** or 907/276-8700; www.sheraton.com), is comparable to the Hilton, but in a less attractive area a few blocks off the downtown tourist area. The advantages of the brand-new **Anchorage Marriott Downtown** (☎ **907/279-8000;** www.marriotthotels.com) are a pool and fabulous views from rooms with wall-sized picture windows.

Copper Whale Inn. 440 L St., Anchorage, AK 99501. ☎ **907/258-7999.** Fax 888/WHALE-IN or 907/258-6213. www.copperwhale.com. 18 units, 16 with private bathroom. High season $110 double with shared bathroom, $135–$160 double with private bathroom. Low season $69 double with shared bathroom, $79 double with private bathroom. Extra person $10. Rates include full breakfast. AE, CB, DC, DISC, MC, V.

A pair of clapboard houses overlook the water and Elderberry Park right on the Coastal Trail downtown, with charming rooms of every shape and size. There's a wonderfully casual feeling to the place. The rooms in the newer building, lower on the hill, are newer, with cherry-wood furniture and high ceilings on the upper level. Two rooms that share a bathroom have great views. Rooms lack TVs and phones, but in some you can get them hooked up by request.

Duke's 8th Avenue Hotel. 630 W. Eighth Ave., Anchorage, AK 99501. ☎ **800/478-4837** or 907/274-6213. Fax 907/272-6308. www.hotel.alaska.com. 28 units. TV TEL. High season $140–$165 suite. Low season $80–$105 suite. Children 12 and under stay free in parents' room. AE, DC, DISC, MC, V.

This cinderblock apartment house downtown was converted into surprisingly light and comfortable one- and two-bedroom suites with full kitchens. Each unit has two telephones and an extra line for your computer. A small, inexpensive laundry is on site. A large party can save a lot of money: The basic rate on two-bedroom units accommodates four adults, and children 12 and under stay free (the one-bedroom unit rates are for two people). On the downside, the four-story building has no elevator, and the 100-level is a half basement.

✪ **The Voyager Hotel.** 501 K St., Anchorage, AK 99501. ☎ **800/247-9070** or 907/277-9501. Fax 907/274-0333. www.voyagerhotel.com. 38 units. A/C TV TEL. High season $169 double. Low season $89 double. Extra person $10. AE, CB, DC, DISC, JCB, MC, V. No smoking.

Thanks to its exacting proprietor, Stan Williams, The Voyager is just right, right down to the quality of the linen. The size is small, the location central, the rooms large and light, all with well-designed kitchenettes, and the housekeeping exceptional. The desks have speaker phones, high-speed data ports, and extra electrical outlets; and the hospitality is warm yet highly professional. There's nothing ostentatious or outwardly remarkable about the hotel, yet the most experienced travelers rave about it the loudest.

Moderate

Here are a few more moderately priced chain-hotel options in downtown: the **Days Inn** (☎ **800/325-2525** or 907/276-7226; www.alaskalife.net/daysinn), which has a courtesy van to the airport and many amenities; the **Holiday Inn of Anchorage**

Downtown Anchorage

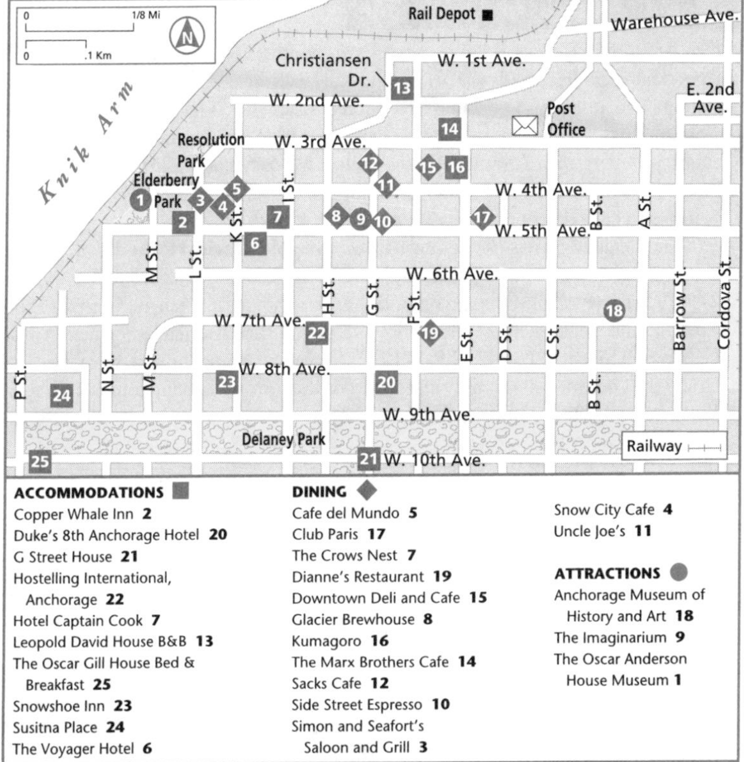

(☎ **800/465-4329** or 907/279-8671; www.holiday-inn.com), which has a pool; the **Clarion Suites** (☎ **888/389-6575** or 907/274-1000; www.hotelchoice.com), across from the Federal Building, with a small pool and suites as standard rooms; and the **Hawthorn Suites** (☎ **888/469-6575** or 907/222-5005; www.hawthorn.com), with similar facilities, plus a Benihana Restaurant on site.

Snowshoe Inn. 826 K St., Anchorage, AK 99501. ☎ **907/258-SNOW.** Fax 907/258-SHOE. E-mail: SnowshoeInnAK@aol.com. 16 units. TV TEL. High season $99–$149 double. Low season $59–$79 double. Extra person $10. Rates include continental breakfast. DISC, MC, V. No smoking.

This cheerful, family run hotel on a quiet downtown street has comfortable, attractively decorated rooms, all perfectly clean. The energetic Zeid family seems to be constantly improving something—Samy does the remodeling work himself—and now every room has a refrigerator, microwave oven, coffeemaker, VCR, HBO, and hair dryer. The $99 rooms are quite small, but the suites are large enough for a family. I've found no better bargain downtown. Freezer and storage space and a coin-op laundry are available.

Inexpensive

✪ **The Oscar Gill House Bed and Breakfast.** 1344 W. 10th Ave. (P.O. Box 200047), Anchorage, AK 99520-0047. ☎ **907/258-1717.** Fax 907/258-6613. www.alaskabandb.com/oscargillindex.html. 3 units, 1 with private bathroom. TEL. High season $85 double with shared bathroom, $95 double with private bathroom. Low season $65 double with shared bathroom, $75 double with private bathroom. Extra person $15. Rates include full breakfast. AE, MC, V.

More Great B&Bs in Anchorage

Here are more excellent B&Bs I didn't have room to list in full. **Birch Trails Bed & Breakfast** (☎ **907/688-5713**), in the Chugiak area a half hour out of town, belongs to a dog-mushing family that offers rides (see "Getting Outside," below). The 24 dogs bed down in the yard right outside the windows of comfortable, country-style rooms. A more upscale choice, **Moosewood Manner,** way up in the mountains at the tree line (☎ **907/345-8788;** e-mail: moosewd@alaska.net), serves gourmet vegetarian food and caters to people with disabilities.

A moderately priced choice downtown, **Leopold David House B&B,** in one of the most historic and interesting houses in Anchorage, at 605 W. Second Ave. (☎ **907/279-1917;** www.alaskaholiday.com), has hosts who speak French, German, Polish, Russian, and Spanish. I also especially like these other affordable downtown places: **G Street House** (☎ **907/258-1717**), an elegant home hosted by a wonderful family (he's on the city assembly and she leads the historic walking tours); and **Susitna Place** (☎ **907/274-3344;** www.susitnaplace.com), overlooking Cook Inlet from atop a bluff on a quiet side street.

On the Delaney Park strip, just a few blocks from downtown, this is truly the oldest house in Anchorage—it was built in 1913, in Knik, before Anchorage was founded, and moved here on a barge a few years later. Oscar Gill was an early civic leader. The house was to be torn down in 1982 but was moved to storage by a historic preservation group; Mark and Susan Lutz saved it in 1994, moving it to its present location and, with their own labor, restoring it authentically as a cozy, friendly bed-and-breakfast. The house is full of appropriate antiques, and manages to be both homey and immaculate. The prices are low—the Lutzes could charge 50% more—but they don't because they are good people. At these rates, however, rooms book up many months ahead. Free bikes are available. There's a 5% surcharge for credit cards.

Hostels

Hostelling International, Anchorage, 700 H St. (☎ **907/276-3635**), is a 95-bed hostel right downtown. A coin-op laundry, kitchen, and baggage storage are available. I found the place more impersonal and gritty than necessary. Members pay $16, nonmembers $19; private rooms are $40 for two. The hostel closes between noon and 5pm daily and the curfew is 1am.

Spenard Hostel International, 2845 W. 42nd Ave. (☎ **907/248-5036;** www.alaskalife.net/spnrdhstl/hostel.html), is a friendly place near the airport, with free phones, inexpensive bike and storage rental, Internet access, a laundry, and a black Lab. There are three lounges for different activities and three kitchens. You can come and go 24 hours. It feels more like communal housing than a hostel. The office is open daily 9am to 1pm and 7 to 11pm in summer, 7 to 11pm winter. Beds are $15.

BEYOND DOWNTOWN

Very Expensive

Regal Alaskan. 4800 Spenard Rd., Anchorage, AK 99517-3236. ☎ **800/544-0553** or 907/243-2300. Fax 907/243-8815. www.regal-hotels.com. 248 units. TV TEL. High season $270–$285 double; $325–$600 suite. Low season $165–$185 double; $250–$400 suite. AE, CB, DC, DISC, EC, JCB, MC, V.

With a good view of the floatplanes on Lake Spenard, near the airport, the large lobby, with its warm colors and the fly rods and animal mounts on display, suggests a huge fishing and hunting lodge. There's a big patio to catch the sun and watch the planes, but the rooms are what's really special—decorated in a style of tasteful opulence and packed with thoughtful details, they're a delight to the eye and an invitation to relaxation. Each has a coffeemaker, fridge, hair dryer, ironing board, clock radio, modem jacks, and a Nintendo game on the TV. The hotel lacks a swimming pool, but does have a health club with a spa and sauna. A courtesy van runs a regular schedule downtown, but this is an airport hotel, and for convenience you really need to rent a car if you stay in this area. The restaurants on-site serve a steak and seafood menu, sandwiches, and the other fare you'd expect.

Expensive

✪ **Aurora Winds Inn B&B Resort.** 7501 Upper O'Malley Rd., Anchorage, AK 99516. ☎ **907/346-2533.** Fax 907/346-3192. E-mail: awbnb@alaska.net. 5 units. TV TEL. High season $125–$175 double. Low season $55–$125 double. Extra person $15 in high season, $10 in low season. Rates include full breakfast. AE, DC, DISC, MC, V.

The rooms in this massive house far up the hillside in South Anchorage are so grand and theatrically decorated you'll feel as if you're in a James Bond movie. Each bedroom has a sitting area, VCR, and decorative details that make it unique, elegant, or even campy. Even the bathrooms are showplaces: Three have Jacuzzis, and one is larger than a lot of hotel rooms, with an "environmental habitat chamber." One lovely room has windows on the deck and forest on three sides. Besides the outdoor hot tub set in luxuriant gardens, they've recently installed a gym with a tiny moving-water swimming pool and a theater with a large video screen.

Moderate

Raven House Bed and Breakfast. 3315 Iliamna Ave., Anchorage, AK 99517. ☎ **907/248-9587.** Fax 907/248-6600. E-mail: ravenbnb@alaska.net. 3 units, one with private bathroom. $85 shared bathroom, $125 private bathroom. Rates include full breakfast. MC.

On a huge, sloping lot on the Coastal Trail in the Turnagain residential area, the house has a sleek, opulently modern style. Maxine Quist's extraordinary housekeeping helps maintain the clean lines—it's as if the place were brand-new. Two nicely decorated bedrooms share a bathroom. A huge and luxuriously appointed suite downstairs has a bar, fridge, entertainment center, and two-person Jacuzzi; it's often used as a honeymoon suite. She lends bicycles, which can quickly and safely get you downtown on the trail.

Inexpensive

Hillside on Gambell Motel and RV Park. 2150 Gambell St., Anchorage, AK 99503. ☎ **800/478-6008** or 907/258-6006. Fax 907/279-8972. 26 units. TV TEL. High season $85–$115 double. Low season $60–$86 double. Extra person $10. AE, DISC, MC, V.

On a busy highway with a car dealership and self-storage business, this funny little hotel is a friendly oasis. Rooms are clean and well maintained and have features—including microwaves, refrigerators and hair dryers—that make them quite practical, if not beautiful or luxurious. A gate in the RV park leads to the Lanie Fleischer Coastal Trail, for biking or Nordic skiing. (Full hookups are $24.) There are coffee machines in the rooms and the lobby, and a coin-op laundry is available.

A Homestead Bed and Breakfast. 6141 Jewel Lake Rd., Anchorage, AK 99502. ☎ **907/243-5678.** Fax 907/248-6184. E-mail: jasper@chugach.net. 2 units. TV TEL. Summer $95 double. Winter $65 double. Extra person $20. Rates include full breakfast. MC, V (5% surcharge for credit cards). No smoking.

This is a real 1930s homestead house built of logs, once remote but now a few minutes from the airport and Kincaid Park. Frank and Patricia Jasper have lived here more

Affordable Rooms Near the Airport

Good, inexpensive standard motel rooms near the airport are rare to the vanishing point, although luxurious rooms (like those at the Regal Alaskan) and B&Bs are readily available. The lowest priced, consistently acceptable standard hotel rooms I could find, after extensive searching, were $129 a night, at peak season, at two places: the **Lakeshore Motor Inn** (☎ **800/770-3000** or 907/248-3485; www.lakeshoremotorinn.com), and the mass-produced **Microtel Inn and Suites** (☎ **888/771-7171** or 907/245-5002; www.microtelinn.com). Various other hotels charge less, but none met my standards to recommend here (I do recommend the Homestead Bed and Breakfast, above). Two new chain hotels stand near the airport, with higher rates: **Courtyard by Marriott** (☎ **800/321-2211** or 907/245-0322; courtyard.com/ANCCY), with many amenities and a pool, and the **Holiday Inn Express** (☎ **800/465-4329** or 907/248-8848; www.holiday-inn.com).

than 30 years, and they've kept it as an authentic slice of Alaska. One of the rooms is a charming log cabin with plank floors, the other is a many-room upstairs suite with four beds, an outside entrance, and many odd corners and pieces of furniture. Both units have kitchenettes and VCRs. It's a great deal. (Beware, an entirely different place on Spenard Road has an almost identical name.)

CAMPING

Anchorage is a big city, so for a real camping experience, you need to head out of town. The State Parks' 28-site, $10-per-night **Bird Creek Campground,** 25 miles south on the Seward Highway next to Turnagain Arm, is one of my favorites. The State Parks' 56-site campground on **Eagle River** also sits in a pleasant spot, and it's well developed with paved roads and large sites with lots of privacy. It costs $15 a night. From the Glenn Highway, 12 miles from Anchorage, take the Hiland Road exit.

Within the Anchorage bowl, there are several camper and RV parks. Near the new Alaska Native Heritage Center, the nicely wooded and landscaped **Anchorage RV Park,** 7300 Oilwell Rd. (☎ **800/400-7275** or 907/338-7275; www.anchrvpark.com), has full services and excellent facilities; they charge $29 per night on the 195 sites. If you don't need full hookups or all the extras, the municipally owned **Centennial Camper Park,** is close by, on Boundary Road at the Muldoon Road exit from the Glenn Highway (☎ **907/333-9711,** or 907/343-4474 off season), just as you enter town from the north, with 83 dry sites, a dump station, and free showers. Camping permits are $13 a night. The **Hillside Motel and RV Park** is listed above under "Inexpensive."

3 Dining

DOWNTOWN

EXPENSIVE

Club Paris. 417 W. Fifth Ave. ☎ **907/277-6332.** Reservations recommended. Lunch $5.75–$15; dinner main courses $14–$44. AE, DC, DISC, MC, V. Summer daily 11:30am–2:30pm and 5–11pm. Winter closing 1 hour earlier Sun–Thurs. STEAK/SEAFOOD.

Walking from a bright spring afternoon, under a neon Eiffel Tower, into midnight darkness, past a smoke-enshrouded bar, and sitting down at a secretive booth for two, I felt as if I should lean across the table and plot a shady 1950s oil deal with my companion. And I would probably not have been the first. In contrast to Sullivan's

Steakhouse, across the street, which contrives a masculine, retro feel, Club Paris is the real thing, decorated with mounted swordfish and other cocktail-era decor. The smoky club is too authentic for some, but it's the essence of old Anchorage boomtown years, when the streets were dusty and an oil man needed a class joint in which to do business. Steak, of course, is what to order, and rare really means rare. Ask for the blue cheese stuffing. Full liquor license.

✪ **The Marx Brothers Cafe.** 627 W. Third Ave. ☎ **907/278-2133.** www.marxcafe.com. Reservations required. Main courses $17.50–$28.50. AE, DC, MC, V. Summer daily 5:30–10pm. Winter, Mon–Thurs 6–9:30pm, Fri–Sat 5:30–10pm. ECLECTIC/REGIONAL.

A restaurant that began as a hobby among three friends 20 years ago is still a labor of love, and has become a standard of excellence in the state. Dinner takes all night—you feel funny not ordering an appetizer—but you can spend the time watching chef Jack Amon pick your herbs and vegetables from the garden behind the historic little building, one of the city's first houses. The cuisine is varied and creative, ranging from Asian to Italian, and every dish is an adventure. It's traditional to order the Caesar salad made at the table by Van, one of the founders and the host. The decor and style are studied casual elegance. One flaw: If your table is not ready, the wait is uncomfortable. Beer and wine license.

Sacks Cafe. 328 G St. ☎ **907/274-4022.** www.sackscafe.com. Reservations required for dinner (reserve a few days ahead for weekend nights). Lunch $5.25–$12.95; dinner main courses $15–$28. AE, MC, V. Mon–Wed 11am–3pm, Thurs–Sun 11am–3pm; Thurs and Sun 5–9:30pm; Fri–Sat 5–11pm. CREATIVE/ECLECTIC.

Anchorage's hippest restaurant also happens to be one of its best. Occupying a small storefront that was recently remodeled by Mike Mense, one of the city's most exciting architects, the dining room, in warm southwest colors and angles, resembles a showcase for the food and diners, who can sit at tables or a tapas bar. The cuisine defies categorization, but is consistently interesting and creative, and rarely fails. The menu constantly changes, but one recent offering was chicken with scallops, shiitake mushrooms, snow peas, udon noodles, ginger cream sauce, and black bean salsa. Vegetarians do as well as meat eaters. For lunch, the sandwiches are unforgettable, with choices such as shrimp and avocado with herb cream cheese on sourdough. They serve beer and wine.

The Best Takeout in Town

Anchorage has great take-out food (as my family's continued survival attests). The best, most original burgers are at **Arctic Roadrunner,** with locations on Arctic Boulevard at Fireweed Lane and on Old Seward Highway at International Airport Road. Try the Kodiak Islander, which has peppers, ham, onion rings, and God knows what else on top.

The best gourmet deli, with legendary sandwiches, is **Atlasta Deli** (☎ **907/563-3354**), in the shopping mall at Arctic Boulevard and Tudor Road. I had a sub that cost $11.50, and I didn't regret it. They deliver.

We get carry-out Chinese from **New Sagaya's City Market** (☎ **907/274-6173**) at the corner of 13th and I streets. It's also a wonderful community grocery and meeting place, and has a good deli and brick-oven gourmet pizza. Pack a picnic there, or eat in the sidewalk dining area.

Order pizza delivery from **Uncle Joe's,** 428 G St. (☎ **907/279-3799**), which serves both traditional New York pizza and Italian-style gourmet pizza.

✪ **Simon and Seafort's Saloon and Grill.** 420 L St. ☎ **907/274-3502.** Reservations required (make dinner reservations a couple of days in advance in summer). Lunch $7–$15; dinner main courses $16–$40. AE, MC, V. Mon–Fri 11:15am–3:30pm and 4:30–11pm, Sat noon–3:30pm and 4:30–11pm, Sun noon–10pm. STEAK/SEAFOOD.

Simon's, as it's known, is a jolly beef and seafood grill where voices boom off the high ceilings. On sunny summer evenings, the rooms, fitted with brass turn-of-the-century saloon decor, fill with light off Cook Inlet, down below the bluff; the views are magnificent. The food is consistently exceptional and sometimes enlightening. At my most recent meal, the long list of nightly specials included a tasty crab- and macadamia-stuffed halibut. The service, too, stands out: warm and professional, and quick enough to allow time for other evening activities. Children are treated well. To enjoy this place on a budget, order a sandwich and soup for lunch in the well-stocked bar.

MODERATE

Glacier Brewhouse. 737 W. Fifth Ave. ☎ **907/274-BREW.** www.glacierbrewhouse.com. Reservations recommended for dinner. Lunch $8–$13; dinner main courses $9–$28. AE, MC, V. High season daily 11am–11pm. Low season Mon–Sat 11am–10pm, Sun 4–9pm. GRILL/SEAFOOD/PIZZA.

A tasty, eclectic, and ever-changing menu is served in a large dining room with lodge decor, where the pleasant scent of the wood-fired grill hangs in the air. They brew eight or more hearty beers behind a glass wall. It's noisy and active, with lots of agreeable if trendy touches, such as the bread, made from spent brewery grain, that's set out on the tables with olive oil. An advantage for travelers is the wide price range—a feta cheese, spinach, and artichoke pizza is $10; crab legs are $30. This is not a good choice for groups, however, as it's too loud to carry on a conversation across a large table; service can be rushed; and a table can take time to acquire, even if you have a reservation.

Kumagoro. 533 W. Fourth Ave. ☎ **907/272-9905.** Lunch $6.50–$14.30; dinner main courses $13.20–$39. AE, CB, DC, JCB, MC, V. Summer daily 11am–11pm. Winter daily 11am–10pm. JAPANESE.

Anchorage has several good, authentic Japanese restaurants, but this one, right on the main tourist street downtown, has the most convenient location. My current favorite lunch anywhere is their lunch box ($14.30), a large sampler of many dishes, including sushi, sashimi, and other tasty things I couldn't identify. The dining room is pleasantly low-key, with tables in rows, so you may have the opportunity to meet those seated next to you. Beer and wine license.

INEXPENSIVE

Dianne's Restaurant. 550 W. Seventh Ave., Suite 110. ☎ **907/279-7243.** All items $4–$7.50. AE, DISC, MC, V. Mon–Fri 7am–4pm. SOUP/SANDWICH.

This is my first choice for a quick, healthful lunch downtown. Located in the base of a tall, glass office building, Dianne's has developed such a reputation for great baking, soups, sandwiches, and specials that it's pretty well clogged with people in suits at lunch hour. The line at the cafeteria moves fast, however, and the bright, casual atmosphere is fun and full of energy. No liquor license.

Downtown Deli and Cafe. 525 W. Fourth Ave. ☎ **907/276-7116.** All items $6.25–$12. AE, CB, DC, DISC, MC, V. Summer daily 6am–10pm. Winter Sun 9am–4pm, Mon 7am–4pm, Tues–Sat 7am–9pm. DELI.

Tony Knowles made his Fourth Avenue sandwich restaurant the place to meet local politicians and people-in-the-know 20 years ago; when he was elected governor in 1994, President Clinton came for dinner. I didn't believe Clinton, however, when he

Coffeehouses

There are coffeehouses all over the city where people go for a cup of java and a pastry, and to meet people and engage in conversation. My favorite is **Side Street Espresso,** on G Street between 4th and 5th, a meeting place for artists, radicals, musicians, and other people who want to trade ideas. **Cafe del Mundo,** at Fourth and K downtown and at Northern Lights and Denali in midtown, gathers an older crowd of businesspeople, yuppies, stay-at-home parents, and anyone else looking for a comfortable meeting place.

---

said he enjoyed the reindeer stew—it's a gimmick. Stick with the quiche, sandwiches, simple entrees, and superior breakfasts. Prices are reasonable—especially for dinner, when downtown is short on inexpensive sit-down places—and kids are treated well. It's just the reliable place you want for a low-key meal. Summer mornings, however, they're overrun with tourists, causing the service to suffer. They serve beer and wine.

Snow City Cafe. 1034 W. Fourth Ave. ☎ **907/272-CITY.** Lunch $5–$10; dinner main courses $9–$15. AE, DISC, MC, V. Summer daily 7am–10pm. Winter Mon–Thus 7am–4pm, Fri 7am–9pm, Sat–Sun 8am–9pm. VEGETARIAN/HOME STYLE.

This is a meeting place for a young, environmentally conscious crowd, and it's also a good restaurant. The food, served by a friendly, committed staff in a light storefront dining room, is laced with interesting flavors and styles of preparation, including many vegetarian dishes. They also serve seafood, chicken, and pasta. For lunch, the sandwiches are filling and various. The Reindeer Reuben, made with reindeer sausage instead of corned beef, is better than an ordinary Reuben on several counts. An excellent stop for breakfast, too. Weekend evenings see acoustic music, poetry, a book club, wine appreciation, and camaraderie.

BEYOND DOWNTOWN

EXPENSIVE

Gesine's. 6700 Jewel Lake Rd. ☎ **907/243-0507.** www.alaska.net/~gesines. Reservations recommended. Lunch $5.55–$13; dinner main courses $24–$36. AE, MC, V. Tues–Sat 11am–10pm, Sun brunch 10am–2pm. Take L St. from downtown until it turns into Minnesota Dr., then turn right on Raspberry and follow it to Jewel Lake Rd. EUROPEAN/ECLECTIC.

When chef John Franschetti comes through the dining room toward the end of the evening, it's the completion of an act of personal expression through food. He and Gesine Marquez transmute their native German, southwest, and Cajun cuisines to create bold new combinations, that, as they say, have "a point of view." The menu comes with a glossary so no one misses the message. High prices are justified by their extraordinary craft and the punctilious service, but it's not the place to go for a simple dinner (stop by for lunch for the scaled-back version). The smoked, grilled artichoke appetizer is not to be missed.

✪ **Jens' Restaurant.** 701 W. 36th Ave. ☎ **907/561-5367.** www.jensrestaurant.com. Reservations recommended. Lunch $8.50–$14.50; dinner main courses $17–$25. AE, CB, DC, DISC, MC, V. Mon–Fri 11:30am–2pm; Tues–Sat 6–10pm. Closed Jan. INTERNATIONAL.

Jens Hansen closes his doors each January to go on a gastronomic working vacation to exotic places, and the tastes he brings back go on display in the restaurant like trophies in a big game hunter's den. Although there are only a few tables, the menu, new every night, goes on and on with new discoveries and ideas, as well as Alaska seafood done in ways ranging from simple to outrageous. A variety of traditional Danish dishes join the menagerie for lunch. I've tried some far-out stuff here, and I've never been less than delighted. While waiting for a table, sip wine from the exceptional list and sample tapas at a counter. Don't bring the kids.

Moderate

Campo Bello Bistro. 661 W. 36th, Suite 10. ☎ **907/563-2040.** Lunch $8–$13; dinner main courses $13–$19.50. CB, DC, MC, V. Mon–Fri 11am–2:30pm; Tues–Sat 5–9pm. NORTHERN ITALIAN/BISTRO.

This quiet little midtown restaurant is amazingly like stepping into northern Italy, except for the Alaska seafood. Even the service has the quality of jocular professionalism I remember from Italy. Unlike most of Anchorage's best restaurants, they don't try to reinvent the cookbook here. Most of the menu consists of recognizable dishes, such as veal Marsala or Italian sausage and polenta, but everything I've had, on many visits, has been bold, highly flavored, and entirely satisfying. Those seeking the bland tomatoes and cheese of a typical Italian family restaurant should go elsewhere (Sorrento's and Romano's, both on Fireweed Lane, each do that tried-and-true formula well). The wine list and food are reasonably priced.

Inexpensive

✪ **The Lucky Wishbone.** 1033 E. Fifth Ave. ☎ **907/272-3454.** All items $3–$9.25. Summer daily 10am–11pm. Winter daily 10am–10pm. MC, V. DINER.

This Anchorage institution ("The Bone") is where the real pioneer Alaska meets families out for a delicious, not-too-greasy fried chicken dinner and famous milk shakes (try the hot fudge) and other delights from the fountain. One section of the counter is reserved for discussion of aviation and golf. When the beloved owners outlawed smoking years ago, it made the front page of the newspaper. You'll see few other tourists, as the location, among the car dealerships at the extreme east end of downtown, is too far to walk from the hotels, but I recently ran into Alaska's senior U.S. senator, Ted Stevens. They have a drive-in.

Mexico in Alaska. 7305 Old Seward Hwy. ☎ **907/349-1528.** Main courses $4.50–$20. AE, MC, V. Mon–Fri 11:30am–3pm, Sat noon–3pm; Mon–Thurs 5–9pm, Fri 5–10pm, Sun 4–9pm. Open until 10pm Mon–Thurs in summer. Take Gambell St. (New Seward Hwy.) south, turn right on Dowling Rd., then left on Old Seward Hwy. MEXICAN.

The down-scale building, location, and decor camouflage Alaska's best Mexican restaurant. It's the food and the service that make it so special. The food—strictly traditional, authentic cuisine of central-west Mexico—is subtle and exciting for anyone used to the heavy flavors of Tex-Mex. The service, carried out by the family of founder Maria-Elena Ball, goes beyond friendly—they seem really interested in sharing their love of their food and culture. The prices are low, and the dining room less than grand. They serve beer and wine.

The Moose's Tooth Pub and Pizzeria. 3300 Old Seward Hwy. ☎ **907/258-2537.** www.moosestooth.net. Large pizza $12.50–$25. DISC, MC, V. Summer, Sun–Thurs 11am–midnight, Fri–Sat 11am–1am. Winter, Sun–Mon 11am–11pm, Tues–Thurs 11am–midnight, Fri–Sat 11am–1am. PIZZA.

The best pizza and beer in Anchorage undoubtedly come from this fun and friendly place. The microbrewery came first, but the pizza really is the greater accomplishment. It has a soft, light crust like Italian pizza, but it has the oomph of American pizza. They offer many ingenious toppings, but not just to dump stuff on: the combinations really work. Dine inside (perhaps in the "hippie pit"), or at picnic tables outside in a tent that's open year-round. That's the best place in town to take kids for dinner. See "Nightlife," below, for their cinema/pub.

Roscoe's Skyline Restaurant. 600 E. Northern Lights Blvd. (in the Sears Mall). ☎ **907/276-5879.** Lunch $4.50–$8; dinner main courses $11–$20. AE, MC, V. Mon–Thurs 11am–9pm, Fri–Sat 11am–10pm, Sun noon–6pm. SOUL FOOD/SOUTHERN.

Roscoe built up this large mall restaurant from a shack where he used to barbecue out back in a cut-off steel barrel. The place hasn't lost any of the authenticity or friendly, homey service in the transition, but now the dining room is comfortable and well appointed. The barbecue and fried chicken are justly famous.

4 Attractions & Activities

I've arranged this section starting with a walking tour through downtown Anchorage, followed by details on the downtown museums and attractions that are farther afield.

The best tour of the historic downtown area is the self-guided walking tour I've outlined just below. If you'd like to go with a group, though, city tours are available from many operators; check with the visitor center to take your choice. **Anchorage City Trolley Tours,** 612 W. Fourth Ave., near the Fourth Avenue Theater (☎ **907/276-5603**), offers hourly tours ($10) in buses that have been made to look like San Francisco streetcars. They leave every hour from 9am to 6pm May to September. Their David and Goliath conflict with the owner of the theater, who built an identical trolley to compete with them, has fascinated Anchorage for several years. The major tour companies described in section 5 of chapter 2 under "Escorted Tour or Do-It-Yourself?" also sell their city tours to independent travelers. **Gray Line of Alaska,** 745 West Fourth Ave. (☎ **800/478-6388** or 907/277-5581; www.graylinealaska.com), charges $40 for its 3-hour tour. **Alaska Tourquest** (☎ **907/344-6667;** www.alaskatourquest.com) charges $39 for half day tours that include the Alaska Zoo.

Anchorage Historic Properties, 645 W. Third Ave. (☎ **907/274-3600;** www.customcpu.com/np/ahpi), a city-endowed historic preservation group, offers a 2-hour, 2-mile guided walking tour of historic downtown Anchorage June to August, Monday to Friday at 1pm. The volunteer guides are fun and knowledgeable. Meet at the lobby of old city hall, 524 W. Fourth Ave., next door to the Log Cabin Visitor Information Center. Tickets cost $5 for adults, $4 for seniors over age 65, and $1 for children. If you can't do the guided tour, pick up their brochure at the visitor center, which tells a little about the buildings and directs you to 11 sequential historical sign kiosks.

Walking Tour: Downtown Anchorage

Start & Finish: Fourth Avenue and F Street.
Time: 2 hours (use the shortcuts noted for a briefer tour).

Start at the **Log Cabin Visitor Information Center** at Fourth Avenue and F Street. Outside is a sign that shows the distance to various cities and a 5,114-pound jade boulder put on display by Stewart's Photo Shop, an Anchorage institution that is just across the street. Walking east, toward the mountains, the:

1. **Old City Hall** (1936), at Fourth Avenue and E Street, is on the right. Recently renovated, its lobby contains a fun display on city history, including dioramas of the early streetscape, old photographs, and the fire bell and fire pole that once were used in this building.

   Crossing E Street, notice on the left side of Fourth Avenue that all the buildings are modern—everything on that side from E Street east for several blocks collapsed in the 1964 earthquake. The street split in half, lengthwise, with the left side ending up a dozen feet lower than the right. That land was later reinforced with a gravel buttress by the U.S. Army Corps of Engineers and the slope below forever set aside from new construction because of the earthquake risk. This stretch of Fourth Avenue is where the **Iditarod Trail Sled Dog Race** and the **Anchorage Fur Rendezvous World Championship Sled Dog Race** start each year in March and February, respectively.

At Fourth Avenue and D Street, the:

2. **Wendler Building** (1915), the old Club 25, is among the oldest buildings in Anchorage. The bronze statue of the dog commemorates the sled-dog races that start here. Across D Street is a mural that depicts a map of coastal Alaska and B.C., with the Iditarod Trail dimly marked.

   Turn right, walking a block south on:

3. **D Street.** Several interesting little businesses and restaurants inhabit this block, sometimes joining together for a street fair. First on the left is **Cyrano's Off-Center Playhouse (☎ 907/274-2599)**, with its Eccentric Theater Company, Bistro Bergerac and film society. Stop in for a snack or cultural offering. On the right, **The Rondy Shop** carries memorabilia from the annual Fur Rendezvous winter carnival and sled dog races, and has a campy little history display.
4. **The 5th Avenue Mall,** a grand, four-story shopping center, faces D from the south side of Fifth.

   Turn left on Fifth.

5. **A series of interesting shops** are on the north side of Fifth, including **Laura Wright Alaskan Parkys,** where seamstresses sew custom Eskimo coats, and **Russian Gift Shop "Aleksandr Baranov"** (www.russiangiftshop.com), which carries an amazing array of nested Russian dolls, lacquered boxes, and the like.

   From Fifth Avenue turn right on C Street and follow it to the corner of Sixth Avenue, where you'll find:

6. **Wolf Song of Alaska (☎ 907/346-3073;** www.wolfsongalaska.org), a museum and gift shop. This nonprofit organization aims to educate and elevate the public about Alaska's most controversial mammal. Inside you'll find dioramas, exhibits, artwork, videos, and eager volunteers. Admission is $3 for adults, $1.50 ages 6 to 18. Unless your interest in wolves is strong, you'll spend only 10 or 15 minutes here. Hours vary, but in summer they're usually open at least 10am to 6pm Monday through Saturday.

   A door or two west (away from the mountains) is the free:

7. **Alaska State Troopers Museum (☎ 907/279-5050;** www.alaska.net/~foast). I don't know why I so enjoy this trove of law enforcement insignia, equipment, a 1952 Hudson Hornet, photographs, and other memorabilia—maybe it's the way these things convey the positive spirit of pioneer Alaska combined with the troopers' obvious pride. It's open year-round Monday to Friday, 10am to 5pm, Saturday noon to 4pm.

   Continue west, past the mall, to Sixth Avenue and E Street, which is one corner of the beautifully planted:

8. **Town square.** The community raised money for the improvements by collecting donations of $40 each for the granite bricks, with an inscription of the contributor's choosing. There are 13,344 (bet you can't find mine). On the east side of the square, behind you, the huge whale mural was painted freehand by Wyland in 1994. He painted similar whale murals in cities all along the West Coast. On the west side of the square, the massive, highly decorated:

Downtown Anchorage Walking Tour

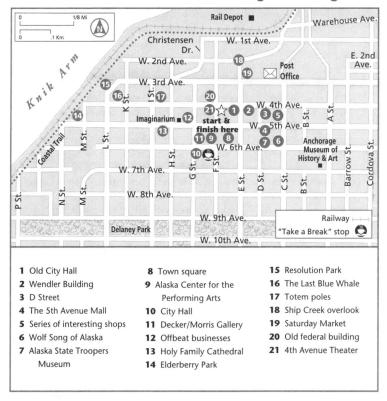

1 Old City Hall	**8** Town square	**15** Resolution Park
2 Wendler Building	**9** Alaska Center for the Performing Arts	**16** The Last Blue Whale
3 D Street	**10** City Hall	**17** Totem poles
4 The 5th Avenue Mall	**11** Decker/Morris Gallery	**18** Ship Creek overlook
5 Series of interesting shops	**12** Offbeat businesses	**19** Saturday Market
6 Wolf Song of Alaska	**13** Holy Family Cathedral	**20** Old federal building
7 Alaska State Troopers Museum	**14** Elderberry Park	**21** 4th Avenue Theater

9. Alaska Center for the Performing Arts dominates; it's Anchorage's most controversial building, completed in 1988 at a cost of over $70 million. The lobby is usually open, and whatever your opinion of the decor, a look inside will spark a discussion. Tours are Wednesday at 1pm; a $1 donation is requested (reach the center's administrative offices at ☎ **907/263-2900**). Thespians believe the building is haunted by the ghost of painter Sydney Lawrence, who makes lights mysteriously vary and elevators go up and down with no one in them. An auditorium demolished to make room for the center was named for Lawrence. Check the box office for current performances in the three theaters, Alaska's premier performance venues; it is operated by **CarrsTix** (☎ **907/263-2787;** see "Performing Arts," below).

TAKE A BREAK From the Alaska Center, cross Sixth Avenue at the F Street light and turn right (west) to **Humpy's,** a popular taver
with a huge selection of microbrews, live music, and g

The square green office building next door to Hun
10. City Hall. Turn left through the pedestrian walkway
Hall. A large mural showing a timeline of the histo
parking lot. A much better mural, by Duke Russell,
outdoor seating area on the near side of the parking

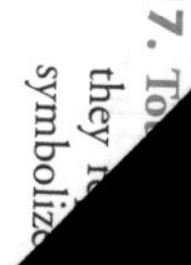

Walk west through the city hall parking lot to G Street, turn right, and proceed to Sixth Avenue and G. On the northeast corner of Sixth Avenue and G Street, in the corner of the Performing Arts Center is the:

11. Decker/Morris Gallery, one of Alaska's best and most uncompromising.

Walk a block north to Fifth Avenue. The west side of G Street between Fourth and Fifth avenues contains some of the downtown's best:

12. Offbeat businesses. First comes **Aurora Fine Arts,** which is hardly offbeat, but is an attractive art and craft shop; next, **Uncle Joe's Pizzeria,** with great pie by the slice; next, **Darwin's Theory,** a friendly, old-fashioned bar with character that shows up in an Indigo Girls song; next, **Suzi's Woolies** (www.suziswoollies.com), a Celtic shop carrying clothing, jewelry, and CDs, and with live Irish music Saturday afternoons; next, **Denali Wear,** which is Tracy Anna Bader's studio and shop of bright, graphic wearable art; next, **Side Street Espresso,** where you can get into a lively discussion on art or politics and make contact with thinking people; next, **Charlie's Alaska Trains** (www.ptialaska.net/~aktrains), a retired couple's labor of love, which sells nothing but Alaska Railroad models and memorabilia.

Shortcut: You can cut an hour off the tour here by continuing north on G Street to Fourth, then turning right and walking 1 block to F Street.

Backtrack to Fifth and G, then proceed west (away from the mountains) on Fifth. **The Imaginarium,** described under "Downtown Museums," below, is on the right. Continuing west on Fifth Avenue and crossing H Street, the:

13. Holy Family Cathedral, a concrete, art deco church, is the seat of the Roman Catholic archbishop. The interior is unremarkable.

Keep going toward the water, crossing L Street and down the hill to:

14. Elderberry Park. The yellow-and-brown house is the **Oscar Anderson House,** described under "Downtown Museums," below. Besides the good playground equipment, the park offers the easiest access point to the **Coastal Trail** (see "Walking & Biking," below). The trail tunnels under the Alaska Railroad tracks from the bottom of the park.

Now hike back up the hill to L Street and turn left. At Third Avenue is:

15. Resolution Park, with the bronze **Captain Cook Monument.** Capt. James Cook stands on a large wooden deck, but he's gazing out to sea—the opposite of the way he was facing when he discovered Cook Inlet in 1778 aboard HMS *Resolution.* Informative signs, powerful mounted binoculars, and a commanding vantage point make this a rewarding stop for gazing out at the water and the mountains beyond. The waters you see are ferocious and wild, with whirlpool currents and a tidal range of almost 40 vertical feet. The shore across the Inlet, about 2 miles away, is virtually uninhabited.

Follow Third Avenue east (back toward the mountains) 1 block and turn right on K Street. On the right is:

16. The Last Blue Whale, Joseph Princiotti's huge 1973 bronze of combat between a whale and whalers in small boats, from the whale's point of view.

Cross K Street to walk through the plaza toward the opposite **Nesbett State Courthouse.** The sinuous shapes of the concrete are supposed to suggest both the flow of people through the court system and the shape of a braided glacial iver. At the courthouse, at 4th Avenue and I Street, take a look at the two:

em poles, carved of red cedar by Lee Wallace, of Ketchikan. Erected in 1997, present the eagle and raven moieties of the Tlingit people, intended to the balance of justice. A Tlingit creation story tells of how raven stole the moon and stars and brought them to mankind; here, the moon and stars are the stars of the Alaska flag.

Walk around past the courthouse on 4th Avenue and turn left onto H Street. Follow H as it crosses 3rd Avenue and becomes Christensen Drive. Descend the hill on Christensen and turn right on 2nd Avenue, toward the mountains. Many of the **old houses** that line 2nd are marked, and a kiosk at Second and F tells some town history. If you imagine houses like this over much of downtown, you'll know what Anchorage looked like before oil.

Continue east on Second Avenue to E Street, where you will find:

18. **A Ship Creek overlook with a monument to President Eisenhower.** The bust commemorates Alaska's 1959 admission to the Union (in fact, Eisenhower was a major barrier to statehood). More interesting is the overlook. You can see the Alaska Railroad yards from here, and part of the port of Anchorage and the neighborhood of Government Hill across the Ship Creek river bottom. This is where the tent city of Knik Anchorage, later shortened to Anchorage, was set up in 1914. An informative set of historic signs on the overlook explains. The Alaska Railroad, which helped build Anchorage, still has its headquarters in a modern brick building that stands by the creek. The nearer concrete building is the railroad's stately depot. The beautifully restored steam engine on the pedestal in front was used on construction of the Panama Canal, then worked in the yard here as a switch engine. The creek itself is full of salmon in June and August (see "Fishing," below), and a walkway that crosses a dam just upstream from here is a good place to watch the fish and to feed ducks. But the walk down the stairs to the river bottom and back is strenuous.

Walk up the hill on E Street to Third Avenue. The extensively landscaped parking lot on the left becomes the:

19. **Saturday Market** every weekend in the summer, a street fair drawing hundreds of vendors and thousands of shoppers. You can buy everything from local vegetables to handmade crafts to somebody's old record collection. There are food booths and music, too.

Turn right on Third Avenue, then left on F Street. **F Street Station,** on the left, is a fun bar with an after-work crowd. Proceed to Fourth Avenue, and you're back at the Log Cabin Visitor Information Center, but don't stop. Turn right on Fourth Avenue. On the right side is the:

20. **Old federal building,** a grand, white, Depression-era structure that now contains the Alaska Public Lands Information Center, with interesting displays and lots of information about the outdoors. Across the street is Anchorage's most attractive historic building, the restored:

21. **4th Avenue Theater.** It was built by Cap Lathrop, Alaska's first business magnate, who created it as a monument to the territory and the permanence of its new society. Today it's a gift store. Don't miss going in and looking at the bas-relief murals and the blinking big dipper on the ceiling, which during many a movie over the years was more entertaining than whatever was on the screen.

DOWNTOWN MUSEUMS

✪ **Anchorage Museum of History and Art.** 121 W. Seventh Ave. ☎ **907/343-4326.** www.ci.anchorage.ak.us. Admission $6.50 adults, $6 seniors 65 and older, free for children 17 and under. June–Aug, Sun–Thurs 9am–9pm, Fri–Sat 9am–6pm. May and early Sept, daily 9am–6pm. Mid-Sept to Apr, Tues–Sun 10am–6pm.

The state's largest museum doesn't have its largest collection, but unlike the Alaska State Museum in Juneau or the University of Alaska Museum in Fairbanks, the

Anchorage museum has the room and staff both to teach and to serve as a center of contemporary culture of a regional caliber. Most visitors tour the Alaska Gallery, an informative and enjoyable walk through the history and some of the anthropology of the state. In the art galleries, you can see what's happening in art in Alaska today; Alaska art isn't all scenery and walrus ivory, but the grandeur of the state does influence almost every work. The Anchorage museum also gets the best touring and temporary exhibits. It's the only museum in Alaska that could require more than one visit. The restaurant, operated by the excellent Marx Brothers Cafe (see "Dining," above), serves some of the best lunches to be had downtown. Call for lectures, openings, and jazz happenings many summer evenings.

The Imaginarium. 737 W. Fifth Ave., Suite G. ☎ **907/276-3179.** www.imaginarium.org. Admission $5 ages 13–64, $4 ages 2–12 and 65 and older. Mon–Sat 10am–6pm, Sun noon–5pm.

This science museum is one of my kids' favorite places. It's geared to children, with not many words and lots of fun learning experiences. The idea is that while they're running around having a great time, the kids may accidentally learn something; at least, the displays will excite a sense of wonder that is the start of science. There's a strong Alaska theme to many of the displays. The saltwater touch tank is like an indoor tide pool.

The Oscar Anderson House Museum. 420 M St. ☎ **907/274-2336** or 907/274-3600. www.customcpu.com/np/ahpi. Admission $3 adults, $2 seniors, $1 children 5–12. Summer Tues–Sat 11am–4pm. Closed in winter.

This house museum, moved to a beautiful site in Elderberry Park over the water, shows how an early Swedish butcher lived. Although far from grand, the house is quaint, surrounded by a lovely little garden. The tour provides a good explanation of Anchorage's short history. Anderson died in 1974, and the house contains many of the family's original belongings, including a working 1909 player piano around which the structure was built. If you come at Christmas, don't miss the Swedish Christmas tours, the first 2 weekends in December.

SIGHTS BEYOND DOWNTOWN

✪ **Alaska Native Heritage Center.** From the Glenn Highway take the North Muldoon exit. ☎ **800/315-6608** or 907/333-8095. www.alaskanative.net. Admission $19.95 adults, $14.95 children 5–12. Summer daily 9am–6pm. Winter at least Sat–Sun noon–5pm; call for additional hours and winter discounts.

Unable to bring visitors to small Alaska villages, Alaska Natives built this extraordinary center to bring their cultures to the visitors. It's Alaska's best Native cultural site. What makes it so is not the graceful building or the professional and informative displays, but the Native people themselves, real village people, who often make a personal connection with visitors and, on our visit, rarely came across as practiced or distant. They seemed really to want to share, and invited visitors' interaction. The three main parts of the center take much of a day to absorb. First, there's a hall where storytellers and dancers perform, with two 30-minute programs rotating through the day. Second, there's a 10-minute film and a gallery of educational displays and a series of workshops, where artisans practice and show off traditional crafts. Finally, there's a pond with five traditional Native dwellings representing each cultural group, each hosted by a member of that group. There's a snack bar for soup and sandwiches and a gift shop, inexplicably stocked with imported junk.

Alaska Aviation Heritage Museum. 4721 Aircraft Dr. ☎ **907/248-5325.** E-mail: aahm@gci.net. Admission $8 adults, $6 active military and seniors over age 62, $4 children under 12. High season daily 9am–6pm. Call ahead in low season. Take International Airport Rd. toward the airport to the Lake Hood exit, then follow the signs.

Big State, Big Movies

Two downtown theaters show large-format films aimed at visitors. **The Alaska Experience Center** (☎ **907/276-3730;** www.alaskaexperiencetheatre.com) is on the northwest corner of Sixth Avenue and G Street, partly in a dome tent. A 40-minute Omnivision wraparound movie about Alaska costs $7 for adults, $4 for children, showing hourly. It's certainly spectacular—too much so for some people, who get motion sickness. Sit toward the center at the back. An Alaska Earthquake display that really shakes is $5 for adults and $4 for children ages 5 to 12. They're open daily from 9am to 9pm in summer, and from 11am to 6pm in winter. In the summer, films often play as well on a large screen in the concert hall of the **Alaska Center for the Performing Arts.** Whether or not they're IMAX films seems to be a matter of dispute, but they're certainly huge and impressive. Recently they've shown *Alaska: Spirit of the Wild,* and a film about wolves, with one or the other on the screen hourly from 9am to 9pm. Tickets are $9.75, adults, $7.75 children, at the center box office (☎ **907/263-2787**).

Hangars house restored classic aircraft and wrecks, with detailed explanatory placards, photographs, and memorabilia of Alaska's Bush pilots posted around. An old advertising sign for the Kantishna-based McGee Airways tells the story: "Fly an Hour or Walk a Week." Aviation was and is the only practical way to most of the state, and pilots are among Alaska's greatest heroes. Not being an expert on old planes, however, I found the living parts of the museum of most interest: the dock on the Lake Hood floatplane base (it's the world's busiest), where you can join a $50 air tour; and the restoration shop, where visitors wander among the works in progress and converse with the volunteers painting, grinding, and putting back together old aircraft. Call ahead, as the museum is chronically in financial trouble, which also may help explain the excessive admission price.

Alaska Botanical Garden. Campbell Airstrip Rd. (off Tudor Rd.). ☎ **907/770-3692.** www.alaska.net/~garden. Free admission. Summer daily 9am–9pm. From downtown, drive out New Seward Hwy. (Gambell St.) to Tudor Rd., exit to the east (left), turn right off Tudor onto Campbell Airstrip Rd., and park at the Benny Benson School. It's 20 minutes from downtown.

The garden is young and the volunteer staff still has a long way to go to fill out the wooded, 110-acre site, but already this is a restful place to learn about native flora and see what else grows here while sitting in peaceful shade on benches and watching birds and squirrels. They've done a good job of integrating the garden into its forest setting while adding a formal herb garden and two perennial gardens. I don't know of many other botanical gardens where you're warned to watch out for moose and bear. A fine nature trail with explanatory signs leaves from the garden down to Campbell Creek, where you may see salmon swimming.

✪ **The Alaska Zoo.** 4731 O'Malley Rd. ☎ **907/346-3242.** Admission $7 adults, $6 seniors, $5 children 12–17, $4 children 3–12. AE, MC, V. Opens daily at 10am; closing time varies by season. Drive out the New Seward Hwy. to O'Malley Rd., then turn left and go 2 miles; it's 25 minutes from downtown, without traffic.

If you're expecting a big-city zoo, you'll be disappointed, but the Alaska Zoo has a charm all its own. Anchorage residents have developed personal relationships with the animals, many of which are named, in their campy little Eden. Watch Oreo and Ahpun, the brown and polar bear buddies, play and swim underwater. Gravel paths wander through the woods past large enclosures with natural flora for bears, seals and otters, musk oxen, mountain goats, moose, caribou, waterfowl—all the animals you were supposed to see in Alaska but may have missed. (Don't get the elephant or Siberian tigers in your snapshots—they'll blow your story.) A snack bar serves basic meals and there is a large gift shop.

Earthquake Park. West end of Northern Lights Blvd. From downtown, take L St. (it becomes Minnesota Dr.) to Northern Lights Blvd. and turn right. The park is on your right after you cross Lakeshore Dr.

The 1964 Good Friday earthquake was the biggest ever in North America, registering at 9.2 on the Richter Scale, killing 131 people, and flattening much of the region. Downtown Anchorage and the Turnagain residential area, near the park, suffered enormous slides that turned neighborhoods into chaotic ruins. A sculpture and excellent interpretive signs commemorate and explain the event and point out its few remaining marks on the land. This also is a good access point to the Coastal Trail.

Eklutna Historical Park. About 25 miles out the Glenn Hwy. ☎ **907/688-6026** or 907/696-2828. Admission $6 adult, $3 children ages 6–12. Summer daily 8am–6pm. Take the Glenn Hwy. to the Eklutna exit, then go left over the overpass.

The Native village of Eklutna has a fascinating old cemetery, still in use, in which each grave is enclosed by a highly decorated spirit house, the size of a large doll house. These little shelters excite the imagination in a way no ordinary marker would. The unique practice evolved in the melding of Athabascan and Russian Orthodox beliefs. There are two small Russian Orthodox churches on the site, including the **St. Nicholas Orthodox Church.** Built north of here of logs sometime before 1870, it is among the oldest buildings in the Southcentral region. Walk through by yourself or take an informative 30-minute tour for the same price. Wear mosquito repellent. If you come out this far, don't miss the Thunderbird Falls, described below under "Hiking."

SPECTATOR SPORTS

Most big events in Anchorage happen at the **Sullivan Arena,** at 16th Avenue and Gambell Street. The main ticket agency in town is **Carrs Tix** (☎ **800/GR8-SEAT** or 907/263-2787; www.carrstix.com), which has counters at most Carrs grocery stores and operates the Alaska Center for the Performing Arts box office.

BASEBALL Anchorage has two semipro baseball teams—the **Anchorage Glacier Pilots** (☎ **907/274-3627;** www.glacierpilots.com) and the **Anchorage Bucs** (☎ **907/561-2827;** www.anchoragebucs.com)—with college athletes playing short midsummer seasons. The quality may be uneven, but you may see diamonds in the rough: Among famed alumni are Mark McGwire, Rick Aguilera, Tom Seaver, Dave Winfield, Barry Bonds, and Wally Joyner. Check the *Anchorage Daily News* for game times. Mulcahy Stadium is at 16th Avenue and A Street, a long walk or a short drive from downtown. Tickets are cheap. Dress warmly for evening games; a blanket is rarely out of order. A weekend day game is warmer, but then you won't get to see baseball played at night without lights.

BASKETBALL The University of Alaska Anchorage men's basketball team (www.goseawolves.com) hosts a major Division I preseason tournament over Thanksgiving weekend, the ✪ **Great Alaska Shootout,** and plays the regular season at the Sullivan Arena and at the University Sports Center, on campus on Providence Drive.

HOCKEY The **Anchorage Aces** (☎ **907/258-2237;** www.anchorageaces.com) compete in the West Coast Hockey League against cities such as Phoenix, Tacoma, and San Diego. The **University of Alaska—Anchorage** (www.goseawolves.com) fields an NCAA Division I hockey team.

5 Getting Outside

Anchorage is unique in Alaska (and anywhere else I know) for the number of places right near town to hike, bike, ski, and otherwise get into the wild. I've broken the options down by activities below. In town, the city's bike trails connect through greenbelts that span the noisy, asphalt urban core with soothing creek-side woods. Kincaid Park and Far North Bicentennial Park are both on the trail system within the city, and encompass scores of miles of trails for Nordic skiing, mountain biking, and horseback riding. The Chugach Mountains, which form the backdrop to the town, offer appealing hiking, backpacking, mountain biking, and climbs that range from easy to technical. More trails and streams, only slightly farther afield, are covered in the "Out from Anchorage" sections later in this chapter.

Many cruises, tours, fishing charters, and sea-kayaking trips leave from nearby **Whittier.** If you'd like to do a long day-trip outing, see section 4 of chapter 7 for details.

INFORMATION The ✪ **Alaska Public Lands Information Center** (☎ **907/271-2737;** www.nps.gov/aplic) offers guidance for all these areas. For information on the bike trails, Nordic skiing parks, and other city recreation, contact the **Municipal Division of Sports & Recreation** at ☎ **907/343-4474** (www.ci.anchorage.ak.us). The **Chugach State Park Headquarters** is in the Potter Section House on the Seward Highway at the south end of town (☎ **907/345-5014;** www.dnr.state.ak.us/parks/parks.htm); get their *Ridgelines* newsprint guide through the public land information center. Chugach National Forest can be reached at ☎ **907/271-2500** or www.fs.fed.us/r10/chugach.

The best trail guide to the entire region is Helen Neinhueser and John Wolfe Jr.'s ***55 Ways to the Wilderness,*** published by The Mountaineers (www.mountaineers.org). It costs $12.95 and is available in any bookstore in the area. The best trail map of the area is published by **Alaska Road and Recreation Maps,** which costs $5 at sporting goods stores, or buy from The Maps Place, 601 W. 36th Ave., Suite 19 (☎ **907/562-7277**). It shows Anchorage roads and bike trails as well as backcountry routes in the Chugach Mountains.

EQUIPMENT You can rent most anything you need for outdoor activities. For bike rentals, see "Getting Around," in section 1 of this chapter. You can get advice and rent kayaks, skis, snowshoes, bear-proof containers, and mountaineering equipment at **Alaska Mountaineering and Hiking,** at 2633 Spenard Rd. (☎ **907/272-1811;** www.alaskan.com/amh). It's a small shop where they will take the time to help you plan a trip. A block away, at 1200 W. Northern Lights Blvd., **REI** has a large store (☎ **907/272-4565;** www.rei.com) that rents a wide range of gear, including canoes with car-top carriers, camping gear, and packs.

WALKING & BIKING

Anchorage has an award-winning network of paved **bike trails** spanning the city along wooded greenbelts. You rarely see a building and almost always cross roads and rail lines through tunnels and over bridges, so you're never in traffic. Here are two of the best.

✪ **TONY KNOWLES COASTAL TRAIL** Leading 10 miles from the western end of Second Avenue along the shore to **Kincaid Park,** the coastal trail is among my favorite things about Anchorage and a unique pathway to the natural environment from the heart of downtown. I've had moose stop me on the trail near the Kincaid

Park end, while closer to downtown, I've ridden parallel to Beluga whales swimming along the trail at high tide. The more popular entry is at **Elderberry Park,** at the western end of Fifth Avenue. **Westchester Lagoon** is 10 blocks south of Elderberry Park, making for a lovely stroll and an equally enjoyable destination for a picnic or to feed the ducks and geese.

LANIE FLEISCHER CHESTER CREEK TRAIL Starting at an intersection with the Coastal Trail at Westchester Lagoon, the trail runs about 4 miles east along the greenbelt to **Goose Lake,** where you can swim in a cool woodland pond at the end of a hot bike ride—still, improbably enough, in the middle of the city. South from the lake, finding your way through the university campus and across Tudor Road, you come to **Bicentennial Park,** with the botanical garden and miles of dirt trails. The paved bike trails, including the Fleischer, stay well back in the trees, so you rarely see a building, and tunnels and bridges span all road and railroad crossings, so you're never in traffic.

HIKING & MOUNTAIN BIKING

✪ **KINCAID PARK** Covered in more detail below, Kincaid Park is an idyllic summer setting for mountain biking and day hikes as well. Moose sightings are a daily occurrence on the wide dirt trails that snake for about 30 miles through the birch and white spruce of the park's hilly 1,400 acres of boreal forest, often with views of the sea and mountains beyond. Within the park, wooded Little Campbell Lake is a picturesque but little-used swimming hole and fun spot for family canoeing; there is no lifeguard.

FAR NORTH BICENTENNIAL PARK The 4,000-acre park, on the east side of town, is a unique patch of urban wilderness, habitat for bears and moose and spawning salmon. People use it for dog mushing and skiing in winter, and exceptional mountain biking and day hiking in summer. The Alaska Botanical Garden, listed above, and the Hilltop Ski Area, below, are both within the park's boundaries. A good place to start a hike or ride through the woods is at the **Campbell Creek Science Center** (☎ **907/267-1257**), an educational facility operated by the Bureau of Land Management, where staff are often on hand to answer questions and where you can consult books and maps. To get there from downtown, take Gambell Street (it becomes New Seward Highway) south to Dowling Road, go east (toward the mountains), turn right on Lake Otis Road and left on 68th Avenue, following it to the end.

✪ **FLATTOP MOUNTAIN & THE GLEN ALPS TRAILHEAD** There are many ways to the alpine tundra, intoxicating fresh air, and cinematic views of the Chugach Mountains, behind Anchorage, but the easiest and best developed are at the Chugach State Park Glen Alps Trailhead. Even those who aren't up to hiking should go for the drive and a walk on a short, paved loop with incredible views and interpretive signs. If you are ready for a hike, you can start at the trailhead for trips of up to several days, following the network of trails or taking off across dry, alpine tundra by yourself, but usually within cell phone range. Camping is permitted anywhere off the trails.

Flattop Mountain is the most popular hike from the Glen Alps Trailhead, and a great family climb, if a bit crowded on weekends. It's a steep afternoon hike, easy for fit adults and doable by school-age children. There's a bit of a scramble at the top, easiest if you stick to the painted markers on the rocks. Dress warmly and don't go in the rain.

For a longer or less steep hike or a mountain-biking trip, follow the broad gravel trail that leads up the valley from the Glen Alps Trailhead. Trails lead all the way over the mountains to Indian or Bird Creek, on Turnagain Arm, up some of the mountains along the way or to round alpine lakes in high, rocky valleys. You're always above the tree line, so you don't need to follow a trail if you have a good map. This is wonderful backpacking country.

To get to the trailhead, take New Seward Highway to O'Malley Road, head east toward the mountains, then turn right on Hillside Drive, and left onto Upper Huffman Road. Finally, turn right on the narrow, twisting Toilsome Hill Drive. Don't forget to bring cash for a self-service day-use fee of $5.

EAGLE RIVER VALLEY & CROW PASS The **Eagle River Nature Center,** at the end of Eagle River Road, 12 miles up Eagle River Valley from the Glenn Highway exit (☎ **907/694-2108;** www.ernc.org), is like a public wilderness lodge, with hands-on naturalist displays about the area and guided nature walks daily in the summer at 1pm and Saturday and Sunday at 2pm all year. Operated by a nonprofit concessionaire for Chugach State Park, it's open in mid-summer daily 10am to 8pm, spring and fall 10am to 5pm except Monday, and winter Friday to Sunday 10am to 5pm. There's a $5 parking fee.

The ¾-mile **Rodak Nature Trail,** with interpretive signs, leads to a viewing platform over a beaver pond. The **Albert Loop Trail** is a 3-mile route; a geology guide from the center matches with numbered posts on the way. Both have good bird and wildlife watching. The 25-mile **Crow Pass Trail,** a portion of the historic Iditarod Trail, continues up the valley into the mountains along the river, eventually surmounting the Chugach in alpine terrain, and passing near Raven Glacier before descending into Girdwood (see "Out from Anchorage: Turnagain Arm & Portage Glacier," later in this chapter). There are campsites with fire rings along the way, and a mile up the trail the center rents out a public-use cabin for $55 a night. A yurt on the Crow Pass Trail and another on the Albert Loop rent for the same price. Reserve well ahead for weekends. Availability is shown on the web site.

THUNDERBIRD FALLS & EKLUTNA LAKE The hike to Thunderbird Falls is an easy, 1-mile forest walk with a good reward at the end; you can see the falls without the steep final descent to their foot. Take the Glenn Highway north to the Thunderbird Falls exit, 25 miles from Anchorage. Continuing 10 miles up the gravel Eklutna Lake Road, you come to a lovely state parks campground ($10 a night, $5 day-use fee) and the beautiful glacial lake for canoeing, hiking, and exceptional mountain biking. You can make a goal of the Eklutna Glacier at the other end. Rental bikes, kayaks, and other equipment, and guided kayak and boat tours, are offered by **Lifetime Adventures,** with a booth at the trailhead (☎ **907/746-4644;** www.matnet.com/~adventures). Rates are reasonable; for $65, they'll drop off a bike at the opposite end of the lake and give you a kayak so you can paddle down and ride back. This glacial melt also is where Anchorage gets much of its city water. People bottle it and sell it as "glacier water."

ARCTIC VALLEY The road to the **Alpenglow Ski Area** (☎ **907/428-1208**) is a wonderful route into mountains of alpine tundra where you can romp on its soft carpet and hike or climb in any direction. Late summer berry picking is excellent. On top of the mountain to the left is an abandoned Cold War–era antimissile emplacement. Take Glenn Highway to the Arctic Valley exit.

FISHING

There are hatchery salmon in many of Anchorage's streams and stocked trout in 28 lakes, so you need not leave town to catch a fish. The **Alaska Department of Fish and Game,** 333 Raspberry Rd., Anchorage, AK 99518-1599 (☎ **907/267-2221;** www.state.ak.us/local/akpages/FISH.GAME/sportf/region2/r2home.htm), publishes informative booklets on the Web and on paper. There's also a recorded information line (☎ **907/267-2510**) with all the details on what's hot and lots of other advice. See chapter 2 for general guidance and license information, and information for planning a fishing vacation, and see chapter 7 for the most-famous fishing opportunities on the Kenai Peninsula.

Although the setting (under a highway bridge in an industrial area) might not be the wilderness experience you've dreamed about, the 40-pound king salmon you pull from **Ship Creek** may make up for it. From downtown, just walk down the hill to the railroad yard. A couple of shacks sell and rent gear in the summer. Fishing for kings is best in June and for silvers in August and September. Fish at or near high tide, especially at the end of the rising tide. You'll need rubber boots, preferably hip waders, for the muddy banks, but don't go too far out, as the mud flats are dangerous.

Bird Creek, 25 miles south of Anchorage on the Seward Highway (see "Out from Anchorage: Turnagain Arm and Portage Glacier"), carries a strong hatchery run of silver salmon, peaking in August. Try to avoid weekends, when it gets crowded and parking is a problem. Pink salmon run from late June to early August. Other creeks along the Arm have similar but smaller runs.

✪ **FLY-IN FISHING** Serious anglers will use Anchorage as a base from which to fly to a remote lake or river with more fish and fewer people. Such a flight can be an unforgettable experience for those who are less than avid about fishing, too. The plane lifts off from Anchorage's Lake Hood floatplane base and within half an hour smoothly lands on a smooth lake or river, often all alone. You climb out and watch as the plane lifts off and disappears, leaving behind the kind of silence unique to true wilderness. It's on these trips that avid anglers are made—or spoiled. I've heard people complain of how sore their arms got from pulling in too many salmon.

Several companies offer fly-in trips; two of the largest and best established are **Ketchum Air Service** (☎ **800/433-9114** or 907/243-5525; www.ketchumair.com) and **Rust's Flying Service** (☎ **800/544-2299** or 907/243-1595; www.flyrusts.com). They can take you out guided or on your own, just for the day or to stay for a while in a cabin or lodge. If you fly to a lake, they'll provide a boat. They can't make fish appear if none are running, but they will try to take you to the hot spots. You can bring your own gear, or they can provide it. Prices start around $200 per person, with a two-person minimum.

OTHER ACTIVITIES

DOG MUSHING In the last 20 years, dog mushing has become a recreational sport as well as the utilitarian transportation it once was in the Bush and the professional sport it has been for years. But keeping a dog team is a more than a hobby—it is a lifestyle revolving around the feeding, care, and exercise of at least a dozen dogs (the pros sometimes have 200). Some mushers offset the great expense by offering rides. In the Anchorage area, among the best are friendly and casual Angie and Tom Hammill, who run two dozen dogs from their home in the Chugiak area, half an hour from downtown on the Glenn Highway. In winter only, they'll take you on as short a ride as two miles, riding in the sled basket while they drive, for $35. For $175, they'll teach you to mush in a 2½-hour session. They do expeditions, too, and have a bed-and-breakfast. The business is called **Birch Trails Adventures,** 22719 Robinson Rd., Chugiak (☎ and fax **907/688-5713**). For other options, see the sections on Girdwood and the Matanuska and Susitna valleys, later in this chapter.

FLIGHTSEEING Small planes are the blood cells of Alaska's circulatory system, and Anchorage its heart. There are several busy airports in Anchorage, and Lake Hood is the world's busiest floatplane base. More than two dozen operators want to take you on a flightseeing tour—check the visitor center for names—but the most comfortable and memorable is probably the restored DC-3 operated by ✪ **Era Aviation** (☎ **800/866-8394** or 907/266-8394; www.era-aviation.com). The plane re-creates the classic days of air travel—you can pretend to be Ingrid Bergman or Spencer Tracy while gazing out the oversize windows at a glacier. The daily summer flights leave from the South Airpark, off Raspberry Road, with itineraries determined by the weather: The plane has the speed and range to go where the best views are, including Mount McKinley, Prince William Sound, or Kenai Fjords National Park's Harding Ice Field. A 90-minute flight is $139 per person. The route is tailored to the weather and viewing opportunities. Era also offers helicopter flightseeing.

ICE-SKATING **Westchester Lagoon,** just 10 blocks from downtown (see "Walking & Biking," above), is a skating paradise in the winter. When the ice gets thick enough, usually by mid-December, the city clears a large rink and long, wide paths on the pond, mopping the ice regularly for a smooth surface. In recent years, a 1-kilometer loop served speed skaters. Skaters gather around burn barrels, well stocked with firewood, to socialize and warm their hands, and on weekends vendors often sell hot chocolate and coffee. Skates are for rent at **Champions Choice,** 3700 Old Seward Hwy. (☎ **907/563-3503**). Or rent skates and skate indoors at one of many rinks in town, including **Ben Boeke Ice Arena,** 334 E. 16th Ave. (☎ **907/274-5715**).

RAFTING There are several white-water rivers within a 90-minute drive of Anchorage. **Nova Raft and Adventure Tours** (☎ **800/746-5753** or 907/745-5753; novalaska.com) has 25 years of experience offering multiday trips all over the state, and four different half-day floats in the Anchorage area. Rafting trips ranging from relatively easygoing Class II and III rapids on the Matanuska River to the Class IV and V white water of Six-Mile Creek, for which you may be required to prove your swimming ability before you can get in the boat. Self-paddling is an option on some trips. White-water rafting always entails risk, but Nova's schedule allows you to calibrate how wild you want to get. The half-day trips range in price from $60 to $135. Children 5 to 11 can go on the calm Matanuska River float; the half-price fare is $30. Other trips are suitable only for older children and adults. You'll need your own transportation to the river and may need to bring your own lunch.

SEA KAYAKING Except at Eklutna Lake (see above), kayaking day trips from Anchorage go through Whittier, on Prince William Sound (see section 4 of chapter 7 for complete details).

SKIING Frequently the site of national competition, ✪ **Kincaid Park** is one of the best **cross-country skiing** areas in the country, and with more than 50 kilometers of trails there's plenty of room. Besides the superb trails, it's a beautiful place to ski, through rolling hills of open birch and spruce, with views of the mountains and ocean. Trails are groomed for skating and classical techniques. Sixteen kilometers are lighted in winter (an important feature on short winter days) and open until 10pm nightly. The **Kincaid Park Outdoor Center** (☎ **907/343-6397**) is open Monday to Friday from 1 to 10pm and on Saturday and Sunday from 10am to 10pm. Skiing often lasts through March. **Far North Bicentennial Park** also has some excellent trails—32 kilometers total, 7 kilometers lighted—and a slightly longer season because of a hillside location. Start at Hilltop Ski Area. Many other parks and the bike trails have kilometers more of skiing, too, much of it lighted.

Anchorage has three **downhill ski areas.** The best, **Alyeska Resort,** is described in the Girdwood section, below. **Alpenglow at Arctic Valley** (☎ **907/428-1208**) is a good local ski area above the tree line, but it is in perennial financial trouble, so you should check before going (take the Glenn Highway to Arctic Valley Road). **Hilltop Ski Area,** in Bicentennial Park in town, is best for beginners, at 7015 Abbott Rd. (☎ **907/346-2169**).

6 Shopping

Some of the most interesting shops are mentioned above, in the walking tour of downtown, where most galleries and gift shops are located.

NATIVE ARTS & CRAFTS Many stores in Anchorage carry Native Alaskan arts and crafts. Before making major purchases, know what you're buying (see "Native Art—Finding the Real Thing," in chapter 2). If you're going to the Bush, you'll find lower prices there but less selection.

Nowhere will you find another business like the **Oomingmak Musk Ox Producers' Co-operative** (☎ **888/360-9665** or 907/272-9225; www.qiviut.com), in the house with the musk ox on the side at Sixth Avenue and H Street. Owned by 250 Alaska Native women in villages across the state, the co-op sells only scarves and items they knit of *qiviut* (*ki*-vee-ute), the light, warm, silky under hair of the musk ox, which is collected from the tundra where the animals shed. Each village has its own knitting pattern. They're expensive—caps can cost over $100—but the quality is extraordinary.

The **Yankee Whaler,** in the lobby of the Hotel Captain Cook, at Fifth Avenue and I Street, is a small but well-regarded shop carrying Native arts. **The Rusty Harpoon,** next door in the yellow Sunshine Mall, at 411 Fourth Ave., also has authentic Native items, less expensive crafts, and reliable, longtime proprietors. Farther afield, the **Alaska Fur Exchange,** at 4417 Old Seward Hwy., near Tudor Road, is a cross between an old-time wilderness trading post and a modern factory outlet. Rural residents bring in furs and crafts to sell and trade, which are displayed in great profusion and clutter. If you're in the market for pelts, go no further.

Probably the best place for Native crafts in Anchorage is the **Craft Shop in the Alaska Native Medical Center,** off Tudor east of Bragaw, where everything is on consignment from the users of the hospital. The shop is open only Monday to Friday 10am to 2pm and some Saturdays. There's exceptional Native art on the walls of the hospital, too.

FURS & KUSPUKS If you're in the market for furs, Anchorage has a wide selection and no sales tax. **David Green Master Furrier,** at 130 W. Fourth Ave., is an Anchorage institution. Others are nearby. **Laura Wright Alaskan Parkys,** at 343 W. Fifth Ave., makes and sells the bright fabric coats called *kuspuks* really worn by Eskimos. Winter-wear *parkys* often have fur trim, but that isn't a requirement for beauty and authenticity. Most of the coats are made to order by the friendly women who work there.

GIFTS There are lots of places to buy both mass-produced and inexpensive handmade crafts that aren't from the Bush. If you can be in town on a Saturday during the summer, be sure to visit the ✪ **Saturday Market** street fair, in the parking lot at Third Avenue and E Street, with food, music, and hundreds of miscellaneous crafts booths. You won't have any trouble finding gift shops on Fourth. Our favorite is the relatively classy **Cabin Fever,** at 650 W. Fourth. Other large, attractive shops include **Once in a Blue Moose,** at Fourth Avenue and F Street, **Grizzly's Gifts,** at Fourth and E, and **Trapper Jacks,** at Fourth and G. The **Kobuk Coffee Company,** at Fifth Avenue and E Street, next to town square, occupies one of Anchorage's earliest commercial buildings; it's a cozy little candy, coffee, and collectibles shop. In midtown, on International Airport Road between the Old and New Seward highways, **Alaska Wild Berry**

Products is a fun store to visit. There's a chocolate waterfall and a big window where you can watch the candy factory at work. The chocolate-covered berry jellies are simultaneously addictive and rich enough to make you dizzy if you eat more than a few.

FINE ART Downtown has several galleries. Openings at all the galleries happen on the first Friday of each month, allowing for an evening of party hopping. The ✪ **Decker/Morris Gallery,** at Sixth Avenue and G Street, shows exciting and adventurous artists, even if they lack broad commercial appeal. **Artique,** 2 blocks north at 314 G St., is Anchorage's oldest gallery and has a much larger selection. Half of the gallery is given over to big oils and other gorgeous originals; the other half is chock-full of prints, less-expensive ceramics, and some mass produced or corny stuff. At Fifth and G, **Aurora Fine Arts** carries more pottery, prints, and gifts.

7 Nightlife

THE PERFORMING ARTS

To find out what's happening, pick up a copy of Friday's edition of the *Anchorage Daily News* for the "8" section, which includes event listings and information on the club and arts scene. Their Web site, **www.adn.com/eight**, allows you to check the calendar and listings from afar, or on days other than Friday. The *Anchorage Press,* the free weekly alternative paper, has a similar service, with a younger slant, at www.anchoragepress.com.

Carrs Tix (☎ **907/263-ARTS;** www.carrstix.com) is the main ticket agency covering Alaska. Their Web site is useful, and they have box offices at the Anchorage Center for Performing Arts and at Carrs grocery stores. The operation may change, as the company was recently bought by Tickets.com, of Concord, California.

The arts season begins in the fall and ends in the spring, but traveling performers often come through in the summer as well. The **Anchorage Concert Association** (☎ **907/272-1471;** www.anchorageconcerts.org) promotes a winter and spring schedule of music, theater, dance, and other performing arts. **Whistling Swan Productions** (www.whistlingswan.net) promotes folk and acoustic alternative performers in intimate venues. The **Anchorage Festival of Music** (☎ **907/276-2465;** www.alaska.net/~anchfest) presents a classical music series in June. The **Anchorage Symphony** (☎ **907/274-8668;** www.alaska.net/~anet/symphony) performs during the winter season. Anchorage also has lots of community theater, opera, and limited professional theater, including the experimental **Out North Theater** (☎ **907/279-8200**), which produces local shows and imports avant-garde performers. **Cyrano's Off Center Playhouse** (☎ **907/274-2599**), at Fourth Avenue and D Street, is a tiny theater featuring art films and semiprofessional theater.

NIGHTCLUBS & BARS

For a fun, funny night out, nothing in town compares to ✪ **Mr. Whitekeys' Fly By Night Club,** on Spenard Road south of Northern Lights Boulevard (☎ **907/279-SPAM**). The goateed proprietor, a consummate vulgarian, ridicules Anchorage in his crude, political, local-humor musical comedy shows, in which he costars with a fallen former Miss Anchorage. If you can laugh at dog poop, you'll love it. The summer show is at 8pm Tuesday to Saturday, with no smoking Tuesday to Thursday; live music follows Fridays and Saturdays. Tickets are $12 to $18, and reservations are necessary well in advance. They serve good food, too.

Blues Central/Chef's Inn, 825 W. Northern Lights Blvd. (☎ **907/272-1341**), is dedicated to showcasing the best blues performers available, virtually every night. Major names come through on a regular basis. Shows start at 9:30pm. They also serve excellent beef. **The Whale's Tail** (☎ **907/276-6000**), at the Hotel Captain Cook, at Fourth and K downtown, has a different band for dancing almost every night. The huge **Chilkoot Charlie's,** at Spenard Road and Fireweed Lane (☎ **907/272-1010**), usually has Top 40 rock playing on various stages. The place is huge, but can be claustrophobic when crowded, with low ceilings and a dark, roadhouse atmosphere. The **Long Branch Saloon,** 1737 E. Dimond Blvd. (☎ **907/349-4142**), east of New Seward Highway, has country music every night and great burgers.

THE MOVIES

The most fun place to see a movie is the **Bear Tooth Theatrepub,** at 1230 W. 27th Ave. (☎ **907/276-4200;** www.beartooththeatre.net), where you can watch art films and second-run movies while sipping craft brews and eating gourmet tacos, pizzas and the like. There are several multiplexes in Anchorage playing all the current Hollywood output; check the *Anchorage Daily News* for listings. The only movie theater downtown is at Cyrano's Off-Center Playhouse "see Performing Arts" above, which has a film society. The closest larger theaters, the **Century 16** (☎ **907/929-FILM;** www.centurytheatres.com) and the **Fireweed Theater** (☎ **907/566-3328;** www.regalcinemas.com), are a short cab ride away in midtown.

8 Out from Anchorage: Turnagain Arm & Portage Glacier

One of the world's great drives starts in Anchorage and leads roughly 50 miles south on the Seward Highway to Portage Glacier. It's the trip, not the destination, that makes it worthwhile. The two-lane highway along Turnagain Arm, chipped from the foot of the rocky Chugach Mountains, provides a platform to see a magnificent, ever-changing, mostly untouched landscape full of wildlife. I've listed the sights in the style of a highway log, for there are interesting stops all the way along the road. It will take at least half a day, and there's plenty to do for an all-day excursion. Use your headlights for safety even in daylight and be patient if you get stuck behind a summertime line of cars—if you pass, you'll just come up behind another line ahead. Mileage markers count down from Anchorage.

Car rental is covered in "Getting Around," in section 1 of this chapter. There are many bus tours that follow the route and visit Portage Glacier (see "Getting There: By Bus," also in section 1 of this chapter). **Gray Line of Alaska** (☎ **800/544-2206** or 907/277-5581; www.graylineofalaska.com) offers a 7-hour trip that includes a stop in Girdwood and a boat ride on Portage Lake for $62, twice daily in summer.

POTTER MARSH (Mile 117) Heading south from Anchorage, the Seward Highway descends a bluff to cross a broad marsh formed by water impounded behind the tracks of the Alaska Railroad. The marsh has a boardwalk from which you can watch a huge variety of birds. Salad-green grasses grow from sparkling, pond-green water.

POTTER SECTION HOUSE (Mile 115) Located at the south end of Potter Marsh, the section house was an early maintenance station for the Alaska Railroad. Today it contains offices of Chugach State Park, open during normal business hours, and, outside, a few old train cars and interpretive displays. Just across the road is the trailhead for the **Turnagain Arm Trail.** It's a mostly level path running down the arm well above the highway, with great views breaking now and then through the trees. You can continue 9 miles to Windy Corner, or break off where the trail meets the McHugh Creek picnic area and trailhead, about 4 miles out.

View of the Chigmit Mountains in Lake Clark National Park, located on the west side of the Cook Inlet at the north end of the Alaska Peninsula. The Chigmits include two active volcanoes, Mt. Redoubt and Mt. Iliamna, and the park's lakes and rivers are crucial salmon habitat to the Bristol Bay salmon fishery, one of the largest sockeye salmon fishing grounds in the world. See chapter 10. © Fred Hirschmann Wilderness Photography.

A pair of tufted puffins at the Walrus Islands State Game Sanctuary in the Bering Sea. Puffins favor the cracks of rugged granite islands and cliffs for nesting and laying their eggs, and they fly better underwater than in the air—something you can see at the Alaska SeaLife Center in Seward. See chapter 7. © Fred Hirschmann Wilderness Photography.

An Alaskan moose up close and personal. They're as big as a large horse and their flanks look like a worn-out shag carpet draped over a sawhorse, but moose are survivors, thriving in land that no one else wants. In the summer, they disperse and are not easily seen in thick vegetation. In the winter, they gather where walking is easy, along roads and in lowlands where people also like to live. See the appendix. © Dorothy Keeler/Ken Graham Agency.

McHUGH CREEK (Mile 111) Four miles south of Potter is an excellent state park picnic area and a challenging day hike with a 3,000-foot elevation gain to Rabbit Lake, which sits in a tundra mountain bowl, or to the top of 4,301-foot McHugh Peak. You don't have to climb all the way; there are spectacular views within an hour of the road.

BELUGA POINT (Mile 110) The state highway department probably didn't need to put up scenic overlook signs on this pull-out, 1½ miles south of McHugh Creek—you would have figured it out on your own. The terrain is simply awesome, as the highway traces the edge of Turnagain Arm, below the towering cliffs of the Chugach Mountains. If the tide and salmon runs are right, you may see beluga whales, which chase the fish toward freshwater. Sometimes they overextend and strand themselves by the dozens in the receding tide, farther along, but usually aren't harmed.

WINDY POINT (Mile 106) Be on the lookout on the mountain side of the road for Dall sheep picking their way along the cliffs. It's a unique spot, for the sheep get much closer to people here than is usual in the wild; apparently, they know they're safe. Windy Point is the prime spot, but you also have a good chance of seeing sheep virtually anywhere along this stretch of road. If cars are stopped, that's probably why; get well off the road and pay attention to traffic, which still will be passing at high speeds.

You may also see windsurfers in the gray, silty waters of the Arm. They're crazy. The water is a mixture of glacial runoff and the near-freezing ocean. Besides, the movement of water that creates the 38-foot tidal difference causes riverlike currents, with standing waves like rapids. At times, rushing walls of water up to 6 feet high, called bore tides, form in the arm with the incoming tide, an incredible sight. You need perfect timing or good luck to see a bore tide.

INDIAN VALLEY (Mile 104) Up the road by the Turnagain House restaurant is the **Indian Valley** trailhead, a gold rush era trail that ultimately leads 24 miles to the other side of the mountains. The path, while often muddy, rises less steeply than other trails along the Arm.

BIRD CREEK (Mile 100) The **Bird Ridge Trail** comes first, at mile 102, a steep alpine climb rising 3,000 feet in a little over a mile. With the southern exposure, it's dry early in the year. An excellent state campground on the right, over the water, costs $10 per night. There also is a short trail, interpretive signs, an overlook, and a platform that makes fishing easier for people with disabilities. Pink salmon run late June to mid-August, silver salmon mid-July to August.

THE FLATS (Miles 96–90) Beyond Bird Creek, the highway descends from the mountainside to the mud flats. At high tide, water comes right up to the road. At low tide, the whole Arm narrows to a thin, winding channel through the mud. Since the 1964 Good Friday earthquake, the Arm has not been navigable; before the earthquake, there was never much reason to navigate it. The first to try was Capt. James Cook, in 1778, as he was searching for the Northwest Passage on his final, fatal voyage of discovery (he was killed by Hawaiians later that year). He named this branch of Cook Inlet Turnagain Arm because he had to keep turning around in its shoal-ridden confines before it petered out.

TURNOFF TO GIRDWOOD (Mile 90) This is the intersection with the road to Girdwood. The attractions of the town, covered below, are worth a visit, but the shopping center here at the intersection is not chief among them. Stop here for a simple meal, a rest room break, or to fill your gas tank for the last time for many a mile.

OLD PORTAGE (Mile 80) All along the flats at the head of Turnagain Arm are large marshes full of what looks like standing driftwood. These are trees killed by saltwater that flowed in when the 1964 quake lowered the land as much as 10 feet. On the right, 9 miles beyond the turnoff for Girdwood, across for the former rail depot, a few ruins of the abandoned town of Portage are still visible, more than 35 years after the great earthquake. There is good bird watching from the turnouts, but don't think of venturing out on Turnagain Arm's tidal mud flats. They suck people up and drown them in the incoming tide. A woman died a few years ago in the arms of rescuers who were not strong enough to pull her out of the quicksandlike mud as the water covered her.

BIG GAME ALASKA (Mile 79) An entrepreneur fenced off 140 acres of this glacial valley to display deer, moose, eagles, owls, elk, bison, musk ox, and caribou—all injured or orphaned—in a more spacious setting than the Alaska Zoo, which has a greater variety of animals. Turn right a mile past the former Portage rail depot (☎ **907/783-2025;** www.biggamealaska.com). Visitors pick up a cassette tape and map and drive the short course looking at the animals in 3- to 5-acre enclosures. A large log gift shop is at the end of the tour. Admission is $5 for adults, $3 for military, seniors and children 4 to 12, with a maximum of $20 per vehicle. In summer, it's open daily from 9:30am to 7:30pm; in winter, daily 10am to 5pm.

PORTAGE GLACIER (Take the 5.5-mile spur road at mile 78) The named attraction at this, the most popular of all Alaska tourist attractions, has largely melted, receding out of sight of the visitor center. (The glacier you can see is Burns.) When the center was built in 1985, Portage Glacier was predicted to keep floating on its 800-foot-deep lake until the year 2020. Instead, it withdrew to the far edge of the lake in 1995. Even so, $8 million spent by the National Forest Service on the **Begich-Boggs Visitor Center** wasn't wasted, and neither is a trip to see where the glacier used to be. If you're in Alaska any length of time, you'll likely be seeing a lot of glaciers, and this glacier museum is an excellent place to learn about what you're looking at.

Several short trails start near the center. Rangers lead nature walks on the ¼-mile, paved Moraine Trail up to six times a day. Another trail leads less than a mile to Byron Glacier, in case you're interested in getting up close to some ice. Always dress warmly, as cold winds are the rule in this funnel-like valley.

A **cruise boat** operated by **Gray Line of Alaska** (☎ **800/478-6388,** 907/277-5581 for reservations, or 907/783-2983 at the lake; www.graylineofalaska.com) traverses the lake to get right up to Portage Glacier on hour-long tours, ice conditions permitting. Sometimes you can see ice fall in the lake. It costs $35 and goes five times daily in summer, every 90 minutes starting at 10:30am. If this is your only chance to see a glacier in Alaska, it's probably a good choice. If your itinerary includes any of the great glaciers in Prince William Sound, Kenai Fjords National Park, or the like, you won't be as impressed by Portage. You can get a free view of the glacier by taking a left just before the visitor center and stopping at a pull-out on the way to the Whittier Tunnel.

Factoid

The **Begich-Boggs Visitor Center** at Portage Glacier is named for Hale Boggs, former U.S. House majority leader, and former Alaska Congressman Nick Begich. They disappeared together in a small plane in 1972 during Begich's first reelection bid. The plane was never found, but Begich, even though declared dead, was reelected anyway. His opponent, Republican Don Young, later won a special election and continues to serve as Alaska's lone congressman.

A restaurant and gift shop near the glacier called the **Portage Lodge** offers basic cafeteria sandwiches. Better meals are to be found at the **Tidewater Cafe** (☎ **907/783-2840;** e-mail: eananook@aol.com), back at the highway junction at mile 78.5. It's a friendly diner with grand views of the valley; the menu includes halibut, steaks, and good hot chili. There are no lodgings in Portage, but two **Forest Service campgrounds** are on the road to the visitor center, with 72 sites between them (more details are in the Chugach National Forest section in chapter 7). At the Williwaw Campground, there's also a place to watch red salmon spawning in mid-August, but no fishing.

9 Out from Anchorage: Girdwood & Mount Alyeska

Girdwood, 37 miles south of Anchorage, is proof that a charming little town can coexist with a major ski resort, as long as the resort goes undiscovered by the world's skiers. Originally a mining community, and more recently a weekend skiing area for Anchorage, Girdwood still has a sleepy, offbeat character. Retired hippies, ski bums, a U.S. senator, and a few old-timers live in the houses and cabins among the big spruce trees in the valley below the Mount Alyeska lifts. They all expected a development explosion to follow the construction of an international resort here a few years ago, but it hasn't happened. That may not be good news for the Japanese investors in the resort, but it is for skiers and other visitors who discover this paradise. They find varied, uncrowded skiing through long winters and an authentically funky community.

The primary summer attractions are the hiking trails, the tram to the top of Mount Alyeska, and the Crow Creek Mine, described below. In winter, it's skiing. Mount Alyeska doesn't have the fame of resorts in the Rockies, but it's large, steep, and uncrowded, half the mountain is above the tree line, and the snow lasts long. Olympian Tommy Moe trained here. Skiers used to tamer, busier slopes Outside rave about the skiing here, with long, challenging downhills and the views of the Chugach Mountains and glistening Turnagain Arm below.

ESSENTIALS

A **rental car** is the most practical route to Girdwood. If you are going just to ski, however, you can take a bus down and back. **The Magic Bus** (☎ **800/836-2006** or 907/441-8420; www.themagicbus.com) charges $25 one way.

The **Girdwood Resort Association** maintains an extensive Web site at **www.girdwoodalaska.com**. For more information, check the Anchorage visitor information listed in section 1 of this chapter.

EXPLORING GIRDWOOD

Crow Creek Mine. Crow Creek Rd. (off the Alyeska Hwy.), Girdwood, AK 99587. ☎ **907/278-8060.** $3 adults, free for children. Gold panning $5 adults, $4 children 11 and under. May 15–Sept 15 daily 9am–6pm.

This mine opened in 1898 and operated until 1940. The Toohey family has turned the paths and 14 small buildings into a charming tourist attraction where you can see the frontier lifestyle and watch the rabbits and ducks wandering around. A bag of dirt, guaranteed to have some gold in it, is provided for gold panning, and you can dig and pan to get more if you have the patience for it, which few people do. Crow Creek Road, off the Alyeska Highway, is quite rough and muddy in the spring.

Mt. Alyeska Tram. At The Westin Alyeska Prince Hotel, 1000 Arlberg Ave. (P.O. Box 249), Girdwood, AK 99587. ☎ **800/880-3880** or 907/754-1111. Fax 907/754-2200. www.alyeskaresort.com. $16 per person for the 7-minute summertime ride.

The tram isn't cheap, but I think it's worth it for anyone who otherwise might not make it to an alpine vista during an Alaska trip. (In winter, the tram is faster and comes with your lift ticket. Alaskans pay only $12 in the summer.) My 3-year-old son called it "the spaceship bus," and that's exactly how it feels to float smoothly from the hotel up into the mountains. At the 2,300-foot level, the tram stops at a station with an attractive but overpriced cafeteria (save greatly by buying a tram/lunch combo ticket). In the evening, the expensive **Seven Glaciers Restaurant,** so named for its view, has great food to go along with the views. Whether or not you eat, the tram presents an opportunity for everyone, no matter how young, old, or infirm, to experience the pure light, limitless surroundings, and crystalline quiet of an Alaskan mountaintop. Dress very warmly.

ACTIVITIES

For additional information about activities in this area, contact the **Alyeska Resort** (see "Accommodations," below).

SKIING Mount Alyeska, at 3,939 feet, has 1,000 acres of skiing, beginning from a base elevation of only 250 feet and rising 2,500 feet. The normal season is early November to April, and it's an exceptional year when there isn't plenty of snow all winter. In 1999, skiing lasted through Memorial Day weekend. The average snowfall is 560 inches, or 46 feet. As it's near the water, the weather is temperate. Light is more of an issue, as the days are short in midwinter.

There are 27 lighted trails covering 2,000 vertical feet on Friday and Saturday evenings mid-December to mid-March, but the best Alaska skiing is when the days get longer and warmer in the spring. There are nine lifts, including the tram. Two chairs serve beginners, with a vertical drop of only around 300 feet. The balance of the mountain is geared to intermediate to expert skiers. Experts skiers love Alyeska the most, because of its many challenging slopes. Helicopter skiing goes right from the hotel, too.

An all-day lift ticket costs $44 for adults, $25 for ages 14 to 17, $18 for those ages 8 to 13 or over 60, and $7 ages 7 and under or over 70. Private and group instruction are available, and a basic rental package costs $20 a day for adults, $10 for age 13 and under.

There are groomed **cross-country trails** as well, and gear for rent, but much better Nordic skiing is to be had in Anchorage.

A utilitarian **day lodge** with snack and rental counters is located at the front of the mountain, but the **Sitzmark Bar** is a more comfortable place for a meal (burgers are around $8). The best approach for day-trippers, however, is to make the hotel your base. Located on the other side of the mountain and connected to the front by the tram to the top and beginner-level chair 7, the hotel has its own, lightly used rental counter and day lockers. Eat lunch there or at the cafeteria up on the mountain.

A center operated by **Challenge Alaska** (☎ **907/783-2925** or 907/344-7399) allows skiers with disabilities to use the mountain without assistance, skiing down to the lift to start and back to the center at day's end.

SNOWMOBILING **Alaska Snow Safaris** (☎ **888/414-7669** or 907/783-7669; www.akadventures.com) offers 3-hour tours for beginners for $95 per person and 5-hour tours to a glacier for those with some experience for $145 per person. This is a chance to get into real, trackless wilderness.

DOG MUSHING **Chugach Express Dog Sled Tours** (☎ **907/783-2266**) offers hour-long rides in the sled basket for $60. Guests get to try driving the team at the end of the tour.

HIKING There are a couple of great trails starting in Girdwood. The **Winner Creek Trail** runs 5 miles through forest from behind the Westin Alyeska Prince Hotel to a roaring gorge where Winner Creek and Glacier Creek meet; it's muddy and snowy in the spring. The winter ski trail takes a separate route, through a series of meadows, to the same destination. The **Crow Pass Trail** rises into the mountains and passes all the way over to Eagle River, after a 26-mile hike that takes a couple of days. But you can make a long day hike of it to the pass and see the glaciers, wildflower meadows, and old mining equipment. The trailhead is up Crow Creek Road, off the Alyeska Highway.

ACCOMMODATIONS

Besides the resort hotel, there are plenty of condos and B&Bs in town. **Alyeska Accommodations,** on Olympic Circle (☎ **907/783-2000;** www.alyeskaaccommodations.com), offers condos, chalets, and houses. Several B&Bs have links to **www.girdwoodalaska.com**.

✪ **Westin Alyeska Prince Hotel.** 1000 Arlberg Ave. (P.O. Box 249), Girdwood, AK 99587. ☎ **800/880-3880** or 907/754-1111. Fax 907/754-2200. www.alyeskaresort.com. 307 units. TV TEL. Summer and Christmas $175–$450 double; $600–$1,600 suite. Winter $175–$300 double; $500–$1,100 suite. Extra adult $25; children stay free in parents' room. AE, DC, MC, V.

The Alyeska Resort's hotel is Alaska's best. The beauty of the building alone separates it from the competition. Studded with dormers and turrets, it impresses on first sight. Inside, sumptuous cherry wood and rich colors unite the welcoming common rooms and elegant guest rooms. Although not large, rooms have every convenience, and the maintenance and housekeeping are exceptional.

Four restaurants vie for attention, two of them—a cafeteria and the gourmet Seven Glaciers Restaurant—2,300 feet above the lobby on Mount Alyeska, at the end of a tram ride. The hotel's Japanese cuisine particularly has developed a reputation. The swimming pool is magnificent, with a cathedral ceiling and windows by the spa overlooking the mountain. As good as the property is, however, the location and activities alone make it worth visiting. To find such a place in a pristine mountain valley is a revelation. To spend a few days there skiing and swimming makes the rest of life seem too drab. One warning: On weekends, especially around holidays, families from Anchorage, like mine, descend on the hotel with noisy children. Couples would do well to come midweek.

DINING

Chair 5. Linblad St., town square. ☎ **907/783-2500.** www.chairfive.com. All meals $6.50–$16.50; large pizza $15.50–$19.75. AE, MC, V. Daily 11am–midnight. SEAFOOD/ BURGERS/PIZZA.

This is where Girdwood locals meet their friends and take their families for dinner, and it's also one of our favorites. One afternoon, Bob Dylan music accompanied a friendly game of pool while baseball played on the TV, and men with ponytails and beards sipped microbrews. Another evening, a guy in the entryway entertained the children with magic tricks and the waitress asked them to draw pictures to enter into a contest. The menu offered choices pleasing to each, including pizza, burgers, fresh fish, and entrees such as the rib eye and mushroom fettuccine, a memorable meal for only $15.50. Every time we've gone, the food has been excellent and inexpensive, and the service friendly and quick.

Double Musky Inn. 3 mile Crow Creek Rd. ☎ **907/783-2822.** www.doublemuskyinn.com. Main courses $18–$32. AE, CB, DC, DISC, MC, V. Tues–Thurs 5–10pm, Fri–Sun 4–10pm. Closed Nov. CAJUN.

The ski-bum-casual atmosphere and rambling, cluttered dining room among the trees match the wonderful Cajun and New Orleans food in a way that couldn't have been contrived—it's at once too improbable and too authentic. Service is relaxed to a fault, and food takes a long time to arrive, but when it does it's flawless. The place isn't to everyone's taste, however; your senses can feel raw after the extreme noise, highly spiced food, and crowds, and parking can be impossible. Loud groups will enjoy it more than couples, and families don't really fit. Full liquor license.

10 Out from Anchorage: The Matanuska & Susitna Valleys

For most visitors, the Mat-Su Valley, as the area is known, will be a place to pass through on the way to somewhere else—along the Glenn Highway to Valdez or the Alaska Highway, or up the Parks Highway to Denali National Park from Anchorage. But the area has some attractions of its own: the sweeping beauty of the Hatcher Pass area, the Matanuska and Knik glaciers, the Iditarod Sled Dog Race, and fishing along the Matanuska and Susitna rivers. This area isn't a destination for visitors with a limited schedule, but it is a worthy day trip from Anchorage or a refreshing stop between the state's major attractions.

The Matanuska Valley developed from the Great Depression until the 1970s as a farming area. The New Deal relocated colonists from other parts of the country to settle the prime growing land. But as transportation links improved both within the state and outside, farming in Alaska lost in competition to shipping goods in from Seattle. Farms became subdivisions, housing a population overflow from booming Anchorage, only an hour's drive south on the Glenn Highway. With its adamantly antigovernment philosophy preventing any community planning, Mat-Su's rush of development produced the worst kind of suburban sprawl. The area along the Parks Highway from its start at the Glenn Highway through Wasilla to Big Lake is truly ugly, the more profoundly so for the beauty it once contained.

The entire area is enormous. The county-level government, the Matanuska-Susitna Borough, covers an area about as large as West Virginia, vaguely defined by the drainages of the Matanuska and Susitna Rivers. Most of the people live in the section near Anchorage, in and around the towns of Palmer and Wasilla. In 1996, the Big Lake area, west of Wasilla, was swept by the costliest forest fire in Alaska history, which destroyed more than 400 buildings and seared 35,000 acres of land. For the casual visitor, however, the fire's ravages are no more than a curiosity.

The borough seat, **Palmer,** is a traditional small town built by the Depression-era colonists. One side of the quiet main street, Colony Way, is lined with little storefront businesses, hotels, and restaurants; the other is an open vista of the mountains. About 10 miles west, **Wasilla** was created mostly by a building boom of the 1970s and 1980s. The town exists primarily as a string of shopping centers along the Parks Highway, and you have to really look to find its center. The area is dotted with lakes surrounded by houses, where people water-ski and fish in the summer and snowmobile and run sled dogs in the winter. **Hatcher Pass** is in the Talkeetna Mountains on the north side of the Matanuska Valley. The Talkeetnas aren't as tall as other ranges, but they have the striking, rugged beauty of cracked rock. A historic mining site nestles up in the pass, and it's a terrific place for summer hikes and winter recreation, including Nordic skiing and snowmobiling. **Talkeetna,** at the northern end of the Susitna Valley, is covered in chapter 8, on Denali National Park.

ESSENTIALS

GETTING THERE & GETTING AROUND You can't get around the broadly spread Valley without a car. Buy a map. The best is the widely available $5 map produced by **Alaska Road and Recreation Maps,** P.O. Box 102459, Anchorage, AK 99510.

VISITOR INFORMATION The **Mat-Su Visitors Center,** Mile 35.5 Parks Hwy., HC 01 Box 6166J21, Palmer, AK 99645 (☎ **907/746-5000;** www.alaskavisit.com), is located on the right side of the Parks Highway just after the intersection with the Glenn Highway, as you enter the area from the south. It's open mid-May to mid-September daily from 8:30am to 6:30pm, closed in winter. The **Palmer Visitor Center,** in the center of town at 723 S. Valley Way, P.O. Box 45, Palmer, Alaska 99645 (☎ **907/745-2880;** www.palmerchamber.org), has a small museum on the 1935 colony project that developed the Valley. It's open mid-April to mid-September daily from 8am to 6pm, and in winter Monday to Friday 10am to 4pm.

FAST FACTS You'll find several **banks** on the Parks Highway in Wasilla and on Bailey Street or S. Colony Way in Palmer; they have **ATMs,** as do most large shopping centers and grocery stores.

The **Valley Hospital** is at 515 Dahlia Ave. in Palmer (☎ **907/746-8600**). **West Valley Medical Campus** is at 950 E. Bogard Rd. in Wasilla (☎ **907/352-2800**).

For nonemergency business with the police, call the **Palmer Police Department** (☎ **907/745-4811**), the **Wasilla Police Department** (☎ **907/373-9077**), or, outside either town, the **Alaska State Troopers** (☎ **907/745-2131**).

Mead's Coffee Shop, 405 E. Herning Ave. (☎ **907/357-5633**), provides **Internet access.**

There's a **post office** in Palmer at 500 S. Cobb St. In Wasilla, it's on Main Street.

Palmer levies a 3% **sales tax;** it's 2% in Wasilla. The Mat-Su borough charges a 5% **bed tax** on top of the sales tax.

SPECIAL EVENTS The ✪ **Iditarod Restart** (☎ **907/376-5155;** www.iditarod.com), on the first Sunday in March, enlivens Wasilla at the end of a long winter. The Iditarod Trail Sled Dog Race starts officially in Anchorage the day before, but then the dogs are loaded in trucks and carried to Wasilla, where the trail becomes continuous to Nome. The restart is the real beginning of the race, and the area makes the most of it.

The ✪ **Alaska State Fair** (☎ **907/745-4827;** www.akstatefair.org) the 11 days leading to Labor Day, is the biggest event of the year for the Valley, and one of the biggest for Anchorage; it's a typical fair, except for the huge vegetables. The good soil and long days in the Valley grow cabbages the size of bean-bag chairs. A mere beach-ball-size cabbage would be laughed off the stage.

EXPLORING THE ROADS OF MAT-SU

A trip to Hatcher Pass combines one of the area's most beautiful drives, access to great hiking and Nordic skiing, and interesting old buildings to look at. If you're headed north to Denali National Park or Fairbanks, the rough, winding gravel road through Hatcher Pass to Willow makes a glorious alpine detour around the least attractive part of your drive. Past the mine and skiing area, the road is open only in summer and is not suitable for large RVs. Just after the Parks Highway branches from the Glenn, exit to the right on the Trunk Road and keep going north on Fishhook Road. From the Glenn near Palmer, take Fishhook just north of town.

The **Independence Mine State Historical Park** (☎ **907/745-2827** or 907/745-3975; www.dnr.state.ak.us/parks/units/indmine.htm) takes in the remains of a hard-rock gold mine operation that closed down in 1943. Some buildings have been restored, including an assay office that's a museum and the manager's house that's a welcoming visitor center, while other structures sag and lean as picturesque ruins. Many details about the park may change, as it is undergoing a renovation. At present, a $3 guided tour ($2 seniors, free under 10) leaves at 1:30pm and 3:30pm weekdays, plus 4:30pm weekends, or you can wander with the help of an excellent walking-tour map. The visitor center is open 11am to 7pm daily in the summer, but closes the week after Labor Day.

The high Talkeetna Mountains valley that the site occupies is idyllic for a summer ramble in the heather or for Nordic or Telemark skiing in winter. There are four hiking trails and two mountain-biking routes in the area—ask at the visitor center. One great hike is the 8-mile **Gold Mint Trail,** which starts across the road from the Motherlode Lodge on Fishhook Road and ends at the Mint Glacier, where you have to turn around to hike back.

The **Musk Ox Farm,** 2 miles north of Palmer on the Glenn Highway and left on Archie Road (☎ **907/745-4151**), raises the beasts for research and breeding, and to provide their underwool for Anchorage's Oomingmak cooperative (see "Shopping," earlier in this chapter). The farm offer tours 10am to 6pm daily in the summer season. It costs $8 for adults, $6.50 seniors and ages 13 to 18, and $5 ages 6 to 12.

The family-operated **Reindeer Farm,** in the Butte area (☎ **907/745-4000**), raises reindeer for pets and puts them in harness each Christmas, and has three Rocky Mountain elk and two moose. The tour teaches all about reindeer and gives you an opportunity to feed them. Take the Old Glenn Highway to the intersection with Bodenburg Butte Road and Plumley Road, going toward the butte less than a mile. It's open 10am to 6pm daily in the summer. Admission is $5 for adults, $4 for seniors, and $3 for children 3 to 11. They offer horseback rides by appointment for $25 an hour. Across the road is a great short hike to the top of the butte.

The **Dorothy G. Page Museum,** at 323 Main St. in Wasilla (☎ **907/373-9071**), preserves the early history of the area in a collection of pioneer buildings. Sometimes real Valley pioneers are on hand to tell their stories. Several buildings are open for tours Tuesday to Saturday from 10am to 6pm in the summer, and the small museum is open Monday to Friday from 9am to 5pm in the winter as well. Admission is $3 for adults, $2.50 for seniors, and free for ages 12 and under.

The **Museum of Alaska Transportation and Industry,** off the Parks Highway at mile 47, west of Wasilla (☎ **907/376-1211;** www.alaska.net/~rmorris/mati1.htm), is a paradise for gear heads and tinkerers. The volunteers have gathered every conceivable machine and conveyance—13 fire trucks and 5 locomotives, for example—and fixed up to running order as many as they can. An indoor museum displays their finished masterpieces, while the 15 acres outside are crammed with future projects—trains, aircraft, fishing boats, and mining equipment—all grist for memories and imagination. It's open summer 9am to 6pm daily, winter Tuesday through Saturday 9am to 5pm. Admission is $5 for adults, $4 for students and seniors, $12 for families, free under age 8.

GETTING OUTSIDE

The Alaska Public Lands Information Center, described in the Anchorage section, is the best place for advice on the outdoors. **Rafting** in the Mat-Su is described under

"Getting Outside" in the Anchorage section, earlier in this chapter. The best **hikes, skiing,** and **snowmobiling** are at Hatcher Pass, described above.

DOG MUSHING The Valley is a center of **sled-dog mushing,** both for racing and recreational dog driving. Raymie Reddington—son of Joe Reddington, father of the Iditarod race—offers trips up the Iditarod Trail, ranging from half an hour to several days, and will teach you to mush as well. The 30-minute ride is $35. Contact **Reddington Sled Dog Tours,** at mile 12.5, Knik–Goose Bay Road (☎ **907/376-6730**). **Lucky Husky Mushing Adventures,** in Willow (☎ **907/495-6470;** www.luckyhusky.com), offers summer and winter rides and lessons. They're located on the Parks Highway north of Willow. The summer rides include a kennel tour, and cost $24 per person. You're bouncing down the trail for about 5 minutes. Winter trips are, of course, longer and more authentic. For most of the ride you'll be in the basket, but they will also teach you to ride the runners, guiding the team with your voice. A 1-hour ride is $120; a 2-hour excursion where you drive is $195. They offer trips of up to 5 days.

FISHING The Mat-Su area has many road-accessible salmon-fishing streams and stocked lakes, as well as plenty of campgrounds to get close to the fishing. Call the **Alaska Department of Fish and Game** (☎ **907/746-6300**) for a recording with current fishing information, or check the Web for most of what you need to know (www.state.ak.us/local/akpages/FISH.GAME/sportf/region2/r2home.htm).

HIKING For a challenging 7- to 10-hour climb, try 6,398-foot Pioneer Peak to the ridge below the top, with stupendous views. The trailhead is on Knik River Road, off Old Glenn Highway. See the description of Hatcher Pass, above for other choices.

HORSEBACK RIDING This is farming country and one of the best places in the state for riding. Near Bodenburg Butte, **Flying G Ranch,** Palmer (☎ **907/745-7258**), offers rides in beautiful country for $25 per person per hour, $15 for children under age 7. The reindeer farm, listed above, also offers rides.

ACCOMMODATIONS

ON THE GLENN HIGHWAY

If you're headed down the Glenn Highway, there are two good remote lodges near the **Matanuska Glacier,** 90 minutes from Palmer.

Majestic Valley Wilderness Lodge. Mile 114.9, Glenn Hwy., HC03, Box 8514, Palmer, AK 99645. ☎ **907/746-2930.** Fax 907/746-2931. www.majesticvalleylodge.com. 10 units, 2 cabins. $80 double; $100 cabin for 2 or more. Extra adult $10 in double; extra child age 4–12 $5 in double. MC, V.

This friendly lodge offers basic rooms with private bathrooms and serves excellent family-style meals if you arrange in advance. While most of the rooms aren't as attractive as those at Sheep Mountain Lodge, they're set back from the highway, and the grounds feature cross-country skiing trails—we enjoy going there for spring skiing weekends in the spectacular terrain. The lodge also offers guided skiing, snowmobiling, and hiking.

Sheep Mountain Lodge. Mile 113.5, Glenn Hwy., HC 03, Box 8490, Palmer, AK 99645. ☎ **907/745-5121.** Fax 907/745-5120. www.alaska.net/~sheepmtl. 10 units. $125 double. MC, V.

This historic lodge, under new, friendlier management, has 10 attractive mountainside cabins with private bathrooms, as well as a hostel. Their cafe has good basic food for a stop on your drive. Hiking trails over tundra mountains and the private road to the Matanuska Glacier are nearby.

AT HATCHER PASS

Hatcher Pass Lodge. P.O. Box 763, Palmer, AK 99645. ☎ **907/745-5897.** Fax 907/745-1200. www.hatcherpasslodge.com. 3 units, 9 cabins. $70 double room; $115 cabin for 2. Extra person $15. AE, CB, DC, DISC, MC, V.

Nine lovely A-frame cabins with chemical toilets sit right in the treeless bowl of the 3,000-foot alpine pass, deeply buried in snow in winter and surrounded by heather in summer. Running water and showers are available in the fun, funky little restaurant. It's a great family place where, in the winter, you can ski out the front door on up to 20 kilometers of Nordic trails.

IN THE MID-VALLEY

Bed-and-breakfasts are a good choice in the Valley. Besides those I've listed, some 30 others book through **Bed and Breakfast Association of Alaska, Mat-Su Chapter,** P.O. Box 873507, Wasilla, AK 99687 (☎ **800/401-7444** or 907/376-4461).

Agate Inn. 4725 Begich Circle, Wasilla, AK 99654. ☎ **800/770-2290** or 907/ 373-2290. Fax 907/376-2294. www.agateinn.com. 8 units. TV TEL. $95 room for 2; $125 apt for 2; $205 cottage. Rates include continental breakfast. AE, DISC, MC, V.

The big, comfortable apartments and two-bedroom cottage come with full kitchens, while the attractive standard rooms have private bathrooms. Originally a home B&B, it's grown to take over two houses and an apartment building, and still growing. Every room has a microwave, fridge, coffeemaker, and iron and ironing board. They've even acquired a couple of reindeer for the guests' amusement and offer weeklong archaeological digs for college credit.

Best Western Lake Lucille Inn. 1300 W. Lucille Dr., Wasilla, AK 99654. ☎ **800/528-1234** for reservations, or 907/373-1776. Fax 907/376-6199. www.bestwestern.com/lakelucilleinn. 54 units. TV TEL. High season $135 double; $175–$195 suite. Low season $89 double; $135–$155 suite. Extra person $10. AE, CB, DC, DISC, MC, V.

This well-run, attractive lakeside hotel right in Wasilla has the best standard hotel rooms in the valley. They're large and well appointed, and those facing the lake have balconies and a grand, peaceful view. Various kinds of boats can be rented for play on Lake Lucille, and flightseeing trips take off right from the dock below the lawn. There's a Jacuzzi, sauna, workout room, self-service laundry, small playground, and coffee in the rooms. The **restaurant** is one of the best in the area, with a light, quiet dining room looking out on the water. It's open for three meals a day, with the beef and seafood dinner menu ranging from $15 to $38.

✪ **Colony Inn.** 325 E. Elmwood, Palmer, AK 99645. ☎ **907/745-3330.** Fax 907/746-3330. 12 units. TV TEL. $80 double; $160 suite. Extra person $5. AE, DISC, MC, V.

This perfect country inn occupies a lovingly restored teacher's dormitory from the New Deal Colony Project, right in the middle of Palmer. The rooms feel fresh and new, yet at the same time wonderfully old-fashioned, with rockers and comforters but also Jacuzzi bathtubs and big TVs with VCRs. A large sitting room and a dining room downstairs are decorated with historic photographs that help tell the building's story. Excellent lunches and inexpensive dinners are served there during the summer at the **Inn Cafe** (☎ **907/746-6118**). A free laundry is available. This is one of the best places to stay in Southcentral Alaska, and an incredible bargain.

DINING

Some of the best restaurants in the Valley are at the **Best Western Lake Lucille Inn,** the **Colony Inn,** and **Hatcher Pass Lodge,** described above.

In **Palmer,** don't miss **Vagabond Blues,** 642 S. Alaska (☎ **907/745-2233**), a great little coffeehouse with hearty soups and breads, and jazz, blues, and other performances on weekend nights. Sometimes nationally known acts show up in the very intimate setting.

In **Wasilla, Mead's Coffee Shop** (☎ **907/357-5633**) is in the historic Teeland's General Store, at 405 E. Herning Ave., by the Dorothy Page Museum (see above). They serve pastries, soups, salads, and vegetarian meals, roast their own coffee, and have entertainment on weekends, as well as Internet access. **The Deli Restaurant and Bakery** (☎ **907/376-2914**), 185 E. Parks Hwy., at the corner of Willow Street, serves good, inexpensive sandwiches, soup, and salad for lunch in a light dining room. **The Windbreak Café** (☎ **907/376-4484**), at 2201 E. Parks Hwy., uphill from Wal-Mart, is one of the area's most popular diners, with solid traditional food in an Alaska-theme dining room.

In **Big Lake, The Islander Lodge** (☎ **907/892-2892**) sits on a tiny island in this large, recreation lake north from Wasilla on the Parks Highway. In summer, guests call for a free boat ride across; in winter, they drive on the ice; during breakup, the restaurant closes. The steak and seafood is fine, but it's the adventure that makes the experience. Call ahead for directions and to arrange for your boat. The ride takes about 5 minutes. Plan to spend the whole evening.

7

The Kenai Peninsula & Prince William Sound

The Gulf of Alaska arcs at its northern edge, forming the rounded northern shore of the Pacific Ocean, a zone of great collisions. This is where the earth's great tectonic plates collide, spewing forth froths of hot lava from dozens of volcanoes and fracturing and folding the earth with titanic earthquakes. Here the ocean's wildest weather collides with mountains jutting miles high from the sea, growing immense prehistoric ice sheets and glaciers that carve the rock into long, deep, intricate fjords. The sea proffers prodigious biological wealth on these shores, including the salmon it unleashes into the rivers in furious swarms of life that climb over the mountains and into the Interior to spawn. Nature seems giant and superabundant in this magnificent arc of land and water.

Geography endowed this one stretch of coast with several of the world's great natural places. On the east, near Cordova, the **Copper River**'s immense, entirely unspoiled delta is the largest contiguous wetlands in the Western Hemisphere. On a day trip, you're immediately alone with flocks of rare, graceful waterfowl that congregate on shallow ponds surrounded by miles of waving grass. **Prince William Sound** is a great protected sea of wooded, uninhabited islands and immense glaciers. On a summer day, I picnicked there with my family on the beach of a deserted bay next to a stream boiling with spawning salmon. A raft of hundreds of sea otters lolled on the sunny water before us while eagles circled low overhead. **Kenai Fjords National Park** takes in bays off the open ocean where the mountains soar a mile straight up from the water. Boats travel there among humpback, gray, and orca whales; spot otters, seals, and sea lions; and visit swarming colonies of puffins and other sea birds. The **Kenai River** harbors the world's biggest salmon, on the western side of the Kenai Peninsula; and on its southern tip, **Kachemak Bay** is like a miniature Prince William Sound. The bay has wildlife and glaciers and all that, but its shores also are dotted by tiny towns with lodges, art galleries on pilings, and some of Alaska's best restaurants.

The whole region is exceptionally accessible, by Alaska standards. The Kenai (*keen*-eye) Peninsula, in particular, is especially easy to get to without the expense and exhausting travel that can make much of the state difficult. Most of what you're looking for in Alaska lies along a few hundred miles of blacktop, within reach of a rental car and perhaps a tour boat ticket: glaciers, whales, legendary sportfishing,

The Kenai Peninsula & Prince William Sound

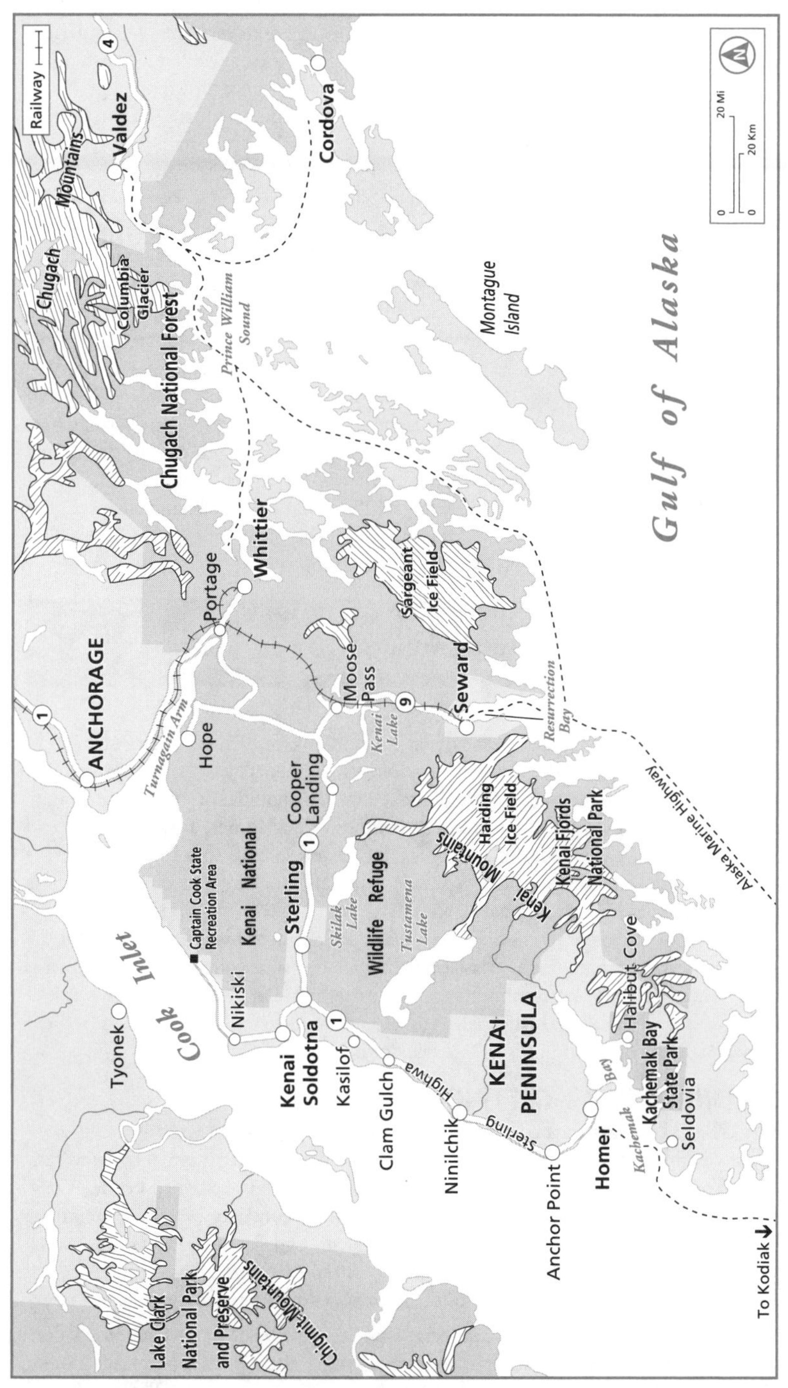

spectacular hiking trails, interesting little fishing towns, bears, moose, and high mountains. People from Anchorage go to the peninsula for the weekend to fish, hike, dig clams, paddle kayaks, and so on, and certain places can get crowded.

There's a special phrase for what happens when the red salmon are running in July on the Kenai and Russian rivers: *combat fishing.* At hot times in certain places, anglers stand elbow to elbow on a bank, each casting into his or her own 1-yard-wide slice of river, and still catch plenty of hefty salmon. The peninsula also exerts a powerful magnetic force on RVs, those road-whales that one finds at the head of strings of cars on the two-lane highways. During the summer, the fishing rivers, creeks, and beaches on the west side of the peninsula and the end of the Homer Spit can become sheet-metal cities of hundreds of Winnebagos and Itascas parked side by side. Often some local entrepreneur will be selling doughnuts or newspapers door-to-door.

Yet the decision is yours as to whether you spend time in the company of tourists. If the roadside fishing is hairy, hiking a little farther down the bank usually means you can be by yourself. In this chapter, I'll describe some towns of unspoiled charm, where you can kayak virtually from your room. Being alone is easy. You can paddle among otters in Resurrection Bay; tramp over the heather in Turnagain Pass; hike, bike, or ski one of the many maintained trails in Chugach National Forest. When you're ready to come back to the comforts of civilization, you'll find that some of the state's best restaurants and most interesting lodgings are here, too.

1 Exploring the Kenai Peninsula & Prince William Sound

THE TOWNS

Kenai, on Cook Inlet on the west side of the Kenai Peninsula, is the largest town in the region. Ten miles up the Kenai River, **Soldotna** is Kenai's twin, and together they form a unit with about a fourth of the Kenai Peninsula's population of 49,000. They're also the least interesting of the peninsula's communities. **Homer,** at the southern end of the peninsula, has wonderful art and character and lots of ways to get out on the water. **Seward,** on the east side, is smaller and quieter, but also charming and a gateway to Kenai Fjords National Park.

There are three major towns on Prince William Sound. **Valdez** is an oil town at the southern terminus of the trans-Alaska pipeline where tankers are loaded. **Cordova** is more attractive, a historic community on the eastern side of the Sound, with outdoor activities close at hand. **Whittier** is a grim former military outpost, but a convenient gateway to the protected fjords and glaciers of the western Sound.

GETTING THERE & GETTING AROUND

BY CAR Highways connect all the region's large towns, except Cordova. Like all of Alaska's main highways, they are paved two-lane roads. The Seward Highway runs south from Anchorage to the Kenai Peninsula. That route is described below. A new road completed in 2000, built in a railway tunnel, connects Whittier, on Prince William Sound, to the Seward Highway. The Glenn and Richardson highways reach from Anchorage to Valdez through Alaska's Interior. Stops along that route are described in chapters 6 and 9, and all the highways are summarized in chapter 9.

BY FERRY The ferry system connects Whittier with Valdez and Cordova. Valdez serves as the hub; ferries run straight between Cordova and Whittier only once a week. The ferry ***Bartlett,*** one of the smallest in the fleet, serves the Prince William Sound towns. There are no sleeping accommodations, but the boat is rarely very full and there is plenty of deck space and recliners for overnight runs. The restaurant has the best views you could hope for, and acceptable food (if short hours). The Chugach National Forest usually has rangers on board offering programs and interpretation in the observation lounge.

The ferry ***Tustumena*** connects Homer and Seward to Seldovia and Kodiak Island and the Aleutian Archipelago (covered in chapter 10), and also runs from Homer to Seldovia, with occasional trips to Seward, Whittier, and Prince William Sound villages as well. The schedule is not convenient for Seldovia, however, and it's much more practical to drive between Homer, Seward, and Whittier. Private passenger ferries serve the towns and remote sites around Kachemak Bay from Homer, described in section 10.

See section 1 of chapter 5 for more information on the ferry system. Call ☎ **800/642-0066** or point your browser to **www.dot.state.ak.us/external/amhs/home.html**.

BY AIR Commuter airlines fan out from Anchorage to Kenai, Homer, Seward, Valdez, and Cordova; their names and phone numbers are given in the relevant sections of this chapter. You can also fly an Alaska Airlines jet to Cordova, with one flight from Anchorage every day, and another daily flight from Yakutat, Juneau, and Seattle. Scheduled and air-taxi services use these smaller towns as bases for the villages, carrying passengers, mail, and cargo, and flying to remote lodges and cabins for fishing or other outdoor activities. Valdez, Cordova, and Anchorage operators serve the Prince William Sound region. Kenai and Anchorage companies cover Cook Inlet and remote public lands such as Lake Clark National Park. Homer is the base for villages around Kachemak Bay and lower Cook Inlet bear viewing sites.

BY TRAIN The **Alaska Railroad** (☎ **800/544-0552** or 907/265-2494; www.akrr.com) runs from Anchorage south to Seward and Whittier daily in the summer.

VISITOR INFORMATION

For information on the peninsula as a whole, contact the **Kenai Peninsula Tourism Marketing Council,** 150 N. Willow St., Kenai, AK 99611 (☎ **800/535-3624** or 907/283-3850; www.KenaiPeninsula.org), which distributes a vacation planner and runs a Web site with information on businesses in the area; the staff will answer inquiries at the toll number during normal business hours. The **Kenai Peninsula Resource Network** (www.kenaipeninsula.com) is a commercial Web site with many links all over the area.

See "Getting Outside," below, for outdoor information.

TRIP PLANNING & ITINERARIES

You'll need to book rental cars and hotel or lodge rooms and wilderness cabins well ahead—certainly by late April. Mid-June to mid-August is the most heavily booked, when finding any decent room can be difficult without reservations. Activities should be reserved a few weeks ahead. Reservations are not necessary for camping. Leave plenty of time in your schedule around any boating or flightseeing excursions. Reputable tour and fishing operators simply won't go out in rough weather. If you have a backup day, you can spend the bad-weather day on shore and try again the next day. Check on weather-cancellation policies before you book any boat excursions.

I've arranged the sections below to match the ways you'll tour the region. First comes general information on the outdoors, next a road guide to the Kenai Peninsula's Seward Highway, a section on Chugach National Forest, then the towns in the region in order of their distance from Anchorage. If you're considering taking a wildlife sightseeing cruise, compare the sections on Seward and Kenai Fjords National Park and the section on Whittier.

BY CAR Driving is the easiest way to get around the region. One good itinerary of 10 days to 2 weeks would be to fly to Anchorage and spend a few days taking in the sights there (see chapter 6). Then rent a car to drive the Seward and Sterling highways, taking plenty of time to get down to Homer, perhaps with a couple of days to stop for fishing or hiking on the way in the Chugach National Forest, in Cooper Landing, or in the Kenai/Soldotna area. In Homer, plan several days, getting out on Kachemak Bay to Halibut Cove, Seldovia, or hiking and boating in Kachemak Bay State Park. Then drive back to Whittier and take the ferry through Prince William Sound to Valdez, seeing the glaciers and wildlife on the way. Spend a day in Valdez, then drive up the Richardson Highway, perhaps making a 2-day side trip to historic Kennicott, in the spectacular Wrangell–St. Elias National Park (see chapter 9), then returning on the Glenn Highway to Anchorage or continuing up to Fairbanks, if there's time.

WITHOUT A CAR A possible 10-day carless itinerary would be to fly to Anchorage, spend a few days sightseeing there, then take the Alaska Railroad to Seward, visiting Kenai Fjords National Park by boat, with a second day in Seward in case of bad weather or for a hike or fishing. Then return to Anchorage and fly to Cordova, taking the tour to Childs Glacier, visiting the quaint and welcoming town, and perhaps getting outdoors on a bike, a hike, a kayak, or a fishing excursion. Then take the ferry to Valdez, spend part of a day there, and board a tour boat to see Columbia Glacier and other glaciers in western Prince William Sound, either going all the way to Whittier and taking the train to Anchorage or returning to Valdez and flying back to Anchorage from there. If there's time left, use Anchorage as a base for further explorations.

GETTING OUTSIDE

The towns of the region are like beads strung along the laces of the highways; everything else is wilderness. You can find all the activities and isolation you seek here, yet the presence of the towns means that comfort is closer at hand than in other parts of Alaska.

Chugach National Forest takes in all of Prince William Sound and most of the eastern Kenai Peninsula. At 5.3 million acres, it's almost three times the size of Yellowstone National Park. Anywhere else but Alaska it would be a national park, and one of the largest and most spectacular, with some of the best sea kayaking, hiking, backpacking, wildlife watching, and scenery anywhere. General information, camping, and ideas on remote areas in the Chugach are covered below, in the Chugach National Forest section. Details about National Forest areas near towns are in the appropriate town sections.

Kenai Fjords National Park, taking in the outer edge and ice cap of the Kenai Peninsula's southern side, is incomparable in its remoteness, stark beauty, and abundance of marine wildlife. Access is though Seward. On the peninsula's western side, **Kenai National Wildlife Refuge** has Alaska's most accessible wilderness lake and river canoeing as well as extraordinary fishing, with access from roads near Soldotna. Each of those areas is covered in its own section, below.

Kachemak Bay State Park offers good sea-kayaking waters and wilderness hiking not connected to any road. The **Alaska Maritime National Wildlife Refuge** protects the wildlife habitat of remote islands and seashores around the state. Both are covered in section 10 of this chapter, on Homer.

VISITOR INFORMATION The best and most central place to get outdoor information is the ✪ **Alaska Public Lands Information Center,** 605 W. Fourth Ave., Suite 105, Anchorage, AK 99501 (☎ **907/271-2737,** or 907/271-2738 TTY; www.nps.gov/aplic/). Since most trips to the region start in Anchorage, the center makes a good first stop. You'll be able to get guidance from residents who have spent time in the places you'll be visiting, and there are exhibits on the wildlife and outdoor opportunities in the region—even maps showing where to find various species of fish. Land agencies present information on the whole state. Pick up books and maps here, too, and buy tickets for the ferries. Summer hours are daily 9am to 7pm, winter Monday to Friday 10am to 5:30pm.

Visitor centers particular to the Chugach National Forest, Kenai Fjords National Park, and Kenai National Wildlife Refuge are included in those sections below. Visitor centers for Kachemak Bay State Park and the Alaska Maritime National Wildlife Refuge are listed in section 10 of this chapter, on Homer.

STATE PARK CABINS Cabins managed by the Alaska Division of Parks stand in beautiful natural spots near Homer, Seward, and Valdez. (Other cabins in Chugach National Forest are covered in section 3, below.) It takes some effort to get to the cabins—either a hike to Caines Head State Recreation Area near Seward or Shoup Bay State Marine Park near Valdez, or a boat to Kachemak Bay State Park near Homer or the marine parks near Seward.

For information about Kachemak Bay, contact the ranger station listed in the Homer section. For Valdez or Seward, go through the **Department of Natural Resources Public Information Center—Anchorage,** 550 W. 7th Ave., Suite 1260, Anchorage, AK 99501-3557 (☎ **907/269-8400,** or 907/269-8411 TDD; fax 907/269-8901; www.dnr.state.ak.us/parks/parks.htm). The Web site is the most complete source of written information about the cabins, with a picture and description of each, a reservation form, and a real-time availability calendar, but at this writing they were accepting reservations only by mail or in person. Cabins generally cost $50 a night and can be reserved up to 6 months in advance.

2 The Seward Highway: A Road Guide

The Kenai Peninsula's main lifeline is the road down from Anchorage, a 127-mile drive to Seward on a good two-lane highway, most of it through public land without development or services. Highway 1, commonly known as the Seward Highway, is more than scenic—it's really a wonderful attraction in itself, designated a National Scenic Byway. There are excellent campgrounds and hiking trails all along the way in the Chugach National Forest, which I've covered in section 3 of this chapter.

The mileposts start in Seward. Here we count backward, since you'll likely start from Anchorage.

MILE 127–79 The highway begins at the south end of Anchorage, the only way out of town in that direction, and runs along Turnagain Arm 48 miles to the Portage Glacier. I've written about that spectacular portion of the drive in chapter 6, in the section on Turnagain Arm and Portage Glacier.

MILE 79–75 Beyond the Portage Glacier turnoff, the road traverses the salt marshes to the south side of the Arm. These wetlands are good bird-watching grounds. The dead trees on the flats are left over from before the 1964 earthquake. The area was inundated in the quake, when the entire region—the Kenai Peninsula and Prince William Sound—sank 7 feet and moved several feet laterally. Besides being the second strongest earthquake ever recorded, the '64 quake moved more land than any other. People who were here tell of their surprise to find the tide coming far higher than they had ever seen it before in the days after the earthquake, until finally they realized that the land itself had sunk. Large parts of Homer, Hope, and Seldovia disappeared under the waves when the land sank. Seward, Whittier, Valdez, and Kodiak were swept by destructive waves.

Why All the Dead Trees?

Whole mountainsides on the Kenai Peninsula and in Anchorage have turned brown. Thousands of dead trees topple in each wind storm. Homeowners all over the region have cleared treasured trees to reduce the fire danger from standing dead spruce.

The culprit? The spruce bark beetle is to blame. Although they're a natural part of the forest ecology, their population exploded in the last 2 decades and swept across Southcentral Alaska, wiping out millions of acres of white spruce (the big Sitka spruce around Resurrection Bay and Prince William Sound aren't susceptible). The beetles have always been present, boring under the outer bark layer to eat the trees' phloem, the soft inner bark that carries food manufactured in the needles down to the roots. The beetles reproduce in the tree, sending the next generation in flight in May and June in search of the next victim.

No one knows why spruce bark beetles have hit so hard now. Dry, stressed trees are more susceptible, because they lack thick-flowing sap that forces the beetles out of healthy trees. Perhaps the drier weather blamed on global warming is a factor. Or the blight may be caused by natural cycles. When Capt. James Cook explored the region in 1778, he purportedly saw treeless vistas quite different than we see today (I have been unable to verify this). Perhaps a spruce beetle epidemic had recently swept through just as today.

MILE 75–69 The highway steeply climbs through the spruce forest to the fresh, towering alpine terrain of the 1,000-foot-elevation **Turnagain Pass.** The vistas here are stupendous year-round, and if you can find dry tundra and avoid rivers, you can hike freely in any direction and appreciate the wildflowers.

MILE 69 At the summit of Turnagain Pass there's a pit toilet and a parking area used by backcountry skiers (on the left side of the road) and snowmobilers (on the right side). An avalanche near here killed five riders in spring 1999, so it's always wise to check with the Forest Service before heading into the backcountry in the winter (see section 3 this chapter, below, for contact info).

MILE 69–57 The pass forms a divide, and now Granite Creek flows down toward the south. The road follows, falling back below the tree line of stunted spruce and then popping back up into sweeping views. Arcing to the northwest after the Granite Creek Campground, the highway follows another north-flowing river, Sixmile Creek.

MILE 57 AND HOPE HIGHWAY The Hope Highway divides off to the north and west along Sixmile Creek while the Seward Highway continues south. Rafting companies based in Anchorage use this wild stretch of water for some of their most challenging rides (see chapter 6).

A SIDE TRIP TO HOPE If you take a break, you'll find **Hope** at the end of the 17-mile Hope Highway. It's a charming gold rush era village with several hiking trails and the Porcupine Campground (the trails and campground are described section 3, on Chugach National Forest). A few white frame buildings remain from the days when Hope was a gold-mining boomtown after a strike in 1895. Many of the newer buildings in the town center are quaint, too. Salmon run in Porcupine Creek, near the main street. Before the 1964 earthquake, the rest of the town used to stand where the creek gives way into a tidal meadow. Today, Hope's year-round population is about 130. The **Hope and Sunrise Historical and Mining Museum** is a one-room log cabin displaying historic objects and photographs. It's open noon to 5pm, Friday to Monday, Memorial Day to Labor Day.

If you need a room for the night in Hope, the best choice is the **Bear Creek Lodge** (☎ **907/782-3141**), with four pleasant cabins around a duck pond and two more on a creek for $80 to $90 double. They have electric heat and wood stoves and share a bathhouse. There's an inexpensive restaurant attached. Check the **Hope Chamber of Commerce** Web site (**www.advenalaska.com/Hope/**) for other choices.

MILE 57–46 The Seward Highway climbs steeply from the Hope Highway intersection, up the canyon of Canyon Creek, before leveling out above the tree line at about 1,400 feet elevation. Next come a series of alpine lakes in a narrow mountain valley.

MILE 46 The first business since the Portage Glacier, and the last for many miles, is on Summit Lake, the **Summit Lake Lodge,** at Mile 45.5 (☎ **907/595-1520**). It's a traditional log roadhouse that's been updated to house a comfortable and modern restaurant, open year-round from 8am to 10pm, and an hour earlier and later in the summer. The food is generally good, but service can suffer badly when weekend highway travelers overwhelm the staff. They do not accept credit cards. There's an ice-cream counter in the log gift shop by the lake. The six-room log motel has rooms for $80 double; they have private bathrooms, but lack TVs or phones. The canoeing photo in the color section at the front of this book was taken in this area; beware, however, of very cold water and sudden winds.

MILE 46–38 The highway continues through similar mountain terrain before descending into the trees again and branching at **Tern Lake.** There's a bird-watching platform with interpretive signs on the lake and, on the west end, a picnic area. This is an unforgettable spot year-round, and a good place to get out and taste the fresh mountain air. To the right at the intersection, the Sterling Highway leads to Cooper Landing, Kenai, Soldotna, and Homer.

MILE 33–18 Trail Lake Fish Hatchery, on Upper Trail Lake, is the first of a string of sparking mountain lakes that the road will follow for the next 15 miles.

MILE 30 The community of Moose Pass, with a population of 120, sits on the shore of Upper Trail Lake.

MILE 18–0 Down among the big spruces of the coastal forest, the highway comes to Seward.

3 Chugach National Forest: Do-It-Yourself Wilderness

I've lived near the Chugach National Forest all my life, but it wasn't until well into adulthood that I had seen all its parts and appreciated its vastness and variety. Still, I doubt I'll ever really know this seemingly infinite land.

Prince William Sound, just one of the National Forest's three parts, has 3,500 miles of shoreline among its folded islands and deeply penetrating fjords and passages. It would take a lifetime to really know all those cove beaches, climb all the island mountains, and explore to the head of every narrow bay under big rain forest trees.

The **Copper River Delta** is another world entirely. Unlike the musty secrets of the Sound's obscure passages, the delta opens to the sky like a heavenly plain of wind and light, its waving green colors splashed by the airiest brushstrokes. It's another huge area: Just driving across the delta and back from Cordova takes most of a day.

Finally, there's the western part of the national forest, on the **Kenai Peninsula.** This is largely an alpine realm. The mountains are steep, their timber quickly giving way to rock, tundra, and wildflowers up above. It's got remote, unclimbed peaks, but also many miles of family hiking trails, accessible fishing streams, and superb campgrounds. This is where you go in Alaska for multiday trail hikes.

The Chugach is managed primarily for recreation and conservation, although there is some logging, too. Visitors today may see large tracts of dead spruce and sometimes areas of cut timber, but these mostly are caused by a blight, the spruce bark beetle. The trees are cut in the forest and on private land to prevent fires in the standing deadwood. Logging in Prince William Sounds was slowed by the *Exxon Valdez* oil spill, when conservationists recognized the need to prevent further environmental damage to support recovery from the disaster. When Exxon was forced to pay $1 billion to a recovery fund, government trustees spent much of the money to buy back timber rights in the Sound and beyond to protect them. So far they've bought roughly as much land as is in all of Yosemite National Park—a lot of land, but only a sixth of what the Chugach already encompassed.

ESSENTIALS

GETTING THERE & GETTING AROUND There are many ways to the Chugach National Forest. For Prince William Sound, use Whittier, Valdez, or Cordova as gateways; for the Copper River Delta, go through Cordova. Trails and campgrounds on the Kenai Peninsula generally meet the Seward or Sterling highways, or spur roads from the highways. The individual town listings later in this chapter provide details on how to get there and into the national forest. Section 2, above describes the Seward Highway.

VISITOR INFORMATION The most central place for information on the national forest is the Alaska Public Lands Information Center in Anchorage, which is listed in full in section 1 of this chapter.

For general forest inquiries, you can also contact the **forest headquarters,** 3301 C St., Ste. 300, Anchorage, AK 99503 (☎ **907/271-2500;** www.fs.fed.us/r10/chugach).

The national forest also has three ranger district offices, where you can get up-to-date local information and personal advice: **Glacier Ranger District,** on Monarch Mine Road, near the Seward Highway off Alyeska Road, Girdwood (☎ **907/783-3242**); **Seward Ranger District,** Fourth Avenue and Jefferson Street, Seward (☎ **907/224-3374**); and **Cordova Ranger District,** Second and Browning streets, Cordova (☎ **907/424-7661**). You can't reserve campground sites and remote cabins through these local offices—for that you must use the national system listed below under "Accommodations"—but you can call them with questions.

GETTING OUTSIDE

HIKING, MOUNTAIN BIKING & BACKPACKING

Alaska's best long trails lead through the mountain passes of Chugach National Forest, including historic gold rush trails and portions of the original Iditarod trail (the race doesn't use these southern portions). The Forest Service maintains **public cabins** on many of these trails, and in other remote spots reachable only on foot or with a boat or small plane. If the nights you need are available, you can use the cabins instead of a tent on a backpacking trip. Or make a cabin your destination and spend a few days there hiking or fishing.

I've covered trails near Cordova in section 14 of this chapter, and some shorter hikes are mentioned below with the campgrounds under "Accommodations." Also check for hikes outside the national forest in the town sections.

The best trail guide covering the peninsula is ***55 Ways to the Wilderness*** by Helen Neinhueser and John Wolfe Jr., published by The Mountaineers (www.mountaineers.org/). ***Kenai Pathways,*** published by the Alaska Natural History Association (www.AlaskaNHA.org/), is available from their Web site or the Public Lands Information Center for $4.95. It contains official guidance for 25 peninsula trails, which coordinate with numbers on the excellent **Trails Illustrated** plastic map (see "Fast Facts: Alaska" in chapter 2).

RESURRECTION PASS TRAIL This gold rush trail begins 4 miles above the town of Hope (mentioned above in the preceding section on the Seward Highway) and runs over the top of the Kenai Peninsula to Cooper Landing (covered in section 7 of this chapter). It's a beautiful, remote, yet well-used trail for hiking, mountain biking, Nordic skiing, or snowshoeing; it rises through forest, crossing the alpine pass, and then descends again to a highway trailhead where you'll need to have transportation waiting. The 39-mile trail has eight public-use cabins, available for $35 to $45 a night. (See "Accommodations," below, for reservation information.) The cabins are well spaced to cover the trail in an easy 5 days, and those on lakes have boats for fishing. They are booked up well ahead winter and summer, but there are lots of good camping spots, too. The **Devil's Pass and Summit Lake trails** cut off from the Resurrection to the Seward Highway south of Summit Lake, shortening the route. The difficulty of doing the whole trail, by any of the entrances, is that you either need two cars or someone willing to drive you back to your starting point.

RESURRECTION RIVER & RUSSIAN LAKE TRAILS These two connected trails begin in Cooper Landing (covered in section 7 of this chapter), near the end of the Resurrection Pass Trail, and ultimately lead to Exit Glacier, outside of Seward, 33 miles away from Cooper Landing. Linked together, the Resurrection Pass and River trails took pioneers 72 miles from Seward to Hope, all the way across the peninsula. This less-used section provides access to excellent fishing and wildlife viewing (bears are common) and has a series of four cabins. Call ahead to the Seward Ranger District to check trail conditions, which can be rough.

JOHNSON PASS TRAIL The 23-mile trail climbs to a pair of lakes above the tree line at the 1,450-foot Johnson Creek Summit, tracing impressively narrow mountain valleys. The route, part of the Iditarod National Historic Trail, leads from near the Trail Lake Fish Hatchery, at mile 32 of the Seward Highway, to near the Granite Creek Campground, on the highway at mile 63, so you do need transportation at each end.

LOST LAKE TRAIL & PRIMROSE TRAIL With their fields of alpine wildflowers and small lakes, these connected trails offer one of the most beautiful hikes in the area. Snow lasts until late in the season up top. The upper, northern trailhead is at the 10-site Primrose Campground, on vast Kenai Lake, 17 miles from Seward off the Seward Highway on Primrose Road. The trail rises through hemlock past a waterfall about 2 miles up (look for the spur to the right when you hear water), past an old mining cabin, and then through ever smaller trees and above the tree line. The Dale Clemens Forest Service cabin stands on a 2-mile spur about 11 miles along the 15.8-mile route; it rents for $45. The south, Lost Lake trailhead is near Seward.

FISHING

The national forest contains some of the most famous, and crowded, fishing banks in Alaska, including the **Russian River,** near Cooper Landing, with its incredible run of red salmon in July and good fishing lasting into September. Easiest access is at the Russian River Campground, just west of the village. There are plenty of other roadside salmon streams and remote fishing rivers and lakes in the national forest where you can lose sight of other anglers, or even be all alone. Some remote lakes have Forest Service cabins for rent on their shores, with rowboats. The Forest Service publishes information on these opportunities. You can also get information or a book from the Alaska Department of Fish and Game before you come; see chapter 2.

SEA KAYAKING & BOATING

A variety of Prince William Sound tour boats are listed in the Whittier, Valdez, and Cordova sections of this chapter. Whittier is the best starting point, with the greatest number of choices.

All three communities also have operators offering sea-kayak rentals and guided outings of various lengths. The best sea kayaking is east of Whittier, an area of long fjords, calving glaciers, narrow passages, and Forest Service cabins, but to get out there you need a boat ride first—the waters right around Whittier aren't as interesting. The local sea-kayaking operators can help you arrange drop-off service. Cordova has more interesting waters right near town, so you can paddle right from the boat harbor. Those who haven't done much sea kayaking should only consider a guided trip; if you're a raw beginner, start with a day trip.

For those who aren't up to paddling but don't want to ride a big tour boat, renting a skiff is a great alternative for an independent day trip. Operators in the Valdez and Cordova harbors offer rentals and fishing gear. My wife and I enjoy taking a boat out just to explore remote beaches with the kids.

ACCOMMODATIONS

REMOTE CABINS

There is no more authentic Alaska accommodation than a pioneer cabin with a wood stove—a place to give you a better feel for the soul of a wild place. Chugach National Forest maintains more than 40 remote recreation cabins for rent to the public. This is simple shelter: Cabins don't have electricity or plumbing, you bring your own sleeping bags, cooking equipment, and other gear, and the cabin is only as clean as the last user left it. But no other room you can rent has a better location or greater privacy. Some cabins are along hiking and skiing trails, others on shores where boats and kayaks can pull up, and others on remote fishing lakes accessible only by floatplane. You can stay up to a week in most, with a summer limit of 3 days in the Resurrection Trail cabins.

The Forest Service prints a free listing of the cabins with short descriptions of each. The maps are rudimentary, so you will need a detailed map such as the Trails Illustrated plastic map mentioned in "Fast Facts: Alaska" in chapter 2, which shows cabin locations and names. Cabins rent for $35 or $45 a night, with most priced at $45 a night. Typically, the price of the cabin itself is not your major expense: You'll need a way to get there, either by plane, boat, or by having a vehicle to drive to a trailhead and then hiking. If you're flying, contact flight services in the nearest town (listed in the sections below) to find out the cost *before* you book the cabin. Flight time is several hundred dollars an hour. You can rent the equipment you'll need at the businesses listed in the Anchorage section, but you should talk to a ranger first to get details about access and what to take.

The National Recreation Reservation Service (NRRS), operated by **Reserve America,** a company in upstate New York, handles the reservation system. Use them to book a cabin, but contact the ranger stations first to choose a cabin that is right for you and to find out what to expect. The easiest way to reserve a cabin is online at **www.reserveusa.com**, because you use its interactive maps and availability calendars to shop for open days at various cabins. To reserve by phone, call ☎ **877/444-6777,** 877/833-6777 TDD, or 518/885-3639 with toll from overseas. In the summer, the lines are open daily 8am to midnight eastern standard time; winter hours are daily 10am to 7pm. They take American Express, Discover, MasterCard, and Visa, or you can reserve on the phone and then pay by certified check. Cabins and campground sites are available for reservation on a first-come, first-served basis. Campsites can be reserved starting 240 days ahead, cabins 180 days ahead.

Campgrounds

Forest Service campgrounds mostly have pit toilets and water from hand pumps, and roads usually are not paved. But some of these places are truly spectacular. I've listed them in order of distance from Anchorage, counting in reverse direction on the Seward Highway mileposts. For information on campgrounds below mile 60, call the Seward Ranger District; for the others, call the Glacier Ranger District, in Girdwood (see "Visitor Information," above). Sites in a few of the following campgrounds, as noted, take reservations through the national system explained above.

Williwaw and Black Bear. Mile 4, Portage Glacier Rd. (turn at mile 78 Seward Hwy.). Williwaw: 60 sites. $10 per night. Reservations accepted with additional fee. Black Bear: 12 sites. $9 per night.

These two campgrounds are next to each other near Portage Glacier, along a creek where you can watch spawning red salmon in mid-August (no fishing is allowed, though). Williwaw, one of the better-developed campgrounds in the national forest, with paved roads and pumped water, is intended primarily for RVs.

Bertha Creek. Mile 65.5, Seward Hwy. 12 sites. $10 per night.

This one's in the high country, near gold-panning sites on the creek.

Granite Creek. Mile 63, Seward Hwy. 19 sites. $10 per night.

Near the Johnson Pass trailhead, this campground offers gold panning on the creek.

✪ **Porcupine.** At the end of the Hope Hwy. 24 sites. $10 per night.

This campground near the gold rush village of Hope is among the most beautiful in the Chugach National Forest, or the state. The sites are on a mountainside overlooking Turnagain Arm, five with sweeping ocean views. The thick trees make for privacy, but also mosquitoes. Bring repellent. Two good day hikes leave from the campground: The level 5-mile trail to **Gull Rock** makes a good family ramble, and with some effort you can scramble down to remote beaches along the way, where we've enjoyed a picnic. The **Hope Point Trail** is a stiff climb that rises 3,600 feet to expansive views. See "The Seward Highway: A Road Guide" above, for more on Hope.

Tenderfoot Creek. Mile 46, Seward Hwy. 27 sites. $10 per night.

This pleasant campground lies across Summit Lake from the Seward Highway as it passes through a narrow mountain valley above the tree line. Campsites look out on the water from a peaceful, sunny hillside. The nearby Summit Lake Lodge, described in section 2 of this chapter on the Seward Highway, offers good meals, and is the only business for many a mile.

Ptarmigan Creek and Trail River. Mile 23, Seward Hwy. 16 and 63 sites, respectively. Reservations accepted, with additional fee. $10 per night.

Near the tiny towns of Moose Pass and Crown Point, the Ptarmigan Creek campground is at the trailhead for the trail to Ptarmigan lake, 4 miles away with only 500 feet elevation gain—a good place for a picnic or fishing for Dolly Varden char and rainbow trout. Trail River campground is a mile away and on the other side of the highway.

✪ **Primrose.** Mile 17, Seward Hwy. 10 sites. $10 per night.

Another favorite, this lovely campground lies on the edge of Kenai Lake and at the base of the Primrose Trail to Lost Lake, one of the area's most beautiful (see "Getting

Outside," above). This campground is the closest to Seward that has a sense of natural isolation.

Russian River. Mile 52, Sterling Hwy., just west of Cooper Landing. Reservations accepted, with additional fee. 84 sites. 3 day limit. Flush toilets. $13 per night.

This large, well-developed campground mainly serves fishermen pursuing red salmon on the river. When the fishing is good, the campground overflows and can be noisy. Overnight parking is $4. Reserve ahead.

Cooper Creek. Mile 50.7, Sterling Hwy. Reservations accepted. 26 sites. $10 per night.

The campground is in Cooper Landing, with 10 sites right on the Kenai River.

Quartz Creek. Quartz Creek Rd., at mile 45 Sterling Hwy. 45 sites. Flush toilets, boat launch. $13 per night.

This campground is on Kenai Lake, in Cooper Landing, with good lake and stream fishing.

Crescent Creek. Mile 3 Quartz Creek Rd., at mile 45 Sterling Hwy. Flush toilets. $10 per night.

A couple of miles short of Cooper Landing, the campground is quieter and more secluded than the others, near the Crescent Lake trailhead. The 6.5-mile trail leads to the Crescent Lake Forest Service Cabin, where a boat is provided for grayling fishing.

4 Whittier: Dock on the Sound

Whittier is Anchorage's portal to Prince William Sound. Although Anchorage itself is on Upper Cook Inlet, that muddy, fast-moving water is little used for recreational boating. Whittier, on the other hand, stands on the edge of a long fjord in the northwest corner of the Sound, whose clear waters are full of salmon, orcas, and otters, and bounded by rain forests and glaciers. In the past, the difficulty of getting to Whittier—through a mountain by train—helped to limit the number of people from Anchorage who would go there. Now they're paved the railway tunnel, creating a one-lane highway and putting Whittier little more than an hour away from the city. The new Anton Anderson Memorial Tunnel is the longest highway tunnel in North America, and among the most inconvenient to use, since it is open to traffic only during certain brief periods during the day. (Anderson was the chief engineer when the tunnel was built during World War II.)

Whittier certainly has major advantages for visitors seeking to get out on the water. The water is calmer here than in Kenai Fjords National Park, so seasickness is rare, and the glaciers are even more numerous. One company's selling point is a "26-glacier cruise," all done in a day trip from Anchorage by rail and large tour boat (see below). Prince William Sound boats also see otters and sometimes whales; Kenai Fjords tours, on the other hand, more often see whales and see more birds. Sea kayakers also have great places to go from Whittier. Almost all of Prince William Sound is in Chugach National Forest, with its public-use cabins in lovely, remote spots on the shores (see section 13 of this chapter).

There's little other reason to go to Whittier—unless you're on a quest to find the oddest towns in America. Most of the 300 townspeople live in a single 14-story concrete building with dark, narrow hallways. The grocery store is on the first floor and the medical clinic on the third. The rest of the people live in one other building. **The Begich Towers,** as the dominant structure is called, was built during the 1940s, when Whittier's strategic location on the Alaska Railroad and at the head of a deep

Prince William Sound fjord made it a key port in the defense of Alaska. Today, with its barren gravel ground and ramshackle warehouses and boat sheds, the town maintains a stark military-industrial character. The pass above the town is a funnel for frequent whipping winds, it always seems to rain, and the glaciers above the town keep it cool even in summer. As one young town ambassador told me once when I was on a visit, "You're thinking, 'Thank God I don't live here,' right?" The official boosters look more on the bright side: Having everyone live in one building saves on snow removal in a place that gets an average of 20 feet per winter. Kids don't even have to go outside to get to school—a tunnel leads from the tower to the school.

An **ATM** is located at the liquor store near the boat harbor, but Whittier lacks a bank and other services, so bring what you need.

ESSENTIALS

GETTING THERE **By Car** Take the Seward Highway to the Portage Glacier Road, at mile 79 (48 miles from Anchorage). The new road through the 2.8-mile long World War II rail tunnel to Whittier is only one lane, so you'll have to wait your turn to go through. Get the schedule through the tunnel's Web site (www.dot.state.ak.us/whittiertunnel/), its toll-free number (☎ **877/611-2586**), or by tuning to 1610AM in the Portage or 530AM in Whittier. It is important to check the schedule, because the tunnel is open to vehicles each way only during certain periods of the day—the rest of the time, the railroad has priority. You could wait for hours if you time it wrong. The tunnel closes altogether at night. Summer hours are daily 6am to 11pm; winter Wednesday to Monday 8am to 5pm, Tuesday 7am to 9pm. The toll is $15 for cars and vans, $40 for RVs, and it is charged only going toward Whittier. Parking in Whittier is $5 a day. A good deal could change, however, as the tunnel opened only in June 2000.

By Train If you plan to take a day trip on the Sound from a base in Anchorage—the way most people use Whittier—you can leave the car behind and take the train straight from the Anchorage depot. The **Alaska Railroad** (☎ **800/544-0552** or 907/265-2494; www.akrr.com) runs a nicely appointed daily train with a dining car timed to match the schedules of Prince William Sound tour boats. Unless you have planned an activity or tour on the water, however, you'll find the 6-hour stay in Whittier is too long to just hang around. The round-trip fare is $52 adults, $26 ages 2 to 11. The train ride is scenic and fun, but if there are more than one of you along, a rental car will save you money.

By Bus To save modestly over the train ride, you can take a Grayline of Alaska bus (☎ **800/544-2206** or 907/277-5581; www.graylineofalaska.com) that leaves from the downtown Anchorage hotels daily at 11am in summer. The fare is $40 for adults, half price for children (I'd spend $12 more to take the train).

By Ferry The **Alaska Marine Highway System** ferry *Bartlett* (☎ **800/642-0066,** or 800/764-3779 TDD; www.dot.state.ak.us/external/amhs/home.html) makes a 6½-hour run to Valdez several times a week, where you can drive north on the beautiful Richardson Highway, completing a circle back to Anchorage in 2 days or more. The fare is $72 for a car up to 15 feet long plus $58 for an adult passenger, with ages 2 to 11 roughly half price. The ferry also runs once a week direct from Whittier to Cordova, a 7-hour trip, or you can go by way of Valdez several times a week in roughly 15 hours. A Chugach National Forest ranger interprets the scenery in the observation lounge, and there is a serviceable little restaurant aboard. See section 1 of chapter 5 for more on the ferry system.

VISITOR INFORMATION Contact the **Greater Whittier Chamber of Commerce,** P.O. Box 607, Whittier, AK 99693 (☎ **907/472-2461**); or you may have more luck calling the city clerk at ☎ **907/472-2327.** There is no visitor center.

GETTING OUT ON THE SOUND

Whittier is the entrance to western Prince William Sound, and home to its most protected waters, with long, deep fjords and tiny islands and passages. You're likely to see marine mammals and eagles. Glaciers lurk at the heads of many of the fjords, dumping ice in the water for the tour boats that cruise from Whittier.

LARGE TOUR BOATS

Several companies, mostly based in downtown Anchorage, compete for your business for day-trip tours to the Sound's western glaciers. Besides the incredible scenery, the water is calm, making seasickness unlikely—for the queasy, this is a much better choice than Kenai Fjords National Park. Each operator times departures to coordinate with the daily Alaska Railroad train from Anchorage, described above, which means they have 6 hours for the trip. Some try to see as much as possible, while others take it slower to savor the scenery and wildlife sightings. Between the train and boat fare, expect to spend $175 per person for this day's outing. You can save some of that by taking the bus or driving (see "Getting There," above). Lunch is generally included on the trips that span the lunch hour, and boats usually also have snack bars.

Besides the listings below, **Prince William Sound Glacier Quest** (☎ **888/305-2515;** www.wildlifequest.com) offers the same service; it is a highly regarded company from Southeast Alaska that recently added service here. The adult fare is $115.

Phillips' Cruises and Tours. 519 W. Fourth Ave., Suite 100, Anchorage, AK 99501. ☎ **800/544-0529** or 907/276-8023. www.26glaciers.com. $119 adults, $59 children ages 2–11.

The 26-glacier cruise travels the Sound on a fast three-deck catamaran, counting the glaciers as they go.

Major Marine Tours. 411 W. Fourth Ave., Anchorage, AK 99501. ☎ **800/764-7300** or 907/274-7300. www.majormarine.com. $99 adults, $49 children ages 11 and under.

This company operates a smaller, 149-passenger vessel at a slower pace than Phillips—they hit a mere 10 glaciers, but spend more time waiting for them to calve. They also put more emphasis on their food, which costs extra; the salmon or prime rib buffet is $10 for adults, $5 for children.

Prince William Sound Cruises and Tours. P.O. Box 1297, Valdez, AK 99686. ☎ **800/992-1297** or 907/835-4731. www.princewilliamsound.com. Sightseeing cruise from Whittier $109 adults, $54 children ages 4–11; free for children under 4. Whittier to Valdez trip (one way): $119 adults, $59 children.

This Native-owned company offers a tour boat ride that connects Whittier and Valdez, with sightseeing along the way, as well as a 6-hour cruise from Whittier like the other operators. See section 13 of this chapter, on Valdez, for more on the company.

SMALL BOAT TOURS

Instead of getting on a giant tour boat with a mob of people, you can go on a small boat with a local who you'll get to know as he shows off favorite places and lands on beaches to picnic and walk. If you see a whale or other point of interest, you stay as long or as short a time as you like. What you give up is the comfort of a large, tour-bus like vessel, and most small boats have a four-person minimum.

Sound Eco Adventures. P.O. Box 707, Whittier, AK 99693. ☎ **888/471-2312** or 888/472-2312. www.SoundEcoAdventure.com/. 10-hour wildlife cruise $175 per person, or rent the whole boat for $100/hour.

Gerry Sanger is a retired wildlife biologist who spent years researching the waterfowl and ecology of Prince William Sound. Now he carries up to six passengers at a time on wildlife and glacier tours and does kayak drop-offs from his 29-foot aluminum boat, which has a large side door for wheelchairs and is perfect for landing on gravel beaches. He claims a 90% success rate on whale-watching trips, quite high for the Sound.

Honey Charters. On the Whittier waterfront (P.O. Box 708), Whittier, AK 99693. ☎ **907/472-2493.** www.honeycharters.com. 3-hour cruise $99 per person, 6 hours $149 per person, 11 hours $199 person.

This family runs small boats licensed for 6 to 10 passengers, specializing in personal tours and water transportation. They operate with a minimum of 4 passengers and a maximum of 10; by paying the four-person minimum, you can have the boat to yourself. They also book fishing charters and drop off kayakers.

Longer Cruises

If you have more time to spend, several operators offer cruises of a few days and longer in the Sound on vessels small enough to allow exploration of its protected waters.

Cruise West. Fourth and Battery Building, Seattle, WA 98121. ☎ **800/888-9378.** www.cruisewest.com. Fares from $775 per person for 3- or 4-night Prince William Sound cruises.

This is the largest of the small-ship cruise companies, offering a full package of tours and cruises statewide (see chapter 4). Their Prince William Sound trips last 3 or 4 nights aboard the 52-passenger *Spirit of Glacier Bay* and 78-passenger *Spirit of Columbia.*

Discovery Voyages. P.O. Box 688, Whittier, AK 99693. ☎ **800/324-7602.** www.discoveryvoyages.com. Basic 5-day cruise $2,250 per person.

For a truly intimate cruise, this company operates a classic 65-foot vessel built in the 1950s for missionary work. There are only six cabins, each sleeping two passengers. Most trips go from Whittier, with itineraries that cover just about every corner of the Sound.

Fishing

More than a dozen charter fishing boats operate out of Whittier, the closest saltwater fishing to Anchorage, targeting salmon and halibut. You can get a list from the visitor center or book through **Bread and Butter Charters** (☎ **888/472-2396** or 907/472-2396; www.alaska.net/~junebbak.com), which represents its own vessel and four other boats. They charge $170 per person for a day of fishing on 35- to 37-foot vessels, and have an office on the waterfront. Honey Charters, listed above under "Tour Boats," has a similar service.

Sea Kayaking

Whittier is a popular starting point for kayak trips to the beautiful and protected western Prince William Sound. Day trips for beginners paddle along the shore near Whittier, often visiting a bird rookery, or take a boat 5 miles from the harbor to Shotgun Cove and paddle back. Longer multiday trips go by boat to even more interesting waters where you can visit glaciated fjords and paddle narrow passages.

Several businesses compete in Whittier. **Alaska Sea-Kayakers** offers 3- and 5-hour day trips, for $60 and $115, respectively, and paddles at Blackstone Glacier that begin with a charter boat ride, for $250. They also have an office in Whittier for kayak rentals. Call them at ☎ **877/472-5753** for day trips, or 907/472-2534 for rentals and custom tours; alaskaseakayakers.com. The **Prince William Sound Kayak Center** (☎ **907/472-2452** in summer or 907/276-7235 year-round; pwskayakcenter.com) offers guided 2-hour trips starting at $65 for a single person or $50 each for a couple, and escorted trips of 2 to 4 days. The 2-day trip is $140 per person, minimum two people. **Alaska Outdoor Adventures** (☎ **888-414-7669** or 907-783-7669; www.seakayakingalaska.com) offers a 5-hour trip for $99, 3 hours for $65, and rents kayaks.

Experienced paddlers can plan their own trip, renting kayaks for out of Whittier for around $40 a day for a single, $60 double. Most people charter a boat to drop them off among the islands beyond the long, deep fjord in which Whittier is located. Honey Charters, listed above under "Tour Boats," offers a drop-off service. There are six Forest Service cabins in this idyllic area off Port Wells. Unfortunately, they're so popular that they must be reserved months ahead. The Forest Service or Alaska Public Lands Information Center in Anchorage can tell you where to find campsites, too. For information and cabin reservations, see section 3, "Chugach National Forest: Do-It-Yourself Wilderness."

ACCOMMODATIONS & DINING

Most meals served in Whittier are for people grabbing a sandwich while waiting for a boat or otherwise passing through. The choice of inexpensive eateries in the shopping area at the east end of the boat harbor seems to change year to year, so I've given up listing them; you will certainly be able to find a sandwich or such.

June's Whittier Bed and Breakfast Condo Suites. P.O. Box 715, Whittier, AK 99693. ☎ **888/472-2396** or 907/472-2396. Fax 907/472-2503. www.alaska.net/~junebbak.com. 7 units. TV TEL. $95–$135 double. Extra person over age 11 $15. AE, MC, V.

These seven units, located right in the Begich Towers, come with full kitchens and one, two, or three bedrooms. Some are nicely remodeled, with great views, VCRs, and other extras. The friendly hostess, June Miller, charges by the person. She and her husband, Ken, also have a fishing charter and sightseeing business, Bread and Butter Charters, listed above.

5 Seward: Gateway to Resurrection Bay & Kenai Fjords

The main reason to go to Seward has always been Resurrection Bay and the access the port provides to Alaska. This agreeable little town started life as a place to fish and to get off the boat for Alaska, then continued as a place for Alaskans and visitors to get *on* boats and see the bay—Kenai Fjords National Park (described in section 6 of this chapter). With the growth of the cruise industry, Seward again is a place to get off the boat. Most cruises that cross the Gulf of Alaska start or end here, with their passengers taking a bus to or from the airport in Anchorage. That flow of people has brought a lot of tourist development to town, mostly of a quality that hasn't damaged the town's character.

Located by the broad fjord of Resurrection Bay, Seward is a mountainside grid of streets lined with old wood-frame houses and newer fishermen's residences. It's long been the sort of place where pedestrians casually wander across the road, hardly glancing for cars, for there likely won't be any, or, if there are, they'll be ready to stop. The growing tourism industry is bringing more traffic, but most of what's new has been good for the town. The largest addition, the Alaska SeaLife Center, is a research

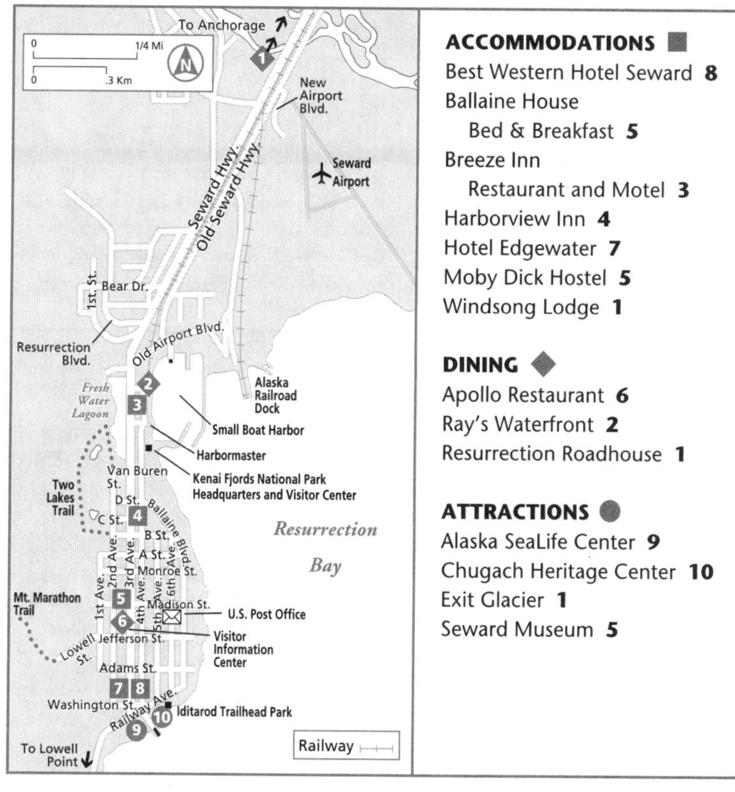

aquarium that's also open to the public; it dominates the waterfront in downtown Seward near a brand-new hotel. Finished in 1998, the center shows off seals, sea lions, marine birds, and the scientists who are studying them in impressive exhibits. Its $50 million price tag was funded mostly by money won from Exxon after the *Exxon Valdez* oil spill. Combined with Seward's excellent ocean fishing, the national park, the wonderful hiking trails, and the unique and attractive town, the new center is helping make this one of Alaska's most appealing towns for a 2-day visit.

Seward's history is among the oldest in Alaska. The Russian governor Alexander Baranof stopped here in 1793, named Resurrection Bay, and built a ship, which later sank, probably because Baranof's workers didn't have proper materials. The town was born in its modern form in 1903, when a company seeking to build a railroad north came ashore. They failed, but Seward still was an important port. Gold prospectors blazed trails from here to finds on Turnagain Arm starting in 1891, and in 1907 the army linked those trails with others all the way to Nome, finishing the Iditarod Trail. Today that route is discontinuous south of Anchorage, but you can follow it through Seward and hike a portion of it through the Johnson Pass north of town (described above in section 3 of this chapter on Chugach National Forest).

More relevant for current visitors and the local economy, the federal government took over the failed railroad-building effort in 1915, finishing the line to Fairbanks in 1923. Until the age of jet travel, most people coming to Alaska arrived by steamer in Seward and then traveled north by rail. The train ride to Anchorage, daily during the summer, is supremely beautiful.

ESSENTIALS

GETTING THERE **By Car** See section 2 of this chapter, on the Seward Highway, for how to make the spectacular 127-mile drive down from Anchorage. All major car-rental agencies are represented in Anchorage.

By Bus The **Seward Bus Line** (☎ **907/224-3608** in Seward or 907/563-0800 in Anchorage; www.sewardbus.com) makes one trip daily, year-round, starting in Seward and going to Anchorage and back; the fare is $35 one way. They'll pick up and drop off passengers anywhere on route and, for an extra $5, take you to the airport.

Gray Line's **Alaskon Express** (☎ **800/544-2206;** www.graylineofalaska.com/alaskon.cfm), operating in summer only, instead leaves Anchorage in the morning and returns in the evening, charging $40.

The Park Connection (☎ **800/208-0200** or 907/245-0200; www.alaska-bus.com/) connects Seward with Anchorage, Talkeetna, and Denali National Park with two buses daily in each direction. The fare is $39 to Anchorage, $98 to Denali.

By Train The train ride between Anchorage and Seward is one of miraculous beauty. The **Alaska Railroad** (☎ **800/544-0552** or 907/265-2494; www.akrr.com) offers passenger service from Anchorage and back daily in summer. The route is even more spectacular than the highway, passing close by glaciers and following a ledge halfway up the narrow, vertical Placer River gorge, where it ducks into tunnels and pops out at bends in the river. The landscape looks just as it did when the first person beheld it. The railroad's young guides are well trained and provide an accurate and not overly verbose commentary. The fare is $50 one way, $86 round-trip; children ages 2 to 11 half price. A rental car will almost always be cheaper, but the train ride is unforgettable. The railroad also offers packages that include a boat tour of Kenai Fjords National Park, but I advise against trying to get down from Anchorage, do the park, and return all in the same day—it's too much.

By Air **F.S. Air** (☎ **907/248-9595** in Anchorage or 907/224-5920 in Seward) serves Seward from Anchorage twice a day for $69 one way, $99 round-trip.

By Ferry The ferry *Tustumena,* of the Alaska Marine Highway System (☎ **800/642-0066** or 907/224-5485; www.dot.state.ak.us/external/amhs/home.html), once a week connects Seward with Valdez (11 hours to the east), with stops by reservation in the Prince William Sound Alaska Native village of Chenega Bay, and Kodiak (14 hours to the southwest). The adult passenger fare for Valdez is $58, Kodiak $54; ages 2 to 11 are about half price. Leaving from Homer cuts off more than 4 hours to Kodiak. Once a month, the *Kennicott* travels from Juneau across the Gulf of Alaska to Valdez and then Seward. The $148 fare is a bargain, but it takes more than 50 hours. The terminal is at the cruise ship dock, on the outside of the small-boat harbor.

GETTING AROUND You can easily cover downtown Seward on foot, although a little help is handy to get back and forth from the boat harbor. If it's not raining, a bike may be the best way. **Seward Mountain Bike Shop** (☎ **907/224-2448**), in a railcar near the depot at the harbor, rents high-performance mountain bikes and models good for just getting around town, plus accessory equipment. A cruiser is $12 half day, $19 full day. The **Chamber of Commerce Trolley** runs every half hour from 10am to 7pm daily in summer; it goes south along Third Avenue and north on Ballaine Street, stopping at the railroad depot, the cruise-ship dock, the Alaska SeaLife Center, and the harbor visitor center. The fare is $2 per trip, or $4 to ride all day. **Independent Taxi** (☎ **907/224-5000**) is one of the cab companies.

VISITOR INFORMATION The **Seward Chamber of Commerce,** P.O. Box 749, Seward, AK 99664 (☎ **907/224-8051;** www.sewardak.org), has four visitor centers.

The one on the right side of the Seward Highway as you enter town is open year-round (summer 8am to 5pm Monday to Friday, 9am to 5pm Saturday, 9am to 4pm Sunday; winter closed weekends). Summer-only centers are in a kiosk at Small Boat Harbor, downtown in an old Alaska Railroad car at the corner of Third Avenue and Jefferson Street, and on the cruise-ship dock. They can help with business information and last-minute help finding a room.

A local Internet provider, Seward Internet Services, has links to many local businesses at **www.seward.net/links.html**.

In addition to these town information sources, don't miss the **Kenai Fjords National Park Visitor Center,** covered in section 6, later in this chapter. For contacts for the Chugach National Forest, see section 3.

SPECIAL EVENTS The ✪ **Fourth of July** is the biggest day of the year in Seward, when the whole town explodes with visitors, primarily from Anchorage. Besides the parade and many small-town festivities, the main attraction is the **Mount Marathon Race,** run every year since it started as a bar bet in 1915. The racers go from the middle of town straight up rocky Mount Marathon to its 3,022-foot peak, then tumble down again, arriving muddy and bloody at the finish line in town. Binoculars allow you to see the whole thing from town, including the pratfalls of the runners on their way down.

The **Silver Salmon Derby** starts the second Saturday of August and runs 10 days, although the peak of silver season comes later. The chamber of commerce visitor centers can provide information.

FAST FACTS There are **ATMs** at the First National Bank of Anchorage, 303 Fourth Ave., in the Eagle Quality Center grocery store at Seward Highway mile 2, and in the Alaska SeaLife Center, among other places.

Providence Seward Medical Center is at 417 First Ave. (☎ **907/224-5205**).

Eagle Eye Photo (☎ **907/224-2022;** www.eagleyephoto.com), at the boat harbor, charges $2.50 for 15 minutes of Internet access on their machine, and has 1-hour photo developing, too.

For nonemergency situations, call the **Seward Police Department** (☎ **907/224-3338**) or, outside the city limits, the **Alaska State Troopers** (☎ **907/224-3346**).

The post office is at Fifth Avenue and Madison Street.

Sales tax is 5%. The **room tax** totals 9%.

GETTING OUTSIDE

Here I've described things to do out of Seward other than the national park, which includes the fjords and Exit Glacier. See section 6, "Kenai Fjords National Park," later in this chapter, for that information.

BOATING & SEA KAYAKING

Introductory sea-kayaking trips stay in Resurrection Bay. **Sunny Cove Sea Kayaking** (☎ **800/770-9119** for reservations, or 907/224-8810; www.sunnycove.com/) offers day trips suitable for beginners as part of the Kenai Fjords Tours trips to its Fox Island (see the Kenai Fjords National Park section below), and also offer their own tours right from Seward. They've earned a good reputation in 5 years of operation. They launch from a base on Lowell Point, about a mile south of the downtown area, following the shore toward Caines Head State Recreation Area, where you can see sea otters, sea birds, intertidal creatures, and other wildlife. Three-hour paddles are $59; 5-hour trips are $99. They also offer multiday trips to the national park and beyond, for those who know they like kayaking. A 2-night trip costs $749; 4 nights cost $1,299.

Also at Lowell Point, **Miller's Landing** (☎ **907/224-5739;** www.millerslandingak.com) is a good place to know about if you intend to spend any time outdoors around Seward. They have a campground (described below), a boat launch with skiffs and sea kayaks for rent, and sea-kayak lessons and tours. Skiffs are $150 a day; kayaks are $45 a day single, $55 double, $10 less after the first day; kayak lessons are $20 an hour; guided day trips are $48 to $98. In the little bait shop and grocery store, a wood stove burns and a coffee pot fuels ongoing discussions on fish and boats. The guys here will teach you how to fish for salmon and send you out on your own or on a guided charter. A water-taxi operation charges flat rates to get to remote beaches and public cabins around the bay or the national park, for sea kayakers or those who just want to get off on their own ($30 one way to Caines Head, $250 round-trip to the park service cabin in Aialik Bay).

Book **sailing charters** on Resurrection Bay through the central agencies that are listed under "Fishing," below. The waters are beautiful, but it's a different experience than sailing in the Lower 48—if there's any wind, it's quite chilly.

✪ FISHING

Seward is renowned for its saltwater silver salmon fishing. The silvers start showing up in the bay in mid-July and last through September. You can catch the fish from shore, from Lowell Point south of town or even near the boat harbor, but your chances of success are far greater from a boat. I prefer small, six-passenger boats because you can get to know the skipper better and use that contact to learn more about fishing. If your party has the whole boat, you can control where it goes, perhaps adding whale watching or sightseeing to the day. The going rate for a guided charter, with everything provided, is around $150 per person for salmon, or $170 for halibut (boats have to go farther for halibut). I've heard good things about Andrew Mezirow's **Crackerjack Sportfishing Charters** (☎ **907/224-2606;** www.outdoorsdirectory.com/akpages/crackerjack). There are several central charter agencies in town, which makes life simpler for visitors. **The Fish House,** located at the Small Boat Harbor, books charters, sells and rents ocean-fishing and spin-casting gear, and carries some fly-fishing supplies. For charters, reserve ahead at P.O. Box 1209, Seward, AK 99664 (☎ **800/257-7760** or 907/224-3674; www.alaskan.com/fishhouse). See "Boating," above, for details about the much less expensive option of renting your own skiff and fishing without a guide.

HIKING

There are several excellent hiking trails near Seward. You can get a complete list and directions at the Kenai Fjords National Park Visitor Center (see the next section).

The **Mount Marathon Trail** is a tough hike to the top of a 3,000-foot mountain. The route of the famous Mount Marathon foot race is the more strenuous choice, basically going straight up from the end of Jefferson Street; the hikers' route starts at the corner of First Avenue and Monroe Street. Either trail rises steeply to the top of the rocky pinnacle and the incredible views there. Allow all day, unless you're a racer; in that case, expect to do it in under 45 minutes.

The **Caines Head State Recreation Area** (www.dnr.state.ak.us/parks/units/caineshd.htm) has a 7-mile coastal trail south of town. Parts of the trail are accessible only at low tide, so it's best done either as an overnight or with someone picking you up or dropping you off in a boat at the far end—the Miller's Landing water taxi, mentioned under "Boating & Sea Kayaking," above, offers this service for $30 per person, one way. The trail has some gorgeous views, rocky shores, and a good destination at the end (a promontory with the concrete remains of a World War II gun emplacement and bunker at Fort McGilvray). Three campsites are at Tonsina Point, 2 miles in, and a state park public-use cabin is 2 miles farther (see "Accommodations," below). At North Beach, 6½ miles from the trailhead, are two camping shelters, a ranger station, and trailheads to the fort, South Beach, and the 3-mile Alpine Trail. It's a beautiful and interesting hike. The trailhead is south of town on Lowell Point Road; pull off in the lot right after the sewage plant, then cross the road through the gate and follow the dirt road a bit until it becomes the actual trail. The state Division of Parks produces a good trail guide you can pick up for free at the Kenai Fjords National Park Visitor Center at the boat harbor; ask there about the tide conditions for your hike.

SLED DOG MUSHING

The dog-driving Seavey family, including the kids, shows off their kennel off Exit Glacier Road in Seward and offers rides in summer and, for groups, in winter. A summertime ride on a cart isn't exactly the real thing, but you'll get a feeling for the dogs' amazing power and intelligence. The 75-minute tour costs $34 for adults, $15 for children 11 and under. Husky puppies are sometimes available for cuddling, too. They call their company **IdidaRide** (☎ **800/478-3139** or 907/224-8607; www.ididaride.com/).

ATTRACTIONS IN TOWN

Besides the Alaska SeaLife Center and the Chugach Heritage Center (see below), most of Seward's attractions are of the modest, small-town variety. Explore downtown with the help of a **walking-tour map** provided by one of the visitor centers.

The **Iditarod Trailhead,** on the water just east of the SeaLife Center, is where pioneers entered Alaska. Walk along the paved path from there to the park, beach, and campground. The broken concrete and twisted metal you see on the beach here are the last ruins of the Seward waterfront, which was destroyed by a tsunami wave in the 1964 earthquake. The campground turns into an RV and tent city in the summer—at times a loud and rowdy one, unfortunately, although the city is cracking down on that. Sometimes you can see sea otters swimming just offshore. During silver salmon season, in August and September, it's possible to catch them casting from shore here, although you're chances are far better from a boat (see "Fishing," above).

The **Seward Museum,** at Third and Jefferson (☎ **907/224-3902**), is a charming grandma's attic of a place, with clippings, memorabilia, and curiosities recalling town history, painter Rockwell Kent, and the ways of the past. Admission is $2 for adults, 50¢ for children, and it's open during the summer, daily from 9am to 5pm.

The steep-roofed **St. Peter's Episcopal Church** is a delightful little chapel under the mountains at First Avenue and Adams Street. Go inside to see the mural in the front of the church, which shows what the Resurrection would have looked like if it had happened in front of Seward locals in the 1930s.

✪ **Alaska SeaLife Center.** Railroad Ave. (P.O. Box 1329), Seward, AK 99664. ☎ **800/224-2525** or 907/224-6300. www.alaskasealife.org. $12.50 adults, $10 children 7–12, free for children 6 and under. Summer daily 8am–8pm. Winter hours vary; open at least Wed–Sat 10am–5pm.

The center is a serious research institution and a superb aquarium of creatures from the nearby Alaska waters. You may have seen puffins diving into the water from a tour boat; here you can see what they look like flying *under* the water. Sea birds, harbor seals, and sea lions reside in three large exhibits that you can see from above or below. There are some smaller tanks with fish, crab, and other creatures, and a touch tank where you can handle starfish and other tide-pool animals. It's not as large as a big-city aquarium, however, and you're not likely to spend more than an hour or two here, despite the high admission price. Programs for kids and adults happen all day. To make the most of your visit, call ahead so you can catch a program on a subject that interests you.

SHOPPING

Chugach Heritage Center, next to the SeaLife Center, at 501 Railway Ave. (☎ **907/224-5065**), occupies the restored railroad depot. Chugach Natives and Aleuts sell traditional crafts and occasionally offer demonstrations and performances. Stop at the **Resurrect Art Coffee House Gallery,** at 320 Third Ave. (☎ **907/224-7161**), in an old church. The fine art is local, but this place is a coffeehouse and meeting place. The **Bardarson Studio,** 1317 Fourth Ave., at the boat harbor (☎ **800/354-0141** or 907/224-5448; www.bardarsonstudio.com), specializes in Dot Bardarson's watercolor prints and has a wonderful, welcoming attitude. There's a children's cave under the stairs and a place to sit upstairs with videos and reading matter. A shopping stop becomes an event. The **Resurrection Bay Galerie,** 500 Fourth Ave. (☎ **907/224-3212;** alaskafinearts.com), shows oils of wildlife and other Alaskan themes in a lovely old shingled house downtown—no prints, only originals.

ACCOMMODATIONS

Connections (☎ **907/224-2323;** www.alaskasview.com) is a Seward hotel and B&B booking agency, and also books some tours and charters. The Web site has an impressive search function for B&B lodgings, but the names of the businesses are not revealed until you buy. You can get a list of B&Bs, including their names, from the Chamber of Commerce Visitor Centers.

A friendly family runs the **Moby Dick Hostel,** at 423 Third Ave. (☎ **907/224-7072**). They charge $16.50 for a bunk, $45 for private hostel rooms, and $60 for kitchenette rooms. They've been renovating and have made it a nice place.

✪ **Ballaine House Bed and Breakfast.** 437 Third Ave. (P.O. Box 2051), Seward, AK 99664-2051. ☎ **907/224-2362.** www.superpage.com/ballaine. 4 units, none with private bathroom. $77 double. Extra person $15. Rates include full breakfast ($16 discount with no breakfast). No credit cards. No smoking. No children under 10.

This 1905 house near the center of downtown is a classic B&B, with its wooden floors, large living room, and tall, double-hung windows. It's on the National Historic Register and the town walking tour. Marilee Koszewski has decorated with antiques and handmade quilts and provides raincoats, binoculars, and other gear for outings, and will even do laundry. She also will give back the commission on boat bookings, normally amounting to a 10% discount. Some of the rooms are small, and all bathrooms are shared.

Best Western Hotel Seward. 217 Fifth Ave. (downtown), Seward, AK 99664. ☎ **800/222-2261** in Alaska only; 800/528-1234 national reservations; 907/224-2378. Fax 907/224-3112. www.bestwesternseward.com. 38 units. TV TEL. High season $192–$212 double. Low season $89–$99 double. Extra person $10. AE, DC, DISC, MC, V.

These rooms, while overpriced, are the best in this small-town selection. Large, solid, and attractively decorated, many have big bay windows and all have VCRs, refrigerators, and coffee makers. The view rooms on the front go for a premium, although the view is largely blocked. A two-story log cabin on a cliff over the boat harbor also is part of the hotel (www.cliffcabin.com). With a large hot-tub spa on the magnificent deck, it's one of the most beautiful and luxurious accommodations in Alaska, renting for $309 a night.

The Breeze Inn. 1306 Seward Hwy. (P.O. Box 2147), Seward, AK 99664-2147. ☎ **888/224-5237** in Alaska only, or 907/224-5237. Fax 907/224-7024. www.sewardalaskamotel.com. 86 units. TV TEL. Summer $119–$160 double. Winter $49 double. Extra person $10. AE, CB, DC, DISC, MC, V.

Located right at the busy boat harbor, this large, three-story, motel-style building offers good standard accommodations with the most convenient location in town for a fishing or Kenai Fjords boat trip. Rooms are constantly renovated, and all have refrigerators. An annex building has superb upscale rooms, some overlooking the harbor. They operate a courtesy van. A restaurant with a full menu and a lounge is across the parking lot.

✪ **Harborview Inn.** 804 Third Ave. (P.O. Box 1305), Seward, AK 99664. ☎ **888/324-3217** or 907/224-3217. Fax 907/224-3218. www.SewardHotel.com/. 35 units, 3 apts. TV TEL. High season $119 double. Off-season $59 double. Extra person $10. AE, MC, V.

The energetic and hospitable Jerry and Jolene King take great pride in their inn, which grew from their bed-and-breakfast operation. And for good reason, as theirs are among the most attractive rooms in town, with lots of light, Mission-style furniture, and Tlingit art based on Jolene's tribal crest. The rates are a bargain by Seward standards, and the location, midway between the Small Boat Harbor and downtown, puts both within long walking distance. Two two-bedroom apartments on the beach along Ballaine Avenue rent for the same price as the motel rooms; they're a great bargain, and perfect for families. There's a nice one-bedroom apartment in the main section, too.

Hotel Edgewater. 200 Fifth Ave. (Box 1570), Seward, AK 99664. ☎ **888/793-6800** or 907/224-2700. Fax 907/224-2701. www.hoteledgewater.com. 76 units. High season $165–$245 double. Low season $65–$105 double. Extra person $10. AE, DISC, MC, V.

Standing right across the street from the ocean and the SeaLife Center, this new hotel has excellent views from two sides and a three-story atrium inside. The rooms have amenities such as VCRs and fine furniture, but they've cut more corners than you would expect in a top-end place (the carpeting and wall coverings aren't the best, there's a lack of space at the vanities, and a utilitarian elevator), so it misses having an opulent feel.

Seward Windsong Lodge. ½ mile, Exit Glacier Rd. (Mailing address: P.O. Box 93330, Anchorage, AK 99509-3330.) ☎ **888/959-9590** or 907/265-4501 in Anchorage, or 907/224-7116 in Seward. www.sewardwindsong.com. 72 units. TV TEL. High season $169 double. Low season $99 double. Extra person $10. Children stay free in parents' room. AE, DISC, MC, V. Closed Oct–Apr.

This hotel is the only one at Kenai Fjords National Park with a national park atmosphere: The 12-unit buildings with mock log siding and the large restaurant and lobby building sit among spruce trees on the broad, unspoiled valley of the Resurrection River. The rooms are crisp and new; all have two queen beds and rustic-style furniture, electric kettles, and VCRs. A driver is on hand to take you a few miles to town and pick you up whenever you like. The Cook Inlet Region Native corporation, which owns this hotel, also owns excellent hotels in Talkeetna and at Denali National Park, and Kenai Fjords Tours and the Park Connection bus (listed above under "Getting There"). The hotel restaurant, the **Resurrection Roadhouse,** is reviewed below, under "Dining."

CAMPING & CABINS

The Alaska State Division of Parks maintains two cabins for rent in the **Caines Head State Recreation Area,** south of town, and two in **Thumb Cove State Marine Park,** across the bay from Caines Head. Details on reserving the cabins are listed in section 1 of this chapter. It's possible to hike to the Caines Head cabins (see "Hiking," above), but to get to Thumb Cove you need a boat. Water taxi service is offered for $50 round trip by Miller's Landing (see "Boating & Sea Kayaking," above).

Cabins in Chugach National Forest and Kenai Fjords National Park are mentioned in those sections, as are the campgrounds in the national forest, but the national park's only campground is quite handy to Seward: near the **Exit Glacier,** at mile 8.5 of Exit Glacier Road. The campground is on willow-covered, gravely ground that plants haven't yet reclaimed from the retreating ice. Sites are far apart and almost completely private, but lack any amenities—no picnic tables, fire grates, or anything. Use the food lockers and central cooking to keep bears away. Snow lingers into early June. There is no fee for the 10 sites, and reservations are not taken. It's open for tents only and has pit toilets and hand-pump water.

The beachfront **Iditarod Trailhead Park** on Ballaine Avenue is acceptable for RV camping, but too crowded and exposed for tenters, especially if the local police lose their new resolve to crack down on the noise and drinking (at best, busy weekends are like a refugee camp). The fee is $6 for tents, $10 for RVs, and showers are $2. It's operated by the city parks and recreation department (☎ **907/224-4055**). A quieter but poorly developed town campground is **Forest Acres Park,** among the spruce trees at Hemlock and Dimond Boulevard, just off Seward Highway near the Coast Guard Recreation Center. Fees are the same.

More appealing is **Miller's Landing,** on Lowell Point Road south of town (☎ **907/224-5739;** www.millerslandingak.com). Sites are along the beach or among large spruce trees. Electric hookups are $25 a night; rustic sleeping-bag cabins are $35 to $55; and cabins with kitchens and bathrooms run $65 to $80. There's lots to do here; see "Boating & Sea Kayaking," above.

DINING

There are various places at the harbor to grab a sandwich or other quick meal on the way out to sea; they change too frequently for me to include here. Downtown, the **Ranting Raven,** at 228 Fourth Ave., downtown (☎ **907/224-2228**), is a great little coffee shop, serving pastries, sandwiches, and soup, as well as a gift shop.

Apollo Restaurant. 229 Fourth Ave. ☎ **907/224-3092.** Main courses $10–$18. AE, MC, V. Daily 11:30am–11:30pm. MEDITERRANEAN/SEAFOOD.

This is a surprisingly good small-town restaurant. Seward families come back for a menu that includes anything they might want: Greek and southern Italian cuisine, seafood, pizza, and much more. But the cuisine is far more sophisticated and expertly turned out that you expect in such a place, especially the seafood dishes, and the service is fast and professional. The dining room, with many booths, takes the Greek theme as far as it will go—I especially enjoyed the miniature Doric columns.

Ray's Waterfront. At the small-boat harbor. ☎ **907/224-5606.** Main courses $14–$20; lunch $6–$10. AE, DC, DISC, MC, V. 15% gratuity added for parties of 6 or more. Daily 11am–11pm. Closed Oct to mid-Mar. STEAK/SEAFOOD.

The lively, noisy dining room looks out from big windows across the small-boat harbor, with tables on terraces so everyone can see. The atmosphere is fun and the food is just right after a day on the water. While not perfect, it's more nuanced than the typical harborside place. Most important, they don't overcook the fresh local fish—and that's really all you can ask. Full liquor license.

✪ **Resurrection Roadhouse.** 7/10 mile Exit Glacier Rd. ☎ **907/224-7116.** Main courses $9–$24; lunch $9–$13. AE, DISC, MC, V. Daily 7am–10pm. Closed mid-Oct to mid-Apr.

Every seasonal restaurant has its ups and downs, but before I dined recently in this hotel dining room I didn't know how high the ups could be. My seafood chowder, soy- and sesame-seasoned grilled halibut and asparagus, and chocolate raspberry torte were a wonderful journey in taste and texture—nothing could be improved. (They also serve hand-thrown gourmet pizzas.) The service was almost too fast. The dining room lacks life, but the mountain view is great and there's plenty of space. The bar's collection of Alaska craft brews on tap is exhaustive. That night, at least, this was one of Alaska's best restaurants.

6 Kenai Fjords National Park

Kenai Fjords is all about remote rocks, mountains, and ice that meet the ocean, and the animals that live there. The park comprises 670,000 acres of the south coast and interior land mass of the Kenai Peninsula. The shore here is exposed to the Gulf of Alaska, whose wild, recurrent storms beat against the mountainous shore unbuffered by any land mass from the vast expanse of the Pacific to the south. Wildlife thrives, but humans have never made a mark.

The geological events that formed this landscape are vast and ongoing. The steep, coastal mountains amount to a dent in the earth's crust where the northward-moving Pacific tectonic plate is colliding and adding land to the southern edge of Alaska. As the Pacific plate pushes under Alaska, it slams islands onto the Alaska coast, then pulls them under into the molten layer down below. These mountains are shrinking measurably as the earth swallows them up. The 1964 earthquake dropped them by 7 feet. As your boat rides past the park's small, sharp, bedrock islands, now populated by sea birds and marine mammals, you are seeing the tips of ancient peaks that once stood far above the shore like today's coastal mountains.

The park's history has barely started. The fjords became a park only in 1980. In 1976, when the National Park Service explored more than 650 miles of coastline, including the park area, they didn't find a single human being. The same was true when geologists came in 1909. British explorer Capt. James Cook made the first maps of the fjords area in 1778, but the coast was too rugged and rocky for him to land. We don't know much about Native Americans who lived in the fjords. Scientists have found some areas where people lived, or at least had camps, but no one knows exactly who they were or what they were doing here. The earth, through earthquakes or glacial action, has erased most remains. Anthropologists call these people Unegkurmiut, and believe they were Alutiiq, Eskimos who lived on the Pacific coast, closely related to the Chugach people of Prince William Sound and the Koniag from Kodiak Island to the south. Those groups are still around; scientists are studying the Unegkurmiut and what happened to them from the little evidence they can find on the fjord's beaches.

The Natives probably never ventured inland, over the impossibly rugged interior of the Kenai Peninsula, leaving its heart to be discovered in 1968, when the first mountain climbers crossed the Harding Ice Field, which covers most of the national park. **Exit Glacier** and all the glaciers of Kenai Fjords flow from this 1,000-foot-thick ice age leftover. The ice field lies in a high bowl of mountains that jut straight out of the ocean to heights of 3,000 to 5,000 feet. When moisture-laden ocean clouds hit those mountains, they drop lots of rain and snow—up on the ice field 40 to 80 feet of snow falls each winter, with a water equivalent of 17 feet. Summer weather isn't warm enough to melt the snow at that elevation, so it packs down ever deeper until it turns into the hard, heavy ice of glaciers and flows downward to the sea.

The area's history finally got an ugly start in 1989, when the tanker *Exxon Valdez* crashed into a rock about 150 miles northeast of the park in Prince William Sound and spilled almost 11 million gallons of oil. Exxon did a poor job of catching the oil before it spread, and by the end of the summer the sticky, brownish-black muck had soiled beaches in the western Sound, across the fjords, and all the way to Kodiak Island

and the Alaska Peninsula. More than 1,000 miles of shoreline were oiled to some degree. Hundreds of sea otters and hundreds of thousands of sea birds were killed in the Sound and on the islands near the fjords. Nature scrubbed the oil off the rocks again, and you will see no evidence of it in the park today; but scientists say most of the affected species of birds and animals haven't come back completely. Nonetheless, you'll still see more wildlife on a boat ride here than anywhere else I know.

Exxon paid over $1 billion to the government in penalties for the oil spill, and that money has done a lot to help the area. Most of it was used to buy land in the spill area that otherwise would have been logged, including 35,000 acres of coastal land in the national park.

Most of the park is remote and difficult to reach. A large vessel, such as a tour boat operating out of Seward, is the only practical way for most people to see the marine portion of the park. That's not cheap or quick, and there are better destinations for people subject to seasickness. The inland portion is accessible only at Exit Glacier, near Seward.

ESSENTIALS

GETTING THERE Seward is the threshold to the park. Exit Glacier is 13 miles from the town by road; the Kenai Fjords National Park Visitor Center is at the Seward Small-Boat Harbor; and the tour boats that visit the park leave from Seward.

Many visitors try to see the park in a day, coming from Anchorage by train or road, touring the park by boat, then returning that evening. I do not recommend this. To really get to the park, you need to be on an all-day boat trip—most half-day trips barely leave Resurrection Bay and hardly see the park proper. More important, a lot of the visitors I saw riding the train back to Anchorage after a 1-day marathon trip to Kenai Fjords were so tired they couldn't keep their eyes open for the extraordinary scenery passing by outside the train. A better plan is to spend a night in Seward and take in the full Kenai Fjords boat trip and Exit Glacier. See section 5.

VISITOR INFORMATION At the **Kenai Fjords National Park Visitor Center,** Seward Small Boat Harbor (P.O. Box 1727), Seward, AK 99664 (☎ **907/224-3175;** www.nps.gov/kefj/), rangers answer questions and provide information on the all-important tour boats. They carry a good selection of books on Alaska natural history and occasionally show films. Call or drop by here for advice on Park Service cabins for rent in the fjords, guidance on a sea-kayaking expedition there, or places in the area to hike and trail conditions. They're open June to August daily from 8am to 7pm, September to May, Monday to Friday from 8am to 5pm.

ACCOMMODATIONS & CAMPING There are no hotels in the park; it's best to base yourself in Seward (see my recommendations earlier in this chapter). The **Exit Glacier Campground,** the only campground in the park, also is listed in section 5.

A free Park Service map shows the location of food lockers and hanging cables to keep your stuff away from bears in the kayaking waters of Aialik Bay and Northwestern Fjord. You can camp anywhere if you observe correct backcountry precautions. Send away for a packet of information from the park. They also rent out four **public-use cabins,** three in the fjords, reachable only by boat or floatplane. One is a mile from Exit Glacier, but is open only during the winter when the road is closed. It's accessible by ski, dogsled, or snow machine. Contact the park headquarters for a $35-a-day cabin permit, open for reservations starting January 2 each year.

SEEING THE PARK

SIGHTSEEING & WILDLIFE CRUISES

Kenai Fjords is essentially a marine park. On a boat tour, you'll see its mountains, glaciers, and wildlife. On any of the tours you're sure to see sea otters and sea lions,

It's Not Easy Being Green

An important factor in choosing your boat tour is your susceptibility to **seasickness.** To reach the heart of the park, vessels must venture into the unprotected waters of the North Pacific. Large, rolling waves are inevitable on the passage from Resurrection Bay to the fjords themselves, although once you're in the fjords, the water is calm. On a rough day, most boats will turn back for the comfort of the passengers and change the full-day trip into a Resurrection Bay cruise, refunding the difference in fare. Of course, they'd rather not do that, and the decision may not be made until the vessel is out there, often after some of the passengers are already vomiting over the side. If you get seasick easily, my advice is to stick to the Resurrection Bay cruise, or take a boat tour in protected Prince William Sound out of Whittier, where the water is smooth. In any event, ask about the tour company's policy on turning back and refunds and take Dramamine *before* you leave the dock (once you're underway, it's probably too late to do any good).

---

and you have a good chance of seeing humpback whales, orcas, mountain goats, and black bears. I saw all those on a recent trip to Aialik Bay. Gray whales come in the early spring and huge fin whales show sometimes, too. Bird watchers will see bald eagles, puffins (both tufted and horned), cormorants, murres, and various other sea ducks and alcids. The farther you go into the park, the more you'll see.

Depending on the time and money you have to spend, you can choose to take a half-day trip (which will stay generally in Resurrection Bay) or a full-day trip that travels to Aialik Bay or Harris Bay, in the heart of the park. Prices are around $115 to $140 to go to Northwestern Glacier, in Northwestern Fjord off Harris Bay, an all-day trip; $100 to $110 to go to Holgate Glacier, in Holgate Arm off Aialik Bay, which takes 6 to 8 hours; and $60 for a 3- to 4-hour Resurrection Bay tour, which doesn't go to the national park at all. Children's prices are around half off.

You can shop for prices, but make sure you compare the same destinations, length of trip, and food service. Look at a map of the route. If you really want to see Kenai Fjords National Park and glaciers that drop ice into the water, the boat has to go at least into **Aialik Bay** to **Holgate Glacier.** Resurrection Bay contains plenty of impressive scenery—its cliffs are as if chiseled from the mountains—but the park is even grander. The half-day cruises do not get close to glaciers, have less of a chance of seeing whales, and see fewer puffins and other birds. The longest trips into the heart of the park proper encounter the greatest variety and number of birds and animals. If you're lucky with the weather, you can make it to the exposed **Chiswell Islands,** which have some of the greatest bird rookeries in Alaska, supporting more than 50,000 seabirds of 18 species. I've seen clouds of puffins swarm here. The day-long trips also allow more time to linger and really see the behavior of the wildlife. Whatever your choice, binoculars are a necessity; you may be able to rent them on board.

Try to schedule loosely, so that if the weather is bad on the day you choose for your boat trip, you can wait and go the next day. If the weather's bad, you'll be uncomfortable, and the animals and birds won't be as evident, or the boat may not go out at all. If you pay up front to hold a reservation on a boat—probably a good idea in the busiest months—find out the company's refund policy.

If you're shopping around, ask how much deck space there is outside so you can really see. What is the seating arrangement inside? How many passengers will be on board and how many crew members to answer questions? Is lunch provided, and what does it consist of? Another important point of comparison is if you have a ranger doing the commentary, or just the captain—some of these captains don't know when to shut up and give inaccurate information.

Most operators offer packages with the Alaska Railroad and the SeaLife Center, which may save money, but make sure you have enough time to do everything you want to do in Seward. All have offices at the Small Boat Harbor in Seward and most have an office in Anchorage, too. In addition to the operators listed in full below, **Renown Charters and Tours** (☎ **907/272-1961;** www.akol.com/renown/) has smaller vessels, offering shorter, lower-priced cruises, and year-round operations. They can get you out on the bay for $49.

Kenai Fjords Tours. At the Seward Small Boat Harbor and at 513 W. Third Ave., Anchorage. ☎ **800/478-8068,** 907/224-8068 in Seward, or 907/276-6249 in Anchorage. www.kenaifjords.com.

This is the largest of the tour operators, with the most daily sailings and choices of destination. The main part of the operation uses 90- to 150-passenger vessels, some of which have forward-facing seats, like an airplane's. They're professionally staffed, but when the ships are crowded, the experience can be impersonal. The captain provides the commentary instead of a ranger. However, the same company also owns **Mariah Tours,** which operates 16-passenger vessels. Their trips are more spontaneous and go farther for a lower fare; the downside is that the smaller boats are less stable in the waves.

Most of the large Kenai Fjords vessels call on a lodge the company owns on **Fox Island,** in Resurrection Bay. It sits on the long cobble beach of **Sunny Cove,** where painter Rockwell Kent lived in seclusion with his son in 1918 and 1919 and produced the art that made him famous, as well as his classic book *Wilderness: A Journal of Quiet Adventure in Alaska* (Wesleyan University Press). It is an inspiring spot. The lodge itself stands on a narrow strip of land between the beach and a pond, which visitors overlook from large wooden decks. Boats stop for lunch of grilled salmon or a family-style dinner, and some passengers spend the night. An overnight package on the island costs $299 per person, meals included. Half-day sea-kayaking paddles from the island are offered for day-trippers or overnight guests: $79 to $89 per person as an add-on for overnighters, or $139 to $159, including the tour boat ride and lunch, for day-trippers.

✪ **Major Marine Tours.** 411 West Fourth Ave., Anchorage. ☎ **800/764-7300** or 907/274-7300, or 907/224-8030 in Seward. www.majormarine.com.

This company pioneered first-class onboard dining and, at this writing, is the only cruise that brings along a park ranger to assure high-quality commentary, a decisive advantage in my judgment (after all, you're here for the park). Their boats are slower than the competition, so they don't make the long trip to Northwest Glacier; they either head into Aialik Bay to see Holgate Glacier or just tour Resurrection Bay around Seward. The trip also takes longer, but that increases your probability of seeing wildlife; animals may also be easier to spot at slower speeds. Instead of bringing sandwiches or stopping for a meal, they serve a fine-dining buffet of salmon and prime rib on board for $10 per person, $5 for children. The food is surprisingly good. While I like their table-seating arrangement to forward-facing seats, it can be an uncomfortable crush when the boat is crowded. Your seat is assigned, so there's no need to rush aboard or try to stake out your spot.

Allen Marine Tours. 519 W. Fourth Ave., Anchorage. ☎ **888/305-2515** or 907/276-5800. www.allenmarine.com.

The company's Wildlife Quest runs into the park on a 78-foot, 150-passenger catamaran they built themselves at their shipyard in Sitka, where they also started a highly regarded marine tour business years ago. Although Allen Marine is new to Kenai Fjords, the boat gives them an advantage: It can get to the glaciers faster and, with its two-hull design, it should be more stable in the waves (although I know some people who disagree with that belief). Rather than puttering slowly along, it shoots quickly from sight to sight.

SEA KAYAKING

The fjords are calm yet rugged, intricate, and full of wildlife and soaring vistas. It's hard to imagine a better place for a sea-kayaking expedition. They also are extremely remote and very rainy, however, so a trip there, which will last at least several days, is not for the beginner paddler or camper, even with a guide. You need to know first that you can enjoy such a venture. Experienced paddlers can rent kayaks and explore on their own, using the Park Service cabins for shelter. I've listed the agencies that rent kayaks and offer guided trips and water taxis under "Boating & Sea Kayaking" in the Seward section, earlier in this chapter. Cabin rental information is below.

✪ EXIT GLACIER

When I visited Italy a few years ago, I got to the point that I thought I'd scream if I saw another painting of the Madonna. If your trip to Alaska is long, you may start to feel the same way about glaciers. But, although relatively small, Exit Glacier really is unique, and my family still enjoys visits there even as jaded lifelong Alaskans. (And I've probably seen even more glaciers than Madonnas.)

You can walk close to Exit Glacier, see its brittle texture, and feel the cold, dense spires of ice looming over you. Cold air breathes down on you like an open freezer door. Approaching the glacier, you can see the pattern of vegetation reclaiming the land that the melting ice has uncovered, a process well explained by interpretive signs and a nature trail. At the same time, however, the area remains refreshingly primitive. The National Park Service's low-key presentation of the site makes it a casual, pleasant visit for a couple of hours (longer if you do a hike).

The easiest way to get to the glacier is to drive. The clearly marked 9-mile road splits from the Seward Highway 3.7 miles north of town. In winter, the road is closed to vehicles. If you don't have a car, van service is usually available; check with the visitor center to see who is currently offering service.

Following the road along the broad bed of the wandering Resurrection River, you'll see in reverse order the succession of vegetation, from mature Sitka spruce and cottonwood trees down to smaller alders and shrubs. It takes time for nature to replace the soil on sterile ground left behind by a receding glacier. As you get closer, watch for a sign bearing the year 1780; more signs count upward through the years, marking the retreat of the glacier through time.

At the end of the road an entrance booth charges a **user fee of $5 per vehicle.** A simple **ranger station** and pit toilets are near the parking lot. **Ranger-led nature walks** start here on a sporadic schedule; check at the visitor center. Often, a spotting scope is set up to see mountain goats up in the rocky cliffs. The short **trail** to the glacier starts here. At the glacier, the trail splits: The steep route goes up along the side of the glacier, and the easy route runs on the flat gravel at its face.

One of the glacier's striking features is a high berm of gravel that fits around its leading edge like a necklace. This is a **moraine,** the glacier's refuse pile. The glacier gouges out the mountains with its immense, moving weight as new ice flows down from the ice field above and melts at this face. It carries along the rock and gravel torn from the mountain like a conveyor belt. This moraine is where the conveyor belt ends and the melting ice leaves the debris behind in a big pile. Probably without knowing it, you've seen hundreds of moraines before all over North America, where the glaciers of the last ice age piled up debris into hills, but this is the most obvious moraine I've ever seen, and it helps you to understand how they work. Don't go beyond the warning signs; ice can fall off and crush you.

An all-day hike, 8 miles round-trip, climbs along the right side of the glacier to the **Harding Icefield**—the glacier gets its name for being an exit from that massive sheet. It's a challenging walk with a 3,000-foot elevation gain, but it's the easiest access I'm aware of to visit an ice field on foot. Because of snow, the trail doesn't open until late June or early July. The ice field itself is cold and dangerous, and there's an emergency shelter maintained by the Park Service. Don't trek out on the ice unless you know what you're doing. The Park Service sometimes guides hikes up the trail.

The **Resurrection River Trail** begins from the road just short of the last bridge to the glacier. It's a pleasant day hike, with lots of wildflowers in the fall, or the start of a long hike on the historic Resurrection Trail, leading 72 miles all the way across the Kenai Peninsula. See section 3 of this chapter, on Chugach National Forest, for backpacking details.

7 Cooper Landing: Road Meets River

The little roadside community of Cooper Landing, in a wooded mountain valley along Kenai Lake and the Kenai River, begins about 8 miles west of Tern Lake, where the Sterling Highway splits from the Seward Highway, and continues sporadically along the highway for about 7 miles. (The Sterling runs generally west until Soldotna, where it heads south again.) The frothing upper **Kenai River** is the community's lifeline, each summer bringing the salmon that in turn draw visitors, who fill hotels, restaurants, and the date books of fishing guides. The **Russian River** meets the Kenai at the western edge of the community, where the mad fishing frenzy of the July red salmon season occurs. A ferry takes anglers across the river from the highway. For information on how to fish the Kenai, see "Fishing" in section 8 of this chapter on Kenai/Soldotna; there's additional information in chapter 2.

If you're not an angler, there's not much here—a couple of operators do rafting trips, some good hiking trails start here, and some of the accommodations could provide a romantic mountain retreat. Cooper Landing is also the starting or ending point for backpacking trips in the Chugach National Forest, described in section 3 of this chapter. Look there also for descriptions of several campgrounds for tents or RVs (there are also RV hookups at the Kenai Princess Lodge, reviewed below).

Cooper Landing has a post office, service stations, and small stores selling fishing gear and essentials, but it's not a real center of commerce. For banking or anything else not directly related to catching a salmon, you'll have to drive to Sterling, 30 miles away to the west, or Soldotna, 14 miles beyond that.

FISHING LODGES

The three lodges below can take care of everything, so you can set up your fishing and other activities with a single phone call. If all you need is a simple, inexpensive room, try **The Hutch Bed and Breakfast,** Mile 48.5, Sterling Highway (☎ **907/595-1270**).

Gwin's Lodge. 14865 (Mile 52) Sterling Hwy., Cooper Landing, AK 99572. ☎ **907/595-1266.** ool.com/gwins/. 11 cabins. High season $99–$139 double. Low season $59 double. DISC, MC, V.

This is the town's old original log roadhouse. Standing just a mile east of the Resurrection trailhead and the Russian River Campground, Gwin's is convenient and has loads of character. The owner, a dynamic former F-15 fighter pilot, keeps it open

24 hours a day all summer long to be the nerve center for the 24-hour fishing on the Russian River (it includes an extensive tackle shop, liquor store, and clothing shops).

Most of the cabins are new. Among other choices, they include trailer-sized units with kitchenettes, mock log exteriors and sleeping lofts with tiny dormers; a small house with a full kitchen and living room; or a real old log cabin. They also book fishing, rafting, and other activities.

Over 50 years, the place has welcomed many a tired angler or backpacker for a hearty meal, including me; after that, it's hard to be objective. Food in the seven-table dining room ranges from burgers to steaks and seafood. Servings are plentiful, satisfying, and generally quite good.

✪ **Kenai Princess Lodge.** Up Bean Creek Rd. above Cooper Landing (P.O. Box 676, Cooper Landing, AK 99572). ☎ **800/426-0500** or 907/595-1425. Fax 907/595-1424. 86 units. High season $229–$249 double. Low season $79–$119 double. AE, DC, DISC, MC, V.

Built for Princess's cruise ship and package-tour business, this hotel also has rooms open for independent travelers. It's the most luxurious choice on the Kenai Peninsula. Each room feels like a remote cabin, with balconies overlooking the wooded valley, wood stoves stocked with firewood, and many unique details; yet they're luxurious hotel rooms at a resort with a gym, spa, and fine restaurant. The restaurant menu is varied and goes well beyond standard "steak and seafood." Even if you have no reason to stay in Cooper Landing, it could be a relaxing overnight stop, or a place to get a meal a few steps up from highway fare. Anchorage couples use the hotel as a romantic getaway. The hotel books guided fishing, horseback riding, tours, and other activities, and there are hiking trails nearby.

An attractive 35-space RV park is on the site of the lodge, with access to the facilities, charging $20 a night for full hookups. For summer, make reservations for rooms or RV sites well ahead.

Kenai River Sportfishing Lodge/Kenai Riverside Lodge. Alaska Wildland Adventures, Sterling Hwy. along the Kenai River, P.O. Box 389, Girdwood, AK 99587-0389. ☎ **800/478-4100** or 907/783-2928. www.alaskasportfish.com. 16 cabins. $450 per person per day, including meals and guided sportfishing; $325 per person per day (based on double occupancy), including meals, river rafting, and other nonfishing activities. MC, V.

This lodge lies between the highway and the river, but down among the trees it feels like a remote lodge. I'd call the cabins faux rustic—I've never seen real bush cabins with smooth walls, wainscoting, and bright rag rugs, but these trim places still feel like the outdoorsy real thing, with no TVs or phones. The plumbing is in a central bathhouse. The location is the real advantage: White-water rafting rides and fishing floats

Floating the Kenai River

The Kenai is more famous for fishing than rafting, but the area is beautiful and the Kenai Canyon, below Cooper Landing and above Skilak Lake, has wild Class III water between vertical canyon walls. **Alaska Wildland Adventures,** at the Kenai Riverside Lodge (☎ **800/478-4100** or 907/595-1279), is the most established operator and has a great reputation. They offer a 7-hour float through the canyon for $110 adults, $69 children, and a placid 2½-hour float down the upper Kenai for $45 adults, $29 children. Their guided fishing is $195 for a full day or $125 for a half day. **Alaska Rivers Co.,** Mile 50, Cooper Landing (☎ **907/595-1226**), also does scenic rafting and guided fishing, and I've heard good things from former customers. They charge $125 for a full day of fishing.

leave right from the riverfront. The lodge also possesses a scarce resource in its coveted guide permits for the hot fishing river section that runs through the Kenai National Wildlife Refuge.

Everything comes with the one price: transportation from Anchorage, meals in a central lodge building, guided salmon fishing or fly-fishing for rainbow trout in drift or jet boats, and halibut fishing (done from boats in saltwater). You provide your own booze and pay the tip. If you don't want to fish, the price drops by $125 and you can join rafting trips and other activities. Most visitors use it as part of a "safari" package that takes them to various outdoor activities and sites; that's described in section 7 of chapter 2.

8 Kenai/Soldotna & Sterling: Giant Salmon

These quintessential western U.S. towns, dominated by shopping malls and fast-food franchises facing broad highways, have a single claim to fame, but it's a pretty good claim: The largest sport-caught king salmon in the world, almost 100 pounds, came from the Kenai River. The Kenai's kings run so large there's a different trophy class for the river—everywhere else in the state, the Alaska Department of Fish and Game will certify a 50-pounder as a trophy, but on the Kenai it has to be at least 75 pounds. That's because kings in the 60-pound class—with enough wild muscle to fight ferociously for hours—are just too common here. Anglers prepared to pay for a charter will be in their element on the river when the fish are running hot. Catching a big king is not easy or quick, however, and success rates vary greatly year-to-year and week-to-week.

Those not interested in fishing will find less than a day's sightseeing in these towns. Instead, use the towns as a base for the outdoors. Kenai has a strangely beautiful ocean beach and the Kenai River mouth, with its exceptional bird watching. Outside town, you'll find a wealth of outdoor activities, primarily in the lake-dotted **Kenai National Wildlife Refuge,** which has its headquarters in Soldotna. The refuge is covered in the next section.

Kenai came into being with the arrival of the Russians at the mouth of the Kenai River more than 200 years ago, but came into its own only with the discovery of oil on the peninsula in 1957. Today its economy relies on oil, commercial fishing, and, to a smaller extent, tourism. Soldotna, a smaller, newer, and less attractive town, is the borough seat, and the primary destination for sportfishermen. Sterling is just a wide place in the road—incredibly wide, as a matter of fact (no one is quite able to explain why such a small town needs such a big road).

ESSENTIALS

GETTING THERE From Anchorage, the drive on the Seward and Sterling highways to Soldotna is 147 miles. Allow 3 hours, without stops: In summer, traffic will slow you down; in winter, speeds are limited by ice and the fear of hitting moose. Most of the major car-rental companies have offices in Kenai, at the airport.

The **Homer Stage Line** (☎ **907/235-7009** or 907/399-1847) connects Anchorage, Homer, and points in between with bus service 6 days a week in the summer, less frequently in the winter. The fare from Anchorage to Soldotna is $35 one way, $60 round-trip. Tickets are for sale in Soldotna at the Goodnight Inn on the highway (☎ **907/262-4584**) or in Anchorage at the Seward Bus Line ticket office at 3339 Fairbanks St. (☎ **907/563-0800**).

Kenai receives as many as a dozen flights a day from Anchorage from **Era Aviation** (☎ **800/866-8394** or 907/283-9091; www.era-aviation.com).

GETTING AROUND The area is so spread out that walking most places really isn't possible, and there's no public transportation. Everyone here owns a car, and you can rent one from most major agencies, located at the Kenai airport. If you plan only to fish, however, you may not need one, instead getting rides from your guide, host, or a taxi cab. There are several cab companies; try **Inlet Taxi Cab** (☎ **907/283-4711** in Kenai or 907/262-4770 in Soldotna).

VISITOR INFORMATION The **Soldotna Visitor Information Center,** 44790 Sterling Hwy., Soldotna, AK 99669 (☎ **907/262-9814** or 907/262-1337; www.SoldotnaChamber.com), is located on the south side of town; drive through the commercial strip and turn right after the Kenai River Bridge. It's open daily in summer from 9am to 7pm; in winter, Monday to Friday 9am to 5pm. Besides the usual brochures, they maintain notebooks full of comparative information about lodgings, camping, and other services, and will help you find a room or charter. Anglers should stop in to see the world-record king salmon, and a 20-pound rainbow trout.

In Kenai, don't miss the **Kenai Visitors and Cultural Center,** at 11471 Kenai Spur Hwy., Kenai, AK 99611 (☎ **907/283-1991;** www.visitkenai.com). It's an attraction in itself. A fascinating free museum does a good job of using artifacts to explain the cultures that passed through the Kenai: the Natives, the Russians who settled in 1791, and the later pioneers and oil workers. A natural history section will help you identify the birds and fish you see. Look for the "King of Snags," an immense conglomeration of lost fishing lures and sticks from the bottom of the river. In the summer, superb temporary art exhibitions are mounted, too. To get there, follow the Spur Highway past Main Street and look for the large, well-landscaped building on your left. They are open Monday to Friday 8am to 7pm, Saturday and Sunday 10am to 7pm in summer; and Monday to Friday 8:30am to 5pm, Saturday 10am to 4pm in winter.

SPECIAL EVENTS May through July, the Kenai Visitors and Cultural Center (see above) will host **2001: A Fish Odyssey,** a show of piscatorial art from all over the United States. The 2000 show, on wildlife in general, was extraordinary. Admission is $3 adults, children and students free. **The Kenai River Festival** (☎ **907/260-5449**), over a weekend in early June, has food, music, crafts, and games.

In Soldotna, the **Tustumena 200 Sled Dog Race** (☎ **907/262-5057**), held in late January, helps kick off the mushing season. **Progress Days** (☎ **907/262-9814**), in July, offers a parade, rodeo, car shows, and other festival events commemorating the completion of a gas pipeline in 1960—that's the area in a nutshell.

In Ninilchik, the **Kenai Peninsula State Fair** (☎ **907/567-3670**), south at mile 136 on the Sterling Highway, is Friday to Sunday the third weekend in August, with a rodeo, crafts, games, agricultural exhibits, and other country attractions, but no rides. Admission is $7 adults, $5 seniors, $4 children aged 6 to 12.

FAST FACTS Kenai has several **banks** on the Kenai Spur Highway in the middle of town; in Soldotna, two banks are on the Sterling Highway commercial strip. In addition, ATMs are in grocery stores all over the area.

The **Central Peninsula Hospital** is in Soldotna at 250 Hospital Place (☎ **907/262-4404**); from the Sterling Highway, take Binkley Street to Vine Avenue.

Golden Tan, Hot Buns and Beans, 10811 Spur Highway, Kenai (☎ **907/283-8495;** golden-tan.com), is a tanning salon, coffee house, and Internet cafe. Connect to the Web for free at the **Kenai public library,** 163 Main St. Loop (☎ **907/283-4378**), or the **Soldotna public library,** 235 Binkley (☎ **907/262-4227**).

Whom to call for nonemergency business with the police depends on where you are: in Kenai, the **Kenai Police Department** (☎ **907/283-7879**); in Soldotna, the

Soldotna Police Department (☎ **907/262-4455**); or outside city limits, the **Alaska State Troopers** (☎ **907/262-4453**).

Sales tax is 5% in Kenai, 3% in Soldotna, and 2% outside city limits.

✪ FISHING

Fishing the Kenai River is the whole point of coming to the area for most visitors. Check at the visitor centers for information and regulation booklets. Or contact the **Alaska Department of Fish and Game,** 43961 Kalifornsky Beach Rd. Suite B, Soldotna, AK 99669 (☎ **907/262-9368** or 907/262-2737, for a recorded fishing report; www.state.ak.us/local/akpages/FISH.GAME/adfghome.htm). Serious anglers shouldn't miss that Web site; navigate through to the Region 2 Sportfish Division and download their treatises on Kenai River biology and fishing techniques. Licenses are for sale on the site, and in virtually any sporting-goods store. Also, read the "Salmon Primer" and "Fishing" in chapter 2.

There are more than two dozen public-access points over the 80 miles of the Kenai River. A **guide brochure** with a map is available from the state **Division of Parks,** P.O. Box 1247, Soldotna, AK 99669-1247 (☎ **907/262-5581;** www.dnr.state.ak.us/parks/parks.htm); you also can pick up a copy at one of the visitor centers.

For anglers interested in less competition and more of a wilderness experience, Kenai is a gateway for vast wild lands accessible by air on the west side of Cook Inlet. There you can fish a stream packed with salmon without competition. Among others, **High Adventure Air** (☎ **907/262-5237;** highadventureair.com) has day trips and packages with fly-in cabins. For a day trip, you'll pay $215 to $280 per person.

KINGS King salmon, the monsters of the river, come in two runs. The early run, which sometimes has been limited to catch-and-release, comes from late May to the end of June, peaking in mid-June. These usually are the smaller fish and less plentiful, in the 20- to 40-pound range. The second run comes during the month of July and includes massive fish that range up to 90 pounds.

Regulations allow only the use of artificial lures with a single hook. Most people fish kings from a boat, floating with the current while the lure bounces along the bottom. Some also keep the boat stationary or back slowly down the river. Your chances from the bank are low; on average, with or without a boat, it takes 29 hours of fishing time to land a king (you'll likely get at least a dozen strikes for every fish that makes it into the boat). With a guide, the average time to land a fish is cut in half, but that still means that if you fish for only 1 day, chances are good that you'll get skunked. A boat of three anglers on a half-day guided charter has roughly a 50% chance of landing king between them. You can increase your chances by fishing for several days, or when king and silver salmon are both in the river, and both biting the same lures—a narrow window in late July.

A guided charter averages $125 to $150 for a 6-hour, half-day trip, $225 to $250 full-day. There are dozens of guides. Contact the visitor center in Kenai or Soldotna to get in touch with a guide; also, many hotels and lodges have their own. It's possible to rent a boat, but advisable only if you are experienced in boats and stay out of the hazardous, faster flowing parts of the river. The **Sports Den,** at 44176 Sterling Hwy. in Soldotna (☎ **907/262-7491;** alaskasportsden.com), is one of the larger charter operators, with river and ocean trips, fly-in fishing, and hunting; they also rent condos, boats, and equipment for many kinds of outdoor activities. I've found them very friendly and helpful.

REDS The area really goes crazy when the red, or sockeye salmon, join the kings in the river, mid-July to early August. You can fish reds from the bank or from a boat.

Reds won't strike a lure—indeed, they don't feed at all in fresh water—and in the best fishing areas, regulations allow only the use of flies, near the confluence of the Russian and Moose rivers with the Kenai. Most people around here cast the flies with spinning gear, weighting the line 18 inches from the fly so it bounces along the bottom. Cast upstream from shore and allowing the fly to drift down, keeping near the bank. The plankton-eating fish probably don't really attack the flies, but get caught when they instinctively move their mouths in an eating motion, which they do in quick-moving water.

SILVERS Silvers come in two runs. The first, lighter run is late July to August, and the larger run arrives in September. They're easiest to catch anchored in a boat, but you can also do well from shore. Lures work well, as does bait of salmon eggs, but eggs aren't always allowed.

OTHER SPECIES Trophy-size rainbow trout and Dolly Varden char also come out of the river. Anglers using light tackle may also get some enjoyment out of catching pink salmon, but most Alaskans turn up their nose at this plentiful, 4-pound fish.

EXPLORING THE TOWNS

Kenai's historic sites, beach walking, and bird watching could occupy you for most of a day. Start at the visitors and cultural center mentioned above and get a copy of the *Old Town Kenai Walking Map*; follow the numbered markers. Not many of the simple, weathered buildings remain from Kenai's life before oil, but those that do are interesting and lie only a few blocks down Main Street from the center, along the Cook Inlet bluff.

The **Holy Assumption Russian Orthodox Church** is the area's most significant building. The parish was founded in 1845 and the present church was built in 1895. It's a quaint, onion-domed church, brightly kept but with old icons. A donation is requested. Several nearby buildings are interesting for their interlocking log construction. Stop at Veronica's Coffee Shop for a cup of java while on the tour—it's located in one of the old, cut-log buildings, with a faded sign out front. Sometimes artists work in Old Town shops in the summer.

The bluff over the beach is nearby. When the salmon are running, you can occasionally see white beluga whales chasing them upstream from here, sometimes in great numbers. To get down to the sandy **beach** itself, go back up to the Kenai Spur Highway, turn to the west (left), then turn left on South Spruce Street. There you'll find a simple beach park and a place to begin a walk. It's easy to imagine the Russians' first arrival. On a calm day the beach sand, mud flats, and the Inlet's gray, glacial water seem to meld together into one vast shimmering plain. Walking south, the beach wraps around and becomes the shore of the Kenai River. The water is far too cold for swimming.

The mouth of the river and the wetlands of its delta make for fine **bird watching,** especially during spring and fall migrations. One of the best places to get to the tidal marshes is along Bridge Access Road, which branches from the Spur Highway. The state of Alaska has developed a viewing area near the bridge.

In Soldotna, there is one modest attraction, on Centennial Park Road, behind the visitor center. The free **Homesteading Soldotna Historical Society Museum** (☎ **907/262-4976**) celebrates the 50-year history of the town with a collection of cabins dating from as recently as the 1960s set among spruce trees to show what the area was like then. They house pioneer artifacts and old photographs. It's open in summer only.

A family looking for something to do while one parent is off fishing may enjoy the magnificent **North Peninsula Recreation Area Nikiski Pool** (☎ **907/776-8472**),

10 miles north of Kenai on the Kenai Spur Road. The facility occupies a large dome and has a 136-foot water slide, mushroom fountains of water, and a raised hot tub from which parents can watch their children play in the pool below. Families travel from other towns just to swim here (including us). Open swimming and water slide use is Tuesday to Sunday 1 to 5pm and 6 to 9pm in the summer; in the winter, they're open the same hours Friday and Saturday and Sunday 1 to 5pm. Pool admission is $3, or $6 to use the slide and pool. Weekends can be crowded.

ACCOMMODATIONS

Rates at all hotels are on seasonal schedules with three, four, or even more levels linked to the salmon runs. I've listed the highest and lowest.

Daniels Lake Lodge Bed and Breakfast. 21 miles north of Kenai (P.O. Box 1444), Kenai, AK 99611. ☎ **800/774-5578** or 907/776-5578. puffin.ptialaska.net/~ducks/. 4 units, 2 cabins. TV. High season $95–$130 double, $125–$100 cabin. Low season $50–$65 any unit. 2-night minimum in cabins. Extra person $15. AE, DISC, MC, V. No smoking.

Located on peaceful and sparsely built Daniels Lake, this lovely, relaxing place has a boat and canoe you can use for trout fishing right out the back door, among the resident ducks. The gregarious hosts share their Christian faith with guests, and, along with their dogs and rabbits, eagerly make friends. It's not a 1-night stopover, but a place to stay for a couple of days of relaxation, closer to the Nikiski Pool and the outlet of the Swanson River Canoe route of the Kenai National Wildlife Refuge than to any town. There's an outdoor Jacuzzi and a laundry, and each room has a VCR.

Great Alaska Adventure Lodge. Moose River, 33881 Sterling Hwy., Sterling, AK 99672 (in winter, P.O. Box 2670, Poulsbo, WA 98370). ☎ **800/544-2261** or 907/262-4515. Fax 907/262-8797 in summer, 360/697-7850 in winter. www.greatalaska.com. 22 cabins. Rates anywhere from $175–$249 for a day trip without lodging to $3,495 for a 7-day package. Rates include all meals, guide service, and travel from Anchorage. AE, MC, V. Closed mid-Oct to mid-May.

For anglers, it's the location that counts: a third of a mile of river frontage where the Moose and Kenai rivers converge, a hot fishing spot since time immemorial, as an ancient Native site attests. In the evening, they keep a guide and campfire on the beach so you can keep casting in the midnight sun. For guests interested in seeing wildlife and the glorious backcountry of the Kenai National Wildlife Refuge, there are cushy tent camps where you can use some muscle but sleep and eat in comfort. A bear camp across Cook Inlet takes 12 visitors a day to watch three dozen resident brown bear up close, engaging in their natural behavior, in June and July. The lodge itself, in Sterling, is nothing remarkable, but perfectly adequate.

Harborside Cottages Bed and Breakfast. 813 Riverview Dr. (P.O. Box 942), Kenai, AK 99611. ☎ **907/283-6162.** www.harborsidecottages.com. 5 cottages. TV TEL. High season $150 double. May and Sept $100 double. Rates include continental breakfast. AE, MC, V. Closed Oct–Apr.

On a grassy compound at the top of the bluff over the mouth of the Kenai River in Old Town, these little white cottages make the most of a perfect site. The view and quiet could keep you occupied all day in a peaceful reverie. Inside, the cottages are as immaculate as if they were brand-new, each with its own light country decoration. Each has a fridge, a microwave oven, and a coffeepot, and the hostess stocks a self-serve breakfast the night before. There are no tubs, just shower stalls. Outside is a deck with a picnic table and gas barbecue.

Kenai River Lodge. 393 Riverside Dr., Soldotna, AK 99669. ☎ **907/262-4292.** Fax 907/262-7332. www.alaskais.com/kenailodge. 25 units. TV TEL. High season $110 double. Low season $60 double. Year-round $240 suite. Extra person $10. Fishing packages available. MC, V.

Overlooking the river, next to the bridge in Soldotna, this roadside motel has the advantages of well-maintained standard rooms (with refrigerators and coffeepots) and a great location for anglers. The grassy front yard descends right to the water, with a barbecue where you can cook up your catch. They operate fishing charters from the hotel.

Log Cabin Inn. 49840 Eider Rd. P.O. Box 2886, Kenai, AK 99611. ☎ and fax **907/283-3653.** www.ptialaska.net/~tedtitus. 9 units, 3 cabins. $80–$90 double. Extra adult $25; extra child $10. Rates include full breakfast. AE, MC, V.

Ted and Carol Titus built this huge log house specifically to be a B&B, but with its huge common room—with a fireplace and towering cathedral ceiling—it feels more like a luxurious wilderness lodge. Located off Kalifornsky Beach Road a little south of the bridge in Kenai, the house stands over an active beaver pond, with a deck and lots of windows to watch the beavers. The upstairs rooms, which cost $10 more, are well worth it—they're large and airy. A room on the main floor has French doors to a deck over the pond. All the rooms are attractively decorated in a country style, although not all are so exceptional. In-room telephones are available, there's a Jacuzzi on the porch, and the hostess cooks a large breakfast at the time of your choosing.

CAMPING

Soldotna's appealing **Centennial Park Campground** lies atop a bluff along the Kenai River among thick spruce and birch trees. Turn right on Kalifornsky Beach Road just past the visitor center. Camping fees are $8 a night; day use is $3. There's a dump station, usable for a $10 fee. **Swiftwater Park** is a similar city-operated riverside campground near the Fred Meyer grocery store and Taco Bell as you enter town from the north.

RV parks are scattered about. **Beluga Lookout RV Park** (☎ **907/283-5999;** e-mail: belugarv@ptialaska.net) is in Kenai's Old Town, at bluff's edge over the Inlet and the river's mouth, at 929 Mission Ave. Full hookups are $25 a night, with phone and cable TV at each site.

DINING

Franchise fast-food and burger-steak-seafood places dominate in Kenai and Soldotna. **Paradisos,** at Main Street and Kenai Spur Highway in Kenai (☎ **907/283-2222**), is a good multiethnic family restaurant.

Charlotte's Bakery, Café, Espresso. 115 S. Willow, Kenai. ☎ **907/283-2777.** All items $5–$8. MC, V. Mon–Fri 7am–4pm, Sat 9am–3pm. Closed Sun. SANDWICHES.

Rich-textured bread from the bakery anchors the sandwiches, and lettuce from a nearby garden fills out the large, filling salads, but the motherly owner doesn't make a point of that—hers is not a trendy or gimmicky place. Locals fill the big wooden chairs in the bright dining room because the food is good, the service sweetly attentive, and the prices reasonable.

Louie's. 47 Spur View Dr., Kenai. ☎ **907/283-3660.** Lunch $6–$11; dinner main courses $13–$26. AE, MC, V. Summer daily 4:30am–11pm. Winter daily 6am–10pm. STEAK/SEAFOOD.

Like the den of a maniacal sportsman, the dimly lit dining room is decorated with moose, bison, mountain goat, shark and even a 326-pound halibut—I kept bumping my head on a caribou's nose—and the televisions are on throughout the day. The service is quick and the soft armchairs and tables with lamps make a cozy place to eat. My halibut was tender and moist. The breakfast menu is an encyclopedia. A glass of wine is $7.

Sal's Klondike Diner. 44619 Sterling Hwy., Soldotna. ☎ **907/262-2220.** Lunch $4.50–$9; dinner main courses $7–$10. AE, MC, V. Daily 24 hours. DINER.

It certainly looks corny and touristy from the outside, but Sal's turns out to be a classic Western highway diner, with huge portions, fast service, and nothing fancy that doesn't have to be. Our meat loaf sandwich and halibut fish-and-chips, served on a plastic tablecloth, were just what we wanted for a quick lunch, and our coffee cups stayed full. The children's menu is good and cheap.

9 Kenai National Wildlife Refuge

Floating through the Kenai National Wildlife Refuge in a canoe narrows the world into a circle of green water, spruce, and birch. You can paddle and hike for days without encountering more than a few other people, your only expense the cost of your canoe and the vehicle that carried you to the trailhead. Out there with my son, I once noticed that, other than his voice, the only sounds I had heard in 2 days were the gurgling of the water and the wind shushing in the birch leaves. You rely on yourself, but your greatest tests are not overly taxing. Trail a line behind the canoe, and, when you catch a rainbow trout, land it and make a fire to cook it. Launch your body into the clear, frigid water to rinse off the sweat on a warm day. Float slowly, watching eagles circle the treetops and puffy clouds drifting like ships past your little world.

Most of the western half of the Kenai Peninsula lies within the 2 million acres of the refuge—it's almost as large as Yellowstone National Park—and much of that land is impossibly remote and truly dedicated to the wildlife. The Kenai River flows through part of the refuge, but the refuge is just a name to the anglers who pursue its salmon. (Information about fishing and rafting the river is above, in the Kenai/Soldotna and Cooper Landing sections.)

Canoeists will be more interested in the lowlands on the west side, west of the Sterling Highway and north of Kenai and Soldotna. The lakes there are as numerous as the speckles on a trout's back, or at least that's how they appears from the air. From the ground, the region is a maze of lakes connected by trails—more than 70 lakes you can reach on canoe routes stretching more than 150 miles. It's the easiest way to real Alaska wilderness I know.

ESSENTIALS

GETTING THERE The refuge surrounds much of the land from Cooper Landing at the north to Homer at the south and Cook Inlet to the west. The Sterling Highway and roads that branch from it are the main ways to the lakes, trails, and rivers, and there is no practical way there without a vehicle.

VISITOR INFORMATION Stop in at the **Kenai National Wildlife Refuge Visitor Center,** Ski Hill Road (P.O. Box 2139), Soldotna, AK 99669 (☎ **907/262-7021;** kenai.fws.gov), for guidance before plunging into the wilderness; they'll tell you about the land and the animals of the refuge. It's open in summer Monday to Friday 8am to 5pm, Saturday and Sunday 9am to 6pm; winter, Monday to Friday 8am to 4:30pm, Saturday and Sunday 10am to 5pm. The U.S. Fish and Wildlife Service, which manages the refuge, exhibits natural history displays here, and shows a film each hour in the afternoon in the summer. A mile-long nature trail has numbered stations. The staff offers advice and sells books and maps that you'll definitely need for a successful backcountry trip. The Web site contains detailed trip-planning information for the canoe routes. To find the center, turn left just south of the Kenai River Bridge, taking the dirt road uphill from the building-supply store.

✪ CANOEING

From 1941 to 1980 the refuge was known as the Kenai National Moose Range. Its brushy wetlands are paradise for **moose,** rich in their favorite foods of willow and birch shoots and pond weeds. Moose like to dine while wading. Waterfowl and other birds, beavers, muskrats, and other aquatic animals are common on the lakes. People also must be partly aquatic to explore the lakes, paddling canoes across their surfaces, pushing through lily pad passages between lakes, and frequently hiking in rubber boots between lakes while carrying the canoe and camping gear.

There are two main canoe routes, both reached from Sterling River and Swan Lake roads, north of the Sterling Highway from the town of Sterling. The **Swan Lake Canoe Route** is a 60-mile network of 30 connected lakes. It meets Swan Lake Road twice, allowing a loop of several days, and in between adventurers can penetrate many lakes deep into the wilderness, visiting remote lakes they'll have all to themselves. It's also possible to canoe through to the Moose River and ride its current 17 miles over a long day back to the Sterling Highway.

Getting anywhere requires frequent portages of a quarter mile or so, and more ambitious routes have mile-long portages. You can skip all the portaging, however, by floating 2 days down the **Swanson River** to its mouth, at the Captain Cook State Recreation Area (see below), joining the river at a landing at mile 17.5 of Swanson River Road. The water is slow and easy all the way.

The most challenging of the routes is the **Swanson River Canoe Route,** which connects to the river's headwaters through a series of lakes and longer portages. The route covers 80 miles, including 40 lakes and the river float. Both routes have many dozens of remote campsites—just lakeside areas of cleared ground with fire rings—and most of the portages are well marked and maintained with wooden planking over the wet areas.

If you go, among your most important tools will be the book ***The Kenai Canoe Trails,*** by Daniel L. Quick, published by Northlite Publishing Company (33335 Skyline Dr., Soldotna, AK 99669-9752). This extraordinary guide contains superdetailed maps and directions, and advice on how to plan your trip and fish and camp on your way—I've never seen a trail guide like it. The author and publisher leads guided canoe trips on the routes; his company is **Northlite** (☎ **800/994-5997** or 907/262-5997; www.alaska.net/~northlit). For around $125 per person per day, you get his personal attention and everything you need but your own clothes. He'll do day trips or paddles of up to a week. Quick shows his gorgeous photography of the area on his Web site, where you can also order the book.

Experienced canoeists don't need a guide, although, of course, you must be prepared before you go off on your own in this wilderness. I haven't provided detailed driving instructions because you'll need detailed maps to go at all. **Trails Illustrated** produces a good detailed map of the whole area, printed on plastic (see "Fast Facts: Alaska" in chapter 2 for details). A serviceable free map is distributed by the refuge visitor center. Coleman canoes and the gear to go with them, including car-top carriers, are for rent from the Sports Den in Soldotna for $35; rental information is listed under "Fishing" in section 8 of this chapter, on Kenai/Soldotna. The refuge can provide you with a list of other rental agencies. But no one in the area I know of rents camping equipment or lightweight canoes, so a better plan might be to rent everything you need, including a canoe and camping gear, in Anchorage (see chapter 6).

There's much more to do in the refuge too, including several upland hiking trails. The refuge visitor center has a free guide map, and can give guidance on where to go.

CAMPING

For car camping, away from all the fishing mayhem, the **Captain Cook State Recreation Area** is a lovely and underused 3,460-acre seaside area on Cook Inlet, 25 miles north of Kenai on the North Kenai Road, at the mouth of the Swanson River. There are lots of attractive sites among large birches, trails, beach walking, a canoe landing at the end of the Swanson River Canoe Route, and lake swimming. The camping fee is $10. **Daniels Lake Lodge,** listed above in section 8 of this chapter, on Kenai/Soldotna, is nearby.

There are many campgrounds within the refuge, too, some of them lovely, quiet spots on the edge of uninhabited lakes, such as the small **Rainbow Lake** and **Dolly Varden Lake campgrounds,** on Swanson River Road near the start of the canoe routes. Get a complete listing from the visitor center. Generally, there is no camping fee.

10 Homer: Cosmic Hamlet by the Sea

Homer's leading mystic, the late Brother Asaiah Bates, always maintained that a confluence of metaphysical forces causes a focus of powerful creative energy on this little seaside town. It's hard to argue. Homer is full of creative people: artists, eccentrics, and those who simply contribute to a quirky community in a beautiful place. Indeed, Brother Asaiah may have been the quintessential Homerite, although perhaps an extreme example, with his gray ponytail, extraordinary openness and generosity, and flowery rhetoric about "the cosmic wheel of life." Homer is full of outspoken, unusual, and even odd individualists—people who make living in the town almost an act of belief. I can say this because I'm a former Homerite myself.

The geography of Homer—physical as well as metaphysical—has gathered certain people here the way currents gather driftwood on the town's pebble beaches. Homer is at the end of the road; the nation's paved highway system comes to an abrupt conclusion at the tip of the Homer Spit, almost 5 miles out in the middle of Kachemak Bay, and believers of one kind or another have washed up here for decades. There were the "barefooters," a communal group that eschewed shoes, even in the Alaska winter (Brother Asaiah came with them in the early 1950s). There are the Russian Old Believers, who organize their strictly traditional communities around their objection to Russian Orthodox church reforms made by Peter the Great. There are the former hippies who have become successful commercial fishermen after flocking here in the late 1960s to camp as "Spit rats" on the beach. And there are even the current migrants—artists and retired people, fundamentalist preachers and New Age healers, wealthy North Slope oil workers and land-poor settlers with no visible means of support—all people who live here simply because they choose to.

The choice is understandable. Homer lies on the north side of Kachemak Bay, a branch of lower Cook Inlet of extraordinary biological productivity. The **halibut fishing,** especially, is exceptional. The town has a breathtaking setting on the Spit and on a wildflower-covered bench high above the bay. The outdoors, especially on the water and across the bay, contains wonderful opportunities. And the **arts community** has developed into an attraction of its own. There are several exceptional galleries and the Pratt Museum, which has a national reputation.

You'll be disappointed, however, if you expect a charming little fishing town. Poor community planning has created a town that doesn't live up to its setting. Homer Spit in summer is a traffic-choked jumble of cheap tourist development and RVs. Homer began to take its modern form after two events: In the 1950s the Sterling Highway connected it to the rest of the world, and in 1964 the Good Friday earthquake sank

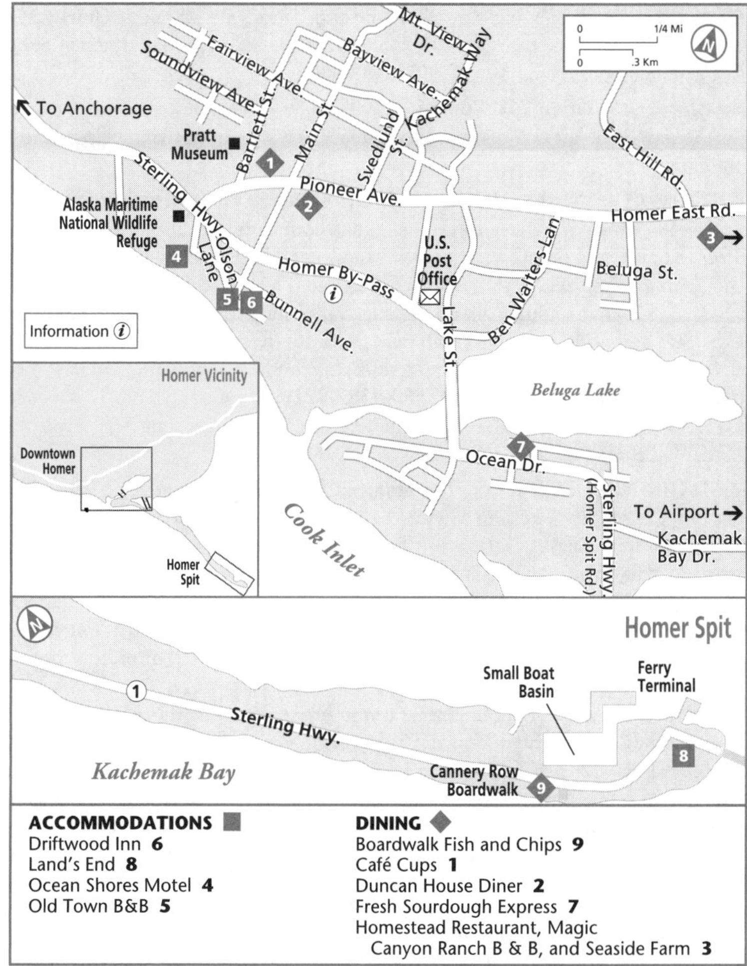

the Spit, narrowing a much larger piece of land with a small forest into the tendril that now barely stands above the water. If not for constant reinforcement by the federal government, the Spit long since would have become an island, and Homer would hardly exist. As long as it survives, however, the town makes the most of that unique finger into the sea. Whether or not it is a cosmic focal, it certainly is an exceptional launching point to one of the world's great marine recreation areas.

ESSENTIALS

GETTING THERE **By Car** At about 235 miles, Homer is roughly 4½ hours from Anchorage by car, if you don't stop at any of the interesting or beautiful places along the way. It's a scenic drive. If you take a rental car, you may want to drive it both ways, as the drop-off fees from Anchorage to Homer are high.

By Bus **Homer Stage Line** (☎ **907/235-7009** or 907/399-1847) runs to Anchorage and back six times a week during the height of summer, and less frequently the rest of the year. The fare is $45 one way, $80 round-trip. Tickets are for sale at **Quicky Mart,** 1242 Ocean Dr., in Homer (☎ **907/235-2252**). In Anchorage, buy tickets at **Seward Bus Line,** 3339 Fairbanks St. (☎ **907/563-0800**).

By Air **Era Aviation** (☎ **800/866-8394**) serves Homer from Anchorage several times a day. Small air-taxi operators use Homer as a hub for outlying villages and the outdoors.

By Ferry The **Alaska Marine Highway System** (☎ **800/642-0066** or 907/235-8449; www.dot.state.ak.us/external/amhs/home.html) connects Homer to Seldovia, Kodiak, and points west along the Alaska Peninsula and Aleutian Archipelago, and Seward to the east, with the ferry *Tustumena.* The run to Kodiak takes 9½ hours and costs $48 for an adult walk-on passenger. It's a long trip, but a memorable one. A U.S. Fish and Wildlife Service naturalist rides the ferries to present programs and answer questions. The **Homer ferry terminal** is run by a contractor, and has its own toll-free number and Web site (☎ **800/382-9229;** www.akmhs.com/), which may make it easier to get through to someone who can answer questions than through the state number above.

VISITOR INFORMATION **The Homer Chamber of Commerce Visitor Information Center,** 135 Sterling Hwy. (P.O. Box 541), Homer, AK 99603 (☎ **907/235-7740;** homeralaska.org/), is on the right as you enter town. In summer, staff is on hand daily from 9am to 8pm to answer questions and to hand out brochures on local businesses—and you can buy tickets for the halibut derby. Winter hours are Monday through Friday 9am to 5pm. Get a copy of the ***Homer Tourism and Recreation Guide,*** published by the *Homer News,* at the center, or order it from the chamber's Web site. It includes a useful map.

On the right side of the highway as you arrive in town, the **Alaska Maritime National Wildlife Refuge Visitor Center,** 451 Sterling Hwy., Ste. 2, Homer, AK 99603 (☎ **907/235-6961;** www.r7.fws.gov/nwr/akmnwr/), is the place to stop for outdoors information wherever you go in the area. It's open in summer daily 9am to 6pm, winter by appointment. The refuge itself consists of islands off Alaska from the Arctic to near British Columbia. The U.S. Fish and Wildlife Service manages these lands for the benefit of birds and marine mammals, and people rarely set foot on their shores, but rangers in Homer also offer bird and beach walks frequently in the summer, and show natural history films and give programs at the center. Call for times.

Call the **Kachemak Bay Bird Alert Information Line** (☎ **907/235-7337**) to find out about recent sightings and upcoming birder events, and leave news of your own observations. It is operated by the wildlife refuge.

The **Kachemak Bay State Park District Office,** Mile 168.5 on the Sterling Hwy., 4 miles from town (P.O. Box 3248), Homer, AK 99603 (☎ **907/235-7024;** www.dnr.state.ak.us/parks/units/kbay/kbay.htm), can help answer questions about planning a trip to the trails and beaches across Kachemak Bay from Homer and book remote cabin rentals.

GETTING AROUND The best way to get to and around Homer is by car. If you didn't bring one, you can rent a car at the airport from **Hertz** (☎ **800/654-3131** or 907/235-0734) or from **Polar Car Rental** (☎ **907/235-5998**). There are several taxi companies in town, including **CHUX Cab** (☎ **907/235-CHUX**).

For strong riders, a bike is a good way around town. You do have to dodge traffic at times, and the Spit is 5 miles long, but it's a great way to experience the outdoors. Some excellent mountain-biking routes are mentioned below. **Homer Saw and Cycle,** 1532 Ocean Dr. (☎ **907/235-8406;** e-mail: homersaw@xyz.net), rents mountain bikes and trailers, starting at $15 half day. They're open Monday to Friday 9am to

5:30pm, Saturday 11am to 5pm. It's wise to reserve bikes a day or two ahead, especially if an outing depends on getting one. **Chain Reaction Sports,** 3858 Lake St. (☎ **907/235-0750**), specializes in high-quality mountain bikes.

Homer Tours (☎ **907/235-6200;** www.ptialaska.net/~ericson/) offers van and bus tours. A 1-hour driving tour is $15 and a 4-hour tour that makes stops is $35.

SPECIAL EVENTS **Homer's Winter Carnival,** in mid-February, is a big community event, a small-town celebration with a beer-making contest, parade, and snow-sculpture competition, among other highlights.

The **Kachemak Bay Shorebird Festival** (☎ **907/235-7740;** homeralaska.org/shorebird.htm), held in early May, includes guided bird-watching hikes and boat excursions, natural history workshops, art shows and performances, a wooden boat festival, and other events. It's organized by Alaska Maritime National Wildlife Refuge and the Homer Chamber of Commerce to mark the return of the annual migration in early May. **The Kachemak Bay Wooden Boat Festival,** which takes place at the same time as the Shorebird Festival, displays handmade boats from around the region and presents workshops and films.

Concert on the Lawn, put on usually the last Sunday in July by KBBI public radio (☎ **907/235-7721**), is a day-long outdoor music, craft, and food festival that brings together the whole town.

The **Jackpot Halibut Derby** (☎ **907/235-7740;** homeralaska.org/halibut-derby.htm) lasting the whole summer long, has a top prize that has surpassed $25,000 for the biggest fish of the summer, and smaller monthly prizes and tagged fish prizes. Winning fish are usually 300 pounds or more. Of course, you must buy your $2 ticket before you fish.

FAST FACTS There are two **banks,** with ATMs, on the Sterling Highway near Heath Street.

The **South Peninsula Hospital** is at the top of Bartlett Street, off Pioneer Avenue (☎ **907/235-8101**).

Eagle Eye Photo and Communications, 639 E. Pioneer Ave. (☎ **907/235-8525;** www.eagleeyephoto.com/), rents computers with Internet access and offers copier and other business services.

For nonemergency needs within the city limits, call the **Homer Police Department** (☎ **907/235-3150**); outside the city, phone the **Alaska State Troopers** (☎ **907/235-8239**). Both have offices located across Pioneer Avenue from the intersection with Heath Street.

The **post office** is on the Sterling Highway at Heath Street.

Within city limits, **sales tax** is 5.5%; there's no room tax. Outside the city limits, you pay only the 2% Kenai Peninsula Borough sales tax.

ATTRACTIONS

Homer's manmade attractions derive from its setting, from walks on the beaches and in the hilltop meadows, and from Kachemak Bay itself. The art this place has inspired is found in more than a dozen galleries and studios in town, not including those across the bay in Halibut Cove and Seldovia (see below). A widely distributed brochure lists most of the galleries in town, with a map. Most of these places feature photography, inexpensive prints, pottery and crafts as well as fine art, and some have other sidelines. Some of the smallest are also the best, where you get to see the mind of the gallery owner at work in his or her creation of a collection. Four good shops are right next to each other on Pioneer Avenue near Kachemak Way: **Fireweed Gallery** (☎ **907/235-7040**), **Picture Alaska Gallery** (☎ **907/235-2300**), **William Henry Gallery**

(☎ **907/235-3411**), and **Ptarmigan Arts,** listed below. New shows open all over town on the first Friday of the month, when restaurants hold special evenings and the entire community comes out for an evening of gallery hopping.

✪ **Pratt Museum.** 3779 Bartlett St. (at Pioneer Ave.). ☎ **907/235-8635.** www.prattmuseum.org. Admission $6 adults, $5.50 seniors, $3 children ages 6–18, $20 family rate. High season daily 10am–6pm. Low season Tues–Sun noon–5pm. Closed Jan.

The Homer Society of Natural History's museum is as good as any you'll find in a town of this size, and it has achieved a well-deserved national reputation. The Pratt displays art and explains local history, too, but it is strongest in natural history. Volunteers pioneered new technology that allows visitors to watch birds inside nesting burrows on Gull Island and bears feeding at the McNeil River State Game Sanctuary (the Gullcam and Bearcam), and you can zoom and pan the cameras live from controls in the museum. There is a saltwater aquarium housing local marine life, and if you're curious about all the fishing boats down in the harbor, you can find out about the different types of gear as well as the fish they catch. The exhibit on the *Exxon Valdez* oil spill, "Darkened Waters," toured nationally, to acclaim. In the garden outside, you can learn to identify all the local wildflowers, and a forest trail teaches about the ecology there. Free garden and forest tours take place daily at 3pm in the summer. There's much more to see, too.

✪ **Bunnell Street Gallery.** 106 W. Bunnell Ave. ☎ **907/235-2662.** www.xyz.net/~bunnell. Summer daily 10am–6pm. Winter, Mon–Sat 10am–6pm. Closed Jan.

This nonprofit gallery, located in a perfect space in an old hardware store near Bishop's Beach at the lower end of Main Street, is my favorite in Alaska. Unlike most other Alaska galleries, which double as tourist gift shops, Bunnell was made by and for artists, and the experience is noncommercial and often challenging. You may be tempted to become a member of the nonprofit corporation that runs it, for membership comes with a one-of-a-kind plate made by one of the artists. As with all Homer art, the themes of the work tend to be fishy, and the medium and style could be anything. The gallery also puts on summer concerts, booking nationally known folk and classical performers into the most intimate of settings. Tickets are $8 to $12. Don't miss the **Two Sisters Bakery** and coffee shop next door.

Ptarmigan Arts. 471 E. Pioneer Ave. ☎ **907/235-5345.** High season, Mon–Sat 10am–7pm, Sun noon–5pm. Low season, Mon–Sat 11am–6pm, Sun noon–5pm.

Often staffed by the artists themselves, Ptarmigan Arts specializes in crafts, especially ceramics and fabrics, which are the most common media in Homer and are generally more affordable than fine art. Occasionally you can see a demonstration by one of the resident artists. There's always a tremendous array of work in various styles.

Sea Lion Gallery. 4241 Homer Spit Rd. (Central Charters Boardwalk). ☎ **907/235-3400.** E-mail: sealion@xyz.net. Summer, Mon–Sat 11am–9pm, Sun noon–6pm. Closed in winter.

Wildlife artist Gary Lyon and his family own and staff this small gallery among the T-shirt shops on one of the boardwalks on Homer Spit. It's pleasant but a little odd to see very valuable works by Lyon and others displayed in this intimate setting. Lyon's work captures Alaska wildlife in spectacular detail, but also transforms his subjects with a distinctively dreamy vision. The rooms they rent upstairs are described under "Accommodations," below.

Norman Lowell Studio & Gallery. ☎ **907/235-7344.** Sterling Hwy. milepost 160.9 (near Anchor Point, about 12 miles out the Sterling Hwy. from Homer. Mon–Sat 9am–7pm, Sun 1–5pm. Closed Oct–Apr.

Lowell built his own huge gallery on his homestead to show his life's work. The immense oils of Alaska landscapes, which are not for sale, hang in a building that counts as one of Alaska's larger art museums. Admission is free, and Lowell or his wife, Libby, often host guests who walk through. Their original homestead cabin also is a museum, showing pioneer life in Alaska as it was when they originally settled here. The studio/gallery sells Lowell's paintings, which range in price from $750 to $30,000; prints start at $100.

GETTING OUTSIDE

The best **map of the Kachemak Bay area** is produced by Alaska Road and Recreation Maps, P.O. Box 102459, Anchorage, AK 99510. Available all over town, it costs around $5, depending on where you buy it.

ON THE HOMER SIDE OF KACHEMAK BAY

✪ **TIDE POOLING** Exploring Kachemak Bay's tide pools is the best way to really get to know the sea and meet the strange and wonderful animals that live in it, and it doesn't cost anything but the price of a pair of rubber boots. First, check a tide book, available for free or for a nominal price in virtually any local store, or ask a local to check one for you. You need a low tide of –2 or lower, meaning that low water will be at least 2 feet below the normal low, some 25 feet below the high. Extralow tides expose more of the lower intertidal zone that contains the most interesting creatures. At a –5 tide, you could find octopus and other oddities. Also, the lower the tide, the more time you'll have to look. Keep track of the time: The tide will come in faster than you imagine, and you could get stranded and quickly drown in the 40°F water.

The best place to go in town is reached from Bishop's Beach Park, near the lower end of Main Street. Walk west on the beach toward the opening of the bay to Cook Inlet. It's at least a half-hour walk to the Coal Point area, where the sand and boulders end, and bedrock makes out from the shore. This is where you'll find pools of water left behind by the receding tide, many full of life. Explore patiently and gently—look at the animals and touch them, but always put them back as they were and be careful not to crush anything underfoot. Marine invertebrate identification keys and many other field guides are sold at **The Book Store** on the Sterling Highway next to Eagle Foods, and the Wildlife Refuge Visitors Center, above under "Visitor Information," is eager to help with advice. If you want to keep going, there's usually a sea otter raft offshore about 3 miles down the beach. Just continue walking, keeping your eyes on the water. As always with watching wildlife, binoculars will improve the experience.

HIKING There are trails on the bench above Homer as well as across the bay at Kachemak Bay State Park (see below). The 6-mile **Homestead Trail** is an old wagon road used by Homer's early settlers. The largely informal trail is lovely and peaceful, tunneling through alders, across fields of wildflowers, and past old homestead cabins. From a hilltop meadow you can see all the way to the Inlet and the volcanoes beyond. A trailhead is at the reservoir on Skyline Drive—drive up West Hill Road from the Sterling Highway, turn right, and follow Skyline, turning left before the pond.

DRIVING OR MOUNTAIN BIKING Several gravel roads around Homer make for exquisite drives or bike rides. Mountain bikers can use the Homestead Trail, above, too. **East End Road** goes through lovely seaside pastures, a forest, and the village of Fritz Creek, then follows the bluff line through meadows toward the head of the bay. The road eventually turns into an all-terrain-vehicle track; don't drive beyond your vehicle's ability to get out, but, of course, a mountain bike can handle it. **Skyline Drive** has extraordinary views of high canyons and Kachemak Bay; drive up East Hill Road just east of Homer. The two bike shops listed above, under "Getting Around," can give you many more ideas. The great mountain biking across the bay is described below.

The nonprofit **Alaska Center for Coastal Studies** (☎ **907-235-6667;** www.akcoastalstudies.org/) leads guided nature walks daily in the summer in the wildflower meadows and woods off Skyline Drive, at the Wynn Nature Center.

HORSEBACK RIDING Ranchers have worked around Kachemak Bay for decades. Drive east of town on East End Road and you can see pastures full of cattle overlooking views that anywhere else would be used for resort hotels. **Trails End Horse Adventures** (☎ **907/235-6393**), 11.2 miles out East End, offers trail rides and overnight trips starting at $20 for the first hour and $15 an hour thereafter; they take all ages and raw beginners.

On & Across Kachemak Bay

Along the south side of the Kachemak Bay, glaciers, fjords, and little wooded islands are arrayed like a smorgasbord before Homer. A quick boat ride puts you there for sea kayaking, mountain biking on unconnected dirt roads, hiking in the mountains, or eating sushi in a top-flight restaurant on pilings. Or gallery hopping, or resting at a remote lodge, or studying at a nature center, or walking the streets of a forgotten fishing village. The far side of the bay has no road link to import the mundane, mass-produced world, but it does have people, and they make the landscape even richer and more enchanting than it would be alone. And underneath the water, there's a wealth of halibut and salmon.

There are two settlements across the bay, **Halibut Cove** and **Seldovia,** each with its own services and lodgings; they are described elsewhere in this chapter. Remote lodgings that aren't in any of the towns are described below under "Accommodations." Here I've covered the many places you can visit for a day trip or longer away from town or lodge.

TRANSPORTATION ACROSS THE WATER The daily **Jakolof Ferry Service** (☎ **907/235-2376;** www.jakolofferryservice.com/) runs to the south side of the bay several times a day all summer with a handsome 34-foot wooden boat. The vessel can carry up to 18 passengers, mostly seated outside, and can pull right up on the beach. It's a great way to get to wilderness cabins and kayaking waters, the hiking and mountain biking roads accessible from the Jakolof Dock (with road access to Seldovia), Halibut Cove, Kachemak Bay State Park, and other remote points. Fares generally are under $50 round-trip, children half price, free age 3 and under—pretty much standard for a water taxi across the bay. Stop by the office on the Spit's Cannery Row Boardwalk for ideas. The Ferry Service also rents remote cabins across the bay for $60 to $75 a night.

Many other water taxis serve the bay, booking through the agencies listed above or directly. **Mako's Water Taxi** (☎ **907/235-9055**) has been around a while and has a good reputation.

JAKOLOF BAY A state-maintained dock opens an area of gentle shorelines, abandoned logging roads, and inexpensive cabins to visitors who seek the wilderness but can't afford to stay at a wilderness lodge. West of Kachemak Bay State Park and east of Seldovia, the lands have roads, but they aren't connected to anything and are used as much by mountain bikers as by anyone else. You can take the Jakolof Bay Ferry straight to the Jakolof dock. The ferry owners rent simple cabins, and the Across the Bay Tent and Breakfast, listed under "Wilderness Lodges" in the "Accommodations" section below, also has inexpensive lodgings.

There's plenty to do in the area. The waters of Jakolof, Little Jakolof, Kasitsna, and Little Tutka bays, and the tiny Herring Islands, are appealing and protected for sea kayaking. Supreme mountain biking trails lead along the shore and right across the peninsula through forest and meadows for berry picking. The Red Mountain and Rocky River roads are prime routes; check with one of the bike shops or the locals to find out about dangerous river crossings and other hazards. A maintained 10-mile road west leads to the charming village of Seldovia, described below.

KACHEMAK BAY STATE PARK The park comprises much of the land across the water that makes all those views from Homer so spectacular. For surprisingly little cost, you can be dropped off there after breakfast, walk the beach, hike in those woods and climb the mountains, then meet your boat in time to be back in Homer for dinner and the first other people you've seen all day. This is heaven, as far as I'm concerned.

The park's main office is at the ranger station listed under "Visitor Information" above. Its center is the summer-only **ranger station** in Halibut Cove Lagoon, where there's a dock and mooring buoys for public use, three public rental cabins over the water, a campsite, and excellent king salmon fishing in mid-June.

The park has about 80 miles of trails, mostly linking here; get a trail guide at the ranger stations or the visitor center. The trails generally start at tidewater among lush, mossy forest of towering spruce and rise into the craggy mountains—up sharp peaks, to a glacier, or, if you don't want to climb, over the hills to the next secluded beach. Bring mosquito repellent and know bear avoidance skills (see "Outdoors Health & Safety" in chapter 2). You can hike to a public rental cabin less than 3 miles from the Halibut Cove dock.

The park's fifth cabin is on Tutka Bay, off the Halibut Cove trail network. You can also use these places as a base for self-guided sea kayaking. Cabin permits are $50 a night and usually must be reserved several months in advance from the ranger station (reservation details are in section 1 of this chapter.

OUTFITTERS

The Bookie. P.O. Box 195, Homer, AK 99603. ☎ **888/335-1581** or 907/235-1581. www.alaskabookie.com.

This newer outfit seems to focus on smaller operators, water taxis, and nonmotorized sports.

Central Charters. 4241 Homer Spit Rd., Homer, AK 99603. ☎ **800/478-7847** or 907/235-7847. www.central-charter.com.

This is the longest established of the booking agents in Homer, and is the place to go for the most popular activities, especially halibut fishing. They have a ticket office on the right side of the Spit as you drive out.

ACTIVITIES

FISHING Homer is known for ✪ **halibut,** those huge, flat bottom fish, and the harbor is full of charter boats that will take you out for the day for around $150 per person. Every day, a few people catch fish that are larger than they are, and halibut over 50 pounds are common. Getting out to where the fish are plentiful requires an early start and a long ride to unprotected waters. People who get seasick easily shouldn't go, as the boat wallows on the waves during fishing. (Take Dramamine *before* you set out; if you wait, it probably won't do any good.) Using gear and lines that look strong enough to pick up the boat, you jig the herring bait (chunks of herring or cod) up and down on the bottom. Halibut aren't wiley or acrobatic, and fighting one can be like pulling up a sunken Buick. One good, large operator is **Silver Fox Charters** (☎ **800/478-8792** or 907/235-8792; silverfoxcharters.com/). Others can be booked through Central Charters, listed above under "Outfitters," or you find one on the **Homer Charter Association** Web site, which has a list and links to dozens of boats, at **homercharterassociation.com/**.

Salmon feed in Kachemak Bay in winter and are fished with trolling gear year-round, not only when they're running in the streams. **Katmai Coastal Tours** (☎ **800/532-8338** or 907/235-7131; www.katmaibears.com) runs those charters, as well as excursions for halibut (their main focus is cruises to see bears on the shore of Katmai National Park). Also, a small lagoon called the Fishing Hole on the Spit is stocked with terminal run king and silver salmon by the Alaska Department of Fish and Game. Silvers arrive early August through early October, and kings are in the lagoon starting in late May for most of the summer. These fish have nowhere to spawn, and some anglers scorn such "fish-in-a-barrel" fishing. At the end of the runs, snagging is permitted, which is something like mugging salmon, and can be a lot of fun, if not something you'll brag about later at the Rod and Gun Club. For more natural salmon fishing, you can surf cast for silvers from the end of the Spit, head over to Halibut Cove Lagoon (see Kachemak Bay State Park, above) or Seldovia, or drive back up the Sterling Highway to the Anchor River, an excellent steelhead trout stream, and the other rivers that flow west into Cook Inlet. The **Alaska Department of Fish and Game** maintains a fishing hot line at ☎ **907/235-6930.** They're located at 3298 Douglas (☎ **907/235-8191**).

Coal Point Trading Co., 4300 Homer Spit (☎ **907/235-3877**), will process, pack, and ship your catch as ordered.

NATURAL HISTORY TOURS Rainbow Tours's twice-a-day **Gull Island** trip is the best deal for getting out on the water in Alaska: For only $20 for an adult, $10 age 12 and under, the comfortable 67-foot *Rainbow Connection* takes passengers on a 90-minute trip to the Gull Island bird rookery, lingering so close to the rocks that it's possible to get a good view of the birds' nests with the naked eye. In season, you can see glaucus winged gulls, tufted puffins, black-legged kittiwakes, common murres, red-faced and pelagic cormorants, horned puffins, pigeon guillemots, and occasionally other species. The boat continues on to drop off visitors at the Alaska Center for Coastal Studies in Peterson Bay, listed below, so you get to see quite a bit of the bay for the price of Gull Island alone. There's a snack and beer and wine bar on board. **Rainbow Tours** has an office on the Spit, at the Cannery Row Boardwalk (☎ **907/235-7272;** www.rainbowtours.net). They also offer tours to Seldovia and fishing charters.

The nonprofit **Center for Alaska Coastal Studies** foundation is dedicated to educating the public about the sea. That means the group's emphasis isn't on making money, but on interpreting Kachemak Bay for visitors on daylong explorations of the Peterson Bay area. If the tides are right, the volunteers will take you on a fascinating guided tide-pool walk; if not, you can take a woodland nature walk. You decide what you want to do. There's also a lodge with saltwater tanks containing creatures from the intertidal zone and microscopes to inspect your finds. **Rainbow Tours** (☎ **907/235-7272**) books the trips and takes passengers at 9am daily on the *Rainbow Connection,* described above. At $63 per adult, $43 ages 6 to 12, it's a bargain. Pack your own lunch, as none is provided, and bring footwear suitable for hiking and beach walks. You can reach the center's office at ☎ **907/235-6667** (www.akcoastalstudies.org/; P.O. Box 2225, Homer, AK 99603).

SEA KAYAKING Silence fell as the boat pulled away from the beach, leaving us behind with the kayaks and our guide. For the rest of the day my son and I absorbed the water-reflected sunlight and glided past fancifully shaped rocks and resident sea otters around Yukon Island. We explored beaches, picnicked, raced, and discovered tiny bays too small for any other craft. At the end of the day, we had a new friend in our quietly cheerful guide, Allison O'Hara, and discovered that she'd imperceptibly taught us a lot about sea kayaking. I certainly can recommend ✪ **True North Kayak Adventures** (☎ **907/235-0708;** www.truenorthkayak.com), which O'Hara runs with Kevin Bell. Their beginner day trips cost $125, including lunch and passage across the bay. Most kayaking day trips in Alaska towns barely get out of the small boat harbor. This trip doesn't feel so tame—it's more like a miniexpedition. They also offer more challenging overnight and multiday trips to remote waters in the area.

The protected waters, tiny islands, and remote settlements on the south side of Kachemak Bay make for perfect sea kayaking no matter whom you go with, or, for experienced paddlers, if you go on your own. Kayakers can take a water taxi across and explore at will, camping on beaches over much of the bay. Check with the Kachemak Bay State Park rangers for guidance. True North Kayak rents to experienced paddlers for $65 a day double, $45 single, with discounts for multiple days. Also see the Halibut Cove and Seldovia sections of this chapter (section 11 and 12) for other rental and guided opportunities.

FLIGHTSEEING & BEAR VIEWING There are several good air taxis in Homer, providing access to the really remote areas of the southern Kenai Peninsula and lower Cook Inlet that you can't easily reach by boat, but **Kachemak Air Service** (☎ **907/235-8924;** www.alaskaseaplanes.com) is really special. It offers spectacular scenic flights over the bay and glaciers starting at $120 per person. The personable Bill de Creeft, flying out of Homer since 1967, is experienced enough to qualify as a pioneer aviator; but he has nothing on his favorite plane, a restored 1929 Travel Air S-6000-B, one of only six remaining examples of the executive aircraft, with mahogany trim and wicker seats. De Creeft also operates rugged DeHavilland Otters and Beavers, which carry fishermen, hikers, kayakers, and those who just want to see the wilderness; the company also offers bear-viewing day trips and boat-based overnights on the west side of Cook Inlet.

ACCOMMODATIONS

Homer has many good B&Bs. About 20 are members of **Homer's Finest Bed & Breakfast Network,** P.O. Box 1909, Homer Alaska 99603 (☎ **907/235-4983;** homeraccommodations.com/), which has links to each on its Web site. The Homer Chamber of Commerce (homeralaska.org) has even more links.

In addition to the places I've listed in detail, **The Sea Lion Cove,** above the Sea Lion Gallery on Homer Spit (☎ **907/235-3400** in summer or 907/235-8767 in winter; www.AlaskaOne.com/sealion/), has two comfortable rooms with kitchens with a deck right over the beach where you can hear the waves roll in at night. **Cranes' Crest Bed and Breakfast,** 59830 Sanford Dr. (☎ **907/235-2969;** www.akms.com/cranes), 5 miles out atop the beach behind the town, has nesting sandhill cranes that wander around like lawn ornaments, and sweeping, cinematic views you can sit and watch all day.

Besides the hotels listed in detail below, you'll find good rooms at the **Bay View Inn,** 2851 Sterling Hwy. (☎ **907/235-8485;** www.bayviewalaska.com), at the top of Baycrest Hill before you come into town on the Sterling Highway, with amazing views, attractive little rooms, peace, and reasonable prices. The **Best Western Bidarka**

Hermits on the Homestead

Late in October, the snow was holding back in the clouds like a strong emotion. The ground was frozen, the swamp grasses stiff, brittle, painted with frost. This was the one time of year when, with a stout four-wheel-drive truck, you could drive in to Ben's cabin. It stood on a small rise amid his hundreds of acres of swampy ground, the only spot where trees could get out of the dampness and grow. The heavy, lovingly peeled logs of the house lay horizontally amid big birch and white spruce trees. Ben had dragged these huge tree trunks from far afield, by himself, when he started his homestead nearly 40 years earlier, so he could keep living trees nearer to his house.

I'm not using his real name. Ben was a private guy. He generously invited us in, offered coffee from the percolator on top of the soapstone wood stove, but it was clear that he wasn't quite sure he remembered how to talk to people—where to look, for example—and he kept mumbling and looking at my feet or the sky. He showed us around the house: the huge rocks he'd dragged in to build a foundation, the cellar where he stored his food, the collection of moose racks. Food tended to walk by each fall—he never had to go far to get his moose, and one of the biggest he shot right on the doorstep. Everything about his home was exactly the way he wanted it, the product of immense effort to make it all with his own hands. I could see plainly how he'd spent his days all these years. But I could only imagine what his nights must have been like, all alone out here—the piles of *Reader's Digest* and *National Geographic* magazines, the insistent silence.

I finally asked Ben why he'd spent his whole adult life on this homestead, so far from other people. Why not move to town, where life is easier and there's someone to talk to? Well, he said, he did work construction in the summer for cash. But I knew that was an evasion. How, I asked, did he first end up out here, in the middle of nowhere, in a huge swamp? What made him want to be off by himself when he first came out here, so long ago? Pause—check the shoes, check the sky—well, he said, it seems there was a woman. She chose the other guy.

Years ago, *U.S. News & World Report* did an article about a homesteader on the Kenai Peninsula who was a Vietnam veteran—just one of the many mad hermits from the war who had hidden off in the Alaska woods by themselves, populating the wilderness with human time bombs. The subject of the story, a well-respected member of his little homesteading community, resented the characterization, and the magazine later paid him to settle his libel suit and printed a retraction. Everyone in the area knew the article was a bunch of baloney; Alaska homesteaders are as varied as people in the city. They aren't all crazed veterans any more than they're all victims of unrequited love, although those make the best stories. What they do have in common is a willingness to invest hard physical labor every day of their lives into the things the rest of us obtain effortlessly by turning a thermostat or a faucet handle.

Alaska's homesteaders came in waves. There were the prospectors from the gold rush who stayed. Then, after World War II, GIs with families looking for broad new opportunities came north and settled more land. The counterculture movement of the 1960s brought yet another group.

Federal homesteading laws written to open the Great Plains to agriculture in the 19th century made getting land difficult and required Alaska homesteaders to do a lot of anachronistic, absurd work—like clearing large tracts for farming that could never occur. The homesteaders had to survey the land, live on it, clear much of it, and then answer any challenges about their accomplishments at a hearing. If they passed the test, they received a patent to up to 160 acres.

The laws allowing homesteading on federal lands in Alaska were all repealed by 1986, but the state government still sometimes provides land to its citizens under laws that allow homesteading, lotteries, and sale of remote land. The parcels are very remote and smaller than the old federal homesteads, and the rules still don't make it easy—for a homestead, you have to live at least 25 months on the land in a 5-year period, for example. Many families try, with a Hollywood dream of living in the wilderness, only to give up when they learn firsthand of the hardship, privations, and cold. I know from experience that I want never again to live in a home where the heating is wood or the water is in jugs, and I've never done anything approaching building a homestead. Homesteading isn't like camping. Outdoor skills won't help unless you also know how to repair engines below zero, build houses without power tools, carry all your own water and firewood, and live poor, largely without an income or any of the things money can buy. You have to be willing to bathe rarely, be cold in winter, and be eaten alive by mosquitoes in summer, and end up with land that isn't really worth anything.

Many successful homesteading experiences end with growing children. A couple may make it in the wilderness before having children, and kids don't care if they can take a bath, so long as the parents don't mind washing diapers by hand and being far from medical care. But when children get to a certain age, they need to go to school and be around other children. The families often expect to go back to the homestead someday, but, somehow, they rarely do. Areas that were thriving little communities of neighbors in the 1950s or 1960s now are deserted, perhaps with one hermit left—like my friend Ben. Only about 160,000 acres of Alaska today—out of a total land mass of 365 million acres—show any signs of human habitation. Less than 1% is in private ownership.

My wife's parents homesteaded in the 1950s and '60s. Her father was a World War II veteran. Today the family still has some acreage, and a treasure trove of great stories—among them the tales of my late father-in-law's feats of strength and endurance, and my wife's memory of playing with dolls as a girl, and looking up to meet the eyes of a bear that had been watching her.

But my favorite is the story of Rose and her lover. They lived in the same area in Northern California where Barbara's parents grew up. Everyone in town knew the story of the red-headed beauty who had an affair with an older man. Rose's parents refused to let her marry him and decreed that the couple couldn't see each other anymore. She entered a convent, and he disappeared, never to be seen in the town again. Many years later, after moving to Alaska, Barbara's parents were boating in Kachemak Bay when they got caught by bad weather on the opposite side of the bay from Homer. On their own in an open boat and looking for shelter, they found a cabin on a remote beach of an otherwise uninhabited island. They were taken in and befriended by the hermit who'd homesteaded there for years. After warming up with a cup of coffee, they got to talking about where they'd come from and how they'd ended up in Alaska. When it came time for their host to tell his story, it was about a beautiful young woman he'd loved, named Rose.

Inn, 575 Sterling Hwy. (☎ **907/235-8148**), on the right as you come into town, has standard motel rooms.

Driftwood Inn. 135 W. Bunnell Ave., Homer, AK 99603. ☎ and fax **907/235-8019.** thedriftwoodinn.com/. 20 units, 11 with private bathroom. TV. High season $59–$124 double. Low season $60 double. Extra person $10. DISC, MC, V. No smoking.

The historic building a block from Bishop's Beach and across from the Bunnell Gallery resembles a lodge or B&B, with its large fireplace of rounded beach rock, the hot coffeepot and inexpensive self-serve breakfast in the lobby, and the owner's roving dog. The smallest rooms resemble Pullman compartments in size and configuration, but they're cute, clean, and have some real style. And they're inexpensive. Nine bedrooms share two bathrooms. Larger rooms have more amenities, but not as much charm. The walls are thin, so there's a no-noise policy during evening hours. There's also an appealing 22-site RV park ($25 per night, full hookups) and a small, grassy tent area ($15 per night), plus a coin-op laundry and free coffee in the lobby.

✪ **Land's End.** 4786 Homer Spit Rd., Homer, AK 99603. ☎ **800/478-0400** in Alaska only, or 907/235-0400. www.lands-end-resort.com/. 82 units. TV TEL. High season $109–$150 double. Low season $75–$120 double. Extra person $10. AE, DC, DISC, MC, V.

Traditionally *the* place to stay in Homer, Land's End would be popular no matter what it was like inside because of its location at the tip of Homer Spit, the best spot in Homer and possibly the best spot for a hotel in all Alaska. It's composed of a line of weathered buildings that straggle along the beach crest like driftwood logs, but the interior has been remodeled into comfortable rooms with occasionally fanciful decoration. There are 11 different classes of rooms, ranging from cute shiplike compartments to two-story affairs, and a complex rate schedule to match. The hotel is near the boat harbor, and you can fish right from the beach in front. There's free coffee and a beachfront spa, with exercise equipment and indoor and outdoor hot tubs.

The **Chart Room restaurant** makes good use of its wonderful location, looking out over the beach and bay, with a casual, relaxing atmosphere. The deck outside has glass wind shields, making it a warm, satisfying place to sit over coffee on a sunny day. You can watch otters, eagles, and fishing boats while you eat. Excellent chefs have passed through from year to year, so its hard to predict the quality of the cuisine. Locals discuss the current food at Land's End the way some towns talk about their baseball players. I've had simply prepared fresh seafood there that couldn't have been better.

Magic Canyon Ranch Bed and Breakfast. 40015 Waterman Rd., Homer, AK 99603. ☎ and fax **907/235-6077.** magiccanyonranch.com. 4 units, 2 with private bathroom. High season $85–$100 double. Low season $55–$70 double. Extra adult $25; extra child $20. Rates include full breakfast. MC, V.

At the top of a canyon road off East End Road, the Webb family shares its charming home, 74 unspoiled acres, a tree house, and sweeping views with guests, a cat, and a herd of retired llamas. The air is mountain clear and quiet between the high canyon walls—you start to relax as soon as you get out of the car. The Webbs serve sherry in the evening and a full breakfast in the morning. The four rooms, some nestled cozily under the eaves, are decorated in country and Victorian style, with some family antiques.

Ocean Shores Motel. 451 Sterling Hwy. #1, Homer, AK 99603 ☎ **800/770-7775** or 907/235-7775. Fax 907/235-8639. www.akoceanshores.com. 32 units. TV TEL. High season $105–$165 double. Low season $70–$75 double. Extra person $5. AE, DISC, MC, V.

Buildings on a grassy compound overlook Kachemak Bay, with a path leading down to Bishop's Beach, yet the location is right off the Sterling Highway as you enter town, within walking distance of downtown Homer. Rooms are fresh and bright, most with private balconies, and many with kitchens. A few less expensive rooms aren't as up-to-date and lack the stunning views, but they still have cute touches. It's a family business, and they've decorated the place with photographs and art collected over five generations in Alaska. The hospitality matches.

Old Town Bed and Breakfast. 106-D W. Bunnell, Homer, AK 99603. ☎ **907/235-7558.** Fax 907/235-9427. www.xyz.net/~oldtown. 3 units, 1 with private bathroom. High season $70–$80 double. Low season 25% discount. Extra person $15. Rates include breakfast. MC, V.

Artist and lifelong Homer resident Asia Freeman and her husband, Kurt Marquardt, casually host a B&B that combines the artiness of the excellent Bunnell Street Gallery downstairs (see "Attractions," above) and the funky, historic feel of the old trading post/hardware store that the building used to house. The wood floors undulate with age and settling, and the tall, double-hung windows, looking out at Bishop's Beach, are slightly cockeyed. Antiques and handmade quilts complete the charming ambience. They serve a full breakfast on weekends, and during the week you get a continental breakfast at the wonderful Two Sisters Bakery, downstairs. Not a good choice for people who have trouble with stairs.

Seaside Farm. 40904 Seaside Farm Rd. (5 miles from downtown off East End Rd.), Homer, AK 99603. ☎ **907/235-7850.** www.xyz.net/~seaside. 4 units, 9 cabins, 12 hostel beds. $55 cabin for 2; $15 per person hostel bunk; $6 campsite. Extra person in room or cabin $12. MC, V.

Take a step back in time—all the way to the 1960s. Mairis Kilcher's farm is populated by Morgan horses, cows, chickens, pigeons, and latter-day hippies, many of whom do chores in exchange for their room: 2½ hours of work equals a night in the hostel bunks, and 90 minutes earns a campsite in the pasture above the bay. Campers have use of an outdoor cooking and washing area, and autumn raspberry picking. Some of the primitive cabins sit in lovely, quiet places. The farm, its meadows dotted with cottonwood trees, slopes spectacularly to Kachemak Bay. Homer's pioneering Kilcher family spawned the singer Jewel (Kilcher), although you're not likely to see her around here anymore.

CAMPING

The most popular place to camp in Homer is out on the Spit. Tenters camp on the southwestern, ocean side, and RVs park around the boat harbor on the opposite side. It can be windy and sometimes crowded, and toilet facilities are minimal; but waking up on a bright, pebbled beach makes up for much. The fee changes annually; at this writing, it's $6 for tents, $10 for RVs, payable at a booth on the right side of the Spit, across from the fishing hole. Tent campers will find a more pastoral setting at Seaside Farm, mentioned above.

If you want hookups for your RV, there are plenty of places to go off the Spit. See the Driftwood Inn, above. **Oceanview RV Park,** 455 Sterling Hwy. (☎ **907/235-3951**), has 110 spaces near the downtown area overlooking the water with a trail to Bishop's Beach. Rates are $26 a night for full hookups, including cable TV and showers.

WILDERNESS LODGES

These four lodges all are based across Kachemak Bay from Homer, each in its own remote cove or bay, and each in its own market niche, from budget family lodgings to upscale accommodations. It's wise to reserve rooms at any of these places months in advance (the preceding winter isn't too soon). More places to stay, some with wilderness-lodge qualities, are listed below under the Halibut Cove and Seldovia sections, later in this chapter.

Across the Bay Tent and Breakfast. On Kasitsna Bay (P.O. Box 81), Seldovia, AK 99663 (winter P.O. Box 112054, Anchorage, AK 99511; ☎ 907/345-2571). ☎ **907/235-3633.** www.tentandbreakfastalaska.com/. 6 tents. $58 per person with breakfast, $85 with all meals. Children 6–11 half price, children 5 and under free. MC, V. Closed mid-Sept to Memorial Day.

Looking like a summer camp, large canvas tents on wooden platforms stand by themselves on a steep hillside among towering spruce trees. There's a central house for meals, an organic garden to produce the food, an outhouse with a stained-glass window, and a forest volleyball court for games. A long beachfront faces placid Kasitsna Bay—that's where water taxis drop off visitors and guided sea-kayaking excursions depart ($95 per person). Up the stairs by the road, mountain bikes are for rent ($25 a day) to explore the area's network of abandoned logging roads or pedal to Seldovia. The tents have beds, but you sleep in your own bag. For families, it's an easy and inexpensive way to the wilderness.

✪ **Kachemak Bay Wilderness Lodge.** China Poot Bay (P.O. Box 956), Homer, AK 99603. ☎ **907/235-8910.** Fax 907/235-8911. www.xyz.net/~wildrnes/lodge.htm. 5 cabins. $2,500 per person for a 5-day stay. Rates include all meals. Mon–Fri package only. No credit cards; checks accepted. Closed Oct 15–May 1.

I can think of no more idyllic way to become acquainted with Alaska's marine wilderness than staying at this intimate, luxurious lodge, run for more than 25 years by hospitable and generous Mike and Diane McBride. I only wish it were affordable for more people, because it's a place of unforgettable experiences. The McBrides' meals are legendary, and their four cabins manage to seem rustic while having every comfort; it's easy to pretend you're the only guest. But their site, on China Poot Bay, is what's really special—it has excellent tide pooling, kayaking, a black-sand beach, and good hiking trails nearby. Experienced, environmentally conscious guide service is included for sea kayaking, hiking, and wildlife watching; outings by boat carry an extra charge.

Sadie Cove Wilderness Lodge. P.O. Box 2265, Homer, AK 99603. ☎ **907/235-2350.** www.sadiecove.com. 4 cabins. $200 per person per night. MC, V.

This place reminded me of *Swiss Family Robinson.* Its weathered buildings of rough-cut lumber—owner Keith Iverson hauled and milled them of driftwood—climb the steep shore of the Sadie Cove fjord amid the sound of clattering water from a creek that provides the electricity and fills the wood-fired hot tub, itself an old boat set into the ground. Keith's wife, Randi, provides the softening touches and cooks the seafood dinners that complete the enchanting experience. Most activities, such as sea kayaking, fishing, and tours, are booked separately.

Tutka Bay Wilderness Lodge. P.O. Box 960, Homer, AK 99603. ☎ **800/606-3909** or 907/235-3905. Fax 907/235-3909. www.tutkabaylodge.com. 5 cabins. TV. $290–$325 per person per night. Rates include all meals. 2-night minimum stay. MC, V. Closed Oct–Apr.

John and Nelda Osgood's personalities are reflected in the amazing place they've built—open and enthusiastic, perfectionist and safety conscious, clean-cut but truly Alaskan. On pilings and on a narrow, grassy isthmus by the green water of the Tutka Bay fjord, they've put together what amounts to an upscale hotel in the wilderness, with cabins connected by long boardwalks, a deck large enough for a helicopter to land on, and a kitchen capable of producing gourmet meals. It's quite a feat—the water system alone is a wonder. There's plenty to do: tide-pool walks, bird watching, hiking, berry picking, and other activities around the lodge, and you can pay extra for guided fishing, kayaking, bear-viewing flights, fishing, and other outdoor experiences that go farther afield.

DINING

Besides those places listed here, don't miss the **Chart Room** at Land's End, described under "Accommodations," above. For good fast food in an attractive beachfront dining room, try **Boardwalk Fish and Chips** (☎ **907/235-7749**), on the boardwalk across from the harbormaster's office on the Spit. The milkshakes are great. **Two Sisters Bakery,** next to the Bunnell Gallery at the bottom on Main Street (☎ **907/235-2280**), is a coffee house with terrific baked goodies and a clientele of interesting folk.

✪ **Café Cups.** 162 W. Pioneer Ave. ☎ **907/235-8330.** Reservations recommended. Lunch $6–$10; dinner main courses $14–$21. MC, V. High season daily 7:30am–10pm. Low season daily 7:30am–3pm. CREATIVE/ECLECTIC.

The facade of the yellow house on Pioneer Avenue, with its elaborate bas-relief sculpture, is truthful advertising for the arty restaurant and creative food to be found inside. Somehow, just sitting in the small, hand-crafted dining room makes you feel sophisticated. The menu specializes in surprises—fresh local seafood is prepared using international cooking styles in ways that no one may have thought of before. The experiments seem to work, and now the restaurant is recognized as one of the very best in the state. The service and hospitality are at once professional and warm. Beer and wine are available. The last time my wife and I dined there, we emerged in the warm, sunny evening with an afterglow of complete relaxation and sensual satisfaction.

Duncan House Diner. 125 E. Pioneer Ave. ☎ **907/235-5344.** Lunch $4–$8.50; dinner main courses $10–$17. DISC, MC, V. Summer, Thurs–Mon 7am–9pm, Tues–Wed 7am–2pm. Winter, Sun–Wed 7am–2pm, Thurs–Sat 7am–8pm. DINER/STEAK/SEAFOOD.

The locals nest on the counter stools to sip coffee and tease the waitresses, who give as good as they get. Most tables are in booths in the open dining room, which is decorated with memorabilia such as old license plates, advertisements, clocks, and the like. The hearty breakfasts and lunches are a cut above typical diner fare, and dinners include steaks, halibut, fettuccini, and other items you'd expect to find only in a fancier place. Breakfast is served all day, and people rave about the deserts, which are baked in-house. The atmosphere can be smoky.

Fresh Sourdough Express Bakery and Cafe. 1316 Ocean Dr. ☎ **907/235-7571.** Lunch $5.50–$7.50; dinner main courses $7.50–$18. MC, V. High season daily 7am–10pm. Low season daily 8am–3pm. Closed Oct–Mar.

Ebullient Donna and Kevin Maltz's organic eatery is quintessential Homer, starting with its motto: "Food for people and the planet." But there's no New Age dogma here. Sourdough Express is fun and tasty, even as it grinds its own grain and recycles everything in sight. An inexpensive lunch menu includes a buffalo burger, halibut hoagie, and reindeer grill, as well as various vegetarian choices. The evening menu has lots of seafood prepared in international styles. The staff will pack lunches for outings, too. Don't miss dessert from the scratch bakery. The aptly named "Obscene Brownie," covered with espresso and ice cream, left me in a happy daze for the rest of the afternoon.

✪ **The Homestead.** Mile 8.2, East End Rd. ☎ **907/235-8723.** Reservations recommended. Dinner main courses $17–$25. AE, MC, V. Summer daily 5–9:30pm. Apr–May Wed–Sat 5–9pm. Closed Oct–Mar. STEAK/SEAFOOD.

The ambience is that of an old-fashioned Alaska roadhouse, in a large log building with spare decoration and stackable metal chairs, but the food is as satisfying as I've had anywhere in Alaska. After a day outdoors, it's a warm, exuberant place for dinner. Many menu items are charbroiled, but the cuisine is far more thoughtful than what you'd find in your typical steak-and-seafood place, including adventurous and creative concoctions along with the simple, perfectly broiled fish and meat. Service is cordial but sometimes slow. Full liquor license.

HOMER NIGHTLIFE

The **Pier One Theatre** (☎ **907/235-7333;** www.pieronetheatre.org) is a strong community theater group housed in a small, corrugated-metal building on the Spit, just short of the small-boat harbor on the left. Instead of the ubiquitous gold rush melodrama and Robert Service readings, Pier One often presents serious drama, musicals, and comedy—not just schlock. They also produce dance, classical music, and youth theater events during the summer. There's generally something playing Thursday to Sunday nights in the summer. Check the *Homer News* or the Web site for current listings. Tickets are available at the door, or can be reserved by phone.

There are lots of bars in Homer. The landmark **Salty Dawg** is a small log cabin on the Spit with a lighthouse on top. It's the place to swap fish stories after a day on the water.

11 Halibut Cove: Venice on Kachemak Bay

A visit to the tight, roadless little community of Halibut Cove, across Kachemak Bay from Homer, encompasses all the best things about a visit to the bay: a boat ride, the chance of seeing otters or seals, a top-notch restaurant, several galleries and open studios with some of Alaska's best fishy fine art, and even cozy, welcoming accommodations. The settlement sits on either side of a narrow, peaceful channel between a small island and the mainland; the water in between is the road. Boardwalks connect the buildings, and stairs reach down to the water from houses perched on pilings over the shore. The post office is on a floating dock. The pace of life runs no faster than the tide.

It's also an essentially private community. Unless you have your own boat, an excursion boat owned by the community's restaurant is the only way to get there. Once there, you have to leave according to plan, as there's no business district and everything is privately owned. You're really a guest the whole time you're in Halibut Cove—the community is open for visitors, however they arrive, only between 1 and 9pm, unless you're staying at the Quiet Place Lodge or the cabins mentioned below. Not all lodges have privileges to take their guests to Halibut Cove, so make sure you ask before booking.

GETTING THERE

The classic wooden boat ***Danny J*** (book through Central Charters at ☎ **907/235-7847**) leaves Homer daily in the summer at noon, brings back day-trippers, and takes over dinner guests at 5pm, then brings back the diners later in the evening. The noon trip includes bird watching at Gull Island. Seating is mostly outdoors, and I wouldn't take the trip in the rain. You also take the *Danny J* if you're spending the night in Halibut Cove. The noon trip is $44 for adults, and the dinner trip is $22, but in the evening you're obliged to buy a meal at the restaurant. Kids 12 and under are $22 both times; seniors $36 at noon and $18 for dinner. The same family operates a steel boat, the *Storm Bird,* which carries passengers at noon in summer, overflow other times, and runs all winter as the mail boat. Reservations and fares are identical to the *Danny J.*

ATTRACTIONS

On an afternoon trip, you can bring lunch or eat at the Saltry, described below, and then explore along the **boardwalk** that runs from the restaurant along Ismailof Island past the galleries, boat shops, and houses. There's also a barnyard where kids, who already will be in heaven, can look at rabbits, chickens, ponies, and other animals.

Fine art is the major industry in this community of fewer than 80 residents, with 16 artists and three galleries. The **Halibut Cove's Experience Fine Art Gallery** (☎ **907/296-2215**) is first past the farm on the boardwalk, on pilings above the water. The airy room contains works by Halibut Cove artists only. Farther on, Diana Tillion, who, with her husband, Clem, pioneered the community, opens her **Cove Gallery** and studio to guests. Since the 1950s, she has worked almost exclusively in octopus ink, painstakingly extracted with a hypodermic needle. **Alex Combs,** a grand old Picasso-like figure among Alaska artists, takes visitors at his studio even though he often isn't there. The building is marked by a huge self-portrait and a sign reading, "Leave money, take pottery and paintings."

ACCOMMODATIONS

Besides the lodge listed below, it is also possible to rent housekeeping cabins in Halibut Cove. **Halibut Cove Cabins** (☎ **907/296-2214** in summer or 808/322-4110 in winter) consists of two quaint cabins on a steep hill overlooking artist Sydney Bishop's private lagoon, at the opposite end of the island from the main part of town. **Cove House** (☎ **907/296-2255;** thecovehouse.com) is near Bishop's place, a two-bedroom house on the water, near the public dock. A brand-new lodge opened too late for me to inspect for this edition; it's the **Halibut Cove Lodge** (☎ **907/299-0100;** www.halibutcovelodge.com).

The Quiet Place Lodge. P.O. Box 6474, Halibut Cove, AK 99603. ☎ **907/296-2212.** www.quietplace.com. Fax 907/296-2241. 5 cabins with shared bathrooms. $185 double. Rates include breakfast. MC, V. Closed Labor Day–Memorial Day.

This family owned B&B sits perched on pilings that seem to climb up the side of the mainland across the water from the Saltry restaurant (see below). The five cabins, linked by stairs and boardwalks, are attractively decorated with local art and quilts and look out on the cove. They share bathrooms in the main lodge, where there's also a large rec room with a library, refrigerator, and microwave and telephone for guests. A full breakfast is served, and dinners are available every other night for $30. Rooms come with a classic wooden row boat to explore the Cove, and they rent kayaks and skiffs from the float below the lodge, essential to explore the area.

DINING

Saltry. On the main channel, Halibut Cove. ☎ **907/235-7847.** Lunch $10–$18; dinner main courses $18–$20. MC, V. In season daily 6am–9pm. Off season call ahead for hours. SEAFOOD.

This restaurant operates in conjunction with the *Danny J,* and sits on pilings in an idyllic setting, over the edge of the smooth, deep green of the cove's main watery avenue. You can sit back on the deck and sip microbrews and eat fresh baked bread, mussels, sushi, and locally grown salads, followed by fresh fish grilled over charcoal. Prices are on the high side, but it's hard to mind. Make reservations with Central Charters at the same time you reserve your *Danny J* tickets.

12 Seldovia

One evening when my family and I were visiting this town of around 300 near the tip of the Kenai Peninsula, a group of children walked up to us in the empty main street and asked, in a friendly way, what we were doing there. That's how quiet Seldovia is. But early in this century, Seldovia was a metropolis, acting as a major hub for the

Cook Inlet area with steamers coming and going with fish and cargo. Unconnected to the road system, the town's decline was steady until 1964, when the Good Friday earthquake destroyed most of what was left. The entire Kenai Peninsula sank, and high tides began covering the boardwalks that comprised most of the city. When the U.S. Army Corps of Engineers came to the rescue, they replaced the boardwalks with rock and gravel and erased much of the waterfront's charm.

A short section of the old boardwalk that remains runs along peaceful **Seldovia Slough,** where you can fish king salmon from shore run in June and a sea otter is in regular residence—you can get a close look at him, if you're patient. The other roads and trails around town make for pleasant walks. Here you can wander in and out of the forest, beach walk, see what a real Alaska fishing town is like without seeing many other tourists, and maybe see wildlife—eagles certainly and maybe bears.

ESSENTIALS

GETTING THERE The trip across Kachemak Bay to Seldovia is one of the best parts of going there. Go at least one way on the **Rainbow Tours** (☎ **907/235-7272**) boat (see the full description in section 10 of this chapter, on Homer, under "Natural History Tours"). You have a good chance of seeing otters, seals, sea lions, puffins, and eagles, and you may see whales. The adult fare is $45, and the boat stays 2 hours in Seldovia—long enough for most people to see the town. Bring your own lunch, however, or you'll spend most of your excursion in one of Seldovia's restaurants.

Flying to Seldovia on one of Homer's air taxis is a cheap way to do a flightseeing trip. **Homer Air** (☎ **907/235-8591;** www.homerair.com/) is one experienced operator, charging $55 round-trip.

The Alaska Marine Highway System ferry *Tustumena* (see section 10 of this chapter, on Homer) also visits Seldovia from Homer, but stays briefly.

VISITOR INFORMATION The **Seldovia Chamber of Commerce,** P.O. Box F, Seldovia, AK 99663-0150 (☎ **907/234-7612;** www.xyz.net/~seldovia), is very helpful. The community also has an astonishingly good Web site at **www.seldovia.com**; it's worth a look as a window into the community even if you don't plan to visit.

FAST FACTS There's no bank, and many businesses don't take credit cards. In a pinch, go to Seldovia Mart, where the cash register takes debit cards and they'll give extra cash in change.

The **Seldovia Medical Clinic** (☎ **907/234-7825**) is at Main Street and Anderson Way; it's open Monday, Wednesday and Friday 9am to 5pm.

For nonemergency help from the **police,** call ☎ **907/234-7640.**

Sales tax is 5%.

ATTRACTIONS & ACTIVITIES

The **Otterbahn Trail,** built by students at the Susan B. English School, leads through woods, wetlands, and beach cliffs to Outer Beach, where there's a picnic shelter. Allow a couple of hours. Unfortunately, there are few other hiking trails, but dirt roads around town lead to some fine **berry picking** grounds, where in late summer and fall you can quickly collect enough berries for a pie. Those roads also make for intriguing and secluded **mountain biking.** There are many miles to explore without encountering another soul. You can rent bikes at The Buzz coffee shop and the Boardwalk Hotel, both listed below. With the lack of hiking trails, bikes really are needed to get into the woods.

The area is good for **sea kayaking. Kayak'atak** (☎ **907/234-7425;** www.alaska.net/~kayaks/), operating out of Herring Bay Mercantile, offers rentals and guided trips. The couple who do the tours, long-time Seldovia residents, take pride in showing off the wildlife and beauty of this little-used area. They charge $110 for a 5-hour tour, including lunch. They also rent kayaks and offer overnight trips.

King salmon spawn in Seldovia Slough, right in the middle of the town. The run peaks in mid-June, and you can fish right from shore. Seldova also has an edge for halibut anglers, because you start out an hour closer to the **halibut** grounds than Homer. Find a charter through the visitor information sources listed above.

There are several **shops** worth visiting, all on the main street. A tiny, picturesque **Russian Orthodox church** stands on the hill above the town, built in 1891. Call the Chamber of Commerce to find out how to get in.

ACCOMMODATIONS

Dancing Eagles Cabin and Bed and Breakfast. On the boardwalk (P.O. Box 264), Seldovia, AK 99663 (in winter, P.O. Box 240067, Anchorage, AK 99524). ☎ **907/234-7627** in summer or 907/278-0288 in winter. Fax 907/278-0289 in winter. www.dancingeagles.com. 5 units, none with private bathroom; 1 cabin. $85 double; $125 cabin for 2. Extra person in cabin $40. Rates include continental breakfast. No credit cards. Closed Oct–Apr.

The boardwalk leads to this large house, cabin, and outbuildings, all nestled on rocks and pilings above the slough and connected by their own boardwalks. Guests can use the hot tub and sauna and watch the otter who lives in the water just outside. Three rooms under the eaves upstairs are cute but very small; two other rooms are larger, as is the cabin, which has a deck, a view of the boat harbor, and its own cooking facilities.

Seldovia's Boardwalk Hotel. 243 Main St. (P.O. Box 72), Seldovia, AK 99663. ☎ **800/238-7862** or 907/234-7816. www.alaskaone.com/boardwalkhotel. 14 units. TEL. $89–$130 double. DISC, MC, V.

This Seldovia institution has light, comfortable rooms with private bathrooms and phones. Despite the name, it isn't on the boardwalk but does stand at the top of the small-boat harbor, so rooms on the water side have a great view. The hotel offers a $129 package from Homer, which includes a boat tour over and a flightseeing trip back—quite a deal. There's a courtesy car and free coffee in the lobby.

DINING

The Buzz Coffeehouse Cafe. 231 Main St. ☎ **907/234-7479.** All meals $3.75–$7.75. MC, V. Daily 6am–6pm daily. CAFE/VEGETARIAN.

This espresso shop and community meeting place also serves meals: tasty quiche, calzone, baked goods, and vegetarian dishes. You can rent bicycles here, too.

Mad Fish Restaurant. At the south end of the harbor on Main St. ☎ **907/234-7676.** Reservations recommended. Lunch $6.25–$13; dinner main courses $11.50–$28.50. MC, V. Summer daily 11:30am–3pm; Sun–Thurs 5–8pm, Fri–Sat 5–9pm. Winter Thurs–Sat noon–2:30pm and 5–8pm. SEAFOOD.

A restaurant like this is rare in a town this small. The dinner menu goes on and on with entrees of beef and seafood—I gave up counting the ways you can have fresh halibut. The lunch menu also is various, with burgers and sandwiches, but also grilled fish, salmon cakes, and bruschetta. The dining room overlooks the harbor.

13 Valdez

Big events have shaped Valdez (val-*deez*). The deep-water port, at the head of a long, dramatic fjord, first developed with the 1898 Klondike Gold Rush and an ill-fated attempt to establish an alternative route to the gold fields from here. Later, the port and the Richardson Highway, which connected Valdez to the rest of the state, served a key role in supplying materials during World War II. On Good Friday, March 27, 1964, all of that was erased when North America's greatest recorded earthquake occurred under Miners Lake, west of town off a northern fjord of Prince William Sound, setting off an underwater landslide that caused a huge wave to sweep over the waterfront, killing 32 people. The town sank and was practically destroyed. The U.S. Army Corps of Engineers rebuilt a drab replacement in a new, safer location that slowly filled with nondescript modern buildings over the next 2 decades. A walking tour provides the locations of a few buildings that were moved to the new town site.

The construction of the trans-Alaska pipeline, completed in 1977, brought a new economic boom to Valdez and enduring economic prosperity as tankers came to fill with the oil. Then, on March 24, 1989, on Good Friday 25 years after the earthquake, the tanker *Exxon Valdez,* on its way south, hit the clearly marked Bligh Reef, causing the largest and most environmentally costly oil spill ever in North America. The spill cleanup added another economic boom.

Today, Valdez is a middle American town, driven by industry but turning to the vast resources of Prince William Sound for outdoor recreation. In town you can tour two small museums and the fish hatchery, and take a hike or a river float, but the city itself is short on charm and would not justify the trip all by itself. The real reasons to come have to do with the setting—the wildlife, fishing, and sightseeing in the Sound, and the spectacular drive down the Richardson Highway.

Because Valdez lies at the end of a funnel of steep mountains that catches moisture off the ocean, the weather tends to be overcast and rainy. For the same reason, the area receives phenomenal snow falls, measured in the tens of feet. Although there is no developed downhill skiing, Valdez attracts many "extreme" skiers for helicopter and snowcat skiing in the mountains behind town in late winter, and a nice network of groomed Nordic ski trails.

ESSENTIALS

GETTING THERE **By Car** The **Richardson Highway,** described in "Alaska's Highways à la Carte," in chapter 9, dramatically crosses Thompson Pass and descends into the narrow valley where Valdez lies. Try to do the trip in daylight, in clear weather, and stop at the Worthington Glacier. This is the only road to Valdez. The drive from Anchorage is 6 hours without stops.

By Bus Gray Line's **Alaskon Express** (☎ **800/544-2206** or 907/835-4391; www.graylineofalaska.com/alaskon.cfm) runs to Anchorage daily in the summer, taking 10 hours for the trip; the fare is $70 and the bus stops at the Westmark Valdez Hotel.

By Ferry The **Alaska Marine Highway System** (☎ **800/642-0066** or 907/835-4436; www.dot.state.ak.us/external/amhs/home.html) calls on Valdez daily in the summer with the *Bartlett,* a ferry connecting Valdez, Whittier, and Cordova. One time-tested way to see the Sound is to put your vehicle on the ferry in Whittier for the 7-hour run to Valdez, then drive north on the Richardson Highway. A forest ranger rides on board to present programs. The fare is $72 for a car up to 15 feet long and $58 for an adult passenger (children half price). The *Tustumena* comes from Seward roughly once a week. The *Kennicott* runs across the Gulf of Alaska between Valdez and Juneau once a month June through September. The 40-hour run costs $90 for adults, $42 to $148 for a cabin. See "Ferry System Booking Tips" in chapter 5 for ways to communicate with the system.

By Tour Boat **Prince William Sound Cruises and Tours** (☎ **800/992-1297** or 907/835-4731; full listing below) offers daily summer cruises between Whittier and

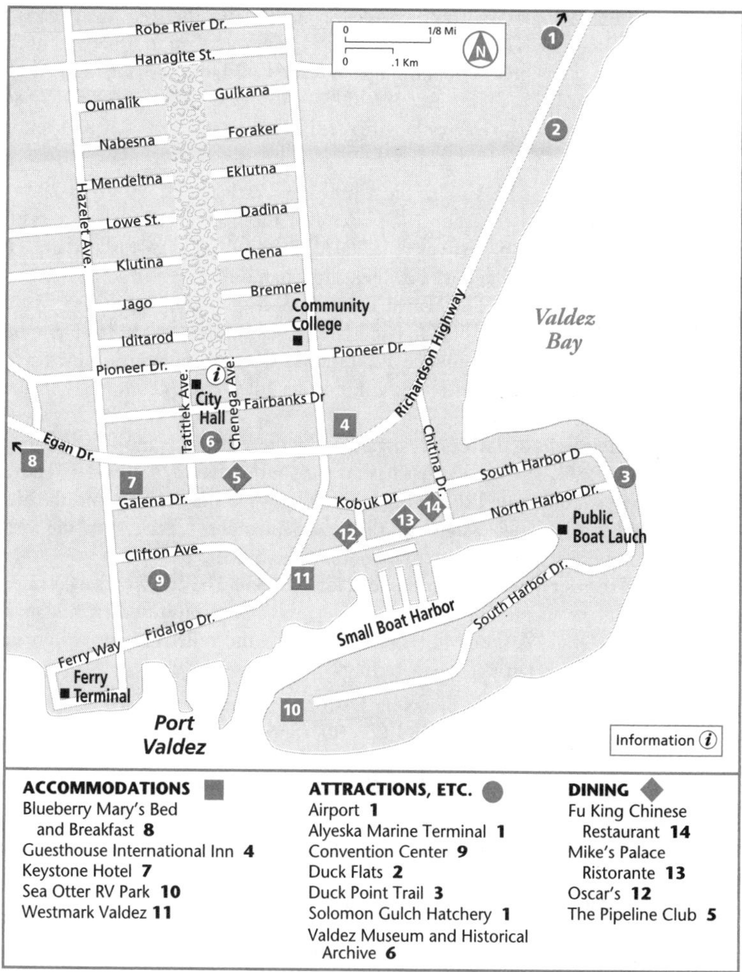

Valdez, including lunch and a tour of the pipeline terminal, for $109 one way ($54 ages 4 to 12). The boat leaves Valdez at 7:15am and leaves Whittier at 2:15pm.

By Air **Era Aviation** (☎ **800/866-8394** or 907/835-2636; www.era-aviation.com) flies several times a day each way between Anchorage and Valdez.

GETTING AROUND A bicycle is a good way to get around the central town area. **Beaver Sports,** 316 Galena St. (☎ **907/835-4727;** www.beaversports.net/), rents mountain bikes for $5 an hour, $16 for 6 hours, and $20 for 24 hours.

To get to the airport, taxis are available from **Valdez Yellow Cab** (☎ **907/835-2500**).

Hertz (☎ **800/654-3131** or 907/835-4378; www.hertz.com/) is the only national car-rental chain with a local office. **Valdez-U-Drive** (☎ **907/835-4402**) also rents cars at the airport.

VISITOR INFORMATION The Valdez Convention and Visitors Bureau maintains a **Visitor Information Center,** at 200 Chenega Ave., a block off Egan Drive (P.O. Box 1603), Valdez, AK 99686 (☎ **800/770-5954,** 907/835-4636, or

907/835-2984 in winter; www.valdezalaska.org/). Pick up the free town map and useful *Vacation Planner.* They're open in summer daily from 8am to 8pm, and normal business hours in the winter. A booking agency, **One Call Does It All,** at 210 N. Harbor Dr. (P.O. Box 2197), Valdez, AK 99686 (☎ **907/835-4988;** fax 907/835-5865; www.alaska.net/~onecall/), reserves lodgings, fishing charters, activities, and tours in the area.

SPECIAL EVENTS **The Valdez Ice Climbing Festival** (☎ **907/835-2984**) is held on Presidents' Day weekend, in February, on the frozen waterfalls of Keystone Canyon. **The Snow Man Festival** (☎ **907/835-2330**), held in early March, is a winter carnival with a food fair, ice bowling, snowman building, and a drive-in movie projected on a snow bank. **The World Extreme Skiing Championships** (☎ **907/835-2108;** www.wesc.com) is held in late March or early April on the faces of mountains north of Valdez, where invited professional skiers from North America and Europe hurl themselves down near-vertical, powder-filled chutes competing in speed and style.

Three **summer fishing derbies** are organized by the Valdez Chamber of Commerce (☎ **907/835-2330**), with prizes that have totaled more than $75,000. The **Halibut Derby** runs all summer, the **Pink Salmon Derby** during most of July, and the **Silver Salmon Derby** is through August until early September. Check with the visitor center or buy a ticket at the boat-rental booth at the harbor.

The Last Frontier Theater Conference (☎ **907/834-1612;** www.uaa.alaska.edu/pwscc/) brings famous playwrights and directors to the community for seminars and performances in June. Arthur Miller, Edward Albee, and other famous writers have met the public here in fairly intimate settings.

FAST FACTS There are two **banks** on Egan Drive, both with ATMs.

The **Valdez Community Hospital** (☎ **907/835-2249**) is located at 911 Meals Ave.

MacCopy's, 354 Fairbanks St. (☎ **907/835-8748**), offers Internet access and fax and copying services.

For nonemergency business with the **Valdez Police Department,** call ☎ **907/835-4560.**

The **post office** is on Galena Drive, 1 block back from the Egan Drive business strip.

Valdez has no **sales tax,** but does charge a 6% bed tax.

GETTING OUTSIDE

SIGHTSEEING & WILDLIFE TOURS

For most visitors, a daylong ride on a tour boat into the Sound is likely to be the most memorable part of a visit to Valdez. After passing through the long fjord of Port Valdez, the boats enter an ice-choked bay in front of **Columbia Glacier.** Some also continue to an active glacier farther west, or continue all the way to Whittier.

Environmental activist Stan Stephens started and still runs the main tour boat company, now owned by the Chugach Alaska Native corporation. **Prince William Sound Cruises and Tours** (☎ **800/992-1297** or 907/835-4731; www.princewilliamsound.com) has its office at the harbor in Valdez, near the Westmark Hotel. Stephens predicted and was working to prevent an accident like the *Exxon Valdez* grounding right up to the eve of the disaster, and he's still working for improved environmental safeguards for the oil companies. The company offers tours of various length to the glacier and other sites, often seeing seals, sea otters, and sea lions, and sometimes whales. Trips go to Whittier and Meares Glacier, but the primary destination is Columbia Glacier and the company's camp there, on Growler Island, where passengers get off and, on some trips, have a meal and can even spend the night and go boating. Prices range from $69 ($34 ages 4 to 12) for a 6-hour cruise to $119 to visit both glaciers and stop for lunch on the island. You can spend the night in a tent cabin on the island for as little as $200, double, meals included. See "Sea Kayaking & Sailing," below, for appealing options to add on a trip to Growler Island.

Sea Kayaking & Sailing

Jim and Nancy Lethcoe are activists for the Sound, like Stephens, and possess an extraordinary store of knowledge about its natural and cultural history—they have written many books about the Sound. They guide sea kayaking, sailing, hiking, and combinations of all three in front of Columbia Glacier, and rent kayaks for self-guided expeditions. Their **Alaskan Wilderness Sailing & Kayaking Safaris** (☎ **907/835-5175;** www.alaskanwilderness.com) operates from Growler Island (see "Sightseeing & Wildlife Tours," above, for how to get there). That gives them a big leg up on sea-kayaking operations based in towns, because they start right at a fascinating and scenic place. Options range from 2 hours to a week. Day trips include kayaking in inflatable kayaks or sailing single-person trimarans; sailing in their 40-foot yacht and then kayaking and hiking; and various combinations. Half-day kayaking or sailing is $65, full day $94 (plus the cost of getting to Growler Island). Chartering the yacht is $250 per person per day, less with larger groups. They rent rigid kayaks to experienced paddlers, $45 single or $65 double. They charge $175 a day to guide kayak/camping expeditions; you bring your own food and camping gear.

Raven Charters, Slip C-25, Valdez Boat Harbor (☎ **907/835-5863;** www. alaska. net/~ravenchr/), is run by a family living on its 50-foot boat who take clients sailing and exploring the Sound. The wind tends to be light and changeable, but a sailboat makes a comfortable base for discovering interesting, isolated places. All-inclusive prices start at $750 per night for up to four passengers, or $600 for a day charter, with discounts for longer trips.

Sea kayaking right around the town of Valdez is not as appealing as some other places you could choose, but experienced kayakers and outdoors people have unlimited possibilities in Prince William Sound. One idea is to take your kayak, perhaps rented in Valdez from **Anadyr Adventures** (☎ **800/TO-KAYAK** or 907/835-2814; www.alaska.net/~anadyr/), on the ferry *Tustumena*'s weekly trip from Valdez to Seward (see "Getting There," above), disembarking at the whistle stop in the village of Chenega Bay. This scheme allows you inexpensively to start out in deep wilderness. The ferry stops in Chenega only when a passenger has a reservation.

Columbia Glacier Pros & Cons

The Columbia Glacier is immense—3 miles across at its face and 30 miles long—and it is retreating fast, dumping thousands of icebergs that float over miles of water in front. The smooth surface and weird white and blue shapes look like a vast Henry Moore sculpture garden that's been invaded by seals and other wildlife. The biggest drawback of visiting the Columbia is that you won't see it calve (when ice falls off the face) because boats can't get close enough through all the icebergs. For that you must go to glaciers in the western Sound, such as Meares. But those glaciers are closer to Whittier.

Fishing & Boating

The ocean waters around Valdez are rich in salmon and halibut. From shore, you can fish for salmon on Allison Point, along Dayville Road on the far side of the port from Valdez. Salmon here are returning to the Solomon Gulch Hatchery and are primarily pinks in June and July and silvers in August and September. The success rate is high when the fish are running—one wild year, fish literally jumped into boats—but it's not the most aesthetic fishing experience, right along a road with many other people. (See "Fishing," in chapter 2, for further advice.)

For more isolated fishing, use one of the **fishing charters** available in the boat harbor. Halibut charters cost around $150 per person, as they have to go a long way. Half-day salmon charters are around $80, and troll right in Port Valdez. Get a referral from the Valdez Chamber of Commerce or check the links on their Web site; you also can book through **One Call Does It All** (both are listed above under "Visitor Information"). **Popeye Charters** (☎ **907/835-2659;** www.alaska.net/~popeyes/) is the best in town.

If you're up for running your own boat, they're for rent from **Valdez Harbor Boat and Tackle Rentals** (☎ **907/835-5002;** www.fishcentral.net/boatrentals.htm); a 16-foot boat costs $125 a day, plus fuel. You can get all the gear you need there. Or use the boat to explore the area, perhaps with a visit to Shoup Glacier, 20 minutes west. Renting a boat overnight, you can pull up on an uninhabited shore and set up camp.

Ketchum Air Service (☎ **800/825-9114** or 907/835-3789; www.ketchumair.com/) offers fly-in fishing starting at $199 per person, and flightseeing trips.

Bird Watching & Beachcombing

Between the airport and downtown Valdez, the **Duck Flats,** a tidal marsh met by a salmon spawning stream, lies along the Richardson Highway. It's a productive bird and marine habitat, busy with activity at spring and fall migrations, and a good place for bird watching or picnicking all summer at one of the two viewing areas. The National Forest Service, which has a ranger station nearby, has set up a salmon-viewing station where you can watch fish do the deed in shallow, clear water. A bird checklist is distributed by the visitor center.

Hiking & Mountain Biking

A pleasant forest and shore walk to **Dock Point** borders the opposite side of the Duck Flats from the road, starting at the east side of the boat harbor, at the end of North Harbor Drive. It's a peaceful, natural walk close to town, with boardwalks and overlooks.

For a longer hike and perhaps an overnight, the new, state-maintained **Shoup Glacier trail** runs 12 miles west from town along the shore of Port Valdez to the glacier. The going is generally flat, and there are many places to get down to the beach. Camping is unrestricted, but be sure to bring mosquito repellent and practice bear avoidance (see "Outdoors Health & Safety" in chapter 2). If you plan to go all the way, reserve the state parks cabin there, which costs $50 a night (details are covered in section 1 of this chapter. The trail starts at the end of West Egan Drive.

Mineral Creek Road, off Hanagita Street, leads 6 miles along the creek up a canyon into the mountains behind town, where the gravel road gives way to a 1-mile trail to a gold rush era stamp mill. It's a good mountain biking route, and in winter the town maintains a fine Nordic ski trail network there.

Rafting

Keystone Raft and Kayak Adventures (☎ **800/328-8460** or 907/835-2606; www.alaskawhitewater.com) takes five trips a day 4½ miles down the amazing Keystone Canyon, a virtual corridor of rock with a floor of frothing water, past the crashing

The *Exxon Valdez*: 12 Years After

I have a friend who has kayaked the whole of Prince William Sound. He knew a place—I don't know if it's still this way—where he would camp just above a pebbled beach and wait for the moon to come out. And in the night, orcas would come, swim up on the beach, scratch their tummies on the rocks, and wriggle back into the ocean. It was their secret spot—his and the killer whales'—and they'd meet there each summer.

That beach was oiled in the *Exxon Valdez* oil spill, and my friend lost the heart to kayak much after all the death he saw there and all over the Sound while trying to save birds and animals that horrible summer of 1989. But now I'm sure the oil is gone from that beach. It's time to get back out there and meet the whales.

The spill coated shores over this entire huge region and beyond, killing birds in the hundreds of thousands and damaging fish and marine mammal populations in numbers and ways that will never be known for sure. Even 10 years later, scientists and subsistence gatherers were still finding buried oil on some pebble beaches. Natives and longtime residents have told me that they can still see a difference in the abundance of animals compared to what was there before the spill, and government studies support the perception that recovery is far from complete. But most everyone else will notice only that a mind-boggling abundance still remains, and on a sunny day on the water nothing could seem more remote than the technological society that could threaten such a place with crude oil.

tumult of the 900-foot Bridal Veil Falls. It's a wild ride, and not without risk—serious mishaps do sometimes occur. They charge $35 per person. The company also has numerous longer trips, ranging from a day to 10 days, on many of the region's rivers.

FLIGHTSEEING

There are several fixed-wing operators at the airport, but I love the extra thrill of helicopters. **Era Helicopters** (☎ **800/843-1947** or 907/835-2595; www.era-aviation.com/helicoptertours) has an office and helipad downtown, near the ferry dock at Hazelet and Fidalgo. A 1-hour, $199 trip overflies Columbia Glacier and lands in front of Shoup Glacier; stay closer to town and land on top of Valdez glacier for $179.

ATTRACTIONS

Valdez recently added a new museum, the **Alaska Cultural Center,** at the airport (☎ **907/834-1690;** www.uaa.alaska.edu/pwscc/), called "The Whitney" by locals for its benefactors, Jesse and Maxine Whitney, who donated a huge collection of Native Alaska arts and crafts and animal mounts. Many details, including the museum's location, were subject to change at this writing; currently, they're open Monday to Friday 9am to 6pm and charge $3 admission.

The Valdez Museum and Historical Archive. 217 Egan Dr. ☎ **907/835-2764.** www.alaska.net/~vldzmuse/. $3 adults, $2.50 over age 65, $2 ages 14–18, free for children under 14. Summer Mon–Sat 9am–6pm, Sun 8am–5pm. Winter Mon–Fri 10am–5pm, Sat noon–4pm.

The museum contains an exceptional history display that follows the story of the area from early white exploration through the oil spill. It's a little light on Alaska Native culture, but there are other museums for that. Each gallery is well designed and some are fun, like the restored bar room. There's also a saltwater aquarium and an area with transportation relics, including shiny fire engines dating from 1886.

The museum recently built a 1/20-scale model of how Valdez looked at its old site, before it was destroyed by the 1964 earthquake. Using photographs, records, and old timers' memories, they have tried to bring that lost city back to life in 400 miniature buildings. The **Historical Old Town Valdez Model** is at 436 S. Hazelet St. It is open in the summer 9am to 4pm and admission is $1.50.

The Solomon Gulch Hatchery. On Dayville Rd. on the way to the tanker terminal. ☎ **907/835-1329.** Free self-guided tours. Daily 9am–9pm.

When the pink salmon are returning from late June to early August, they swarm on the hatchery in a blizzard of fish. The hatchery releases more than 200 million pinks each year, as well as millions of chums and silvers (or coho). There is no stream for the salmon to return to, so they try to get back into the hatchery, crowding together in a solid sea of fighting muscle. Seals and birds come in to feed, and you can stand on shore and watch the spectacle. (Surefire fishing is allowed up the shore—see "Fishing" in section 14, below.) A self-guided walking tour leads through the hatchery and into some buildings, getting up close to tanks and pools where workers raise and breed millions of fish.

Alyeska Pipeline Marine Terminal Bus Tour. Operated by Valdez Tours, corner of Pioneer and Tatitlek sts. ☎ **907/835-2686.** $16 adults, $8 children ages 6–12; free for children ages 5 and under. May–Sept.

The 2-hour ride visits the terminal where tankers carrying much of the nation's oil supply are loaded. You can't enter any of the buildings. The highlights are a chance to see the big ships and an impressive scenic overlook, the only point where you can get off the bus.

ACCOMMODATIONS

In addition to the hotels listed, you'll find standard motel rooms at the **Rodeway Inn,** 210 Egan Dr. (☎ **888/835-4485**), and the **Totem Inn,** 144 E. Egan Dr. (☎ **907/835-4443**).

Blueberry Mary's Bed and Breakfast. Blueberry Hill Rd., off West Egan Dr. (P.O. Box 1244), Valdez, AK 99686. ☎ **907/835-5015.** www.alaska.net/~bmary. 2 units. TV TEL. $80 double. No credit cards. Closed in winter.

A lucky few get to sleep under Mary Mehlberg's handmade quilts on her feather beds, gaze at the ocean views, bake in the sauna, and breakfast on her blueberry waffles made from wild berries that grow just outside the house. She only takes parties of two or less and sometimes closes for breaks. Those who do stay here get a terrific deal on immaculate, hand-crafted rooms with VCRs, refrigerators, microwaves, coffeemakers, private entrances, and a prime location.

GuestHouse International Inn. 100 Meals Ave., Valdez, AK 99686. ☎ **888/478-4445.** 77 units. TV TEL. High season $139 double. Low season $99 double. AE, DC, MC, V.

This hotel already had the best standard rooms in town, such as you'd find in a mid-scale chain; then, in 2000, it changed hands and name, and the building was gutted for a complete remodel, with completion too late for our inspection.

Keystone Hotel. 401 W. Egan Dr. (P.O. Box 2148), Valdez, AK 99686. ☎ **888/835-0665** or 907/835-3851. Fax 907/835-5322. www.alaskan.com/keystonehotel. 105 units. TV TEL. $95 double. Extra person over age 12 $10. Rates include continental breakfast. AE, MC, V. Closed in winter.

This building, made of modular units, was built by Exxon to serve as its offices for the oil-spill cleanup operation but wasn't completed until late summer 1989, so the company occupied it for only about a month. In 1994, after standing vacant, a new owner remodeled it into a hotel, with small rooms that mostly have two twin beds or one double bed, though some have two doubles. Select a room when you check in, as they vary in decor; some have dark paneling, some are more modern. All the rooms I saw were clean and pleasant. A coin-op laundry is available.

Westmark Valdez. 100 Fidalgo Dr. (P.O. Box 468), Valdez, AK 99686. ☎ **800/544-0970** for reservations, or 907/835-4391. Fax 907/835-2308. www.westmarkhotels.com. 97 units. TV TEL. High season $155 double. Low season $95 double. Extra adult $15. AE, CB, DC, DISC, MC, V.

This is the only Valdez hotel on the water. There's a pleasant grassy area with tables where you can watch the boats come in the entrance to the small-boat harbor, and the office for Prince William Sound Cruises and Tours is just outside on a dock. Most rooms lack views, but all rooms and bathrooms were all newly refurbished, bringing them up to par for a standard high-end motel. Don't be scared off by the rack rates; call and find out what they really charge, which may be as little as half.

The hotel maintains a tour desk, gift shop, and fuel dock. The hotel's **Captain's Table Restaurant** has the only waterfront dining in Valdez, overlooking the harbor, and was recently remodeled. Unfortunately, the food and service have been inconsistent year to year.

Wild Roses by the Sea B&B Retreat. 620 Fiddlehead Ln. (P.O. Box 3396), Valdez, AK 99686. ☎ **907/835-2930.** Fax 907/835-4966. www.bythesea.alaska.net. 3 units. TV TEL. Summer $125–$145 double, including full breakfast. Winter $89 double, no breakfast. Extra person $10. MC, V.

Light pours from bay windows that overlook the water and surrounding woods into large, elegantly appointed rooms with high ceilings, decorated with Asian and contemporary art, and finished in light colors, wood floors and Berber style carpets. Best of all is the spacious and private "Ocean View Guesthouse," a downstairs suite with a kitchen, living room, and VCR. All rooms have modem lines. The hostess, Rose Marie Fong, prepares elaborate breakfasts in the summer.

CAMPING

Valdez is a popular RV destination. When the salmon are running, RVs can park, self-contained, at the **Allison Point** fishing area (☎ **907/835-2282**) for $10 a night; water and portable toilets are available. The **Sea Otter RV Park,** P.O. Box 947, Valdez, AK 99686 (☎ **800/831-2787** in Alaska only, or 907/835-2787), sits on the outside of the boat harbor breakwater, with views and beachfront where you can fish for salmon or watch the harbor sea otters. They have a laundry and other facilities, and charge $20 for full hookups.

The town's **Valdez Glacier Campground** has 101 well-separated sites among alder and cottonwood trees near the airport, but the trees also make it a mosquito haven. They have pit toilets and well water. The fee is $10 a night.

The best campground in the area is the state's **Blueberry Lake Campground,** 24 miles out of town on the Richardson Highway, just below Thompson Pass. The campground is above the tree line, with mountaintop views and access to limitless alpine hiking. It can be windy and cold. The small lake is stocked with trout. Fifteen well-screened sites are $12 on a self-serve system. There are pit toilets.

DINING

I'm not enthusiastic about any restaurant in Valdez, but you can find decent food to sustain you. I like the deep-fried fish at the **Alaska Halibut House,** a fast-food joint at Fairbanks and Meals Avenue. It's open all day. **Oscar's,** on the waterfront at

143 N. Harbor Dr. (☎ **907/835-4700**), is a serviceable if gritty diner, open early and late for boaters. The outdoor seating area is pleasant. The restaurant at the **Totem Inn** (☎ **907/834-4443**), on the Richardson Highway as it comes into town, is the main local hangout. The service is friendly and the lunch specials satisfying, the TV is always on, and coffee cups are never empty. A mural of Port Valdez on one wall seems to show the smoggy haze emitted by the pipeline terminal.

Fu Kung Chinese Restaurant. 207 Kobuk Dr. (1 block from the boat harbor). ☎ **907/835-5255.** Lunch $6.75–$8.75; dinner main courses $11–$16,. MC, V. Daily 11am–11pm. CHINESE.

This long-established family restaurant in a Quonset hut near the harbor is consistently good. The interior of the old metal building is clean and pleasant, with a fish tank, warm colors and plenty of room. The food is plentiful and tasty, especially the kung pao chicken. Service is fast and attentive. In winter, they often close earlier than the hours listed above.

Mike's Palace Ristorante. 201 N. Harbor Dr. ☎ **907/835-2365.** Lunch $5–$9; dinner main courses $9–$25. MC, V. Daily 11am–11pm. PIZZA/STEAK/SEAFOOD.

This is a good family pizza restaurant, a place where Valdez residents come for a casual evening out. The calzone is good, the service skilled, and everything consistent. It's a warm, cheerful place, my favorite in Valdez. Mike's also has a place in history: Capt. Joseph Hazelwood was waiting for a take-out pizza here when he slipped next door to the Club Bar for his last drink before starting the fateful voyage of the *Exxon Valdez* that hit Bligh Reef. Mike also serves his national Greek cuisine. Beer and wine license.

The Pipeline Club. 112 Egan Dr. ☎ **907/835-4332.** Main courses $7.50–$23.75. AE, DISC, MC, V. Sun–Thurs 5:30–11pm, Fri–Sat 5:30pm–midnight.

This traditional beef-and-seafood house is something of a time capsule from the 1970s with its very dark cocktail-bar ambience, booths, and at least one kidney-shaped table. Our meals showed no flaws, but were unmemorable. You can get lunch in the lounge, with its two TVs, karaoke, and golf simulator. If asked, the bartender will point out the stool where Capt. Joe Hazelwood got loaded on vodka tonics before taking command of the *Exxon Valdez.* Full liquor license.

14 Cordova: Hidden Treasure

The first time I ever went to Cordova, my companion and I arrived at the Mudhole Smith Airport in a small plane and happened upon an old guy with a pickup truck who offered to let us ride in back with some boards the 10 miles to town. The highway led out onto a broad, wetland plain—the largest contiguous wetland in the Western Hemisphere, as it happens. Our guide's voice, studded with profanity, boomed through the back window as he told us proudly about the diversity of the wildlife to be found out there. Then, absolutely bursting with enthusiasm, he leaned on the horn and bellowed, "Look at them fucking swans!" We looked; trumpeters paddling in the marsh looked back. He would have invited them along to the bar, too, if he'd known how.

Every time I've been to Cordova since, I've been taken under the wings of new friends. Although they usually don't express themselves the same way that first gentleman did, they are just as enthusiastic to show off the amazing natural riches of their little kingdom. Tourists are still something of a novelty here, for Cordova isn't just off the beaten track—it's not on the track at all. There's no road to the rest of the world and the town is an afterthought on the ferry system. Boosters call their town "Alaska's Hidden Treasure." For once, they're right.

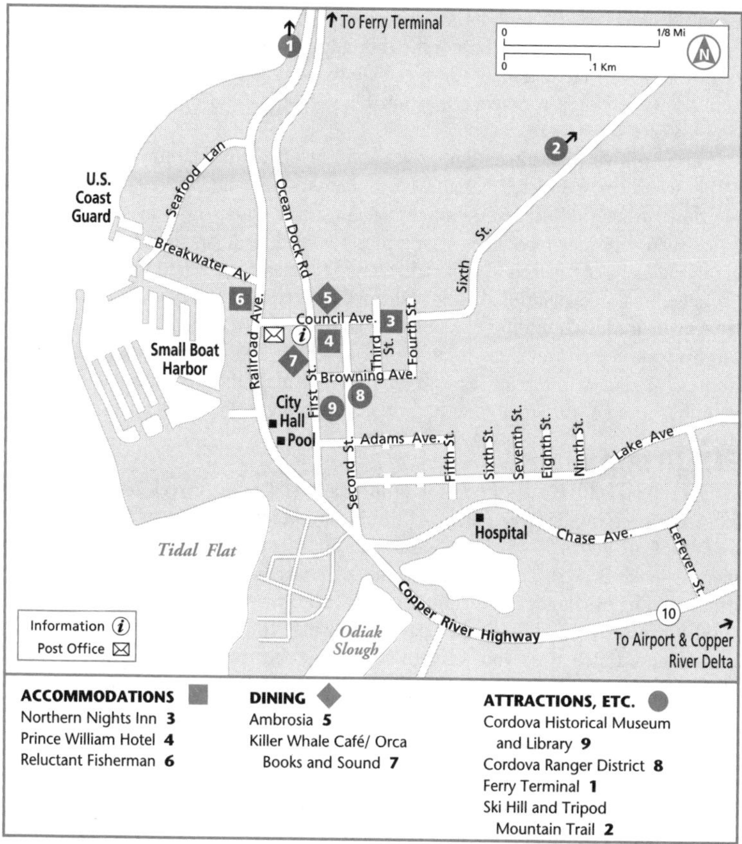

Our family has had some of our happiest times in Cordova. Visiting the **Childs Glacier** and seeing the swans and geese on the delta, hiking into the mountains behind town, boating on the Sound to meet the sea otters and sea lions, eagles and spawning salmon, hiking and canoeing at a remote lake cabin—and meeting no other people at all. In town, we have made new friends whenever we turned around, and received hearty greetings from old friends from previous visits. Leaving on the ferry for Valdez, I've watched Cordova shrinking behind us with a wistful hope that it would never change.

So far, I've gotten my wish. You can feel a bit like an anthropologist discovering a tribe lost to time, for Cordova has the qualities small towns are supposed to have had but lost long ago in America (if they ever did have them). Walking down First Street, you pass an old-fashioned independent grocery store, the fishermen's union hall, and Steen's gift shop, run by the same family since 1909—no chains or franchises. People leave their keys in the car and their doors unlocked at night. When a friend of mine bought one of the quaint, moss-roofed hillside houses a few years ago, he didn't receive a key—the simple reason was that the front door didn't have a lock.

The commercial fishermen who power the economy have fought to protect Cordova from change. They pushed for the oil industry to improve its shipping practices years before the 1989 oil spill and then, after the disaster (which hurt

Cordova worst of all), lobbied for the money won from Exxon to be spent on the Sound's environment. They have resisted building a road to Cordova, as well. Another faction in town, the merchants and tourism workers, want a road. The debate is hot, and a few years ago a mayoral election between pro- and antiroad candidates was decided by a single vote.

This controversy has been going on for 50 or 60 years. The town's heyday was in 1911, when the Copper River and Northwestern Railroad opened, carrying copper ore down from the mine at Kennicott; it hit a low when the mine closed in 1938. Since then, boosters have been trying to get a road built on the old rail line, north along the Copper River to Chitina (that fascinating area is covered in chapter 9, under "Wrangell–St. Elias National Park and the Copper River Valley"). The road builders have made it only about 50 miles out of town so far. From Cordova, the **Copper River Highway** provides access to the best bird watching and, in my judgment, the most impressive glacier in Alaska, as well as trails and magnificent vistas and areas to see wildlife. In town, the small-boat harbor is a doorway to Prince William Sound.

ESSENTIALS

GETTING THERE **By Ferry** Cordova is served twice a week from Valdez, once from Whittier, by the ferry *Bartlett* of the **Alaska Marine Highway System** (☎ **800/642-0066** or 907/424-7333; www.dot.state.ak.us/external/amhs/home.html). If you plan to make this trip, study the schedule carefully before planning the rest of your itinerary. The passenger fare for the 5½-hour run from Valdez is $30, while the 7-hour trip from Whittier is $58; children pay roughly half. It may pay to bring a car, depending on how much time you want to spend out the road, on the delta, and at the glacier. Taking a vehicle under 15 feet one way from Valdez to Cordova is $64. See "Ferry System Booking Tips" in chapter 5 for ways to communicate with the system.

By Air **Alaska Airlines** (☎ **800/426-0333** or 907/424-7151; www.alaskaair.com) flies one jet daily each direction, from Anchorage to the west and Yakutat, Juneau, and Seattle to the southeast, with two more flights to Anchorage operated by **Era Aviation** (☎ **800/866-8394;** www.era-aviation.com).

The **Airport Shuttle** from the Reluctant Fisherman Hotel (☎ **907/424-3272**) meets all planes and charges $10 one way. Taxis are usually available as well from **Wild Hare Cab** (☎ **907/424-3939**). Formerly, a free van picked up passengers at the ferry dock, but that arrangement may not continue in 2001; ask the purser.

GETTING AROUND You can easily walk around downtown Cordova, but that's not where the most interesting sights are. To get out on the Copper River Highway, you'll need a car, bus, or, if you're vigorous, a bike.

Cars are for rent from the Reluctant Fisherman Hotel (listed below) for $75 a day, without mileage charges; the airport shuttle is free when you rent a car. **Cordova Auto Rentals** (☎ **907/424-5982;** www.ptialaska.net/~cars) rents cars, vans, and four-wheel-drive vehicles at the airport.

Rent bikes, kayaks, skiffs, canoes, and fishing and camping gear at **Cordova Coastal Outfitters,** at the boat harbor below the fishermen's memorial (☎ **800/357-5145** or 907/424-7424; www.cdvcoastal.com). They're described in full below.

VISITOR INFORMATION A new **Cordova Chamber of Commerce Visitor Center** (☎ **907/424-7260;** www.cordovachamber.com) is at 404 First St., north of Council Avenue (P.O. Box 99, Cordova, AK 99574). They're open Monday to Friday from 10am to 3pm. Besides the usual information, the center has a 60-minute recorded walking tour that you can listen to as it guides you around town.

The folks at the museum and library also provide **visitor information** at 622 First St. (☎ **907/424-6665**). Summer hours are Monday to Saturday 10am to 6pm, Sunday 2 to 4pm; winter Tuesday to Friday 1 to 5pm.

The **Cordova Ranger District** of the Chugach National Forest, upstairs in the old white courthouse at Second Street and Browning (P.O. Box 280), Cordova, AK 99574 (☎ **907/424-7661**), has displays and provides maps and guide information that's indispensable for planning outdoor activities. The staff will sit down and help you figure out what you want to do.

SPECIAL EVENTS **The Cordova Ice Worm Festival** is a winter carnival the first full weekend in February; the big ice worm—or, to be precise, ice centipede—marches in a parade. **The Copper River Delta Shorebird Festival** (**907/424-7260;** www. ptialaska.net/~midtown) revolves around the coming of dizzying swarms of shorebirds—estimates range from 5 to 22 million—that use the delta and beaches near the town as a migratory stopover in early May. It's an opportunity to see immense waves of birds. The whole community gets involved to host bird-watchers and put on a full schedule of educational and outdoor activities that lasts 5 days.

FAST FACTS Two banks on First Street have **ATMs,** as does the Alaska Commercial grocery store at the boat harbor.

Internet access is available at the **Cordova Public Library** (☎ **907/424-6665**) and at **Laura's Liquor Shoppe** (☎ **907/424-3144**), both on First Street.

The **Cordova Community Medical Center** is on Chase Street (☎ **907/424-8000**), off the Copper River Highway near the slough.

For nonemergency **police** calls, dial ☎ **907/424-6100.**

The **post office** is at Railroad Avenue and Council.

Sales tax in Cordova is 6%; rooms and car rentals carry an additional 6%.

HIKING AROUND CORDOVA

Cordova has more good hiking trails per capita than any place I know. The Cordova Ranger Station can provide you with a free trail-guide booklet with lots of ideas and maps. There are three close to town (trails farther out are listed below, in the section on the Copper River Delta).

The **Tripod Mountain Trail** begins right from town and climbs 1,255 feet over less than a mile up the first mountain back from the shore, a half-day hike with views that present the Sound and Cordova like a map below you. The trail begins at the foot of the town ski lift, on Sixth Street—take Browning up the hill.

Partway up Tripod Mountain, near the middle drop off of the ski lift, a 1-mile trip links to the **Crater Lake Trail,** which eventually joins the **Power Creek Trail** on a loop of 12 miles. An easier start for that route is the Power Creek Road—take it along the north side of Eyak Lake to the end, 7 miles from town. The creek has spawning red salmon in July and attracts a lot of bears; watch, but don't get out of your car if you come upon one. The trail follows the creek through dramatic scenery 4.2 miles to the Power Creek Forest Service cabin, with a great view (reserve through the system described in section 3, Chugach National Forest, above).

✪ THE COPPER RIVER DELTA

The delta and its star attraction, the **Childs Glacier,** make an unforgettable day trip by car or tour bus from Cordova, but if you have a couple of days, you can do more. The backwaters, sloughs, and ponds beg to be explored by canoe. Bird-watchers will especially enjoy such a paddle, or visits to the boardwalks and blinds set up by the Forest

Service. You can raft the rivers. There are excellent hiking trails and mountain-biking routes branching from the road, and Forest Service cabins to stay in.

The delta seems to go on forever, a vast patchwork of marsh, pond, small hills of trees, and the huge, implacable gray river itself. The glacial silt it carries away—some 2 million tons a day—has built this 700,000-acre wetland. A well-maintained gravel road leads across it, all in Chugach National Forest, and the rangers have done a good job of providing ways and places to enjoy and learn about the area. The road itself is the old bed of the Copper River and Northwestern Railroad. It leads 48 miles to the **Million Dollar Bridge.** Built by Michael Heney, a magician of a 19th-century railroad builder who also constructed the White Pass and Yukon Route in Skagway, the 200-mile Copper River line was an engineering triumph that brought the mind-boggling wealth of the Kennicott Copper Mine to ships in Cordova (read more about the mine in the section on "Wrangell–St. Elias National Park and the Copper River Valley" in chapter 9). The bridge over the Copper River went up in a race against time between two surging glaciers in 30-foot-deep, fast-flowing glacial water, in winter. The bridge stood 56 years, until the 1964 earthquake knocked down one end of one of the spans, augering it into the riverbed. But you can still drive across on a jerry-built ramp and go a few miles farther on unmaintained road.

Getting There

BY CAR Driving gives you the most freedom. The road is gravel, but it's wide and level. Beyond the Million Dollar Bridge, however, it's a rough four-wheel-drive track at best, and if you get stuck you'll be there for a long time. Pick up the road guide from the Forest Service Cordova Ranger Station, and read the highlights below.

BY BIKE Mountain biking the highway is the adventurous way to travel, camping or staying in a Forest Service cabin on the way. The drawbacks are the distances, the delta's strong winds, and a lot of road dust. Of course, you don't have to ride all the way to see lots of birds and wildlife, and there are good mountain biking routes on the delta away from the road. The 3-mile **Saddlebag Glacier Trail,** at mile 25 of the Copper River Highway, leads to a stunning vista of a glacial lake surrounded by rocky peaks. Bikes are for rent from Cordova Coastal Outfitters (see "Out On the Sound," below) for $15 a day.

Along the Road

Keep your eyes scanning the wetlands and mountains around you as you drive out the road. The **wildlife** you may see along the way includes black and brown bears, wolf, coyote, moose, and mountain goats. The entire world population of dusky Canada geese nests on the delta, and you're likely to see eagles and trumpeter swans without really looking. The ranger station provides a wildlife-viewing guide and several places to stop along the way designed for bird watching. The first is a platform with interpretive signs as you leave town, as sort of an introduction to the delta; this stretch of the road is fine for bird watching.

Don't miss the **Alaganik Slough Boardwalk.** Take the 3.2-mile spur road to the right 16.8 miles out the Copper River Highway; it's marked. The sky here is big and certain while the land is ambivalent—it doesn't know if it wants to be waving grass of green and gold or shallow, shimmering ponds and tendrils of water. The road leads out to a parking lot and small, free campground, the start of the 1,000-foot boardwalk. One part leads to a large blind where you can watch the ponds and brush for birds. The other takes you above a large pond that reflects the sun and the colors of the marsh. We were speechless when we stood there one evening at sunset, even in the complete absence of birds. Often in the summer you can see breeding trumpeter swans, ducks, and grebes, and in the spring and fall migrating waterfowl and shorebirds.

The highway ends with its best attraction, the ✪ **Childs Glacier.** This is the most amazing glacier I've ever seen, and no one seems to know about it outside Cordova. The wall of ice, 300 feet tall, comes right down to the quarter-mile-wide river, where flowing water cuts it off like a knife, eroding the base and bringing down huge chunks. As you sit on the opposite bank, the glacier on the opposite side is too large to see—it completely fills your field of vision, creating an eerie and hypnotic sense of scale. On a warm summer day, you can feel the glacier's thunder as the ice shifts, and see pieces fall off. A chunk the size of a car barely registers, but when an office building–size hunk falls, there's a roar and gray breakers radiate out across the river. Falling glacier pieces have made waves large enough to uproot trees here, not to mention hurling a few fish around—at the Forest Service viewing and picnic area across the river, salmon have been found high up in the trees and boulders in odd places. Several years ago, such a wave injured some visitors, and now the Forest Service warns that anyone who can't run fast should stay in the observation tower. A bit farther from shore there's a campground with pit toilets.

Don't miss seeing and at least walking on the **Million Dollar Bridge,** less than a mile from the glacier-viewing area.

ACTIVITIES

HIKING The Forest Service maintains several trails on the delta. The **Alaganik Slough Boardwalk** and **Saddlebag Glacier Trail** are mentioned above.

The **Haystack Trail,** starting on the right just past the 19-mile marker on the highway, climbs through mossy rain forest from the delta's floor onto an odd little hill. The glaciers that once covered the delta spared this bedrock outcropping. The trail is steep in places but only 0.8 mile in length, and it leads to an overlook.

The **McKinley Lake Trail,** at mile 21.6 on the highway, leads 2.4 miles through rain forest vegetation to a lake bearing trout (although we got no bites), and a little further to the overgrown ruins of a gold mine. You can also get there by canoe (see below). There are two Forest Service cabins on the trail, the small McKinley Trail Cabin near the highway and the McKinley Lake Cabin, beautifully situated among big trees above the lake. Each costs $35 a night and can be reserved through the national system described in section 3 of this chapter, on the Chugach National Forest.

CANOEING The delta's canoe routes are little used, leading to remote places where birds and aquatic animals rule. You can launch on Alaganik Slough at a picnic area right at mile 22 on the Copper River Highway, padding placid waters into stunningly beautiful marsh lands. Taking the "Wrong Way" route that starts a couple of miles up the road, you can float several miles of more challenging water down to McKinley Lake, stay at the cabin, then float downstream again to the slough launch, back at the road. It's ideal overnight, or you could do it in a day, or, as we did, spend an extra day and night at the cabin. The couple who run **Cordova Coastal Outfitters** (see below, under "Out on the Sound") rents canoes for $30 a day and drops them off, and will help you decide what route to take. You can ride out on one of their bicycles and pick up the canoe already at the launch site. They rent camping gear, too.

RAFTING The immense quantity of water draining the Wrangell–St. Elias Mountains through the Copper River Delta, and the Copper River Highway that provides river access, make this a perfect venue for rafting. **Alaska River Rafting** (☎ **800/776-1864** or 907/424-7238; www.alaskarafters.com) is well regarded by locals. Their diverse territory means they can offer quite a range of trips, from easy floating to white water, or even rafting right in front of the Childs Glaciers. Trips last from 3 hours to all day, or overnight. A 3-hour trip is $60 per person; all-day, with flightseeing, $250.

FISHING The delta's lakes and streams harbor all five species of Pacific salmon, as well as Dolly Varden and cutthroat trout. The Cordova Ranger Station can offer guidance and regulation booklets, and the Cordova office of the **Alaska Department of Fish and Game** is at 401 Railroad Ave. (☎ **907/424-3212;** www.state.ak.us/local/akpages/FISH.GAME/sportf/region2/r2home.htm). See "Fishing" in chapter 2 for general guidance.

OUT ON THE SOUND

The waters of Prince William Sound around Cordova, although lacking the tidewater glaciers found in the western Sound, are protected and rich in marine life. Sea otters are so common as to no longer receive a second glance from locals, congregating in rafts of many dozens or even hundreds. Sea lions can be found predictably, too, and orcas and humpback whales are not out of the ordinary. Bird watchers can expect harlequin ducks and many other marine birds. Getting out on the water is easy, too, either on your own or with a guide, by boat or by sea kayak.

Cordova Coastal Outfitters is a good place to start for any outdoor activities (☎ **800/357-5145** or 907/424-7424; www.cdvcoastal.com). Andy Craig and Seawan Gehlbach know the equipment, the skills, and the area, and they convey that knowledge with casual enthusiasm. Their booth is on the dock below the Alaska Commercial grocery store, on the south side of the boat harbor. They guide sea kayaking and rent kayaks and fully equipped motorized boats. If your group isn't up to kayaking, **renting a boat** might be the way to go—you won't believe the sense of freedom you feel clearing the harbor breakwater to explore Orca Inlet and the bays of Hawkins Island, on the far side. Boats rent for $95 a day, fishing gear included. They also offer water taxi or guided boat tour service in the Sound and on the Copper River Delta.

The **guided sea-kayaking trip** for beginners lasts 4 hours and costs $60, concentrating on wildlife sightings. A 4-hour trip for the same price paddles on Eyak Lake to see brown bears and great blue herons. They offer all-day and multiday trips, too. Single kayaks rent for $35 a day, doubles $50.

Dave Janka runs the classic wooden ***Auklet*** (☎ **907/424-3428;** www.auklet.com), a 58-foot former U.S. Fish and Wildlife Service patrol boat, to carry scientific researchers and visitors into the Sound from Cordova, Valdez, and Whittier. He doesn't enjoy fishing and doesn't believe in hunting, so this is a wildlife and scenery experience. You design your own trip with him, paying $180 per person per day, with a minimum of three passengers. You can start or end in any of the three towns, saving the cost of transportation between the communities. The accommodations on board are nautical, not luxurious. Other businesses offering cruises are listed in section 4 of this chapter, on Whittier.

Several vessels are available for fishing charters, or day trips to see whales and other wildlife. **Alaska's Beyond Boundaries Fishing and Hunting** (☎ **907/766-2610;** www.akbeyondboundaries.com) is run by Ray Staska, a retired fisheries biologist. He charges $110 for a day of whale watching, $160 to $190 for a trip to fish halibut, salmon, or sharks. The Chamber of Commerce (see "Visitor Information," above) has links to other charter operators on its Web site, or call them for a referral.

ATTRACTIONS

Save some time to wander around town, possibly with the help of the **historic walking tour booklet** produced by the historic society, available from the chamber of commerce. Cordova is full of little discoveries to make on your own.

In the Air

Cordova is all by itself, with untouched wilderness in all directions. The most inexpensive way to see it from the air is to take a **mail plane** to one of the villages or fish hatcheries. **Cordova Air** (☎ **907/424-3289**) is the largest operator, based on Eyak Lake. **Fishing and Flying** (☎ **907/424-3324**), located at the airport, is a friendly operation and has remote cabins for rent. Either one can fly you out to an extremely remote Forest Service cabin, where you can fish, explore, or just discover what it's like to be totally alone.

The **Cordova Historical Museum,** at 622 First St., is a well-presented one-room display with some valuable artifacts reflecting Cordova's eventful past. The three-seat kayak and other artifacts of Prince William Sound Native peoples are of particular interest. Cordova is the home of the last few Eyak, a Native people whose language now has only one speaker left. There's also a Linotype machine, the interior of a fishing boat, and photographs of fishing and historic scenes. The museum is open summer Monday to Saturday 10am to 6pm, Sunday 2 to 4pm; winter Tuesday to Friday 1 to 5pm, Saturday 2 to 4pm. Admission is $1, free under age 18.

ACCOMMODATIONS

✪ **The Northern Nights Inn.** 500 Third St. (P.O. Box 1564), Cordova, AK 99547. ☎ **907/424-5356.** Fax 907/424-3291. E-mail: alaskan@cordovanet.com. 5 units. TV TEL. $60–$75 double. Extra adult $5. Children stay free in parents' room. AE, DISC, MC, V.

These large rooms, with private bathrooms, antiques, quilts, VCRs, coffeemakers, microwaves, refrigerators, and views, are an almost unreal value. All but one has a full kitchen, and breakfast supplies are provided. They're upstairs in Becky Chapek and Bill Myers's historic 1906 house, a couple of blocks above the main street. Each room has been lovingly renovated, and three have kitchenettes. One room is essentially an entire apartment. There are five bicycles for guests' use, a coin-op laundry, and a freezer for your fish. The family also operates the well-run tour business in town.

Prince William Motel. Second St. and Council (P.O. Box 908), Cordova, AK 99574. ☎ **907/424-3201.** Fax 907/424-2260. PWMOTEL@yahoo.com. 16 units. TV TEL. Summer $80–$100 double. Winter $75–$95 double. Extra adult $10. Children 11 and under stay free in parents' room. AE, MC, V.

A friendly and helpful family renovated this old building into a clean, comfortable, modern motel. The lower rooms look out onto an airshaft, but that may be an advantage if you're trying to get to sleep when it's still light out. All rooms have coffee machines, microwaves, and small refrigerators, and seven have kitchenettes (these rooms go for $20 more). There's a coin-op laundry, a barbecue, and a freezer for fish. Not a good choice if you have trouble with stairs.

✪ **The Reluctant Fisherman.** 401 Railroad Ave. (P.O. Box 150), Cordova, AK 99574. ☎ **800/770-3272** or 907/424-3272. Fax 907/424-7465. E-mail: reluct@ptialaska.net. 50 units. TV TEL. High season $75–$125 double. Low season $75–$95 double. Extra person $10. AE, CB, DC, DISC, JCB, MC, V.

Margy Johnson presides at Cordova's main hotel with limitless energy. She and her husband, Dick Borer, have created one of the best waterfront lodgings in Alaska, overlooking the small-boat harbor. The decor in the lobby, lounge, and restaurant capture the town's railroad and copper-mining history, with rich wood and pressed-copper ceilings, stained glass, and mementos of the couple's history here. The rooms are comfortable and modern, with coffee machines, VCRs, and local art. Those on the water side have good views, while an economy wing on the parking lot rents for only $75 a night. There's a gift shop and travel agency in the hotel; they also rent cars and operate the airport shuttle.

The ✪ **restaurant** serves the town's best dinners. Main courses of fish, steaks, and pasta range from $15 to $27. Lunch is $4 to $10. A small deck overlooks the harbor for outdoor dining. Order the Copper River king or red salmon in season, broiled—the river produces exceptionally rich fish, a real delicacy that's made into delicious chili for lunch.

DINING

Other than the restaurants listed here, try the **Reluctant Fisherman.** Also, the **Flying Dutchman Pub and Grill,** 531 First St. (☎ **907/424-3248**), serves good burgers, fish-and-chips, and soup at a counter overlooking the harbor. It's one of the least smoky bars in town. Some of Cordova's best lunches come from **Baja Taco** (☎ **907/424-5599**), a bus at the boat harbor with a covered dining area elevated on a small tower. The proprietor, who lives in Baja in the winter, specializes in salmon tacos and operates here May to September.

Ambrosia. 410 First St. ☎ **907/424-7175.** Main courses $5.75–$18.75. MC, V. High season daily 4–11pm. Low season daily 4–9pm. ITALIAN.

This is a comfortable family restaurant with an extensive menu and pizza. It's the kind of place that stays in business in a small town: The food is reliable and the portions large, but nothing too challenging or unusual. Beer and wine license.

Killer Whale Cafe. In Orca Book and Sound, 507 First St. ☎ **907/424-7733.** All items $6–$9. No credit cards. Mon–Fri 7am–4pm, Sat 8am–3:30pm.

The food has not been consistent, and at this writing the place was up for sale, but this cafe is still worth a stop for the atmosphere. It's the loft above a bookstore that is a nexus of local ecopeople. Oil-spill hero Kelly Weaverling owns Orca Book and Sound, and was the only member of the Green Party to hold elective office in the United States when he was Cordova's mayor a few years ago. (He later lost to Margy Johnson, of the Reluctant Fisherman, by one vote, but refused to ask for a recount.) Order soups, sandwiches, and the like at the counter. No liquor license.

8

The Denali National Park Region

Denali (den-*al*-ee) stands alone among the nation's parks: It gives regular people easy access to real wilderness, with sweeping tundra vistas, abundant wildlife, and North America's tallest mountain. Other wilderness areas in Alaska may have equally inspiring scenery and even more animals, but Denali is unique because of its accessibility to visitors—and because that accessibility hasn't spoiled the natural experience, as it has at so many other parks.

It's a sad truth that even the largest national parks in the Lower 48 are too small to comprise complete ecosystems. The dream of leaving nature undisturbed is essentially lost in those places, and only through human intervention do the natural systems within the parks stay as close to their primeval state as they do (this is illustrated by the work of rangers at Yellowstone to drive bison back within park boundaries so they won't come to harm outside). Millions of people driving through the parks in cars adds greater interference. At Rocky Mountain National Park, there's a crossing guard for big horn sheep. At Yosemite Valley and the Grand Canyon, they're figuring out ways to get rid of the cars, recognizing that the vehicles themselves can spoil the experience of nature.

On the other end of the spectrum, Alaska has many parks with immense intact ecosystems that have remained unchanged, still existing as they did before white men made contact. More than two-thirds of America's national park acreage is in Alaska, taking in inconceivably huge swaths of land without roads, buildings, or landing strips. They're natural all right, but almost no one goes there. Some of these parks receive a few hundred visitors a year—only the Alaska Natives of the surrounding region and perhaps the hardiest and wealthiest outdoors people. Just chartering a plane to get out to some of these places can cost as much as most of us spend on our whole vacation. With as many people on the earth as we've got, wilderness survives only when it's rationed somehow. In most of Alaska, the rationing system is simply the expense and difficulty of getting to the wild.

At Denali, on the other hand, you can see the heart of the park for little more than it would cost you to visit Yellowstone. And when you get there, it's a pristine natural environment where truly wild animals live in a complete ecosystem pretty much without human interference. A single national park service decision makes this possible: The only road through the park is closed to the public. This means that to get into the park, you must ride a crowded bus over a dusty gravel road hour after hour, but it also means that the animals are still there to watch, and their behavior remains essentially normal. From the window of the bus, you're likely to see grizzly bears doing what they would be doing even if you weren't there. It may be the only $20 safari in the world.

What's even more unique is that you can get off the bus pretty much whenever you want to and walk away from the road across the tundra, out of sight of the road, and be alone in this primeval wilderness. Unfortunately, many Denali visitors never take advantage of the opportunity, which normally would cost a lot of money or require a lot of muscle and outdoor skill. Being alone under God's big sky makes many people nervous. Most of us have never been really away from other people, much less apart from anything people have made. But that's the essence of Alaska—learning, deep down, how big creation is and how small you are, one more mammal on the tundra under the broad sky. At Denali, you can experience that wonder, and then, when you're ready to return to civilization, you can just walk to the road and catch the next bus—they come every half hour.

The Denali experience spreads beyond the park. After all, the park boundary is an artificial line—the wildlife and the scenery of the Alaska Range don't observe its significance. To the east, the **Denali Highway** runs through the same extraordinary terrain, with opportunities for hiking over the tundra and canoeing on the lakes managed by the Bureau of Land Management. To the south, **Denali State Park** and the town of **Talkeetna** provide another vantage on Mount McKinley, with the advantage of salmon fishing in the rivers and remote lake recreation. The construction of comfortable new lodges and a variety of good outdoor guides have helped make Talkeetna a popular alternative gateway to Denali. Even though it's 150 miles from the park entrance by car, Talkeetna is physically closer to the mountain than is the park headquarters.

Visitors often skip all the area's other attractions, however, and focus instead on **Mount McKinley,** which, at 20,320 feet, is the tallest mountain in North America. It is an impressive peak, but you don't need to go to the park to see it—in fact, most people who do go *don't* see it. Summer weather patterns usually sock in the mountain by midafternoon, at least as seen from the ground in the park.

Unfortunately, Denali has become a thing people feel they must do, and seeing Mount McKinley is a thing they must do when they visit Denali. Many package tours rush the park so quickly it becomes just a blur outside a window rather than an experience. If they miss the mountain, passengers may wonder why they traveled so far to stay at the ticky-tacky roadside development at the park's entrance and then ride on a bus over a bumpy road. A friend swears she overheard a tourist ask, as she boarded the train leaving Denali, "Why did they put the park way out here in the boondocks?"

The answer is there for you to find, at the bottom of the steps of the shuttle bus door.

1 Planning a Visit to the Park

ORIENTATION

The park is like a pivot in the center of Alaska, a huge slice of the Alaska Range—rock and ice robed in tundra and stunted black spruce. Denali National Park and Preserve encompasses 6 million acres, a roughly triangular polygon about 20% larger than Massachusetts. The only park entrance is 230 miles north of Anchorage and 120 miles south of Fairbanks on the paved George Parks Highway or the Alaska Railroad.

Denali National Park

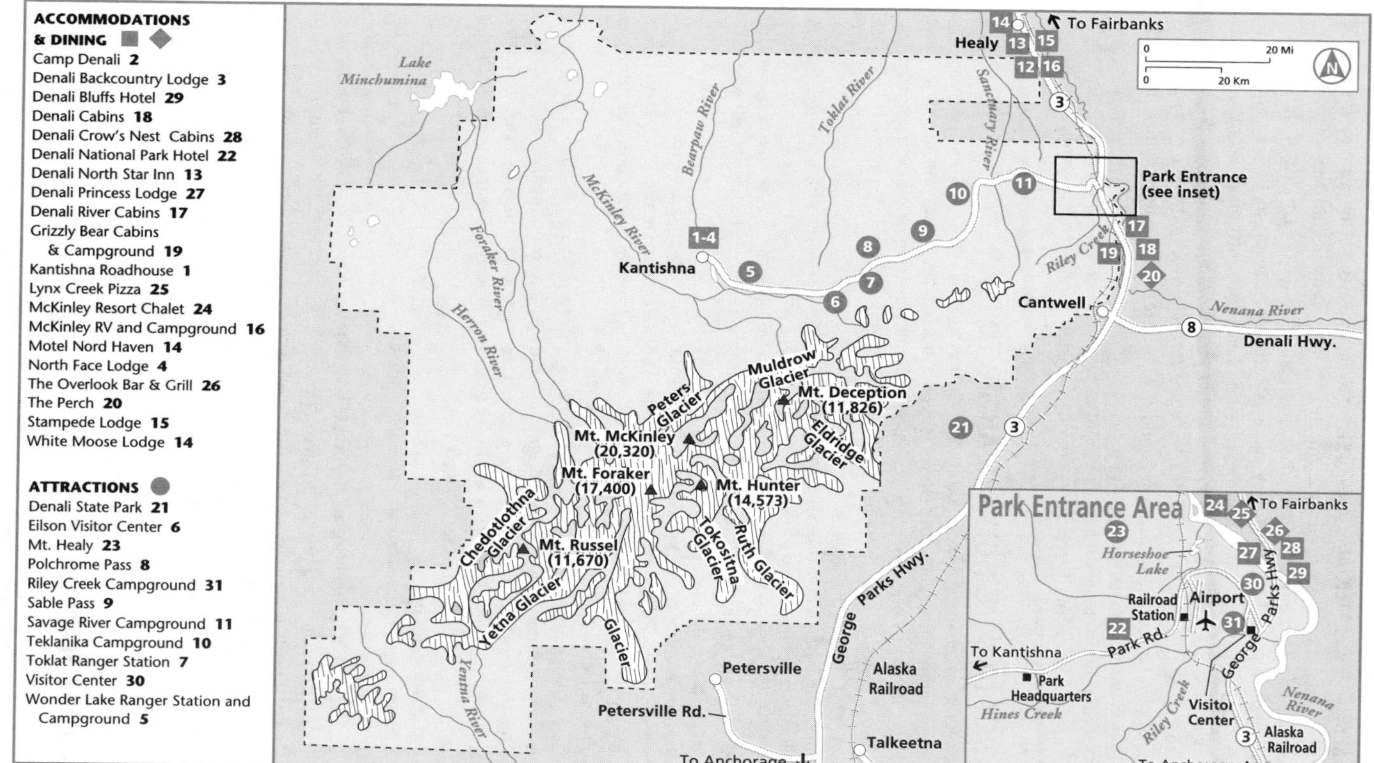
ACCOMMODATIONS & DINING
Camp Denali 2
Denali Backcountry Lodge 3
Denali Bluffs Hotel 29
Denali Cabins 18
Denali Crow's Nest Cabins 28
Denali National Park Hotel 22
Denali North Star Inn 13
Denali Princess Lodge 27
Denali River Cabins 17
Grizzly Bear Cabins & Campground 19
Kantishna Roadhouse 1
Lynx Creek Pizza 25
McKinley Resort Chalet 24
McKinley RV and Campground 16
Motel Nord Haven 14
North Face Lodge 4
The Overlook Bar & Grill 26
The Perch 20
Stampede Lodge 15
White Moose Lodge 14
ATTRACTIONS
Denali State Park 21
Eilson Visitor Center 6
Mt. Healy 23
Polchrome Pass 8
Riley Creek Campground 31
Sable Pass 9
Savage River Campground 11
Teklanika Campground 10
Toklat Ranger Station 7
Visitor Center 30
Wonder Lake Ranger Station and Campground 5
Lake Minchumina
Bearpaw River
Toklat River
Sanctuary River
McKinley River
Foraker River
Herron River
Healy
To Fairbanks
0 20 Mi
0 20 Km
Park Entrance (see inset)
Kantishna
Riley Creek
Cantwell
Nenana River
Denali Hwy.
Muldrow Glacier
Mt. Deception (11,826)
Peters Glacier
Mt. McKinley (20,320)
Eldridge Glacier
Mt. Foraker (17,400)
Mt. Hunter (14,573)
Chedotlothna Glacier
Mt. Russel (11,670)
Tokositna Glacier
Ruth Glacier
Yetna Glacier
Glacier
Yentna River
George Parks Hwy.
Petersville
Petersville Rd.
Alaska Railroad
Talkeetna
To Anchorage
Park Entrance Area
To Fairbanks
Horseshoe Lake
Railroad Station
Airport
Parks Hwy
Park Rd.
To Kantishna
Park Headquarters
Hines Creek
Riley Creek
George
Visitor Center
Nenana River
Alaska Railroad
To Anchorage

Although **Mount McKinley** is visible from as far away as Anchorage, you can't see it at all from the area near the park entrance (where you will find the railroad depot and all services accessible by private vehicle), since it's on the far side of the park. A mile north on the Parks Highway, along a cliff-sided canyon of the Nenana River, hotels and restaurants have developed a kind of seasonal town on private land in the immediate area of the **park entrance.** Other services are at **Carlo Creek,** 13 miles south on the Parks, or at another gathering of roadside development 7 miles south of the park entrance, and in the year-round town of **Healy,** 10 miles north of the park entrance. From the park entrance, a road accessible only by shuttle bus leads west 89 miles through the park, past a series of campgrounds and a visitor center, and ending at the **Kantishna district,** a patch of park-surrounded private lands inholdings with wilderness lodges.

WHEN TO GO & HOW FAR AHEAD TO PLAN

Crowding is relative. Once you're out in the park, Denali is never crowded. A transportation bottleneck, the shuttle system, protects the park from overuse. What makes the July-to-mid-August busy season difficult is getting through that bottleneck from the crowded park entrance into the wilderness. At that time, travelers who just show up at the visitor center without any reservations often have to spend a day or two outside the park before they can get a seat on a shuttle bus, a campground site, or a backcountry permit.

The flow of visitors seems to vary greatly from year to year. Some years, you've needed to make **reservations** by March for a July visit; other years, a few weeks of advance planning will do. To be on the safe side, get your shuttle tickets and campsites as soon as you know the dates of your visit. Lodgings also get tight in July, but are not as critical to the success of your visit. Reserve as far ahead as you can, but don't worry about getting stuck in a dive if you don't get your first choice of rooms or cabins, as I've found no really bad places there.

The park is populated by people beginning in mid-May, when there still is some snow; the humans migrate south again in mid- to late September, when winter is closing in. In the off-season, only a few dozen residents remain—caretakers who watch over the hotels and other buildings and sled-dog-driving rangers who patrol the backcountry. The visitor season gets into high gear in mid-June and starts to wind down in mid-August, providing a month of relative quiet and often reduced prices at the beginning of the season and another at the end. Reservations are easy to come by at those times.

Access within Denali doesn't begin until Memorial Day, so May is out, but fall is a wonderful time to go. The weather gets nippy at night, and there can be surprise snowfalls, but rain is less likely, and the trees and tundra turn wonderful colors. By early September, visitors are so few that the park no longer takes telephone reservations. By mid-September, private cars can drive on the park road for a few days—the park service holds a lottery in September to determine who will get that treat.

Another way to avoid the crowds is to book a stay in a **wilderness lodge.** Three lodges in Kantishna, listed in section 7 of this chapter, have the right to carry clients to their businesses over the park road in buses and vans, avoiding the bottleneck.

SAMPLE ITINERARIES

The more you're willing to rough it, the closer you get to the real Denali. There are no hotels in the heart of the park.

The Hotel-Stay Itinerary

Arrive by train at the park, checking into accommodations nearby—shuttles and courtesy vans will get you around. Attend a ranger talk, the *Cabin Nite* dinner-theater show, or go on a short **nature walk** around the park hotel in the evening. Get to bed early, and the next morning take a shuttle bus before 7am into the park, riding to the **Eielson Visitor Center** to see the terrain and animals, and possibly to get a view of the mountain (arriving there in late morning). Now ride partway back toward the entrance before getting off the bus at a place of your choosing for a walk and to eat the bag lunch you've brought along with you (pack out all trash, of course), or take one of the **park service guided walks.** After enjoying the wilderness for a few hours, head back on the bus, finishing a long day back at the hotel. Next day try a rafting ride, a flightseeing trip, or another activity near the entrance to the park before reboarding the train.

The Family Camping Itinerary

Arrive at the park entrance by car with your camping gear and food for a couple of nights. (You can rent the camping gear and car in Anchorage.) Camp that evening at the **Riley Creek Campground** near the visitor center and enjoy the evening ranger program or a nature walk, or go straight to a campsite farther within the park (either way, you'll need to reserve well ahead). Next day, catch a shuttle bus or camper bus to get deeper into the park for sightseeing and **hiking.** If you have another day after that within the park, you can do more hikes and have the cushion of a weather day. If you're staying 3 nights, you can drive your car to the **Teklanika Campground,** which offers good hiking on the Teklanika riverbed, and the advantage of having your home base well within the park. Finally, break camp early on the third or fourth day and return to the entrance. Add a rafting or horseback excursion at the park entrance before driving on, if you like, and possibly a night at a hotel to get washed up.

The Backcountry Camping Itinerary

Arrive by train, bus, or car with your backpack, camping gear, and food for at least several days' hiking. Go immediately to the visitor center to orient yourself to the backcountry permit process, buy the information you need for your trek (see section 4 of this chapter), and choose the unit area that looks most promising. **Backcountry permits** cannot be reserved in advance; you can only apply for them in person for the next day, and they go fast. If you're lucky, permits will be left for the day after you arrive; more likely, you'll need to camp at the **Morino Backpacker's Campground,** 1.9 miles on the park road from the highway, and arrive at the visitor center by the 7am opening to get your permit for the following day. Now you've got another day to wait; if you've reserved a shuttle-bus seat, you can get a preview of the park and see some wildlife, or, outside the park, go on a rafting trip. The next morning you can start your backcountry hike, taking the camper bus to your unit, then traveling for up to 2 weeks in a huge area of wilderness reserved almost exclusively for your use.

The Wilderness Lodge Itinerary

For those who can afford it, this may be the best way to see Denali. The lodge will fly you in—or, if it's in Kantishna, drive you through the park—and you'll immediately be away from the crowds in remote territory. The lodges all have activities and guides to get you out into the wilderness. If you're not staying in Kantishna, you may want to schedule a day to ride the shuttle bus into the park to see the mountain and wildlife anyway, with an evening in a hotel near the park or in Healy.

The Denali Highway: The Drivable Denali

From Cantwell, 27 miles south of the Denali National Park entrance, the Denali Highway leads 133 miles east to another tiny village, Paxson, on the Richardson Highway. The little-known road is a lesson in how we're influenced by labels. It runs due east from the Denali National Park border, a natural extension of the park over the Alaska Range, with scenery that's equal to and in some ways more impressive than the park's. Yet without the national park name, the terrain along the Denali Highway is comparatively little used, even by Native Alaskans.

The Bureau of Land Management controls the land along the Denali Highway, and it's pretty much open for any recreational activity. The **Tangle Lakes** start a 3-day, 35-mile float trip to the Richardson Highway and host fine lake canoeing, where you can see an extraordinary variety of waterfowl, including trumpeter swans, sandhill cranes, and loons. Much of the highway passes through high, alpine terrain, with views that extend infinitely into the distance and good chances of seeing caribou, moose, and black and grizzly bear. At **Maclaren Pass,** at 4,086 feet, you stand in high Alaska Range terrain of tundra and rock, with views of Maclaren Glacier. The land invites you to walk at least a little way out across it.

Simply driving the road is an experience. If you're traveling to Denali National Park from Anchorage or Fairbanks, consider making a return trip via the Denali Highway and Richardson Highway. The road is gravel (plans are in the works to pave it, unfortunately), but you can cover its length in less than 4 hours. (Check with your car-rental agency to find out if you are allowed to drive on gravel highways; agencies that do allow it are listed under "Getting There" in both the Fairbanks section of chapter 9 and in Anchorage, chapter 6.) Small roadhouses are along the way. **Biking** the road is one of the best ways to see it. Trails and remote roads from the highway offer some exceptional mountain biking and hiking routes, especially in the Tangle Lakes National Register Archaeological District. There are three **Bureau of Land Management campgrounds** along the highway, and you can camp anywhere you want outside a campground.

Be sure to get the BLM's *Denali Highway Points of Interest* road guide and *Trail Map and Guide to the Tangle Lakes National Register District.* They're available at the Alaska Public Lands Information Centers in Fairbanks, Anchorage, or Tok, or directly from the **Bureau of Land Management.** Their Glennallen District Office, P.O. Box 147, Glennallen, AK 99588 (☎ **907/822-3217;** www.glennallen.ak.blm.gov/), open Monday to Friday 8am to 4pm, manages the area, and rangers there can give you guidance on where to go.

Alaskan Bicycle Adventures (described in chapter 2; ☎ **800/770-7242** or 907/243-2329; www.alaskabike.com) leads a variety of bike tours that include the Denali Highway, generally starting from Anchorage, looping up the Parks Highway and returning south on the Richardson and Glenn highways. They provide the bikes and all the gear, as well as the van and trailer carrying the gear to make the trip comfortable. **CampAlaska Tours** (also described in chapter 2; ☎ **800/376-9438** or 907/376-9438; e-mail: campak@alaska.net) covers this ground, too, with group camping excursions.

THE TALKEETNA OPTION

Drive only as far as Talkeetna, about 110 miles north of Anchorage, and board a flightseeing plane from there to the park, perhaps **landing on a glacier** on Mount McKinley itself. You'll stand a better chance of seeing the mountain than anyone else, since the weather tends to be better on the south side and you can fly above most clouds when they do come. You'll also save yourself hours of driving to the park and the bus ride into the park, and you'll have the pleasure of staying in a town with some character, unlike the park entrance area. But you'll miss the wildlife-viewing opportunities that can be had only on the ground in the park. (See section 10 of this chapter for more info.)

2 Park Essentials

VISITOR INFORMATION

Getting the information you need to plan your visit is especially important at Denali because of the need for advance reservations. Besides the centers here, you can stop by at an interagency **Alaska Public Lands Information Center;** there are locations in Anchorage, Fairbanks, and Tok, all listed in chapters 6 and 9.

The easiest places to make contact with the park service are via their handy Web site and in person at the information desk at the **Denali National Park Visitor Center,** Denali Park Rd., one-half mile from the park entrance (P.O. Box 9), Denali National Park, AK 99755 (☎ **907/683-2294;** fax 907/683-9612; www.nps.gov/dena). Since there's no park entrance station, stop here for the park map, a copy of the *Alpenglow* park newspaper, and other handouts. A small bookstore offers a limited selection on the area, and films and programs take place in an auditorium. It's open June to mid-September, daily from 7am to 8pm; May and late September, daily 10am to 4pm. It's closed October to April.

The park's nonprofit publishing arm is the **Alaska Natural History Association,** Denali Branch. P.O. Box 230, Denali National Park, AK 99755 (☎ **907/683-1272;** www.alaskanha.org). They operate the shops in the park visitor centers, and you can use their Web site to order books and maps before coming.

At the **Eielson Visitor Center,** on Denali Park Road, more than 60 miles inside the park (accessible only on the shuttle bus), rangers answer questions about Mount McKinley, which on clear days presents a dramatic view from the center. There are displays on wildlife and geology, and a seismograph constantly measures earthquake activity. A ranger allocates open seats on in-bound buses for passengers who want to go back on a bus different than the one they rode into the park on. Picnic tables outside make a good place to eat your sack lunch before boarding the bus back. Closed October to mid-June.

Most important for planning your trip is the concessionaire, **ARAMARK/Denali Park Resorts,** 241 W. Ship Creek Ave., Anchorage, AK 99501 (☎ **800/622-7275** or 907/272-7275; fax 907/264-4684; www.denalinationalpark.com). They handle the reservation system for the campgrounds and shuttle buses, plus three hotels, bus tours, a rafting operation, and a dinner theater you can reserve. They have a desk in the main visitor center. The workings of the reservation system are covered below.

THE RESERVATION SYSTEM

Here's the system for reserving shuttle bus tickets and spots at the developed campgrounds. This section may look long, but paying attention to the details of the reservation system greatly improves your chances of a good visit to the park. (The backcountry permit system is covered later in section 4 of this chapter.)

FOR ADVANCE RESERVATIONS

Sixty-five percent of shuttle-bus seats and all campground sites (except Morino, Sanctuary, and Igloo) are offered for booking by telephone, fax, or mail; the balance are held back for walk-ins.

Reservations by mail or fax open for the whole summer on December 1 of the preceding year. Reservations by phone open sometime in February. After that date, lines are answered daily 7am to 5pm Alaska time (remember, that's 4 hours earlier than eastern standard time), but at times it has been impossible to get through. By faxing, you bypass this problem and can get in before the phone lines open. Reservation forms to fax or mail are available on the park's Web site (**www.nps.gov/dena**) or the concessionaire's Web site (**www.denalinationalpark.com**), or you can just use a blank piece of paper, making sure to include the dates, times, and campgrounds you want, plus alternate dates; the names and ages of the people in your party; and entrance and reservation fees (see "Fees" below) along with a Visa, MasterCard, American Express, or Discover Card number, with expiration and signature. You don't have to figure out the total. You can also pay by check if reserving by mail. But don't use the mail unless you're writing *well ahead* of your trip—more than a month, certainly—otherwise, you could miss getting a reservation at all (mail to Alaska takes about 5 days from the East Coast).

A **confirmation** should be sent out by mail or fax within 2 days of receipt. Take the confirmation to the "will call" desk at the visitor center when you arrive to exchange it for a camping permit and bus ticket. If you'll be arriving after the center closes at 8pm, you must call ☎ **907/683-1266** in advance to avoid losing your site or shuttle seat.

For Walk-Ins

Phone, mail, and fax orders shut down the day before the visit starts, but walk-in reservations begin 2 days out, offering the remaining 35% of the shuttle bus seats and any leftover car-camping sites, and all sites in two primitive backcountry campgrounds, Igloo and Sanctuary. If it's a busy time of year, desirable shuttle reservations are snapped up early in the day. That means you may not get a good reservation for the day of your arrival or even the day after, only the next day after that. That's why it's so critical to reserve in advance.

On the other hand, don't despair if you arrive without reservations, as the flow of visitors rises and falls unpredictably. It's perfectly possible you'll walk into the visitor center and get a shuttle seat on the same day.

FEES

The **park entrance fee** is $10 per family, or $5 per person, good for 7 days. There is no entrance station to collect the fee, but it is automatically added to your bill when you make shuttle or campground reservations. If you have a Golden Eagle, Golden Age, or Golden Access national pass, mention it when you call in order to get your discount.

Campground fees are $12 per night. In addition, a campground **reservation fee** of $4 is charged for the first night of any campground stay.

Another $6 fee is charged for canceling or changing a campsite or bus ticket, except for free children's tickets. You can cancel until 6pm for campground reservations, or 2 hours before departure for bus tickets.

Various bus fees are listed in the chart in section 3 of this chapter.

GETTING THERE

By Train

The **Alaska Railroad** (☎ **800/544-0552** or 907/265-2494; www.akrr.com) pioneered tourism to the park before the George Parks Highway was built in 1972. In summer, trains leave both Anchorage and Fairbanks daily at 8:15am, arriving at the park from Anchorage at 3:45pm and from Fairbanks at noon, crossing and going on to the opposite city for arrival at 8:15pm in each. The fare from Anchorage to Denali is $120 one way for adults, half price for children. The full train runs only from mid-May to mid-September, with somewhat lower fares in the first and last few weeks of the season. During the winter, the Alaska Railroad runs a single passenger car from Anchorage to Fairbanks and back once a week—a truly spectacular, truly Alaskan experience.

The advantages of taking the train to Denali are that it's a historic, unspoiled route through beautiful countryside; there's a good chance of seeing moose and caribou; it's fun and relaxing; there's commentary along the way; and the food is good. There are disadvantages, too. The train is very expensive. You can almost rent a car for a week for the same price as one round-trip on the train. It's slow, adding 3 hours to a trip from Anchorage to the park, and when it's late, it can be very late. And, once you arrive, you have to rely on shuttles and courtesy vans to get around outside the park—not a big drawback, since shuttles are frequent.

The Alaska Railroad's locomotives also pull two sets of cars with full domes owned by **Princess Cruises and Tours** (☎ **800/835-8907;** www.princess.com), and **Holland America–Westours/Gray Line of Alaska** (☎ **800/544-2206** or 907/277-5581; www.hollandamerica.com). Each provides separate, distinct service and operates independently. You can't walk from one kind of car to another. Fares on these two operations run about 25% above the railroad's fares, but they're mainly sold, and much more advantageously priced, as lodging packages in the company's Denali hotels. Essentially, they are intended to be part of their package tours.

The Princess and Holland America cars offer a luxurious but controlled experience wherein each passenger has his or her own dome-car seat on a unique, beautifully appointed cars that resembles a lounge more than a railcar. You have assigned seats and eat during a scheduled dining seating. The Alaska Railroad cars are traditional railroad cars, with seats facing forward, and you can sit anywhere you want, move between cars and stand in the breezeway between cars, and eat when you want to. The food is served in an old-fashioned dining car with tablecloths and flowers. Limited dome-car seats are available, often with a time limit on staying in them—not the dome-to-yourself arrangement of the cruise-line cars. Well-trained guides provide intermittent commentary and answer questions in each car. Children will enjoy the Alaska Railroad cars more; adults can judge for themselves which approach is more appealing.

By Car

Renting a car and driving from Anchorage is far cheaper than taking the train. The drive is about 4½ hours from Anchorage, 2½ from Fairbanks, on a good two-lane highway. Many of the views along the **Parks Highway** are equal to the views on the train, but large stretches, especially in the Matanuska and Susitna Valleys, near Anchorage, have been spoiled by ugly roadside development (which you don't see on the train). A long but spectacular detour around the mess leads through **Hatcher Pass** on a mountainous gravel road open only in the summer. See section 10 of chapter 6, on the Matanuska & Susitna Valleys. Farther north from Anchorage, the Parks Highway passes through Denali State Park. If the weather's clear, you can see Mount McKinley from the pull-outs there. The state park also contains several campgrounds and hiking trails and a veterans memorial.

By Bus

Several van and bus services inexpensively connect Anchorage and Fairbanks to Denali. Most will carry bikes and other gear for an additional fee.

The **Parks Highway Express** (☎ **888/600-6001;** www.AlaskaShuttle.com/) offers daily service between Anchorage and Fairbanks, with one bus each way, stopping at

Denali, Talkeetna, and any other point. In Anchorage, it leaves from the downtown Anchorage Youth Hostel, and in Fairbanks, from the visitor center. The fare is $40 from Anchorage, $25 from Fairbanks.

The Park Connection (☎ **800/208-0200,** or 907/683-1240 at Denali, 907/245-0200 in Anchorage; www.alaska-bus.com/) runs to Seward and Anchorage, with two buses daily in each direction. The fare is $59 to Anchorage, $98 to Denali. Children ride for half price.

BY AIR

Flightseeing trips to Denali from Anchorage are listed in section 5, "Getting Outside," under Flightseeing. You also can charter to Denali from Anchorage or Fairbanks, although it's costly.

GETTING AROUND

If you take the train or bus, you'll find that most accommodations have arrangements to get you around, although this becomes less convenient as you get farther from the park entrance. Ask how it works when you book your room. The summer-only **Caribou Cab** (☎ **907/683-5000**) charges on a per person basis ($6 from Healy to Denali, for example), with a $13 minimum.

If you drive to the park, you'll still need to take the shuttle bus, described below, to get into its heart, except under certain circumstances. You can drive past mile 14 on the park road only if you have a 3-day camping permit at Teklanika Campground, 29 miles in; then your vehicle must remain parked at the campground for the entire 3 days. The rules also loosen at the end of the season, when winners of a drawing can drive the road for a few days in late September (check with the Park Service for lottery details). After the permit driving is over, the road is open to anyone as far as mile 30 until the snow flies; then it's maintained only as far as the headquarters, 3 miles from the entrance.

Bicycles have free access to the park road. For that option, see section 5 of this chapter.

FAST FACTS

Banks An **ATM** is located at Wally's Service Station in Healy, 12 miles north of the park. But do your banking before leaving Anchorage or Fairbanks.

Emergencies Call ☎ **911** outside the park, ☎ **907/683-5900** within the park.

Hospital A **health clinic** (☎ **907/683-2211**) is located in Healy, 10 miles north of the park entrance; it's open 24 hours a day for emergencies, or normal office hours for nonemergencies.

Police The police agency for the area is the **Alaska State Troopers** (☎ **907/683-2232** or 907/768-2202), which handles nonemergency calls from Cantwell, 28 miles south.

Post Office The post office is near the park hotel, a mile within the park entrance.

Stores The small **McKinley Mercantile** (☎ **907/683-9246**) should be at the Riley Creek Campground, near the park entrance, by 2001 (if not, check across from the train depot). It's open daily from 7:30am to 8pm in the summer. Besides convenience groceries, they have firewood, some basic camping supplies, and showers. A larger convenience store and gas station, the **Park Mart** (☎ **907/683-2548**), is on the Parks Highway in the Nenana Canyon area, just north of the park entrance. Do major shopping before coming to the park.

Taxes The local bed tax is 7%. There is no sales tax.

3 Denali by Shuttle Bus

Your visit to Denali will likely revolve around your ride on the shuttle bus into the park to see the wildlife and to stop for a walk in the wilderness. Some planning will make it a more successful trip.

CHOOSING YOUR DESTINATION

You can buy shuttle tickets to the Toklat (*toe*-klat) River, 53 miles into the park; the Eielson (*aisle*-son) Visitor Center at 66 miles; Wonder Lake at 85 miles; or Kantishna, at 89 miles (fares are listed in the "Denali Park Road Bus Facts" chart that accompanies this section). On any day trip, you have to go both ways, so you're in for a long drive. If you don't get off the bus along the way, the round-trip takes 6½ hours to Toklat, 8 hours to Eielson, 11 hours to Wonder Lake, and 12 hours to Kantishna.

In choosing your destination, you need to balance your stamina, your desire to save time for a day hike, and your desire to see wildlife. There are no firm rules about where wildlife shows up, but my own observations are that in the early morning, you can often see moose on the first part of the road; in midsummer, brown (grizzly) bears seem to appear most in the higher country, beyond Toklat, which also is the best area for caribou; in the fall berry season, the grizzlies show up all along the drive.

The best views of Mount McKinley show up after mile 61, also beyond Toklat. The mountain is most likely to be visible in the morning, as clouds often pile up during the day. Going beyond Eielson to Wonder Lake provides more amazing views, including the land-covered Muldrow Glacier and many classic images of Mount McKinley. There's really no reason to go as far as Kantishna unless you are headed to a lodge there (see "Wilderness Lodges" in section 7 of this chapter). In general, I think **Eielson** is the best destination for most people, offering both the chance to see the mountain and some wildlife while leaving some time to get out and walk (I've included some ideas on where to hike below).

You won't be able to time your trip for **good weather,** as you need to book ahead. But don't despair if it rains—the sun may be out at the other end of the park. The best weather for wildlife sightings is cool overcast skies without rain. One trick of the system that allows visitors to wait for sun is to stay at Teklanika Campground. If you drive to a campsite there, agreeing to stay for 3 days, you're eligible to buy a special shuttle ticket for $21 that is good for rides deeper into the park the entire time you're staying at the campground. Wherever you stay, you can buy a three-trip pass from the park service for the price of two.

Denali can be a challenge for families. Young children will go nuts on an 8-hour bus ride, and often can't pick out the wildlife—this isn't a zoo, and most animals blend into their surroundings. Older children also have a hard time keeping their patience on these trips, as do many adults. The only solution is to get off the bus and turn your trip into a romp in the heather. When you've had a chance to revive, catch the next bus. Besides, just because you buy a ticket to Eielson doesn't mean that you have to go that far. Also, if your child normally needs a car seat, you must bring it along on the bus, or borrow one from the park service.

ARAMARK also operates narrated bus tours, booked mostly as part of package tours. The **Natural History Tour** provides just a taste of the park, going 17 miles down the park road. The **Wildlife Tour** goes to Toklat when the mountain is hidden by clouds, and 8 miles farther, to Highway Pass, when it is visible. Food is provided, but you can't get off the bus along the way, and the route skips the beautiful grizzly and caribou habitat toward the Eielson Visitor Center. The **Kantishna Roadhouse**

Bus Concerns & Complaints

ARAMARK, the Denali concessionaire, uses only school bus–type vehicles over the park road. We've received complaints from readers who allegedly were stuck on these buses while other visitors toured the park in luxury motor coaches, but this just isn't so: Only these tough, lightweight buses are allowed on the narrow, gravel park road. I've also heard from visitors complaining of white knuckles on the ride. It's true the buses act a bit like mountain goats on the heights of Polychrome Pass and near Eielson Visitor Center. The road climbs without guard rails, and if you're afraid of heights, it might not be to your liking.

(listed in section 7 of this chapter) offers a 190-mile, 13-hour marathon with lunch and a dogsled and gold panning program at the halfway mark, at the lodge. It's well done, with commentary, but you can't get off the bus along the way, and the return trip may be too rushed to stop for all wildlife sightings. The cost is $109.

GETTING READY

Reserve your shuttle ticket for as early as you can stand to get up in the morning. This strategy will give you more time for day hikes and enhance your chances of seeing the mountain and wildlife. Many animals are more active in the morning, especially on hot days. During peak season, the first bus leaves the visitor center at 5:15am and then roughly every 15 minutes in the morning. A few buses leave in the afternoon, mostly to pick up stragglers on the way back, returning late under the midnight sun.

By taking an early bus, you have more time to get off along the way for a hike, walking back to the road and getting the next bus that comes along with a spare seat. Time it right, and you could have more than 8 hours for hiking plus a tour of most of the park road before returning on a late bus. (To be on the safe side, don't push it to the very last bus.) The sun won't set until after 11pm May to July and it will be light all night. If you need to get back to the park entrance at a certain time, leave yourself plenty of time, because after getting off your westbound bus, you can't reserve seats going back the other way, and you may have to wait an hour for a bus with room to take you.

Before you leave for the visitor center to get on your shuttle bus, you need a packed lunch and plenty of water; you should be wearing sturdy walking shoes and layers of warm and lighter clothing with rain gear packed; you should have binoculars or a spotting scope at the ready; and you should have insect repellent. You may also want a copy of Kim Heacox's worthwhile booklet ***Denali Road Guide,*** available for $6 at the visitor center bookstore, published by the Alaska Natural History Association, listed above under "Visitor Information." It provides a milepost commentary you can follow as you ride. ANHA also publishes guides to Denali birds, mammals, geology, and trails. If you'll be doing any extensive day hiking, you may also want to bring a detailed topographic map printed on waterproof plastic (published by Trails Illustrated and sold for $9.95 from the visitor center or ANHA) and a compass; if you're just going to walk a short distance off the road, you won't need such preparations.

ON YOUR WAY

There are no reserved seats on the bus, but if you arrive early you can find a place on the left side, which has the best views on the way out. Shuttle-bus etiquette is to yell out when you see wildlife. The driver will stop, and everyone will rush to your side of

Denali Park Road Bus Facts

Bus	Purpose	Route	Frequency	Fare
ARA courtesy shuttle	Links hotels to park entrance	Hotels 1 mile north and 7 miles south and within park	Continuous loop	Free, even if not staying at an ARA hotel
Riley Creek Loop	Links facilities within park entrance area	Visitor Center, Riley Creek Campground, rail depot, Park Hotel	Continuous loop	Free
Savage River Shuttle	Public transport to hiking near the Savage River, which can also be reached by car	From Visitor Center to Savage River Day use area, about 14 miles into the park	Every 2 hours	$2, paid to driver
Camper shuttle	Access to campgrounds beyond the park entrance	From the visitor center to Wonder Lake Campground, 85 miles into the park	Several times a day	$15.50 adults, $7.75 children 13–16, free children 12 and under
Backcountry shuttle (or just "the shuttle")	General access to the park and wildlife viewing; limited commentary, depending on the driver; no food service	From the visitor center as far as Kantishna, 89 miles away through the park	Every 30 minutes to Eielson Visitor Center, every hour to Wonder Lake, once daily to Kantishna	$12.50 to Toklat, $21 to Eielson, $27 to Wonder Lake, $31 to Kantishna; children 13–16 half price, children 12 and under free
Tundra Wildlife Tour	7-hour guided bus tour with lunch provided; passengers may not get off en route	From the visitor center to the Toklat River or Highway Pass, 53 to 61 miles into the park	Twice daily	$64 adults, $34 ages 12 and younger
Natural History Tour	3-hour guided bus tour at the edge of the park	From the visitor center 17 miles into the park	Three times daily	$35 adults, $20 age 12 and younger
Kantishna Roadhouse bus	All-day bus tour to a lodge in Kantishna and back (see section 7 of this chapter)	From the park entrance 95 miles to Kantishna	Once a day	$109, no discount for children, no children under 5

the bus. After you've had a look, give someone else a chance to look out your window or to get a picture. Try to be quiet and don't stick anything out of the bus, as that can scare away the animals. Of course, you have to stay on the bus when animals are present. Most buses will see grizzly bears, caribou, Dall sheep, and moose, and occasionally wolves, but, as one driver said, the animals aren't union workers, and it's possible that you won't see any at all.

The shuttle bus drivers generally offer commentary about the sights on the road, but they don't have to and haven't specifically been trained to teach about natural history. Some do a great job, some pass on inaccurate information, and some don't say much. The tour bus drivers are trained to give commentary.

A ROAD LOG

Here are some of the highlights along the road (check the visitor center or the park service information handouts to confirm times of the guided walks):

MILE 9 In clear weather, this is the closest spot to the park entrance with a view of Mount McKinley. This section also is a likely place to see moose, especially in the fall rutting season.

MILE 14 The end of the paved road at the Savage River Bridge. This generally is as far as private vehicles can go. A park service checkpoint stops anyone who doesn't have a proper permit. From the parking lot by the bridge, a simple climb over dry tundra leads to Primrose Ridge, also known as Mount Wright.

MILE 17 The portable toilets here are as far as the Natural History Tour bus goes.

MILE 29 An hour and 10 minutes into the drive, a large rest stop overlooks the Teklanika River, with flush toilets, the last plumbing until the Eielson Visitor Center. The Teklanika, like many other rivers on Alaska's glacier-carved terrain, is a braided river—a stream wandering in a massive gravel streambed that's much too big for it. The braided riverbeds, sometimes miles wide, were created by water from fast-melting glaciers at the end of the last ice age. Each is kept free of vegetation by its river, which constantly changes course as it spreads the rock and dust debris carried down from the glaciers. Flat plains in glacial terrain usually are laid down by this mechanism.

MILE 34 Craggy Igloo Mountain is a likely place to see Dall sheep. Without binoculars, they'll just look like white dots. Manageable climbs on Igloo, Cathedral, and Sable mountains take off along the road in the section from Igloo Creek to Sable Pass.

MILE 38–43 Sable Pass, a critical habitat area for bears, is closed to people. A half-eaten sign helps explain why. Bears show up here mostly in the fall. This is the start of the road's broad alpine vistas.

MILE 46 The top of 5-mile-wide Polychrome Pass, the most scenic point on the ride, and a toilet break, 2 hours and 25 minutes into the trip. Caribou look like specks when they pass in the great valley below you, known as the Plain of Murie after Adolph Murie, a biologist who pioneered study here and helped develop the park service's scientific ethic (the name does not always appear on maps, however). Note how the mountains of colored rock on either side of the plain match up—they once connected before glacial ice carved this valley. Huge rocks on its floor are glacial erratics, plucked from the bedrock by moving ice and left behind when it melted.

MILE 53 The Toklat River, another braided river, is a flat plain of gravel with easy walking. The glaciers that feed the river are 10 miles upstream; the river bottom is habitat for bears, caribou, and wolves, and a good place for picnics.

MILE 58 Highway Pass, the highest point on the road. In good weather, dramatic views of Mount McKinley start here. The alpine tundra from here to the Eielson Visitor Center is inviting for walking, but beware: Tundra is soft underfoot and can conceal holes and declivities that can twist an ankle.

MILE 64 Thorofare Pass, where the road becomes narrow and winding, is a good area to look for bears and caribou. Bus drivers know best where the animals are on any particular day; they exchange information among themselves.

MILE 66 The **Eielson Visitor Center,** the end of most bus trips, has flush toilets, a covered picnic area, and a small area of displays where rangers answer questions. Among the exhibits is one explaining why you probably can't see the mountain from this best of vantage points, just 33 miles from its summit (Mount McKinley creates its own weather and is visible only about a third of the time in the summer). There's also a seismograph on display, registering the frequent small earthquakes that accompany McKinley's prodigious growth—about an inch every 3 years. This region is a jumble of rocks pushed together by the expanding Pacific tectonic plate; the mountain, and the whole Alaska Range, are folding upward in that great collision. Starting late in June, a ranger-guided tundra walk occurs daily at 1:30pm, lasting no more than an hour; take a 9am or earlier bus to be there on time. If you leave the bus here for a hike, you can get a ride back later by signing up on the standby list kept by a ranger.

MILE 68.5 The incredibly rugged terrain to the north is the earth and vegetation covering Muldrow Glacier. The ice extends to McKinley's peak, and was the early and arduous route for climbers; these days, they fly to a base camp at 7,200-feet elevation on the Kahiltna Glacier, on the south side. McKinley's glaciers, falling 15,000 vertical feet and extending up to 45 miles in length, are among the world's greatest. The Ruth Glacier has carved the Great Gorge on the south side, which is almost 6,000 feet deep above the ice and another 4,000 below—almost twice the depth of the Grand Canyon. The park road comes within a mile of the Muldrow's face, then continues through wet, rolling terrain past beaver ponds, and finally descends into a small spruce patch near mile 82.

MILE 86 Wonder Lake campground is the closest road point to Mount McKinley, 27 miles away. Some buses continue another half hour to Kantishna. The fact that McKinley looks so massive from this considerable distance, dominating the sky, is a testament to its stupendous size. You'll likely never see a larger object on this planet. From its base (your elevation here is only 2,000 feet) to its top is an elevation gain greater than any other mountain on earth. Other mountains are taller overall, but they stand on higher ground.

4 Denali on Foot: Day Hiking & Backpacking

DAY HIKING IN THE BACKCOUNTRY

One of the unique aspects of Denali is the lack of developed trails—you really can take off in any direction. I've covered some of the best hiking areas above, in "A Road Log," including Primrose Ridge, Teklanika River, Igloo and Sable mountains, and the Toklat River. The park service long resisted building any trails, but is giving in and recognizing some trails visitors have created. A mile-long, accessible tundra loop trail is under construction at the Eielson Visitor Center and a new 2-mile path leads from the Wonder Lake Campground to the McKinley River Bar, which extends far to the east and west. You can drive or take a $2 shuttle to the Savage River Day Use Area, at mile 15, which has a 1-mile loop trail, and longer, informal routes for great alpine tundra hiking. No permit is needed for day hiking.

Ranger Programs in the Park

Check the park newspaper, *The Alpenglow,* for ranger talks and slide shows that happen as often as several times a day at the Park Hotel auditorium, at the visitor center, and at the Riley Creek, Savage River, and Teklanika campgrounds.

The broad, hard gravel flats of the **braided riverbeds,** such as the McKinley, Toklat, Teklanika, and Savage, are among the best routes for hiking in the park. **Stony Creek,** leading up a gorge to the north from the road at mile 60, is an excellent walk into the mountains. You can also hike on the tundra, of which there are two varieties: The **wet tundra** lies on top of permanently frozen ground called permafrost; it's mushy at best, like hiking on foam rubber laid over bowling balls. At worst, it's swamp. **Dry tundra** clothes the mountainsides, and generally makes for firmer footing and easier walking. The brush and stunted forest of the region are virtually impenetrable.

The major risks of hiking here relate to the weather and rivers. It can get cold and wet in the middle of summer, and if you're not prepared with warm, waterproof clothing, you could suffer the spiraling chill of hypothermia. The rivers are dangerous because of their fast flow and icy cold water. See the note on river crossings in the "Outdoors Health & Safety" section of chapter 2; better yet, avoid crossing any sizable rivers. Bears, which people worry most about, have never killed a Denali visitor. Tips on avoiding them are in chapter 2, and are widely distributed at the park.

For a first foray beyond the trails, consider joining one of the park service guided hikes. Two daily ✪ **Discovery Hikes** go somewhere near the Eielson Visitor Center and another route nearer the entrance end of the park. A ranger takes only 15 hikers, leading them into wilderness while teaching about the nature of the places they visit. Plan a 5- to 11-hour day, including the shuttle ride; actual hiking time is about 4 hours. The hikes generally are not too strenuous for families with school-age children, although it is wise to inquire how steep it will be if you have any doubts. They cost no more than the price of your shuttle ticket. You need to wear hiking shoes or boots and bring food, water, and rain gear. Reserve a place in advance, as the hikes fill up during July and you'll need to know when and where to catch the special bus. Rangers also lead walks on the short Savage River Loop, 15 miles into the park. The **Eielson Stroll,** at 1:30pm daily starting in early June, is a short guided stroll from the Eielson Visitor Center, at mile 66 on the park road. Check in at the visitor center for late word on all the hikes before heading out on a long bus trip.

DAY HIKING IN THE PARK ENTRANCE AREA

There are six short trails at the park entrance, weaving through the boreal forest around small lakes, and one steep and spectacular hike to the **Mount Healy overlook,** a 5-mile round-trip. That trail breaks through the tree line to slopes of tundra and rock outcroppings, where you can see just how small the pocket of human infestation is at the park entrance area: The Alaska Range and its foothills extend far into the distance. If you were to continue on an all-day hike right to the top of Mount Healy, you could see all the way to McKinley on a clear day. The *Alpenglow* park newspaper contains a brief guide for these trails, and you can get a natural history guide, *The Nature of Denali,* at the visitor center.

BACKPACKING

Imagine backpacking over your own area of wilderness, without trails, limits, or the chance of seeing other people. There's no need to retrace your route to get back:

Anywhere you meet the 89-mile Denali Park Road you can catch a bus back to the world of people. Any experienced backpacker should consider a backcountry trek at Denali.

Yes, it can be challenging. Hiking on the tundra, broken rock mountainsides, and braided rivers is tiring and it's easy to fall or turn an ankle. You must be prepared for river crossings and cold weather, know how to find your way with a map and compass, and know how to avoid attracting bears. But if you've done a backpacking trip in a less challenging area, you surely can manage it here, so long as you prepare and don't underestimate the additional time you'll need in trail-less terrain. Nor do you need to trek far—you could camp just a few miles off the road and still be in a place that looks like no one has ever been there before.

You must be flexible about where you're going and be prepared for any kind of terrain, because you can't choose the **backcountry unit** you will explore until you arrive at the backcountry desk at the visitor center and find out what's available. This information, and a map of the units, is posted on a board behind the desk. Groups of four or more may have a hard time finding a place to hike, but there's almost always *somewhere* to go. You can reserve permits only 1 day in advance; you're unlikely to get one for the day you arrive, but you can reserve permits for continuation of your trip for up to 14 days at the same time. The first night of a trip is the hard one to get—for one thing, you can reserve only units that are contiguous to the park road for the first night—but after that, each night gets progressively easier. A couple of rangers are there to help you through the process. Buy the ***Denali National Park and Preserve* topographical map,** published by Trails Illustrated, available for $9.95 from the Alaska Natural History Association, listed above under "Visitor Information." Printed on plastic, the map includes the boundaries of the 43 backcountry units and much other valuable information. Also, you'll want a copy of ***Backcountry Companion,*** by Jon Nierenberg, a book selling for $8.95 that describes conditions and routes in each area, published and sold by ANHA. It's for sale at the visitor center, or you can look at a well-thumbed copy kept at the backcountry desk.

The alpine units from the Toklat River to Eielson Visitor Center are most popular. That's where you get broad views and can cross heathery dry tundra, walking in any direction. But to go far, you'll also have to be ready to climb over some rugged, rocky terrain, and the tundra itself is deceptively difficult walking—it's soft and hides ankle-turning holes. The wooded units are the least popular, since bushwhacking through overgrown land is anything but fun. The best routes for making time here (and anywhere in the Alaska Bush) are along the braided river valleys and streambeds. You need to be ready for stream crossings.

Before venturing into the backcountry, everyone is required to watch an **orientation film** called the *Backcountry Simulator.* It's intended to teach you how not to attract bears, but it's intimidating enough to scare you out of the park—don't let it. The park service provides bear-resistant food containers in which you are required to carry all your food. Guns are not permitted in the park; a pepper spray for self-defense from bears is allowed. You'll have to take the **camper bus** to get to your backcountry unit, at a cost of $15.50 for each adult.

Before you decide to go backpacking at Denali, however, you may want to broaden your thinking—if you're up to a cross-country hike without a trail, there are tens of millions of acres in Alaska available for backpacking that don't require a permit. Check with the Alaska Public Lands Information Center in Anchorage or Fairbanks for ideas about road-accessible alpine wilderness in Gates of the Arctic National Park, on the Denali Highway (see above); and in Wrangell–St. Elias National Park (in chapter 9). I've listed some great trail hikes in chapter 7, under Chugach National Forest, and in chapter 9, in the sections on Chena Hot Springs Road and the Steese Highway.

5 Activities Within the Park

MOUNTAIN BIKING

A bicycle provides special freedom in the park. Bicyclists can ride past the checkpoint where cars have to turn back, at mile 14 on the park road. Park campgrounds have bike stands, and you can take a bike on the shuttle or camper bus, so you can get a lift when needed, or ride one way. The longest stretch on the park road between campgrounds is 52 miles. On the downside, the buses kick up a lot of dust, and bikes may not go off-road. Pick up a copy of the bicycle rules from the backcountry desk before you start. **Denali Outdoor Center** (☎ **888/303-1925** or 907/683-1925; www.denalioutdoorcenter.com), located right in the heart of things, just north of the overlook in the canyon area, rents front-suspension bikes for $40 for 24 hours, $25 for 6 hours, with discounts for longer rentals. Or shop for a better price or bike in Anchorage and bring it up with you.

SLED DOG DEMONSTRATIONS

In the winter, rangers patrol the park by dogsled, as they have for decades. In the summer, to keep the dogs active and amuse the tourists, they run a sled on wheels around the kennel, and a ranger gives a talk two to three times a day. Although there's no substitute for seeing dogs run on snow, you can get a sense of the dogs' speed and enthusiasm from this show. It was the highlight of my son's trip to Denali when he was 3 years old. There's a shortage of parking at the kennels, near the headquarters at mile 3.4 on the park road, so take a free bus from the visitor center a half hour before each show. Times are listed in the *Alpenglow* park newspaper.

FISHING

Fishing is quite poor at Denali. There are grayling in some rivers, but the water is too cold and silty for most fish. Those who don't care if they catch anything, however, do enjoy fishing in this wonderful scenery. You don't need a fishing license within park boundaries, but you do have to throw back everything you catch. Bring your own gear, as it's unavailable in the park area.

CLIMBING MOUNT MCKINLEY

Mount McKinley, because of its altitude and weather, is among the world's most challenging climbs. Summer temperatures at the high camp average 20° to 40°F below zero. If you're looking here for advice, you're certainly not up to an unguided climb. A guided climb is a challenging and expensive endeavor requiring months of conditioning and about a month on the mountain. Get names of guides from the Park Service's **Talkeetna Ranger Station,** P.O. Box 588, Talkeetna, AK 99676 (☎ **907/733-2231**). The climbing season lasts from late April or early May until the snow gets too soft, in late June or early July. Climbers fly from Talkeetna to a 7,200-foot base camp on Kahiltna Glacier. About 1,000 climbers attempt the mountain annually in about 300 parties; about half typically make it to the top each year, and usually a few die trying.

6 Attractions & Activities Outside the Park

FLIGHTSEEING

Getting a good, close look at Mount McKinley itself is best accomplished by air. Frequently you can see McKinley from above the clouds even when you can't see it from the ground. Best of all, some Talkeetna operators that fly mountaineers also land visitors on the mountain itself, a unique and unforgettable experience (see section 10 of this chapter; also see chapter 6, on Anchorage, for an air excursion from there). Regardless of how close you approach the mountain, however, a flight does show how incredibly rugged is the Alaska Range.

Small planes and helicopters fly from the park airstrip, private heliports and airstrips along the Parks Highway, and the Healy airstrip. **Denali Air** (☎ **907/683-2261;** www.denaliair.com) has an office in the Nenana Canyon area, and flight operations at mile 229.5 of the Parks Highway. An hour-long flight going within a mile of the mountain costs $175 for adults, $90 for children age 12 and under. **Era Helicopters** (☎ **800/843-1947** or 907/683-2574; www.era-aviation.com) has hour-long flights for $195, including van pickup from the hotels. Their helihikes land for a 3-hour hike on a mountain ridgeline, the difficulty tailored to the customer's ability; it costs $285. A 75-minute glacier-landing flight costs $295.

RAFTING

Rafting on the Nenana River, bordering the park along the Parks Highway, is fun and popular. Several commercial guides float two stretches of the river: an upper portion, where the water is smoother and the guides explain passing scenery; and the lower portion, where the river roars through the rock-walled Nenana Canyon, and rafts take on huge splashes of silty, glacial water through Class III and IV rapids. Guides take children as young as 5 on the slow trip (although I don't know if I'd let my kid go at that age); the youngest accepted for the fast portion is age 12. White-water rafting carries risks you shouldn't discount just because a lot of people do it, as a fatal accident on the supposedly easy tour confirmed in 1999. Each session takes 2 to 2½ hours, including safety briefings, suiting up, and riding to and from the put-in and take-out points. Prices are around $55 for adults, with discounted rates for children (from $10 less to half off).

Denali Outdoor Center (☎ **888/303-1925** or 907/683-1925; www.denalioutdoorcenter.com) is a professional operation, offering rafting trips and instruction in river techniques. There are five firms in competition, however, so you may be able to save by shopping around. When reserving, make sure to ask what kind of gear is provided: Dry suits will keep you comfortable, while you're likely to get drenched if all they give you is rain gear or Mustang floatation suits. If you're camping, plan a shower afterward, as the silt in the river water will stick to your skin and hair.

HORSEBACK RIDING

There is no riding in the park itself, but you have several opportunities in similar terrain outside its boundaries. Various companies offer rides, although the lineup of firms seem to change every year. One- to 2-hour rides cost from $55 to $85. Among the operators are **Cripple Creek Ranch** (☎ **907/683-7670**) and **Denali Saddle Safaris** (☎ **907/683-1200;** www.denalisaddlesafaris.com), which also offers pack trips and extended journeys.

7 Accommodations

PARK SERVICE CAMPGROUNDS

I've explained how to make camping reservations in section 2 of this chapter, under "The Reservation System." Note that reservation fees are added to camping fees.

Only Riley Creek Campground is open after September (water is off in winter). The rest reopen when the snow is gone, in May for all but Wonder Lake, which opens in June.

First to the Top

It's the biggest. That's why climbers risk their lives on Mount McKinley and why politicians fight over its name. You can see the mountain from Anchorage, more than 100 miles away. On a flight across Alaska, McKinley stands out grandly over waves of other mountains. It's more than a mile taller than the tallest peak in the other 49 states. It's a great white triangle, always covered in snow, tall but also massive and strong.

The Athabascans of Interior Alaska named it Denali, translated as "the high one," or "the great one," but spent little time in the immediate area, where the weather is too severe and the rivers too silty to produce much fish or game. (At least that's what we've always thought: Recently a historian pointed out that the word *Denal'iy* actually was referring to a mountain near Anchorage, now known as Pioneer Peak, and means "one that watches." The word for McKinley, "the high one," was *Doleika.*) The first white men to wander into the area were looking for gold; in 1896, a prospector named the mountain after William McKinley of Ohio, who was elected president of the United States that year. Native Alaskans prefer the Athabascan name, and since 1975 have petitioned to change it officially back. Ohio won't allow it. In 1980, congressmen from Alaska and Ohio compromised on the issue, changing the name of the national park to Denali but leaving the mountain named McKinley.

Alaskans still want the mountain's name changed, but the U.S. Board on Geographical Names has refused to take up the issue. They have a rule against considering an issue that is also before Congress, and Rep. Ralph Regula of Ohio has repeatedly introduced a one-paragraph bill saying the name should stay the same. His bill never goes anywhere, but just having it introduced has been enough to stop the name board. In 1999, Alaska representative Don Young brought the issue back to life with an opposing bill to change the name to Denali. He said Regula should name something in Ohio for McKinley. Young's bill, however, also died quietly.

The first group to try to climb Mount McKinley came in 1903, led by Judge James Wickersham, who also helped explore Washington's Olympic Peninsula before it became a national park. His group made it less than halfway up, but on the trip they found gold in the Kantishna Hills, setting off a small gold rush that led to the first permanent human settlement in the park area. Wickersham later became the Alaska Territory's nonvoting delegate to Congress and introduced the bill that created the national park, but the government was never able to get back land in the Kantishna area from the gold miners. Today, that land is the site of four luxurious wilderness lodges, right in the middle of the park.

On September 27, 1906, renowned world explorer Dr. Frederick Cook announced to the world by telegraph that he had reached the summit of Mount McKinley after a lightning-fast climb, covering more than 85 miles and 19,000 vertical feet in 13 days with one other man, a blacksmith, at his side. On his return to New York, Cook was lionized as a conquering explorer and published a popular book of his summit diary and photographs.

Car-Accessible Campgrounds

In addition to these, see **Teklanika River campground** under "Bus-Accessible Campgrounds," below; you can drive to it as long as your stay is 3 days long.

In 1909, Cook again made history, announcing that he had beat Robert Peary to the North Pole. Both returned to civilization from their competing treks at about the same time. Again, Cook was the toast of the town. Then his Eskimo companions mentioned that he'd never been out of sight of land, and his story began to fall apart. After being paid by Peary to come forward, Cook's McKinley companion also recanted. A year later, Cook's famous summit photograph was re-created—on a peak 19 miles away and 15,000 feet lower than the real summit.

In 1910, disgusted with Cook, four prospectors from Fairbanks took a more Alaskan approach to the task. Without fanfare or special supplies—they carried doughnuts and hot chocolate on their incredible final ascent—they marched up the mountain carrying a large wooden flagpole they could plant on top to prove they'd made it. But on arriving at the summit, they realized that they'd climbed the slightly shorter north peak. Weather closed in, so they set up the pole there and descended without attempting the south peak. Then, when they got back to Fairbanks, no one could see the pole, and they were accused of trying to pull off another hoax.

In 1913, Episcopal archdeacon Hudson Stuck organized the first successful climb to reach the *real* summit—and reported he saw the pole on the other peak. Harry Karstens led the climb (he would become the park's first superintendent in 1917), and the first person to stand at the summit was an Alaska Native, Walter Harper.

McKinley remains one of the world's most difficult climbs, even with modern, lightweight gear, but since 1980 the number of climbers has boomed and it's become crowded at the top (garbage disposal has even become a problem). In 1970, only 124 made the attempt; now more than 1,000 people try to climb the peak each year, with about half making it to the summit. The cold and fast-changing weather is what usually stops people. From late April into early July, climbers fly from the town of Talkeetna to a base camp at 7,200 feet elevation on the Kahiltna Glacier. From there, it takes about a month to get to the top, through temperatures as cold as –40°F.

During the season, the Park Service stations rescue rangers and an emergency medical clinic at the 14,200-foot level of the mountain, and keeps a special high-altitude helicopter ready to go after climbers who get in trouble. They and the military spend about half a million dollars a year rescuing climbers, and sometimes much more. In 1998, a volunteer ranger lost his life trying to save a Canadian who had fallen; he was one of three people who died that year, bringing the total who have perished on McKinley to 91. None died in 1999, but in 2000, three volunteer rangers and their pilot died trying to fly into the Kahiltna Glacier base camp, and one climber was killed in an avalanche on nearby Mount Johnson. Most died in falls, but cold and altitude also took many, and may have contributed to the falls. Climbers lose fingers, toes, and other parts to frostbite every year, or suffer other, more severe injuries.

About 10,000 people have made it to the top since Hudson Stuck's party. Monuments to those who never returned are in the cemetery near the airstrip in Talkeetna.

Morino Backpacker Campground. 1 mile from park entrance, near railroad depot. $6 per night; tents only.

This campground is simply an area of trees near the entrance where you can self-register, put up a tent, and use a portable toilet. There's no parking, and only two people are allowed per site.

Keeping Clean at Denali

None of the campgrounds at Denali have showers. The larger campgrounds have the typical cold-water bathrooms found in the national parks. Better bathrooms are at the hotels and visitor center. You can grab a shower at **McKinley Mercantile,** at the Riley Creek Campground; its showers cost $3, with a $5 key deposit (assuming its planned move is complete). There has been no time limit or coin machine to feed. You also can take showers, even if you're not a guest, at **McKinley RV and Campground** (listed below) for $2.50. It has a token-operated laundry, too.

Riley Creek. Near the visitor center. $12 per site. 150 sites; RVs or tents. Campfires allowed; flush toilets, dump station.

This large campground right across the road from the visitor center is best for those who want to be in the middle of things. It's near the store, showers, a bus stop for the free front-country shuttle, and a pay phone. Sites are wooded with small birch and spruce, and they're adequately separated, but this isn't exactly wilderness camping. Reservations are relatively easy to get. The park's only sewage dump station is here.

✪ **Savage River.** On Denali Park Rd., 13 miles from entrance. $12 per site. 33 sites; RVs or tents. Campfires allowed; flush toilets.

On the *taiga*—the thin spruce forest and tundra—this is a wonderful campground with unforgettable views. Campers can wander from their sites on some of the park's best hikes. This is the only campground you can readily drive to that's away from the activity at the park entrance. There is no telephone.

Bus-Accessible Campgrounds

To use these campgrounds, you'll need a camper ticket on the shuttle bus, which costs $15.50 for adults, $7.75 ages 13 to 16, free 12 and under. There are no businesses and no phones beyond the park entrance area; you must bring everything you need.

Igloo Creek and Sanctuary River. On Denali Park Rd., 23 miles and 34 miles from park entrance, respectively.

These two primitive campgrounds, each with seven tent sites, offer a backcountry experience, away from cars. There's a $6 camping fee and no campfires are allowed, only stoves. You can't reserve sites in advance; you can only reserve in person at the visitor center when you arrive. Both campgrounds have only chemical toilets.

Teklanika River. On Denali Park Rd., 29 miles from entrance; access by camper bus, or drive in with a minimum 3-day stay. $12 per site. 53 sites; RVs or tents. Campfires allowed; flush toilets.

This is the only car campground that's beyond the checkpoint on the Park Road. You can drive in only if you don't move your vehicle for 3 days; otherwise, take the camper bus. Sites are among the small trees of the boreal forest. One big advantage of staying here is that you begin the morning much closer to the heart of the park, cutting the time you have to spend on the bus, and one bus ticket lasts your whole 3-day stay. Using this base for 3 days, you could really explore different areas of the park in different kinds of weather.

✪ **Wonder Lake.** On Denali Park Rd., 85 miles from entrance. $12 per site. 28 sites; tents only. No campfires, stove only; flush toilets.

It takes almost 6 hours to get here on the bus, but this campground by placid Wonder Lake, at the foot of Mount McKinley, puts you in the most beautiful and coveted area of the park. Sites are among a patch of spruce trees on the mountain side of the lake. Sites can be tough to get.

COMMERCIAL CAMPGROUNDS

There are two commercial campgrounds in the area. **Denali Grizzly Bear Cabins and Campground** (☎ **907/683-2696;** www.AlaskaOne.com/dengrzly) is about 7 miles south of the park entrance, and has some exposed sites and others on a hillside among small trees. Small cabins and tent cabins dot the property, too. There is a coin-operated shower. Tent sites are $17 for up to four people, with electrical and water hookups $6 more.

A better-developed campground is 10 miles north of the park, in Healy. **McKinley RV and Campground,** at mile 248.5 on the Parks Highway (☎ **800/478-2562** or 907/683-2379; e-mail: rvcampak@mtaonline.net), has a deli and espresso bar, gas station, token-operated laundry, hot showers, and a small playground. Basic tent sites are $16.25 to $18.25, full hookups $27.

HOTELS

Patterns of land ownership and the uncontrolled development around Denali have led to a hodgepodge of roadside hotels, cabins, lodges, campgrounds, and restaurants in pockets arrayed along more than 20 miles of the Parks Highway. There are rooms of good quality in each of the pockets, but the going rates vary widely.

The most expensive rooms, and the first booked, are in the immediate area of the park entrance. Next are the hotels south of the park. Both these areas are entirely seasonal. The best deals are in **Healy,** 10 miles north of the park, where you can find a room for $50 less than a comparable room near the park entrance. Of course, if you don't have a car, it's most convenient to stay in or near the park.

The other choices are to stay in **Talkeetna,** the back door to the park (described in section 10 of this chapter); at a wilderness lodge in the **Kantishna** or outside the park. I've listed each of the choices separately.

Despite their high prices, rooms can be hard to find in the high season, and it's wise to book well ahead. If you don't mind gambling, however, you can often get great last-minute deals from hotels that have had large cancellations from their package-tour clients.

NEAR THE PARK

This area, sometimes known as Denali or Nenana Canyon, or as "Glitter Gulch," extends about a mile north of the park entrance on the Parks Highway. Two huge hotels that primarily serve package-tour passengers dominate the area, the **Denali Princess Lodge,** Mile 238.5, Parks Hwy. (☎ **800/426-0050;** fax 206/336-6100; www.princess.com), and the **McKinley Resorts Chalets,** Mile 238.5, Parks Hwy. (book through Denali Park Resorts, under "Visitor Information," above). If they have a cancellation, you may be able to get attractive rooms at one of these places at the last minute for a fraction of their astronomical rack rates. The McKinley Resorts Chalets also is a good place to book activities.

Since most readers of this book are independent travelers, I've concentrated instead on smaller lodgings that cater to individual bookings. In addition to those I've listed, you'll find good standard rooms at **Denali River View Inn,** Mile 238.4, Parks Hwy. (☎ **907/683-2663**), for $134 double; and at **Sourdough Cabins,** Mile 238.5, Parks Hwy. (☎ **907/683-2773**), which has comfortable little cabins in the woods below the highway for similar prices.

All of the hotels in this area are open only during the tourist season, roughly May 15 to September 15.

Denali Bluffs Hotel. Mile 238.4 Parks Hwy. (P.O. Box 72460, Fairbanks, AK 99707). ☎ **907/683-7000.** Fax 907/683-7500. denalibluffs.com. 112 units. TV TEL. High season $179 double. Low season $126 double. Extra person $10. AE, DISC, MC, V.

A series of 12 buildings on a steep mountainside looks down on the Nenana Canyon area from above the highway. The light, tastefully decorated rooms have two double beds, coffeemakers, and small refrigerators, and those on the upper floor have vaulted ceilings and balconies with great views. A courtesy van will take you anywhere in the area, and a token-operated laundry is available. A dining room serves simple meals for breakfast and lunch.

Denali Crow's Nest Cabins. Mile 238.5, Parks Hwy. (P.O. Box 70), Denali National Park, AK 99755. ☎ **888/917-8130** outside Alaska only, or 907/683-2723. Fax 907/683-2323. www.denalicrowsnest.com. 39 cabins. High season $154 cabin for 2. Low season $75 cabin for 2. Extra person $10. MC, V.

Perched in five tiers on the side of a mountain above the Nenana Canyon area, looking down on Horseshoe Lake and the other, larger hotels, the cabins are roomy and comfortable, especially those on the 100 and 200 level. A log cabin and the warmth of the Crofoot family create more of an appropriate, Alaskan feeling than the modern, standard rooms that have filled the canyon. You spend a lot of time climbing stairs, however, and despite the great views and the price, the cabins are simple, not luxurious; the rooms have shower enclosures, not tubs. The staff will book tours, and they offer a courtesy van, free coffee, and an outdoor Jacuzzi. All rooms are no-smoking. The restaurant, **The Overlook,** is recommended separately under "Dining," later in this chapter.

Denali National Park Hotel. Mile 1.5, Denali National Park Rd. (P.O. Box 87), Denali Park, AK 99755. (For reservations, contact Denali Park Resorts, 241 W. Ship Creek Ave., Anchorage, AK 99501; ☎ **800/276-7234;** fax 907/258-3668.) www.denalinationalpark.com. 100 units. High season $152 double. Low season $111 double. Extra person $10. AE, DISC, MC, V.

The original park hotel burned down in 1972, replaced by this "temporary" structure, which was cobbled together from old railroad cars and modular housing units. It will close for good in September 2001 as part of a long-term park plan; the alternative was to build a new, permanent structure, and the Park Service rightly took the opportunity instead to eliminate lodgings from within park boundaries. Despite its flawed pedigree, the doomed structure has quirky, oddly historic character beyond most of the bland, standard places outside the park. Staying here puts you at the center of park activities, with the front-country hiking trails leaving out the back door. The rooms need remodeling, however, and have no views. There's a courtesy shuttle, coffee in the rooms, and a tour desk.

The attractive **dining room** serves large portions. The lounge, in a pair of railroad cars, has a good, campy feel. Smoking is permitted in only one of the two rail cars it occupies, a fair arrangement for both sides of that debate. For fast food, the snack bar is quite adequate and probably the best place for takeout in the area. The gift shop has reasonable prices, regulated by the park service.

IN HEALY

Healy is 10 miles north of the park entrance, but a world away. It's a year-round community with an economy based primarily on a large coal mine and only secondarily on the park. It sits in a large, windy valley with a few patches of stunted trees and big, open spaces of tundra. There are many hotels and B&Bs with rooms that cost from

$20 to $90 less than those near the park. They say the water tastes better, too. On the downside, you need a car to stay in Healy.

Besides my two favorites listed below, you'll find hundreds of small, serviceable rooms with twin beds at a converted pipeline camp, the **Denali North Star Inn,** Mile 248.5, Parks Hwy., Healy (☎ **800/684-1560** or 907/683-1560; www.alaskan.com/denalinorthstar), for $110 double. They also serve terrific meals. Across the highway, the **Stampede Lodge,** Mile 248.8, Parks Hwy., Healy (☎ **907/683-2242;** www.AlaskaOne.com/stampede), has small but attractively decorated rooms in a renovated 1946 railroad building; they go for $89 double in summer. There's a reasonably priced restaurant inside serving three meals a day.

✪ **Motel Nord Haven.** Mile 249.5, Parks Hwy. (P.O. Box 458), Healy, AK 99743. ☎ **800/683-4501** or 907/683-4500. Fax 907/683-4503. www.motelnordhaven.com. 24 units. TV TEL. High season $108–$117 double. Low season $70 double. AE, MC, V.

This fresh little gray hotel with a red roof has large, immaculate rooms, each with one or two queen-size beds. They're equal to the best standard rooms in the Denali Park area and a lot less expensive. Bill and Patsy Nordmark offer free newspapers, coffee, tea, and hot chocolate, extra phone lines for the Internet, and a sitting room with a collection of Alaska books. The rooms, decorated with Alaska art and oak trim, all have interior entrances and have been smoke-free since their construction. Up to four people can stay in the rooms with two beds for the price of a double. The Nordmarks hope to complete four kitchenette units by 2001. They'll also pack a sack lunch for $8, or you can eat breakfast or lunch indoors from a menu of soup, salad, or sandwiches.

White Moose Lodge. Mile 248, Parks Hwy. (P.O. Box 68), Healy, AK 99743. ☎ **800/481-1232** or 907/683-1231. Fax 907/683-1232. www.mtaonline.net/~mooseinn. 12 units. TV. High season $90 double. Low season $70 double. Extra adult $10, extra child $5. Rates include continental breakfast. AE, DC, DISC, MC, V. Closed Oct to mid-May.

This old, low-slung building among stunted black spruce contains an unlikely find—comfortable, cheerfully decorated rooms with flower boxes, and a small greenhouse. The breakfast served in the small lobby consists of coffee, tea, orange juice, and pastries.

SOUTH OF THE PARK

Lodgings south of the park are in widely separated pockets of private land concentrated 7 and 14 miles south of the park. (Anything south of that is in Talkeetna, covered in section 10 of this chapter.) I've listed just two of the best in detail below, but you may also want to try these others: **McKinley Creekside Cabins,** 13 miles south at Mile 224, Parks Hwy. (☎ **907/683-2277**), which has cabins with private or shared bathrooms starting at $99 double, including a hot breakfast; or **Denali Cabins,** Mile 229, Parks Hwy. (☎ **907/683-2643,** or 907/258-0134 in winter; www.alaskan.com/denalicabins).

Denali River Cabins. Mile 231, Parks Hwy. (mailing address: P.O. Box 81250, Fairbanks, AK 99708). ☎ **800/230-7275** or 907/683-2500. Fax 907/683-2502. (Winter ☎ 907/456-5200; fax 907/456-5212.) www.denalirivercabins.com. 54 cabins. High season $149–$159 cabin for 2. Low season $95–$105 cabin for 2. Extra person $10. AE, DISC, MC, V.

These cedar cabins along boardwalks above the Nenana River feel fresh and luxurious. They are arrayed on a maze of boardwalks. They have shower stalls, not tubs, and lack closets. Those on the river, with decks over the water, are $10 more. The sauna has a picture window on the river and there's a Jacuzzi and a comfortable lobby. It's owned by the same Native corporation that owns the Kantishna Roadhouse, listed under "Wilderness Lodges," below. Don't confuse this place with Denali Cabins.

The Perch. Mile 224, Parks Hwy. (P.O. Box 53) Denali National Park, AK 99755. ☎ **888/322-2523,** or phone/fax 907/683-2523. www.AlaskaOne.com/perchrest. 21 cabins, 14 with private bathroom. $65–$95 cabin for 2. Extra person $10. AE, DISC, MC, V.

In the trees along rushing Carlo Creek, 13 miles south of the park entrance, a variety of cabins range from large, modern units with private bathrooms to adorable if Spartan little A-frames with lofts that share a bathhouse. There's a sense of privacy and of being out in the woods along the wooden and gravel walkways. It's an exceptional value, open year round. You will need a car to stay here. Atop a steep hill, the **restaurant and bar,** is among the best in the area, described below under "dining."

WILDERNESS LODGES

For those who can afford it, a lodge allows you to experience real wilderness in complete comfort. Here I've listed the three lodges in the Kantishna district, an old gold mining inholding near McKinley, and one fly-in lodge east of the park. All are open only in summer. You get to Kantishna on a private bus or van over the 89-mile park road, guided by your host. Once there, you can explore the park using a special pass for shuttle rides starting in Kantishna, which costs $15.50, available from your lodge, space available. See section 10 of this chapter, on Talkeetna, for other choices.

✪ **Camp Denali/North Face Lodge.** Kantishna District (P.O. Box 67), Denali National Park, AK 99755. ☎ **907/683-2290** or 907/683-1568. www.campdenali.com. 17 cabins, none with private bathroom (Camp Denali); 15 units with bathroom (North Face Lodge). $325 per person per night, double occupancy. Rates include all meals. Minimum stay 3 nights. No credit cards.

At this pioneering ecotourism establishment, you can wake to the white monolith of Mount McKinley filling your window. The naturalist guides here have the right to use the park road free of the shuttle system for hikes, biking, lake canoeing, bird watching, photography sessions, and other outdoor learning activities. During some sessions, nationally reputed academics and other experts lead the program. All arrivals and departures are on fixed session dates and start with a picnic on the park road on the way out of camp. The Camp Denali cabins each have their own outhouse and share a central bathhouse and wonderful lodge common rooms—it would be my first choice for anyone who can stand not having his or her own flush toilet. North Face Lodge has smallish traditional rooms with private bathrooms. A conservation ethic pervades the operation, from the homegrown vegetables to the proprietors' efforts to preserve the natural values of private land in the park.

Denali Backcountry Lodge. Kantishna District (P.O. Box 189), Denali National Park, AK 99755. ☎ **800/841-0692** or 907/683-2594. Fax 907/683-1341. (In winter: P.O. Box 810, Girdwood, AK 99587; ☎ **907/783-1342;** fax 907/783-1308.) www.denalilodge.com. 30 cabins. $315 per person per night, double occupancy. Rates include all meals. 3-night minimum recommended. MC, V.

Thirty comfortable, modern, cedar cabins sit in rows on a deck next to babbling Moose Creek and a two-story lodge building. Guests can sit in a screened porch away from the mosquitoes and watch the day go by, or join a choice of guided hikes, natural history programs, or other activities around the lodge each day. To go out into the park, you're on your own, either on a lodge mountain bike or the shuttle, although the ride in from the entrance is treated as a safari. It's run by Alaska Wildland Adventures, which offers a variety of well-regarded ecotourism packages all over the state, including some that include a stay at the lodge.

Kantishna Roadhouse. Kantishna District, Denali National Park (mailing address: P.O. Box 81670, Fairbanks, AK 99708). ☎ **800/942-7420** or 907/683-1475. Fax 907/683-1449.

(Winter: ☎ 907/479-2436; fax 907/479-2611.) www.kantishnaroadhouse.com. 27 units. $295 per person per night, double occupancy. Rates include all meals. 2-night minimum. AE, DC, DISC, MC, V.

This well-kept property of many buildings along Moose Creek in the old Kantishna Mining District trades on both the mining history and outdoor opportunities of the area. Some rooms are large and luxurious, while others are in smaller single cabins with lofts. The log central lodge has an attractive lobby with people coming and going—it's got more of a hotel feel and might be more attractive to an older, less active set or to families than the other lodges in the Kantishna District. It's also less expensive than the other lodges at Kantishna and accommodates 2-night stays. Daily activities (some with an added fee) include guided hikes, wagon rides, horseback riding, biking, and gold panning.

A sled-dog demonstration (denaliwildlifetour.com) coincides with the arrival of a day trip the lodge offers (the same bus brings lodge guests). That ride is the only choice in the park for a narrated day tour that covers the entire park road. At 13 hours, it's a marathon, and not suitable for children. The fare, including lunch at the lodge, is $109.

Denali Wilderness Lodge. Wood River (P.O. Box 50), Denali Park, AK 99755. ☎ **800/541-9779** year-round or 907/683-1287 summer only. www.DenaliWildernessLodge.com. (In winter: P.O. Box 120, Trout Lake, WA 98650) 22 units. $330 per person per night, double occupancy. Rates include all meals. Plane fare from Denali $65 one way. MC, V.

The extraordinary log buildings were built by the late big-game guide Lynn Castle along the Wood River, but they don't kill the animals anymore: Now they're more valuable to look at alive, and the lodge has become an ecoestablishment, flying guests in for horseback riding, hiking, talks by naturalists, and other activities. This is the best place for riders, with a sizable stable and a daily ride included in the price. The cabins, while not luxurious, are quite comfortable and have private bathrooms. There's a 2.3% surcharge for credit cards. The location is distant from Mount McKinley, in a remote valley 30 miles east of the park entrance.

8 Dining

Since Denali is entirely seasonal, it lacks the range of inexpensive family restaurants that develop in year-round communities. For that, head north to Healy, where the **Denali North Star Inn,** a retired Alaska pipeline construction camp, contains the locals' favorite priced restaurants. Across the highway, the **Stampede Lodge** also has reasonably priced burgers, sandwiches, and steaks.

Nearer the park, most meals are overpriced by 25% to 50%, a cost of the short season and captive audience. The large hotels in the canyon each have fine dining and casual restaurants. The restaurants at the Denali Princess Lodge have beautiful dining rooms with great views. The **Chalet Center Cafe** at the McKinley Resorts Chalets serves casual meals in a large, light room (a ham sandwich is $9). You can't miss the tacky highway frontage of the **McKinley Denali Salmon Bake** in the Nenana Canyon area. Although casual to the point of indifference, it can be a fun place to eat in a picnic setting, and the food is adequate and relatively inexpensive. There is also a full-service restaurant at the **Denali River Cabins,** and there are other places in the works which are not ready to be reviewed; ask around.

Lynx Creek Pizza. Mile 238.6, Parks Hwy. ☎ **907/683-2547.** All items $3.25–$22.95. AE, DISC, MC, V. Daily 11am–11:30pm. Closed late Sept to early May. PIZZERIA.

This ARAMARK-managed pizza restaurant is a center of activity for the less-well-heeled visitors to Denali, as it is the only place to get a slice and a beer. The food isn't anything special, and there often are lines to order, but the dining room is a relatively nontouristy place to meet young people, since it has a TV and evening activities such as "open mike." An 18-inch pepperoni pizza costs $20.

The Overlook Bar and Grill. Mile 238.5, Parks Hwy., up the hill above the Denali Canyon area. ☎ **907/683-2641.** Lunch main courses $9–$15, dinner main courses $16–$30. MC, V. 11am–11pm. Closed mid-Sept to mid-May. BURGERS/STEAK/SEAFOOD.

This fun, noisy place has the feeling of a classic bar and grill, with a vaulted ceiling of rough-cut lumber and a spectacular view of the Nenana Canyon. There are two dining rooms, one with the bar, and another, behind a glass partition, which is quieter and has tablecloths. A huge variety of craft beers is available, with several on tap. At times I've gotten superb fare here, but at other times it has been merely acceptable, and not worth the prices, which are high.

The Perch. Mile 224, Parks Hwy., 13 miles south of the park. ☎ **907/683-2523.** Lunch main courses $7.50–$8.50, dinner main courses $14–$40. Summer daily 6am–10pm. Winter hours vary. AE, DISC, MC, V. STEAK/SEAFOOD.

The odd, knoblike hill the restaurant stands on provides reason for the name (the attractive cabins described above sit below the restaurant). It's a friendly, family run place serving a straightforward steak and seafood menu—they don't try anything fancy, but they do what they do right. The home-baked bread is noteworthy. The dining room is light, with well-spaced tables, and makes up for a somewhat stark quality with big picture windows on three sides.

9 Denali Nightlife

The main evening event is the concessionaire's **Cabin Nite Dinner Theater,** at the McKinley Resorts Chalets (☎ **800/276-7234** or 907/683-8200), a professionally produced musical revue about a gold rush era woman who ran a roadhouse in Kantishna. You can buy the $39 tickets (half price for kids under age 11) virtually anywhere in the area. The actors, singing throughout the evening, stay in character to serve big platters of food to diners sitting at long tables, doing a good job of building a rowdy, happy atmosphere for adults and kids. You go for the show, not the all-you-can-eat salmon and ribs, which were plentiful but less than memorable when we visited.

Princess Cruises and Tours puts on a similar evening show, **Mt. McK's Roadhouse Review,** in a big wall tent at the Denali Princess Lodge. (The local rap says: better food, worse show.) Tickets are for sale at the hotel's tour desk (☎ **800/426-0500** or 907/683-2282) for $35 (half price 12 and younger), or $14 for the show without the meal.

10 Talkeetna: Back Door to Denali

Talkeetna, a historic and funky little town with a sense of humor but not much happening, slept soundly from its decline around World War I until just a few years ago. Now there are paved streets (both of them), a new National Park Service building, a new railroad depot, and two large new luxury lodges. It seems that while Talkeetna slumbered in a time capsule, an explosion of visitors was happening at Denali National Park. Now, not entirely voluntarily, Talkeetna finds itself enveloped in that boom.

As a threshold to the park, Talkeetna has significant pros and cons that you should take into account. On the positive side, it's closer to Anchorage; the development is much more interesting and authentic than that at the park entrance; there's lots to do in the outdoors; and great views of the mountain are less frequently obscured by clouds. On the negative side, a big minus: You can't get into the park from here. That means you miss the dramatic scenery, easy backcountry access, and unique wildlife viewing on the park road.

The town itself dates from the gold rush, and there are many charming log and clapboard buildings. With 15 sites of historic note, the entire downtown area has been listed on the National Register of Historic Places. You can spend several hours looking at two small museums and meeting people in the 2-block main street, then go out on the Talkeetna or Susitna river for rafting, a jet-boat ride, or fishing, or take a flightseeing trip to the national park.

ESSENTIALS

GETTING THERE Talkeetna lies on a 13-mile spur road that branches from the Parks Highway 99 miles north of Anchorage and 138 miles south of the park entrance.

The **Alaska Railroad** (☎ **800/544-0552** or 907/265-2494; www.akrr.com) serves Talkeetna daily on its runs to Denali National Park during the summer, and weekly in the winter. (See section 2 of this chapter for additional details.) The summer fare from Anchorage to Talkeetna is $70 one way for adults, half price for children.

The **Talkeetna Shuttle Service** (☎ **907/733-1725** office, or 907/355-1725 cellular) runs back and forth to and from Anchorage for $40 one way. The **Parks Highway Express** (☎ **888/600-6001;** www.AlaskaShuttle.com/), listed earlier in section 2, also serves Talkeetna.

VISITOR INFORMATION Built to serve people aiming to climb Mount McKinley, the **Denali National Park Talkeetna Ranger Station,** downtown Talkeetna (P.O. Box 588), Talkeetna, AK 99676 (☎ **907/733-2231;** www.nps.gov/dena), makes a fascinating stop for anyone curious about mountaineering. Inside the handsome structure, you'll find a large sitting room with a river rock fireplace, climbing books, and pictures of the mountain—it's like an old-fashioned explorers' club. Records open for inspection cover the history of McKinley climbs. Rangers are on hand to answer questions, too. It's open April to summer, daily 8am to 6pm; winter, Monday to Friday 8am to 4:30pm.

The **Denali/Talkeetna Visitor Center,** located in a tiny cabin at the intersection of the Parks Highway and Talkeetna Spur Road (P.O. Box 688), Talkeetna, AK 99676 (☎ **800/660-2688,** 907/733-2688 summer, or 907/733-2499 winter; www.alaskan.com/talkeetnadenali/), is a commercial center providing brochures, information, and advice while earning commissions from bookings. They represent everyone in Talkeetna. It's the handiest commercial information stop in the region. The center is open daily 8am to 8pm in summer, and they respond to inquiries year-round with free trip-planning help.

GETTING AROUND You can walk everywhere in Talkeetna, but there are good **mountain biking** routes, too. **CGS Bicycles,** on Main Street (☎ **907/733-1279**), is a full-service bike shop, renting mountain bikes for $15 a day and leading trail tours starting at $20 per person.

FAST FACTS The coin-operated laundry and store at the Three Rivers gas station on Main Street in Talkeetna has an **ATM.**

The **Sunshine Community Health Center** is located at mile 4.4 on the Talkeetna Spur Road (☎ **907/733-2273**).

The **Alaska State Troopers** (☎ **907/733-3513**), at mile 97.8 on the Parks Highway, are just south of the intersection with the Talkeetna Spur Road.

The **post office** is in the town center, near the intersection of Talkeetna Spur Road and Main Street.

There is no **sales tax. Bed tax** in the area is 5%.

SPECIAL EVENTS **The Talkeetna Moose Dropping Festival,** held over the second weekend in July, is the big event of the year, a community fair finishing its third decade as a fundraiser for the Talkeetna Historical Society (☎ **907/733-2487;** www.moosedrop.com, though note that the site is dead in the off-season). The main event doesn't involve dropping moose, as an aggrieved animal lover once complained, but dropping moose droppings. There's also a parade and many other events.

ATTRACTIONS & ACTIVITIES IN TOWN

Talkeetna is famous for its laid-back atmosphere and outdoors, not for "attractions," but there are several places to stop in to get the sense of the place. One is the ranger station mentioned above in section 5, "Climbing Mount McKinely." If you come in May or June, you're sure to meet many international mountain climbers; you'll have no difficulty picking them out.

The **Fairview Inn** is a historic bar with the rough edges still in place. Along Main Street, artists and craftspeople have shops where you can often find them at work.

The **Talkeetna Historical Society Museum,** in three buildings on the Village Airstrip a half block south of Main Street (☎ **907/733-2487**), is well worth a stop. The first building contains artifacts and displays on the local mining history, including engaging photographs and biographies of individual characters. The second is an attempt to re-create the old railroad depot. The third holds climbing displays and a huge scale model of Mount McKinley and the nearby mountains (don't miss it if you will fly over the mountain). The museum also is a handy information stop. It is open daily in summer, 10:30am to 5:30pm, winter weekends only. Admission is $2.50.

I've found the most affecting site in town to be the **mountain climbers' memorial** at the town cemetery, near the airstrip on the east side of the railroad tracks. Besides a granite memorial of plaques for lost mountaineers, there is a small garden of monuments to many individual climbers, some in Japanese. The bodies of 34 climbers who died on the mountain have never been recovered.

GETTING OUTSIDE

✪ FLIGHTSEEING

The only way you'll get into the park from Talkeetna is by flying with one of the glacier pilots who support McKinley climbs, which typically begin with a flight from here to the 7,200-foot level of the Kahiltna Glacier. There is no more dramatic or memorable experience available to the typical tourist in Alaska. These immense mountains grow ever larger as you fly toward them until, like a tiny insect, you fly among their miles-tall folds, watching the climbers toiling on the ice below you. I was simply speechless.

Several operators with long experience offer the flights. The least expensive excursions cost around $100 (if the plane is full) and approach McKinley's south face. Rates often depend on how many are going, so if you can put together a group of four or five, or the operator can add you to a group, you can save as much as half. If at all possible—and if the weather is good—buy an extended tour that circles the mountain and flies over its glaciers, for $120 to $200 with a full plane. Best of all, in May and June you can arrange a landing on the mountain itself, just as the climbers do (the snow is too soft starting in July). The Don Sheldon Amphitheater on the Ruth Glacier is a stunning spot high on McKinley; only after you stand there do you realize the incredible scale of what you have seen from above. These landings are usually treated as add-ons to the tours mentioned above, for an additional price of around $40 per person.

Try any of these three renowned glacier pilot operations, all operating out of the Talkeetna airport: **Talkeetna Air Taxi** (☎ **800/533-2219** or 907/733-2218; www.talkeetnaair.com); **K2 Aviation** (☎ **800/764-2291** or 907/733-2291; www.alaska.net/~flyk2); and **Doug Geeting Aviation** (☎ **800/770-2366** or 907/733-2366).

FISHING & JET BOAT TOURS

Talkeetna is at the confluence of the wild Talkeetna and Susitna Rivers. **Mahay's Riverboat Service** (☎ **800/736-2210** or 907/733-2223; www.alaskan.com/mahays/) is a top guide, with 2-hour tours on a unique 51-foot jet boat for $45 per person, operating several times a day from a dock near the public boat launch on the Talkeetna River. Owner Steve Mahay is legendary, the only person ever to shoot Devil's Canyon in a jet boat. He offers fishing charters as well.

RAFTING

Talkeetna River Guides, on Main Street (☎ **800/353-2677** or 907/733-2677; www.talkeetnariverguides.com/), offers a 2-hour wildlife river-rafting tour, without white water, over 9 miles of the Talkeetna three times a day for $44 adults, $15 children under 12. They also offer longer trips and guided fishing.

ACCOMMODATIONS & DINING

NEAR TOWN

Besides the hotels listed in full below, good budget rooms are for rent from the **Talkeetna Motel,** at the west end of Main Street (☎ **907/733-2323**). The clean, basic rooms go for $62 to $95 double. In a small A-frame, the motel also operates the TeePee restaurant, with three hearty, inexpensive meals a day in an eight-table dining room that's a slice of the old Talkeetna.

Mt. McKinley Princess Lodge. Mile 133.1, Parks Hwy., Denali State Park, AK 99755 ☎ **800/426-0500** or 907/733-2900. Fax 907/733-2904. www.princesstours.com. 162 units. TV TEL. Summer $179 double; $275 suite. Spring and fall $99 double; $199 suite. AE, DISC, DC, MC, V. Closed mid-Sept to mid-May.

The Princess Cruise Line built the main lodge building to take advantage of a striking view of the mountain, only 42 miles away as the crow flies. The property isn't really near anything—100 miles south of the park entrance and about 45 road miles from Talkeetna—but, like a resort, they offer everything you need on-site and a full set of activities, including a short network of trails. The design and decoration are an inspired modernization of the classic national park style.

Swiss-Alaska Inn. F St., near the boat launch (P.O. Box 565), Talkeetna, AK 99676. ☎ **907/733-2424.** Fax 907/733-2425. www.swissalaska.com/. 20 units. $100 double. Extra person $10. AE, DISC, MC, V.

This place is more the essence of Talkeetna than the flashy newer places above. It's a friendly family business with a small restaurant serving good, familiar American meals, plus a few German dishes. There are large, attractive rooms with oak furniture and Jacuzzis in the newer of the two buildings. The rooms for smokers in the old building are clean but quite small.

Talkeetna Alaskan Lodge. Mile 12.5, Talkeetna Spur Rd. (P.O. Box 93330, Anchorage, AK 99509-3330). ☎ **888/959-9590** or 907/265-4501. Fax 907/263-5559. www.talkeetnalodge.com. 99 units. TV TEL. Summer $179 double. Winter $99 double. Extra person $10. AE, DISC, MC, V.

Built of big timbers and river rock, this sumptuous hotel was opened in 1999 by Cook Inlet Region, a Native corporation. It stands just 2 miles from the town but feels like it's out in the wilderness. The view from on top of a high river bluff is a broad-canvas masterpiece of the Alaska Range, with McKinley towering in the center. Unlike other large hotels in the area, this place is open year-round and employs mainly local people; its philosophy shows in the Alaska art and style of the place—it's not faked. Rooms and hallways are thoughtfully crafted with regional birch trim and understated stylish touches. Those in the main building are somewhat larger and have queen-size beds. There's a good restaurant, sharing the stupendous view, and a small bar.

A Wilderness Lodge

Caribou Lodge. 20 miles east of Talkeetna (P.O. Box 706) Talkeetna, AK 99676. ☎ and fax **907/733-2163.** 3 cabins. Summer $250 per person per day. Winter $210 per person per day. Rates include all meals and are based on double occupancy. No credit cards.

This lodge sits on an alpine lake amid the tundra of the Talkeetna Mountains with Mount McKinley looming out back. The location, far from any road, offers an opportunity to live for a few days in terrain much like Denali's, with only a few other people in many a mile, while you're hosted by a family who've made a life in this remote wilderness. They'll guide you hiking, canoeing on the lake, and watching the wildlife of the area. In the winter, come for cross-country skiing, snowshoeing, dog mushing, and snowmobiling, when the endlessly rolling hills are buried in snow. The accommodations are simple, with shared bathrooms. Access is by air only—a floatplane or ski plane from Talkeetna is $125.

9

The Alaskan Interior

A warm summer evening in a campground; a slight breeze rustling the leaves of ghostly paper birches, barely keeping the mosquitoes at bay; the sounds of children playing; a perpetual sunset rolling slowly along the northern horizon—this is Interior Alaska. You know it's time to gather up the kids, separate them according to who belongs to whom, and put them to bed; it's 11 o'clock, for heaven's sake. But it's too difficult to feel that matters, or to alter the pace of a sun-baked day that never ends, meandering on like the broad, silty rivers and empty two-lane highways. Down by the boat landing, some college kids are getting ready to start on a float in the morning. An old, white-bearded prospector wanders out of the bar and, offering his flask to the strangers, tries out a joke while swatting the bugs. "There's not a single mosquito in Alaska," he declares. Waits for the loud, jocular objections. Then adds, "They're all married with big, big families." Easy laughter; then they talk about outboard motors, road work, why so many rabbits live along a certain stretch of highway. Eventually, you have to go to bed, and leave the world to its pointless turning as the sun rotates back around to the east. You know it'll all be there tomorrow, just the same—the same slow-flowing rivers, the same long highways, the same vast space that can never be filled.

Interior Alaska is so large—it basically includes everything that's not on the coasts or in the Arctic—you can spend a week of hard driving and not explore it all. Or you could spend all summer floating the rivers and still have years of floating left to do before you'd seen all the riverbanks. It's something like what the great mass of America's Midwest once must have been, perhaps a century and a half ago, when the great flatlands had been explored but not completely civilized and Huckleberry Finn could float downriver into a wilderness of adventures. As it happens, I have a friend who grew up on a homestead in the Interior and ran away from home at age 15 in that exact same fashion, floating hundreds of miles on a handmade raft, past the little river villages, cargo barges, and fishermen. During an Interior summer, nature combines its immensity with a rare sense of gentleness, patiently awaiting the next thunderstorm.

Winter is another matter. Without the regulating influence of the ocean—the same reason summers are hot—winter temperatures can often drop to –30°F or –40°F, and during exceptional cold snaps, much lower. Now the earth is wobbling over in the other direction, away from the sun. The long, black nights sometimes make Fairbanks, the region's dominant city, feel more like an outpost on a barren planet, far off in outer space. That's when the northern lights come, spewing swirls of color across the entire dome of the sky and crackling with electricity. Neighbors get on the phone to wake each other and, rising from bed to put on their warmest parkas and insulated boots, stand in the street, gazing straight up. Visitors lucky enough to come at such times may be watching from a steaming hot-spring tub. During the short days, they can bundle up and watch sled-dog racing or race across the wilderness themselves on snowmobiles.

Fairbanks stands second in Alaska in population, with over 80,000 in the greater area, but the Interior otherwise is without any settlements large enough to be called cities. Instead, it's defined by roads, both paved and gravel, which are strands of civilization through sparsely settled, often swampy land. Before the roads, development occurred only on the rivers, which still serve as thoroughfares for the **Athabascan villages** of the region. In the summer, villagers travel by boat. In the winter, the frozen rivers become highways for snowmobiles and sled-dog teams. White homesteaders and gold miners live back in the woods, too. Gold rush history is written on the land in piles of old gravel tailings and abandoned equipment, as well as in the prettier tourist attractions and historic sites. Gold mining goes on today, in small one-man operations and huge industrial works employing hundreds.

1 Exploring the Interior

Having your own car in the Interior, more than anywhere else in Alaska, provides the freedom to find the out-of-the-way places that give the region its character. Bus service connects Fairbanks with the Alaska Highway, including the ferry terminus at Haines or Skagway, and trains run between Fairbanks and Anchorage. But that will show you only the larger, tourist-oriented destinations.

If you have the time and money, you may enjoy driving one of the remote gravel highways, or just poking along on the paved highways between the larger towns, ready to stop and investigate the roadhouses and meet the people who live out in the middle of nowhere. You'll find them mostly friendly and, often, downright odd—*colorful,* to use the polite term. As I drove an abandoned highway recently, I saw a hand-lettered sign advertising coffee. It wasn't your typical espresso stand, just a log cabin dozens of miles from the next nearest building. A squinting high plains drifter stepped out, wearing a cowboy hat on his head and a huge revolver on his hip, and asked, "Yeah?" The coffee came from a percolator warming on the wood stove, and the proprietor and I struck up a good conversation in his dark little dwelling. He was living the life of the old-time frontier. Another favorite roadside sign, sighted on the Alaska Highway, in spray paint on plywood: SALE—EEL SKINS—ANVILS—BAIT. I've always wished I'd stopped in to window-shop and meet the man or woman who came up with that business plan.

Of course, not every mile of back road is scenic, nor are all the stops interesting. Driving a car through Alaska takes a long time, including many hours spent in dull, brushy forest, and calls for a high tolerance for greasy hamburgers. Paved highway sections can develop frost heaves in this often-frozen land—backbreaking dips and humps caused by the freeze and thaw of the road base and ground underneath. The gravel roads generate clouds of dust and quickly fatigue drivers, and windshield and headlights often succumb to their flying rocks.

Rollin' on the River

Floating any of the thousands of miles of the Interior's rivers opens great swaths of wilderness. Beginners will want to take a guided trip before venturing on their own. (See the lists of operators in chapter 2.) For Yukon River day trips, see the sections on Dawson City or the Dalton Highway. To plan your own trip, get Karen Jettmar's *The Alaska River Guide,* published by Alaska Northwest Books, P.O. Box 10306, Portland, OR 97210-0306 (☎ **800-452-3032,** ext. 272), which includes details for floats on more than 100 river trips across the state. Also, check with the **Alaska Public Lands Information Center** in Fairbanks, Tok, or Anchorage for guidance on setting up your trip. Among the most accessible and historic rivers in the region are the Chena, Chatanika, Yukon, and Fortymile (see the sections on Chena Hot Springs Road, the Steese Highway, Dawson City, and Eagle in this chapter, respectively).

LIKELY ITINERARIES

You can shorten your driving time by flying or taking the train to Fairbanks, then renting a car for an exploration. Renting a car one way is a good way to go, too, if you can stand the drop-off fee.

One itinerary that makes sense is to rent a car in Fairbanks, explore eastward to Dawson City along the Alaska Highway and Taylor and Top-of-the-World highways, then drive south through the Yukon Territory to drop the car in Skagway. There you can board the ferry south to fly out from Juneau, Sitka, or Ketchikan. I'd allow a good 10 days for such a plan, and expect a drop-off fee of around $300. If you prefer to return the car to the starting point in Fairbanks, take it on the ferry from Skagway to Haines, then follow the Alaska Highway back.

Another idea is to make a loop through Anchorage. From Fairbanks, take the Richardson Highway to Kennicott, in Wrangell–St. Elias National Park, then continue to Valdez, take a ferry to Whittier, and drive back north on the Seward Highway to Anchorage, continuing on the Parks Highway to Denali National Park and back to Fairbanks. That would take 10 days to 2 weeks, depending on how long you stayed in each place. For a shorter loop, cross through the Alaska Range on the Denali Highway, which links the Richardson and Parks highways at their midpoint.

Or simply base yourself in Fairbanks and take a few days to experience the Steese or Dalton highways or Chena Hot Springs Road, perhaps with hot springs soaking, hiking, or canoeing on the way.

An especially fun way to go is with an **RV.** They're everywhere on these highways, so services are well developed even in many remote areas. An RV offers much of the freedom of camping, but sidesteps a lot of the problems of tent camping in a cool climate so far from home. Perhaps most important, it allows spontaneity. You don't have to stick so closely to an itinerary tied to hard-to-get hotel reservations. But RVs are expensive: Just the rental can cost as much as staying in hotels, renting a car, and eating out for your meals. High-season rates are around $200 a day, plus the large amount of fuel you use and mileage charges of over 30¢ a mile beyond certain minimums. Campgrounds with full utility hookups cost $20 to $30 a night, or you can go self-contained at public campgrounds that cost half as much, dumping your tanks later.

Morris Communications' ***The Milepost*** (www.themilepost.com/), a highway guide to Alaska and northwestern Canada, has long been considered the indispensable handbook for Alaska drivers. It has mile-by-mile descriptions of all the major roads and is

Alaska's Highways à la Carte

You won't need a detailed highway map of Alaska, because Alaska doesn't have detailed highways. A single triangle of paved two-lane highways connects Tok, Fairbanks, and Anchorage. From this triangle, a few routes reach to discrete destinations, and gravel roads penetrate the periphery of the Bush. Beyond a few miles around Fairbanks and Anchorage, our highways are narrow strips of asphalt or gravel through the wilderness.

MAIN HIGHWAYS

Alaska Highway (Route 2 from the border to Delta Junction) Running nearly 1,400 miles from Dawson Creek, British Columbia, to Delta Junction, Alaska, a couple of hours east of Fairbanks on the Richardson Highway, this World War II road is paved, but that doesn't mean it's always smooth. Like other northern highways, it's subject to bone-jarring frost heaves and spring potholes. Two tiny towns lie on the Alaska portion of the road, Delta Junction and Tok. The prettiest part is on the Canadian side, in the Kluane Lake area. Driving the highway all the way to Alaska is still a real adventure, covered later in this chapter.

Denali Highway (Route 8) I simply couldn't believe my eyes when I first drove this 133-mile gravel road connecting the midpoints of the Parks and Richardson highways. The stunning alpine vistas high in the Alaska Range rival those within Denali National Park, but are open to all drivers, with a rich network of trails and mountain lakes and a good chance to see caribou, bears, moose, and waterfowl. It's popular with mountain bikers, canoers, anglers, and hunters. See chapter 8.

Glenn Highway (Route 1 from Anchorage to Tok) This is the road you'd take if you were coming from the Alaska Highway on your way to Southcentral Alaska, including Prince William Sound, Anchorage, and the Kenai Peninsula. It connects Tok to Anchorage, 330 miles southwest. (The section between Glennallen and Tok is sometimes called the "Tok Cut-Off.") The northern section, from Tok to Glennallen, borders Wrangell–St. Elias National Park, with broad tundra and taiga broken by high, craggy peaks. That area is covered below, in this chapter. Glennallen to Anchorage is even more spectacular, as the road passes through high alpine terrain and then close by the Matanuska Glacier, where it winds through a deep canyon valley carved by the glacier's river. That part of the road is covered in chapter 6.

Parks Highway (Route 3) The George Parks Highway is a straight line from Anchorage to Fairbanks, 358 miles north, providing access to Denali National Park. There are some vistas of Mount McKinley from south of the park, but the Parks Highway is mostly just a transportation route, less scenic than the Richardson or Glenn highways. From the northern (Fairbanks) end, the highway passes Nenana (covered in section 3 of this chapter), then Denali and Talkeetna (chapter 8), and finally the towns of the Matanuska and Susitna Valleys (chapter 6).

Richardson Highway (Route 4 from Valdez to Delta Junction, Route 2 from Delta Junction to Fairbanks) The state's first highway, leading 364 miles from tidewater in Valdez to Fairbanks, has lost much of its traffic to the Parks Highway, which saves more than 90 miles between Anchorage and Fairbanks, and the Glenn

Highway, which saves about 120 miles from Glennallen to Tok. But it's still the most beautiful paved drive in the Interior. From the south, the road begins with a magnificent climb through Keystone Canyon and steep Thompson Pass, just out of Valdez (see chapter 7), then passes the huge, distant peaks of southern Wrangell–St. Elias National Park. North of Glennallen, the road climbs into the Alaska Range for a series of broad vistas as the road snakes along the shores of a series of long alpine lakes. Finally, it descends again to the forested area around Delta Junction and meets the Alaska Highway before arriving in Fairbanks.

Seward Highway (Route 1 from Anchorage to Tern Lake, route 9 from Tern Lake to Seward) The highway leaves Anchorage on the 127-mile drive to Seward following the rocky edge of mountain peaks above a surging ocean fjord. Abundant wildlife and unfolding views often slow cars. Later, the road climbs through high mountain passes above the tree line, tracing sparkling alpine lakes. Alaska's best trail hikes are here. The section from Anchorage 50 miles south to Portage Glacier is covered in chapter 6, the remainder, to Seward, in chapter 7.

Sterling Highway (Route 1 from Tern Lake to Homer) Leading 142 miles from the Seward Highway to the tip of the Kenai Peninsula, the highway has some scenic spots, but mostly is a way to get to the Kenai River, the Kenai National Wildlife Refuge, Kachemak Bay, and the towns of Cooper Landing, Soldotna, Kenai, and Homer.

RURAL ROADS

Each of these mostly gravel roads is covered in detail later in this chapter.

Chena Hot Springs Road A more civilized road into the outdoors, this paved 57-mile highway east of Fairbanks meets hiking and river routes on the way to Chena Hot Springs.

Dalton Highway (Route 11) Built to haul equipment to the Prudhoe Bay oil fields, about 500 miles north of Fairbanks, the Dalton punctures the heart of the wilderness, crossing the Brooks Range and the North Slope.

Edgerton Highway & McCarthy Road (Route 10) Running east from the Richardson Highway south of Glennallen, the Edgerton leads to the tiny town of Chitina, where the McCarthy Road, a muddy one-lane track, penetrates Wrangell–St. Elias National Park to the historic sites at McCarthy and Kennicott. The journey of 93 miles takes half a day.

Steese Highway (Route 6) This gravel road climbs the rounded tundra mountains 162 miles east of Fairbanks to the Native village of Circle, on the Yukon River. It's a route to the real Alaska.

Taylor Highway (Route 5) At times rough, narrow, and a little scary, this dirt road leads 161 miles from a junction on the Alaska Highway east of Tok to the fascinating Yukon River village of Eagle, an island in time.

Top of the World Highway (Yukon Route 9) Connecting to the Taylor Highway and crossing the Canadian border to Dawson City, a distance of 79 miles, the road rides mountaintop to mountaintop, above the tree line nearly the entire way.

available for sale everywhere along the Alaska Highway and at many major bookstores throughout the U.S. Most of the book, however, is taken up by advertisements that are included in the text as listings, so don't expect objective descriptions.

2 Fairbanks: Alaska Heartland

If the story of the founding of Fairbanks had happened anywhere else, it wouldn't be told so proudly, for the city's father was a swindler, and its undignified birth contained an element of chance not usually admitted in polite society. As the popular story goes (and the historians' version is fairly close), it seems that in 1901, E. T. Barnette decided to get rich by starting a gold-mining boom town like the others that had sprouted from Dawson City to Nome as the stampeders of 1898 sloshed back and forth across the territory from one gold find to the next. He booked passage on a riverboat going up the Tanana with his supplies to build the town, having made an understanding with the captain that, should the vessel get stuck, he would lighten the load by getting off with the materials on the nearest bank. Unfortunately, the captain got lost. Thinking he was heading up a slough on the Tanana, he got sidetracked into the relatively small Chena River. That was where the boat got stuck and where Barnette got left, and that was where he founded Fairbanks.

Fortunately for Barnette, an Italian prospector named Felix Pedro had been looking for gold in the hills around the new trading post, and made a strike on the Tanana. On that news, Barnette dispatched his cook off to Dawson City to spread the word. The cook's story showed up in a newspaper that winter, and a stampede of hundreds of miners ensued, heading toward Fairbanks in weather as cold as –50°F. Barnette's town was a success, but the cook nearly got lynched when the stampeders found out how far he'd exaggerated the truth. Much more gold was found later, however, and half the population of Dawson City came down river to Fairbanks. Barnette had made it big.

The town's future was assured thanks to a political deal. Barnette did a favor for the territory's judge, James Wickersham, by naming the settlement for Wickersham's ally in Congress, Sen. Charles Fairbanks of Indiana, who later became vice president. Wickersham then moved the federal courthouse to Fairbanks from Eagle—he loaded his records on his dogsled and mushed here, establishing the camp as the hub of the region. Wickersham's story is interesting, too. He was a notable explorer, Alaska's first real statesman as a nonvoting delegate to Congress, and father of the Alaska Railroad. Houses he lived in are preserved at Alaskaland in Fairbanks and in Juneau just up the hill from the capitol building. Barnette didn't do as well in history's eyes: He was run out of the town he founded for bank fraud.

Fairbanks is Alaska's second-largest city now, with a population of about 32,000 in the city limits and 84,000 in the greater metropolitan area, but it has never learned to put on airs. It sprawls, broad and flat, along big highways and the Chena. It's a friendly, easygoing town, but one where people still take gold and their independence seriously. They're still prospecting and mining for gold around here, fighting off environmental regulation, and maintaining a traditional Alaskan attitude that it's us against the world. Fairbanks is the birthplace of strange political movements, including the secessionist Alaskan Independence Party. It's an adamant, loopy, affable place; it doesn't seem to mind being a little bizarre or residing far from the center of things. And that makes it an intensely Alaska city, for those are the qualities Alaskans most cherish in their myth of themselves.

Fairbanks could strike a visitor a couple of ways, depending on what you expect and what you like. Fairbanks could come across as a provincial outpost, a touristy cross between Kansas and Siberia. Driving one of the franchise-choked commercial strips, you could wonder why you went out of your way to come here, and the deserted downtown area can be downright depressing. Or you could relax and take Fairbanks on its own terms, as a fun, unpretentious town, full of activities and surprises, that never lost its sense of being on the frontier.

My children love it there. There's plenty for families to do in Fairbanks, much of it at least a little corny and requiring drives to widespread sites at the University, on the Chena River, in the gold mining area north of town, and at a big town park called Alaskaland. (You *must* have wheels in Fairbanks.) There are good opportunities for hiking and mountain biking, and great opportunities for canoeing and slow river float trips.

ESSENTIALS

GETTING THERE **By Car or RV** Fairbanks is a transportation hub. The Richardson Highway heads east 98 miles to Delta Junction, the end point of the Alaska Highway, then south to Glennallen and Valdez. The Parks Highway heads due south from Fairbanks to Denali National Park, 120 miles away, and Anchorage, 358 miles south.

By Bus Gray Line's **Alaskon Express** (☎ **800/478-6388** or 907/451-6835; www.graylinealaska.com/alaskon.cfm) offers service 3 days a week from Skagway, up the Alaska Highway to the Westmark Fairbanks (the fare is $212), with stops along the way. **Alaska Direct Bus Line** (☎ **800/770-6652** or 907/277-6652) runs to and from Whitehorse and Skagway for slightly lower fares. The **Parks Highway Express** (☎ **888/600-6001;** www.AlaskaShuttle.com/) offers daily service in summer to and from Denali National Park and Anchorage (one-way fares are $25 and $60 respectively), and less frequent service to and from Valdez and even Dawson City and other remote spots.

By Train The **Alaska Railroad** (☎ **800/544-0552** or 907/456-4155; www.akrr.com/) links Fairbanks with Denali National Park and Anchorage, with tour commentary provided along the way. The high-season one-way fare is $48 to Denali and $160 to Anchorage. See a detailed description of the services available in section 2 of chapter 8.

By Air **Fairbanks International Airport** has direct jet service from Anchorage on several airlines, with **Alaska Airlines** (☎ **800/252-7522** or 907/474-9175; www.alaskaair.com) having the most flights. Round-trip fares are generally under $200. The airport is a hub for various small carriers to Alaska's Interior and Arctic communities. A cab downtown from the airport is about $15 with **Yellow Cab** (☎ **907/455-5555**).

VISITOR INFORMATION The **Fairbanks Log Cabin Visitor Information Center** is in a large log building at 550 First Ave., on the Chena River at the center of town, at Cushman Street, Fairbanks, AK 99701 (☎ **800/327-5774** or 907/456-5774; fax 907/452-2867; www.explorefairbanks.com). The staff provides maps, including a road map and detailed walking and driving tour maps, and will help you find a room with their daily vacancy listing. They also book activities. The Web site contains many useful links and is easy to use. The center is open daily 8am to 8pm in summer, Monday to Friday 10am to 5pm in winter. When you stop by, take a look at nearby Golden Heart Plaza for a shot of civic pride.

The **Alaska Public Lands Information Center,** 250 Cushman St. (at Third Avenue), Suite 1A, Fairbanks, AK 99701 (☎ **907/456-0527;** TTY 907/456-0532; fax 907/456-0514; www.nps.gov/aplic), is an indispensable stop for anyone planning to spend time in the outdoors, and an interesting one even if you're not. The staff is remarkably knowledgeable and can tell you about trips and activities based on their own first-hand experience. Besides providing maps and other details, the center houses a small museum about the state's regions and the gear needed to explore them. Daily films and naturalist programs show in a small auditorium. Open daily 9am to 6pm in summer, Monday to Friday 10am to 6pm in winter.

GETTING AROUND It's possible to see much of Fairbanks without a car, staying in the downtown area and making excursions by bus or shuttle; but the city is designed around the car, and that's the easiest way to get around. Good road maps are available free at the visitor center. The city is too spread out to use taxis much.

If you flew in and need to rent a car, you'll find many agencies. **Avis** (☎ **800/230-4898** or 907/474-0900) is located at the airport. **National Car Rental** is downtown, at 1246 Noble St. (☎ **800/227-7368** or 907/451-7368), and rents SUVs and will allow some vehicles to go on gravel roads such as the Dalton and Steese highways, an important consideration in this region. Several local firms rent RVs in Fairbanks, including **Diamond Willow RV Rentals,** 350 Old Steese Hwy. N. (☎ **888/724-7373** or 907/457-2814).

The Fairbanks North Star Borough's **MACS bus system** links the University, downtown, the nearby North Pole community, and shopping areas, and some hotels. Service is every 30 minutes, at best, and virtually nonexistent on weekends. Pick up timetables at the visitor center. All buses connect at the transit park downtown, at Fifth Avenue and Cushman Street.

Fairbanks' car-oriented layout does not lend itself to using bikes as your primary means of transportation. But bicycles, and other outdoor equipment, are for rent from **Beaver Sports,** 3480 College Rd. (☎ **907/479-0876;** www.beaversports.net). Downtown you can rent bikes by the hour at the **Fairbanks Hotel,** 517 Third Ave. (☎ **907/456-6411**).

FAST FACTS Fairbanks has numerous banks with **ATMs** in the downtown area and along the commercial strips; you can also find ATMs in many grocery stores. **Key Bank** (☎ **907/452-2146**) is at 100 Cushman.

A **Kinko's Copy Center** is at 418 Third St. (☎ **907/456-7348**). Also downtown, **Café Latte,** 519 6th Ave. (☎ **907/455-4898**), offers Internet access.

Fairbanks Memorial Hospital is at 1650 Cowles St. (☎ **907/452-8181**).

For nonemergency police business, call the **Alaska State Troopers** (☎ **907/451-5100**) or the **Fairbanks Police Department** (☎ **907/459-6500**).

The **post office** is at 315 Barnette St.

There is no **sales tax** in Fairbanks, but the North Pole suburb charges 3%. The local **bed tax** is 8%.

A recorded **weather forecast** is available at ☎ **907/452-3553.**

SPECIAL EVENTS A recording of current local happenings can be reached at ☎ **907/456-INFO,** maintained by the Fairbanks Convention and Visitors Bureau, which also posts an event calendar at **www.explorefairbanks.com**.

The **Yukon Quest International Sled Dog Race** (☎ **907/452-7954;** www.yukonquest.org/), held in mid-February, starts or finishes in Fairbanks (Fairbanks has the start in even-numbered years; Whitehorse, Yukon Territory, hosts the start in odd-numbered years). Mushers say this rugged 1,000-mile race is even tougher than the Iditarod.

The **Nenana Ice Classic** (☎ **907/832-5446;** www.ptialaska.net/~tripod), held the first weekend in March, in Nenana, starts with a weekend celebration of dance performances, dog mushing, and other activities; the classic is a sweepstakes on who

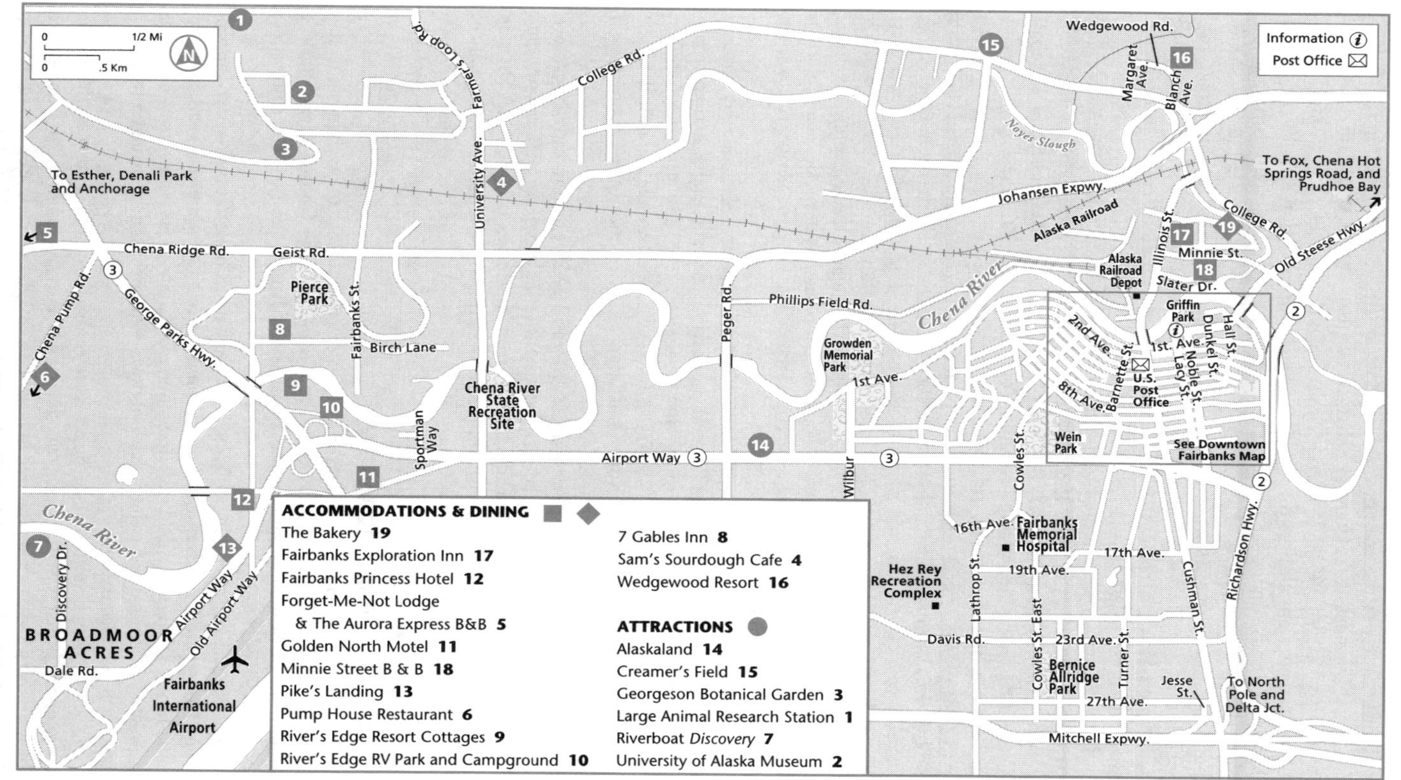
ACCOMMODATIONS & DINING
The Bakery 19
Fairbanks Exploration Inn 17
Fairbanks Princess Hotel 12
Forget-Me-Not Lodge
& The Aurora Express B&B 5
Golden North Motel 11
Minnie Street B & B 18
Pike's Landing 13
Pump House Restaurant 6
River's Edge Resort Cottages 9
River's Edge RV Park and Campground 10
7 Gables Inn 8
Sam's Sourdough Cafe 4
Wedgewood Resort 16
ATTRACTIONS
Alaskaland 14
Creamer's Field 15
Georgeson Botanical Garden 3
Large Animal Research Station 1
Riverboat Discovery 7
University of Alaska Museum 2
Information
Post Office
0 1/2 Mi
0 .5 Km
To Fox, Chena Hot Springs Road, and Prudhoe Bay
To Esther, Denali Park and Anchorage
To North Pole and Delta Jct.
See Downtown Fairbanks Map
Fairbanks International Airport
BROADMOOR ACRES
Chena River
Noyes Slough
Alaska Railroad
Alaska Railroad Depot
Griffin Park
U.S. Post Office
Wein Park
Fairbanks Memorial Hospital
Hez Rey Recreation Complex
Bernice Allridge Park
Growden Memorial Park
Chena River State Recreation Site
Pierce Park
College Rd.
Wedgewood Rd.
Johansen Expwy.
Old Steese Hwy.
Richardson Hwy.
Cushman St.
Airport Way
Old Airport Way
George Parks Hwy.
Chena Pump Rd.
Chena Ridge Rd.
Geist Rd.
University Ave.
Farmer's Loop Rd.
Phillips Field Rd.
Peger Rd.
Cowles St.
Lathrop St.
Davis Rd.
Mitchell Expwy.
Sportsman Way
Birch Lane
Fairbanks St.
Discovery Dr.
Dale Rd.
Wilbur
Minnie St.
Illinois St.
Slater Dr.
Hall St.
Dunkel St.
Noble St.
Lacy St.
1st Ave.
2nd Ave.
8th Ave.
Barnette St.
16th Ave.
17th Ave.
19th Ave.
23rd Ave.
27th Ave.
Turner St.
Jesse St.
Cowles St. East
Margaret Ave.
Blanch Ave.

can guess closest to the exact date and time when the ice will go out on the Tanana River (see "Nenana: Parks Highway Sidetrack," below). The ✪ **World Ice Art Championships** (☎ **907/451-8250;** www.icealaska.com/), held in early to mid-March, brings carvers from all over the world to sculpt immense, clear chunks cut from a Fairbanks pond. Among ice carvers, Fairbanks' ice is famous for its clarity and the great size of the chucks. Some spectacular ice sculptures stand as tall as a two-story building, and businesses all over town commission works to go out front, too. Check the Web site for pictures of past winners. The **North American Sled Dog Championships** (☎ **907/488-1357**) is the oldest running, taking place over a weekend in mid-March.

Lots of events happen around the **summer solstice,** usually June 21. A street fair happens downtown (☎ **907/452-8671**), there's a big 10K race open to walkers and people in funny costumes (☎ **907/452-7211**), and the **Midnight Sun Baseball Game** is hosted by the semipro Fairbanks Goldpanners (☎ **907/451-0095**); it begins at 10:30pm, and there are no artificial lights.

Golden Days, over 2 weeks in late July, includes crafts fairs and a parade (☎ **907/452-1105**). Visitors to Fairbanks flock to corny gold rush melodramas in the evening; instead, you can take in real performing art at ✪ **The Fairbanks Summer Arts Festival,** on the University of Alaska Fairbanks campus (☎ **907/474-8869;** www.fsaf.org/). Over 2 weeks in late July and early August, the festival brings artists of international reputation for workshops and performances in music, dance, theater, opera, and the visual arts. Check their remarkable Web site for performances when you will be visiting.

The **Tanana Valley Fair** (☎ **907/452-3750;** www.tananavalleyfair.org/), in early August, shows off the area's agricultural production, arts and crafts, and entertainment, and includes rides, a carnival, and a rodeo. Late August to mid-September, Friends of Creamers Field (☎ **907/452-5162**) hosts an annual **Sandhill Crane Festival,** with nature walks, lectures, and other activities, mostly at Creamers Field (see "Special Places," below).

The **Athabascan Fiddling Festival** (☎ **907/452-1825**), held in early November, draws together musicians and dancers from the Interior region for performances and workshops. The **Top of the World Classic,** late in November, brings NCAA Division I basketball teams to the University of Alaska—Fairbanks for a weekend tournament (☎ **907/474-6830**).

ATTRACTIONS & ACTIVITIES

STROLLING AROUND DOWNTOWN

If you want to explore downtown for an hour or two, pick up the walking tour map available at the visitor center. Among the highlights is the **Golden Heart Park,** a waterfront plaza with a fountain and a bronze of a Native family, where community events often occur.

The town's most interesting building is the Roman Catholic **Church of the Immaculate Conception,** across the river on Cushman Street. The white clapboard structure, built in 1904, has ornate gold rush decoration inside, rare for its authenticity, including a pressed-tin ceiling and stained-glass windows—an appealing if incongruous mix of gold rush and sacred decor.

At First Avenue near Kellum Street, east from the visitor center, **St. Mathew's Episcopal Church** is a cute old log church with a working rope-pull bell. It was founded by missionary and dogsled explorer Hudson Stuck in 1904, an early advocate for Alaska's Natives. The original church burned; the present structure dates from 1948.

Seeing the Aurora Borealis

One fall evening I left the house of friends in Fairbanks to the sight of a swirling green glow that filled the dark sky. I knocked on the door and brought them out to see, only to have my friends laugh in my face. They informed me, with mock contempt for my Anchorage home, that in Fairbanks they don't even bother to bend their necks back for northern lights as dim as these. It's true—a bright aurora borealis is routine in Fairbanks. Some of the world's top experts on the phenomenon work here, at the University of Alaska's Geophysical Institute (their Aurora predictions and background on the Aurora are posted at **www.gi.alaska.edu/**). The hours-long displays can be incredibly spectacular and even moving.

Unfortunately, few visitors ever see these wild strands of bright colors whipping across the sky, because when most visitors come, the sky is never dark. Alaskans rarely see the stars from late May through early August, and to see the aurora well you need an especially dark night sky. To improve your chances, plan your trip in the fall or winter. An early September trip offers brilliant fall foliage, dark night skies, and the remnants of summer weather. In midwinter, the sky is dark all night and most of the day, too. Many hotels and resorts cater to travelers coming to see the aurora in winter, and also will introduce them to winter sports, including dog mushing and snowmobiling. See chapter 2 for tips on planning a winter trip.

At Second Avenue and Lacey Street, the **Fairbanks Ice Museum** (☎ **907/451-8222**) aims to show summer visitors what winter is like, with a freezer you can enter to feel the cold and 40,000 pounds of carved ice animals. A striking high-tech slide show plays hourly, explaining the annual World Ice Art Championships (see "Events," above), and freezers contain impressive ice tableaux. Admission is $6 for adults, $4 ages 6 to 12. It's open 10am to 6pm daily June to mid-September.

At 410 Cushman St., the former city hall contains the volunteer-operated **Fairbanks Community Museum** (☎ **907/452-8671**), which shares quarters with the Yukon Quest International Sled Dog Race (see "Events," above) and displays dog-mushing material, a miner's cabin, and old Fairbanks photographs. Hours are Monday to Saturday 10am to 6pm, Sunday noon to 4pm.

ALASKALAND

Built for the Alaska purchase centennial in 1967, **Alaskaland** is the boiled-down essence of Fairbanks on grounds at the intersection of Airport Way and Peger Road (☎ **907/459-1087**). It's called a theme park, but don't expect Disneyland or anything like it. Instead, Alaskaland is a city park with a theme. It's relaxing and low-key, entrancing for young children and interesting for adults if you can give in to the charm of the place. Admission to the park is free, and the tours and activities are generally inexpensive. The park is open year-round, but the attractions operate only Memorial Day to Labor Day, daily from 11am to 9pm. Pick up a map and schedule when you arrive; here I've listed the highlights, but there is more to see. Depending on the pace you like to keep and the age level of your group, you could spend anything from a couple of hours to most of a day here.

The ✪ **SS *Nenana*** (☎ **907/456-8848**) is the park's centerpiece. Commissioned by the federally owned Alaska Railroad in 1933, the large stern-wheeler plied the Yukon and Tanana rivers until 1952. In 1967 the *Nenana* came to Alaskaland, but was unmaintained and had nearly collapsed from rot when it was saved by a community restoration effort, completed in 1992. There are five decks of sumptuous mahogany, brass, and white-painted promenades. The wheelhouse and engine room remain well preserved, too. A tour is $5 for adults, $3 children, and goes to the fascinating upper decks only in dry weather—the steps and decks get slippery in rain. You can see the ground-floor cargo deck anytime without paying, and it contains an amazing set of dioramas showing all the riverside towns and villages where the boat called, modeled as they looked in its heyday.

Most of Fairbanks's history has been moved to Alaskaland. A village of log cabins contains shops and restaurants, each marked with its original location and place in Fairbanks's history. **Judge Wickersham's house,** circa 1904, is kept as a museum, decorated appropriate to the period of the town's founding. The house is less than grand—it may remind you of your grandmother's—but it's worth a stop to strike up a conversation with the historical society volunteers who keep it open. **Pres. Warren Harding's fancy rail car,** from which he stepped to drive the golden spike on the Alaska Railroad, sits near the park entrance. The **Pioneer Air Museum** (☎ **907/451-0037**) is housed in a geodesic dome toward the back of the park. Besides the aircraft, some of which are open to climb into, there are displays and artifacts of the crashes of Alaska's aviation pioneers. Admission is $2.

If you have children, you certainly won't escape Alaskaland without a ride on the **Crooked Creek and Whiskey Island Railroad** that circles the park twice, with a tour guide pointing out the sights; rides cost $2 for adults, $1 for children, free for senior citizens and children under age 4. Kids also will enjoy the large **playground,** with equipment for toddlers and older children, where lots of local families come to play, and the 36-hole miniature golf course. The only carnival ride is a nice old **merry-go-round.** There's a boat landing and a mining display with a mechanical waterfall.

Tour groups generally come to Alaskaland in the evening mid-May to mid-September for the **Alaska Salmon Bake,** at the mining display (☎ **907/452-7274**), and the **Golden Heart Revue,** at the Palace Theater (☎ **907/456-5960;** www.alaskasbest.com/ester). The all-you-can-eat halibut, ribs, or brown-sugar salmon costs $21.95, or you can get a steak for $22.95. Beer and wine are available. The revue, nightly at 8:15pm, mid-May to mid-September, covers the amusing story of the founding of Fairbanks with comedy and song in a nightclub setting; admission is $14 for adults.

University of Alaska—Fairbanks

The state university's main campus contains several interesting attractions, and the administration makes a point of attracting and serving tourists. The campus is on the west side of town; look for University Avenue. A widely distributed brochure lists tours, hours, and fees. A free 2-hour **walking tour,** led by students, meets at the museum Monday through Friday at 10am, June to August except July 4. Call ahead (☎ **907/474-7581**) to confirm the time and any weather cancellations. (See www.uaf.edu/univrel/Tour/index.html for information on all University tours and maps.) Besides the full campus tour, the **Geophysical Institute** (☎ **907/474-7558;** www.gi.alaska.edu/) offers tours of its seismology lab, radar facility, and a talk on the aurora Thursdays at 2pm in July and August. Anyone interested in earth science shouldn't miss it.

✪ **University of Alaska Museum.** 907 Yukon Dr. (P.O. Box 756960), Fairbanks, AK 99775-6960. ☎ **907/474-7505.** www.uaf.alaska.edu/museum. June–Aug daily 9am–7pm; May and Sept daily 9am–5pm; Oct–Apr, Mon–Fri 9am–5pm, Sat–Sun noon–5pm. Admission $5 adults, $4.50 ages 60 and older, $3 ages 7–17, ages 6 and under free.

This rich, interdisciplinary museum explains the nature and culture of each of the state's regions. It's Alaska's best natural history museum, and its most scholarly, with information presented at advanced as well as elementary levels. Some of the objects have a real wow factor, such as Blue Babe, the petrified Steppe Bison, and a 5,400-pound copper nugget. Despite the museum's small size, a curious person could spend most of a day here. The only major weakness is that it tries to do so much in too small a space and seems cluttered. A display on emission spectrums is side by side with a stuffed lynx, a woven root basket, and a broad-view aurora camera. They're working on that problem, raising money for an expansion. In the summer, catch the shows in the auditorium.

UAF's scientists lead the world in the study of **the northern lights,** and their aurora show depicts and explains the phenomenon daily at 10am and 3pm; admission is $4 adults, $3 youth (7 to 17), $2 children. A show on Alaska Native culture is at 11am and 2pm and costs $6.50 for adults, $4 youth, $2 children.

Georgeson Botanical Garden. W. Tanana Dr. ☎ **907/474-1944.** www.lter.alaska.edu/~salrm/GBG_WWW/GBG.html. Suggested donation $1. Open daylight hours; store open May 15 to Labor Day daily 10am–6pm; free guided tours Fri at 2pm.

I really enjoy the mix of science and contemplation I find at this relaxed working garden. Plots are laid out to compare seeds and cultivation techniques, usually well posted with explanatory information on the experiment; but at the same time the flowers and vegetables are spectacular, and there are peaceful memorials and places to picnic. You don't need a tour to enjoy the garden. Nearby, the barn of the university's experimental farm is open for visitors to wander through and view the cows, pigs, and reindeer.

Large Animal Research Station. Yankovich Rd. (drive north from campus, turn left on Ballaine Rd., left again on Yankovich). ☎ **907/474-7207.** Tours June–Aug Tues, Thurs, and Sat 11am and 1:30pm; Sept Sat 1:30pm. Admission $5 adults, students $2, ages 6 and under free.

The university studies captive musk ox and caribou here, on a property more commonly known as the musk ox farm. Tours are given five times a week in the summer, but just walking along the fence you can see the animals behaving naturally in the large pastures. With a long lens, you can get a good picture.

COMMERCIAL TOURIST ATTRACTIONS AROUND FAIRBANKS

Three major for-profit attractions around Fairbanks pack in visitors by the hundreds of thousands, most of them on group tours. These places are educational and fun, as I've described below, but I think they all charge excessive prices; whether they're worth your money depends on how much you've got and your level of interest.

The Riverboat *Discovery*. 1975 Discovery Dr., Fairbanks, AK 99709. ☎ **907/479-6673.** www.riverboatdiscovery.com. Sailings at 8:45am and 2pm, with a less crowded evening sailing sometimes added. Admission $39.95 adults, $36.95 teens, $29.95 ages 3–12.

The *Discovery* belongs to the pioneering Binkley family, which has been in the riverboat business since the Klondike gold rush and whose family members still run the boat. The *Discovery* is a real stern-wheeler, a 156-foot steel vessel carrying 700 passengers on as many as three trips a day. There's nothing intimate or spontaneous about the 3½-hour ride, which mostly carries package-tour passengers off fleets of buses, but the Binkleys still provide a fun, educational experience that doesn't feel cheap or contrived. After loading at a landing with shops off Dale Road, near the airport, the boat cruises down the Chena and up the Tanana past demonstrations on shore—among others, a bush plane taking off and landing, fish cutting at a Native fish camp, and a musher's dog yard (in recent years, it was five-time Iditarod champion Susan

Butcher's yard, and she'd often show off the dogs herself). Finally, the vessel pulls up at the bank for a tour of a mock Athabascan village.

The El Dorado Gold Mine. Off the Elliot Hwy., 9 miles north of town. ☎ **907/479-7613.** www.eldoradogoldmine.com/. Tours daily; call for times. Admission $27.95 adults, $19.95 ages 3–12.

A train such as you would find at an amusement park carries visitors though an impressively staged educational tour, much like the Riverboat *Discovery* tour operated by the same family, but the gold miners who act as hosts are the real attraction here. Visitors gather around a sluice to hear the amusing and authentic Dexter and Lynette (aka Yukon Yonda) Clark and watch a swoosh of water and gold-bearing gravel rush by. You pan the resulting pay dirt, and everyone goes home with enough gold dust to fill a plastic locket—typically $5 to $35 worth. Drive out to the mine after making reservations, or take a free shuttle.

Gold Dredge Number 8. 1755 Old Steese Hwy., Fairbanks, AK 99712. ☎ **907/457-6058.** Mid-May to mid-Sept daily 9am–6pm; tours hourly 9:30am–3:30pm. Admission $17 adults, $13 children age 4–12; add $4 for gold panning; add another $8.50 for a cafeteria lunch. To get there, go north on the Steese Expressway from town, turn left on Goldstream Rd., and again on the Old Steese Hwy.

This is the area's best gold-mining historic site, because it's real. The centerpiece is a 1928 gold dredge, similar to machines in Dawson City and Nome, that stands five decks tall on a barge floating in a pond it created. When it operated, huge scoops would dig from one end, the mechanism inside would digest the gold from the gravel, and then it would dump the spoils out the back—in this way, the pond and the dredge it supports crept 21 miles across the frozen ground north of Fairbanks. Many sterile areas you see in this area were created by these earth-eaters, for nothing grows on their tailings for decades after. The tour company that bought the historic site added to the dredge with museums housed in relocated gold camp buildings, showing the drab life lived by the miners and the tools they worked with. A 90-minute tour starts with a film, then a half hour on the dredge, and finally a chance to pan for gold yourself, with success assured. A large cafeteria is mostly for package-tour bus passengers.

SHOPPING

Fairbanks has a few good shops downtown. **New Horizons Gallery,** at 519 First St. (☎ **907/456-2063**), occupies a large space with a combination of large oils by Alaska's best serious artists, inexpensive prints, and gifts. The **Arctic Travelers Gift Shop,** at 201 Cushman St. (☎ **907/456-7080**), specializes in Native crafts, carrying both valuable art and affordable but authentically Alaska gifts. The staff is friendly and knowledgeable. The **Yukon Quest Store,** at 558 Second Ave. (☎ **907/451-8985;** www.shopyukonquest.com/), supports the incredible 1,000-mile sled dog race between Whitehorse and Fairbanks; you'll find race memorabilia and a little museum.

Near the airport, at 4630 Old Airport Rd., the **Great Alaskan Bowl Company** (☎ **907/474-9663;** www.woodbowl.com) makes and sells bowls of native birch—salad bowls, of course, but also for many other purposes. They can carve up to eight nested bowls from one piece of wood. One side of the shop is a glass wall looking into the shop, where you can see workers and their power tools cutting the bowls from raw logs.

GETTING OUTSIDE

In this section, I've described the outdoor opportunities local to Fairbanks, but some other choices are barely farther afield: Check out sections 4 and 5 of this chapter, on Chena Hot Springs Road and the Steese Highway.

The **Alaska Public Lands Information Center,** 250 Cushman St. (at Third Avenue), Suite 1A (☎ **907/456-0527;** www.nps.gov/aplic), is a great resource. The staff will advise you on outings, outfitters, and where to find rental equipment.

Special Places

✪ CREAMER'S FIELD At 1300 College Rd., right in Fairbanks, this migratory waterfowl refuge is a 1,800-acre former dairy farm that was saved from development in 1966 by a community fund drive. The pastures are a prime stopover point for Canada geese, pintails, and golden plovers in the spring and fall. Sandhill cranes, shovelers, and mallards show up all summer. The **Friends of Creamers Field** (☎ **907/452-7307;** www.state.ak.us/local/akpages/FISH.GAME/wildlife/region3/refuge3/creamers.htm) operates a small visitor center with bird and history displays, open June through August Tuesday through Friday from 10am to 5pm and on Saturday from 10am to 4pm, and offers guided nature walks in summer Saturday and Wednesday at 9am and Tuesday and Thursday at 7pm. You don't need a guide, however; I especially enjoyed the boreal forest nature walk, interpreted by an excellent booklet you can pick up at the visitor center or from a stand at the trailhead when the visitor center is closed.

CHENA LAKES RECREATION AREA This is a wonderful and unique place for a family camping trip. A birch-rimmed lake created for a flood-control project has been developed by the local government to provide lots of recreational possibilities: flat walking and bike trails; a swimming beach; fishing; a place to rent canoes, sailboats, and paddleboats; a self-guided 2½-mile nature trail; a playground; big lawns; and the terrific campground, with 80 camping sites, from pull-throughs for RVs to tent sites on a little island you can reach only by boat. In the winter, it's a popular cross-country skiing area. Drive 17 miles east of Fairbanks on the Richardson Highway and turn left on Laurance Road as you leave North Pole. For information, contact Fairbanks North Star Borough Chena Lakes Recreation Area (☎ **907/488-1655;** co.fairbanks.ak.us/parks&.htm).

Activities

CANOEING The Chena River is slow and meandering as it flows through Fairbanks, and you have your pick of restaurants on the bank. Farther up river, the canoeing passes wilder shores, and near its headwaters becomes more challenging (covered in the "Chena Hot Springs Road" section, below). For beginners, try the wilderness section from the Chena Lakes Recreation Area downstream (see above). It's about 12 hours from there all the way into town, or you can take out at one of the roads that crosses the river along the way. The **U.S. Army Corp of Engineers** (☎ **907/488-2748**) produces a float map with take-out points and float times, available at the Alaska Public Lands Information Center (see "Visitor Information," above). The Public Lands Center can provide guidance for all the trips, and a list of companies that rent equipment. **7 Bridges Boats and Bikes** rents canoes and kayaks for $35 per day, $100 per week, and provides the valuable service of dropping you off at the river and picking you up at your destination for $1.50 per mile out of town, with a $10 minimum. They're at the 7 Gables Inn, 4312 Birch Lane (☎ **907/479-0751;** www.7gablesinn.com/7bbb/).

BIKING & HIKING **7 Bridges Boats and Bikes** (see contact info immediately above) rents bicycles: street bikes are $15 a day; mountain bikes, $20. Also see "Getting Around," above. Traffic goes fast in Fairbanks, and the separated bike trails are few, but strong cyclists can get by. Mountain biking and hiking is good on the remote dirt roads and trails out of town. Some of Alaska's best are off the Steese

Highway and Chena Hot Spring Road, described below. Ask at the Alaska Public Lands Information Center for more ideas (see "Visitor Information," above).

FISHING Salmon fishing isn't as good here as nearer the coast, where the fish are brighter, and the season is brief. Most fishing is in the streams and stocked lakes for pike, grayling, and various kinds of trout. You can fish right in the Chena as it flows through town, although getting out of town and hiking away from a road yields better results. Fly-in fishing will further increase your chances, but the expense of around $300 a day is easier to justify from Anchorage, where you can target salmon as well as fresh water fish. The Alaska Public Lands Information Center (see above) offers guidance, or contact the **Alaska Department of Fish and Game,** at Creamer's Field, 1300 College Rd., Fairbanks, AK 99701 (☎ **907/459-7207;** sportfish information recording 907/459-7385; www.state.ak.us/local/akpages/FISH.GAME/adfghome.htm).

WINTER RECREATION Fairbanks has real Jack London winters, with long darkness and temperatures that commonly linger well below zero, but that doesn't stop people from getting outdoors for Nordic skiing, snowmobiling, and sled-dog mushing. You can count on snow and have excellent chances of seeing the Northern Lights. Many local dog mushers offer rides; get a referral from the visitor center. There are several cross-country ski trail networks, including a 50-mile groomed network at the University of Alaska and hilly, well-maintained trails at the **Birch Hill Recreation Area,** off Farmers Loop Road just east of the Steese Highway. Both have lighted loops for after-dark skiing.

ACCOMMODATIONS

Fairbanks is a popular destination in the peak summer season, and a good hotel room can be hard to find on short notice. Besides the establishments described in full below, try the **Comfort Inn Chena River,** 1908 Chena Landings Loop (☎ **800/201-9199** or 907/479-8080), with attractive rooms and a small pool in a lovely wooded site near the river; and the **7 Gables Inn,** 4312 Birch Lane (☎ **907/479-0751;** www.7gablesinn.com/), in a subdivision near the university. They rent canoes and other outdoor gear, with discounts for guests.

Going the bed-and-breakfast route is a good choice in Fairbanks. At the B&Bs I've listed below, you can save money over a hotel and get just as good a private room while staying in a unique place with interesting people. The **Fairbanks Association of Bed and Breakfasts,** P.O. Box 73334, Fairbanks, AK 99707-3334, lists many more on its Web site at **www.ptialaska.net/~fabb/**. You also can get B&B information at the Fairbanks Log Cabin Visitor Information Center, where the staff keeps a daily tally of vacancies (see "Visitor Information" at the beginning of this section).

VERY EXPENSIVE

Fairbanks Princess Hotel. 4477 Pikes Landing Rd., Fairbanks, AK 99709. ☎ **800/426-0500** or 907/455-4477. Fax 907/455-4476. www.princessalaskalodges.com. 325 units. TV TEL. High season $199–$209 double. Low season $129–$139 double. Year-round $199–$349 suite. Extra person $10. AE, DISC, MC, V.

This well-thought-out gray clapboard structure in a wooded area on the banks of the Chena, near the airport, was built to serve Princess cruise line passengers. The rooms, while not large, are trim and stylish, and many look out on the river. Besides the convenient location, newspapers and data ports make it a good choice for business travelers. The lobby is attractive, and the bar and Edgewater Restaurant have a large deck. The dinner menu is short, with entree prices in the $20 to $25 range, but the

Downtown Fairbanks

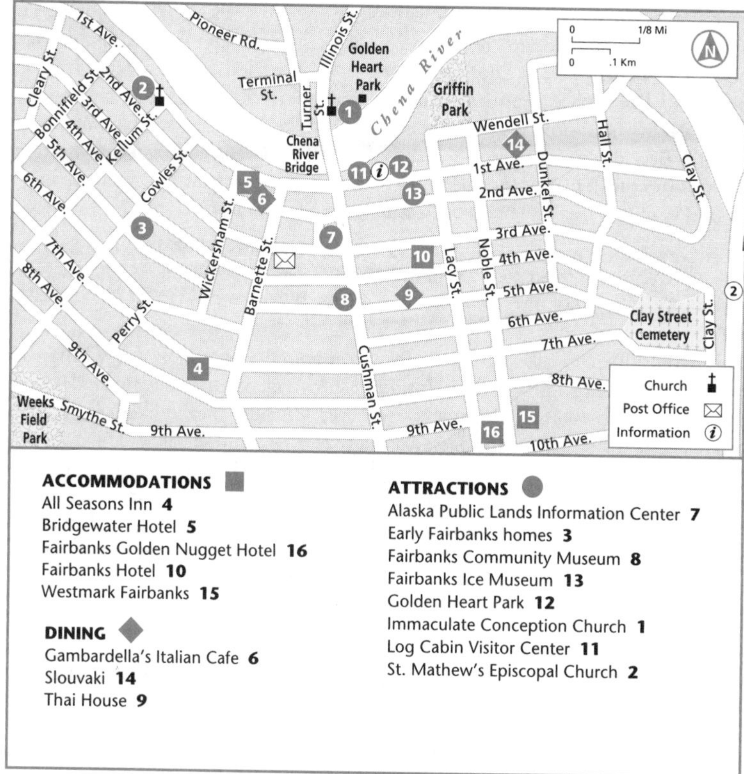

food is consistent. The hotel also offers an airport shuttle, health club, steam room, and tour desk.

Expensive

All Seasons Inn. 763 Seventh Ave., Fairbanks, AK 99701. ☎ **888/451-6649** or 907/451-6649. Fax 907/474-8448. www.alaska.net/~inn. 8 units. TV TEL. High season $135 double. Low season $75 double. Extra person $25. Rates include full breakfast. CB, DC, DISC, MC, V.

This charming and comfortable country inn stands on a pleasant residential street a couple of blocks from the downtown core. Each cozy room has its own inspired decorative details, and the housekeeping has always been perfect when I have visited. For socializing, a series of large, elegant common rooms connect downstairs, where you'll find a bar with hot drinks and a sun porch with books and games. Complimentary newspapers come with the full breakfast and there is a self-service laundry. No smoking.

✪ **Fairbanks Exploration Inn.** 505 Illinois St., Fairbanks, AK 99701. ☎ **888/452-1920** (outside Alaska) or 907/451-1920. Fax 907/455-7317. www.feinn.com. 16 units, 14 with private bathroom. TEL. Summer $130 double, $175 suite. Winter $85 double; $105 suite. Extra person $25. Rates include breakfast. AE, MC, V.

Executives of the Fairbanks Exploration Co. lived in these bungalows—the inn takes its name from that early gold mining operation—then left them vacant for 20 years to be rescued, lovingly restored, and made into Alaska's best historic accommodation, near the rail depot. Light streams in through screen porches and big, double-hung windows onto wood floors. There are white walls framed with varnished moldings and hung with contemporary fine art, as well as crisp period furnishings and working fireplaces. The service is professional. Port and sherry in the evening and breakfast delicacies in the morning are included in the price of the room. It's not flawless, though. Besides the high prices, the rooms can be too cool, most rooms have only showers (no tubs), many lack closets, all have only one bed (you can get a roll-away in a suite), and you may have to request a TV and VCR.

✪ **River's Edge Resort Cottages.** 4200 Boat St., Fairbanks, AK 99709. Take Sportsman Way off Airport Way to Boat St. ☎ **800/770-3343** or 907/474-0286. Fax 907/474-3665. www.riversedge.net. TV TEL. 86 cottages, 8 suites. High season $165–$180 double. Low season $89 double. Extra person age 12 and over $10. AE, MC, V.

These trim little cottages stand in a grassy compound along the gentle Chena River, where guests can fish for grayling. Inside, each cottage is an excellent standard hotel room, with high ceilings and two queen beds. Outside, they're like a little village, where guests can sit on the patio, watch the river go by, and socialize. The owners got the idea for the place from their RV park next door, when they noticed how their guests enjoyed visiting together in the open with their own private units to retreat to. It's perfect for families, as the outdoor areas are safe for playing and noise inside won't bother the neighbors. A large restaurant sits at river's edge, with dining on a deck or inside at round, oak tables. Dinner entrees are $8 to $20—steak, seafood, and down-home cooking. A breakfast buffet is served in the summer for $8.95.

A Taste of Alaska Lodge. 551 Eberhardt Rd. (turn right 5.3 miles out Chena Hot Springs Rd.), Fairbanks, AK 99712. ☎ **907/488-7855.** Fax 907/488-3772. www.tasteofalaska.com. 8 units, 2 cabins. TV TEL. $150 double; cabin $175–$200. Extra person $25. Rates include full breakfast. AE, MC, V.

Situated atop a grassy slope on 220 acres, facing Mount McKinley, the hand-crafted log main building feels like a wilderness lodge, but is less than half an hour from Fairbanks. You can enjoy a hot tub while taking in the view. Rooms are decorated with handmade quilts, brass beds, and other reproductions; and each has a door straight onto the grounds, where moose are often seen wandering. The cabins are large and especially luxurious.

Wedgewood Resort. 212 Wedgewood Dr., Fairbanks, AK 99701. ☎ **800/528-4916** or 907/452-1442. Fax 907/451-6376. www.fountainheadhotels.com. 157 units, 294 apts. A/C TV TEL. High season $182 double; $160 apt for 2. Low season $80 apt for 2, regular double rooms not offered. Extra person in apt $10. AE, DC, DISC, MC, V.

Off College Road near the Creamer's Field Refuge, this huge, well-kept hotel sprawls across a grassy, 23-acre complex in eight large buildings. Seven of them are converted three-story apartment buildings, newly remodeled, without elevators but with large living rooms, separate dining areas, fully equipped kitchens, air conditioners, TVs, and phones with voice mail in both the living room and bedroom, and balconies. The convenience of this kind of suite is hard to exaggerate—the main difference from home is that someone else cleans up after you. Another 157 standard hotel rooms are large and thoughtfully designed, if somewhat antiseptic. They mostly house package tour groups in summer and are closed in winter. (I would choose an apartment, but if you don't have your own car, you'll be hiking back and forth to the buildings and up the stairs a lot, so travelers with mobility issues might prefer the more centrally located though smaller regular rooms.) All units have irons, coffeemakers, and hair dryers. There are two restaurants, one with pleasant outdoor tables, sharing a brief menu (entrees $16 to $25) and are open only in the summer. A scheduled courtesy van runs to the airport and train depot. Another van runs in the evening, traveling to various sites for a small fee. Coin-op laundries are scattered around the property.

Westmark Fairbanks. 813 Noble St., Fairbanks, AK 99701-4977. ☎ **800/544-0970** (reservations), or 907/456-7722. Fax 907/451-7478. www.westmarkhotels.com. 244 units. TV TEL. High season $179–199 double. Low season $99–$129 double. Extra person $15. AE, DC, DISC, MC, V.

Taking up a full block downtown, the Westmark Fairbanks (not to be confused with the seasonal and somewhat less expensive Westmark Inn on South Cushman Street) fulfills the role of the city's grand, central hotel. A recent remodeling helps it hold that image, with an impressive lobby on Tenth Street, but the rooms, in a series of buildings surrounding a central courtyard, remain uneven in quality. Some are large and fresh, with new furniture, while others are worn, dated, and grossly overpriced. Make a choice when you check in. Facilities include a courtesy van, tour desk, cafe, lounge, and gift shop.

MODERATE

Cloudberry Lookout Bed and Breakfast. Off Goldhill Road (P.O. Box 84511), Fairbanks, AK 99708. ☎ **907/479-7334.** www.mosquitonet.com/~cloudbry. 5 units, 4 with private bathroom. $85–$105 double. Extra person $25. Rates include full breakfast. AE, DISC, MC, V. Closed Dec–Feb.

Back amid the spruces on the edge of town, near its own small pond, a house with a 60-foot wooden tower in its center rises up like a vision. Sean McGuire and Suzi Lozo took 7 years to build this masterpiece of log carpentry, with huge, airy common rooms that radiate from a central spiral staircase that ascends to a high perch for viewing the aurora and countryside. Rooms vary greatly in size, but all are comfortable and decorated with family antiques. The couple serves a large breakfast and can tell you about their work in the local environmental community. Since the house is on wetland, it has finicky marine toilets.

Fairbanks Hotel. 517 Third Ave., Fairbanks, AK 99701. ☎ **888/329-4685** or 907/456-6411. Fax 907/456-1792. www.alaska.net/~fbxhotl. 35 units, 11 with private bathroom. TV TEL. High season $85–$109 double. Low season $40–$55 double. AE, DISC, MC, V.

Four women transformed a notorious flophouse into a trim art deco–style historic hotel, in the core of downtown. The proprietors aim for the feel of a small European hotel. Although quite small, the rooms are light and attractively decorated, including brass beds and other period touches. The neighborhood remains gritty, however, and the building has quirks, so it's wise to choose your room when checking in. The hotel offers a courtesy shuttle to the airport and railroad station, and rents bicycles.

✪ **Forget-Me-Not Lodge and the Aurora Express Bed and Breakfast.** 1540 Chena Ridge Rd. (P.O. Box 80128), Fairbanks, AK 99708. ☎ **800/221-0073** or 907/474-0949. Fax 907/474-8173. www.aurora-express.com. 10 units, 8 with private bathroom. $85–$150 double. Extra person $25. Rates include full breakfast. MC, V. Closed Nov–Apr.

Susan Wilson's late grandmother appeared to her in a dream and told her there would be a train on a bank below her house, on the family's 15 acres high in the hills south of Fairbanks. So Wilson went out and got a train—a still-growing collection that includes a pair of 1956 Pullman sleepers, a locomotive, a caboose, a dining car, and a World War II hospital car—and her husband, Mike, brought it all up the mountain to install below the house, right in the spot indicated. Some cars are close to their original form, and Susan says older guests weep over the memories they bring back. Others were elaborately remodeled into small rooms on themes related to Fairbanks history. One 85-foot-long car is meant for families, with railroad-theme decor, puzzles, and toy trains. Then there's the incredible caboose, dedicated to Grandma. Three rooms in the house are sumptuous. The family often serves breakfast in gold rush costumes. They're located 6.5 miles out of town, so you will need your own car if you stay here.

Minnie Street Bed & Breakfast Inn. 345 Minnie St., Fairbanks, AK 99701. ☎ **888/456-1849** or 907/456-1802. Fax 907/451-1751. www.minniestreetbandb.com. 10 units, 6 with private bathroom. TV TEL. High season $100–$130 double; $145–$195 suite. Low season $50–$75 double; $100 suite. Extra person $20. Rates include full breakfast. AE, DISC, MC, V.

Just across the river from the downtown center, near the rail depot, two buildings around a garden courtyard contain clean, brightly decorated rooms with many amenities. In a new building, there's a dining room with a high vaulted ceiling and rooms supplied with robes, alarm clocks, hair dryers, closets, custom designed carpeting, handmade quilts, and stylish furniture. Every room has its own outside phone line. Suites have kitchens, and one is a full two-bedroom apartment.

INEXPENSIVE

Golden North Motel. 4888 Old Airport Way, Fairbanks, AK 99709. ☎ **800/447-1910** or 907/479-6201. Fax 907/479-5766. www.akpub.com/goldennorth. 62 units. TV TEL. $69 double; $99 suite. Rates include continental breakfast. AE, CB, DC, DISC, MC, V.

The Baer family, owners since 1971, keep the rooms in this two-story motel clean and up-to-date, making it a good bargain favored by Alaskans who've come to town from the Bush to shop or just visit by car. The standard rooms are quite small, but the reasonably priced suites are a good choice for families. The building is a nondescript brown rectangle, but bright flower boxes lighten the outdoor walkways and the location is near the airport. The motel provides a courtesy van to the airport or railroad station and free continental breakfast and coffee in the office.

Grandma Shirley's Hostel. 510 Dunbar St., Fairbanks, AK 99701. ☎ **907/451-9816.** 14 bunks. $16.25 per person.

Shirley runs a really exceptional hostel, competing with four others in town to be the most comfortable and hospitable. Instead of sleeping bags, she puts linen on the beds, and instead of a coin-op laundry, she washes your stuff and brings it back folded for $4 a load. Guests can come and go at any hour and use the kitchen until 10pm; she provides free coffee and cocoa. She loans bikes free, too, with a $10 deposit. Men and women sleep in the same bunk rooms, and share a single shower.

CAMPING

Tent camping is a good way to go in Fairbanks, with its mild summers and ample public lands. Right in town, the **Chena River State Recreation Site** (not to be confused with the recreation "area" of the same name described in the next section of this chapter), is located where University Avenue crosses the river. Riverside sites are surrounded by birch. The self-service fee is $15, $10 for walk-in camping. Getting a bit out of town, there are superb public campgrounds at Chena Lakes Recreation Area (see "Special Places" under "Getting Outside," above) and along Chena Hot Springs Road (covered in section 4 of this chapter).

Fairbanks has plenty of RV parks, some with full service and then some. Pick up a list at the visitor center. Among the best is **River's Edge RV Park and Campground,** at a wooded riverside bend of the Chena at 4140 Boat St., off Airport Way and Sportsman Way (☎ **800/770-3343** or 907/474-0286; www.riversedge.net), with lots of services, including free shuttles and organized tours. Full hookups are $25 and tent camping $15.50. The same people operate the cottage resort and restaurant next door.

DINING

DOWNTOWN

✪ **Gambardella's Italian Cafe.** 706 Second Ave. ☎ **907/456-3417.** www.gambardellas.com. Main courses $9.50–$17; lunch $6–$10. 15% gratuity added for parties of 5 or more, or for split checks. AE, MC, V. Mon–Sat 11am–10pm, Sun 4–10pm. ITALIAN.

Gambardella's doesn't disappoint—it's one of Alaska's best restaurants. My halibut was very fresh, deftly seasoned, on light, rich pasta, with mixed vegetables that miraculously were all done perfectly, even mushrooms and carrots side by side. The lasagna is justly famous. Dining rooms are narrow and long, with high ceilings and well-scuffed wooden floors, and bend around a corner—pleasingly noisy but intimate at the same time. On a sunny day, eat on the patio among the hanging flowers. The service is quick and professional, the prices reasonable, and the desserts, baked in-house, not to be missed. Beer and wine are served.

Souvlaki. 310 First Ave. ☎ **907/452-5393.** Main courses $5.25–$6.25. MC, V. Summer, Mon–Fri 10am–9pm, Sat 10am–6pm. Winter, Mon–Sat 10am–6pm. GREEK.

Drop in here for a quick, inexpensive lunch or dinner. Besides the tasty Greek dishes, this place serves sandwiches, salads, and some Mexican food from a brief menu. Servings are light. Families will do well, occupying one of the small, single-party rooms off the main dining room. The desserts, baked in-house, are memorable. Souvlaki also operates a take-out place at Alaskaland in the summer.

✪ **Thai House.** 526 Fifth Ave. ☎ **907/452-6123.** Lunch items $6.25–$8; dinner main courses $9–$11. MC, V. Mon–Sat 11am–4pm and 5–10pm. THAI.

In a small, brightly lit storefront in the downtown area, this is a simple, family run restaurant with authentic Thai cuisine. The last time I ate there, the food came quickly, it was deftly seasoned and cooked to a turn, and the bill was so small I thought it was a mistake. Such gems may be common in cities with large ethnic communities, but in Fairbanks, this place stands out.

WITHIN DRIVING DISTANCE

Besides the restaurants listed here, there's the salmon bake at Alaskaland, described above, and the Ester Gold Camp, below. Also, in town, near the university at 3702 Cameron Street, off University Road, **Sam's Sourdough Cafe** (☎ **907/479-0523**) is a masterpiece in the art of the greasy spoon, with quick, friendly service, creative burgers, great milk shakes, and breakfast all day. They're open 6am to 10pm, and it's a bit smoky.

The Bakery. 69 College Rd. ☎ **907/456-8600.** Lunch items $4–$8; dinner main courses $7.25–$17. MC, V. Mon–Sat 6am–9pm, Sun 7am–4pm. DINER.

There are an infinite number of old-fashioned coffee shops in and around Fairbanks—the kind of place where a truck driver or gold miner can find a big, hearty meal, a motherly waitress, and a bottomless cup of coffee. This is the best of the lot, which is really saying something. The sourdough pancakes are memorable, the menu is long and inexpensive, the service is friendly, and the quality of the baked goods testified to by the number of police cars always in the parking lot. The Formica tables are worn down from years of wiping. No liquor license.

Pike's Landing. 4438 Airport Way. ☎ **907/479-6500.** Main courses $20–$55; lunch items $9–$13.50. AE, DC, DISC, MC, V. Daily 11:30am–2:30pm and 5–11pm. STEAK/SEAFOOD.

The large dining room overlooking the Chena River near the airport is primarily a place for straightforward steak and seafood. It's all well prepared, with huge servings and occasional flashes of creativity in the more sophisticated fish dishes. For an inexpensive meal, the bar serves basic food on the deck over the river from 2:30pm to closing time. It's a pleasant choice on a sunny day, less so in cool or rainy weather, when it remains in operation behind plastic.

The Pump House Restaurant and Saloon. 1.3 Mile, Chena Pump Rd. ☎ **907/479-8452.** www.pumphouse.com. Main courses $15–$25. AE, DISC, MC, V. Summer daily 11:30am–1am; winter Mon–Fri 4pm–1am, Sat noon–1am, Sun 10am–1am. STEAK/SEAFOOD.

The historic, rambling building on the Chena River is elaborately decorated and landscaped with authentic gold rush relics. Sitting on the deck, you can watch the riverboat paddle by or a group in canoes stop for appetizers and drinks from the full bar. It's a jolly place, good for groups. The dinner menu includes the usual steak and seafood, which are the best items to choose (a more ambitious entree I ordered was overseasoned and inappropriately doused in cheese).

✪ **Two Rivers Lodge/Tuscan Gardens.** 4968 Chena Hot Springs Rd. ☎ **907/488-6815.** Main courses $12–$27. AE, DC, DISC, MC, V. Mon–Fri 5–10pm, Sat–Sun 3–10pm. STEAK/SEAFOOD/NORTHERN ITALIAN.

Inside the log lodge building, chef Tony Marsico brings interesting touches to a steak and seafood menu—such as his wonderful soups, about which he's published a cookbook. The creamy, complex king crab bisque, in a bowl of sourdough bread with a layer of cheese on top, put me in a contemplative reverie. Service is friendly but not necessarily quick—it's a place to settle in for an evening of dining. Outside, on a deck over the duck pond, a whole separate operation serves meals from a brick Tuscan oven in the open air, operating only in fine weather. Start there for appetizers, or eat a whole inexpensive Tuscan meal under the evening sun. There are full bars at both spots. The drive from Fairbanks is about 25 minutes.

NIGHTLIFE

Fairbanks has a lot of tourist-oriented evening activities, as well as entertainment also attended by locals. Call the 24-hour event recording of what's playing currently (☎ **907/456-INFO**) or get a copy of the *Fairbanks Daily News-Miner.* The best of the summer arts scene is at the ✪ **Fairbanks Summer Arts Festival** (☎ **907/474-8869;** see "Special Events" under "Essentials," at the beginning of this section). There also are **movie theaters**—a large multiplex is located on Airport Way. The evening show at the **Palace Theater** is discussed above under "Alaskaland."

The Ester Gold Camp (☎ **800/676-6925** or 907/479-2500; www.alaskasbest.com/ester) is an 11-building historic site, an old mining town that's been turned into an evening tourist attraction. The main event is a gold rush theme show at the Malamute Saloon, with singing and Robert Service poetry, nightly at 9pm; admission is $14. A "photosymphony" slide show about the aurora takes place every summer evening at 6:45 and 7:45 and costs $8. There's also a restaurant that serves a buffet and has mess-hall seating for $15.95 for adults, $7.95 for big kids, and $4.95 for little kids. If you have crab, it's $25.95 for adults. The gift shop is open in the evening, and there are simple, inexpensive rooms in the old gold-mine bunkhouse. A free bus is available from major hotels in Fairbanks.

The **Howling Dog Saloon,** north of town in Fox (☎ **907/457-8780**), claims to be the "farthest north rock 'n' roll club in the world." That's questionable, but the bar with the dancing dog on the roof does have a reputation for a rowdy good time. The music is classic rock and blues; a selection of 17 craft brews is on tap at $4 each, while regular American beer is $2.75; and there's no cover charge. Outside there are volleyball nets, horseshoe pits, and the like. The saloon usually closes for a few months in midwinter.

3 Nenana: Parks Highway Sidetrack

Although there's little to justify a special trip, you might spend a pleasant hour or two wandering the deserted streets of Nenana, a little riverside town an hour's drive south of Fairbanks, as you travel the Parks Highway to Denali National Park or Anchorage. The town has a unique memory, keeping alive a sleepy, riverbank lifestyle Samuel Clemens might have found familiar. The Tanana River docks still serve barges pushed by river tugboats, carrying the winter's fuel and supplies to roadless villages across the region. The Alaska Railroad still rumbles through, although it made its last stop at the depot in 1983, passing the spot where President Warren G. Harding drove the golden spike marking the line's completion on July 15, 1923. (The first president to visit Alaska, Harding died soon after the trip, supposedly from eating some bad Alaska shellfish—but we don't believe that, now *do* we?)

A log cabin **visitor center** stands at the intersection of the highway and A Street, the main business street. The friendly hosts will engage you in conversation and try to entice you farther into the town. At the other end of A Street, by the river, the old railroad station has been made, with little meddling, into the **Nenana Depot Museum** (☎ **907/832-5500**), with a gift shop chock-full of Alaska Railroad memorabilia. Time seems to have simply stopped in the museum, where you'll find old documents, scales, and other items from the past era. The golden spike is displayed outside.

A block down Front Street, along the river, **St. Mark's Episcopal Church** is the town's most historic and loveliest building; its 1905 log cabin construction remains unspoiled, even though the church is still in use. The church predates most of the town, which was built as a railroad camp. You'll probably have to track down a key to get a look inside at the hand-carved pews and moose-hide altar cloth; ask at the visitor center.

On the left of Front Street, you can see the **barge docks,** and a block farther on the riverfront, the **Alfred Starr Nenana Cultural Center** (☎ **907/832-5520**). The center is a meeting and display venue for local art and cultural history, with a strong emphasis on the Athabaskan people of the area. Besides the museum displays—an engaging set of items that locals feel are important enough to share—don't miss the **Alphonse Demientieff Wheelhouse Gift Shop.** Much of the Athabaskan art and craft work there is of exceptional quality, and items are displayed with biographies of their makers. Prices were low when I visited.

Nenana's main claim to fame is the **Nenana Ice Classic** (☎ **907/832-5446;** www.ptialaska.net/~tripod), a traditional statewide gambling event since 1917 in which contestants try to predict the exact date and time of the ice breakup on the Tanana. The pot of $2 tickets builds to over $100,000 by spring, but it's generally shared among several winners who pick the same time. The town kicks off the classic each February with a celebration that includes dancing and dog-mushing races and the raising of the "four-legged tripod," a black-and-white log marker whose movement with the ice indicates that spring has arrived and that someone, somewhere, has won a lot of money. Usually it happens sometime in May. You can consult a thick book of past guesses at the visitor center.

4 Chena Hot Springs Road

The 57-mile paved road east from Fairbanks is an avenue to an enjoyable day trip or a destination for up to a week's outdoor activities and hot-spring swimming. Of all the roads radiating from Fairbanks, this short highway will be most rewarding to most outdoors people, as well as providing some of the best remote lodgings accessible on the Interior road system.

The road travels through the Chena River State Recreation Area, with spectacular hikes and float trips and well-maintained riverside campgrounds, and leads to the Chena Hot Springs, where there's a year-round resort perfect for soaking in hot mineral springs and for use as a base for summer or winter wilderness day trips. The resort is open to people who want to rent one of the comfortable rooms or to campers and day-trippers, and it's equally as popular in the winter as in the summer (the slow seasons are spring and fall). Japanese visitors especially make the pilgrimage in winter to see the northern lights, but Americans are discovering it as well.

The paved road leads through a forest of birch, spruce, and cottonwood, first passing an area of scattered roadside development and then following the Chena River through the state recreation area. It's a pleasant drive, around 1¼ hours each way from Fairbanks, but not particularly scenic. On a sunny summer weekend, the people of Fairbanks migrate to the riverside and the hiking trails; on a sunny winter weekend, they take to the hills on snowmobiles, cross-country skis, or dog sleds.

A pair of prospectors, the Swan brothers, discovered the hot springs in 1905, having heard that a U.S. Geological Survey crew had seen steam in a valley on the upper Chena. Thomas Swan suffered from rheumatism; incredibly, he and his brother poled up the Chena River from Fairbanks, found the hot springs, built a cabin and rock-floored pool, and spent the summer soaking. He was cured! More visitors followed, drawn by stories that whole groups of cripples were able to dance all night after soaking in the pools—by 1915 a resort was in operation, drawing worn-out miners and gold rush stampeders and many others as well. The resort has been in constant use ever since, and recently was bought by an aggressive new owner who is improving the fading accommodations.

ESSENTIALS

GETTING THERE The Chena Hot Springs Road meets the Steese Expressway about 10 miles north of downtown Fairbanks. (Details on renting a car in Fairbanks can be found at the beginning of section 2 of this chapter.) The resort offers rides from Fairbanks for $30 per person round-trip with a minimum of two passengers; one-way fares are not available.

VISITOR INFORMATION For outdoors information, check the Fairbanks **Alaska Public Lands Information Center,** 250 Cushman St. (at Third Avenue), Suite 1A, Fairbanks, AK 99701 (☎ **907/456-0527;** TTY 907/456-0532; fax 907/456-0514; www.nps.gov/aplic).

The **Alaska Division of Parks,** at 3700 Airport Way, Fairbanks, AK 99709 (☎ **907/451-2695;** www.dnr.state.ak.us/parks/parks.htm), manages the area and produces trail, river, and road guides, which are available at trailhead kiosks or from the public lands center. Contact them, also, to rent the public cabins in the area, which are described below. Call or check the Web site for information and availability, and then reserve by mail or in person up to 6 months ahead. Full payment is required to hold the reservation.

The **Chena Hot Springs Resort** owns and operates the springs; they're discussed below.

STOPS ALONG THE ROAD

Don't miss a stop at **Tacks General Store,** at mile 23.5, in Two Rivers (☎ **907/488-3242**). The old-fashioned country store and post office is a center of the rural community, a friendly place to stop for breakfast, lunch, or pie. Only one item is on the menu for each meal, but there may be a dozen or more kinds of pie. The pie is so good Fairbanks families drive out on the weekend just for a slice. The crude dining room is like a picnic area. They're open 8am to 8pm daily.

Also on the road are the **Two Rivers Lodge,** a fine-dining establishment and bar, and **A Taste of Alaska Lodge,** a bed-and-breakfast. They are listed in "Dining" and "Accommodations" respectively in section 2 of this chapter, on Fairbanks.

THE CHENA RIVER STATE RECREATION AREA

The recreation area takes in 254,000 acres along the river valley and over the rolling mountains of heather around it. Some of Interior Alaska's best hiking and floating are found here. As everywhere in the Interior, the mosquitoes are brutal.

ACTIVITIES

HIKING & BACKPACKING The best trail hikes in the Fairbanks area are in the Chena Hot Springs State Recreation Area. Backcountry camping requires no permit, and many of the trails go above the tree line, so it's a good area for backpackers to get into the wilderness.

The **Angel Rocks Trail** is a sometimes steep 3½-mile loop to an immense granite outcropping, an impressive destination with good views of the valley below. The trail mostly stays below the tree line. The trailhead is well marked, at mile 48.9 of the road.

The 15-mile loop of the **Granite Tors Trail,** starting at mile 39 of the road, is a challenging day hike, rising through forest to rolling alpine terrain, but the towering tors more than reward the effort. Like surrealist experiments in perspective, these monolithic granite sentinels stand at random spots on the broad Plain of Monuments, at first confounding the eye's attempts to gauge their distance and size. Like the Angel Rocks, they were created when upwelling rock solidified in cracks in the surrounding earth, which then eroded away. Water is scarce, so bring along plenty. This is an excellent overnight hike, with the driest ground for camping right around the tors, and there is also a public shelter halfway along.

For a longer backpacking trip, the **Chena Dome Trail** makes a 30-mile loop, beginning at mile 50.5 and ending at mile 49. The 3 miles nearest the road at either end pass through forest, but the remaining 23 miles are above the tree line, marked with cairns, and with expansive views, summiting 4,421-foot Chena Dome after the 10-mile mark. The trail can be quite wet and muddy in parts and steep and rocky elsewhere. Two public shelters are on the trail.

RIVER FLOATING The Chena is a lovely river, growing from a clear, frothy creek near the end of the road to a lazy Class I river as it flows off toward Fairbanks, several days downstream. Where you choose to start depends on your experience. Easier water is downstream from Rosehip Campground (mile 27), with the slowest of all nearer Fairbanks, but the upper portion is more popular if you are up for something a bit more challenging. The road crosses the river several times, and the state park system has developed other access points, so it's possible to plan a float that exactly matches your time and abilities. Use the State Parks river guide to choose your route.

Canoe Alaska (☎ **907/479-5183**) offers instruction and guided trips; an introductory clinic is $165. **7 Bridges Boats and Bikes,** 4312 Birch Lane, Fairbanks (☎ **907/479-0751;** www.7gablesinn.com/7bbb/), rents canoes for $35 per day, and will drop you off and pick you up for $1.50 per mile out of town.

FISHING Several of the ponds are stocked with trout, which you can keep; signs along the road mark access points. You can catch-and-release arctic grayling in the Chena, depending on the current regulations and bait restrictions. Check with the

Alaska Department of Fish and Game, 1300 College Rd., Fairbanks, AK 99701 (☎ **907/459-7207**).

CAMPING & CABINS

Three beautiful campgrounds with water and pit toilets lie along the road by the Chena River, managed by the Alaska Division of Parks (see "Visitor Information," above). Although they can't be reserved ahead, the campgrounds are unlikely to be full. The **Rosehip Campground,** at mile 27, has 37 sites, well separated by spruce and birch, with six suitable for RVs. Some sites are right on the river, and some are reserved for more private tent camping, back in the woods. The **Granite Tors Campground** is across the road from the trailhead at mile 39; it has 24 sites, seven suitable for RVs. Some sites have river frontage, and, as at Rosehip, float trips start here. Sites at each of those campgrounds are $10 a night. The **Red Squirrel Campground,** at mile 42.8, has 12 sites and a pleasant picnic area on the grassy edge of a small, placid pond, where swimming is permitted. Camping is $5 per vehicle.

There are several public-use cabins in the recreation area, two of them easily accessible to summer visitors. (See "Visitor Information," above, for reservation information.) These are small, primitive cabins, and you must bring your own sleeping bags, lights, and cooking gear. The **North Fork Cabin** is at mile 47.7 of the road and the large, new **Chena River Cabin** faces the river at mile 32.2. You can get to either by car or canoe, and they cost $35 a night. Other public cabins in the area primarily serve winter users and are difficult to reach when the ground thaws.

THE HOT SPRINGS

Our family has enjoyed wonderful days here swimming and exploring, but this is not a sophisticated resort. It's a place to romp in the pool, hike through the woods, and enjoy the sound of the wind in the trees. The hot springs heat the buildings and, mixed with cold water, supply an indoor pool and a series of hot tubs and spas. A large outdoor pool has been built but is not in use at this writing because of problems with government regulators. The existing indoor swimming pool is kept cool enough to swim, but it's small and can be overcrowded and noisy with children during the day. The locker rooms are undersized, so guests will want to change in their rooms. Having various hot tubs and spas allows you to soak at your chosen temperature, inside or outside. The swimming facility is open daily 7am to midnight; no one under age 18 allowed after 10pm. Swim passes come with your room if you're staying at the resort; for campers or day-trippers, a day pass is $8 for ages 13 to 55, $6 for age 6 to 12 and over 55, free children 5 and under.

ACCOMMODATIONS

The resort has an RV parking area with electric hookups and two campgrounds. A tent campground with outhouses wraps itself around the bends in a creek. All camping sites are $20 per night. Campers can use a dump station free.

✪ **The Chena Hot Springs Resort.** Mile 56.5, Chena Hot Springs Rd. (P.O. Box 73440), Fairbanks, AK 99707. ☎ **800/478-4681** or 907/452-7867. Fax 907/456-3122. www.chenahotsprings.com. 80 units, 11 cabins. $125–$170 double; $190–$200 suite. Extra person $20. AE, DC, DISC, MC, V.

The resort, set on 440 acres of land in a bowl of mountains, invites a slow pace, with plenty of time spent soaking or walking. Families love it, while couples may prefer to go during school days when the pool is quieter. In the winter, the aurora viewing is exceptional here, away from city lights, and you can enjoy Nordic skiing, snow-cat and snow-machine tours, skating, sled-dog rides, and more. In the summer, you can go horseback riding, rafting, hiking, gold panning, or mountain biking. There's also a large new activity building. A 6-mile alpine ridge trail links to the Angel Rocks trail described above.

The rooms range from the crude, original cabins built by the prospectors who discovered the area to large new hotel rooms with television, phones, and coffeemakers. The larger cabins—not the prospectors' originals—are crude but adequate for a family or group looking for inexpensive lodgings and not particular about indoor plumbing. The lodge building contains the restaurant and bar, with a brief but sufficiently varied menu with prices only slightly above town. I've eaten well there; however, staffing appears to be a problem of late, and my last meal was poor.

5 The Steese Highway

The Steese Highway leads from Fairbanks 162 miles northeast to Circle, a village on the Yukon River about 50 miles south of the Arctic Circle (they were mistaken about the town's exact location when they named it—oh well). The historic gold rush route parallels the Davidson Ditch, a huge aqueduct and pipe that carried water to the mining operations near Fairbanks. Small-time miners and prospectors still scratch the hills. They bring their gold into the bar in Central, where they can get a shower and the current metal price is posted on the wall. **Arctic Circle Hot Springs** is out here, too, with a big, hot outdoor pool.

There are a couple of good hikes from the road, and it provides many access points to **river floats.** The clear, Class I water of the Chatanika River is perfect for day trips or relaxed expeditions of a week or more. And the road meets two National Wild and Scenic Rivers: Beaver Creek, for trips of a week or more over easy Class I water, and Birch Creek, for more experienced paddlers. Get *The Alaska River Guide,* mentioned at the beginning of this chapter in a sidebar called "Rollin' on the River," for detailed guidance, and check with the Alaska Public Lands Information Center, below.

The Steese is paved only for the first 40 miles, and you can drive only so fast on these rural gravel roads without bouncing into a ditch. Besides the bumps, you must go slowly and pull to the side to avoid rocks thrown up by vehicles going the other direction. Consequently, you'll spend much of your day in the car going out the highway—driving both ways in one day would be absurd. On the other hand, the overnight accommodations to be had on the highway are below many people's standards, and if you're not interested in a hike, float trip, or hot springs soak, there isn't that much to do. Arctic Circle Hot Springs is the main attraction—more on that below. If you go, above all, take mosquito repellent.

ESSENTIALS

GETTING THERE The Steese turns to gravel 40 miles out of Fairbanks. Most car rental agencies won't allow their vehicles to drive gravel roads, but **National Car Rental,** at 1246 Noble St. in downtown Fairbanks (☎ **800/227-7368** or 907/451-7368), is an exception.

VISITOR INFORMATION For information on the outdoors, check with the **Alaska Public Lands Information Center,** 250 Cushman St. (at Third Avenue), Suite 1A, Fairbanks, AK 99701 (☎ **907/456-0527;** TTY 907/456-0532; fax 907/456-0514; www.nps.gov/aplic).

The federal **Bureau of Land Management (BLM),** 1150 University Ave., Fairbanks, AK 99709 (☎ **907/474-2200;** wwwndo.ak.blm.gov), manages most of the land and campgrounds. Their Web site contains detailed information about campgrounds, trails and rivers (click on "Site Map" and scroll down to "Recreation"), and even a Web cam of the view outside the office.

Check for business information with the **Fairbanks Convention and Visitors Bureau,** at 550 First Ave. (at Cushman Street), Fairbanks, AK 99701 (☎ **800/327-5774** or 907/456-5774; www.explorefairbanks.com).

A HIGHWAY LOG

11 MILES The Steese and Elliot highways split, the Steese heading east into hilly, wooded land. The big piles of gravel and the machinery you may see in the trees are the many-years-old remains of the environmentally destructive form of mining practiced in this region, which requires the excavation and sorting of large amounts of gravel.

28 MILES **Chatanika,** an old gold-mining settlement, has a couple of roadhouses where you can stop for a burger, a beer, and, if necessary, a room or place to park your RV. **Chatanika Lodge,** 5760 Old Steese Hwy. N. (☎ **907/389-2164**), is a thriving and authentic roadhouse with a large bar in which to immerse yourself in local ways amid every kind of animal trophy, a collection of signed dollar bills, and 21,000 Christmas lights (we didn't count them, but the proprietor seemed honest). This place serves good, simple food and rents clean rooms with TVs for $60 a night double. It's a popular snowmobiling hangout and the scene of an **Outhouse Race** during Chatanika Days, the second weekend in March. Snowmobiles rent next door, at **Snow RV** (☎ **907/389-7669**) for $55 for 2 hours, and you can hire a guide for $65 for that time.

Beyond Chatanika, there's little more in the way of any kind of services from here to Central.

30 MILES The University of Alaska's **Poker Flat Research Range** (☎ **907/474-7558**) is marked by a small rocket by the road. This is where the Geophysical Institute launches rockets to study the aurora and other high-altitude phenomena. Tours are scheduled every other Friday in the summer at 1:30pm. Call to confirm before making the drive.

39 MILES The inviting state parks' **Upper Chatanika River Campground** sits on the river below a bridge on the highway, with 35 sites, pit toilets, and a hand pump for water. Camping is $10. There are grayling in the river, and it's a good spot to start or end a Chatanika float trip. State Parks produces a brochure covering the 12-hour float to the Elliot Highway, available from the Alaska Public Lands Information Center. The road is paved for another 5 miles, slowly rising along the Chatanika with some good views.

42.5 MILES A pull-out here at the McKay Creek Trailhead offers access to the **White Mountains National Recreation Area,** a 1-million-acre area managed by the BLM with some summer hiking trails, lots of rafting opportunities, more than 200 miles of winter trails with cabins, and extensive recreational gold mining.

57 MILES The 1928 **Davidson Ditch** water pipeline is along here—it's not much to look at, just a big rusted pipe. It siphoned water 80 miles to mining operations nearer Fairbanks. The U.S. Creek Road intersects to the left, or north, branching after 6 miles into the Nome Creek Road, which runs east and west along the creek to two campgrounds, trails, and river recreation within the BLM's White Mountains National Recreation Area. It's a well-maintained gravel way over scenic hills. The 19-site **Ophir Creek Campground** is 12 miles west of the T (18 miles from the Steese Highway), a put-in for a long float of Beaver Creek. The self-service camping fee is $6. At the other end of the road, 4 miles east of the T (10 miles from the Steese), is the

Mt. Prindle Campground, with 13 treeless sites and a $6 fee. The high country beckons here by way of the 16-mile Quartz Creek Trail, open to all-terrain vehicles and hikers.

60 MILES The 12-site BLM campground at **Cripple Creek** has a ½-mile nature trail and put-in for Chatanika River floats. This is the last public campground on the highway. The fee is $6.

86 MILES The drive becomes really spectacular from here to just short of Central, as it climbs over rounded, windblown, tundra-clothed mountaintops at **Twelvemile Summit.** There's a parking lot for interpretive signs and the lower end of the BLM's 28-mile **Pinnell Mountain Trail,** a challenging 3-day hike over this amazing terrain. (The upper trailhead is at Eagle Summit.) There are two emergency shelters on the way for protection from the ferocious weather that can sweep the mountains. Get the free BLM trail guide from one of the agencies listed above. Over the next 20 miles, the scars you see in the land are from gold mining.

94 MILES The **Upper Birch Creek** wayside is the put-in point for a challenging 126-mile wild river float trip, taking out at mile 140. For a more doable trip, put in at mile 140 and float an easy 15 miles of Birch Creek through scenic country to a bridge at mile 147.

107 MILES **Eagle Summit,** at 3,624 feet, is the highest place on the highway, and the best place to be on June 21 each year (the summer solstice). Although still a degree of latitude below the Arctic Circle, the sun never sets here on the longest day because of the elevation and atmospheric refraction. People come out from Fairbanks and make a celebration of it. The midnight sun is visible for about 3 days before and after the solstice, too, assuming the sky is clear. The BLM has installed a toilet and a viewing deck on a 750-foot loop trail.

CENTRAL

After descending from the mountains and entering a forest of spruce that continues to the Yukon, the road at mile 128 suddenly reaches a stretch of pavement and is surrounded by the spectral white trunks of paper birches—like a breath of fresh air after hours bouncing over gravel. You're in the friendly little gold-mining town of Central. We were made to feel like we were the first tourists ever to come this far. From Central you can turn right for the 8-mile drive to Arctic Circle Hot Springs, or continue straight on the Steese for a featureless 34-mile drive to Circle.

The big annual event is the **miners picnic** in August. The town's main attraction is the **Central Museum** (☎ **907/520-1893**), which concentrates on the gold mining that has sustained the area since 1893. It's surprisingly good for a town of this size. Admission is $1 for adults, 50¢ for children; it's open Memorial Day to Labor Day, daily from noon to 5pm.

There are two restaurants, both with acceptable rural diner food. The **Central Motor Inn** (☎ **907/520-5228**) is a bit more ambitious in its menu, although smoky and dark when we visited. They serve food daily from 7am to 11pm all year (the bar is virtually always open). Its six rooms, with TVs and private bathrooms, rent for $60 as a double. A shower is $3, and there's a coin-op laundry and a gas pump. The other establishment, **Crabb's Corner** (☎ **907/520-5599**), at the corner of Circle Hot Springs Road and the Steese, has good, basic food in the bar as well as a tiny grocery, liquor store, and gas station. It seemed the cleaner of the two restaurants. Their pleasant campground among the birches costs $7 a night. Both places accept MasterCard and Visa.

Don't miss taking the 8-mile side trip to **Arctic Circle Hot Springs,** mile 8, Circle Hot Springs Rd. (☎ **907/520-5113**). The main draw is the large outdoor pool, fed directly by the hot springs. (A daily pool pass is $5; families of four or more pay $16.) In wintertime, Fairbanksans like to come out here for snowmobiling and to swim outdoors in subzero weather, toasty warm in the water while their hair freezes. The hotel offers massage and can arrange flightseeing and dog sledding, but it's not a center of resort activities as much as a place to taste, for a day or two, a slice of Alaska's rural past. The patched authenticity of the big, frame lodge is undeniable, confirmed by the blend of lacy antiques and simply old stuff dating from the 1940s through the 60s. The main house has 24 rooms with shared bathrooms; there are 12 cabins, some with water and some without; and five hostel cubbyholes in the eaves of the lodge. Everything is unique, but the hospitable management will try to suit your taste. Rates in the main building range from $74 to $125; cabins are $85 to $110 and hostlers pay $20. They accept MasterCard and Visa, and it's wise to reserve ahead for holiday periods. The camping area is suitable only for self-contained RVs. The comfortable dining room is typically open 8am to 9pm, year-round, and was serving excellent home-style meals from a short menu when we last visited.

CIRCLE

Another 34 miles past Central along the winding gravel road is a collection of log buildings and fewer than 100 people—mostly Athabascans—at the town of Circle. The Yukon flows by, broad and flat like a big field of water; it looks as if you could walk right across it, but the gray water is moving swiftly westward. As broad as it is, you can see only the nearest channel from Circle. The boat launch has a sign with facts about the river. Boaters can put in here bound for the town of Fort Yukon or the Dalton Highway to the west; the Dalton Highway bridge is 300 miles downstream. Or you can use Circle as a take-out after coming down from Eagle, 550 miles away by road but only about 158 miles and 5 days to a week over the water. The village has basic services, but nothing in itself worth a visit.

6 The Dalton Highway

Although it was built to service the trans-Alaska pipeline, one of humankind's largest private construction projects, the glory of the 414-mile Dalton Highway is the wilderness it passes through. Running straight through Interior Alaska to the Arctic coast, the Dalton crosses all kinds of scenic terrain, including forested rounded hills, the rugged peaks of the Brooks Range, and the treeless plains of the North Slope. This is still some of the most remote and untouched land on the globe. To the west of the highway, Gates of the Arctic National Park protects 8.4 million acres of the Brooks Range, part of protected wilderness that spans from the Canadian border to the Chukchi Sea. Beyond the thin ribbon of the gravel highway, only a few thousand human beings a year venture into that vastness.

Wildlife shows up all along the road, from grizzly bears to sport fish to songbirds. The road passes through Alaska's history of mineral extraction, too—there's the gold rush era town of Wiseman and the current oil industry complex at Prudhoe Bay. Also, the Dalton provides Fairbanks's closest access to the Yukon River. But surely the reason most people drive all the way on the Dalton is because of where it goes, and not what's there. It goes to the very end of the earth, as far north as you can drive. It's quite a rough trip to nowhere, but a dramatic one if you have the time and endurance.

The Dalton is known to most Alaskans as the Haul Road—it was built to haul supplies to the Prudhoe Bay oilfield and the northern half of the 800-mile pipeline. It remains a wilderness route, with little in the way of human habitation along the way. Coldfoot is the northernmost truck stop in the United States. Just 15 miles up the road from Coldfoot, Wiseman now is home to 20 people year-round.

That's it for settlement until you reach the modern industrial complex at Prudhoe Bay, where you must join a shuttle or tour to see the Arctic Ocean or the oilfield.

DALTON HIGHWAY ESSENTIALS

PRACTICAL TIPS You can drive the highway yourself, staying in the few motels along the way or in a tent or motor home. **National Car Rental,** in downtown Fairbanks at 1246 Noble St. (☎ **800/227-7368** or 907/451-7368), will allow renters to take some of its vehicles on the Dalton, though most other firms do not. The highway starts north of Fairbanks at mile 73 of the Elliot Highway—take the Steese Highway north from town until it becomes the Elliot. The total road distance from Fairbanks to the Arctic Ocean is 497 miles. Road conditions are notorious on the gravel-and-dirt Dalton, but now much of it is kept in good condition. Speeds of 50 miles per hour are possible on some of the road, while doing 35 will keep you in one piece on rougher spots. The drive takes 12 hours each way, without stops. It's dusty, shoulders are soft, and flat tires are common. For **road conditions,** call the state hot line (☎ **907/456-7623**).

Driving the Dalton Highway gets you into some remote territory, and you must take **precautions.** Services are up to 240 miles apart. Drive with your headlights on at all times. Bring at least one full-sized spare tire and extra gasoline. Insect repellent is an absolute necessity. Truck traffic is dominant. Slow down or even stop to allow trucks to pass you either way, and be careful on bridges, as some are not wide enough for two vehicles to pass safely. Also, pull off for views or pictures—don't just stop in the middle of the road, as some people do.

For those who want to let someone else do the driving, several companies offer a variety of bus packages. See section 9 of chapter 10, on Prudhoe Bay, for details.

VISITOR INFORMATION The best source of information on the Dalton Highway is Fairbanks's **Alaska Public Lands Information Center,** at 250 Cushman St. (at Third Avenue), Suite 1A, Fairbanks, AK 99701 (☎ **907/456-0527;** TTY 907/456-0532; fax 907/456-0514; www.nps.gov/aplic). Rangers there drive the road annually to keep their advice up to date.

Much of the road runs through land managed by the **Bureau of Land Management,** 1150 University Ave., Fairbanks, AK 99709 (☎ **907/474-2200;** aurora.ak.blm.gov/arcticinfo/). They publish extensive information for driving and recreation on the highway on their Web page and in the ***Dalton Highway Road Guide,*** which includes an indispensable map.

For information specific to Gates of the Arctic National Park, contact the **Park Headquarters,** at 201 First Ave., Fairbanks, AK 99707-4680 (☎ **907/456-0281;** www.nps.gov/gaar).

For information about businesses along the highway, try the **Fairbanks Convention and Visitors Bureau,** at 550 First Ave. (at Cushman Street), Fairbanks, AK 99701 (☎ **800/327-5774** or 907/456-5774; fax 907/452-2867; www.explorefairbanks.com).

Along the highway, there are two visitor information stops, both open summer only. A cabin **contact station** at the Yukon crossing is staffed by BLM volunteers and open daily in summer 9am to 6pm. It has no phone. A larger, **interagency center** is in Coldfoot (☎ **907/678-5209**), open 10am to 6pm daily.

ON THE ROAD

The bridge over the Yukon River at mile 56 is the only crossing in Alaska, and many people drive the Dalton just to get to the **Arctic Circle** at mile 115, where you'll find a colorful sign for pictures as well as a crude camping area. A number of places along the highway have incredible views, including Finger Mountain at mile 98; Gobbler's Knob at mile 132, which offers the first view of the Brooks Range; and 4,739-foot Atigun Pass at mile 245, where the road crosses the Brooks Range, winding through impossibly rugged country. The pass is the highest point on the Alaska road system, and you may find summer snow. All along the highway are opportunities to see birds and animals, including rabbits, foxes, wolves, moose, Dall sheep, bears, and caribou. Sit still if you want to see the skittish caribou, as they may wander closer to an unmoving vehicle.

The road parallels the 4-foot-wide **trans-Alaska pipeline.** The line, completed in 1977, serves America's largest and second-largest oil fields, Prudhoe Bay and Kuparuk, carrying the hot crude 900 miles from the Arctic Ocean to docks in Valdez, where tankers pick it up for shipment primarily to the West Coast. The public road ends before reaching the Prudhoe Bay complex and the Arctic Ocean. The only way through the gate is with a tour operator. See section 9 of chapter 10, on Prudhoe Bay, for details.

HIGHWAY SERVICES: FOOD, FUEL & LODGINGS

Among the three places offering services along the 414 miles of the Dalton, you won't find anything luxurious, or even similar to budget chains.

Yukon Ventures Alaska, at mile 56, just past the Yukon River Bridge (☎ **907/655-9001**), has a motel, a restaurant, a gift shop, fuel, and tire repair. The motel is a former pipeline construction camp and the food includes salmon, halibut, and Italian dishes.

The truck stop in Coldfoot, run by **Sourdough Fuel,** at mile 175 (☎ **907/678-5201**), offers a variety of services, including lodging, a 24-hour restaurant, fuel, minor repairs, towing, RV hookup, laundry, a post office, and a gift shop. As at Yukon Ventures, the inn is made of surplus construction worker housing—not fancy, but the rooms are clean and have private bathrooms. The park service has a small campground 5 miles north.

After Coldfoot, the next service area is at **Deadhorse,** at the end of the road 240 miles north, with rooms, fuel, restaurants, a post office, vehicle maintenance, a general store, and an airport. See the Prudhoe Bay section in chapter 10.

GETTING OUT OF THE CAR

ACTIVITIES

BOATING River tours from the Dalton Highway bridge are offered by **Yukon River Tours** (☎ **907/452-7162;** www.mosquitonet.com/~dlacey/). The 90-minute trips include a visit to a working fish camp and to a culture center in Stevens Village. They run three times a day from June 1 to September 1 and cost $25 for adults, $15 under 12. You can buy a ticket at the bridge. The company also offers transportation along the river. The bridge is a take-out for floats on the Yukon River.

HIKING The road has no established hiking trails, but most of the area is open to self-reliant hikers who are willing to pick their own route. The country opens up in the alpine **Brooks Range,** north of the Chandalar Shelf at mile 237. At upper elevations, you can avoid the vast swamps of the wet tundra, but you still will run into tussocks and stream crossings. Forests and brush make cross-country traveling more difficult south of the shelf. A popular destination is the **Gates of the Arctic National Park and Refuge,** to the west of the road, but consider going east. The country is more open, and major rivers lie between the road and the park. Topographical maps and advice on hiking the Brooks Range are available at the sources listed under "Visitor Information," above. Remember, this is remote wilderness; do your research, be prepared, and tell someone where you're going and when you'll be back.

FISHING The Dalton is not a top fishing area, but there are fish in streams and lakes along the highway. Many of the streams have grayling, but you'll want to hike farther than a quarter mile from the road to increase your chances. A good bet is the **Jim River area** between mile 135 and 144, where the river follows the road and fishing pressure is more spread out. Many of the lakes along the road have grayling, and the deeper ones have lake trout and Arctic char. For detailed information, contact the Alaska Public Lands Information Center, or the **Alaska Department of Fish and Game,** 1300 College Rd., Fairbanks, AK 99701 (☎ **907/459-7207;** www.state.ak.us/local/akpages/FISH.GAME/sportf/region3/rgn3home.htm).

CAMPING

The Bureau of Land Management has several camping sites along the road, mostly just gravel pads left over from construction days. They are at:

- **Mile 60:** artesian well, outhouses, and dump station.
- **Mile 98** (Finger Mountain): nice views, outhouse, and wheelchair-accessible trail with interpretive signs.
- **Mile 115** (Arctic Circle): outhouses and picnic tables, an interpretive display, and undeveloped campground without water.
- **Mile 150** (Grayling Lake): Pull-out with outhouse.
- **Mile 175** (Coldfoot): A private campground with hookups is part of the truck stop described above.
- **Mile 180** (Marion Creek): A developed BLM campground with 27 campsites, 11 of them for large RVs (no hookups). The campground has a well and outhouses; the self-service fee is $8.
- **Mile 235** (Arctic tree line): Outhouses.
- **Mile 275** (Galbraith Lake): Undeveloped campground with outhouses about 5 miles off-road; landing strip.

7 The Alaska Highway

I can't fit all the advice you need for a 2,400-mile drive to Alaska in this book, but chapter 2's "Getting There" section provides the planning basics. Here I've covered the towns on the Alaska portion of the road.

The 200 miles of the Alaska Highway running from the border with Canada to the terminus, in Delta Junction, is mostly boring driving—hours of stunted black spruce and brush, either living or burned out. It's a relief when you hit the first major town, **Tok** (rhymes with Coke), 100 miles along. Don't get your hopes up, though. This is the only place where I've ever walked into a visitor center and asked what there is to do in town, only to have the host hold up her fingers in the shape of a goose egg and say, "Nothing." Another 100 miles (I hope you brought plenty of cassette tapes, because no radio station reaches out here) and you've made it to **Delta Junction.** There's a little more to do here, but it's still not a destination. Another 100 miles, and you're in Fairbanks.

The main sources of information for the drive are based in Tok, the first town you hit after you cross the border. It acts as a threshold for the entire state. To plan the journey ahead, contact them, and see "Exploring the Interior," at the beginning of this chapter. One useful Web site, with many links, specializes in advice for Alaska Highway travelers: **www.alcanseek.com**.

I've arranged this section in order from the border with Canada heading west.

CROSSING THE BORDER

Remember to set your watch back an hour when crossing the border east to west—it's an hour later in Yukon Territory. Also, if you make significant purchases or rent rooms in Canada, you may be able to get a refund on the 7% goods and services tax (GST). See section 8 of this chapter, on Dawson City, for details.

CUSTOMS Crossing the U.S./Canadian border either way is usually as simple as exchanging a few pleasantries with a smiling guard, but occasionally it can get more complicated. Going into Canada, **firearms** other than hunting rifles or shotguns may cause you problems; it's wise to call ahead if you plan to take any guns over the border. Visas are unnecessary going either way, but U.S. and Canadian citizens should carry **proof of citizenship** and **proof of residence.** A driver's license is usually enough, but a passport, voter's card, or birth certificate could be required. **Children** with their parents may need a birth certificate; children or teens under 18 unaccompanied by parents may need a letter from a parent or guardian, and children with a single parent should carry a letter from the other parent. There are no duties on products made in the United States or Canada; for items that you buy that originated in other countries, or alcohol or smoking supplies, see chapter 3. Products you buy in Alaska made of **ivory, fur, or other wildlife** will probably require special permits to be taken out of the United States, and it's easiest to have the store where you bought the item take care of it (see chapter 3 for details). **Dogs and cats** require rabies certificates. If in doubt, call **Canadian Customs** in Whitehorse (☎ **867/667-3943**) or **U.S. Customs** in Anchorage (☎ **907/271-2675**).

FROM THE BORDER TO TOK

The first 60 miles after entering the United States, the road borders the Tetlin National Wildlife Refuge. A **visitor center,** 7 miles past the border, at mile 1,229 (☎ **907/774-2245**), overlooks rolling hills and lakes. It is open Memorial Day to Labor Day daily 8am to 5pm. The U.S. Fish and Wildlife Service also has two small campgrounds over the next 27 miles, Deadman, at mile 1,249, with 16 sites, and Lake View, at mile 1,256, with 8.

TOK

Originally called Tokyo Camp, a construction station on the highway, the name was shortened to Tok when it became unpopular after Pearl Harbor. Since then, Tok's role in the world hasn't expanded much beyond being a stop on the road. With its location at the intersection of the Alaska Highway and the Glenn Highway to Glennallen—the short way to Anchorage and Prince William Sound—the town has built an economy of gas stations, gift stores, cafes, and hotels to serve highway travelers.

ESSENTIALS

GETTING THERE You're surely passing through Tok with your own set of wheels. If you get stuck for some reason, the Gray Line **Alaskon Express** (☎ **800/478-6388** or 907/883-2291; www.graylinealaska.com/alaskon.cfm) stops most days during the summer at the Westmark Inn.

VISITOR INFORMATION Local boosters and public land agencies have combined to operate a large, informative visitor center to introduce highway travelers to Alaska. The government's part, the **Alaska Public Lands Information Center,** P.O. Box 359, Tok, AK 99780 (☎ **907/883-5667;** www.nps.gov/aplic), is open daily from 8am to 8pm in summer and from 8am to 4:30pm in winter. Besides answering questions, rangers offer talks and nature walks in the summer. The commercial portion, the **Main Street Visitor Center,** operated by the Tok Chamber of Commerce, P.O. Box 389, Tok, AK 99780 (☎ **907/883-5775;** www.TokAlaskaInfo.com), provides information on Tok and anywhere else you may be bound on the highway. They're open Memorial Day to September 15 daily 8am to 8pm.

FAST FACTS An **ATM** is to be found at the bank in Frontier Foods, near the center of town, and at the Texaco station across the road from Fast Eddy's restaurant.

The **Tok Clinic** is on the Tok Cut-Off across from the fire station (☎ **907/883-5855**).

The **Alaska State Troopers** (☎ **907/883-5111**) police the region; they maintain an office near the intersection of the Alaska Highway and Glenn Highway.

The **post office** is at the highway junction next to the Westmark Hotel.

There are no **taxes** in the region.

ATTRACTIONS

Mukluk Land, under the big fiberglass mukluk 3 miles west of town (☎ **907/883-2571**), is a homemade theme park that may amuse young children or even adults in a certain frame of mind; admission is $5 for adults, $4 senior citizens, $2 children and teens. It's open June to August, daily from 1 to 9pm. Gold panning is an extra $5. The **Burnt Paw Gift Shop** has a free sled-dog demonstration on wheels June to August, Monday to Saturday at 7:30pm.

ACCOMMODATIONS

The motels are numerous and competitive in Tok. There also are many B&Bs; check at the visitor center.

The **Tok International Youth Hostel** (☎ **907/883-3745**) occupies a wall tent a mile off the Alaska Highway, 8 miles west of town on Pringle Drive. There is a shower, laundry machines, and limited cooking facilities. There are 10 beds for $10 apiece. It's closed September 15 to May 15.

Be sure to get the 25¢ state highway and campground map from the public lands center, which includes all the public campgrounds in Alaska. Three attractive state parks campgrounds lie near Tok on the three highway links that radiate from the town. Each has a $10 self-service fee. There are lots of competitive RV parks in Tok. One that has wooded sites suitable for tent camping, too, is the **Sourdough Campground,** 1½ miles south of town on the Glenn Highway (☎ **907/883-5543**). They charge $22 for full hookups, $16 dry.

Snowshoe Motel & Fine Arts and Gifts. Across the highway from the information center (P.O. Box 559), Tok, AK 99789. ☎ **800/478-4511** in Alaska, Yukon, and part of B.C., or 907/883-4511. Fax 907/883-4512. E-mail: snowshoe@ptialaska.net. 24 units. TV TEL. High season $68 double. Low season $48–$58 double. Rates include continental breakfast in summer. Extra person $5. DISC, MC, V.

The 10 newer no-smoking rooms near the front are a real bargain. Each is divided into two sections by the bathroom, providing two separate bedrooms—great for families. The housekeeping seemed exceptionally good when I visited, and the outside walkways were decorated with flowers. The gift shop carries some authentic Native art as well as highway kitsch.

Westmark Tok. Intersection of Alaska Hwy. and Glenn Hwy. (P.O. Box 130), Tok, AK 99780-0130. ☎ **800/544-0970** (reservations) or 907/883-5174. Fax 907/883-5178. www.westmarkhotels.com. 92 units. TV TEL. $129 double. AE, DC, DISC, MC, V. Closed Sept 16–May 15.

The central hotel in town is closed in the winter, as its clientele is primarily the package tour bus trade. It's made up of several buildings connected by boardwalks. The older rooms are narrow, without enough room at the foot of the bed for the TV, but they're comfortable and up-to-date. The new section has larger, higher-priced rooms. Ask for the "highway rate," $99 for a double. There's a "factory outlet" gift store in the lobby that sells remainders from Westmark's other shops for lower prices. A greenhouse grows huge vegetables. The restaurant serves three meals a day, with dinners in the $14 to $20 range.

Young's Motel. Behind Fast Eddy's Restaurant on the Alaska Hwy. (P.O. Box 482), Tok, AK 99780. ☎ **907/883-4411.** Fax 907/883-5023. 43 units. TV TEL. High season $73 double. Low season $55 double. Extra person $5. AE, DISC, MC, V.

Good standard motel rooms occupy three one-story structures on the parking lot behind Fast Eddy's restaurant, where you check in. Eighteen newer, smoke-free rooms are the pick of the litter, but all are acceptable.

DINING

The only noteworthy restaurant in town is **Fast Eddy's** (☎ **907/883-4411**), on the right as you enter town from the east. Begun as a typical roadside cafe, it has developed into a place where a wine list and fine-dining entrees don't seem out of place. Yet the proprietor knows that most highway travelers just want a simple, relaxing meal, and the varied menu offers anything they might have in mind. I relish the salad bar and light dishes that offer a break from the usually carnivorous greasy spoon choices found elsewhere along the highway. The dining room is decorated in dark wood and brass. They're open in summer 6am to midnight, in winter 7am to 11pm.

DELTA JUNCTION

This intersection with the Richardson Highway, which runs from Valdez to Fairbanks, is the official end of the Alaska Highway. It's an earnest little roadside town set in a broad plain between the Delta and Tanana Rivers. People make their living from farming and tourism, and at a trans-Alaska pipeline pump station south of town. Locals hope that Fort Greely, long the core of the town but now closing, will survive as a high-tech missile defense base or as a prison, or maybe both. For visitors, there are two historic roadhouse museums and several good campgrounds, but not enough to hold most for more than a few hours.

ESSENTIALS

VISITOR INFORMATION A helpful **visitor center** run by the Delta Chamber of Commerce, P.O. Box 987, Delta Junction, AK 99737 (☎ **877/895-5068** or 907/895-5068; www.wildak.net/chamber/), stands at the intersection of the Alaska and Richardson highways, in the middle of town; it's open May to mid-September. The Delta Junction Convention and Visitors Bureau has an extensive Web site at **www.alaska-highway.org/delta/**.

FAST FACTS The **National Bank of Alaska** has a branch right at the center of town, on the Richardson Highway, with an ATM.

The **Family Medical Center** is at mile 267.2 on the Richardson Highway, 2 miles north of the visitors center (☎ **907/895-4879** or 907/895-5100).

The **Alaska State Troopers'** emergency number is ☎ **907/895-4800.** For non-emergencies, call ☎ **907/895-4344.**

The **post office** is on the east side of the Richardson, 2 blocks north of the visitor center.

Delta has no **taxes** of any kind.

Attractions & Activities

Before construction of the first road to Fairbanks in 1917 (today's Richardson Highway), travelers to the Interior followed a trail on basically the same route by horse in summer and dog sled in winter, stopping at roadhouses that provided food and shelter a day apart on the 2-week trip. Two well-preserved examples of the roadhouse system survive near Delta Junction.

In 1996, the Army saved the 1905 **Sullivan Roadhouse,** which had stood, abandoned since 1922, on what became an Army bombing range. Today the log building stands next to the town visitor center and is open in summer 9am to 5:30pm Monday through Saturday as a free museum (call the chamber of commerce for information). Many of the Sullivan's original belongings have been set back in their original places, giving a strong feel for frontier life, but the heart of the restoration is the authentic hospitality of the local volunteers who show off the place with great pride.

The next stop on the trail was 16 miles toward Fairbanks. **Rika's Roadhouse and Landing,** 10 miles northwest of Delta on the Richardson Highway (☎ **907/895-4201**), still makes a pleasant stop on your drive. This roadhouse lasted later than the Sullivans' because drivers had to board a ferry here to cross the Tanana River until the 1940s, and the shore was the end of the line for Tanana sternwheelers. The state historical park preserves a 1917 log building and its lovely grounds. The main building has been altered too much to feel real, but the grassy compound completes a fascinating picture of Alaska pioneer life with surviving out buildings, a gorgeous vegetable garden and a pen of domestic fowl. A restaurant serves soups, salads, and sandwiches daily 9am to 5pm; the grounds and museum are open 8am to 8pm, May 15 to September 15. An impressive suspension bridge carries the trans-Alaska pipeline over the Tanana River, and boaters use the shoreline, at the confluence of the Tanana and Delta rivers, as a landing. The campground is best for RVs.

Accommodations

In addition to the two somewhat idiosyncratic places listed here, you'll find inexpensive basic rooms at **Alaska 7 Motel,** 3548 Richardson Hwy. (☎ **907/895-4848;** www.alaskan.com/ak7motel).

Bed and Breakfast at the Home of Alys. 2303 Alys Ave., Delta Junction, AK 99737. ☎ **907/895-4128.** 2 units. TV. $75 double. Extra person $15. Rates include breakfast. No credit cards.

As the name says, these rooms are fully part of Henry and Alys Brewis's home, but that's good, because you wouldn't want to come to Delta Junction without meeting this fascinating couple, hearing their stories of a lifetime pioneer homesteading in Alaska, and being treated like a member of their family. Henry's parents both came to Alaska in the Klondike gold rush. The comfortable rooms look out on a yard with a greenhouse and impressive gardens, where moose often wander through. Take Brewis road off the Richardson Highway just north of town.

Kelly's Country Inn. Intersection of Richardson and Alaska hwys. (P.O. Box 849), Delta Junction, AK 99737. ☎ **907/895-4667.** Fax 907/895-4481. www.knix.net/kellys. 21 units. TV TEL. $90 double. Extra person $5. AE, MC, V.

This funny little motel, in town, has always had clean, charming rooms. The owner is a real Alaska pioneer who has projected her personality into the place. All rooms have refrigerators and free coffee, and most have microwave ovens.

CAMPING

Alaska State Parks maintains five campgrounds on the rivers and lakes in and around Delta Junction and a couple of public cabins. Right on the highway near town, the **Delta State Recreation Area campground** lies among large spruce and birch trees, the sites well separated, some with walk-in privacy. It is the most attractive campground on the highway. The **Quartz Lake State Recreation Area,** 11 miles northwest of town on the Richardson Highway and down a 3-mile turn-off, has an 80-site campground on the shallow fishing lake. The camping fee at each is $10. For information, contact the **Department of Natural Resources Public Information Center,** 3700 Airport Way, Fairbanks, AK 99709 (☎ **907/451-2705;** www.dnr.state.ak.us/parks/parks.htm)

To park an RV, or if you're tent camping and need a shower, **Smith's Green Acres RV Park and Campground,** 1½ miles north on the Richardson Highway from the visitor center (☎ **800/895-4369** or 907/895-4369; www.akpub.com/akbbrv/smith.html), has grassy sites and tent sites among the trees, as well as a small playground and laundry.

DINING

Buffalo Center Diner. 1680 Richardson Hwy. ☎ **907/895-5089.** Main courses $6.25–$25. MC, V. Summer, Sun–Thus 6am–9pm, Fri–Sat 6am–10pm. Winter daily 6am–9pm. DINER.

The locals eat here, for good reason. The dining room is light and clean and the menu covers everything you would hope for in a simple family restaurant—plus a seasonal list of buffalo dinners in honor of the Delta herd. Service is friendly and quick, and the waitress called me Hon.

8 Dawson City: Gold Rush Destination

A gold rush scatters the seeds of civilization promiscuously. It is an irrational force of history, driven by hysterical greed for a metal that could show up almost anywhere, and its unpredictable results have the dramatic allure of madness, leaving cities behind on the landscape as if at random. Dawson City's presence at the confluence of the Yukon and Klondike Rivers is just such a historic accident. Certainly, no other chain of events could have built it here, in such a remote place, nor filled it with such an extraordinary cast of characters. Today, no other town I know of preserves so well the true look and setting of a gold rush city. Being so far from the rest of the world, Dawson City never had the chance to change.

Approaching by road accentuates the town's weird isolation, especially coming from the west over the Top of the World Highway. By the third hour of bouncing over gravel road, orange midnight twilight falls to the north and a huge moon rises to the east, lighting the silhouettes of rounded mountains that stand all around in countless, receding layers, all quiet, all empty. The border to Canada is closed for the night; camping by the road, no vehicles pass in the alpine silence. Next morning, passing through Customs, you go on for 1½ hours without signs of humankind within the broad horizon, only the thread of gravel you're following. Turn another corner, and there it is. Down below, a grid of city streets at river's edge: Dawson City, once the second largest city on the west coast of North America, and still way out in the middle of nowhere 100 years later.

In town, there are people all over wide, straight streets, looking at well-kept old buildings. Inside a museumlike visitor center, guides dressed in period costumes are

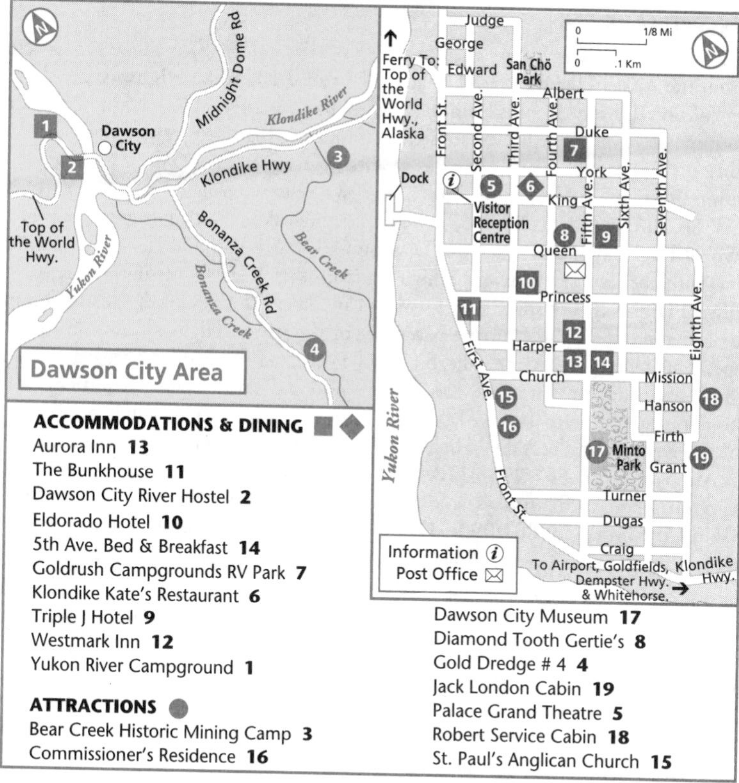

providing tourists with directions and selling them tickets to shows. Looking back at the hill across the river, at the wilderness so close at hand, it's suddenly easy to understand the incongruity and shock of the gold rush. A little more than 100 years ago, the world suddenly went mad and rushed to this riverbank beyond the edge of civilization and created an instant city. It arrived as suddenly as it arrives in your windshield on the highway.

Dawson City was the destination for some 100,000 stampeders hoping to strike it rich on the Klondike River in 1898, about 30,000 of whom actually made it here. Mining for gold and other minerals continues today, but the town's main focus is on the visitors who come to see a well-preserved gold rush boom town. Parks Canada does a good job of keeping up the buildings that make up part of the **Klondike National Historic Sites** and providing activities that bring history alive; you can easily spend 2 full days here, if you're interested in the period the town celebrates. Dawson City sometimes feels like one big museum, and it doesn't suffer from the commercialism that pervades Skagway, the other major gold rush town in the region.

Since winter temperatures can drop to –40°F, Dawson gets mighty quiet in the off-season. Before the second week of May or after the second week of September, you're unlikely to find any attractions open, and few other businesses. The town wakes a little for winter dog mushing and snowmobiling events, but a visit then wouldn't include the historic aspect more people go for.

ESSENTIALS

GETTING THERE Most visitors drive to Dawson City by making a long detour from the Alaska Highway into Canada. The paved **Klondike Highway,** also known as **Yukon Highway 2,** splits from the Alaska Highway a few miles west of Whitehorse, heading 327 miles north over scenic, fairly smooth road to Dawson City. For guidance on that part of the trip, get the excellent *Canada's Yukon Official Vacation Guide* from **Tourism Yukon,** P.O. Box 2703, Whitehorse, Yukon, Canada Y1A 2C6 (☎ **867/667-5340;** fax 867/667-3546; www.touryukon.com). The gravel **Top of the World Highway** heads west from Dawson City, crossing the border before connecting with the **Taylor Highway,** which leads north to Eagle and south to rejoin the **Alaska Highway,** 175 miles after Dawson City. The 502 miles for the detour compare to 375 miles if you stay on the pavement of the Alaska Highway. You do miss the spectacular vistas on Kluane Lake, but maybe you can see that on the way back. Below, you'll find a description of the Top of the World and Taylor highways and Eagle. The border is open 5am to 10pm Alaska time, and the road closes in winter. See section 7 of this chapter, on the Alaska Highway, for a note on Customs.

Air North (☎ **867/993-5110**) flies round-trip between Fairbanks and Dawson City on Tuesdays, Thursdays, and Sundays, with fares starting at around US$200. **Gold City Tours** (☎ **867/993-5175**) offers an airport limousine, $10 one way.

VISITOR INFORMATION The **Parks Canada Visitor Reception Centre,** King and Front streets (P.O. Box 390), Dawson City, YT, Canada Y0B 1G0 (☎ **867/993-5566;** www.harbour.com/parkscan/khs/), is a mix of information center, museum, and theater of historic films, and is an indispensable stop. The hosts are knowledgeable and provide free maps and guides, as well as selling tickets to all the Klondike National Historic Sites tours, events, and shows. They're open daily in summer from 8am to 8pm. If you plan to do all or most of the gold field attractions, the five-tour pass sold here for Can$15 is a good deal.

The **Klondike Visitors Association,** housed in the same building as the Parks Canada center, above (P.O. Box 389P, Dawson City, YT, Canada Y0B 1G0; ☎ **867/993-5575;** fax 867/993-6415; www.DawsonCity.com), offers information on local businesses, accommodations, and community events.

GETTING AROUND You probably got to Dawson City in a car or RV. If not, cars are for rent from **Budget** (☎ **867/993-5644**). Dropping off in Whitehorse adds around $100.

Bikes are a fun way to get to the outlying sights for strong riders and are available for rent at the **Dawson City River Hostel,** listed below.

The free **George Black Ferry** crosses the Yukon 24 hours a day May to September, except for servicing early Wednesday mornings. The landing is at the north end of Front Street. On the other side is the Top of the World Highway, a provincial campground, and the hostel.

FAST FACTS The **Canadian Imperial Bank of Commerce** at Second Avenue and Queen Street has an ATM. The next closest bank machine is 330 miles southeast in Whitehorse or 175 miles southwest in Tok.

Except as noted, ***the prices in this section are listed in Canadian dollars.*** At this writing, a U.S. dollar would buy about Can$1.50. Current rates are listed in the newspapers or check CNN's currency converter at www.cnn.com/travel/currency. It's wise to exchange your currency at a bank or using an ATM, or to use credit cards, rather than at a point of sale. Most Alaska businesses will accept Canadian small change at face value, but not dollar coins or bills.

In an emergency, call the **Royal Canadian Mounted Police,** on Front Street near Turner (☎ **867/993-5555**), or the **ambulance** (☎ **867/993-4444**). A **nursing station** is located at Sixth and Mission streets (☎ **867/993-4444**).

The **post office** is on Fifth Avenue near Princess Street, and a historic post office, with limited services, is at Third Avenue and King Street.

You'll pay the 7% **goods and services tax (GST)** for almost everything, but if you're not a Canadian, you can apply to get up to Can$500 of it back at a duty-free shop or from **Visitor Rebate Program,** Revenue Canada, Summerside Tax Centre, Summerside, PE, C1N 6C6 Canada (☎ **800/668-4748** in Canada; 902/432-5608 outside Canada; www.ccra-adrc.gc.ca/tax/nonresidents/visitors/index-e.html). Pick up a booklet containing the rules and an application from the visitor center. The rebate counts only if you spent more than Can$200, and only on taxes paid for goods and accommodations, not food, services, rentals, transportation, fuel, and the like. Save your receipts. You may need to present the goods and receipts for verification at the border.

Dawson City is on Pacific time, 1 hour later than Alaska. The time changes at the border.

SPECIAL EVENTS Check the Klondike Visitor Association Web site for a complete events calendar (**www.DawsonCity.com**).

The Yukon Quest International Sled Dog Race runs between Fairbanks and Dawson City, starting in Fairbanks on odd-numbered years, and in Dawson in even-numbered years. It's held, naturally, in the deep cold of February. A huge snowmobile trek connects Dawson City and Tok later in the month, called **Trek Over the Top.**

The **Commissioner's Grande Ball,** in early June, is the social event of the year in Dawson City. **The Yukon Gold Panning Championships** and **Canada Day Celebrations** are on July 1. **The Dawson City Music Festival,** a miniature Woodstock (but better behaved), occurs in late July.

GOLD RUSH ATTRACTIONS

It makes sense to start off your visit at the **Parks Canada Visitor Reception Centre,** at King and Front streets (see "Visitor Information," above), where you can get advice and maps and buy tickets to attractions. It's open daily in summer from 8am to 8pm. Parks Canada leads a daily **town walking tour** from here for Can$5. The guides are well trained and can open historic buildings you won't get to look inside otherwise. They also lend a 90-minute cassette tape version with headphones. Or you can use one of the maps they distribute to make up your own walking tour; there are interesting buildings almost anywhere you wander. Here are some of the highlights.

On Front Street, just south of the visitor center, the newly restored steamer ***Keno*** sits on timbers. At Third Avenue and Princess Street, **Bigg's Blacksmith Shop** is next to a gold rush era building that is slowly sinking into the permafrost. At Front and Church streets, 2 blocks south, **St. Paul's Anglican Church** is a charming, creaky 1902 structure on the riverfront. Next door, the **Commissioner's Residence,** an impressive mansion with a wraparound porch, standing amid beautifully planted grounds, has been restored with mostly original furnishings. A tour goes through daily at 4pm for Can$5. In back of the house, you'll find a log building that was part of the 1897 **Fort Herchmer,** and later a jail.

The ✪ **Dawson City Museum,** on Fifth Avenue between Church and Turner streets (☎ **867/993-5291**), is the best-presented gold rush museum I've seen. The fascinating, tin-roofed neoclassical building housed the Territorial Government from 1901 until it moved to Whitehorse, and upstairs one of the galleries still doubles as an impressive courtroom. The galleries downstairs display gold rush artifacts in a way that

The Gold Rush in Context

The biggest event in Alaska history happened just over 100 years ago: the 1898 Klondike Gold Rush. If you're coming to Alaska, you'll be hearing a lot about it. Here's some of the context for the barrage of anecdotes you can expect.

Prospectors sought gold in small numbers even before Russia sold Alaska to the United States in 1867, but the Russians' main interest in Alaska was sea otter pelts, and they made few forays beyond the coast, leaving the great mass of the North and Interior unexplored. When the United States took over, Alaska had virtually no white population, and what it had was concentrated in the Southeast—in Sitka, the Russian capital, a few other Russian settlements, and at the trading post of Wrangell, which miners used as a jumping-off point for gold fields up the Stikine River in British Columbia.

After the American flag went up over Sitka, prospectors slowly worked their way into Alaska's vastness, often led or in partnership with Natives who knew the country. Called **sourdoughs** for the live yeast and flour mixture they carried to make their bread, these were tough wilderness men living way beyond the law or communication with the outside world. A few of them struck it rich. In 1880, a major find on the Gastineau Channel started the city of Juneau and decades of industrial, hard-rock mining there. Finds followed on the Fortymile River in 1886 (on the Taylor Highway), near Circle in 1893 (on the Steese Highway), and near Hope on the Kenai Peninsula in 1895 (on the Seward Highway). Gold slowly brought more people to Alaska, but not enough to catch the nation's attention.

In 1896, white prospector **George Carmack** and his Native partners, Tagish Charlie and Skookum Jim, found gold on the Klondike River, a tributary to the Yukon in Canada. Word traveled downriver to the gold fields in the Fortymile Country, and within 48 hours that area was empty and claims on the Klondike were being staked. The miners dug gravel from the creek that winter, and when they washed it in the spring, it yielded big hunks of solid gold, a massive discovery. They were instant millionaires in a time when a million dollars meant something.

It's hard to imagine today the impact of the news on the outside world. The U.S. economy was deeply in depression. The dollar was on a gold standard, and the scarcity of gold had caused a deflationary vise that in 1893 brought a banking collapse and unemployment of 18%. Suddenly, in 1897, a steamer arrived in Seattle bearing men from a place called the Klondike with trunks and gunny sacks full of gold. The supply of money suddenly grew and economic confidence returned. The national economy turned around on the news, and some 100,000 people set off for Alaska to get rich, too, plunging off into a trackless wilderness for which most were completely unprepared.

Contemporary Alaska marks the **Klondike Gold Rush** as the start of its history. Before the gold rush, Alaska largely remained as it had been for thousands of years, ruled and inhabited by its indigenous people. As late as 1880, the territory had fewer than 500 white residents, and only 4,000 by 1890—it was virtually empty from the point of view of those who discounted the Alaska Natives. In 1898, the

makes them seem immediate and alive. Guides dressed in costume lead tours further expanding on the teaching power of the objects and excellent placards. The clutter common to this kind of museum is confined to the "visible storage" gallery upstairs, where a rich collection is housed inside glass-fronted cabinets. A cafe serves soup, stampede began, bringing an instant population. Even the mayor of Seattle left for Alaska. Within a few years, Alaska had cities, telegraph lines, riverboats, and sled dog mail routes. About 30,000 made it all the way to Dawson City. Few of that number struck it rich, but those who built the towns and businesses to serve them did—there were suddenly saloons and brothels, dress shops and photo studios. Promoters sold a credulous public newly laid-out towns on supposed routes to the gold fields, including routes that were essentially impassable.

The **White Pass** above Skagway and the **Chilkoot Pass** above Dyea carried the most stampeders. Gold seekers arrived in the crazily lawless settlements by steamer from Seattle, got robbed and cheated, and then ferried their goods over the passes to **Lake Bennett.** (Upon completion of the railroad through the White Pass in 1901, Dyea and the Chilkoot Pass were abandoned, but Skagway lives on—see chapter 5.) The Canadian authorities wisely required each stampeder to bring a ton of supplies, a rule that undoubtedly prevented famine but made the single-file journey over the passes a miserable ordeal. Prospectors sometimes had to make dozens of trips up the trail to get their supplies up. At Lake Bennett, the stampeders built boats, crossed the lake, and floated down the Yukon River, through the dangerous Five Finger Rapids, to **Dawson City,** a 500-mile journey from the sea.

Imagine their disappointment to find, on their arrival, that the gold claims had all been staked, and big companies were taking over. The prospectors looking to strike it rich had humbling choices. The smart ones started businesses to make money off the other stampeders, and some of them did quite well. Others worked for wages or went home. But many continued in pursuit of the next find. Their wild chase for gold drew the modern map of Alaska, founding dozens of towns. Many of these towns disappeared as soon as the frenzy cooled and now are entirely forgotten or live on only as place names, but some became real cities. **Nome** came in 1899, **Fairbanks** in 1902, **Kantishna,** now within Denali National Park, in 1905, **Iditarod** in 1908, and many others, until the rush finally ended with the start of World War I in 1914.

Even without a rush, there's still gold to be dug. Ever larger and more sophisticated machinery worked the Klondike claims and washed the gravel until the 1960s, and gold mining remains an important part of that area's economy to this day. Small-time prospectors are still looking all over Alaska and working their claims, and sometimes someone does make a significant new strike. A 1987 find north of Fairbanks, developed at a cost of $400 million, brings out more than 1,000 ounces a day.

But there's a much bigger and safer business in mining the tourist trade. The rush of visitors each summer dwarfs the number who came in 1898, and, in the true spirit of the event whose history they celebrate, the gold rush towns of Skagway, Dawson City, Fairbanks, and Nome know there's more money to be made from people than from gold.

muffins, coffee, and tea, and there's a gift shop. Admission is Can$4; the museum is open Victoria Day to Labour Day, daily from 10am to 6pm. Next door is a free display of 19th-century locomotives from the short-lived Klondike Mine Line Railway, which ran 32 miles up Bonanza Creek.

The **Jack London Cabin,** at Eighth Avenue and Grant Street along the foot of the bluff, is a replica with some logs from the original cabin where London probably spent his winter in the Klondike. (The rest of the logs are in a replica in Oakland, California, where London also lived.) A small museum with a guide is at the site, and readings are given at 11:30am and 2:30pm. London found a gold mine of material for his classic adventure stories, but little actual gold, when he stampeded north.

Poet **Robert Service** spent more time at his cabin, at Eighth Avenue and Hansen Street, just down the road. Service wrote his ballads about the North while working as a bank clerk in Dawson City, reciting them for free drinks in the bars. Today you can hear them in tourist shows all over Alaska and the Yukon.

After the initial gold rush, the Rothschilds and Guggenheims financed large-scale industrial gold mining here. The remains of that amazing technical effort are preserved outside of town. **Gold Dredge No. 4,** 8 miles down Bonanza Creek Road south of town, is maintained by Parks Canada to show how these incredible earth-eating machines worked their way across the landscape, sifting gold out of the gravel; similar dredges are in Fairbanks and Nome. Hour-long tours, which circle the outside of the machine but don't go inside, take place hourly June to mid-September from 9am to 5pm and cost Can$5. Another 7 miles up the road, the site of the original Klondike strike is marked. Parks Canada also manages the **Bear Creek Historic Mining Camp,** 7 miles up the Klondike Highway. The camp was headquarters for the company that owned the gold diggings. It's been kept as if the workers just left, including warehouses and workshops full of odd and interesting mechanical relics. The highlight is the gold room, where the gold was melted into bricks. At the end, you can watch a documentary film about the mining made before the operation shut down in 1966. The tour takes place twice daily, at 1:30 and 3pm, and costs Can$5.

Gold City Tours (☎ **867/993-5175**), on Front Street across from the riverboat *Keno,* offers a 3½-hour tour that includes Gold Dredge No. 4 and gold panning every day in the summer for Can$36.

ON THE RIVER

Dawson City is the largest town on the Yukon River after Whitehorse, and the most developed access point near Alaska. The Yukon, flowing 5 to 10 miles per hour, is a slow-paced westward-flowing highway. Here you can join its journey, either on a tour boat or on your own, floating with the current in a canoe.

Gray Line Yukon operates the new high-speed ***Yukon Queen II*** catamaran (☎ **867/993-5599**), which runs daily from late May to early September 108 miles downriver to Eagle. The modern 115-passenger boat leaves at 8am for a 4-hour, narrated ride to Eagle; once there, you can eat at the cafe and visit the museum. It returns at 2pm, going upstream in 5 hours and serving dinner before arriving back in Dawson City. Most passengers are on Holland America–Westours packages, but you can book a place if space is available. It's US$120 one way, double round-trip; or you can fly back. The office is across Front Street from the Visitor Reception Centre.

One popular trip is to float 3 or 4 days in a canoe or raft to Eagle (you can come back on the *Yukon Queen II,* but not with the canoe). There are other, more remote floats in the area, or you can keep floating down the Yukon to Circle, or even farther. A company offering gear for one-way floats to Eagle is listed below, in section 9 of this chapter, on Eagle. The **Dawson Trading Post** (☎ **867/993-5316**) rents canoes and camping gear, and operates a shuttle that can drop you off on the more remote Stewart River for Can$175. Canoes rent for Can$150 a week.

ACCOMMODATIONS

In addition to the hotels listed below, there are several good B&Bs in Dawson City, including the **5th Avenue Bed and Breakfast,** on Fifth Avenue next door to the museum (☎ **867/993-5941**). It has seven fresh, basic rooms. Three have their own bathrooms, and there are two kitchens for guests to use.

Dieter Reinmuth operates the **Dawson City River Hostel** (☎ **867/993-6823**), across the Yukon from Dawson City on the free ferry mid-May through September. Bunks in cabins, private rooms, and camping are available, as well as a sweat lodge and cold showers. A bunk is Can$16 for nonmembers, a private room Can$32 double. He also rents bicycles and canoes for Can$20 a day.

The wooded provincial **Yukon River Campground,** just down the road, has 98 sites; the fee is Can$8. The **Goldrush Campground RV Park,** at Fifth Avenue and York Street (☎ **867/993-5247**), is a conveniently located lot right downtown.

Aurora Inn. Fifth and Harper sts. (P.O. Box 1748), Dawson City, Yukon Y0B 1G0. ☎ **867/993-6860.** Fax 867/993-5689. www.wildandwooly.yk.net. 10 units. High season Can$119 double; Can$180 suite. Low season Can$80 double; Can$140 suite. MC, V.

This pleasant little inn behind a false front on a boardwalk street has the added advantage of proprietors, Romy and René Jansen, who value an uncluttered atmosphere and immaculate housekeeping. When I visited, everything was new and perfectly kept. Rooms have their own tiled bathrooms and are decorated with quilts and stripped-log furniture. To watch television or use the phone or Internet, you must visit the comfortable front room. Guests remove their shoes before entering.

The Bunkhouse. Front and Princess sts. (Bag 4040), Dawson City, YT, Canada Y0B 1G0. ☎ **867/993-6164.** Fax 867/993-6051. 31 units, 5 with private bathroom. Can$50 double without bathroom, Can$80–$95 double with bathroom. Extra person Can$5. MC, V. Closed in winter.

This is a unique place—it looks like a riverboat from the outside, and is fresh and trim, but it's intended for budget travelers. The rooms, all no-smoking and each with its own exterior entry, have varnished wooden floors and attractive fabrics. The beds are really bunks—no bed springs. Those that share bathrooms are quite small; the bathrooms are clean, but the showers for men and women are in the same room, shielded only by stalls with doors. The rooms with private bathrooms have telephones and TVs.

Triple J Hotel. Fifth Ave. and Queen St. (P.O. Box 359), Dawson City, YT, Canada Y0B 1G0. ☎ **867/993-5323.** Fax 867/993-5030. 47 units, 18 cabins. TV TEL. High season Can$109–$119 double or cabin for 2. Low season Can$74–$79 double or cabin for 2. Extra person Can$10. AE, DC, EC, MC, V. Closed Nov–Apr.

This rambling set of structures has three different kinds of rooms: large hotel rooms in the old, wooden main building; smallish rooms in the low-slung motel building; and cabins with kitchenettes and little porches. Some of the rooms are excellent; others are nothing to brag about but are still clean and serviceable. All rooms have fans and coffeemakers, and the hotel also provides a courtesy car and a coin-op laundry. The **restaurant** has a menu with a broad range of prices and varied cuisine, and they hold a popular barbecue on the deck of the lounge.

Westmark Inn Dawson. Fifth Ave. and Harper St. (P.O. Box 420), Dawson City, YT, Canada Y0B 1G0. ☎ **800/544-0970** (reservations) or 867/993-5542. Fax 867/993-5623. www.westmarkhotels.com. 131 units. TV TEL. Can$139–$179 double. AE, CB, DC, EC, MC, V. Closed Sept 15–May 15.

The modern, well-run Westmark is the best hotel in town. I especially liked the newer Jack London and Robert Service wings, where wide, well-lit hallways lead to large rooms with crisp gold rush–theme decorative touches. The older rooms are good, too, but are smaller and have older decor. All rooms have fans and clocks, and there's a coin-op laundry. Ask for the "highway rate." A patio in the grassy courtyard is the site of a daily barbecue. **Belinda's Restaurant,** with light-wood decor and well-spaced tables, is open daily from 6am to 10pm; there's also a lounge.

DINING & NIGHTLIFE

I've described restaurants at the Westmark and Triple J hotels, above. Also try **Klondike Kate's Restaurant,** in a historic building at Third Avenue and King Street (☎ **867/993-6527**), with decent food for low prices, and a fully licensed bar. The patio is pleasant.

Some of Dawson City's most famous and fun activities are in the evening. **Diamond Tooth Gertie's,** at Fourth Avenue and Queen Street (☎ **867/993-5575**), operated by the Klondike Visitors Association, is a gambling hall and bar, with tame cabaret singing and cancan dancing floor shows. It's a fun place to go with a group. The shows, each different, play three times nightly. It's open Tuesday to Sunday from 7pm to 2am, and admission is Can$6 for all evening, with only those at least 19 years old admitted.

The *Gaslight Follies* is a 2-hour vaudeville show nightly at 8pm in the **Palace Grand Theatre,** a historic building at Second Avenue and King Street that has been renovated by Parks Canada. Tickets (Can$16 to Can$18 for adults, Can$8 for children) are on sale at the box office from 3pm. Parks Canada also leads tours through the theater at 11am daily; it costs Can$5 at the Visitors Reception Centre.

9 A Detour to Eagle via the Top of the World & Taylor Highways

Sometime before World War I, the tiny town of Eagle got lost in an eddy in the stream of history, where it still awaits discovery by the outside world. The town was founded in 1898 as a subtle fraud, when a group of prospectors staked out the land then cleverly created a buzz in Dawson City, just upriver across the border, of a gold discovery. The federal government followed the rush, and in 1900, Judge James Wickersham chose Eagle for a new courthouse to try to bring law to the wild country. But when gold really was found in Fairbanks, the attention of prospectors and of Wickersham moved on, leaving Eagle slowly to decline to a ghost town of only nine residents by 1953.

But that's where the really exceptional part of the story begins. The few remaining people recognized the value of the history that had been left behind—Wickersham's papers were still in his desk where he'd left them—and formed the historical society that today is the main activity for the town's 150 residents. Visitors can tour the courthouse, customs house, and five museums, and use Eagle for the start or end of a history-drenched Yukon River float. You'll also see the places John McPhee wrote about in his classic *Coming into the Country.*

The reason Eagle is still so interesting is that it's still isolated, 173 dusty miles from Tok or 144 from Dawson City. It's a major side trip from the route between the two cities, which are 187 road miles apart, adding at least a day to your trip.

The **Taylor Highway** runs 160 miles north from the Alaska Highway just east of Tok to Eagle, 4 or 5 hours over a rough gravel road that's open only in summer. This is the Fortymile Country, around the past and current gold mining of the Fortymile River drainage. It's a remote country, mostly managed by the **Bureau of Land Management,** Tok Field Office, P.O. Box 309, Tok, AK 99780 (☎ **907/883-5121;**

wwwndo.ak.blm.gov/fortymile/FMwelcome.html). There are no services or signs of human development on the way except at the town of **Chicken,** barely a wide spot in the road 66 miles north, with gas, a couple of shops, a bar, and a cafe, but no phone. The drive does have impressive views in spots, and at mile 96, the Taylor meets the Top of the World Highway, described below. That's the road more traveled. If you instead choose to go on to Eagle, you turn to the north for the last 66 miles of rough, winding road through lovely canyons and forest. That distance doesn't sound great, but at best it takes the better part of 2 hours, one way, on this crude dirt road. There are two **campgrounds** along the Taylor, at mile 49 and mile 82, maintained by the BLM office mentioned above. The fee for each is $6. The BLM also is responsible for the **Fortymile National Wild and Scenic River,** a system with several floats of various lengths and levels of difficulty. The BLM or the public land information center in Tok can provide a river guide brochure and advice, or get *The Alaska River Guide,* mentioned at the beginning of this chapter in a sidebar called "Rollin' on the River." The BLM also produces a Taylor Highway road guide that's worth picking up.

The **Top of the World Highway** connects mile 96 of the Taylor with Dawson City, 79 miles east. If you're starting this drive in Dawson City, you might take the Top of the World to connect with the Taylor, which continues on to Eagle. The Canadian part of the gravel highway is better maintained and stunningly beautiful on a clear day. You drive over the tops of mountains, treeless alpine vistas spreading far to the horizon. Just west of the border, 13 miles from the junction, there's a small roadhouse at a place called Boundary, the only habitation on the way. The border is open 5am to 10pm Alaska time. (Don't forget that it's an hour later in Yukon.) The road closes entirely in winter. See section 7, "The Alaska Highway," above, for information on Customs.

Don't plan on making 60 miles an hour on any of these unpaved roads. In the Canadian section, most of the road is fairly broad and smooth, but speeds over 45 or so contribute to losing control or losing a headlight or windshield to a rock from a passing vehicle. On the U.S. side, the road is poorly maintained in places, and you sometimes have to go quite slowly. Part of the Taylor Highway itself was mined for gold a few years ago.

Eagle has the historic sites and the Yukon River. The **Eagle City Historical Society** (☎ **907/547-2325**) offers town walking tours Memorial Day to Labor Day, daily at 9am; the 3-hour tour costs $5. Or for the admission plus $10 more for a group, they'll do the tour anytime you like, winter or summer. The guides are local people, brimming with pride and knowledge about the area. Find them at the courthouse at Second and Berry streets. Even if you don't take the tour, a great little museum downstairs is open around the middle of the day. The tour takes you through various historic buildings loaded with the original materials left behind after the gold rush, including five buildings in the army's 1899 Fort Egbert, where Gen. Billy Mitchell had his first major assignment, in 1901 (before he was a general), to build a telegraph line to Valdez. You'll also notice the monument to Norwegian explorer Roald Amundsen, who stopped off in Eagle in 1905 during his journey through the Northwest Passage—400 miles away by dogsled—to use the telegraph.

The office of the **Yukon–Charley Rivers National Preserve** is across the airstrip on the west side of town. The preserve starts a few miles downstream on the Yukon and extends almost to Circle. The **National Park Service field office,** P.O. Box 167, Eagle, AK 99738 (☎ **907/547-2233;** www.nps.gov/yuch/), is a good place to get information on floating the river and to register your journey. It's open Memorial Day to September, daily from 8am to 5pm, and normal business hours year-round. The staff can also provide lots of information on the natural history of the area and historic sites downstream.

You can start or finish a **river float** in Eagle. From Dawson City to Eagle is 108 miles and takes 3 or 4 days, and from Eagle to Circle is 158 miles and 5 to 7 days. Mike Seger's **Eagle Canoe Rentals,** based in Eagle (☎ **907/547-2203** in Eagle or 867/993-6823 in Dawson City), allows you to drop off the canoe at the end of your float, and also rents rafts. The Dawson City office is located at the Dawson City River Hostel on the west side of the river next to the free ferry landing. The price, including return of the canoe, is $110 for up to 4 days to Eagle, $165 up to 5 days to Circle, and additional days are $20. You can take the *Yukon Queen* tour boat back upriver (see section 8 of this chapter, on Dawson City).

The **Eagle Trading Company** (☎ **907/547-2220**) is the main business in town, with a grocery store, gas station, public showers, restaurant, and motel. Their **Riverside Cafe** is good for the Bush, with tasty, inexpensive food and a dining room overlooking the river. The nine **motel rooms** also are good, with TVs and phones, tubs with showers, two queen beds in each, and a rate of only $60 double.

An attractive **BLM campground** with well-wooded sites is located in the woods above Fort Egbert. It costs $6 per night. Contact the BLM for information.

10 Wrangell–St. Elias National Park & the Copper River Valley

Looking at a relief map of Alaska, you'd think the portion drained by the Copper River was so overweighted with mountains that it might topple the whole state into the Pacific. The Alaska Range, in the center of the state, has the tallest mountain, but this Gulf of Alaska region, straddling the Alaska-Yukon border, has more mass—the second- and fourth-tallest mountains in North America (Logan and St. Elias), plus 9 of the tallest 16 peaks in the United States. Four mountain ranges intersect, creating a mad jumble of terrain covering tens of millions of acres, a trackless chaos of unnamed, unconquered peaks. The Copper River and its raging tributaries slice through it all, swallowing the gray melt of innumerable glaciers that flow from the largest ice field in North America. Everything here is the largest, most rugged, most remote; words quickly fall short of the measure. But where words fail, commerce gives a little help: These mountains are so numerous and remote that one guide service makes a business of taking visitors to mountains and valleys that no one has ever explored before.

Ironically for such a wild land, the area's main attraction for visitors is its history. The richest copper deposit in the world was found here in 1900 by a group of prospectors who mistook a green mountaintop for a patch of green grass where they could feed their horses. It was a mountain of almost pure copper, with metallic nuggets the size of desks (one is at the University of Alaska Museum in Fairbanks). The deposit produced trainloads of 70% copper ore so rich it required no processing before shipping, lots more copper that did need minimal processing, and much more lower-grade ore still left underground. The Alaska Syndicate, an investment group that included J. P. Morgan and Daniel Guggenheim, built the Kennecott Copper Corporation from this wealth (its name was a misspelling of Kennicott, where the copper was found). To get the copper out, they paid for an incredible 196-mile rail line up from Cordova (see chapter 7), and created a self-contained company town deep in the wilderness, called **Kennicott.** When the high-grade ore was gone, in 1938, they pulled the plug, leaving a ghost town of extraordinary beauty that still contains machinery and even documents they left behind.

Wrangell–St. Elias National Park and Preserve now owns Kennicott and more than 13 million acres across this region of Alaska. It's the largest national park in the United States by a long shot, six times the size of Yellowstone and about 25% larger than the entire country of Switzerland. The protected land continues across the border in Canada, in **Kluane National Park,** which is similarly massive. Most of that land is impossibly remote, but Wrangell–St. Elias has two rough gravel roads that allow access to see the mountains from a car. The main route is the abandoned roadbed of the Copper River and Northwestern Railroad leading to Kennicott and the historic sites there. It's an arduous but rewarding journey by car, requiring at least 2 days to do it right. Air taxis, river guides, and remote lodges offer other ways into the park's untouched wilderness, mostly starting from **McCarthy,** a historic village near Kennicott. There are a few trails near Kennicott, but only for day hikes. Rare in the world, this is a country where experienced outdoors people can get away from any trace of humans for weeks on end.

THE KENNICOTT & MCCARTHY AREA

This historic copper area is the only part of the park most visitors see, as it's the most accessible and has the most services, interesting sites, and paths to explore. It's still not easy to get to, however—that's why it's still so appealing—and there's little point in going without adequate time and planning. You can hit the highlights at Kennicott and McCarthy in one long, full day, but just getting there takes time, too. My family and I spent 3 nights on our last visit and could have stayed longer.

The main event is the ghost town at **Kennicott,** whose red buildings gaze from a mountainside across the Kennicott Glacier in the valley below. Now owned by the Park Service, the buildings made up an isolated company town until 1938, when it abruptly shut down. Tourists coming here as late as the 1960s saw it as if frozen in time, with breakfast dishes still on the tables from the day the last train left. Most of that was looted and destroyed in the 1970s, but when I toured the company store recently, old documents still remained, and the powerhouse and 14-story mill buildings still had their heavy iron and wood equipment. Besides the buildings, there are excellent hiking trails, including one that traverses the glacier. The town now has only a few year-round residents, but in summer there's a lodge, a couple of bed-and-breakfasts, guide services, and a Park Service meeting hall.

Five miles down the road, Kennicott's twin town of **McCarthy** served the miners as a place to drink, gamble, and hire prostitutes on their rare days off—the company didn't allow any frivolity in Kennicott or in the bunkhouses high up on the mountain. McCarthy retains the relaxed atmosphere of its past, with businesses and residents living in false-front buildings not much changed from Wild West days. More of a year-round community, McCarthy has restaurants, lodging, flight services, and other businesses.

Yet even this most populous part of the park is isolated and sparsely inhabited, with few services. Only 37 people live in the greater area year-round. You will find no banking services, real stores, gas stations, clinics, police, or anything else you're used to relying on. Phones came to McCarthy and Kennicott only within the last few years; there still are few, and none along the McCarthy Road. Bring what you need.

ESSENTIALS

GETTING THERE **By Car** The **Edgerton Highway** starts 17 miles south of Copper Center on the Richardson Highway, then runs east for 33 miles to the tiny, dried-up mining town of **Chitina** (*chit*-na), the last reliable stop for groceries, gas, and other necessities until you return here. Do fill your tank; prudence also demands a full-sized spare tire. Heading east, into the park, the **McCarthy Road** continues along the roadbed of the Copper River and Northwestern Railroad. It's 60 miles of narrow dirt road, rutted and prone to mud holes in wet weather, but the drive is a fun adventure. The road passes through tunnels of alders and crosses rivers on 100-year-old wooden railroad trestles, one of which spans a canyon more than 200 feet deep. (Most car-rental agencies won't let you bring their vehicles here, but I've listed two that will: one is in section 2 of this chapter, on Fairbanks, and the other is an obscure agency in Anchorage, **Levi Car Rental** at ☎ **907/563-2279.**) There are virtually no services and no more than two or three buildings on the entire 3-hour drive. There's a good chance you won't encounter another vehicle. The road ends at a crude campground, a parking lot, and collection of temporary businesses on the banks of the Kennicott River. Here you must leave your vehicle (parking costs $5 a day) and proceed across a foot bridge or two. Late in the summer the Kennicott Glacier releases a flood from an underground lake, but at other times the second channel is a dry wash and the second bridge isn't used. Handcarts are available to move your luggage across, and on the other side you can catch a van. The place you are staying will send one, or you can buy a ticket on an **hourly van** operated by **Wrangell Mountain Air** (☎ **907/554-4411**) or **McCarthy Air** (☎ **907/554-4440**). Each charges $5 per person, one way. A free public telephone has been installed along with an information kiosk near the bridge; use the phone to call the van or your lodgings.

By Bus The **Backcountry Connection** (☎ **800/478-5292** within Alaska, or 907/822-5292; e-mail: backcntry@alaska.net) runs a van from Glennallen and Chitina to the footbridge daily in summer except Sunday, leaving at 7am and 8:30am, respectively, arriving at the bridge at 11:45am and returning at 4pm. The fare is $80 round-trip from Chitina, $99 from Glennallen, and $10 more if you return on a different day. I think a 4-hour stay would be too brief.

By Air The simplest way to Kennicott and McCarthy is to fly there on one of the air taxis, then get around on one of the vans that shuttles back and forth over 5 miles of dirt road. **Wrangell Mountain Air** (☎ **800/478-1160** or 907/554-4411; www.wrangellmountainair.com/) offers twice-daily service from Chitna for $140 round-trip. You can charter from anywhere. A five-passenger plane is $795 from Anchorage, $495 from Valdez, one way. Another reputable operator is **McCarthy Air** (☎ **888/989-9891** from outside Alaska only, or 907/554-4440; 316/758-2512 in winter; www.mccarthyair.com). Both operators also offer charters to remote park valleys and glaciers for backcountry trips, covered below under "Getting Outside: Hiking & Backpacking." It's also possible to fly straight from Anchorage to McCarthy on the twice-weekly mail plane operated by **Security Aviation** (☎ **907/248-2677**), for $225 one-way.

VISITOR INFORMATION The park visitor center is just north of Copper Center, a mile off the Richardson Highway on the old Richardson Highway (☎ **907/822-5234;** www.nps.gov/wrst). A new center, right on the highway, should be completed by September 2001. Stop in to buy maps and publications or get advice from a ranger on outdoor treks. The office is open Memorial Day to Labor Day, daily from 8am to 6pm; in winter, Monday to Friday from 8am to 4:30pm. You can write for information at P.O. Box 439, Copper Center, AK 99573.

The **Chitina Ranger Station** (☎ **907/823-2205**) is along the most popular way to the park, in the old mining town of Chitina, 33 miles down the paved Edgerton Highway, which starts about 17 miles south of Copper Center on the Richardson Highway. The center is arranged like a reading room, with lots of material to consult, historic photographs on display, and rangers who help visitors figure out backcountry trips. There's a picnic table out front. Like almost all visitor services in the area, it is closed in winter. Summer hours are 10am to 6pm daily.

The Park Service is just starting to develop **visitor services in Kennicott** itself. Usually you'll find a ranger there during the day, often giving a talk in the evening in the hall across the road from the lodge. There's a summer kiosk at the foot bridge. A visitor center is planned, but hadn't gotten much beyond the idea stage at this writing.

The **Kennicott-McCarthy Chamber of Commerce,** P.O. Box MXY, McCarthy, AK 99588 (**www.mccarthy-kennicott.com/cc**) provides information on every business, whether or not a member; they have no phone or office. Check out the local newspaper at **www.mccarthy-kennicott.com**.

GETTING AROUND A great way to get around on your own is by bicycle; the rental agency by the bridge recently closed up, but I'm sure someone else will pick up the business. You also can rent bikes at the **Glacier View Campground,** a half mile short of the footbridge on the McCarthy Road (☎ **907/554-4490**).

Attractions & Activities in the Towns

CHITINA A town of around 50 people, Chitina has a post office and limited services, but not much to hold you. It's a desiccated outpost, with a row of historic buildings that stand empty and decaying. One stop is worth making, besides the ranger station, mentioned above: **Spirit Mountain Artworks** (☎ **907/823-2222;** e-mail: uncleart@igc.org), where an old building has been lovingly restored into a historic landmark to house fine art and crafts. Heading a little to the east, the McCarthy Road crosses the **Copper River,** which is full of red salmon in season. It's also possible to get to fishing waters to the south, along the unfinished and abandoned Copper River Highway. Check at the ranger station for guidance.

McCARTHY McCarthy feels authentic as soon as you walk down the dirt main street between the false fronts. On a summer evening young backpackers and locals stand in the road—there is no traffic, since there are almost no vehicles—meeting and talking, carrying their glasses of beer from the lodge over to the ice cream shop, laughing loudly, walking around the dogs that are having their own party. Along the street, there are flight service offices to arrange a trip out, a couple of restaurants, a lodge. Then, a street beyond, unbroken wilderness for hundreds and perhaps thousands of miles. The people here know it's unique, and everyone hopes it doesn't change. No one wants a big flood of tour-bus visitors—that's why they fought the state government when it wanted to build a road bridge over the Kennicott; they prefer to have the McCarthy Road rough instead of smooth. The foot bridge should keep too many casual visitors at bay. Those who do make it are treated well—like one of the community. If you need help, you just walk up to anyone you see and he or she will help you.

The town's one formal visitor attraction is the **McCarthy-Kennicott Historical Museum,** housed in a couple of rooms and a railroad car at the edge of town. The exhibits of historic photographs help put the stories you'll hear in perspective, and there are some interesting artifacts. You'll likely be the only visitor when you arrive, so you can ask the volunteer questions you may have saved up. They're open Memorial Day to Labor Day, 10am to 6pm daily; admission is free, but a donation is requested.

To learn the natural history of the area, pick up a copy of *Learning the Landscape: An Interpretive Dayhike from McCarthy to the Kennicott Glacier Face,* sold at the ranger stations and footbridge kiosk for $3. It explains the botany and extraordinary geology of the area in a walking tour beginning from the footbridge.

KENNICOTT This has got to be one of the world's greatest ghost towns, with some 40 buildings, mostly in good enough condition to be reused today—indeed, they still play basketball in the community hall, some buildings have become lodgings, and the Park Service is planning to move into the store. Locals still pick rhubarb and chives from the company garden. History has the same kind of immediacy here that you get from holding an old diary in your hand, quite different from the sanitized history-through-glass that you're used to at more accessible sites.

The Park Service only completed purchase of the buildings recently, and still needs to secure the artifacts. When we visited around the time of the purchase, items remained out on the ground or on store shelves that would be in museums in many places. If Kennicott were an ordinary industrial site, that would be interesting enough, but this place was something well out of the ordinary: an outpost beyond the edge of the world where men built a self-contained city almost a century ago. The hardship of the miners' lives and the ease of the managerial families' lives also presents a fascinating contrast.

You can take in a lot of it by wandering around with a walking tour booklet (available at a park service kiosk in the ghost town) and reading signs. You can look inside some buildings on your own, but to go into the really impressive mill building and several other remarkable structures, you need to join a ✪ **guided tour** offered by **St. Elias Alpine Guides** (☎ **888/993-4537** or 907/544-4445; full listing below under "Hiking and Backpacking") for $25 per person. The park service may also contract with a concessionaire to offer tours. The St. Elias Alpine tour I joined lasted much of the afternoon and went into real scholarly depth on the geology and history, as well as climbing to the perilous 14th floor of the mill building. It's something not to miss.

GETTING OUTSIDE

HIKING & BACKPACKING There are a few trails radiating from Kennicott, for which crude maps are available from the rangers and others around town, or buy the **Trails Illustrated** topographic map, printed on plastic, also for sale at the ranger stations (see "Fast Facts: Alaska" in chapter 2). An impressive walk or challenging mountain-bike ride continues through the ghost town up the valley, paralleling the Kennicott Glacier and then its tributary, the Root Glacier. You can either climb along the Root's edge to a towering ice fall, or traverse the glacial ice itself on a trail branch. It's wise to join a group if you want to walk on the glacier, as it can be dangerous: A couple of different guides in Kennicott accept walk-ins for daily glacier day hikes and other hikes and tours. A half day on the glacier goes for around $50 a person, while all-day hikes or ice climbing lessons cost about $80 to $100. Try St. Elias Alpine Guides, listed below, or **Kennicott-McCarthy Wilderness Guides** (☎ **800/664-4537** or 907/554-4444). Another fascinating hike leads straight up the mountain behind the Kennicott buildings to the old mines and miner bunkhouses, 3,000 feet higher on the alpine tundra.

Beyond the trails, the park is endless miles of trackless wilderness—one of earth's last few places that really deserves that name. Fit hikers without the backcountry experience to mount their own expedition should join one of the guides who work in the area. **St. Elias Alpine Guides** (☎ **888/933-5427** or 907/554-4445; winter 907/345-9048; www.steliasguides.com) offers day hikes, mountain biking, rafting, backpacking trips, and alpine ascents, but specializes in guiding extended trips to unexplored territory. Bob Jacobs, president of the company, stopped guiding on Mount McKinley years ago because of the crowds. He claims never to have seen another party in more than 20 years of guiding expeditions in Wrangell–St. Elias, and has led more than 45 parties of customers up previously unclimbed peaks. By definition, you can't get farther from civilization. A 2-week trek and climb, including 4 days of mountaineering instruction, is a big commitment, and costs $3,000 and up, but then, first ascents are a finite resource. The St. Elias catalogue will make anyone who loves backpacking drool. Trips begin at $775 for a 4-day Donohoe Peak trek. They are all-inclusive, but not without hardship and risk—nothing can take away from the severity of this wild country.

Hiking on your own in a wilderness largely without trails is a whole new kind of experience for experienced backpackers and outdoors people who are used to more crowded parts of the planet. You feel like an explorer rather than a follower. At times, there's a fairy-tale sense of the world unfolding around you, as fresh as creation. If you're not prepared to select your own route—a task only for those already experienced in trackless, backcountry traveling—there are various established ways through the park you can follow with a topographic map. The Park Service publishes **trip synopses** of many of the routes, and rangers will help you choose one to suit your party—although none are easy. Get a Trip Synopsis List from the headquarters. Some routes start from the roads, but a better way to go is to charter a flight into a remote valley from one of the two **air services** in McCarthy. The planes land on gravel strips, river bars, glaciers, and any other flat places the pilots know about. These companies make a business of flying out backpackers, and so have established rates for different landing sites and can help with determining a route that's right for you, as well as providing a list of supplies. You can do it for $100 per person, with at least two passengers. Or fly in to a lake or river for fishing and exploring from a base camp, eliminating some of the worry about how much you pack. Two operators are listed above, under "Getting There."

I wouldn't want to scare off anyone who would really be able to manage one of these trips, but people do get in trouble in the Alaska wilderness every year, and some of them don't come back. Before you head out into the backcountry, you must know how to take care of yourself where help is unavailable, including how to handle river crossings, bear avoidance, preventing hypothermia, basic first aid, and other issues. Some of this is covered in chapter 2, but you can't get all you need to know from this book. Unless you have plenty of backpacking experience in less remote areas, I wouldn't recommend starting here.

MOUNTAIN BIKING Anywhere else, the 60-mile road that leads to this area would be considered a mountain-biking trail. You also can make good use of bikes between McCarthy, Kennicott, and the footbridge. An old **wagon road** parallels the main road that connects the two towns, 4.5 miles each way; the road itself is a one-lane dirt track. Advanced cyclists can also ride the trails around Kennicott described above under "Hiking & Backpacking."

RAFTING Many great, wild rivers drain these huge mountains, which are still being carved by enormous glaciers. The **Kennicott River,** starting at the glacier of the same name, boils in Class III rapids for some 40 minutes starting right from the footbridge at the end of the McCarthy Road. As the area lacks roads, however, most trips must include a plane ride at least one way, and that makes white-water rafting day trips here more expensive than outings near Anchorage or Valdez. At times, hour-long, drive-back floats have been available on a walk-in basis at the footbridge, but most trips punch deeper into the backcountry. The Kennicott River meets the Nizina, passing through a deep, dramatic canyon; then the Nizina River flows into the Chitina River, which meets the Copper River near the town of Chitina, 60 miles from the starting point. The Copper River flows to the ocean. A float from the footbridge through the Nizina Canyon takes all day, with lunch and bush plane flightseeing back, which could include a glacier fly-over. Two firms offer this unforgettable float and flight. Family operated **Copper Oar Adventures** (☎ **800/523-4453** or 907/554-4453; www.alaskan.com/copper_oar/) does it for $225 per person, and St. Elias Alpine Guides (see "Hiking & Backpacking," above) charges $285. Other trips continue 3 or 4 days to Chitina, for $575 to $850 per person; or 10 to 13 days, 180 miles all the way to the Copper River Delta and the sea (see "Cordova" in chapter 7), for $2,500 to $2,900 per person. I've never done that trip, but I dream about it. This is Alaska on its largest and most grandiose scale, accessible only from the banks of these great rivers.

ACCOMMODATIONS

There's not a hotel room with a private bathroom for 100 miles, but the Kennicott-McCarthy area has several attractive places to stay, all thick with the history the towns represent. Besides the three recommended below, I was impressed with houses for rent behind the Kennicott ghost town. The two I saw were **Kennicott Cottage** (☎ **907/242-1392** in Kennicott or 907/345-7961 in Anchorage), and, right next door, **17 Silkstocking Row** (☎ **907/338-5859,** or 907/554-1717 summer only; www.alaska.net/~lei). You can rent one room, a two-bedroom suite, or the whole three-bedroom house. The only drawback of the attractively restored houses is a lack of flush toilets or electricity, although they do have running water and showers.

Historic Kennicott Bed and Breakfast. Silk Stocking Row, Kennicott. (McCarthy no. 4 P.O. Box MXY, Glennallen, AK 99588). ☎ **907/554-4469.** 1 unit. $175 for 2, $250 for 4. Extra person $25. Rates include full continental breakfast. No credit cards.

A family that lives here year-round hosts guests in a house next door to their own, a historic, unspoiled residence in the woods behind the ghost town, once the home of the family of a Kennecott Copper manager. Their warmth is infectious—the kids will try to sell you pieces of copper ore they found—giving guests a chance to make friends of people living a real pioneer lifestyle. The rental unit even has plumbing. As with the two nearby houses listed above, you must be able to walk up a hill to get there from the main road.

Kennicott Glacier Lodge. P.O. Box 103940, Anchorage, AK 99510. ☎ **800/582-5128** or 907/258-2350. In season only, 907/554-4477. Fax 907/248-7975. www.KennicottLodge.com. 25 units, none with private bathroom. $179 double. AE, DISC, MC, V. Closed mid-Sept to mid-May.

This is the area's largest and most comfortable accommodation, a first-class place that takes the edges off the isolation. The lodge accurately re-creates an old Kennicott building, with the same red-and-white color scheme, right amid the historic structures of the ghost town. You can't get any closer to what you want to see. Guests can sip drinks on a long front porch overlooking the glacier, or relax on a lawn with the same view. The rooms are not large, and bathrooms are down the hall—although all were quite clean when we visited.

Filling meals are served family style, at long tables, with a fixed menu for a fixed price (a turkey dinner was $22.50, for example). There's nowhere else to eat right in Kennicott, so plan to spend about $40 per person on food, or simply book the package that includes meals, for $127.50 per person per night. A brief tour of the ghost town and bicycles is available.

McCarthy Lodge. P.O. Box MXY, McCarthy, AK 99588. ☎ **907/554-4402.** Fax 907/554-4404. 18 units, none with private bathroom. $115 double. MC, V. Rates include continental breakfast. Closed Oct to Memorial Day.

The lodge is the center of the relaxed village of McCarthy, 5 miles from the historically more buttoned-up Kennicott. The small rooms are in a false-front building that you might see in an old Western movie, except that it's real and unrestored. The decor is lace and rough-cut lumber. The shared bathroom was clean when I visited.

The lodge is an authentic Bush roadhouse, serving dinner family style. You must make reservations for the single 7pm seating. Dinners range from $16 to $22.

Camping & Hostelling

There is no campground on the Kennicott-McCarthy side of the Kennicott River footbridge. The Park Service allows camping anywhere in the park without a permit, but there are few appropriate spots on public land (remember, much of the land along the roads is private).

A couple of primitive private campgrounds, and a hostel, are at the end of the McCarthy Road. **Kennicott River Lodge and Hostel** (☎ **907/554-4441** summer, 907/479-6822 winter; www.ptialaska.net/~grosswlr/) is just up the road, with bunks for $25 per person and cabins for $85 double plus $15 for each additional person. Showers and bedding cost extra, as they have to haul their water.

There are three campgrounds on the way to the footbridge. The most attractive is the State Parks' **Liberty Falls Campground,** at mile 23 on the Edgerton Highway, which is set among big trees at the foot of a crashing waterfall. Many of the sites are walk-ins, with wooden tent platforms and lots of privacy. The self-service camping fee is $10 per vehicle; the day use fee is $1. There are pit toilets, and no running water. A mile or two beyond Chitina, across the Copper River on the McCarthy Road, a primitive **state campground** at riverside has pit toilets and dusty sites among cottonwoods. At mile 11 on the McCarthy Road, the 30-site **Silver Lake Campground** (no telephone) sits in a lovely, peaceful spot along the shore of a lake with Rainbow trout. Skiffs with outboards and canoes are for rent. The sites are most attractive for RVs, and there is an outhouse. The camping fee is $10.

DINING

The main restaurants in the Kennicott area are at the Kennicott Glacier Lodge and McCarthy Lodge, described above. I also enjoyed pizza and beer in a screened porch at **Taylor-Made Pizza** in McCarthy (☎ **907/554-1155**). It's open 10am to 10pm daily in the summer. There's a food stand at the footbridge, too.

11 Glennallen & the Copper River Country

The people of the Copper River Country, as this cold, arid region along the great river is known, live on homesteads and tiny settlements, and in a couple of towns near the regional hub of **Glennallen,** at the intersection of the Glenn and Richardson highways. It's a sparsely settled land for rugged outdoor activities. The volunteer-run **Copper River Visitor Center** is in a log cabin right at the intersection of the highways (P.O. Box 469, Glennallen, AK 99588; ☎ **907/822-5555;** www.traveltoalaska.com); in summer it's open daily from 8am to 7pm. (The Web site is still under construction.) Glennallen has a bank with an ATM, a post office, a medical center, and government offices.

The best standard accommodations in the area are at the **New Caribou Hotel,** at mile 187 of the Glenn Highway (☎ **800/478-3302** or 907/822-3302). The rooms are the equal of a good chain. A double is $130 in the summer. Unfortunately, the hotel books up many months ahead with bus tours. Their **Caribou Restaurant** is inexpensive and good for comfort food—meat loaf, roast beef, pork chops. The other place where my family likes to eat while passing through Glennallen is the **Tastee**

Freez (☎ **907/822-3923**), a clean burger joint and local hangout with wallpaper and fine art on the walls. Besides big burgers and soft ice cream, they also serve chicken and Mexican dishes, and good milk shakes.

Fourteen miles south of Glennallen, **Copper Center** is a tiny Athabascan community on the old Richardson Highway. A historic roadhouse, the **Copper Center Lodge** (☎ **888/822-3245** or 907/822-3245; www.alaska.net/~ccl/) is worthy of a stop for dinner or even overnight, if it's time for a rest on your drive. Rooms in the big old log building rent for $89 a night with a shared bathroom, $99 with a private bathroom. The restaurant here has a good reputation all over the region for hearty, satisfying meals. It's open 7am to 9pm, and the staff brags especially of its sourdough pancakes, made with starter 100 years old. (Gold rush prospectors carried sourdough starter, a mixture of live yeast and flour, always growing more so they never ran out. Alaskans sometimes track their pedigree by the lineage of their sourdough starter.) The history of the lodge dates from the bizarre gold rush origins of Copper Center and Valdez, when about 4,000 stampeders to the Klondike tried a virtually impossible all-American route from Valdez over the glaciers of the Wrangell–St. Elias region. Few made it, and hundreds who died are buried in Copper Center. The original lodge was built of the stuff they left behind. The existing building dates from 1932.

Other than Wrangell–St. Elias National Park, most of the public land in the Copper River Country is managed by the **Bureau of Land Management Glennallen District,** with a log cabin office in town on the north side of the Glenn Highway, P.O. Box 147, Glennallen, AK 99588 (☎ **907/822-3217;** www.glennallen.ak.blm.gov/), open Monday to Friday 8am to 4pm. Information also is available from the public land information centers in Anchorage, Fairbanks, and Tok. This huge area, about the size of a midsized eastern U.S. state, is more accessible than the park, an advantage for outdoor recreation, but it's still a rough, remote land with few high-quality visitor facilities. There are several large alpine lakes, two National Wild Rivers, many hiking trails, and five campgrounds, all reached on the Richardson, Glenn, and Denali highways. Guides are available for **rafting** and **fishing** in the rivers. Check at the visitor center or BLM office for referrals. The salmon are not as desirable this far inland as they are near the coast, as they've begun to turn red, soften, and lose oil content with their spawning changes.

The Bush 10

The Bush is most of Alaska. On a map of the state, the portion with roads and cities is a smallish corner. Yet most visitors—and, indeed, most Alaskans—never make it beyond that relatively populated corner. Recently a lifelong Anchorage resident was elected to the legislature and appointed chair of its rural issues committee, only to admit he had never been to the Bush. It's common for children to grow to adulthood in Anchorage, Fairbanks, or Southeast Alaska without traveling to the Arctic, the Aleutians, or the vast wetlands of western Alaska. It happens for the same reason most tourists don't go to Bush Alaska—getting there is expensive, and there's not much in the way of human activity once you arrive. Bush Alaska is one of the planet's last barely inhabited areas. But that's a reason to go, not a reason to stay away. You can meet indigenous people who still interact with the environment in their traditional way, and see virgin places that remain to be explored by self-reliant outdoors people.

Although there are few people in the Bush, the hospitality of those you do meet is special and warming. In Bush Alaska, where the population is overwhelming Alaska Native, it's not uncommon to be befriended by total strangers simply because you've taken the trouble to come to their community and are, therefore, an honored guest. Even in the larger towns, people look you in the eye and smile as you pass in the street. If you have a questioning look on your face, they'll stop to help. Living in a small place where people know each other and have to work together against the elements makes for a tight, friendly community.

Alaska's Native culture is based more on cooperative than competitive impulses. Honesty, respect, and consensus carry greater weight than in white society. Cooperation requires slowing down, listening, not taking the lead—people from our fast-paced culture can leave a village after a visit wondering why no one spoke to them, not realizing that they never shut up long enough to give anyone a chance. The cultural differences here are real, unlike the shadows of past differences we celebrate in most regions of the homogenous United States. Long pauses in conversation are normal, looking down while addressing a person demonstrates respect, punctuality is highly relative, child care is a community function, and when gifts are offered people really mean it—turning down even a cup of coffee is gauche. (For more on the culture of Alaska's Native peoples, see the appendix.)

The Native people of the Bush also have terrible problems trying to live in two worlds. There's too much alcohol and too many drugs in the Bush, too much TV, but not enough of an economic base to provide for safe drinking water or plumbing in many villages. Even in some of the relatively prosperous village hubs described in this chapter, visitors will glimpse a kind of rural poverty they may not have seen before—where prices are extremely high, and steady jobs are scarce and interfere with traditional hunting and food gathering. But if you ask why they stay, you're missing something. In a world where so few indigenous cultures survive, people here are working to retain traditions that give their lives meaning while also adopting what they need from modernity. It's a work in progress, but there's no question they're slowly succeeding. They control their own land, they're building an economic base, and Native ways are being passed on to younger generations.

The Natives' physical environment is extreme in every respect—the weather, the land, even the geography. There's a special feeling to walking along the Arctic Ocean, the virtual edge of the earth, on a beach that lies between flat, wet tundra and an ocean that's usually ice. The quantity and accessibility of wildlife are extreme, too, as are the solitude and uniqueness of what you can do. Unfortunately, the prices also are extreme. With few exceptions, getting to a Bush hub from Anchorage costs more than getting to Anchorage from Seattle. And once you're at the hub, you're not done. Getting into the outdoors can cost as much again. Many travelers can't afford to make a Bush sojourn, instead satisfying their curiosity about the state's unpopulated areas on Alaska's rural highways. Most who can afford the trip usually make the most of their time and money with brief prearranged tours or trips directly to wilderness lodges. Only a few explorers head for the Bush unguided, although there are some good places to go that way—Nome, Kodiak, and Unalaska among them.

Covering the Bush also is a challenge for the writer of a book like this one. There are more than 200 Alaska villages, many lodges, camps, and guides, and a vast, undefined territory to describe. All that information would fill a larger book than this one, but would be of little use to the great majority of readers. I've taken the approach, instead, of providing sections on those few Bush hubs that are most accessible and popular with visitors, that have modern facilities, and can be used as gateways to much more of the state for those who want to step out beyond the fringe of civilization.

If you find yourself in a town such as **Nome, Kotzebue, Barrow,** or **Kodiak,** all hubs for outlying Native villages, there's a simple and relatively inexpensive way to get out and see how village people live: Mail and scheduled passenger planes, typically small, single-engine craft, make daily rounds of the villages from each hub. Without the difficulty, expense, and dubious interest of going for a longer trip to a village, you can fly out on one of these planes for a quick day trip, walk around and meet people, then fly back to the hub city on the next flight to come through. *One warning:* Don't make such an excursion in lowering weather, as you could get weathered in at a remote village. A journalist friend of mine was weathered in for more than 2 weeks on one occasion. You'll find the air-taxi operators—true bush pilots—friendly, informal, and most willing to oblige you in working out your Bush adventure. To find out where to go, just walk into the office and tell them what you're interested in seeing and how much time and money you want to spend. It's also an inexpensive way to go flightseeing.

1 Exploring the Bush

Alaska's Bush is better defined by what it's like there than where it is. The most common and convenient conception says the Bush is everything beyond the road system. On a map, everything north and west of Fairbanks obviously meets that definition, but many Bush villages lie elsewhere in the Interior, in Southcentral, and in Southeast Alaska. In fact, there are some Bush villages you can drive to. No simple definition works. You know a Bush community by how it feels. It's a place where the wilderness is closer than civilization, where people still live off the land and age-old traditions survive, and where you have to make a particular effort to get in or out.

THE REGIONS

THE ARCTIC The Arctic Circle is the official boundary of the Arctic. The line, at 66° 33' north latitude, is the southern limit of true midnight sun—south of it, at sea level, the sun rises and sets, at least a little, every day of the year. But in Alaska, people think of the Arctic as beginning at the **Brooks Range,** which is a bit north of the circle, including **Barrow** and **Prudhoe Bay.** The northwest Alaska region, which includes **Kotzebue** and, slightly south of the Arctic Circle, **Nome,** also is Arctic in climate, culture, and topography. The biggest geographic feature in Alaska's Arctic is the broad **North Slope,** the plain of tundra that stretches from the northern side of the Brooks Range to the Arctic Ocean. It's a swampy desert, with little rain or snowfall, frozen solid all but a couple of months a year.

WESTERN ALASKA This is the land of the massive, wet **Yukon-Kuskokwim Delta** and the fish-rich waters of Bristol Bay. The Y-K Delta, as it's known, was never really exploited by white explorers, and the Yup'ik people who live there have maintained some of the most culturally traditional villages—in some, Yup'ik is still the dominant language. **Bethel** is the main hub city of the delta, but holds little attraction for visitors. **Bristol Bay** is known for massive salmon runs, and avid fishers may be interested in its wilderness lodges, using **Dillingham** as a hub.

SOUTHWEST ALASKA Stretching from the Aleutians—really a region of their own—to the Alaska Peninsula, Kodiak Island, and the southern part of the mountainous west side of Cook Inlet, this is a maritime region, like Southeast, but far more remote. The hub of the wet, windy **Aleutians** is **Unalaska and its port of Dutch Harbor. Katmai National Park** and the adjoining wild lands are the main attraction of the Alaska Peninsula, although there also are fishing lodges on the salmon-rich rivers and on the lakes to the north, including areas in **Lake Clark National Park** and **Iliamna Lake.** The lakes and west side of **Cook Inlet** are accessed primarily by Kenai, Homer, and Anchorage flight services for fishermen and hunters. **Kodiak** is hardly a Bush community, but fits better in this chapter than anywhere else.

GETTING AROUND

With a few exceptions for strongly motivated travelers, who can take the ferry to Kodiak and Unalaska or drive to Prudhoe Bay, getting to each town in this chapter will require flying. **Alaska Airlines (☎ 800/252-7522;** www.alaskaair.com) jets fly to all the towns described in this chapter. Other, smaller operators serve each town as well, mostly with prop aircraft. Throughout the chapter, I've listed the plane fare to various communities from Anchorage, based on flying coach and getting a significant discount for advance purchase and some restrictions. Full Y-class fares are more. With the way airfares fluctuate, it would be unwise to use these numbers as anything more than rough guides. To get the current best fare, use a travel agent or the Internet (check the Online Directory for tips).

Kodiak, which barely fits in a chapter on the Bush, is the most accessible of the communities in this chapter, but it still requires either a 10-hour ferry ride from Homer or a $200 round-trip plane ticket from Anchorage. This charming, historic town is similar to towns in Southeast Alaska or Prince William Sound; but it is also a hub for Native villages on the island. **Unalaska/Dutch Harbor,** in the Aleutian Islands, is an interesting place to go way off the beaten path while staying in complete comfort, but is short on the Native culture you may be looking for. A visit requires a $700 to $800 round-trip plane ticket. **Kotzebue** and **Barrow** are the most purely Native of the communities in the chapter. **Nome** has the advantages of Arctic surroundings easily accessible on gravel roads, but is more of a gold rush town than a Native village. **Prudhoe Bay,** at the end of the Dalton Highway, is an industrial complex without a real town associated with it. Fares range from $360 to $700 for these communities. Buying an **Alaska Airlines package tour** saves a lot of money to Nome, Kotzebue, or Barrow, and gives you something to do when you arrive.

2 Kodiak

The habitat that makes Kodiak Island a perfect place for bears also makes it perfect for people. Runs of salmon clog unpopulated bays and innumerable, unfished rivers; the rounded green mountains seem to beg for someone to cross them; the gravel beaches and protected rocky inlets are free of people, but full of promise. But, in this respect, bears are smarter than people. Brown bears own the island, growing to prodigious size and abundant numbers, but Kodiak is as yet undiscovered by human visitors. That's a part of the wonder of the place. I'll never forget flying over the luxuriant verdure of Kodiak's mountains and the narrow string of glassy Raspberry Strait on a rare sunny day, seeing no sign of human presence in the most beautiful landscape I had ever beheld. That's something the bears will never experience, despite their superior collective intelligence.

The streets of the town of Kodiak are a discovery, too. Narrow and twisting over hills with little discernible order, they were the original stomping grounds of **Lord Alexander Baranof,** the first Russian ruler of Alaska, who arrived here in 1790—and before Baranof, of the **Koniag,** the first people who lived off the incomparable riches of the island, and who today recover their past in a fascinating little research museum. The Russian heritage includes the oldest Russian building in North America. It was nearly lost in the 1964 Good Friday earthquake, which destroyed most of the town (that explains the general lack of old buildings). The quake brought a 30-foot wave that washed to the building's doorstep. A marker near the police station on Mill Bay Road shows the wave's incredible high-water point.

The town still looks to the sea. Along with the Coast Guard base, fishing makes Kodiak prosperous, creating a friendly, energetic, unpolished community. Kodiak is separate from the rest of Alaska, living its own commercial fishing life without often thinking of what's going on in Anchorage or anywhere else. It's off the beaten path because it doesn't really need anything the path provides.

For the visitor, Kodiak is an undiscovered gem. When I took my family there on the ferry recently, our 3-day visit just scratched the surface of the charming, vibrant town and the easily accessible wild places around it. In the middle of the summer, other tourists were barely in evidence.

There are seven **Native villages** on the island—a flight to one of them and back on a clear day is a wonderful, low-cost way to see remote areas of the island and to get a taste of how Alaska Natives live. **Ranches** on the road system around town offer riding and lodging. You can fly out to see the famous bears on a day trip, or stay at one of several **wilderness lodges** for wildlife watching, fishing, sea kayaking, and hunting, and even participating in a Native-led archaeological dig.

ESSENTIALS

GETTING THERE It's a 1-hour flight from Anchorage to Kodiak on **Alaska Airlines** (☎ **800/252-7522;** www.alaskaair.com). **ERA Aviation** (☎ **800/866-8394;** www.eraaviation.com) also serves the route. A round-trip ticket costs $200 to $250, depending on how far ahead you buy. A **cab,** from **Ace Mecca** (☎ **907/486-3211**) or **A and B Taxi** (☎ **907/486-4343**), runs around $13 from the airport.

The ferry *Tustumena,* of the **Alaska Marine Highway System** (☎ **800/642-0066** or 907/486-3800; www.dot.state.ak.us/external/amhs/home.html), serves Kodiak from Homer and Seward. If you have the time for the 10-hour run from Homer—the closest port with a road—this boat ride is truly memorable. The vessel leaves land behind and threads through the strange and exposed Barren Islands. The ocean can be quite rough, and when it is, lots of passengers get seasick; take Dramamine *before* boarding. A cabin is a good idea for an overnight run. The U.S. Fish and Wildlife Service staffs the trips with a naturalist. The adult passenger fare is $48, children half price. The Kodiak terminal is in the same building as the visitor center.

VISITOR INFORMATION The **Kodiak Island Convention and Visitors Bureau,** 100 Marine Way, Kodiak, AK 99615 (☎ **907/486-4782;** fax 907/486-6545; www.kodiak.org), occupies a small building on the ferry dock. The staff is helpful and the Web site is exceptional. Hours vary according to the ferry schedule, but essentially follow this pattern: summer Monday 8am to 8:30pm, Tuesday to Friday 8am to 5pm, Saturday 10am to 4pm, Sunday 1 to 8:30pm; winter Monday to Friday 8am to 5pm, closed for lunch.

The **Kodiak National Wildlife Refuge Visitors Center,** Buskin River Road, near the airport 4 miles south of town (☎ **907/487-2600;** alaska.fws.gov/nwr/kodiak/kodnwrt.html), is headquarters for a refuge that covers most of the island and is home of the famous Kodiak brown bear. There are remote public-use cabins all over the refuge, reachable by chartered plane. Permits are $30, available by phone or lottery 3 months in advance. The center has interesting exhibits and is a good place to stop for outdoors information. They're open mid-June to August daily 8am to 4:30pm; the balance of the year Monday to Friday only.

ORIENTATION The Kodiak Archipelago contains Kodiak, Shuyak, and Afognak islands, and many other, smaller islands. Kodiak is the nation's second-largest island (after Hawaii's Big Island). The city of Kodiak is on a narrow point on the northeast side of Kodiak Island, surrounded by tiny islands. There are seven Native villages on other parts of the island. The airport and Coast Guard base are several miles southwest of town on **Rezanof Drive,** which runs through town and comes out on the other side. The center of Kodiak is a hopeless tangle of steep, narrow streets—you need the excellent map given away by the visitor center, but it's all walkable. The ferry dock is on **Marine Way,** and most of the in-town sights are right nearby. Several gravel roads, totaling 100 miles, make wonderful exploring from Kodiak to deserted shorelines, gorgeous views, pastures, recreation areas, and salmon streams. The visitors guide contains a mile-by-mile guide to each drive.

GETTING AROUND Several companies rent cars, including **Budget** (☎ **800/527-0700** or 907/487-2220; www.budget.com), which has offices at the airport or downtown.

If it's not raining, a bike is a great way to get around Kodiak, and strong riders will enjoy touring the roads out of town. Bikes are for rent at **Fifty-Eight Degrees North,** a full-service bike shop at 1231 Mill Bay Rd. (☎ **907/486-6249**). Front-suspension mountain bikes rent for $30 for 24 hours, tandems for $40.

FAST FACTS There are several **banks** downtown with ATMs, including Key Bank on the mall at the waterfront.

The **Providence Kodiak Island Medical Center** is at 1915 E. Rezanof Dr. (☎ **907/486-3281**).

Sweets-N-More, 117 Lower Mill Bay Rd. (☎ **907/481-1630**), charges $6 per hour for Internet access. **Mail Boxes Etc.,** 202 Center St. (☎ **907/486-8780**), also offers access.

The number for the **Kodiak Police Department** is ☎ **907/486-8000.**

The **post office** is near Lower Mill Bay Road and Hemlock Street, with stations at the Safeway and Alaska Commercial grocery stores.

Sales tax is 6% within city limits. The **room tax** inside the Kodiak city limits totals 11%, while outside the city it's 5%.

SPECIAL EVENTS **Russian Orthodox Christmas,** coming about 2 weeks after the Roman Catholic and Protestant celebration, includes the **Starring Ceremony,** in which a choir follows a star in the evening to sing at the homes of church members. The late-March **Pillar Mountain Golf Classic** (☎ **907/486-4782**) is played on a one-hole par-70 course that climbs 1,400 feet from tee to flag; dogs, chain saws, two-way radios, and tracking devices are prohibited, and cursing the officials carries a $25 fine. Hand saws and hatchets are allowed. The 5-day **Kodiak Crab Festival** (☎ **907/486-5557;** www.kodiak.org/crabfest.html), on Memorial Day weekend, is the big event of the year and includes a carnival, parade, ultramarathon, and rubber duck race, and also the solemn blessing of the fleet and memorial service for lost fishermen. In early September, the **Kodiak State Fair and Rodeo** (☎ **907/485-4959**) has all kinds of small-town contests. The **Harbor Stars** (☎ **907/486-8085**), in mid-December, is a fleet parade of vessels decorated for Christmas. The visitor bureau maintains a complete community calendar online at **www.kodiak.org/calendar.html**.

ATTRACTIONS & ACTIVITIES

A **walking tour** in the local visitors guide will show you what's available in town (a version is on the Web at **www.kodiak.org/walk.html**). The highlights include the **Fishermen's Memorial,** near the harbormaster's office at the head of the St. Paul Harbor, where a soberingly long list of Kodiak fishermen who have lost their lives at sea is posted on plaques. The warship set in concrete on Mission Way is the ***Kodiak Star,*** the last World War II Liberty Ship built. It came here as a fish processor after the 1964 earthquake destroyed the canneries, and is still in use. At Kashevarof and Mission, the **Holy Resurrection Russian Orthodox Church** was founded in 1794, although the present building dates only to 1945, when it was rebuilt after a fire.

Half-hour **Native dance performances** take place June to August daily at 2pm at the Kodiak Tribal Council Barabara, at 713 E. Rezanof Dr. (☎ **907/486-4449**). Admission is $15 adults, kids half price.

Alutiiq Museum. 215 Mission Rd. ☎ **907/486-7004.** www.alutiiqmuseum.com/. Admission $2 adults, free for kids under age 12. Summer, Mon–Fri 9am–5pm, Sat 10am–5pm. Winter, Tues–Fri 9am–5pm, Sat 10:30am–4:30pm.

This exceptional Native-funded and -governed museum seeks to document and restore the Koniag Alutiiq people's culture, which the Russians virtually wiped out in the 18th century. Besides teaching about Alutiiq culture in a single gallery, the museum manages its own archaeological digs (see "Getting Outside," below) and repatriates Native remains and artifacts, which researchers removed by the thousands in the 1930s. The archaeological repository now includes 100,000 objects. In 2001, this renaissance should take another step forward when the museum hosts a major exhibit, *Looking Both Ways: Heritage and Identity of the Alutiiq People,* which will include holdings from the Smithsonian Institution and is being organized with help from their Arctic Studies Center. If all goes as planned (dates have been postponed once already), the exhibit will open in September 2001 with a Gathering, a meeting and celebration by Native peoples from the entire Alutiiq region, from Prince William Sound to the tip of the Alaska Peninsula.

The Baranov Museum. 101 Marine Way. ☎ **907/486-5920.** Admission $2; free for children 12 and under. Summer, Mon–Sat 10am–4pm, Sun noon–4pm. Winter, Mon–Wed and Fri–Sat 10am–3pm. Closed Feb.

The museum occupies the oldest Russian building of only four left standing in North America; it was built in 1808 by Alexander Baranof as a magazine and strong house for valuable sea otter pelts. It stands in a grassy park overlooking the water across from the ferry dock. Inside is a little museum rich with Russian and early Native artifacts. The guides know a lot of history and show 30 educational albums on various topics. The gift store is exceptional, selling antique Russian items and authentic Native crafts.

GETTING OUTSIDE

TWO RECREATION AREAS

A couple of miles north of town on Rezanof Drive, the **Fort Abercrombie State Historical Park** encompasses World War II ruins set on coastal cliffs amid huge trees. Paths lead to the beaches and good tide-pool walking, a swimming lake, and lots of other discoveries. The gun emplacements, bunkers, and other concrete buildings defended against the Japanese, who had seized islands in the outer Aleutians and were expected to come this way. A group of local World War II buffs, led by Joe Stevens, known as Crusty Old Joe, have built a museum of war artifacts from the Alaska fighting in one of the bunkers (see "The Aleutians: The Quiet After War," below), as well as other military operations in Alaska. Hours hadn't been set at this writing, but will be posted at www.kAdiak.org; you can also call at ☎ **907/486-7015.** A wonderful 13-site campground sits atop the cliffs among the trees and ruins. Camping is $10. The **Division of State Parks,** Kodiak District Office, 1400 Abercrombie Dr., Kodiak, AK 99615 (☎ **907/486-6339;** fax 907/486-3320; www.ptialaska.net/~kodsp/), maintains an office here where you can pick up a walking-tour brochure or, during the summer, join the Saturday-night interpretive program or a guided tide-pool walk, scheduled to coincide with the tides. Or investigate the tide pools on your own, picking up an identification guide at a bookstore or the Fish and Wildlife Service visitor center.

The **Buskin River State Recreation Site,** 4 miles south of town off Rezanof Drive near the Fish and Wildlife Service visitor center, has 15 sites, a hiking trail, and access to fishing. Camping is $10.

ACTIVITIES

ARCHAEOLOGY **Dig Afognak,** 215 Mission Rd., Suite 212 (☎ **800/770-6014** or 907/486-6014; www.afognak.com/dig/), operated by the Afognak Native Corporation, offers visitors a chance to help in scientific excavations of Koniag sites on Afognak Island, an effort by the Native group to reassemble their cultural heritage. Visitors are instructed in the natural history of the beautiful area as well as archaeology, but they're also expected to work, digging and working in a remote lab. Each weeklong session has a different educational emphasis, with scientists or elders on hand to enrich the learning. Accommodations are in heated tents, and you have to bring your own sleeping bag. Dinner often is seafood caught in nets at the beach. A 7-day session is $1,650, including transportation from Kodiak.

✪ **BROWN BEAR VIEWING** To see Kodiak's famous bears, you need to get out on a plane or boat. The easiest way is a Kodiak-based floatplane; expect to pay at least $400 per person, with a two- or three-person minimum (prices can fluctuate depending on the size of your party, the type of plane, how far you have to fly, and so on). Landing on the water, you may watch from the safety of the plane's floats, or put on rubber boots to get closer. Bears congregate only when salmon are running, so the timing of your visit is critical. If seeing bears on Kodiak is an important element of your trip, call ahead to the Kodiak National Wildlife Refuge (☎ **907/487-2600;** see "Visitor Information," above) to make sure you come at the right time, since salmon runs and the hot bear-viewing spots can vary from year to year. If you go at an off time, you're liable to waste a lot of money (although you'll still enjoy the scenery). When the salmon aren't running, Kodiak flight services fly over to the east coast of the Alaska Peninsula to watch bears digging clams from the tidal flats; it's fascinating behavior and a spectacular flight, but flying that far is expensive. If bear viewing is the whole reason you're going to Kodiak, it makes more sense to time your visit for the salmon run, or to try to see bears from a base in Homer (see chapter 7) or King Salmon (see section 3 of this chapter, on Katmai National Park) instead. Several small flight services offer bear viewing, including (I have no preference): **Highline Air** (☎ **907/486-5155;** www.ptialaska.net/~highline), **Sea Hawk Air** (☎ **800/770-4295** or 907/486-8282; www.seahawkair.com), or **Andrew Airways** (☎ **907/487-2566;** www.andrewairways.com), which also has an overnight option.

FISHING The roads leading from Kodiak offer access to terrific salmon and trout fishing. You can get a guidebook, including where to fish and the names and addresses of guides for remote fishing, from the visitor center. The **Alaska Department of Fish and Game** is at 211 Mission Rd., Kodiak, AK 99615 (☎ **907/486-1880;** www.state.ak.us/local/akpages/FISH.GAME/adfghome.htm). To fish the remote areas, you'll need to charter a plane to a remote public-use cabin or go to a wilderness lodge. Several boats are available for ocean salmon and halibut fishing. Check with the visitors center.

HIKING & BIRD WATCHING There aren't a lot of trails on Kodiak, but there are some good day hikes. Pick up a copy of the *Kodiak Hiking Guide* at the visitor center for a variety of mountain climbs and day hikes from the road system. They'll also have the field-trip program of the **Kodiak Audubon Society,** which includes guided hikes and bird-watching trips.

HORSEBACK RIDING The lush green hills that cover much of the island are idyllic grounds for riding. The **Kodiak Cattle Co.** (☎ **907/486-3705**) is one of several outfits offering rides. They often see deer, eagles, and bears on their day trips, which start at $45 per person with a two-person minimum.

✪ **SEA KAYAKING** The Kodiak Archipelago, with its many folded, rocky shorelines and abundant marine life, is a perfect place for sea kayaking; after all, kayaks were invented here and on the Aleutian Islands to the west. Several operators offer kayaking services and tours in and around Kodiak, and on the shore of Katmai National Park. **Mythos Expeditions** (☎ **907/486-5536;** www.mythos-expeditions.com) offers introductory paddles from the boat harbor—surprisingly complex and attractive waters for kayaking—starting at $40 per person. Longer excursions of various kinds, for experienced kayakers, seek bears on the Katmai coast or the peace of **Shuyak Island State Park,** 54 miles north of Kodiak. The park is a honeycomb of islands and narrow passages in virgin Sitka spruce coastal forest. The Division of State Parks (see addresses under "Two Recreation Areas," above) maintains four public-use cabins, which rent for $65 a night, and distributes a free kayaking guide with route descriptions. Mythos Expeditions rents kayaks for use in the park, as well as offering custom kayaking and ecotours from a sturdy boat.

ACCOMMODATIONS

Besides the hotels listed below, you'll find good standard rooms for around $70 a night at **Shelikof Lodge,** 211 Thorsheim Ave. (☎ **907/486-4141** or 907/486-4116; www.ptialaska.net/~kyle), and the **Russian Heritage Inn,** 119 Yukon (☎ **907/486-5657;** www.ak-biz.com/russianheritage/). I've listed places in town, but there also are more than two dozen wilderness lodges on and around Kodiak Island. You can get a list from the visitor center, and their Web site contains links to most of them.

Best Western Kodiak Inn. 236 W. Rezanof Dr., Kodiak, AK 99615. ☎ **888/563-4254** or 907/486-5712. Fax 907/486-3430. www.ptialaska.net/~kodiakin/. 81 units. TV TEL. High season $139–$149 double. Low season $99 double. Extra person over age 12 $15. AE, CB, DC, DISC, MC, V.

This is the best hotel in downtown Kodiak, with attractive, up-to-date rooms perched on the hill overlooking the boat harbor, right in the center of things. Rooms in the wooden building vary in size and view, although all are acceptable and have refrigerators, microwaves, and coffeemakers. There's an outdoor spa in a sort of courtyard and a tour desk in the pleasant lobby. A free shuttle picks up guests at the airport. The **Chart Room** restaurant, specializing in seafood and with a great view of the water, is a good choice for a nice dinner out, with entrees in the $15 to $25 range.

Buskin River Inn. 1395 Airport Way, Kodiak, AK 99615. ☎ **800/544-2202** or 907/487-2700. www.kodiakadventure.com. 50 units. TV TEL. High season $145 double. Low season $125 double. Extra person over age 12 $15. AE, DC, DISC, MC, V.

This quiet, well-kept hotel with standard rooms is near the airport, not the downtown sights; you will need a rental car if you stay here. Rooms on one side look out on the parking lot. It's near the wildlife refuge visitor center, a hiking trail, and the nine-hole golf course at the Coast Guard base. The Buskin makes a specialty of booking activities and offering package discounts for outdoor explorations of the island. The rooms all have coffeemakers, refrigerators, voice mail, and hair dryers; there's a self-service laundry, and they'll pick you up at the airport. The **Eagle's Nest Restaurant** has reliable food from a complete beef and seafood menu, and a pleasant setting.

Kodiak Bed and Breakfast. 308 Cope St., Kodiak, AK 99615. ☎ **907/486-5367.** Fax 907/486-6567. www.ptialaska.net/~monroe. 2 units, both with shared bathroom. $88 double. Rates include breakfast. MC, V.

Hospitable, active Mary Monroe runs this comfortable, homey place with a big, friendly golden retriever, Buffy. There is a porch where you can eat breakfast on sunny mornings, overlooking the harbor (fish is often on the morning menu). The location is convenient, right downtown, and the entry for the bedrooms and shared sitting room downstairs doesn't require you to walk through Monroe's own living quarters.

Wintels Bed and Breakfast. 1723 Mission Rd. (P.O. Box 2812), Kodiak, AK 99615. ☎ and fax **907/486-6935.** www.wintels.com. 3 units, 1 with private bathroom. TEL. $80–$100 double. Extra person $35. Rates include breakfast. AE, MC, V.

A long walk from downtown (you'll need a car if you stay here), this house stands with the ocean on one side and a lake on the other, so all rooms have water views. The owners, a family of longtime residents, can tell you a lot about Alaska and show off their mounted sea ducks and furs. The rooms are attractive, the breakfasts large, and there's a sauna and a Jacuzzi surrounded by potted plants. Laundry facilities are available.

DINING

Besides the hotel restaurants listed above at the Best Western Kodiak Inn and Buskin River Inn, Kodiak has a selection of family restaurants.

Downtown, **El Chicano,** at 103 Center St. (☎ **907/486-6116**), is a good Mexican family restaurant, with friendly service and reasonable prices. **The Captain's Restaurant,** upstairs at 202 E. Rezanof St. (☎ **907/486-4144**), serves tasty, inexpensive breakfast and lunch items. The friendly owner and chef, Father Jonas Worsham, teaches at the local Russian Orthodox seminary, St. Innocent Academy, and students often work as servers. **Beryl's** is a nice little sandwich and breakfast shop on a pedestrian way at 202 Center St. (☎ **907/486-3323**). It started out as a candy and ice-cream place, but now serves meals all day until 6pm. **Harborside Coffee and Goods,** at 216 Shelikof St. (☎ **907/486-5862**), on the south side of the boat harbor, is a comfortable coffee house with soup and bagels, popular with commercial fishermen and young people. **Henry's Great Alaskan Restaurant,** at 512 Marine Way (☎ **907/486-8844**), on the waterfront mall, is a popular but very smoky bar and grill.

A mile from downtown, **Mongolian Barbecue,** 1247 Mill Bay Rd. (☎ **907/486-2900**), is the best family restaurant in town. Diners choose their thinly sliced meat and vegetables raw and watch the chef toss them on the grill. An all-you-can-eat dinner is $13, half-price for kids. It's fun and the food is great.

3 Katmai National Park

Most of the land of the Alaska Peninsula, pointing out to the Aleutian Archipelago, is in one federally protected status or another, centering on Katmai National Park, which was originally set aside in 1918. Katmai (*cat*-my) lies just west of Kodiak Island, across the storm-infested Shelikof Strait. Bears and salmon are the main attractions today. **Brooks Camp,** with a campground and lodge within Katmai, is probably the most comfortable place for foolproof bear viewing in Alaska. Here, in July and September only, you can sit back on a deck and watch 900-pound brown bears walk by, going about their business of devouring the spawning salmon that contribute to their awesome size. (A brown bear is the genetic twin of the grizzly, but generally larger due to its coastal diet of salmon.) Staying the night will require you to reserve a place in the 16-space campground the previous winter (see "Reservations & Fees," below) or stay in the pricey lodge, where rooms book up over a year ahead for the bear season. You can go for a day trip, too, if you can afford round-trip airfare of around $500 from Anchorage and reserve a day-use permit (see "Reservations & Fees," below).

Katmai originally exploded into world consciousness in 1912, with the most destructive volcanic eruption to shake the earth in 3,400 years. When Katmai's Novarupta blew, it released ten times more energy than Mount St. Helens's eruption of 1980 and displaced twice as much matter as 1883's Krakatoa. In Kodiak, the sky was black for three days and two feet of ash crushed houses and choked rivers. People could clearly hear the blast in Juneau; acid rain melted fabric in Vancouver, British Columbia; and the skies darkened over most of the northern hemisphere. At ground zero, all life was wiped out in a 40-square-mile area and buried as deep as 700 feet. But so remote was the area, then still unnamed, that not a single human being was killed. The **Valley of Ten Thousand Smokes,** the vast wasteland created by the blast, belched steam for decades after. Today Novarupta is dormant and the steam is gone, but the area is still a barren moonscape, making a fascinating day tour or hiking trip.

ESSENTIALS

GETTING THERE The most common way to get to Katmai is to fly from Anchorage to the village of **King Salmon,** which lies just west of the park, and then continue by air taxi to **Brooks Camp. Alaska Airlines** (☎ **800/252-7522;** www.alaskaair.com) flies to King Salmon, charging around $290 to $350 round-trip. A floatplane from there to Brooks Camp is about $140, round-trip. Various air taxis make that jump, including **Katmai Air,** operated by park concessionaire Katmailand (☎ **800/544-0551** or 907/243-5448; www.bear-viewing.com/). This company also offers round-trip airfare packages that may save money.

As an alternative to Brooks Camp, more and more visitors are exploring the supremely rugged wilderness on the east side of the park from the beaches along **Shelikof Strait.** Air-taxi operators make drops-offs and do bear-viewing day trips from Homer or Kodiak (see section 2 of this chapter, above, on Kodiak, or see the Homer section in chapter 7), and boats out of Kodiak go across for extended cruising and kayak expeditions. In this park, with more than 2,000 brown bears resident (the world's largest protected population), it's easy for pilots to find them digging clams on the tidal marshes, then land on floats for a good, close look.

RESERVATIONS & FEES To go to the bear-viewing area at Brooks Camp, you must first make a reservation and pay the use fee of $10 per person, per day. Camping costs $5 per person per night. There are only 16 sites, and they are in very high demand during the bear season in July. The crowds are less in September, but the bears are not quite as numerous. All sites become available for the entire summer on January 15. There are no limits on day-use permits, so everyone gets in. To reserve, call the **Park Service national reservation system,** which is operated by Biospherics (☎ **800/365-2267** or 301/722-1257; reservations.nps.gov). You can reserve online (note, there is no "www" on the URL). If you're using the phone system, enter **KAT#** at the prompt. If reserving a campsite, make sure also to get a day-use permit. Lodge guests get their permit automatically.

VISITOR INFORMATION Besides the **Katmai National Park Headquarters,** P.O. Box 7, King Salmon, AK 99613 (☎ **907/246-3305;** www.nps.gov/katm), there's also a **visitor center** at the airport in King Salmon (☎ **907/246-4250**), staffed jointly by the National Park Service, U.S. Fish and Wildlife Service, and the local government. At Brooks Camp the park service has a center where all visitors are required to attend a 20-minute orientation called "The Brooks Camp School of Bear Etiquette," designed to train visitors (not bears) and keep them out of trouble. In Anchorage, you can get information at the **Alaska Public Lands Information Center,** at Fourth Avenue and F Street (☎ **907/271-2737;** see the complete listing in section 1 of chapter 6).

GETTING AROUND Once you've made it to Brooks Camp, a **bus** carries visitors to the Valley of Ten Thousand Smokes, 23 miles by gravel road from the camp. The park concessionaire, **Katmailand,** charges $72 per person, round-trip, for the all-day excursion, plus $7 more for lunch. One-way transfers for hikers are $42.

FAST FACTS A **bank** with an ATM is ¼ mile west of the King Salmon Airport on the town's one paved road.

You can call the **police in King Salmon** at ☎ **907/246-4222.** Reach the **Alaska State Troopers** at ☎ **907/246-3346** or 907/246-3464.

Note that there are no phones or cellular service out in the park.

The **Camai Clinic,** in Naknek (☎ **907/246-6155**), is open during normal business hours; calls to the number go to emergency dispatchers after hours.

EXPLORING KATMAI

Katmai's famous bear viewing occurs at **Brooks Camp** when the bears congregate near the Brooks River to catch salmon, during July and September, and maybe the last week of June or the first week of August. This is when you're assured of seeing bears from the elevated platforms near the Brooks River falls, half a mile from Brooks Camp, even on a day trip. Forty to sixty bears feed here. Other times in the summer, you might see a bear, or you might not; don't spend the money.

The Brooks Camp area has a small park service campground, visitor center, and a lodge, located where the Brooks River flows into Naknek Lake. Unfortunately, when the area was first developed for fishing in the 1950s, the camp was placed in the middle of a bear corridor and on top of a valuable archaeological site. The park service plans to move facilities and people to the south side of the Brooks River and to impose limits on how many visitors can come, but that probably won't happen for a few years. The most comfortable way to stay in the camp is at the **Brooks Lodge,** operated by Katmailand (see contact info under "Getting There," above). The lodge has 16 units, with private bathrooms with shower stalls. To save money, book the lodge rooms as packages with air travel. The least expensive, 1-night visit is $663 per person, double occupancy, meals not included; 3 nights is $1,078. A double room without airfare is $396. The place books up a full year ahead; reservations open January of the year before the visit. Three buffet-style meals are served daily for guests and visitors who aren't staying in the lodge. Breakfast is $10, lunch $12, and dinner $22. For food, they take plastic at the lodge: American Express, MasterCard, and Visa. Also at Brooks Camp, there's a small store, the park service visitor center, and the 16-site campground. See "Reservations & Fees," above, for info on campground reservations, which should be made 6 months in advance. The rangers require special precautions to keep bears away from campers.

The rivers and lakes of Katmai lure human anglers as well as ursine ones. Katmailand operates two lodges within the park other than Brooks Lodge for remote fishing, the **Kulik and Grosvenor lodges.** Check their Web site at www.katmailand.com/ for fishing details. The park service also has a list of dozens of fishing, hiking, and air guides. There is no central clearinghouse for remote fishing, but you can find and book a good place through an agency such as **Sport Fishing Alaska,** 9310 Shorecrest Dr., Anchorage, AK 99515 (☎ **907/344-8674;** www.alaskatripplanners.com), listed in full under "Planning an Outdoor Vacation" in chapter 2.

Backcountry hiking in Katmai means crossing a wilderness without trails, and only experienced backpackers should plan extended trips. The park service asks hikers to obtain a voluntary permit for backcountry travel, thereby clueing them in to your plans in case you need to be rescued. Anyone can walk for the day without such precautions in the desolate **Valley of Ten Thousand Smokes.** This 40-square-mile plain remains a moonscape almost 90 years after the titanic volcanic blast that buried it, little changed except that the famous plumes of smoke are gone and rivers have sliced through the debris in places to create narrow, white-walled canyons. Although it looks like a desert and is subject to dust storms, rain is common and temperatures rarely go higher than 65°F. Katmailand operates a tour bus from Brooks Camp, mentioned above under "Getting Around." The visitors on those tours usually stay to a short trail on the valley's rim. Longer hikes into the valley bring you into contact with more of the bizarre landforms created by the eruption.

4 Dutch Harbor/Unalaska: Aleutian Boom Town

After a lifetime of hearing how desolate the Aleutians (uh-*loo*-shuns) were, I felt like I was leaving the edge of the earth the first time I traveled to Unalaska (oon-ah-*las*-ka). Shortly after I arrived, a storm started slinging huge raindrops horizontally through the air so hard that they stung as they splattered on my face. People went on about their business as if nothing special was happening—stormy weather constantly batters these rocks that pop up from the empty North Pacific. My expectations seemed justified.

But the next day, the storm cleared like a curtain opening on a rich operatic scene—simultaneously opening the curtain of my dark expectations. Unalaska may lack trees, but it's not a barren rock. The island is covered with heather and wildflowers. Rounded mountains that invite wandering exploration rise from the ocean like the backs of huge beasts. For sightseeing, it has only a half a day's attractions, but for outdoor exploring, bird watching, and halibut fishing, few places come close.

With the protected port of Dutch Harbor so far out in a ferocious ocean habitat rich in crab and bottom fish, Unalaska has grown in three decades from a tiny, forgotten Native village to the nation's largest fishing port. The pattern of growth followed the form of the early gold rushes. There was a wild, lawless time in the 1970s when crab fishermen got rich quick and partied like Old West cowboys. Then the overfished crab stocks crashed, only to be replaced, starting in the mid-1980s, by an even bigger boom, when waters within 200 miles of the U.S. shore were rid of foreign vessels and American bottom fishing took off. Big factory ships began unloading here, and huge fish plants were built on ground chipped from the rock. Today that expansion has reached a more steady state, and more women and families are coming to town—another part of the gold rush pattern. But domestication isn't done yet. Most of the population lives in bunk houses and flies back to Seattle when the processing plants close for the season. Housing and public services still lag far behind the boom, in part because it's hard to build on the Aleutians' volcanic bedrock and there's such a lack of flat land. Unalaska may be the best current example of the American cultural phenomenon of the frontier boomtown.

Ironically, Unalaska is Alaska's oldest town as well as its newest city. The value of a good port out in the middle of the ocean was recognized from the beginning by the Aleuts. In 1759, the Russians began trading here, and fought a war with the Aleuts from 1763 to 1766, the outcome of which was slavery for the Aleut hunters and the massacre of their people. The Russians built a permanent settlement here in 1792, their first in Alaska. Unalaska also was a key refueling stop for steamers carrying gold rush stampeders to Nome a century ago, which brought an epidemic that killed a third of the indigenous population. In 1940, Dutch Harbor—the seaport on Amaknak Island associated with the town and island of Unalaska—was taken over by the U.S. Navy to defend against Japanese attack. That attack came: In June 1942, Japanese planes bombed Unalaska, killing 43. The Aleut people were removed from the islands for the duration of the war and interned in inadequate housing in Southeast Alaska, where many died of disease. The military pulled out in 1947, but the remains of their defenses are interesting to explore. Today, thanks to a 1971 act of Congress settling Native claims, the Aleut-owned Ounalashka Corporation owns much of the island.

ESSENTIALS

GETTING THERE Several operators fly to Dutch Harbor from Anchorage, including **Alaska Airlines** (☎ **800/252-7522;** www.alaskaair.com). You're likely to pay $740 to $800 round-trip. An air/hotel package makes sense and saves money—see the Grand Aleutian Hotel, described under "Accommodations," below.

The Aleutians: The Quiet After War

In 1995, the navy deactivated the secret naval base at **Adak,** in the outer Aleutian Islands, leaving only a few caretakers. Few civilians had ever seen the base, which had been hurriedly built more than 50 years before to fight back a Japanese invasion. With its closing, the book closed on a bizarre and bitter tale with few parallels in American history. The battle for the Aleutians was costly, pointless, and miserable, bringing ruin and disease to the Aleuts and death to thousands of Japanese and American soldiers. What began as a diversion became a ferocious fight for honor with little strategic meaning. When the fighting was done, it turned out that no one even wanted the land enough to stay. With the 50th anniversary of the war, Japanese and American soldiers met on the deserted islands they'd fought for and dedicated a monument. Then they left again—leaving behind the site of death and struggle to the fog, whipping wind, and migrating geese.

The Japanese attacked the islands of **Kiska** and **Attu** at the start of the Pacific war to divert the main core of the American navy away from what became the Battle of Midway. But the Americans had intercepted and decoded Japanese transmissions, and weren't fooled. Meanwhile, the Japanese had sent 24 ships, including two aircraft carriers, on a fool's errand to bomb the new American naval base at Dutch Harbor/Unalaska and occupy islands in the western Aleutians. Those ships could have tipped the balance at Midway, among the most important battles of the war. Instead, the Japanese met stiff antiaircraft fire in 2 days of bombing at Dutch Harbor; although 43 Americans were killed, the defensive function of the base was not greatly impaired.

The Japanese then took Kiska and Attu, meeting no resistance from 10 Americans staffing a weather station or from a small Aleut village whose few inhabitants were all—even the children—sent to a prison camp in Japan to mine clay for the duration of the war. About half the prisoners survived to return to Alaska.

The Americans had their own plan to remove the Aleuts, but the idea of depopulating all the islands had been turned down. Now, with the Japanese attack, it was swiftly put into effect. All the Aleuts were rounded up and put on ships. As they pulled away from their ancestral islands, they could see the glow of huge fires destroying their villages—the U.S. military had torched the villages to deny the modest assets of the islands to the Japanese, should they advance farther. With little thought given to their living conditions, the Aleuts were interned in abandoned summer camps and similarly inadequate facilities in Southeast Alaska. Shunned by the local communities and without the basic necessities of life, many died of cold and disease. The U.S. Fish and Wildlife Service took Aleut hunters to hunt furs as virtual slaves, much as the Russians had done 200 years before.

The Japanese and American military fared not much better on their new real estate. Although the Aleutians quickly became irrelevant to the rest of the war, significant resources were committed to a largely futile air and sea battle in the fog and endless storms. Flying at all was difficult and extremely dangerous, and finding the enemy in the fog over vast distances close to impossible. The Americans couldn't spare a land invasion force at first, and had to rely on bombing Kiska and Attu to punish the Japanese and try to deter a further advance up the chain. To that end, they built the base at Adak, among others, so shorter-range fighter escorts could accompany the bombers. Construction in the spongy tundra was difficult in any case, made more so by the length of supply lines.

The Japanese high command never had any intention of advancing up the chain, but also saw no reason to abandon their new Kiska air base when it was causing the Americans to exert such effort—even if it had no strategic value to either side. The Japanese concentrated on fortifying Kiska, which became a honeycomb of underground bunkers and heavy antiaircraft guns and withstood constant bombing raids from the Americans.

Finally, on May 11, 1943, almost a year after the Japanese took the islands, Americans landed on Attu, and a brutal 18-day battle for the rugged island began. The Japanese were massively outnumbered but heavily dug in. Finally, with only 800 soldiers left from an original force of 2,600, the Japanese mounted a banzai attack. Only 28 were taken prisoner—the rest were killed in battle or committed suicide. The Americans lost 549 killed, 1,148 wounded, and 2,132 injured by severe cold, disease, accident, mental breakdown, or other causes. In the end, it was the second most costly island battle in the Pacific, after Iwo Jima.

The battle for Kiska was less dramatic. The Japanese withdrew under cover of fog. After a massive bombardment of the empty island and the rallying of heavy reinforcements, the Americans landed to find that no one was there. Still, 105 American soldiers died in the landing in accidents and fire from their own forces.

After the Aleutian battle was over, American forces in Alaska declined drastically, but never went away altogether. Before the war, the absurd little Fort William Seward, in Haines, had been the totality of Alaska's defenses, with a couple of hundred men armed with Springfield rifles and no reliable means of transportation. Afterward there were large bases in several areas of the state. Military spending became the biggest economic boom the territory had ever seen, connecting it by a new road to the Lower 48 and bringing precious year-round jobs. A new wave of postwar settlers, many former GIs looking for a new, open field of opportunity, brought a population boom. The advent of the Cold War, and Alaska's prime strategic location in defense against the Soviet Union, brought ever-greater increases in military spending in Alaska. To this day, the military is one of the largest sectors of the Alaska economy, and the state has been relatively unscathed in base closures except for remote outposts like Adak.

The end of the war was more bitter for the Aleuts. Everything they had in their villages had been destroyed. Many who had survived the terrible period of internment never returned to the islands where their villages had once stood, and some of the villages never revived. Some were wiped off the map as a cost-saving measure by the bureaucrats who managed the evacuation. Aleuts who were able to return found belongings, subsistence gear, and religious icons destroyed. "When I came back to Atka after World War II, my buddy said, 'Why are you going back to the Aleutians? They say even the sea gulls are leaving there,'" villager Dan Prokopeuff has been quoted as saying. "I told him I was going because it's peaceful and quiet."

Today Atka is the westernmost village remaining in the Aleutians. On Kiska there are only ruins of the Japanese fortifications. As for Adak and the assets the U.S. military left behind, it's being taken over by the Aleut Corporation, the regional Native corporation, which hopes to redevelop it as a commercial fishing port.

The **Alaska Marine Highway System** ferry *Tustumena* (☎ **800/642-0066;** www.dot.state.ak.us/external/amhs/home.html) runs once a month from Homer, leaving Tuesday morning and arriving in Unalaska on Saturday morning after stopping in Kodiak and the villages along the way. The passenger fare is $242, and an outside cabin, with facilities, is $328 more. I don't know anyone who has actually done this long open-sea passage, but it must be an adventure. Of course, unless you want to spend only 5 hours on a Saturday morning in Unalaska and then make the long return trip, you'll need to fly back.

VISITOR INFORMATION The **Unalaska/Port of Dutch Harbor Convention and Visitors Bureau,** P.O. Box 545, Unalaska, AK 99685 (☎ **907/581-2612;** arctic.net/~updhcvb), is at Fifth Street and Broadway, in the old part of town. The Web site has many useful links.

GETTING AROUND The main historic part of the town is a tiny street grid on a narrow peninsula facing Iliuliuk Bay. The **Bridge to the Other Side** (that's the official name) leads to Amaknak Island, the site of the airport, the Grand Aleutian Hotel, and the fishing industrial area of Dutch Harbor. Traveling down the road in the other direction leads a little way up into the mountains, a starting point for walks.

Van taxis are the main way of getting around town for the hordes of fishermen. One company is **Blue Checker Taxi** (☎ **907/581-2186**).

You can rent a car, truck, or forklift from **North Port Rentals** (☎ **907/581-3880**) or a couple of other companies. Cars rent for $40 a day.

In good weather, bikes are a good way to cover the town, which has only a few miles of road. **Aleutian Adventure Sports** (☎ **888/581-4489** or 907/581-4489; www.aleutianadventure.com), in a two-story former grocery store, rents bikes for $30 a day. They also rent camping gear, sea kayaks, and fishing gear.

FAST FACTS A **Key Bank** branch is near the Alaska Commercial Store.

Iliuliuk Family and Health Services (☎ **907/581-1202**) offers complete clinic services.

You can log on to the Internet or check your e-mail at the **public library** (☎ **907/581-5060**).

The **Unalaska Department of Public Safety** (☎ **907/581-1233**) is just above the bridge on the Unalaska side.

Sales tax is 3%; **room tax** is 8%.

ATTRACTIONS & ACTIVITIES

Unalaska's main historic site is the **Holy Ascension Cathedral.** Completed in 1896 on the site of churches that had stood since 1808, the white church with green onion-shaped domes contains 697 icons, artifacts, and artworks—a significant collection that has been continuously in use by the Aleut congregation. The congregation was founded by Fr. Ivan Veniaminov, who translated the Gospel into Aleut and has been canonized as St. Innocent. The building was not well maintained, and the buffeting of rugged weather and history put it in peril, but a $1.3 million restoration completed in 1996 has left it looking bright and trim. Sitting on the edge of sparkling Iliuliuk Bay, the church and its cemetery are a picturesque cultural gem.

The new, professionally curated **Museum of the Aleutians,** next door to the Ounalashka Corporation on Margaret Bay in Dutch Harbor (☎ **907/581-5150;** www.aleutians.org), contains some of the Aleuts' best artifacts anywhere, including some from North American's oldest coastal sites, on Umnak and Unalaska islands. Exhibits also cover the town's history with World War II artifacts and other items left behind by the successive waves of occupiers, and the museum has temporary exhibits, too. Admission is $2. It's open daily in summer from 10am to 4pm, in winter Wednesday to Sunday 11am to 4pm.

Right outside the museum, an archaeological dig has unearthed more than 100,000 objects from layers of Aleut villages 3,000 to 5,500 years old. Work continues at the **Margaret Bay Archeological Project,** and the scientists invite visitors to join in the work, earning college credit while digging, working to clean the artifacts in the museum, and hearing evening lectures. To volunteer, call Museum of the Aleutians Director, Dr. Rick Knecht (☎ **907/581-5150;** e-mail: knecht@arctic.net).

There are several **World War II military ruins** around town, including some that are still in use—like a submarine dry dock that today fixes fishing boats. The activity at the port is interesting to see, too, if only for the size of the vessels and harvest and the incredible investment in buildings and equipment.

Aleut Tours (☎ **907/581-6001;** e-mail: akaleut@arctic.net) offers town tours in the summer, including all the major sights, with an Aleut guide driving the van. It lasts 2 to 3 hours, with pickup wherever you are, and costs $40.

GETTING OUTSIDE

✪ BIRD WATCHING Flip through the crisp, unused pages of your bird book to find out what you may see in the Aleutians. Several rare bird species nest in the area, and Asian birds occasionally drop in as accidentals. The whiskered auklet and red-legged kittiwake are among the birds commonly found around Unalaska that don't show up anywhere else. You have greatest success taking a boat to a sea bird colony. The Grand Aleutian Hotel (below, under "Accommodations") offers packages; it's also possible to combine halibut fishing and bird watching on your own chartered boat (see "Fishing"). You're also likely to encounter sea lions and other marine mammals.

FISHING You can fly out for salmon fishing from black-sand beaches, but Unalaska has become more famous for huge **✪ halibut.** In 1995, a local sport fisherman caught a 395-pound halibut from an 18-foot skiff within a half mile of town; to kill the behemoth he had to beach it and beat it over the head with a rock. The next year, Fairbanks angler Jack Tragis landed the world's record halibut here, which weighed 459 pounds. If you're having trouble imagining a fish that big, drop by City Hall, where it hangs stuffed in the lobby. If you plan to fish, buy a $7 derby ticket from the visitor center; if you break the world record, you could win $100,000. (The world record was broken twice here recently.) John Lucking's **Far West Outfitters** (☎ **907/581-1647**) brought in the 459-pounder. Charters are around $165 per person for a 4- to 6-hour trip, with a two-person minimum. Also check on packages with the place where you are staying, which can save money.

SEA KAYAKING The Aleuts invented the kayak to hunt and travel. **Aleutian Adventure Sports** (see "Getting Around" above) rents kayaks and offers daily beginners' harbor tours (3½ hours, $50) as well as longer day trips and multiday expeditions. They also lead treks and volcano climbs, and rent mountain bikes.

HIKING The island's green heather and rounded mountains of wildflowers are inviting for unguided day hiking, too. You can walk pretty much in any direction, looking at the abandoned World War II defenses; making a goal of a beach or one of the small peaks around the town; or, for the ambitious, even heading to the top of an active volcano, Mount Makushin. There are no bears and not many bugs, but there's great berry picking and beachcombing. The weather can be a threat, however, and fox holes can trip you up. As always in remote outdoor areas, you must be suitably dressed, know how to take care of yourself, and leave word of where you're going and when you'll be back.

For extended hikes, go to the Department of Public Safety (see "Fast Facts: Dutch Harbor/Unalaska," above) for a travel-planning guide and to report your route on a travel plan that will assist with a search if you don't come back (not necessary if you're just going for a short ramble in the hills around town). You'll also have to pay a fee to the **Ounalashka Corp.,** at 400 Salmon Way near the Grand Aleutian Hotel (☎ **907/581-1276**), the Native village corporation that owns much of the island. Hiking is $6 per person per day, camping $11. They're open Monday to Friday from 8am to 5pm; if you arrive when they are closed, you can get a permit from OC Security (the guys driving around town in the white pickup trucks with "Security" written on the side in blue).

ACCOMMODATIONS

Carl's Bayview Inn. 606 Bayview (P.O. Box 730), Unalaska, AK 99685. ☎ **800/581-1230** or 907/581-1230. Fax 907/581-1880. E-mail: bayview@arctic.net. 47 units. TV TEL. $90 double, $125 double with kitchenette; $150 suite. Extra person $20. AE, DISC, MC, V.

The building, in town on Iliuliuk Bay, looks a bit like a Dutch Harbor warehouse from the outside, but the eight kitchenette units and six suites inside, all newly remodeled and with every amenity, come closer to *Better Homes and Gardens,* with their pastel colors and sweeping views. The double rooms, although very clean, showed more signs of wear and are not as attractive. Few rooms are reserved for nonsmokers. The staff will pick up guests at the airport.

✪ **Grand Aleutian Hotel.** 498 Salmon Way (P.O. Box 921169), Dutch Harbor, AK 99692. ☎ **800/891-1194** or 907/581-3844. Fax 907/581-7150. 112 units. TV TEL. $150 double; $225–$250 suite. Extra person $15. Packages available. AE, CB, DC, DISC, JCB, MC, V.

It's almost unreal to arrive in this big, luxurious hotel in a hard-driving Alaska Bush community. The Grand Aleutian is among the best hotels in Alaska, to say nothing of the Bush. For the same room in Anchorage, you'd pay considerably more. There's a courtesy van; the rooms are well designed and comfortable, many with good water views; the lobby is grand, with a huge stone fireplace; and there's a piano bar. As you walk outside into a driving gale, it's like teleporting from a big city hotel back to an exposed rock out in the North Pacific. Why build such a grand hotel in such a remote place? I don't know, but I've heard it called the "Grand Illusion."

The **Chart Room** restaurant, on the second floor, allows bird watchers to see waterfowl in the bay while dining on steak, seafood, or pasta. The menu, although brief, is Unalaska's most sophisticated. Dinner entrees range from $18 to $28. The **Margaret Bay Cafe,** downstairs, also has a good view, with a menu of grilled sandwiches and some lighter fare. A hamburger is $8.

The Japanese-owned UniSea fish-processing company (which built the hotel) has developed a full scope of sportfishing and birding packages to entice visitors, and booking one of those packages, including airfare, should save money. A 2-night package, which includes a boat visit to the Baby Islands bird colony to see the whiskered auklet, tufted and horned puffin, albatross, and other creatures, starts at about $1,300 per person, double occupancy. Longer packages with more birding trips are available, as well as fishing packages at about the same price.

DINING

Two of the town's best restaurants are at the **Grand Aleutian Hotel,** described above. Here's the other contender.

Tino's Steak House. N. 2nd St. at Broadway. ☎ **907/581-4288.** Lunch items $9–$12; dinner main courses $16–$40. AE, MC, V. Daily 8am–11pm. AMERICAN.

They pack in the commercial fishermen and other locals by serving huge portions of authentic Mexican food fast, as well as steaks, a few seafood items, and lots of sandwiches and burgers. I'm told you save money but get virtually the same meal by ordering from the lunch menu—the dinner prices are on the Unalaska scale, with most over $20.

5 The Pribilof Islands: Birder's Paradise

The Pribilof Islands of St. Paul and St. George sit out in the middle of the Bering Sea, due north of Unalaska, teeming with marine mammals and seabirds. Some 600,000 fur seals meet at the breeding rookeries in the summer, and 2 million birds of more than 200 species use the rocks. Bird watchers visit St. Paul for one of the most exotic and productive ✪ **birding and wildlife-viewing opportunities** in Alaska. It's best during the spring migration, from mid-May to mid-June, when great numbers of birds show up, including rare Asian accidental species; the fall migration comes in late July and August. You can count on making rare sightings any time during the summer. Indeed, the National Audubon Society's *Field Guide to North American Birds* calls this "perhaps the most spectacular seabird colony in the world."

However, the islands are extremely remote and the accommodations simple; if you're not interested in birding or spending a lot of time watching wildlife, it's probably too much money and trouble. There is only one hotel, the **King Eider,** which has basic rooms and shared bathrooms. There is no restaurant on the island, so guests are issued food vouchers for the mess hall at the Trident Seafoods fish-processing plant, near the hotel. Three meals a day come from a buffet there, and cost $10 to $17; you settle up at the end of your stay depending on how many vouchers you used. There is also a grocery store across from the hotel.

Visitors generally come on tours, which are sold as a package with airfare and guiding by Aleuts and expert birders. With the guides' help and radio communication, your chances of seeing exotic species are much enhanced. The tours are offered by **Tanadguix Corp.,** 1500 W. 33rd Ave., Anchorage, AK 99503 (☎ **877/424-5637;** www.alaskabirding.com). Check the Web site for birding news and species details. Packages from Anchorage start at $1,069 for a 2-night visit. Travelers can choose to ride on a bus, as a group, or hike on their own. Permanent blinds are in place for watching birds and seals. The weather is always cool and damp.

6 Nome: Arctic Frontier Town

The accidents of history deposited the streets and buildings of this lusty little town on the shore of Norton Sound, just south of the Arctic Circle in Northwest Alaska, and gave it qualities that make Nome an exceptionally attractive place for a visitor to go. For once, the local boosters' motto—in this case, "There's no place like Nome"—is entirely accurate, and that's because Nome, although itself nothing special to look at, combines a sense of history, a hospitable and somewhat silly attitude, and an exceptional location on the water in front of a tundra wilderness that's crossed by 250 miles of road. Those roads are the truly unique thing, for Nome is the only place in Arctic

Alaska where a visitor can drive or bike deep into the open country, coming across musk ox, reindeer, rarely seen birds, Native villages, undeveloped hot springs, and even an abandoned 1881 elevated train from New York City. Elsewhere, you're obliged to fly from rural hubs to get so far into the Bush, a more expensive and ambitious undertaking for casual explorers.

The accidents of history have been rather frequent in Nome—history has been downright sloppy. Start with the name. It's essentially a clerical error, caused by a British naval officer who, in 1850, was presumably in a creative dry spell when he wrote "? Name" on a diagram rather than name the cape he was sailing past. A mapmaker interpreted that as "Cape Nome." The original gold rush of 1898 was caused by prospectors in the usual way, but a much larger 1899 population explosion happened after one of the '98 stampeders, left behind by an injury in a camp on the beach, panned the sand outside the tent—and found that it was full of gold dust. By 1900, a fourth of Alaska's white population was in Nome, sifting the sand. Small-time operators and tourists are still at it. A huge floating gold dredge of the kind that makes for major historic sites in Fairbanks and Dawson City sits idle on the edge of town. In Nome, it stopped operation only in recent years. There are two other, smaller dredges in town, too. Historic structures are few, however, as fires and storms have destroyed the town several times since the gold rush.

Nome has a particular, broad sense of humor. It shows up in the *Nome Nugget* newspaper and in silly traditions like the Labor Day bathtub race, the pack ice golf tournament, and the Memorial Day polar bear swim. The population is half white and half Native, and the town is run largely by the white group. Some see Nome as a tolerant mixing place of different peoples, while the town strikes others as a bit colonial. Booze is outlawed in Kotzebue, the Native-dominated city to the north; but in Nome there is still a sloppy, gold rush style saloon scene. That sort of thing is prettier as historic kitsch than when it shows up in the form of a staggering Front Street drunk.

But you can ignore that, instead taking advantage of the great bargains to be had on **Inupiat arts and crafts.** And, most important, you can use one of the pleasant little inns or bed-and-breakfasts as a base to get into the countryside that beckons, down one of the gravel roads. Nome is popular with bird watchers, who find the roads especially useful.

ESSENTIALS

GETTING THERE Flying is the only way to get to Nome. **Alaska Airlines** (☎ **800/252-7522** or 907/443-2288; www.alaskaair.com) flies 90 minutes by jet either direct from Anchorage or with a brief hop from Kotzebue. Prices range $350 to $600. Many visitors come on a package sold by **Alaska Airlines Vacations** (☎ **800/468-2248**), which first visits Kotzebue, starting at $496 per person, double occupancy; it is described in section 7 of this chapter, on Kotzebue.

All taxis operate according to a standard price schedule you can get from the visitor center. A ride to town from the airport is $5. Call **Nome Cab** (☎ **907/443-3030**).

VISITOR INFORMATION The **Nome Convention and Visitors Bureau,** Front and Hunter streets (P.O. Box 240), Nome, AK 99762 (☎ **907/443-6624;** www.nomealaska.org), is exceptionally well run, providing maps and detailed information for diverse interests, and screening videos for those interested. The office is open mid-May to mid-September daily 9am to 7pm, mid-September to mid-May daily 9am to 6:30pm.

The **Bering Land Bridge National Preserve Headquarters,** Front Street (P.O. Box 220), Nome, AK 99762 (☎ **907/443-2522;** www.nps.gov/bela), is a good source of outdoors information from the rangers who staff a desk and are responsible for a rarely visited 2.3-million-acre national park unit, which covers much of the Seward Peninsula north of the Nome road system.

Also check the *Nome Nugget* Web site, at **www.nomenugget.com/**, a real window into the community.

GETTING AROUND The town is a mostly unpaved grid along the ocean. **Front Street** follows the sea wall, **First Avenue** is a block back, and so on. A harbor is at the north end of town, and the gold-bearing beach is to the south. You can mostly walk to see this area. Three roads branch out from Nome. I've described them below, under "On the Road." To get out on the roads, you need to take a tour or rent a car, or bring a bike with you.

Several local car-rental agencies operate in town; the visitor center maintains a list, with rates. **Stampede Rent-A-Car,** 527 Front St. (☎ **800/354-4606** or 907/443-3838), charges $75 a day for a SUV, $115 for a van. The same people operate the Aurora Inn (see "Accommodations," below).

FAST FACTS A **bank** with an ATM is at Front Street and Federal Way.

The **Norton Sound Regional Hospital** is at Fifth Avenue and Bering Street (☎ **907/443-3311**).

The **Nome Public Library,** 200 Front St. (☎ **907/443-5133**), offers Internet access.

The **police and fire station** is at Bering Street and Fourth Avenue (☎ **907/443-5262**).

The **post office** is at Front Street and Federal Way.

The **sales tax** is 4% and the **room tax** is also 4%.

SPECIAL EVENTS The **Iron Dog Classic Snowmachine Race** (☎ **907/563-4414;** irondog.ptialaska.net/), in mid-February, is the world's longest, covering the Iditarod Trail twice, a distance of 2,274 miles. Nome is the halfway point.

The biggest event of the year is the ✪ **Iditarod Trail Sled Dog Race** (☎ **907/376-5155;** www.iditarod.com/), a marathon of more than 1,000 miles that ends in Nome in mid- to late March. The sled dog racers and world media descend on the town for a few days of madness, with lots of community events planned. The activities last for the whole month; contact the Nome visitors center for a calendar. Among the most exciting vacations you could plan would be to volunteer to help run the Iditarod; call the race headquarters at the number above well in advance to get the information you need. One of the March Iditarod events, showcasing Nome's well-developed sense of humor, is the **Bering Sea Ice Golf Classic** (☎ **907/443-5162**)—six holes are set up on the sea ice. The pressure ridges constitute a bad lie.

Various similar silly events take place all year, including the **Polar Bear Swim,** which occurs in the Bering Sea on Memorial Day, ice permitting, and the Labor Day **Bathtub Race.** The **Midnight Sun Festival** (☎ **907/443-5535**) celebrates the summer solstice, around June 21, when Nome gets more than 22 hours of direct sunlight, with a parade, softball tournament, bank holdup, raft race, and similar events.

ATTRACTIONS & ACTIVITIES IN TOWN

Most of Nome's original buildings were wiped out by fires or by storms off Norton Sound that tore across the beach and washed away major portions of the business district. A seawall, completed in 1951, now protects the town. An interesting **Historical Walking Tour,** produced by the Alaska Historical Commission and the Lion's Club, is available from the visitor center; it covers 20 sites, including a turn-of-the-20th-century church and saloon, and a bust of Roald Amundsen, who landed near Nome, in

Teller, after crossing the North Pole from Norway in a dirigible in 1926. Below the library, at Front Street and Lanes Way, the small **Carrie M. McLain Memorial Museum** (☎ **907/443-2566**) has mounted a gold rush exhibit for the town's centennial. I also was fascinated by 100-year-old copies of the *Nome Nugget.* It still sells for the same price, 50¢, indicating just how inflated the town local economy was back then. The museum is free and open summer daily noon to 8pm, winter Tuesday to Saturday from noon to 6pm.

In good weather, a pleasant walk is to be had southeast of town, along the **beach.** Small-time miners may be camped there, but the gold-bearing sand extends for miles more of solitary walking. You can buy a gold pan in town and try your luck, but the sand has been sifted for nearly 100 years, so don't expect to gather any significant amount of gold. The **Swanberg Dredge** you can see from here operated until the 1950s; a large dredge north of town worked into the mid-1990s. The 38 gold dredges that once operated on the Seward Peninsula crept across the tundra, creating their own ponds to float in as they went. The **cemetery,** with white, wooden crosses on top of a little hill just out of town, also is worth a look.

Several companies offer **organized tours. Nome Discovery Tours** (☎ **907/443-2814;** e-mail: Discover@dwarf.nome.net) has the asset of talented professional actor Richard Beneville as the van driver and tour guide. He'll pick you up and drive you anywhere in the area, sharing his quirky enthusiasm and extensive knowledge of the surroundings. The highlight is the wildlife and scenery on the roads out of town, and he also visits an ivory carver and working gold mine. Half days are $45 per person, full days $85. **Nome Tour and Marketing,** at the Nugget Inn, at Front and Bering streets (☎ **907/443-2651**), is a more traditional tour, with a dog sled demonstration and gold panning. It is timed to meet flights bringing in visitors on packages, running in the summer only, and costs $52 per person. Bike tours are listed below under "On the Road."

If you're in the market for walrus ivory carvings and other **Inupiat arts and crafts,** you'll find low prices and an extraordinary selection in Nome. Jim West has a legendary collection for sale, assembled in the bar room of the historic **Board of Trade Saloon** that is attached to a shop on Front Street. The **Arctic Trading Post** is more of a traditional gift shop and also has a good ivory collection, and try **Sitnasuak Heritage Gallery** and **Maruskiya's,** both also on Front Street. **Chukotka-Alaska,** at 185 West First Ave., is an importer of art and other goods from the Russian Far East, and is really worth a look. Alaska Native art you find in Nome is likely to be authentic, but still ask; see "Native Art—Finding the Real Thing" in chapter 2. Foreign visitors should see chapter 3 to find out about the special permit you need to carry ivory out of the United States.

ON THE ROAD

The modest attractions downtown would hardly justify a trip to Nome, but the city's surroundings do. The roads provide unique access to a large stretch of the Seward Peninsula. Unlike other Arctic Bush areas, where you need to have someone take you where you want to go, in Nome, all you have to do is rent a car and go. There are few cars in Nome (they have to be shipped in by barge), so you won't see many other vehicles on a huge expanse of spectacular territory, with wildlife-viewing opportunities as good as anywhere in the state.

Most of the land is managed by the **Bureau of Land Management (BLM),** P.O. Box 925, Nome, AK 99762 (☎ **907/443-2177;** wwwndo.ak.blm.gov/). The **Alaska Department of Transportation** (☎ **907/443-3444**) can provide current information on road conditions. You have a good chance to see moose, reindeer, owls, foxes, bears, and musk ox anywhere you drive, but check in with the visitor center or the **Alaska Department of Fish and Game,** at Front and Steadman streets, for where you're most likely to see animals. They can also give you guidance on fishing along the roads and a "Nome Roadside Fishing Guide," or download it from www.state.ak.us/local/akpages/FISH.GAME/sportf/region3/nwmgt/nwhome2.htm. Check "Getting Around," above, for how to get out on the roads.

✪ **ROAD HIGHLIGHTS** None of the three roads radiating from Nome have services of any kind—just small Native villages, a few dwellings, and some reindeer herders—so you must be prepared and bring what you need with you, including insect repellent. The visitor center provides a good road guide. Here are some highlights:

The **Nome-Council road** heads 72 miles to the east, about half of that on the shoreline. It turns inland at the ghost town of Solomon, an old mining town with an abandoned railroad train, known as the Last Train to Nowhere. The engines were originally used on the New York City elevated lines in 1881, then were shipped to Alaska in 1903 to serve the miners along this line to Nome. This is a great scenic spot for bird watching, and fishing is good in the Solomon River, all along the road. Council, near the end of the road, has a couple of dozen families in the summer; you have to get a boat ride across a river just short of the village.

The **Nome-Taylor road,** also known as the Kougarok road, runs north of town into the Kigluaik Mountains, 85 miles from Nome, eventually petering out and becoming impassable. About 40 miles out, you reach lovely Salmon Lake, with a lakeshore campground with picnic tables, grills, and outhouses. A few miles farther, a road to the left leads to the 125° Pilgrim Hot Springs, near the ruins of a Catholic church and orphanage. Access is limited to when the caretaker is on hand, so check with the visitor center before going.

The **Nome-Teller road** leads 73 miles to the village of Teller, which has 266 residents, a gift shop, and a store. It's an opportunity to see an authentic Arctic Native village.

✪ **MOUNTAIN BIKING** The roads of Nome are one of the world's great, undiscovered mountain biking destinations—where else can you bike past musk oxen and reindeer? Keith Conger's **Bering C Bikes** (☎ **907/443-4994**) offers guided bike day trips and van-supported multiday camping expeditions. Keith, a biologist, leads the tours and teaches about the ecology of the land they peddle through. He also sells and fixes bikes, but, unfortunately, no one in town rents bikes. For bike enthusiasts, it may be worth renting one in Anchorage or bringing yours from home.

BIRD WATCHING Bird-watchers will make many discoveries out on the Nome roads, using new pages of their bird books. A bird list is available at the visitor center, and they can tell you where to look—each of the three roads has different habitat. The best times to visit for birding are right around Memorial Day, and from July to mid-August. Lana and Richard Harris are Nome's leading birders of long standing, and the only local members of the American Birding Association. Lana can most easily be reached at the visitor center, where she now works, but the couple also maintains a **birders' hot line** on their home phone recorder (☎ **907/443-5528**); please don't call before 6am or after 10pm, Alaska time. There's a chance to see Siberian birds, and you can count on bluethroats, yellow wagtails, wheatears, Arctic warblers, and Aleutian and Arctic terns. Nome is the only place to see a bristle-thighed curlew without chartering a plane. You don't need a guide, although guided trips are available (check with the visitor center). As Lana put it, "If you haven't found a yellow wagtail, you haven't left the bar yet."

IN THE AIR

Nome is a hub for Bush plane operators. Flightseeing charters are available, or you can fly on one of the mail-run routes out to the villages and spend a couple of hours touring for as little as $90; check how long the plane will stay in the village, as you may want to fly back on a different run to get more time. The visitor center or the flight services will help you figure it out. Among the operators are **Olson Air** (☎ **800/478-5600** in Alaska only, or 907/443-2229; e-mail: drdonny@nook.net) or **Cape Smythe Air** (☎ **800/78-5125** in Alaska only, or 907/443-2414). Don't go in bad weather, as you'll see little and may get stuck in a tiny village. You can also fly 150 miles over the International Dateline and see Russia from the air and the narrow water that divides our two nations. **Bering Air** (☎ **800/443-5465** in Alaska only, or 907/443-5620; www.beringair.com/) specializes in these trips, which cost $150 for a 2-hour flight.

ACCOMMODATIONS

There are two larger hotels in town, which I do not recommend; the rooms are better at the smaller places listed below.

Aurora Inn and Executive Suites. Inn is located at 527 Front St.; Executive Suites is located at 226 W. D St. (P.O. Box 1008), Nome, AK 99762. ☎ **800/354-4606** or 907/443-3838. Fax 907/443-6380. 35 units. www.aurorainnome.com. TV TEL. Summer $125 double; $165 suite. Winter $90 double; $150 suite. Extra person over age 12 $10. AE, MC, V.

Choose, at the same price, among these two comfortable buildings with different styles of accommodations under the same ownership. The Aurora Inn offers the best traditional hotel rooms in town in a brand-new mock country inn on the town's main street. The Executive Suites is comprised of a dozen apartmentlike units, ranging from rooms with kitchenettes to two-bedroom apartments with full kitchens and living areas. All have cable with HBO, coffeepots, and popcorn for the microwave. That building, too, is only a couple of years old. Uniquely in town, they have lots of no-smoking rooms. They also operate Stampede Rent-A-Car and have a self-service laundry on site.

June's Bed and Breakfast. 231 E. Fourth Ave. (P.O. Box 489), Nome, AK 99762. ☎ **800/494-6994** or 907/443-5984; Oct–May 206/547-7826. www.gold-digger.com/. 3 units, none with private bathroom. $80 double. Rates include breakfast and airport pickup. No credit cards. Closed Oct–May.

June Engstrom hosts this traditional little B&B, proudly declaring, "I really am a gold digger's daughter." Her sourdough pancake starter came over the Chilkoot Trail in 1898, and she gives it and the recipe away to guests (the starter is the yeast concoction that prospectors cultivated on the trail). The rooms are cozy, not commodious, but June's gregarious hospitality makes it special. Each has one of her handmade quilts and use of the laundry is free.

Nanuaq Manor. Kings Place and Spokane St. (P.O. Box 850), Nome, AK 99762. ☎ **907/443-5296.** Fax 907/443-3063. 15 suites. TV TEL. $95–$175 double. AE, MC, V.

These are simply light, roomy two- and three-bedroom apartments with full kitchens and their own laundry machines in buildings with permanent residents in other units. Everything was very clean and up-to-date when we visited. Few are reserved for nonsmokers. Rates depend on the number of bedrooms in the apartment you use.

DINING

There's not a selection of places where you'd go out of your way to dine, but you can find an adequate family meal at various establishments in Nome, all along Front Street.

There are several restaurants operated by immigrant families, offering their national cuisine and something else, often with servers who speak broken English. **Nachos,** at 503 Front St. in the Old Federal Building (☎ **907/443-5503**), has OK American-style Mexican food and good Chinese. **Milano's Pizzeria** (☎ **907/443-2924**), in the same building, serves Italian and Japanese meals; its pizza gets a thumbs-up from the locals. **Twin Dragons,** on Front Street near Steadman Street (☎ **907/443-5552**), has made it for years with Chinese food alone, which is consistently good, although the service isn't so reliable. The other ethnic place is **Pizza Napoli,** on Front between Hunter and Lanes Way (☎ **907/443-5300**), a Greek/Italian combination serving good pizza and great Greek salads. It doesn't take credit cards; all the others take Visa and MasterCard.

The other flavor of restaurant in Nome is the classic American greasy spoon. The ethnic restaurants mentioned above all have a way to escape the smoke; these burger habitats tend to be smoky throughout. The **Polar Cub Restaurant,** at 225 Front St. (☎ **907/443-5191**), has an extensive dinner menu and prices that, for the Alaska Bush, are quite reasonable. **Fat Freddy's Restaurant,** in the Nugget Inn (☎ **907/443-5899**), serves more expensive fare in the evening, such as steaks and fried fish, in addition to the usual sandwiches; their prices are higher than those in the Polar Cub.

The **Fort Davis Roadhouse,** on the beach about a mile east of town (☎ **907/443-2660**), is more of a fine-dining experience, with open views of the tundra and water, but currently it's open only on Friday and Saturday evenings.

7 Kotzebue

Although its 3,000 residents make Kotzebue (*kotz*-eh-biew) a good-sized town, with a bank, a hospital, and a couple of grocery stores, I've heard it called a village instead. A "village," in Alaskan parlance, is a remote Native settlement in the Bush, generally with fewer than a few hundred residents, where people live relatively close to the traditional lifestyle of their indigenous ancestors. Kotzebue is a support hub for the villages of the Northwest Arctic, with jet service and a booming cash economy, but it's populated and run by the Inupiat—fish-drying racks and old dog sleds are scattered along the streets, and Native culture is thriving. It does feel like a village.

For visitors, this characteristic makes Kotzebue unique because you can see real **Eskimo culture** without leaving the comforts of jet travel and standard hotel rooms behind. Or, if you don't mind giving up some of those comforts, you can get even closer to the Inupiat way of life. For adventurous outdoors people, Kotzebue offers access to huge areas of remote public land through which you can float on a raft or canoe. **Kobuk Valley National Park,** with its bizarre sand dunes, **Noatak National Preserve,** and **Cape Krusenstern National Monument** are among the largest national park units in the country, and among the least visited.

It's important to realize from the outset, however, that outside of an organized bus tour, there's absolutely nothing to do in Kotzebue. As I was told, "You have to shoot something or burn a lot of gas to have any fun around here." Kotzebue is not set up for independent travelers except those of the most intrepid ilk, and they will most likely use the town as a way to get into the remote public lands. Nome offers more for the independent traveler interested in something in between an organized tour and a wilderness expedition.

The dominant business in town is the **NANA Corporation,** a regional Native corporation representing the roughly 7,000 Inupiat who live in this Northwest Arctic region the size of Indiana. NANA, which stands for Northwest Arctic Native Association, is a successful example of how the 1971 Alaska Native Claims Settlement Act gave the indigenous people control over their own destiny. With huge land and resource holdings and the cash to develop them, NANA is making money for its Inupiat shareholders and providing them with jobs in institutional catering and oil drilling, and at the Red Dog zinc mine near Kotzebue, the world's most productive. More relevant for visitors, NANA also owns the main hotel and tourist businesses in Kotzebue.

ESSENTIALS

GETTING THERE The only way to Kotzebue is by air. **Alaska Airlines** (☎ **800/252-7522;** www.alaskaair.com) has several daily jets from Anchorage and Fairbanks in the summer. You'll pay in the range of $350 to $600 round-trip from Anchorage. They also fly from Kotzebue to Nome. Once in Kotzebue, there are many air taxis and commuter lines to the outlying villages (more on that below). The cheapest and most convenient way for most tourists to go to Kotzebue is to take a package offered by **Tour Arctic** and **Alaska Airlines Vacations,** described under "Attractions & Activities," below.

VISITOR INFORMATION There is no town visitor center. The National Park Service staffs the **Iññaigvik Education and Information Center** at Second Avenue and Lake Street (P.O. Box 1029), Kotzebue, AK 99752 (☎ **907/442-3760,** or 907/442-3890 for headquarters; fax 907/442-8316; www.nps.gov/noaa), providing information and displays on the immense area of protected land in the region and offering classes in topics such as basket weaving or medicinal plants. Employees will answer questions about the town as well. It's open in summer daily from 8am to 6pm, by appointment in winter.

The local headquarters of the park service, Fish and Wildlife Service, and Bureau of Land Management are open during normal business hours all year. The **Park Service headquarters** is in the post office on Shore Avenue, and the other agencies are at 120 Second Ave.

GETTING AROUND Kotzebue is 26 miles north of the Arctic Circle on the Chukchi Sea. About a mile by 2 miles in size, it sits on a low spit of land extending into the shallow Kotzebue Sound. You can walk pretty much everywhere you need to go or take a cab if you have luggage. The main hotel is a 15-minute walk from the airport, and taxis are available from **Polar Cab** (☎ **907/442-2233**). If you're on the Tour Arctic package, buses will pick you up at the plane and deliver you and your luggage to the hotel. The gravel streets are on a warped grid radiating from **Shore Avenue,** also known as **Front Street,** which runs along the water. Roads extend only a few miles out of town.

FAST FACTS The sale of **alcohol** is illegal in Kotzebue, but possession for personal use is permitted, a legal status known as "damp."

A **bank** with an ATM stands at the corner of Lagoon Street and Second Avenue.

The **Maniilaq Medical Center,** with a 24-hour emergency room, is located at Fifth Avenue and Mission Street (☎ **907/442-3321**).

For nonemergency matters, call the **Kotzebue Police Department** at ☎ **907/442-3351** or the **Alaska State Troopers** at ☎ **907/442-3222.**

The **post office** is at Shore Avenue and Tundra Way.

The **sales tax** is 6%; the **tax on rooms** totals 12%.

SPECIAL EVENTS The **Fourth of July** is something special in Kotzebue. Besides the Independence Day celebration, it's as early as you can count on all the snow being gone.

ATTRACTIONS & ACTIVITIES

There is only one activity in town, and it's part of an organized tour. **Tour Arctic** (☎ **907/442-3441**) hosts around 10,000 visitors annually in its cultural and natural-history program, the centerpiece of which is the seasonal **NANA Museum of the Arctic,** across from the airport (☎ **907/442-3747**). For most people, the packages, also sold through **Alaska Airlines Vacations** (☎ **800/468-2248**), are the only sensible way to go to Kotzebue. You'll learn about the Arctic and Native culture, but the tour is scripted and there are no spectacular sights on the way. Owned and operated by the Inupiat, the company employs real Eskimo guides who offer commentary for about 5 hours while keeping customers comfortable, mostly in buses and indoors. A show at the museum includes children dancing, a blanket toss, and a high-tech slide show about the struggle to save Inupiat culture. The tour also includes a talk and demonstration in a tent about the clothing and survival techniques of the Eskimos. There's also a brief opportunity to walk on the tundra. Independent travelers in town for outdoor activities can attend the hour-long museum program only for $35, the culture camp for $20, or the whole tour for $90; museum shows are timed to match the arrival of flights, at 4 and 6:30pm. The price is high, but it's the only thing to do in town.

Day trip packages are $366 from Anchorage—less than a full-fare ticket. The same tour with an overnight stay and a day in Nome is $496, double occupancy. You can choose to spend the night in Kotzebue at NANA's Nullagvik Hotel or in Nome at the Nugget Inn; choose Kotzebue. Any of those visits will feel brief, with little time for anything but the structured tours. A 2-night trip, one each in Nome and Kotzebue, is $547, and adds more free time. Adding an excursion to the village of Kiana and a lengthy flightseeing trip over the Northwest Arctic region, including the Kobuk Sand Dunes, requires another night and an additional $350.

GETTING OUTSIDE

A FISH CAMP Some rugged and curious travelers may want something a bit less pampered and scripted than the Tour Arctic program. **Arctic Circle Educational Adventures** (☎ **907/442-3509** in summer, 907/276-0976 in winter; fishcamp.org) offers a chance to stay at a camp similar to the fish camps where Native people spend the summer gathering food for the winter—and participate in set-net fishing, fish cutting, food gathering, and other traditional subsistence activities, as well as hiking, town tours, and bird watching. The camp on the beach 5 miles south of town is crude, and only for people who don't mind using an outhouse or sleeping in a plywood cabin. Elderhostel groups sometimes come for a week. Rates are $150 to $250 a day for the tour activities plus $95 per person per day for lodgings and meals. The season is mid-June to late August.

Which Arctic Tour to Choose

Visitors can encounter Alaska Native culture on guided tours in Kotzebue, with an optional add-on to Nome, or in Barrow. Nome is best visited as an independent traveler, but the tours make more sense in the other two communities. The tours are similar, involving a ride in a small bus and indoor presentations of Inupiat dance, culture, and crafts. Kotzebue's tour was more informative and seemed better thought out when I took it, but Barrow has the better sights: the nation's northernmost point, the brand-new Inupiat Heritage Center, and the chance, at least, of seeing a whale landed on the beach.

FLIGHTSEEING You can get an idea of what Native villages look like and see the **Kobuk Valley National Park,** including the Great Kobuk Sand Dunes, a desertlike area of shifting 100-foot dunes, from the air by buying a round-trip seat on one of the scheduled bush planes that serve the area. **Cape Smythe Air** (☎ **907/442-3020;** capesmythe.com) charges $171 for its loop that includes Shungnak and Kobuk and overflies the dunes (make sure to tell the pilot what you want to see). For $107, you can fly a shorter, northern loop to Noatak and Kivalina, over the **Cape Krusenstern National Monument.**

FLOAT TRIPS There are several remote rivers near Kotzebue with easy self-guided floating for experienced outdoors people. This is a rare chance to get deep into the Arctic on your own. The great Noatak River originates in the Brooks Range and flows 450 miles through America's largest undisturbed wilderness, in the impressive scenery of the Noatak National Preserve. The Selawik, Squirrel, and Kobuk rivers all have long sections of easy water. **Nova Raft and Adventure Tours, Alaska Discovery,** and **Equinox Wilderness Expeditions,** listed in chapter 2 under section 7, "Planning an Outdoor Vacation," have float trips in the area, although not necessarily every year. Expect to pay $2,500 to $3,000 per person, including air travel. Most river running in the region is self-guided. Get details from ***The Alaska River Guide,*** by Karen Jettmar, director of Equinox, published by Alaska Northwest Books, P.O. Box 10306, Portland, OR 97210-0306 (☎ **800/452-3032,** ext. 272). Obviously you should be experienced in the outdoors and in river floating before heading out for a multiday trip in the Arctic. And plan ahead, arranging details well in advance with the Park Service and your pilot. Most visitors bring all their gear from Anchorage, but Buck Maxson, of **Arctic Air Guides Flying Service** (☎ **907/442-3030**), rents rafts and canoes for $35 a day. An experienced bush pilot, he also will fly you out; how much you pay depends on where you go, but charter rates are typically $300 an hour. You can minimize your costs by putting in or taking out at villages along the river and using scheduled air services.

ACCOMMODATIONS & DINING

Dining options in Kotzebue are limited. Besides the hotel restaurant listed below, you'll find good breakfasts and great burgers at the **Bayside Inn,** right next door (☎ **907/442-3600**). I cannot recommend their rooms, however. There is also **Mario's Pizza and Deli,** at 606 Bison St. (☎ **907/442-2666**), a Japanese-Chinese-pizza-burger take-out place that serves sushi.

To save some money and meet friendly local people, stay at **Lagoon Bed and Breakfast,** 227 Lagoon St. (☎ **907/442-3723;** e-mail: mar81wsw@ptialaska.net).

Nullagvik Hotel. Shore Ave. and Tundra Way (P.O. Box 336), Kotzebue, AK 99752. ☎ **907/442-3331.** Fax 907/442-3340. 73 units. TV TEL. High season $130 double. Low season $95 double. AE, DC, DISC, MC, V.

The NANA-owned hotel is thoughtfully designed and comfortably furnished. The clean, up-to-date rooms have all the features of a good chain hotel. Their windows angle out from the building so that all get at least some ocean view. It can be startling to see Eskimo women wearing summer parkas called kuspuks cleaning in the halls; they certainly do a thorough job. By booking with an Alaska Airlines Vacations package, you save considerable money on stays here.

The **restaurant** is clean and nicely decorated, with a good view and flowers on the table. Certainly it is the best in town. Reindeer steak and Arctic salmon are on the menu for the tourists. Locals are more likely to come in for the popular Sunday breakfast, or order the less expensive sandwiches and beef for lunch. They serve dinner only Memorial Day to Labor Day, and close entirely October to April.

8 Barrow: Way North

The main reason visitors go to Barrow is its latitude. The Inupiat town is the northernmost settlement on the North American continent, above the 71st parallel. Here half-liquid land comes to an arbitrary point at the north tip of Alaska. The tundra around Barrow is dotted with lakes divided by tendrils of swampy tundra no more substantial than the edges of fine lace. On this haven for migratory waterfowl, the flat, wet land and the ocean seem to merge. Indeed, for all but a few months, it's all a flat, frozen plain of ocean and land. For 65 days in the winter, the sun never rises. In the summer, it doesn't set, and the ice recedes from the shore only for the months of the brief summer. Such extreme geography is a magnet—people want to stand in such a place, perhaps dip a toe in the Arctic Ocean.

And then what do you do next? If you're on a package trip, you can see an Eskimo blanket toss and dancing, look at whale bones and maybe buy Native crafts, and see some other manifestations of traditional Inupiat life amid a modern, oil-enriched town. An **Inupiat Heritage Center,** completed in 1999, exhibits and teaches about the culture. But there's no need to spend the night if your only interest is sightseeing. You can do it in a day and be back in Fairbanks or Anchorage in the evening.

The village of 4,500 is culturally unique. It's ancient, and still a center of whaling from open boats, with a summer festival celebrating a successful hunt and distribution of the meat to the community. But Barrow also is the seat of the North Slope Borough, a county government encompassing a larger area than the state of Nebraska, in which lies North America's largest oil field. The borough has everything money can buy for a local government, yet the people of the villages still must contend with crushing ice, snooping polar bears, and utter isolation.

ESSENTIALS

GETTING THERE **Alaska Airlines** (☎ **800/252-7522;** www.alaskaair.com) flies to Barrow daily from Anchorage and Fairbanks, and offers 1-day and overnight tour packages, described in "Attractions & Activities," below. The packages are a good deal, competitive with round-trip tickets alone from Anchorage, which range from $425 to $800. Book them through **Alaska Airlines Vacations** (☎ **800/468-2248**).

VISITOR INFORMATION A chamber of commerce **visitor center,** at Momegana and Ahkovak streets, near the airport, operates in the summer only, with a guide to talk to but little else. The town lacks a central tourism authority, but you can write ahead for information from the City Barrow, Office of the Mayor, P.O. Box 629, Barrow, AK 99723 (☎ **907/852-5211;** fax 907/852-5871; e-mail: barrowmayor@barrow.com).

GETTING AROUND Facing on the Chukchi Sea, Barrow has two sections, lying on each side of Isatkoak Lagoon. **Browerville,** to the east, has the Inupiat Heritage Center and the Alaska Commercial store, with a food court and many services. **Barrow,** containing the offices and most businesses, is to the west. The northern tip of Alaska, **Point Barrow,** is north of the town on a spit. The road leads 6 miles in that direction to a point tour companies advertise as the "farthest north point navigable by bus," but the absolute end is farther out, beyond the road. **All-terrain vehicles** are for rent in town, if you're going to be compulsive about it. Gas Field Road is the only other route out of town, leading 10 miles out onto the tundra.

Taxis are handy, charging a flat $5 anywhere in town ($3 for seniors), plus $1 for each additional passenger. **Polar Taxi** (☎ **907/852-2227**) is one cab service.

Barrow has an extraordinary bus system. The exact location of the buses is broadcast on TV channel 57 so riders can step right out the door without waiting;

Bush Softball

Barrow is mad for the game. You can hear the play-by-play on the radio, but to attend you will need a car: that's how the spectators watch on the chilly Arctic evenings, honking for good plays. And remember: If a ball disappears completely from view in a puddle, runners can advance no more than two bases.

On the rocky, mountainous Aleutian island of Unalaska their problem was too small a field, so home runs carried heavy penalties. Hit three in a season and you were permanently expelled from the league. But that's all past: They recently built a new, larger field, at a cost of nearly $3 million, including the cost of bringing nine shipping van containers of sod out from Palmer.

---

this saves them from standing in –40° weather in the company of polar bears. The fare is $1.

Jim Vordestrasse, the mayor (☎ **907/852-5211**), rents bicycles for $20 a day and offers tours by appointment for $20 an hour.

SPECIAL EVENTS The return of the sun after 2 months below the horizon is met by traditional celebrations on **January 21.** The **Piuraagiaqt,** a spring festival, takes place in mid-April. If the traditional bowhead whaling season is a success, the **Nalukataq festival** in late June celebrates the event. The length of the celebration depends on the number of whales landed. If you're very lucky, as I once was, you'll be there when a whale is landed, pulled up on the town beach, and butchered by the community.

FAST FACTS At this writing, the sale of **alcohol** was illegal in Barrow, and importation for personal use limited.

There is a **bank** at Agvik and Kiogak streets. An ATM is located in Browerville at the Stuaqpaq Alaska Commercial general store, inside the front door.

The **hospital** is on Agvik Street (☎ **907/852-4611**).

The borough **Department of Public Safety** is at ☎ **907/852-6111.**

Thanks to all that oil, there is **no sales or bed tax** in Barrow.

ATTRACTIONS & ACTIVITIES

The new ✪ **Inupiat Heritage Center** (☎ **907/852-4584**) is the town's main attraction. Completed in 1999, it is part museum, part gathering center, and part venue for living culture. Inside is a workshop for craftsmen and a performance space for storytellers and dancers—there's a gift shop to buy the artists' output. In the museum area, Inupiat artifacts include items recovered from the "Frozen Family," a precontact home that was found, with its occupants, in the permafrost near Barrow. If you have time, you can even join **classes** on skin sewing, carving, kayak building, or learn to speak Inupiaq. The center is open Monday to Friday 8:30am to 5pm, except during the midday Tundra Tours cultural show (see below). Admission is $5 adults, $2 ages 15 to 17, $1 ages 6 to 14, and free under age 6 or over age 55.

The main business in town, Native-owned **Tundra Tours** (☎ **800/882-8478** or 907/852-3900; www.AlaskaOne.com/topworld), along with the Top of the World Hotel, is owned by the Arctic Slope Regional Corp., a Native corporation covering the region. Their tour (the same one sold through Alaska Airlines Vacations) presents the town to visitors who arrive with little idea of what to expect. The 6-hour summer tour, in a small bus, drives around the town to show off the modest sights, including the school, an Eskimo boat, the cemetery, a stop for a dip of toes in the Arctic Ocean at the farthest north point, and so on. It's interesting to drive one of the short roads out of town to find snowy owls and Arctic fox. The owls stand still out on the flat tundra like bowling pins. The tour visits the new Inupiat Heritage Center for a blanket toss and cultural presentation, with a drumming and dance performance, and a chance to buy gifts from local craftspeople.

The day trip tour is $395, including airfare from Fairbanks, or $440 (double occupancy) to spend 1 night in Barrow at the Top of the World Hotel, giving you a chance to walk around a bit on your own. Book the tour through Alaska Airlines Vacations or with Tundra Tours at the numbers listed above. If you buy the tour separately, it's $58. They also offer a more expensive winter tour for seeing the Aurora.

ACCOMMODATIONS

If you spend the night on the package tour, you'll stay at the **Top of the World Hotel,** 1200 Agvik St. (☎ **907/852-3900;** www.AlaskaOne.com/topworld), which has standard hotel rooms, some overlooking the water. Here are choices for independent travelers.

Barrow Airport Inn. 1815 Momegana St. (P.O. Box 933), Barrow, AK 99723. ☎ **907/852-2525.** Fax 907/852-2528. 16 units. TV TEL. $115 double. Extra person $10. Rates include breakfast bar. CB, DC, DISC, MC, V.

These relatively economical rooms in a family operated establishment are clean and come with microwave ovens and small refrigerators; nine have full kitchens.

King Eider Inn. 1752 Ahkovak St. (P.O. Box 1283), Barrow, AK 99723. ☎ **907/852-4700.** Fax 907/852-2025. www.kingeider.net. 19 units. TV TEL. Summer $185 double. Winter $160 double. Extra person $30. AE, MC, V.

The best rooms in town are found in this new building near the airport. With the large stone fireplace in the lobby and large seating area, it feels like a lodge. The rooms are fresh and attractive; nine have kitchenettes, stocked with microwave popcorn. There's a sauna on-site, and the staff will pick you up at the airport.

DINING

There are several decent restaurants in Barrow. Generally, they stay open very late, have TVs always on, offer free delivery, and don't offer decaffeinated coffee—I have no idea why.

Adjoining the Top of the World Hotel, **Pepe's North of the Border,** at 1204 Agvik St. (☎ **907/852-8200**), is the most famous place in town, serving large portions of familiar American-style Mexican food. The tours come here for lunch, and host Fran Tate hands out souvenirs.

We found better food at **Arctic Pizza,** at 125 Apayauk St. (☎ **907/852-4222**). It's a regular pizzeria downstairs and a white-tablecloth Italian and steak/seafood place upstairs, with a gorgeous view of the Arctic Ocean; children are forbidden—they can stay downstairs and have pizza. The charbroiled halibut was excellent, and a bargain at $15.50.

You'll find a menu with something for everyone in a fine dining atmosphere at **Northern Lights Restaurant,** at 5122 Herman St. (☎ **907/852-3300**). **Teriyaki House,** 1906 Takpuk St. (☎ **907/852-2276**), serves good Japanese, Chinese, and Korean food in a well-worn dining room.

9 Prudhoe Bay: Arctic Industry

The Prudhoe (*prew*-dough) Bay complex is no ordinary oil field: It's a historic and strategic site of great importance and a major technological achievement. It was built the way you'd have to build an oil field on the moon, with massively complex machinery able to operate in winters that are always dark and very, very cold. But in some ways, it might be simpler to build on the moon—here, the industry has to coexist with a fragile habitat for migrating caribou and waterfowl, on wet, fragile tundra that permanently shows any mark made by vehicles. It works, and that's quite an achievement. Workers are forbidden even to set foot on the tundra, and as you look from the edge of one of the gravel pads the heathery ground looks as undisturbed as a calm sea.

To see Prudhoe Bay, you have to sign up for a tour. Everything is behind chain-link fences and security checkpoints. The tour visits the Arctic Ocean and gives you a chance to see the tundra and touch the pipeline, but it doesn't go inside any of the buildings where the heavy-duty, high-tech equipment handles the oil and readies it for passage down the line. From the outside, these buildings and the oil wells don't look like much—just metal-sided industrial buildings. The grim town of **Deadhorse,** which serves the oil facility, is really more of an industrial yard, barely deserving to be called a town; it certainly isn't anything you'd travel to see. Frankly, I can't recommend taking the time and expense required for a Prudhoe Tour. If you're curious about the Arctic, a trip to Barrow, Kotzebue, or Nome makes more sense. (The oil companies' VIP tours, which do go inside, are fascinating, but you have to be a VIP.)

If you still want to go, fly up from Fairbanks or Anchorage for the day and take the tour from Deadhorse. There's no need to spend the night if you fly, as the tour takes less than 3 hours and there's nothing else to do and nowhere else to go. Or, if you drive up on the Dalton Highway, you can engage a tour in Deadhorse, or just get a lift to the water, through the oil complex. See chapter 9, on the Interior, for information on driving the Dalton. **Alaska Airlines** (☎ **800/252-7522;** www.alaskaair.com) serves Prudhoe Bay. A round-trip ticket costs around $600 from Anchorage.

Once at Prudhoe, the **Arctic Caribou Inn,** P.O. Box 340112, Prudhoe Bay, AK 99734 (☎ **907/659-2368** in summer or 907/659-2840 in winter), provides visitor services, including a hotel and cafeteria, plus tours and a shuttle service to the Arctic Ocean. Rooms start at $120 double. The restaurant has a buffet for breakfast ($10.50) and dinner ($18), and menu service for lunch. The hotel is near the airport in Deadhorse and serves as the starting point for the tours. The oil complex tour costs $50. It includes a video and lasts 2½ hours. It doesn't go inside any of the buildings, but does stop at the shore of the Arctic Ocean. The 1½-hour round-trip just to touch the ocean costs $25.

Gray Line of Alaska (☎ **800/544-2206,** or 907/277-5581 in Anchorage; www.graylinealaska.com) operates summer trips from Fairbanks that fly one way and drive the other over the Dalton Highway in buses. The 3-day, 2-night trip costs $805, and can be added to a longer tour or a cruise. Other tour companies offer similar services.

Appendix: Alaska in Depth

An old photo album opens, emitting a scent of dust and dried glue. Inside, pale images speak wanly of shrunken mountains and glaciers, a huge blue sky, water and trees, a moose standing way off in the background. No family photographer can resist the urge to capture Alaska's vastness in the little box of a camera, and none, it seems, has ever managed it. Then, turning the page, there it is—not in another picture of the landscape, but reflected in a small face at the bottom of the frame: my own face, as a child. For anyone who hasn't experienced that moment, the expression is merely enigmatic—slightly dazed, happy but abstracted, as if hearing a far-off tone. But if you've been to Alaska, that photograph captures something familiar: It's an image of discovery. I've seen it on the fresh, pale faces in photographs stamped with the dates of my family's first explorations of Alaska 35 years ago. And then, researching this book, I got to see it once again, on my own young son's face. And I knew that, like me, he had discovered something important.

So what am I talking about? Like anything worth experiencing, it's not simple to explain.

Tour guides try to get it across with statistics. Not much hope of that, although some of the numbers do give you a general idea of scale. Once you've driven across the continental United States and know how big that is, seeing a map of Alaska placed on top of the area you crossed, just about spanning it, provides some notion of size. Alaskans always like to threaten that we'll split in half and make Texas the third-largest state. Alaska has about 600,000 residents. If you placed each of them an equal distance apart, no one would be closer than a mile to anyone else. Of course, that couldn't happen. No one has ever been to some parts of Alaska.

But none of that expresses what really matters. It's not just a matter of how big Alaska is or how few people it contains. It's not an intellectual conception at all. None of that crosses your mind when you see a chunk of ice the size of a building fall from a glacier and send up a huge splash and wave surging outward, or when you feel a wave lift your sea kayak from the fall of a breaching humpback whale. Or when you hike for a couple of days to stand on top of a mountain, and from there see more mountaintops, layered off as far as the horizon, in unnamed, seemingly infinite multiplicity. A realization of what Alaska means can come in a simple little moment. It can come at the end of a long day driving an Interior Alaska highway, as your car climbs into yet another mountain range, the sun still hanging high in what should be night, storm systems arranged before you across the landscape, when you realize that you haven't seen another car in an hour. Or standing on an Arctic Ocean beach, it could happen when you look around at the sea of empty tundra behind you, the sea of green water before you, and your own place on what seems to be the edge of the world. Or you might simply be sitting on the sun-warmed rocks of a beach in Southeast or Southcentral Alaska when you discover that you're occupying only one of many worlds—a world of intermediate size, lying in magnitude between the tiny tide-pool universes of life all around you and the larger world seen by an eagle gliding through the air high above.

What's the soul alchemy of such a moment? I suppose it's different for each person, but for me it has something to do with realizing my actual size in the world, how I fit in, what it means to be just another medium-sized mammal, no longer armed with the illusions supplied by civilization. On returning to the city from the wilderness, there's a re-entry process, like walking from a vivid movie to the mundane, gray street outside—it's the movie that seems more real. For a while, it's hard to take human institutions seriously after you've been deep into Alaska.

Some people never do step back across that boundary. They live their lives out in the wilderness, away from people. Others compromise, living in Alaskan cities and walking out into the mountains when they can, the rest of the time just maintaining a prickly notion of their own independence. But anyone can make the same discovery, if he or she has the courage to come to Alaska and the time to let the place sink in. You don't have to be an outdoors enthusiast or a young person. You only have to be open to wonder and able to slow down long enough to see it. Then, in a quiet moment when you least expect it, things may suddenly seem very clear and all that you left behind oddly irrelevant.

How you find your way back to where you started is your affair.

1 Natural History: Rough Drafts & Erasures

THE SURGING ICE

In 1986, **Hubbard Glacier,** north of Yakutat, suddenly decided to surge forward, cutting off Russell Fjord from the rest of the Pacific Ocean. A group of warm-hearted but ill-advised wildlife lovers set out to save the marine mammals that had been trapped behind the glacier. Catching a dolphin from an inflatable boat isn't that easy—they didn't accomplish much, but they provided a lot of entertainment for the locals. Then the water burst through the dam of ice and the lake became a fjord again, releasing the animals anyway.

Bering Glacier can't decide which way to go. Apparently surging and retreating on a 20-year cycle, it recently reversed course after bulldozing a wetland migratory bird stopover and speedily contracted back up toward the mountains. **Meares Glacier** has plowed through old-growth forest. On the other hand, some glaciers are so stable they gather a layer of dirt where trees and brush grow to maturity. When **Malspina Glacier** retreated, the trees on its back toppled. And on a larger scale, all the land of **Glacier Bay**—mountains, forests, sea floor—is rising 1½ inches a year as it rebounds from the weight of melted glaciers that 100 years ago were a mile thick and 65 miles longer.

Yet these new and erased lands are just small corrections around the margins compared to what the earth has done before in setting down, wiping out, and rewriting the natural history of Alaska. In the last Ice Age, 15,000 years ago, much of what is Alaska today was one huge glacier. At the tops of granite mountains in Southeast Alaska, especially in the northern Lynn Canal, it's possible to see a sort of high-water mark—the highest point the glaciers came in the Ice Age. Even looking from the deck of a boat, thousands of feet below, you can see where mountain shoulders, rounded by the passage of ice, are much smoother than the sharp, craggy peaks just above, which stuck out of that incredible sheet of ice.

Some 7-year-old children worry about the bogeyman or being caught in a house fire. When I was that age, living with my family in Juneau, I learned how Gastineau Channel was formed and then went to see Mendenhall Glacier. I was told how it was really a river of ice, advancing and retreating, and with this knowledge I developed a deeper fear: ice. I was afraid that while I slept, another Ice Age would come and grind away the city of Juneau.

It's possible that a glacier *could* get Juneau—the city fronts on the huge Juneau Ice Field—but there would be at least a few centuries' warning before it hit. Glaciers are essentially just snow that doesn't get a chance to melt. It accumulates at higher altitudes until it gets deep enough to compress into ice and starts oozing down the sides of the mountain. When the ice reaches the ocean, or before, the melt and calving of icebergs at the leading edge reaches a point of equilibrium with the snow that's still being added at the top. The glacier stops advancing, becoming a true river of ice, moving a snowflake from the top of the mountain to the bottom in a few hundred years. When conditions change—more snow or colder long-term weather, for example—the glacier gets bigger; that's called advancing, and the opposite is retreating. Sometimes, something strange will happen under the glacier—in the case of Bering Glacier, it started to float on a cushion of water—and it will surge forward, several feet or even dozens of feet a day in extreme cases. But most of the time, the advance or retreat is measured in inches or feet a year.

It took some time to figure out how glaciers work, and the living glaciers of Alaska, like living fossils from the last Ice Age, helped show the way. In the 1830s, scientists in Switzerland found huge rocks (now called glacial erratics) that appeared to have moved miles from where they had once been a part of similar bedrock. They developed the theory that ancient glaciers shaping the Alps must have moved the rocks. **John Muir,** the famous writer and naturalist, suggested in the 1870s that the granite mountains of Yosemite National Park had been rounded and polished by the passing of glaciers that melted long ago. He traveled to Alaska to prove it. Here, glaciers were still carving the land—they had never finished melting at the end of the last glacial period—and Muir could see shapes like those at Yosemite in the act of being created. Glacier Bay, which Muir "discovered" when guided there by his Alaska Native friends, was a glacial work in progress, as it is still today.

When you visit, you'll see for yourself how the heavy blue ice and white snow are streaked with black rock and dust that was obviously gouged from mountains and left in hills at the face and along the flanks of the glaciers, debris piles called moraines. At Exit Glacier in Kenai Fjords National Park, you can stand on a moraine that wraps the leading edge of the glacier like a scarf, and feel the cold streaming off spires of clicking ice—it feels like standing in front of a freezer with the door open. Find another hill like that, no matter where it is, and you can be pretty sure a glacier once came that way. Likewise, you can see today's glaciers scooping out U-shaped valleys in the mountains. Fjords and valleys all over Alaska in those same shapes surely were made by the glaciers of the 50 ice ages that have covered North America in the last few million years.

Today, Alaska's 100,000 glaciers cover about 5% of its land mass, mostly on the southern coast. There are no glaciers in the Arctic because the climate there is too dry to produce enough snow. The northernmost large glaciers are in the Alaska Range, such as those carving great chasms in the side of Mt. McKinley. The **Kahiltna Glacier** flows 45 miles from the mountain, losing 15,000 feet downhill over its course. The mountain's height creates its own weather, wringing moisture out of the atmosphere and feeding its glaciers. Will global warming shrink Alaska's glaciers? No one knows for sure, but it could make some larger if a change in climate brings greater precipitation.

THE TREMBLING EARTH

Despite my early glacier phobia, I never had a similar fear of earthquakes. Living in Anchorage, I'd been through enough of them that, as early as I can remember, I generally didn't bother to get out of bed when they hit.

It's all part of living in a place that isn't quite done yet. Any part of Alaska could have an earthquake, but the Pacific Rim from Southcentral Alaska to the Aleutians is the shakiest. That's because this is where Alaska is still under construction. The very rocks that make up the state are something of an ad hoc conglomeration, still in the process of being assembled. The floor of the Pacific Ocean is moving north, and as it moves, it is carrying islands and mountains along with it. When they hit the Alaska plate, these pieces of land, called **terranes,** dock like ships arriving, but very slowly—an island moving an inch a year takes a long time to travel thousands of miles. Geologists studying rocks near Mount McKinley have found a terrane that used to be tropical islands. In Kenai Fjords National Park, fossils have turned up that are otherwise found only in Afghanistan and China. The slowly moving crust of the earth brought them here on a terrane that makes up a large part of the south coast of Alaska.

Here's how it works. Near the center of the Pacific, underwater volcanoes and cracks that constantly ooze molten new rock are adding to the tectonic plate that forms the ocean floor. As it grows from the middle, the existing sea floor spreads, at a rate of perhaps an inch a year. At the other side of the Pacific plate, where it bumps up against Alaska, there's not enough room, so the crust bends and cracks as it's forced downward into the planet's great, molten recycling mill of magma. Land masses that are along for the ride smash into the continent that's already there. When one hits—the so-called Yakutat block is still in the process of docking—a mountain range gets shoved up. Earthquakes and volcanoes are a by-product.

Living in such an unsettled land is a matter of more than abstract interest. The Mount Spurr volcano, which erupted most recently in 1992, turned day to night in Anchorage, dropping a blanket of ash all over the region, choking lungs and machines. A Boeing 747 full of passengers flew into the plume and lost power in all its engines, falling in darkness for several minutes before pilots were able to restart the clogged jets. After that incident, the airport was closed until aviation authorities could find a way to keep volcanic plumes and planes apart. More than 80 volcanoes have been active in Alaska in the last 200 years. Earthquakes over 7 on the Richter scale—larger than the 1994 Los Angeles quake—have occurred every 15 months, on average, over the last century. The worst of the quakes, on March 27, 1964, was the strongest ever to hit North America. It ranked 9.2 on the Richter scale, lowering an entire region of the state some 10 feet and moving it even farther laterally. No other earthquake has ever moved so much land.

There are lots of tales about what people did when the quake hit—it lasted a good 5 minutes, long enough for a lot to happen. My wife, Barbara, a

1-year-old at the time, is said to have found it hilariously funny while everyone else ran around in panic. A family friend rushed out into the street from bathing, stark naked; a neighbor who had been doing laundry when the earth started shaking met him there and handed him a pair of socks she had happened to carry with her.

The earthquake destroyed much of Anchorage and several smaller towns, and killed about 131 people, mostly in sea waves created by underwater landslides. In Valdez, the waterfront was swept clean of people. In the Prince William Sound village of Chenega, built on a hill along the water, people started running for higher ground when the wave came. About half made it. Families were divided by just yards between those who ran fast enough and those who were caught by the water and disappeared. But the earthquake could have been much worse—it occurred in the early evening, on Good Friday, when most public buildings were empty. An elementary school in Anchorage that broke in half and fell into a hole didn't have anyone inside at the time.

But even that huge earthquake wasn't an unusual occurrence, at least in the earth's terms. Geologists believe the same Alaska coast sank 6 feet in an earthquake in the year 1090. Big earthquakes happen every year in Alaska, but so few people live here that most of them don't bother anyone. The earth's crust is paper thin compared to the globe's forces, and, like paper, it is folding where the two edges meet. At the edge, Alaska's coast is bending down; and farther inshore, where McKinley stands, it is bowing up. The steep little rock islands you see flocking with birds at Kenai Fjords National Park are old mountain tops; the monolith of McKinley a brand new one.

THE FROZEN TUNDRA

The Interior and Arctic parts of the state are less susceptible to earthquakes and, since they receive little precipitation, they don't have glaciers, either. But there's still a sense of living on a land that's not quite sure of itself, as most of northern Alaska is solid only by virtue of being frozen. When it thaws, it turns to mush. The phenomenon is caused by **permafrost,** a layer of earth a little below the surface that never thaws—or at least, you'd better hope it doesn't. Buildings erected on permafrost without some mechanism for dispersing their own heat—pilings, a gravel pad, or even refrigerator coils—thaw the ground below and sink into a self-made quicksand. You occasionally run across such structures. There's one in Dawson City, Yukon Territory, still left from the gold rush, that leans at an alarming angle with thresholds and lower tiers of siding disappearing into the ground.

Building sewer and water systems in such conditions is a challenge still unmet in much of Alaska's Bush, where village toilets are often "honey buckets" and the septic systems are sewage lagoons on the edge of town where the buckets are dumped. Disease caused by the unsanitary conditions sweeps the villages as if rural Alaska were a Third World country, but the government has been slow to provide the funds required to solve the problem.

Permafrost makes the land do other strange things. On a steep slope, the thawed earth on top of the ice can begin to slowly slide downhill like a blanket over a pile of pillows, setting the trees at crazy angles. These groves of black spruce—the only conifer that grows on this kind of ground—are called **drunken forests,** and you can see them in Denali National Park and elsewhere in the Interior. Permafrost also can create weird ground sometimes called **muskeg,** where shaky tussocks the size of basketballs sit a foot or two apart on a wet, muddy flat. From a distance it looks smooth, but walking on real basketballs would be easier.

The Arctic and much of the Interior are a sort of swampy desert. Most of the time, the tundra is frozen in white; snow blows around, but not much falls. That snow melts in the summer and the water stands on the surface, on top of the permafrost, creating ponds—Alaska is a land of 10 million lakes, with 3 million larger than 20 acres. Migratory birds arrive to feed and paddle around those shallow circles of deep green and sky blue. Flying over the Arctic in a small plane is disorienting, for no pattern maintains in the flat green tundra, and irregularly shaped patches of water stretch as far as the eye can see. Pilots find their way by following landmarks like tractor tracks etched into the tundra. Although few and far between, the tracks remain clearly delineated for decades after they're made, appearing as a pair of narrow, parallel ponds reaching from one horizon to the other.

The permafrost also preserves much older things. The meat of prehistoric mastodons, still intact, has been unearthed from the frozen ground. On the Arctic Coast, the sea eroded ground near Barrow that contained ancient ancestors of the Eskimos who still inhabit the same neighborhood. In 1982, they found a family that apparently was crushed by sea ice up to 500 years ago. Two of the bodies were well preserved, sitting in the home they had occupied and wearing the clothes they had worn the day of the disaster, perhaps around the time Columbus was sailing to America.

Sea ice is the frozen ocean that extends from northern Alaska to the other side of the world. At the very top of the world it never thaws, but the water opens for a few months of summer along the shore. Then, in September, when the ocean water falls below 29°F, ice forms along the beach and expands from the North Pole's permanent ice pack until the two sides meet. The clash of huge ice floes creates towering pressure ridges, small mountains of steep ice that are difficult to cross. The Eskimo blanket toss—the game of placing a person in the center of a walrus-skin blanket and bouncing him or her high in the air—traditionally got hunters high enough to see over the pressure ridges so they could spot game. At its extreme, in March, the ice extends solidly all the way south to the Pribilof Islands, when it's possible to drive a dog team across the Bering Sea to Siberia. The National Weather Service keeps track of the ice pack and issues predictions you can find on the Internet (www.alaska.net/~nwsar). Crab boats like to tempt its south-moving edge in the fall and shippers look for the right moment in the summer to venture north with barges of fuel and other supplies for the coast of the Arctic Ocean—they barely have time to get there and back before the ice closes in again in the fall. Ice even interferes with shipping in Cook Inlet, around Anchorage, although the floes never form a solid pack. Walking on the downtown coastal trail, you can hear their eerie crunch and squeal as they tumble together in the fast tidal currents.

The Arctic and Interior are relatively barren biologically compared to the southern coastal areas of the state. Polar bears wander the Arctic ice pack, but they, like the Eskimos, feed more on marine mammals than on anything found on the shore. A 1,200-pound adult polar bear can make a meal of a walrus, and they're expert at hunting seal. In the summer, herds of caribou counted in the tens of thousands come north to their eastern Arctic calving grounds, but they migrate south when the cold, dark winter falls unremittingly on the region.

In Barrow, the sun doesn't rise for more than 65 days in the winter. In February, the average daily high temperature is –12°F, and the average low is –24°F. The Inupiat people learned to survive in this climate for millennia, but life was short and terribly hard. Today they've made some sensible allowances while holding onto many cultural traditions. For example, the school in Barrow has wide, light hallways and a large indoor playground.

THE RAIN FOREST

By comparison, southern coastal Alaska is warm and biologically rich. Temperate rain forest ranges up the coast from Southeast Alaska into Prince William Sound, with bears, deer, moose, wolves, and even big cats living among the massive western hemlock, Sitka spruce, and cedar. This old-growth forest, too wet to burn in forest fires, is the last vestige of the virgin, primeval woods that seemed so limitless to the first white settlers who arrived on the east coast of the continent in the 17th century. The trees grow on and on, sometimes rising more than 200 feet high, with diameters of 10 feet, and falling only after hundreds of years. When they fall, the trees rot on the damp moss of the forest floor and return to soil to feed more trees, which grow in rows upon their nursery trunks.

Standing among these giants, entirely shielded from the sky, one feels dwarfed by their age and size, living things of so much greater life span and magnitude than any person. Part of the mystery and grandeur also comes from the knowledge that, here at least, Alaska *does* seem permanent. That sense helps explain why cutting the rain forest is so controversial. Just one of these trees contains thousands of dollars worth of wood, a prize that drives logging as voraciously as the federal government, which owns most of the coastal forest, may choose to allow.

The rivers of the great coastal forests bring home runs of big **salmon,** clogging in spawning season like a busy sidewalk at rush hour. The fish spawn only once, returning by a precisely tuned sense of smell to the streams where they were hatched as many as 7 years before. When the fertilized eggs have been left in the stream gravel, the fish conveniently die on the beach, making a smorgasbord for bears and other forest animals. The huge **Kodiak brown bear,** topping 1,000 pounds, owes everything to the millions of salmon that return to the island each summer. By comparison, the grizzly bears of the Interior—the same species as browns, but living on grass, berries and an occasional ground squirrel—are mere midgets, their weight counted in the hundreds of pounds. Forest-dwelling black bears grow to only a few hundred pounds.

TAIGA & FIRE

Rain forest covers only a small fraction of Alaska. In fact, only a third of Alaska is forested at all, and most of this is the boreal forest that covers the central part of the state, behind the rain-shadow of coastal mountains that intercept moist clouds off the oceans. Ranging from the Kenai Peninsula, south of Anchorage, to the Brooks Range, where the Arctic begins, this is a taiga—a moist, subarctic forest of smaller, slower-growing, hardier trees that leave plenty of open sky between their branches. In well-drained areas, on hillsides and southern land less susceptible to permafrost, the boreal forest is a lovely, broadly spaced combination of straight, proud white spruce and pale, spectral paper birch. Along the rivers, cottonwood (also known as poplar) grow, with deep-grained bark and branches that spread in an oaklike matrix—if they could speak, it would be as wise old men. Where it's wet and swampy—over more and more land as you go north—all that will grow is low, brushy willow and the glum black spruce, which struggles to become a gnarled stick a mere 3 inches thick in 100 years, if it doesn't burn first. As the elevation grows, the spruce shrink, these trees turn into weirdly bent, ancient shrubs just before the tree line and the open alpine tundra.

Forest fires tear through as much as a million acres of Alaska's boreal forest each summer. In most cases, forest managers do no more than note the occurrence on a map. Unlike the rain forest, there's little commercially valuable timber in these thin stands, and, anyway, it isn't possible to halt the process of nature's self-immolation over the broad expanse of Alaska. The boreal forest regenerates through fire—it was made to burn. The wildlife that lives in and eats it needs new growth from the burns as well as the shelter of older trees. When the forest is healthiest and most productive, the dark green of the spruce is broken by streaks and patches of light-green brush in an ever-changing succession.

This is the land of the **moose.** They're as big as large horses, with long, bulbous noses and huge eyes that seem to know, somehow, just how ugly they are. Their flanks look like a worn-out shag carpet draped over a sawhorse. But moose are survivors. They thrive in land that no one else wants. In the summer, they wade out into the swampy tundra ponds to eat green muck. In the winter, they like nothing better than an old burn, where summer lightning has peeled back the forest and allowed a tangle of willows to grow—a moose's all-time favorite food. Eaten by wolves, hunted and run over by man, stranded in the snows of a hard winter, the moose always come back. In the summer, the moose disperse and are not easily seen in thick vegetation. In the winter, they gather where walking is easy, along roads and in lowlands where people also like to live. Encounters happen often in the city, until, as a resident, you begin to take the moose for granted. Then, skiing on a Nordic trail one day, you round a corner and come face to face with an animal that stands 2 feet over you. You can smell the beast's foul scent and see his stress, the ears pulled back on the head and the whites of the eyes showing, and you know that this wild creature, fighting to live until summer, could easily kill you.

THE LIGHT & THE DARKNESS

There's no escaping the stress of winter in Alaska—not for moose or people—nor any shield from the exhilaration of the summer. In summer it never really gets dark at night. In Fairbanks in June, the sun sets in the north around midnight, but it doesn't go down far enough for real darkness to settle, instead rising again 2 hours later. It's always light enough to keep hiking or fishing, and, in clear weather, always light enough to read by. You may not see the stars from early May until sometime in August (the climate chart in chapter 2 gives seasonal daylight for various towns). Visitors have trouble getting used to it: Falling asleep in broad daylight is hard. Alaskans deal with it by staying up late and being active outdoors. In the winter, on the other hand, you forget what the sun looks like. Kids go to school in the dark and come home in the dark. The sun rises in the middle of the morning and sets after lunch. At high noon in December, the sun hangs just above the southern horizon with a weak, orange light, a constant sunset. Animals and people go into hibernation.

As you go north, the change in the length of the days gets bigger. In Ketchikan, the longest day of the year, the June 21 summer solstice, is about 17 hours 20 minutes; in Fairbanks, 22 hours; and in Barrow, the longest day is more than 2 months. In contrast, in Seattle the longest day is 16 hours 15 minutes, and in Los Angeles 14 hours 30 minutes. On the equator, days are always the same length, 12 hours. At the North Pole and South Pole, the sun is up half the year and down the other half.

The best way to understand this is to model it with a ball and a lamp. The earth spins on its axis, the North and South poles, once a day around. When the axis is upright, one spin of the ball puts light on each point on the ball equally—that's the spring and fall equinox, March 21 and September 21, when the day is 12 hours long everywhere. In the summer, the North Pole leans toward the light and the Northern Hemisphere gets more light than darkness, so during the course of one rotation each northern spot is lighted more than half the time. In winter, the Southern Hemisphere gets its turn, and more than half the Northern Hemisphere is in shadow, meaning shorter days. As you go farther north in winter, the shadow gets larger, and the day in any one spot shorter. But no matter how the axis leans, the equator is always half light and half dark, like the entire globe as a whole.

In the North, on a long, summer evening, you can almost feel the planet leaning toward the sun. Come feel it for yourself.

2 Politics & History: Living a Frontier Myth

The occupations of prospector, trapper, and homesteader—rugged individualists relying only on themselves in a limitless land—would dominate Alaska's economy if the state's image of itself were accurate. Alaskans talk a lot about the Alaskan spirit of independence, yearn for freedom from government, and declare that people from "Outside" just don't understand us when they insist on locking up Alaska's lands in parks and wilderness status. The bumper sticker says, simply, "We don't give a damn how they do it Outside." A state full of self-reliant frontiersmen can't be tied down and deterred from their manifest destiny by a bunch of Washington bureaucrats. At the extreme, there has even been a movement to declare independence as a separate nation so Alaskans could extend the frontier, extracting its natural resources unfettered by bunny-hugging easterners.

But just because you wear a cowboy hat doesn't mean you know how to ride a horse. In Las Vegas you find a lot more hats than horsemen, and Alaska is full of self-reliant frontier pioneers who spend rush hour in traffic jams and worry more about urban drug dealing and air pollution than where to catch their next meal or dig the mother lode. As for self-reliance and independence from government, Alaska has the highest per capita state spending of any state in the nation, with no state income or sales taxes and an annual payment of more than $1,700 a year to every man, woman, and child just for living here. The state government provides such socialistic benefits as retirement homes and automatic income for the aged; it owns various businesses, including a dairy, a railroad, and a subsidized mortgage lender; it has built schools in the smallest communities, operates a state ferry system and a radio and television network,

Dateline

- **Approximately 15,000 years ago** First human explorers arrive in Alaska from Asia.
- **1741** Vitus Bering, on a mission originally chartered by Peter the Great, finds Alaska; ship's surgeon and naturalist Georg Steller goes ashore for a few hours on Kayak Island, the first white to set foot in Alaska.
- **1743** Enslaving the Aleuts, Russian fur traders enter the Aleutian Islands; Aleuts are massacred when they try to revolt—their cultural traditions are eliminated, and over the coming decades they are relocated as far south as California for their hunting skills.
- **1772** Unalaska, in the Aleutian Islands, becomes a permanent Russian settlement.
- **1776–79** British Capt. James Cook makes voyages of exploration to Alaska, seeking the Northwest Passage from the Pacific to the Atlantic, and draws charts of the coast.
- **1784** Russians build settlement at Kodiak.
- **1799** Russians establish a fort near present-day Sitka, which will later become their capital; Tlingits attack and destroy the fort, but are later

continues

driven off in a counterattack; the Russian-America Company receives a 20-year exclusive franchise to govern and exploit Alaska.

- **1821** Russian naval officers are placed in control of Russian-America Company, which begins to decline in profitability.
- **1824** Boundaries roughly matching Alaska's current borders are set by treaty between Russia, Britain, and the United States.
- **1839** The British Hudson's Bay Company, surpassing Russia in trade, begins leasing parts of Southeast Alaska and subsequently extends trading outposts into the Interior.
- **1843** First overtures are made by American officials interested in buying Alaska from the Russians, so U.S. instead of British power could expand there.
- **1867** In need of money and fearful that Russia couldn't hold onto Alaska anyway, Czar Alexander II sells Alaska to the United States; Secretary of State William Seward negotiates the deal for a price of $7.2 million, roughly 2¢ an acre; the American flag is raised in Sitka, and the U.S. military assumes government of Alaska.
- **1870** The Alaska Commercial Company receives a monopoly on harvesting seals in the Pribilof Islands and soon expands across the territory (the company remains a presence in the Alaska Bush today).
- **1879** Naturalist and writer John Muir explores Southeast Alaska by canoe, discovering Glacier Bay with Native guides.
- **1880** Joe Juneau and Richard Harris, guided by local Natives, find gold on

continues

and owns nearly a third of the land mass of Alaska. And although the oil money that funds state government has been in decline in recent years, forcing the legislature to dig into savings to balance its books, the independent, self-reliant citizens have successfully resisted having to pay any taxes.

That conflict between perception and reality grows out of the story of a century of development of Alaska. The state is a great storehouse of minerals, oil, timber, and fish. A lot of wealth has been extracted, and many people have gotten rich. But it has always been because the federal government let them do it. Every acre of Alaska belonged to the U.S. government from the day Secretary of State William Seward bought Alaska from Russia in 1867. Since then, the frontier has never been broader than Uncle Sam made it.

Yet the whole conception of ownership didn't fit Alaska well from the first. Did the Russians really own what they sold? Alaska Natives didn't think so. They'd been living on this land for more than 100 centuries, and at the time of the purchase, most had never seen a white face. How could Russia hold title to land that no Russian had so much as explored? As Americans flooded into Alaska to search for gold at the turn of the century, and settled on some of the land, this conflict became obvious. Alaska Natives, never conquered by war or treaty, began their legal and political fight to recover their land early in the century—a fight they would eventually win.

The concept of ownership has changed in other ways, too. When the United States bought Alaska and for the next 100 years afterward, the vast majority of the state was public domain—like the Old West of frontier lore, federal land and its surface and hard-rock resources were there for the taking. They belonged to everyone, but only until someone showed up to lay private claim. Today, amid deep conflicts about whether areas should remain natural or be exploited for natural resources, federal control stands out far more clearly than it did during the gold rush, when the land's wealth was free to anyone with strength enough to take it. Alaskans who want to keep receiving the good things that government brings today equate the frontier spirit of the past with their own financial well-being, whether that means working at a mining claim or at a desk in a glass office tower. But other Americans feel they own Alaska, too, and they don't necessarily believe in giving it away anymore. They may want the frontier to stay alive in another sense—unconquered and still wild.

White colonization of the territory came in boom-and-bust waves of migrants arriving with the goal of making a quick buck and then clearing out—without worrying about the people who already lived there. Although the gold rush pioneers are celebrated today, the **Klondike rush** of 1898 that opened up and populated the territory was motivated by greed and was a mass importer of crime, inhumanity, and, for the Native people, terrible epidemics of new diseases that killed off whole villages. Like the Russians 150 years before, who had made slaves of the Natives, the new white population considered the indigenous people less than human. Segregation was overcome only after World War II. Until Franklin Roosevelt became president, federal policy was to suppress Alaska Native cultures; missionaries forbade Native peoples telling the old stories or even speaking in their own languages. Meanwhile, the salmon that fed the people of the territory were overfished by a powerful, outside-owned canning industry with friends in Washington, D.C. Their abuses destroyed salmon runs. Formerly rich Native villages faced famine when their primary food source was taken away.

It was only with **World War II,** and the Japanese invasion of the Aleutian Islands, that Alaska developed an industry not based on exploitation of natural resources: the military industry. It was another boom. To this day, the federal government remains a key industry whose removal would deal the economy a grievous blow.

The fight for **Alaska statehood** also came after the war. Alaskans argued that they needed local, independent control of natural resources, pointing to the example of overfishing in the federally managed salmon industry. Opponents said that Alaska would never be able to support itself, always requiring large subsidies from the federal government, and therefore should not be a state. But the advocates pointed out that Alaska's lack of self-sufficiency came about because its citizens did not control the resources—Alaska was a colony, with decisions and profits taken away by the mother country. If Alaskans could control their own land, they

Gastineau Channel and found city of Juneau; gold strikes begin to come every few years across the state.

- 1884 Military rule ends in Alaska, but residents still have no right to elect a legislature, governor, or congressional representative, or to make laws.
- 1885 Protestant missionaries meet to divide up the territory, parceling out each region to a different religion; they begin to fan out across Alaska to convert Native peoples, largely suppressing their traditional ways.
- 1897 After prospectors arrive in Seattle with a ton of gold, the Klondike gold rush begins; gold rushes in Nome and Fairbanks follow within a few years; Americans begin to populate Alaska.
- 1906 Alaska's first (nonvoting) delegate in Congress takes office; the capital moves from Sitka to Juneau.
- 1908 The Iditarod Trail, a sled dog mail route, is completed, linking trails continuously from Seward to Nome.
- 1913 The first territorial legislature convenes, although it has few powers; the first automobile drives the Richardson Highway route, from Valdez to Fairbanks.
- 1914 Federal construction of the Alaska Railroad begins; the first tents go up in the river bottom that will be Anchorage, along the rail line.
- 1917 Mount McKinley National Park is established.
- 1920 The first flights connect Alaska to the rest of the United States; aviation quickly becomes the most important means of transportation in the territory.

continues

could use the resources to fund government. The discovery of oil on the Swanson River, on the Kenai Peninsula, in 1957, helped win that argument. Here was real money that could fund a state government. In 1959, Alaska finally became the 49th state. Along with the rights of entering the union, Alaska received a dowry, an endowment of land to develop and pay for all future government. The Statehood Act gave the new state the right to select 103 million acres from a total land mass of 365 million acres. Indeed, that land does pay for state government in Alaska, in the form of oil royalties and taxes—but, to this day, the federal government still spends a lot more in Alaska than it receives.

Oil revenues supported the new state and it began to extending services to the vast, undeveloped expanse of Alaska. **Anchorage** boomed in the 1960s in a period of buoyant optimism. Leaders believed that the age-old problems of the wide-open frontier—poverty, lack of basic services, impenetrable remoteness—would succumb to the new government and new money, while the land still remained wide open. Then the pace of change redoubled with the discovery of the largest oil field in North America at **Prudhoe Bay** in 1968—land that had been a wise state selection in the federal land-grant entitlement. The state government received as much money in a single oil lease sale auction as it had spent in total for the previous 6 years. This was going to be the boom of all booms.

The oil bonanza on the North Slope would change Alaska more than any other event since the gold rush. Once, opening the frontier had only meant letting a few prospectors scratch the dirt in search of a poke of gold—nothing to make a federal case over. But getting this immense pool of oil to market, from one of the most remote spots on the globe, would require allowing the world's largest companies to build across Alaska a pipeline that, when completed, could credibly claim to be the largest privately financed construction project in world history. With the stakes suddenly so much higher, it came time to figure out exactly who owned which parts of Alaska. The land couldn't just be public domain any longer. That division wouldn't be easy. Much of the state had never even been mapped, much less surveyed, and there were some large outstanding claims that had to be settled.

- **1923** Pres. Warren Harding drives final spike on the Alaskan Railroad at Nenana, then dies on the way home, purportedly from eating bad Alaska seafood.
- **1925** Leonhard Seppala and other dog mushers relay diphtheria serum on the Iditarod Trail to fight an epidemic in Nome; Seppala and his dog, Balto, become national heroes.
- **1934** Federal policy of forced assimilation of Native cultures is officially discarded, and New Deal efforts to preserve Native cultures begin.
- **1935** New Deal "colonists," broke farmers from all over the United States, settle in the Matanuska Valley north of Anchorage.
- **1940** A military buildup begins in Alaska; bases built in Anchorage accelerate city's growth into major population center.
- **1942** Japanese invade Aleutians, taking Attu and Kiska islands and bombing Dutch Harbor/Unalaska (a U.S. counterattack the next year drives out the Japanese); Alaska Highway links Alaska to the rest of the country overland for the first time, but is open to civilians only after the war.
- **1957** Oil is found on Kenai Peninsula's Swanson River.
- **1959** Alaska becomes a state.
- **1964** The largest earthquake ever to strike North America shakes Southcentral Alaska, killing 131 people, primarily in tsunami waves.
- **1968** Oil is found at Prudhoe Bay, on Alaska's North Slope.
- **1970** Environmental lawsuits tie up work to build the Alaska pipeline, which is needed to link the North Slope oil field to markets.

continues

Alaska Natives, who had lost land, culture, and health in 2 centuries of white invasion, finally saw their luck start to turn. It wouldn't be possible to resolve the land issues surrounding the pipeline until their claims to land and compensation were answered. Native leaders cannily used that leverage to assure that they got what they wanted. In the early 1970s, America had a new awareness of the way its first people had been treated in the settlement of the West. When white frontiers expanded, Native traditional homelands were stolen. In Alaska, with the powerful lure of all that oil providing the impetus, Native people were able to insist on a fairer resolution. In 1971, with the support of white Alaskans, the oil companies, and Pres. Richard Nixon, who threatened to veto any settlement that Natives did not support, Congress passed the **Alaska Native Claims Settlement Act,** called ANCSA. The act transferred 44 million acres of land and $962.5 million to corporations whose shareholders were all the Native people of Alaska. The new Native corporations would be able to exploit their own land for their shareholders' profit. In later legislation, Natives also won guaranteed subsistence hunting and fishing rights on federal land. Some Natives complained that they'd received only an eighth of the land they had owned before white contact, but it was still the richest settlement any of the world's indigenous people had received.

It was a political deal on a grand scale. It's unlikely that Natives would have gotten their land at all but for the desire of whites to get at the oil, and their need for Native support. Nor could the pipeline have overcome environmental challenges without the Natives' dropping their objections. Even with Native support in place, legislation authorizing the pipeline passed the U.S. Senate by only one vote, cast by Vice President Spiro Agnew.

But there were other side effects of the deal that white Alaskans didn't like so well. After the Native settlement passed, the state—which still hadn't received a large portion of its land entitlement—and the Native corporations both had a right to select the land they wanted. There still remained the question of who would get what—and of the wild lands that Congress, influenced by a strong new environmental movement, wanted to maintain as national parks and wilderness and

- **1971** Congress acknowledges and pays the federal government's debt to Alaska's indigenous people with the Alaska Native Claims Settlement Act, which transfers 44 million acres of land and almost $1 billion to new Native-owned corporations.
- **1973** The first Iditarod Trail Sled Dog Race runs more than 1,000 miles from Anchorage to Nome.
- **1974** Congress clears away legal barriers to construction of the trans-Alaska pipeline; Vice Pres. Spiro Agnew casts the deciding vote in the U.S. Senate.
- **1977** The trans-Alaska pipeline is completed and begins providing up to 25% of the U.S. domestic supply of oil.
- **1980** Congress sets aside almost a third of Alaska in new parks and other land-conservation units; awash in new oil wealth, the state legislature abolishes all taxes paid by individuals to state government.
- **1982** Alaskans receive their first Alaska Permanent Fund dividends, interest paid on an oil-wealth savings account.
- **1985** Declining oil prices send the Alaska economy into a tailspin; tens of thousands leave the state and most of the banks collapse.
- **1989** The tanker *Exxon Valdez* hits Bligh Reef in Prince William Sound, spilling 11 million gallons of North Slope crude in the worst oil spill ever in North America.
- **1994** A federal jury in Anchorage awards $5 billion to 10,000 fishermen, Natives, and others hurt by the Exxon oil spill; Exxon appeals continue today.

continues

- **1996** Wildfire rips through the Big Lake area, north of Anchorage, destroying 400 buildings.
- **1999** Alaskans vote 87% against a plan to use Permanent Fund earnings to cover a state budget cap.

not give away. That issue wasn't settled until 1980, when the **Alaska National Interest Lands Conservation Act** passed, setting aside an additional 106 million acres for conservation, an area larger than California. Alaska's frontier-minded population screamed bloody murder over "the lock-up of Alaska," but the act was only the last, tangible step in a process started by the coming of big oil and the need its arrival created to draw lines on the map, tying up the frontier.

When construction of the $9 billion pipeline finally got underway in 1974, a huge influx of new people chasing the high-paying jobs put any previous gold rush to shame. The newcomers were from a different part of the country than previously, too. Alaska had been a predominately Democratic state, but oil workers from Texas, Oklahoma, and other Bible-belt states helped shift the balance of Alaska's politics, and now it's solidly Republican. In its frontier days, Alaska had a strong Libertarian streak—on both the liberal and the conservative side—but now it became more influenced by fundamentalist Christian conservatism. A hippie-infested legislature of the early 1970s legalized marijuana for home use. Conservatives at the time, who thought the government shouldn't butt into its citizens' private lives, went along with them. After the pipeline, times changed, and Alaska developed tough antidrug laws.

Growth also brought urban problems, just as it has anywhere else. As the pipeline construction boom waned with completion in 1977, a boom-town atmosphere of gambling and street prostitution went with it, but other big-city problems remained. No longer could residents of Anchorage and Fairbanks go to bed without locking their doors. Both cities were declared "nonattainment" areas by the Environmental Protection Agency because of air pollution near the ground in cold winter weather, when people leave their cars running during the day to keep them from freezing. We got live television but also serial murderers.

But the pipeline seemed to provide limitless wealth to solve these problems. For fear that too much money would be wasted, the voters altered the state constitution to bank a large portion of the new riches. The new Permanent Fund would be off limits to the politicians in Juneau, with half the annual earnings paid out to citizens as dividends. The fund now contains more than $26 billion in savings and has become one of the largest sectors of the economy simply by virtue of paying out more than $1 billion a year in dividends to everyone who lives at least a year in the state. All major state taxes on individuals were canceled, and people got used to receiving everything free from the government.

Then, in 1985, oil prices dropped, deflating the overextended economy like a pin in a balloon. Housing prices crashed, and thousands of people simply walked away from their mortgages. All but a few of the banks in the state went broke. Condominiums that had sold for $100,000 sold for $20,000 or less a year later. It was the bust that always goes with the boom; but even after so many previous examples, it still came as a shock to many. The spending associated with the ***Exxon Valdez* oil spill** in 1989 restarted the economy, and it continued on an even keel for a decade after, but the wealth of the earlier oil years never returned.

Meanwhile, the oil from Prudhoe Bay started running out. Oil revenues, an irreplaceable 85% of the state budget, started an irrevocable downward trend in the early 1990s. The oil companies downsized. Without another boom on the horizon, the question became how to avoid, or at least soften, the next bust. At this writing, that question remains unanswered. In 1999, the governor and legislature asked the voters to approve reducing their Permanent Fund dividends to cover a $1 billion budget gap. Conservatives said the state should just cut the budget; liberals said reducing the dividend would amount to a head tax, hitting hardest the poor people who have come to rely on the money for necessities. The plan failed with 87% voting no. The legislature, with a temporary budgetary reprieve provided by higher oil prices, backed away from doing anything. With the political system in deadlock, the disadvantages of individualism seemed apparent, and some asked if Alaskans had lost their capacity for collective sacrifice.

Culture moves slower than politics or events, and Alaskans still see themselves as those gold rush prospectors or wildcat oil drillers, adventuring in an open land and striking it rich by their own devices. Even as Alaska's economy blends ever more smoothly into the American corporate landscape, Alaskans' myth of themselves remains strong. Today, the state's future is as little in its own hands as it has ever been. There may be more oil in protected wilderness areas on the North Slope, and there certainly is plenty of natural gas that could be exploited. But whether or not to explore those resources will be decided in corporate board rooms in London and Houston, and in Congress—not in Alaska. Ultimately, an economy based on exploiting natural resources is anything but independent.

Haggling over one plot of land or another will always continue, but the basic lines have been drawn on the map. The frontier has been carved up. Today it's mostly just a state of mind. Or a myth we like to believe about ourselves.

3 The People: Three Ways to Win an Argument in Alaska

NUMBER ONE: WAIT FOR SPRING

A small town in Alaska in March. Each time it snows, you have to throw shovels of it higher over your head to dig out. The air in the house is stale, and out the window all you see is black, white, and gray. Everyone's ready to go nuts with winter. It's time for a good political ruckus.

No one can predict exactly what will set it off—it could just be an ill-considered letter to the editor in the local newspaper, or it could be something juicier, like a controversial development proposal. At some point, when the cabin fever gets bad enough, it almost doesn't matter what sparks the inferno. Alaskans can generate outrage about almost anything, with a ritual of charges and countercharges, conspiracy theories, and impassioned public testimony.

It's particularly amusing when some outsider is involved, thinking he's at the town council meeting in a normal political process to get some project approved, only to wind up on the receiving end of a public hearing from hell. I'll never forget a sorry businessman who was trying to lease some land from the town of Homer. He endured hours of angry public testimony one night. He was sweating, the only person in the packed city hall meeting room wearing a tie, surrounded by flannel shirts, blue jeans, and angry faces. Finally, he stood up at his chair and, in a plaintive tone of frustration and near tears, declared, "You're not very professional as a community!" For once, no one could disagree.

He gave up. He didn't know that if he had only waited a couple of months, the opposition would dry up as soon as the salmon started running. Then most of the city council meetings would be canceled, and those that weren't would be brief and sparsely attended. If anything really important came up, the council would be smart enough to postpone it till fall. In the summer, Alaskans have more important things to attend to than government.

The sun shines deep into the night so you can catch fish and tourists, not sit inside. It's the season when the money is made. The streets are full of new people, like a bird rookery refreshed by migrants. Everyone stays awake late pounding nails, playing softball, and fly-casting for reds. Office workers in Anchorage depart straight from work for a 3-hour drive down to the Kenai Peninsula, fish through the night, catch a quick nap in the car in the wee hours, and make it to work on time the next morning, with fish stories to share at the coffee machine. Sleep is expendable—you don't seem to need it that much when the sky is light all night.

In the Native villages of the Bush, everyone has gone to fish camp. Families load everything in an aluminum river boat and leave town, headed upriver and back to a time of purer cultural traditions. On the banks and beaches, they set up wall tents and spruce-log fish-drying racks, maybe a basketball hoop and campfire, too. Huge extended families work as a unit. Men gather in the salmon, and the women gut them with a few lightning strokes of a knife and hang them to dry on the racks. Children run around in a countryside paradise, watched by whatever adults are handiest.

Suddenly, August comes. For the first time in months, you can see the stars. It comes as a shock the first time you have to use your car headlights. The mood gets even more frantic. There's never enough time in the summer to do everything that needs to get done. Construction crews can count the days now till snow and cold will shut them down. Anything that's not done now won't be done until next May. Labor Day approaches as fast as 5pm on a busy business day.

As September turns to October, everything had better be done. The last tourists are gone, and T-shirt shops are closed for the season. The commercial fishing boats are tied up back in the harbor, and the fishermen prepare for vacation. Cannery workers are already back at college. For the first time in months, people can slow down long enough to look at each other and remember where they left off in the spring. It's time to catch up on sleep, think longer thoughts, make big decisions. The hills of birch turn bright yellow, the tundra goes brick red, and the sky turns gray—there's the smell of wood smoke in the air—and then, one day, it starts to snow.

It's not the velvet darkness of midwinter that gets you. December is bearable, even if the sun rises after the kids get to school, barely cruises along the horizon, and sinks before they start for home. Nowhere is Christmas more real than Alaska, where residents sing carols with cheeks tingling from the cold. January isn't so hard. You're still excited about the skiing. The phone rings in the middle of the night—it's a friend telling you to put on your boots and go outside to see the northern lights. February is a bit harder to take, but most towns have a winter carnival to divert your attention from the cold.

March is when bizarre things start to happen. People are just holding on for the end of winter, and you never know what will set them off. That's when you'd better hunker down and lay low, watch what you say, bite your tongue when your spouse lets hang a comment you'd like to jump on like a coho hitting fresh bait. Hold on—just until the icicles start to melt, the mud shows around the snowbanks, and the cycle starts fresh.

NUMBER TWO: BE HERE FIRST

There's a simple and effective way to win an argument in Alaska—state how long you've lived here. If it's longer than your adversary, he'll find it difficult to put up a fight. This is why, when speaking in public, people will often begin their remarks by stating how many years they've been in Alaska. It's a badge of authenticity and status in a place with a young, transient population that's grown fast. No one cares where you came from, or who you were back there, and there's no such thing as class in Alaska—anyone who tries to act superior will quickly find that no one else notices. But if you haven't made it through a few winters, you probably don't know what you're talking about.

It's also traditional—although, sadly, a fading tradition—to treat strangers as friends until they prove otherwise. The smaller the town you visit, the more strongly you'll find that hospitality still alive. Visitors can find it pleasantly disorienting to arrive in a small town and have everyone in the street greet them with a smile. These traditions of hospitality and respect for experience run deepest in Alaska's **Native people.** (Alaskans use the word *Native* to mean all the indigenous peoples of Alaska.) But instead of beginning a conversation by stating how long they've lived here, Natives—who've always been here—try to find a relation with a new person by talking about where their families are from.

Theories differ about how North America was originally populated. The traditional notion is that the first people walked across a land bridge from Asia through the dry Bering Sea around 15,000 years ago in pursuit of migrating game. The bridge, up to 1,000 miles wide, would have lasted longest in the area between Nome and Kotzebue and, at its largest size, included the entire west coast of Alaska. But new archaeology and geology throw doubt on the theory, suggesting a migration story that's much more complex. People who know the Arctic know the land bridge simply wasn't necessary: In the winter you can walk between Siberia and Alaska even today, and the seafaring skills of Alaska's Aleuts and Eskimos would have enabled them to travel back and forth to Asia at any time. Siberian and Alaskan Natives share language, stories, and kin. Perhaps the connection across the north was continuous and followed many routes after northern people learned to sew skin boats and clothing about 15,000 years ago. Certainly, the idea they walked seems increasingly questionable. Geologists now believe the route south was an impassable sheet of ice during the Ice Age; if migrants did use it, they could only have done so by making a tricky sea journey connecting coastal pockets that remained green.

However and whenever the first people arrived, they quickly spread through the Americas, creating cultures of incredible complexity and diversity. Those who kept going south from Alaska were the ancestors of all the indigenous people of the hemisphere, from the Inca to the Algonquin. Those who stayed in Alaska became the Eskimos, who include the Inupiat of the Arctic, the Yup'ik of the Southwest, and the Alutiiq of the Gulf of Alaska coastline. They also became Indians: the Athabascans of the Interior and the Tlingit, Haida, and Tsimshian of Southeast Alaska and British Columbia. And seafaring Pacific people landed in the Aleutian Chain, becoming the Aleuts, who are neither Eskimo nor Indian.

The Native groups of Alaska have a lot in common culturally, but before the white invasion, they had well-defined boundaries and didn't mix much. They didn't farm, and the only animal they domesticated was the dog—dog teams and boats were the primary means of transportation and commerce. But they generally were not nomadic, and no one in Alaska lived in igloos. Where there

An Alaska Glossary

If Alaska feels like a different country from the rest of the United States, one reason may be the odd local usage that makes English slightly different here—different enough, in fact, that the Associated Press publishes a separate style-book dictionary just for Alaska. Here are some Alaskan words you may run into:

break up When God set up the seasons in Alaska, He forgot one: spring. While the rest of the United States enjoys new flowers and baseball, Alaskans are looking at melting snowbanks and mud. Then, in May, summer miraculously arrives. Break up officially occurs when the ice goes out in the Interior's rivers, but it stands for the time period of winter's demise and summer's initiation.

bunny boots If you see people wearing huge, bulbous white rubber boots in Alaska's winter, it's not necessarily because they have enormous feet. Those are bunny boots, superinsulated footwear originally designed for Arctic air force operations—and they're the warmest things in the world.

cheechako A newcomer or greenhorn. Not used much anymore, because almost everyone is one.

dry or damp Many towns and villages have invoked a state law that allows them to outlaw alcohol completely (to go dry) or to outlaw sale but not possession (to go damp).

Lower 48 The contiguous United States.

Native When capitalized, the word refers to Alaska's indigenous people. "American Indian" isn't used much in Alaska, "Alaska Native" being the preferred term.

Native corporation In 1971, Congress settled land claims with Alaska's Natives by turning over land and money; corporations were set up, with the Natives then alive as shareholders, to receive the property. Most of the corporations still thrive.

was no wood, houses were built of whale bone and sod; where wood was plentiful, large and intricately carved houses sheltered entire villages. Typically, a family connected tribal group would have a winter village and a summer fish camp for gathering and laying up food. Elders guided the community in important decisions. A gifted shaman led the people in religious matters, relating to the spirits of ancestors, animals, trees, and even the ice that populated their world. Stories passed on through generations explained the universe.

Those oral traditions kept Native cultures alive. Twenty distinct **Native languages** were spoken—some elders still speak only their Native language yet today, and only one language, Eyak, is essentially extinct. The languages break into four major families: Eskimo-Aleut, Athabascan-Eyak-Tlingit, Haida, and Tsimshian (the last two are primarily Canadian). The Eskimo-Aleut language group includes languages spoken by coastal people from the Arctic Ocean to the Gulf of Alaska, including Inupiaq, in the Arctic; Yup'ik, in the Yukon-Kuskokwim and Bristol Bay region; Aleut, in the Aleutian Islands; and Alutiiq, on the Alaska Peninsula, Kodiak, and Prince William Sound. There are 12 Athabascan and Eyak languages in Alaska, and more Outside, including Apache and Navajo. In Southeast Alaska, Tlingit was spoken across most of

oosik The huge penile bone of a walrus. Knowing this word could save you from being the butt of any of a number of practical jokes people like to play on cheechakos.

Outside Anywhere that isn't Alaska. This is a widely used term in print, and is capitalized, like any other proper noun.

PFD No, not personal flotation device; it stands for Permanent Fund Dividend. When Alaska's oil riches started flowing in the late 1970s, the voters set up a savings account called the Permanent Fund. Half the interest is paid annually to every man, woman, and child in the state. With more than $26 billion in investments, the fund now yields more than $1,700 in dividends to each Alaskan annually.

pioneer A white settler of Alaska who has been here longer than most other people can remember—25 or 30 years usually does it.

salmon There are five species of Pacific salmon, each with two names. The king or Chinook is the largest, growing up to 90 pounds in some areas; the silver or coho is next in size, a feisty sport fish; the red or sockeye has rich red flesh; the pink or humpy and the chum or dog are smallish and not as tasty, mostly ending up in cans and dog lots.

Southeast Most people don't bother to say "Southeast Alaska." The region may be to the northwest of everyone else in the country, but it's southeast of most Alaskans, and that's all we care about.

tsunami Earthquake-caused sea waves are often called tidal waves, but that's a misnomer. The destructive waves of the 1964 Alaska earthquake were tsunamis caused by underwater upheavals like landslides.

village A small, Alaska Native settlement in the Bush, usually tightly bound by family and cultural tradition.

the Panhandle. Haida was spoken on southern Prince of Wales Island and southward into what's now British Columbia, where Tsimshain also was spoken.

The first arrival of whites was often violent and destructive, spanning a 100-year period that started in the 1740s with the coming of the Russian fur traders, who enslaved and massacred the Aleuts, and continued to the 1840s, when New England whalers and other mariners first met the Inupiat of the Arctic. There were pitched battles, but disease and nonviolent destruction of oral traditions was more influential. Christian missionaries, with the support of government assimilation policy, drove the old stories and even Native languages underground. Lela Kiana Oman, who has published traditional Inupiat stories to preserve them, told me of her memories of her father secretly telling the ancient tales at night to his children. She was forbidden to speak Inupiaq in school and did not see her first traditional Native dance until age 18.

Oman's work is part of today's **Native cultural renaissance.** It's not a moment too soon. In some villages, children know more about the geography of Beverly Hills, which they see on television, than about their own culture. Some don't share a language with their own grandparents. But schools in many areas have begun requiring Native language classes, or even teach using language immersion techniques. For the Aleut, whose cultural traditions were almost completely wiped out, the process of renewal involves a certain amount of invention. On the other hand, some traditional villages remain, especially deep in the country of the Yukon-Kuskokwim Delta, where Yup'ik is still the dominant language and most of the food comes from traditional subsistence hunting and gathering, altered only by the use of modern materials and guns.

Alaska Natives also are fighting destruction fueled by alcohol and other substance-abuse problems. Rates of suicide, accidents, and domestic violence are very high in the Bush. Statistically, virtually every Alaska Native in prison is there because of alcohol. A sobriety movement is attacking the problem one person at a time. One of its goals is to use traditional Native culture to fill a void of rural despair where alcohol now flows in. Politically, a "local option" law provides individual communities the choice of partial or total alcohol prohibition; it has been successfully used in many villages and towns but remains controversial in others, where repeated local option elections sometimes divide Native and white residents, with whites more often voting against prohibition.

There are social and political tensions between Natives and whites on many levels and over many issues. The lives of the Alaskan city and village share less in common than do most different nations. Although village Natives come to the city to shop, get health care, or attend meetings, urban Alaskans have no reason to go to the villages, and most never have made the trip. The most contentious rural-urban issue concerns allocation of fish and game. Some urban outdoorsmen feel they should have the same rights to hunt and fish as the Natives, and the state Supreme Court has interpreted Alaska's constitution to say they're right. Rural Natives have federal law on their side, however, and Alaska faced the prospect of a federal takeover of fish and game management unless the Alaska constitution was amended to provide a rural preference for fish and game. Over a decade of political stalemate, a legislative minority was able to block any constitutional amendment, and in 2000 the feds finally stepped in. Many Natives were glad to see it finally happen, as humiliating as the move was for independent-minded Alaskans. Natives feel subsistence hunting and fishing are an integral part of their cultural heritage, far more important than sport, and should take priority. Darker conflicts exist, too, and it's impossible to discount the charges of racism that Native Alaskans raise.

Alaska Natives have become a minority in their own land. In 1880, Alaska contained 33,000 Natives and 430 whites. By 1900, with the gold rush, the numbers were roughly equal. Since then, whites have generally outnumbered Natives in ever greater numbers. Today there are about 94,000 Alaska Natives—22,000 of whom live in the cities of Anchorage and Fairbanks—out of a total state population of more than 600,000 people of all races. Consequently, Alaska Natives must learn to walk in two worlds. The North Slope's Inupiat, who hunt the bowhead whale from open boats as their forefathers did, must also know how to negotiate for their take in international diplomatic meetings. And they have to use the levers of government to protect the whale's environment from potential damage by the oil industry. The Alaska Native Claims Settlement Act created a new class, the corporate Native, responsible for representing rural needs but also obliged to function as an executive for large, far-reaching business concerns. Outnumbered by white voters, Bush politicians in the legislature must be especially skilled, sticking together, crossing political boundaries, and forming coalitions to protect their constituencies.

Non-Natives traveling to the Bush also walk in two worlds, but they may not even know it. In a Native village, a newly met friend will ask you in for a cup of coffee; it can be rude not to accept. Looking a person in the eye in conversation also can be rude—that's how Native elders look at younger people who owe them respect. If a Native person looks down, speaks slowly, and seems to mumble, that's not disrespect, but the reverse. Fast-talking non-Natives have to make a conscious effort to slow down and leave pauses in conversation, because Natives usually don't jump in or interrupt—they listen, consider, and then respond. Of course, most Native people won't take offense at your bad manners—they're used to spanning cultures, and they know whites may not know how to act in a village. When I was in a village recently, I looked in confusion at a clock that didn't seem right. "That's Indian time," my Athabascan companion said. Then, pointing to a clock that was working, "White man time is over there."

Urban visitors who miss cultural nuances rarely overlook the apparent poverty of many villages. Out on a remote landscape of windswept tundra, swampy in summer and frozen in winter, they may secretly wonder why Natives stay there, enduring the hardships of rural Alaskan life when even the most remote villager can see on cable television how easy it is in Southern California. Save your pity. As Yup'ik social observer Harold Napoleon has said, "We're poor, all right, but we've got more than most people. Our most important asset is our land and our culture, and we want to protect it come hell or high water."

Alaska's Natives may be outnumbered, but they've been here a lot longer than anyone else. My money is on them.

NUMBER THREE: BE A REAL ALASKAN

Alaska's history books are full of the stories of economic booms, the people who came, what kind of wealth they were after, and how they populated and developed the land. In a largely empty place, you can make it into history just by showing up. But every wave is followed by a trough, the bust that comes after the boom when those who came just for the money go back where they came from. Those are the times when the real Alaskans—those who live here for the love of the place, not only the money—are divided from the rest. The real Alaskans stay; the others leave. It's the perfect way to settle an argument.

Other people have other definitions of what it takes to be a real Alaskan. One definition, which I once read on a place mat in a diner in Soldotna, holds that to be a real Alaskan, you have to know how to fix a Caterpillar tractor. Similar definitions require various feats in the outdoors—hunting, fishing, or shooting—and even acts in the barroom or the bedroom. They all assume that a real Alaskan is a big, tough, white, male, bulldozer-driving type of guy. But those can be the first to leave when the economy goes down the tubes.

The first group to leave were the Russians sent by the czar and the Russian-America Company. On October 18, 1867, their flag came down over Castle Hill in Sitka in a solemn ceremony, got stuck, and had to be untangled by a soldier sent up the pole. The territory was virtually empty of Russians before the check was even signed, as Congress didn't much like the idea of the purchase and took a while to pay. The gold rush stampeders were the next to leave. The population of Nome went from 12,500 to 852 after the stampede was over. The oil years have seen the same phenomenon, as people who can't find work in the bust years pack up and leave.

But each time the boom has gone bust, enough have stayed so that Alaska ended up with more people than it had before. Over the long term, the population has kept growing dramatically. It doubled from 1890 to 1900 (the gold rush); doubled again by 1950 because of World War II and the Cold War; doubled again by 1964, with statehood and the early oil years; and doubled again by 1983, because of the trans-Alaska pipeline and the arrival of big oil. Since then, it has grown another 20%.

Each set of migrants has been similar—young, coming mostly from the West, but from other parts of the United States, too. Most people who have come to Alaska have been white—minority populations are smaller than in the nation as a whole—but there are strong minority communities in Anchorage. In Kodiak, the canneries are run by a tight Filipino community started by just a few pioneer immigrants. Today the population of Alaska as a whole is young and relatively well paid and educated. Six times as many babies are born as people die.

Historically, old people often moved somewhere warmer when they retired. Some snowbirds migrate annually, spending only the summer in Alaska. Over the years, the state government set out to keep more old people in the state, to help build the continuity and memory a community needs. Special retirement homes were built, local property-tax breaks were granted to the elderly, and the legislature created a "Longevity Bonus" entitlement whereby elders who'd been in the state at least 25 years were automatically paid $250 a month for life. When a court ruled that the state couldn't impose a residency requirement of more than 1 year for the program, Alaska began to import thousands of new elderly people who were coming north to take advantage of the handouts. Now the bonus is being phased out.

It wasn't the first time Alaska has tried to reward real Alaskans just for staying. When the Permanent Fund Dividend program started in the 1970s, to distribute some of the state's new oil riches to the citizens, it was designed to provide more money for each year of residency. A 1-year greenhorn would get $50 and a 20-year pioneer $1,000. The Supreme Court threw out the plan—apparently being a "real Alaskan" isn't a special category of citizen in the U.S. Constitution.

Alaskans have always been well paid. Until recently, the popular explanation always held that prices are higher because of shipping costs, so salaries needed to match. That's still true in rural Alaska and for some purchases in the large cities. But generally, fierce competition in the retail trade has driven prices down. Large national chains moved in all at once in 1994. Today the cost of living in Anchorage, Fairbanks, and Juneau compares to most parts of the country, and Wal-Mart has even moved into such remote towns as Ketchikan and Kodiak. Wages have gone down a little, largely because all those new retail jobs lowered average pay, but the federal government still pays a premium to its Alaskan employees, and oil workers, fishermen, and other skilled workers make a very good living.

Prices for hotel rooms and restaurant meals also remain quite high. The best explanation is the seasonal nature of the economy—tourism operators need to make their full income in the summer season. The other explanation is that they'll charge what the market can bear, and empty hotel rooms are in high demand in summer.

The non-Native part of Alaska, 100 years old with the anniversary of the gold rush in 1998, hasn't had time to develop a culture of its own, much less an Alaskan accent. It's a melting pot of the melting pot, with a population made up of odds and ends from all over the United States. People tend to judge each other on the basis of their actions, not on who they are or where they came from. New arrivals to Alaska have been able to reinvent themselves since the days when Soapy Smith, a small-time con man, took over Skagway with a criminal gang and was offered the job of town marshal by the territorial governor—all in a year. Everyone arrives with a clean slate and a chance to prove himself or herself, but on occasion, that ability to start from scratch has created some embarrassing discoveries, when the past does become relevant.

There have been a series of political scandals uncovered by reporters who checked the résumés of well-known politicians, only to find out they had concocted their previous lives out of thin air. One leading legislative candidate's husband found out about his wife's real background from such a news story.

If an Alaskan culture hasn't had time to develop, Alaska does have traditions, or at least accepted ways of thinking—among them tolerance and equality, hospitality, independence, and a propensity for violence. In the late 1980s in Homer, there was a gunfight over a horse that left a man lying dead on a dirt road. In the newspaper the next week, the editorial called for people not to settle their differences with guns. A couple of letters to the editor shot back, on the theme, "Don't you tell *us* how to settle our differences." Guns are necessary tools in Alaska. They're also a religion. I have friends who exchanged handguns instead of rings when they got married.

The tradition of tolerance of newcomers has made Alaska a destination for oddballs, religious cults, hippies, and people who just can't make it in the mainstream. Perhaps the most interesting of the **religious groups** that formed its own community is the Old Believers, who in recent decades have built villages of brightly painted, gingerbreadlike houses around Kachemak Bay, near Homer. Their resistance to convention dates from Peter the Great's reforms to Russian Orthodoxy in the 18th century, which they reject. After centuries of persecution, in Alaska they've found a place where they can live without interference—in fact, they've thrived as fishermen and boat builders. You see them around town, in their 18th-century Russian peasant dress. Even the girls' high-school basketball team wears long dresses, with their numbers stitched to the bodice.

Nikolaevsk was the first of the Russian Old Believer villages. In the public school there, they don't teach about dinosaurs or men landing on the moon—that's considered heresy. Yet other Old Believers rebelled, convinced that Nikolaevsk was making too many compromises and was bound to lose the next generation to decadent American ways. They broke off and formed another village, farther up the bay, unreachable except by all-terrain vehicle, and adhered to stricter rules. They, in turn, suffered another schism and another village was formed, farther up the bay, virtually inaccessible and with even stricter rules. The process continues. The fight against assimilation may be hopeless, as children will ultimately do as they please, but it's the Old Believers' own struggle. No one in Homer pushes them to change. No one pays any attention at all, except to buy their fish and their top-quality boats.

After several decades, it looks as if the Old Believers are here to stay. Whether they speak English or not, I'd say they're real Alaskans.

4 Alaska Wildlife

For anyone interested in the natural world, using a field guide will greatly deepen the enjoyment of this unfamiliar land. It's easy and fun to identify Alaska plants and trees because the biodiversity is less than in southern latitudes. A good bird book adds much depth to any sea tour. Tide pooling or fishing demand some knowledge or a guidebook. The **Alaska Department of Fish and Game's *Wildlife Notebook Series,*** available in book form or online (www.state.ak.us/local/akpages/FISH.GAME/notebook/notehome.htm), is a fascinating and educational reference covering common land and marine mammals, birds, fish, and shellfish. It and many other Alaska-specific books are for sale from the **Alaska Natural History Association,** 750 W. Second Ave., Suite 100, Anchorage, AK 99501-2167 (☎ **907/274-8440;** www.alaskanha.org).

My favorite color field guides, covering many North American subjects, are in the National Audubon Society's multivolume set published by Knopf; they'll work for birds, but you need an Alaska-specific book for flowers.

If your interest isn't so deep, here are a few facts about some of Alaska's biggest and most spectacular mammals.

WHALES

The sight of a leaping humpback whale is the sort of experience that can instantaneously change the way you see the world around you, changing the sea from a familiar plain of light and motion into a hidden universe of surging giants. The whale shoots upward without warning, then seems to hang a moment and twist in the air—there's plenty of time for those facing the other direction to turn around and look—and then splashes down with a sound we once mistook for thunder. Whales that surface during their feeding and cruising behavior patterns also can make you catch your breath at first, then, over extended viewing, give you a chance to appreciate the whale: how the texture of its skin is rough yet slick, how it moves gracefully despite its incredible size.

HUMPBACK These migratory whales spend their summer in Alaska feeding, then swim to Mexican or Hawaiian waters for the winter, where they give birth to their young and then fast until going north again in spring. Cold water contains more dissolved carbon dioxide than southern oceans can hold; that makes them a richer ground for the photosynthesis of phytoplankton (tiny plants in the water), the basic food for the marine ecosystem. Humpbacks feed on small fish and other tiny creatures that feed on phytoplankton, taking in a million calories a day through the filter of their mouth baleen—strips of stiff, fibrous material that substitute for their teeth. A humpback is easy to recognize by its huge, mottled tail; by the hump on its back, just forward of its dorsal fin; and by its armlike flippers, which can grow to be 14 feet long.

The Humpback Whale. Max. length: 53 ft.

Most humpback sightings are of the whales' humped backs as they cruise along the surface, resting, and of the flukes of the tail as they dive. Humpbacks know how to weave nets of bubbles around their prey, then swim upward through the schooled fish, mouths wide open, to eat them in a single swoop, sometimes finishing with a frothy lunge through the surface. Feeding dives can last a long time and often mean you're done watching a particular whale, but if you're lucky the whale may be just dipping down for a few minutes to get ready to leap completely out of the water, a practice called breaching. No one knows for sure why they do this; it may simply be play.

Humpbacks tend to congregate to feed, making certain spots with rich supplies of food reliable places to watch them. In Southeast Alaska the best spots include the waters of Icy Strait, just outside Glacier Bay; Frederick Sound outside Petersburg; and Sitka Sound. In Southcentral Alaska, Resurrection Bay, outside Seward near Kenai Fjords National Park, has the most reliable sightings.

ORCA (KILLER WHALE) The starkly defined black-and-white patches of the orca recall the sharp graphic look of the Native American art of the Pacific Northwest and Southeast Alaska. It's as if the whales were painted by their creator to reflect the speed, agility, and fierceness of the ocean's top predator. Largest of the dolphins, most orcas live in highly structured family groups called pods that cooperate in feeding. Resident pods feed mostly on salmon and other fish. Transient pods and lone orcas are the wolves of the sea, using their swimming speed of up to 30 miles per hour to hunt porpoises, seals, sea lions, and even other whales; there's never been a report of one attacking a human being. Most often, you see orcas' long dorsal fin; sometimes they pop above the surface in a flash of a graceful arc when they travel, and occasionally they breach.

The Orca, or Killer Whale. Max. length: 30 ft.

Orca sightings depend on where their food is that day, but pods often have been sighted in Resurrection Bay and Prince William Sound in the summer; we saw a pod of orcas from the beach in Gustavus; and they could show up anywhere in Southeast Alaska waters. For cruisers coming to Alaska, a top spot to see orcas is Robson Bight, an area in Johnstone Strait (between Vancouver Island and mainland British Columbia).

BELUGA This small, white whale with the cute rounded beak lives in Alaska coastal waters year-round, making it an important traditional food source for Alaska Natives. Adults are all white, while juveniles are gray. Belugas swim in large packs that can number a thousand, but more often are in the dozens.

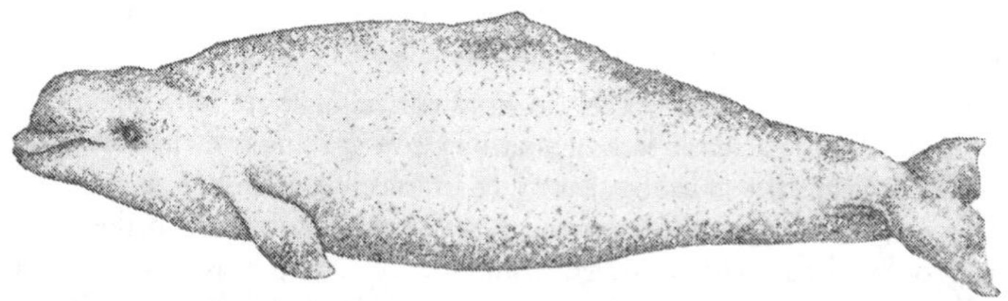

The Beluga Whale. Max. length: 16 ft.

Belugas have teeth like orcas and dolphins, feeding on salmon and other seasonal fish, making the mouths of spawning rivers the best places to see them. Occasionally, a group will strand itself chasing salmon on a falling tide, swimming away when the water returns. The Cook Inlet group of belugas is the most often seen: Watch the waters of Turnagain Arm while driving the Seward Highway just south of Anchorage, or watch from the beach near the mouth of the Kenai River in Kenai.

MINKE The smallest of the baleen whales, the minke is generally under 26 feet long and has a blackish-gray body with a white stomach, a narrow triangular head, and white bands on its flippers. Along with the humpback and the gray whale, it is the only baleen whale commonly seen in Alaska's southern coastal waters. Minkes leap like dolphins, gracefully reentering the water head first, and are easily confused with them: Watch for the dark skin color.

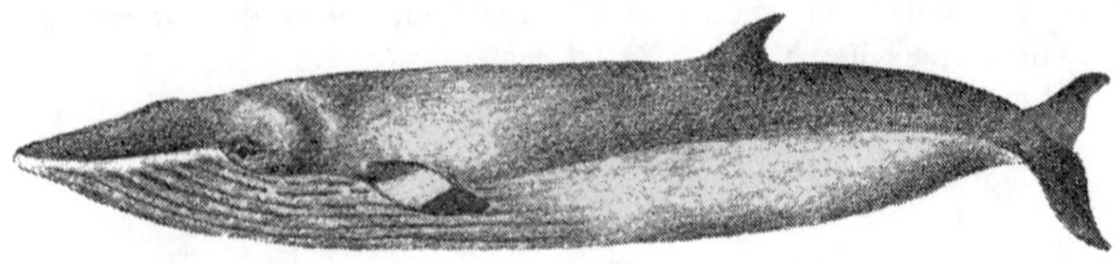

The Minke Whale. Max. length: 26 ft.

LAND ANIMALS

Large mammals other than humans still rule most of Alaska. Even in the urban areas there sometimes remains a question of who's in charge, as moose snarl winter traffic and bears and wolves prey on family pets at the edge of town. Your chances of seeing the animals described below are excellent. Here are a few of the more common.

BALD EAGLE Now making a comeback all over the United States, the bald eagle always was extremely common in Alaska: In most coastal towns, a pigeon would cause a greater stir among bird fanciers. Eagles soar over the high-rise buildings of downtown Anchorage, and every fishing town is swarming with them. Only adult eagles have the familiar white head and tail; juveniles less than 5 years old have mottled brown plumage and can be hard to tell from a hawk or golden eagle. Eagles most often are seen soaring on rising air over ocean or river waters, where they are likely looking for fish to swoop down and snatch, but you also can often see them perched on beach driftwood or in large trees. Haines is a prime eagle-spotting area, where thousands congregate in the fall; Sitka and Ketchikan both have raptor centers where you can see eagles in enclosures. (See chapter 5.)

The eagle represents one of the two main kinship groupings, or moieties, in the matrilineal Tlingit culture (the other is the raven), so eagles frequently appear on totem poles and in other Southeast Native art.

RAVEN Common throughout the northern hemisphere and ubiquitous Southeast Alaska, you can tell the all-black raven from a crow by its larger size, heavy bill, shaggy throat feathers, and its unmistakable voice, a deep and mysteriously evocative "kaw" that provides a constant soundtrack to the misty forests of Southeast. The raven figures importantly in Southeast Alaska Native stories, and in the creation myths of many other Native American peoples; its personality is of a wily and resourceful protagonist with great magical powers, an understandable match for this impressive and intelligent scavenger.

Bald Eagle

Raven

BLACK BEAR Black bears inhabit forests all over Alaska, feeding on fish, berries, insects, vegetation, and anything else handy. In Southeast Alaska, they can be so common as to be a pest, and many communities have adjusted their handling of garbage to keep the bears out of town. Although not typically dangerous, blackies still deserve caution and respect: They stand about a yard tall at the shoulders and measure 5 or 6 feet from nose to tail, with an average male weighing about 200 pounds. Black bears are usually black, but can also be brown, blond, or even blue—color is not the best way to tell a black bear from a brown bear. Instead, look at the smaller size, the narrower, smoother face, and the shape of the back, which is straight and lacks the brown bear's large shoulder hump. One of the best places to see black bears is the remote Anan Bear Observatory, reached from Wrangell or Ketchikan by floatplane or boat (see chapter 5).

BROWN BEAR Also known as the grizzly bear when found inland, brown bears are among the largest and most ferocious of all land mammals. Size depends on the bears' food source. In coastal areas where salmon are plentiful, such as Southeast Alaska or Katmai National Park, brown bears can grow well over 1,000 pounds and up to 9 feet tall. The largest of all are found on salmon-rich Kodiak Island, a genetically isolated subspecies. Inland, at Denali National Park and on similar tundra landscape, where they feed on rodents, berries, insects and the like, brown bears (called grizzlies) top out below 500 pounds. They can also take larger prey, but that's less common. Recognize a brown bear by the prominent shoulder hump, more rounded face, and large size; color can range from almost black to blond. Among the best places to see brown bears are Pack Creek on Admiralty Island near Juneau, at Denali and Katmai national parks, or on bear viewing floatplane excursions from Homer or Kodiak. Of these, Denali is the only inexpensive option.

Black Bear

Brown Bear

MOOSE In winter, when they move to the lowlands, moose can be a positive pest, blocking roadways and eating expensive shrubbery. In the summer, they're a little more elusive, often seen standing in forest ponds eating the weeds from the bottom or pruning willows from stream banks or disturbed roadsides. But even in summer gardeners can often be heard cursing these animals, which, despite their immense size, can neatly chomp the blossom off each tulip in a flower bed. Moose are the largest member of the deer family, and the Alaska race of moose are the largest of the species, with males reaching 1,200 to 1,600 pounds. They live all over Alaska, thriving in the boreal forest that covers Interior and Southcentral Alaska. They are unmistakable. As big as a large horse, with bristly, ragged brown hair; a long, bulbous nose; and huge, mournful eyes, moose seem to crave pity—through they get little from the wolves and people who hunt them, and the trains and cars that run them down, and they give little to anyone in their way when they're on the move. Males grow large antlers, which they shed after battling for a mate every fall. Females lack antlers and are smaller, having one to three calves each year.

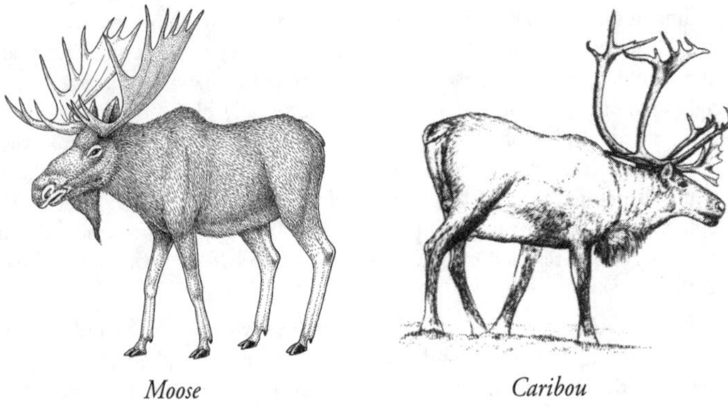

Moose *Caribou*

CARIBOU Alaska's barren-ground caribou are genetically identical to reindeer, but were never domesticated as reindeer were in Europe. For Inupiat and Athabaskan people, they were an essential source of food and hides, and the hunt remains a cultural mainstay. Both males and females have antlers that they shed annually. Reindeer travel the arctic tundra and Interior foothills in herds of up to hundreds of thousands of animals, a stunning sight witnessed by only a lucky few, as the migration routes lie in remote regions. You can, however, often see caribou in smaller groups of a few dozen at Denali National Park, along the Dalton and Denali highways, and on other northern rural roads above the tree line. They're skittish, so the best technique is to stop and let them approach you.

SITKA BLACK-TAILED DEER This is a relatively small deer found in the coastal rain forests of Alaska and British Columbia. Adults weigh in around 80 to 120 pounds and the male's antlers also are small. The coat is reddish-brown in summer. They can be found throughout Southeast and have been successfully transplanted to Prince William Sound and Kodiak Island.

DALL SHEEP Resembling the more familiar bighorn, Dall sheep are smaller, weighing up to 300 pound for males, 150 for females. Males and females have horns, but only the males' horns curl into powerful fighting tools for establishing dominance in head-butting contests. Sheep stay in high, rocky places, where their incredible agility makes them safe from predators. Except in a few exceptional spots, such as on the cliffs above the Seward Highway just south of Anchorage on Turnagain Arm, you almost always need strong binoculars to see them. Their range extends north from Southcentral Alaska. Denali National Park is a good place to see them from afar. Scanning the gray rock of the mountains, pick out white spots, then focus in on them.

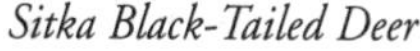

Sitka Black-Tailed Deer

Dall Sheep

MOUNTAIN GOAT Another animal you won't see well without binoculars, the mountain goat inhabits the same craggy mountain habitat as Dall sheep, but farther south, from Alaska's Southcentral region south to Montana. Alaska's prime viewing area is on Turnagain Arm; they're also seen on the mountainsides of Resurrection Bay, Kenai Fjords, and other areas where you can see sheer cliffs. Mountain goats are big, shaggy beasts with two small, nearly straight horns on males and females.

Mountain Goat

Index

Index

Index

Frommer's® Complete Travel Guides

Alaska
Amsterdam
Arizona
Atlanta
Australia
Austria
Bahamas
Barcelona, Madrid & Seville
Beijing
Belgium, Holland & Luxembourg
Bermuda
Boston
British Columbia & the Canadian Rockies
Budapest & the Best of Hungary
California
Canada
Cancún, Cozumel & the Yucatán
Cape Cod, Nantucket & Martha's Vineyard
Caribbean
Caribbean Cruises & Ports of Call
Caribbean Ports of Call
Carolinas & Georgia
Chicago
China
Colorado
Costa Rica
Denmark
Denver, Boulder & Colorado Springs
England
Europe
European Cruises & Ports of Call
Florida
France
Germany
Greece
Greek Islands
Hawaii
Hong Kong
Honolulu, Waikiki & Oahu
Ireland
Israel
Italy
Jamaica
Japan
Las Vegas
London
Los Angeles
Maryland & Delaware
Maui
Mexico
Montana & Wyoming
Montréal & Québec City
Munich & the Bavarian Alps
Nashville & Memphis
Nepal
New England
New Mexico
New Orleans
New York City
New Zealand
Nova Scotia, New Brunswick & Prince Edward Island
Oregon
Paris
Philadelphia & the Amish Country
Portugal
Prague & the Best of the Czech Republic
Provence & the Riviera
Puerto Rico
Rome
San Antonio & Austin
San Diego
San Francisco
Santa Fe, Taos & Albuquerque
Scandinavia
Scotland
Seattle & Portland
Shanghai
Singapore & Malaysia
South Africa
Southeast Asia
South Florida
South Pacific
Spain
Sweden
Switzerland
Thailand
Tokyo
Toronto
Tuscany & Umbria
USA
Utah
Vancouver & Victoria
Vermont, New Hampshire & Maine
Vienna & the Danube Valley
Virgin Islands
Virginia
Walt Disney World & Orlando
Washington, D.C.
Washington State

Frommer's® Dollar-a-Day Guides

Australia from $50 a Day
California from $60 a Day
Caribbean from $70 a Day
England from $70 a Day
Europe from $70 a Day
Florida from $70 a Day
Hawaii from $70 a Day
Ireland from $60 a Day
Italy from $70 a Day
London from $85 a Day
New York from $80 a Day
Paris from $80 a Day
San Francisco from $60 a Day
Washington, D.C., from $70 a Day

Frommer's® Portable Guides

Acapulco, Ixtapa & Zihuatanejo
Alaska Cruises & Ports of Call
Bahamas
Baja & Los Cabos
Berlin
California Wine Country
Charleston & Savannah
Chicago
Dublin
Hawaii: The Big Island
Las Vegas
London
Los Angeles
Maine Coast
Maui
Miami
New Orleans
New York City
Paris
Puerto Vallarta, Manzanillo & Guadalajara
San Diego
San Francisco
Sydney
Tampa & St. Petersburg
Venice
Washington, D.C.

Frommer's® National Park Guides

Family Vacations in the National Parks
Grand Canyon
National Parks of the American West
Rocky Mountain
Yellowstone & Grand Teton
Yosemite & Sequoia/Kings Canyon
Zion & Bryce Canyon

Frommer's® Memorable Walks

Chicago
London
New York
Paris
San Francisco
Washington, D.C.

Frommer's® Great Outdoor Guides

New England
Northern California
Southern California & Baja
Southern New England
Washington & Oregon

Frommer's® Born to Shop Guides

Born to Shop: France
Born to Shop: Italy
Born to Shop: London
Born to Shop: New York
Born to Shop: Paris

Frommer's® Irreverent Guides

Amsterdam
Boston
Chicago
Las Vegas
London
Los Angeles
Manhattan
New Orleans
Paris
San Francisco
Seattle & Portland
Vancouver
Walt Disney World
Washington, D.C.

Frommer's® Best-Loved Driving Tours

America
Britain
California
Florida
France
Germany
Ireland
Italy
New England
Scotland
Spain
Western Europe

The Unofficial Guides®

Bed & Breakfasts in California
Bed & Breakfasts in New England
Bed & Breakfasts in the Northwest
Bed & Breakfasts in Southeast
Beyond Disney
Branson, Missouri
California with Kids
Chicago
Cruises
Disneyland
Florida with Kids
Golf Vacations in the Eastern U.S.
The Great Smoky & Blue Ridge Mountains
Inside Disney
Hawaii
Las Vegas
London
Miami & the Keys
Mini Las Vegas
Mini-Mickey
New Orleans
New York City
Paris
San Francisco
Skiing in the West
Southeast with Kids
Walt Disney World
Walt Disney World for Grown-ups
Walt Disney World for Kids
Washington, D.C.

Special-Interest Titles

Frommer's Britain's Best Bed & Breakfasts and Country Inns
Frommer's Britain's Best Bike Rides
The Civil War Trust's Official Guide to the Civil War Discovery Trail
Frommer's Caribbean Hideaways
Frommer's Adventure Guide to Central America
Frommer's Adventure Guide to South America
Frommer's Adventure Guide to Southeast Asia
Frommer's Food Lover's Companion to France
Frommer's Gay & Lesbian Europe
Frommer's Exploring America by RV
Hanging Out in Europe
Israel Past & Present
Mad Monks' Guide to California
Mad Monks' Guide to New York City
Frommer's The Moon
Frommer's New York City with Kids
The New York Times' Unforgettable Weekends
Places Rated Almanac
Retirement Places Rated
Frommer's Road Atlas Britain
Frommer's Road Atlas Europe
Frommer's Washington, D.C., with Kids
Frommer's What the Airlines Never Tell You